Lecture Notes in Computer Science 9058

Commenced Publication in 1973
Founding and Former Series Editors:
Gerhard Goos, Juris Hartmanis, and Jan van Leeuwen

More information about this series at http://www.springer.com/series/7408

Klaus Havelund · Gerard Holzmann
Rajeev Joshi (Eds.)

NASA
Formal Methods

7th International Symposium, NFM 2015
Pasadena, CA, USA, April 27–29, 2015
Proceedings

 Springer

Editors
Klaus Havelund
Jet Propulsion Laboratory
Pasadena, California
USA

Rajeev Joshi
Jet Propulsion Laboratory
Pasadena, California
USA

Gerard Holzmann
Jet Propulsion Laboratory
Pasadena, California
USA

ISSN 0302-9743   ISSN 1611-3349   (electronic)
Lecture Notes in Computer Science
ISBN 978-3-319-17523-2   ISBN 978-3-319-17524-9   (eBook)
DOI 10.1007/978-3-319-17524-9

Library of Congress Control Number: 2015935615

LNCS Sublibrary: SL2 – Programming and Software Engineering

Springer Cham Heidelberg New York Dordrecht London

Printed on acid-free paper

Springer International Publishing AG Switzerland is part of Springer Science+Business Media
(www.springer.com)

Preface

This volume contains the papers presented at NFM 2015, the 7th NASA Formal Methods Symposium, held during April 27–29, 2015 in Pasadena. The NASA Formal Methods Symposium is a forum for anyone interested in the development and application of formal methods, both theoreticians and practitioners, from academia, industry, and government. The goal of the symposium is to identify challenges and provide solutions that can help us achieve greater reliability of mission- and safety-critical systems.

Within NASA, such systems include manned and unmanned spacecraft, orbiting satellites, and aircraft. Rapidly increasing code size and new software development paradigms, including the broad use of automatic code generation and code synthesis tools, static source code analysis techniques, and tool-based code review methods, all bring new challenges as well as new opportunities for improvement. Also gaining increasing importance in NASA applications is the use of more rigorous software test methods, often inspired by new theoretical insights.

The focus of the symposium is understandably on formal methods, their foundation, current capabilities, and limitations. The NASA Formal Methods Symposium is an annual event, which was created to highlight the state of the art in formal methods, both in theory and in practice. The series started as the Langley Formal Methods Workshop, and was held under that name in 1990, 1992, 1995, 1997, 2000, and 2008. In 2009 the first NASA Formal Methods Symposium was organized by NASA Ames Research Center, which also organized the 2013 symposium. In 2010 the symposium was organized in Washington DC by the Formal Methods Group of NASA Langley Research Center with the collaboration of NASA Goddard and NASA Headquarters; and in 2012 it was organized by NASA Langley Research Center in Norfolk, Virginia. In 2011 the organization was done by JPL's Laboratory for Reliable Software, in Pasadena, California. In 2014 it was organized by NASA's Johnson Space Center in collaboration with NASA Ames Research Center and Lero (Ireland), in Houston, Texas. Finally, the organization of the current 2015 symposium returned to JPL's Laboratory for Reliable Software in Pasadena, California.

The topics covered by the NASA Formal Methods Symposia include: theorem proving, logic model checking, automated testing and simulation, model-based engineering, real-time and stochastic systems, SAT and SMT solvers, symbolic execution, abstraction and abstraction refinement, compositional verification techniques, static and dynamic analysis techniques, fault protection, cyber security, specification formalisms, requirements analysis, and applications of formal techniques.

Two types of papers were considered: regular papers describing fully developed work and complete results or case studies, and short papers on tools, experience reports, or work in progress with preliminary results. The symposium received 108 submissions (77 regular papers and 31 short papers) out of which 33 were accepted (24 regular papers and 9 short papers), giving an acceptance rate of 30.6%. All submissions went through a rigorous reviewing process, where each paper was read by three reviewers.

In addition to the refereed papers, the symposium featured three invited presentations: by Dino Distefano from Facebook, USA, and Professor at Queen Mary University of London, UK, titled Moving Fast with Software Verification; by Viktor Kuncak, from the Laboratory for Automated Reasoning and Analysis at EPFL, in Lausanne, Switzerland, on Developing Verified Software using Leon; and by Rob Manning, from NASA's Jet Propulsion Laboratory, on Complexity Tolerance: Dealing with Faults of Our Own Making.

The organizers are grateful to the authors for submitting their work to NFM 2015 and to the invited speakers for sharing their insights. NFM 2015 would not have been possible without the collaboration of the outstanding Program Committee and external reviewers, the support of the Steering Committee, and the general support of the NASA Formal Methods community. The NFM 2015 website can be found at http://nasaformalmethods.org.

Support for the preparation of these proceedings was provided by the Jet Propulsion Laboratory, California Institute of Technology, under a contract with the National Aeronautics and Space Administration.

February 2015   Klaus Havelund
                                                                      Gerard Holzmann
                                                                      Rajeev Joshi

Organization

Program Committee

Erika Ábrahám	RWTH Aachen University, Germany
Julia Badger	NASA Johnson Space Center, USA
Christel Baier	Dresden University of Technology, Germany
Saddek Bensalem	VERIMAG/University Joseph Fourier, France
Dirk Beyer	University of Passau, Germany
Armin Biere	Johannes Kepler University, Austria
Nikolaj Bjørner	Microsoft Research, USA
Borzoo Bonakdarpour	McMaster University, Canada
Alessandro Cimatti	Fondazione Bruno Kessler, Italy
Leonardo De Moura	Microsoft Research, USA
Ewen Denney	NASA Ames Research Center, USA
Ben Di Vito	NASA Langley Research Center, USA
Dawson Engler	Stanford University, USA
Jean-Christophe Filliatre	Université Paris-Sud, France
Dimitra Giannakopoulou	NASA Ames Research Center, USA
Alwyn Goodloe	NASA Langley Research Center, USA
Susanne Graf	VERIMAG, France
Alex Groce	Oregon State University, USA
Radu Grosu	Vienna University of Technology, Austria
John Harrison	Intel Corporation, USA
Mike Hinchey	University of Limerick/Lero, Ireland
Bart Jacobs	Katholieke Universiteit Leuven, Belgium
Sarfraz Khurshid	University of Texas at Austin, USA
Gerwin Klein	NICTA and University of New South Wales, Australia
Daniel Kroening	University of Oxford, UK
Orna Kupferman	Hebrew University Jerusalem, Israel
Kim Larsen	Aalborg University, Denmark
Rustan Leino	Microsoft Research, USA
Martin Leucker	University of Lübeck, Germany
Rupak Majumdar	Max Planck Institute, Germany
Panagiotis Manolios	Northeastern University, USA
Peter Müller	ETH Zürich, Switzerland
Kedar Namjoshi	Bell Laboratories/Alcatel-Lucent, USA

Corina Pasareanu	NASA Ames Research Center, USA
Doron Peled	Bar-Ilan University, Israel
Suzette Person	NASA Langley Research Center, USA
Andreas Podelski	University of Freiburg, Germany
Grigore Rosu	University of Illinois at Urbana-Champaign, USA
Kristin Yvonne Rozier	NASA Ames Research Center, USA
Natarajan Shankar	SRI International, USA
Natasha Sharygina	University of Lugano, Switzerland
Scott Smolka	Stony Brook University, USA
Willem Visser	Stellenbosch University, South Africa
Mahesh Viswanathan	University of Illinois at Urbana-Champaign, USA
Michael Whalen	University of Minnesota, USA
Jim Woodcock	University of York, UK

Additional Reviewers

Alberti, Francesco
Alt, Leonardo
Arlt, Stephan
Astefanoaei, Lacramioara
Bartocci, Ezio
Bourke, Timothy
Bozga, Marius
Bozzano, Marco
Cattaruzza, Dario
Chamarthi, Harsh Raju
Chang, Yen Jung
Cholewa, Andrew
Christ, Juergen
Corzilius, Florian
Dangl, Matthias
David, Cristina
Decker, Normann
Duan, Lian
Duggirala, Parasara Sridhar
Dutertre, Bruno
Farkash, Monica
Fedyukovich, Grigory
Ferrara, Pietro
Fiadeiro, José Luiz
Frömel, Bernhard
Ghassabani, Elaheh
Greenaway, David
Griggio, Alberto
Harder, Jannis

Hyvärinen, Antti
Isakovic, Haris
Jain, Mitesh
Jovanović, Dejan
Juhasz, Uri
Kahsai, Temesghen
Kandl, Susanne
Katz, Guy
Kesseli, Pascal
Kim, Chang Hwan Peter
Li, Wenchao
Li, Yilong
Luckow, Kasper
Luo, Qingzhou
Löwe, Stefan
Mahboubi, Assia
Markin, Grigory
Mehta, Farhad
Melnychenko, Oleksandr
Melquiond, Guillaume
Mentis, Anakreon
Mery, Dominique
Miyazawa, Alvaro
Moore, Brandon
Moy, Yannick
Munoz, Cesar
Murali, Rajiv
Narkawicz, Anthony
Neogi, Natasha

Neville, Daniel
Nouri, Ayoub
Olivo, Oswaldo
Owre, Sam
Pais, Jorge
Papavasileiou, Vasilis
Prokesch, Daniel
Radoi, Cosmin
Ratasich, Denise
Rodriguez-Navas, Guillermo
Rozier, Eric
Scheffel, Torben
Schrammel, Peter
Schupp, Stefan
Schönfelder, René

Selyunin, Konstantin
Stefanescu, Andrei
Sticksel, Christoph
Stümpel, Annette
Taha, Walid
Thoma, Daniel
Tixeuil, Sebastien
Van Glabbeek, Rob
Vizel, Yakir
Wachter, Björn
Weissenbacher, Georg
Wendler, Philipp
Westphal, Bernd
Yang, Junxing
Zalinescu, Eugen

Contents

Invited Papers

Moving Fast with Software Verification

Cristiano Calcagno, Dino Distefano[✉], Jeremy Dubreil, Dominik Gabi,
Pieter Hooimeijer, Martino Luca, Peter O'Hearn, Irene Papakonstantinou,
Jim Purbrick, and Dulma Rodriguez

Facebook Inc., Cambridge, USA
ddino@fb.com

Abstract. For organisations like Facebook, high quality software is
important. However, the pace of change and increasing complexity of
modern code makes it difficult to produce error-free software. Available
tools are often lacking in helping programmers develop more reliable and
secure applications.

Formal verification is a technique able to detect software errors statically, before a product is actually shipped. Although this aspect makes
this technology very appealing in principle, in practice there have been
many difficulties that have hindered the application of software verification in industrial environments. In particular, in an organisation like
Facebook where the release cycle is fast compared to more traditional
industries, the deployment of formal techniques is highly challenging.

This paper describes our experience in integrating a verification
tool based on static analysis into the software development cycle at
Facebook.

1 Introduction

This is a story of transporting ideas from recent theoretical research in reasoning
about programs into the fast-moving engineering culture of Facebook. The context is that most of the authors landed at Facebook in September of 2013, when we
brought the INFER static analyser with us from the verification startup Monoidics
[4,6]. INFER itself is based on recent academic research in program analysis [5],
which applied a relatively recent development in logics of programs, separation
logic [10]. As of this writing INFER is deployed and running continuously to verify select properties of every code modification in Facebook's mobile apps; these
include the main Facebook apps for Android and iOS, Facebook Messenger, Insta-
gram, and other apps which are used by over a billion people in total.

In the process of trying to deploy the static analyser the most important issue
we faced was integration with Facebook's software development process. The
software process at Facebook, and an increasing number of Internet companies,
is based on fast iteration, where features are proposed and implemented and
changed based on feedback from users, rather than wholly designed at the outset.
The perpetual, fast, iterative development employed at Facebook might seem

© Springer International Publishing Switzerland 2015
K. Havelund et al. (Eds.): NFM 2015, LNCS 9058, pp. 3–11, 2015.
DOI: 10.1007/978-3-319-17524-9_1

to be the worst possible case for formal verification technology, proponents of which sometimes even used to argue that programs should be developed only after a prior specifications had been written down. But we found that verification technology can be effective if deployed in a fashion which takes into account when and why programmers expect feedback. INFER runs on every "diff", which is a code change submitted by a developer for code review. Each day a number of bugs are reported on diffs and fixed by developers, before the diff is committed and eventually deployed to phones. Technically, the important point is that INFER is a compositional[1] program analysis, which allows feedback to be given to developers in tune with their flow of incremental development.

2   Facebook's Software Development Model

Perpetual Development. As many internet companies Facebook adopts a continuous development model [9]. In this model, software will never be considered a *finished product*. Instead features are continuously added and adapted and shipped to users. Fast iteration is considered to support rapid innovation. For its web version, Facebook pushes new changes in the code twice a day.

This perpetual development model fits well with the product and its usecase. It would be impossible to foresee a-priori how a new feature would be used by the hundreds of million of people using Facebook services every day. The different uses influence the way a new feature is shaped and further developed. In other words, Facebook prioritises people using the product rather than an initial design proposed in some fixed specification by architects at the company.

Perpetual Development on Mobile Versus Web. In the last couple of years, Facebook has gone through a shift. From being a web-based company Facebook transitioned to embrace mobile. Use of its mobile applications on the Android and iOS platforms has increased substantially, reflecting a global trend for consumers of Internet content.

For mobile applications, Facebook applies a continuous development model as well. However there are some fundamental differences w.r.t. web development. Although the development cycle is the same, the deployment is fundamentally different. In web development the software runs on Facebook servers in our datacenters, and in the client on code downloaded from our servers by a browser. New code can, therefore, be deployed directly to the servers, which then serves the users (including by serving them Javascript); new versions of the software are deployed without the users getting involved.

On the contrary, mobile applications run on users' phones. Therefore, it is up to the user to update to a new version of the app implementing new features

---

[1] A compositional analysis is one in which the analysis result of a composite program is computed from the results of its parts. As a consequence, compositional analyses can run on incomplete programs (they are not whole-program analyses), are by their nature incremental, scale well, and tolerate imprecision on parts of code that are difficult to analyse [5].

or fixing existing bugs. Facebook can only distribute a new version to the Apple App Store or Google Play, but Facebook is not anymore in control of which version a user is running on her mobile device.

This difference has dramatic impact on bug fixes. On web when a bug is discovered a fix can be shipped to the servers as part of a periodic release or in exceptional cases immediately via a "hotfix". And on the web mechanisms exist to automatically update the JavaScript client software running in the browser, allowing fixes to quickly and automatically be deployed as soon as they have been developed. On current mobile platforms updates must typically be explicitly authorised by the device owner, so there is no guarantee that a fix will be deployed in a timely manner, if ever, once it is developed.

The sandboxes provided by modern web browsers also make it easier to isolate the effects of a bug in one part of the interface from another, allowing the experience to gracefully degrade in the face of runtime errors. Current mobile platforms typically provide a model closer to processes running on a traditional operating system and will often terminate the entire app when a runtime error is detected in any part of it. This lower fault tolerance increases the potential severity of bugs which would have a minor impact on the web.

Thus mobile development at Facebook presents a strong dichotomy: on one hand it employs continuous development; on the other hand it could benefit from techniques like formal verification to prevent bugs before apps are shipped.

When the INFER team landed at Facebook there was a well developed version of INFER for C programs, and a rudimentary version for Java. Facebook has considerable amounts of C++, Javascript, php, objective-C and Java code, but less development is being done in pure C. This, together with the above discussion determined our first targets, Android and iPhone apps.

3 Software Verification in the Perpetual Development Era

As we have seen, Facebook employs a perpetual development model both for web and mobile software. While in such an environment it is difficult to envisage requiring specs to always be written before programming starts, a common approach in static analysis has been to work towards the implicit specification that (certain) runtime errors cannot occur. Of course, when an assertion is placed into code it can help the analysis along. In INFER's case at the beginning the implicit safety properties were null pointer exceptions and resource leaks for Android code, and additionally memory leaks for iOS.

Unlike many other software companies, Facebook does not have a separate quality assurance (QA) team or professional testers. Instead, engineers write (unit) tests for their newly developed code. But as a part of the commit and push process there is a set of regression tests that are automatically run and the code must pass them before it can be pushed. This juncture, when diffs are reviewed by humans and by tests, is a key point where formal verification techniques based on static analysis can have impact.

There are several features that the verification technique should offer to be adopted in such different environment:

- *Full automation and integration.* The technique should be push-button and integrated into the development environment used by programmers.
- *Scalability.* The technique scales to millions of lines of code.
- *Precision.* Developers' time is an important resource. An imprecise tool providing poor results would be seen as a waste of that resource.
- *Fast Reporting.* The analysis should not get in the way of the development cycle; therefore it has to report to developers in minutes, before programmers commit or make further changes. As we will see in Section 5, fast reporting is not only about analysing code fast, but it also involves good integration with the existing infrastructure where many other tasks need to be performed.

These requirements are challenging. In our context we are talking about analysis of large Android and iPhone apps (millions of lines of code are involved in the codebases). The analysis must be able to run on thousands of code diffs in a day, and it should report in under 10 minutes on average to fit in with the developer workflow. There are intra-procedural analyses and linters which fit these scaling requirements, and which are routinely deployed at Facebook and other companies with similar scale codebases and workflows. But if an analysis is to detect or exclude bugs involving chains of procedure calls, as one minimally expects of verification techniques, then an inter-procedural analysis is needed, and making inter-procedural analyses scale to this degree while maintaining any degree of accuracy has long been a challenge.

4   Background: the INFER Static Analyser

INFER [4] is a program analyser aimed at verifying memory safety and developed initially by Monoidics Ltd. It was first aimed at C code and later extended to Java. After the acquisition of Monoidics by Facebook, INFER's development now continues inside Facebook.

INFER combines several recent advances in automatic verification. It's underlying formalism is separation logic [10]. It implements a compositional, bottom-up variant of the classic RHS inter-procedural analysis algorithm based on procedure summaries [11]. There are two main novelties. First, it uses compact summaries, based on the ideas of footprints and frame inference [2] from separation logic, to avoid the need for huge summaries that explicitly tabulate most of the input-output possibilities. Second, it uses a variation on the notion of abductive inference to discover those summaries [5].

Bi-abduction. INFER computes a compositional shape analysis by synthesising specification for a piece of code in isolation. Specifications in this case are Hoare's triples where pre/post-conditions are separation logic formulae. More specifically, for a given piece of code C, INFER synthesises pre/post specifications of the form

$$\{P\} \; C \; \{Q\}$$

by inferring suitable P and Q. A crucial point is that such specifications do not express functional correctness but rather memory safety. The consequence is that they relates to a basic general property that every code should satisfy.

The theoretical notion allowing INFER to synthesise pre and post-conditions in specifications is *bi-abductive inference* [5]. Formally, it consists in solving the following extension of the entailment problem:

$$H * A \vdash H' * F$$

where H, H' are given formulae in separation logic describing a heap configuration whereas F (frame) and A (anti-frame) are unknown and need to be inferred. Bi-abductive inference is applied during an attempted proof of a program to discover a collection of anti-frames describing the memory needed to execute a program fragment safely (its footprint).

Triples of procedures in a program are composed together in a bottom-up fashion according to the call graph to obtain triples of larger pieces of code.

Soundness. The soundness property for the algorithm underlying INFER is that if INFER finds a Hoare triple $\{P\} \, C \, \{Q\}$ for a program component C then that triple is true in a particular mathematical model according to the fault-avoiding interpretation of triples used in separation logic [10]: any execution starting from a state satisfying P will not cause a prescribed collection of runtime errors (in the current implementation these are leaks and null dereferences) and, if execution terminates, Q will be true of the final state. Soundness can also be stated using the terminology of abstract interpretation (see [5], section 4.4).

Soundness can never be absolute, but is always stated with respect to the idealization (assumptions) represented by a mathematical model. In INFER's case limitations to the model ([5]) include that it doesn't account for the concurrency or dynamic dispatch found in Android or iPhone apps. So interpreting the results in the real world must be done with care; e.g., when an execution admits a race condition, INFER's results might not over-approximate. Note that these caveats are given even prior to the question of whether INFER correctly implements the abstract algorithm. Thus, soundness does not translate to "no bugs are missed." The role of soundness w.r.t. the mathematical model is to serve as an aid to pinpoint what an analysis is doing and to understand where its limitations are; in addition to providing guarantees for executions under which the model's assumptions are met.

Context. In this short paper we do not give a comprehensive discussion of related work, but for context briefly compare INFER to several other prominent industrial static bug catching and verification tools.

- Microsoft's Static Driver Verifier [1] was one of the first automatic program verification tools to apply to real-world systems code. It checks temporal safety properties of C code. It assumes memory safety and ignores concurrency, so is sound with respect to an idealized model that doesn't account for some of the programming features used in device drivers. Driver Verifier uses a whole-program analysis which would be challenging to apply incrementally, with rapid turnaround on diffs for large codebases, as INFER is at Facebook. In INFER we are only checking memory properties at present.

We could check temporal properties but have not surfaced this capability to Facebook code as of yet.

- Astrée has famously proven the absence of runtime errors in Airbus code [8]. Strong soundness properties are rightfully claimed of it, for the kinds of program it targets. It also does not cover programs with dynamic allocation or concurrency, which are areas that Driver Verifier makes assumptions about. Astrée has a very accurate treatment of arithmetic, while INFER is very weak there; conversely, INFER treats dynamic allocation while Astrée does not. Astrée is a whole-program analysis which would be challenging to apply incrementally as INFER is at Facebook.
- Microsoft's Code Contracts static checker, Clousot, implements a compositional analysis by inferring preconditions in a way related to that of INFER [7]; consequently, it can operate incrementally and could likely be deployed in a similar way to INFER. Beyond this similarity, its strong points are almost the opposite of those of INFER. Clousot has a precise treatment of arithmetic and array bounds, but its soundness property is relative to strong assumptions about anti-aliasing of heap objects, where INFER contains an accurate heap analysis but is at present weak on arithmetic and array bounds. And, INFER focusses on preconditions that are *sufficient* to avoid errors, where Clousot aims for preconditions that are *necessary* rather than sufficient; necessary preconditions do not guarantee safety, but rather provide a novel means of falsification.
- Coverity Prevent has been used to find bugs in many open source and industrial programs. We are not aware of how Prevent works technically, but it has certainly processed an impressive amount of code. Coverty do not claim a soundness property, and a paper from Coverity questions whether soundness is even worthwhile [3].

5   Integration with the Development Infrastructure

Part of deploying formal verification in this environment of continuous development was the integration of INFER into the Facebook development infrastructure used by programmers. In this environment it was desirable that the programmer does not have to do anything else than his/her normal job, they should see analysis results as part of their normal workflow rather than requiring them to switch to a different tool.

At a high-level, Facebook's development process has the following phases:

1. The programmer develops a new feature or makes some change on the codebase (a.k.a. *diff*).
2. Via the source-control system, this diff goes to a phase of peer-reviews performed by other engineers. In this phase the author of the diff gets suggestions on improvement or requests for further changes from the peer reviewers. Thus, the author and the peer reviewers start a loop of interactions aimed at making the code change robust and efficient as well as being understandable, readable and maintainable by others.

3. When the reviewers are satisfied, they "accept" the code change and the diff can be then pushed via the source-control system to the main code-base.
4. Every two weeks a version of the code base is frozen into the *release candidate*. The release candidate goes into testing period by making it available to Facebook employees for internal use. During this period, feedback from employees helps fixing bugs manifesting at runtime.
5. After two weeks of internal use, the release candidate is deployed to Facebook users. First to a small fraction of users and, if it doesn't raise any alert, it is finally deployed to all users.

During phase 2, regression tests are automatically run and before accepting any code change a reviewer requires that all the tests pass. Tests run asynchronously and the results are automatically available in the collaboration tool phabricator (http://phabricator.org) used for peer review.

INFER is run at phase 2. The process is completely automatic. Once the code is submitted for peer review, an analysis is run asynchronously in one of Facebook's datacenters and results are reported on phabricator in the form of comments. INFER inserts comments on the lines of code where it detects a possible bug. Moreover, we have developed tools to navigate the error trace and make it easier for the developer to inspect the bug report. To provide useful commenting on bugs we had developed a *bug hashing* system to detect in different diffs, whether two different bugs are actually the same bugs or not.

Going forward a goal is to reduce the 2 week period in step 4. There will however still remain a period here with scope for analyses and are longer-running than a per-diff analysis should be.

Incremental Analysis. On average INFER needs to comment on a diff within ten minutes, and for this the incremental analysis aspect of INFER is important. We have implemented a caching system for analysis results. The latest Android/iOS code base is fully analysed nightly. A full analysis can take over 4 hours. This analysis produces a database of pre/post-condition specifications (a cache). Using the mechanism of bi-abduction (see Section 4) this cache is then used when analysing diffs. Only functions modified by a diff and functions depending on them need to be analysed.

The Social Challenge. Ultimately, one of the biggest challenges we faced was a *social challenge*: to get programmers to react to bugs reported by the tool and fix genuine errors. Programmers need to accumulate trust in the analyser and they should see it as something helping them to build better software rather than something slowing them down. All the features listed in Section 3 (scalability and precision of the analysis, full automation and integration, fast reporting) are important for the social challenge.

This challenge suggested to us that we should start small to build trust gradually, and this determined our attitude on what to report. Facebook has databases of crashes and other bugs, and many on Android were out-of-memory errors and null pointer exceptions. We concentrated on these initially, targeting false positives and negatives for resource leaks and null dereferences, and we wired INFER up to the internal build process. We trained INFER first on Facebook's Android apps to improve our reports.

Having a dedicated static analysis team within Facebook helps tremendously with the social challenge.

6   Conclusions

INFER is in production at Facebook where it delivers comments on code changes submitted by developers. INFER's compositional, incremental, nature is important for this means of deployment. This stands in contrast to a model based on whole-program analysis/verification, where long runs produce bug lists that developers might fix outside of their normal workflow. We have run INFER in a whole-program mode to produce lists of issues but found this to be less effective, because of the inefficiency of the context switch that it causes when taking developers out of their flow (amongst other reasons).

Just as the apps are, INFER itself is undergoing iterative development and changing in response to developer feedback; the number of bugs reported is changing, as is the proportion of code where specs are successfully inferred. And, in addition to null dereference and leak errors, we will be extending the kinds of issues INFER reports as time goes on.

Finally, although there have been some successes, we should say that from an industrial perspective advanced program analysis techniques are generally underdeveloped. Simplistic techniques based on context insensitive pattern matching ("linters") are deployed often and do provide value, and it is highly nontrivial to determine when or where many of the ingenious ideas being proposed in the scientific literature can be deployed practically. Part of the problem, we suggest, is that academic research has focused too much on whole-program analysis, or on specify-first, both of which severely limit the number of use cases. There are of course many other relevant problem areas – error reporting, fix suggestion, precision of abstract domains, to name a few – but we believe that automatic formal verification techniques have the potential for much greater impact if compositional analyses can become better developed and understood.

References

1. Ball, T., Bounimova, E., Cook, B., Levin, V., Lichtenberg, J., McGarvey, C., Ondrusek, B., Rajamani, S.K., Ustuner, A.: Thorough static analysis of device drivers. In: Proceedings of the 2006 EuroSys Conference, Leuven, Belgium, April 18-21, pp. 73–85 (2006)
2. Berdine, J., Calcagno, C., O'Hearn, P.W.: Smallfoot: modular automatic assertion checking with separation logic. In: de Boer, F.S., Bonsangue, M.M., Graf, S., de Roever, W.-P. (eds.) FMCO 2005. LNCS, vol. 4111, pp. 115–137. Springer, Heidelberg (2006)
3. Bessey, A., Block, K., Chelf, B., Chou, A., Fulton, B., Hallem, S., Gros, C.-H., Kamsky, A., McPeak, S., Engler, D.R.: A few billion lines of code later: using static analysis to find bugs in the real world. Commun. ACM 53(2), 66–75 (2010)

4. Calcagno, C., Distefano, D.: Infer: an automatic program verifier for memory safety of C programs. In: Bobaru, M., Havelund, K., Holzmann, G.J., Joshi, R. (eds.) NFM 2011. LNCS, vol. 6617, pp. 459–465. Springer, Heidelberg (2011)
5. Calcagno, C., Distefano, D., O'Hearn, P.W., Yang, H.: Compositional shape analysis by means of bi-abduction. J. ACM **58**(6), 26 (2011)
6. Constine, J.: Facebook acquires assets of UK mobile bug-checking software developer Monoidics. http://techcrunch.com/2013/07/18/facebook-monoidics
7. Cousot, P., Cousot, R., Fähndrich, M., Logozzo, F.: Automatic inference of necessary preconditions. In: Giacobazzi, R., Berdine, J., Mastroeni, I. (eds.) VMCAI 2013. LNCS, vol. 7737, pp. 128–148. Springer, Heidelberg (2013)
8. Cousot, P., Cousot, R., Feret, J., Mauborgne, L., Miné, A., Monniaux, D., Rival, X.: The ASTREÉ analyzer. In: Sagiv, M. (ed.) ESOP 2005. LNCS, vol. 3444, pp. 21–30. Springer, Heidelberg (2005)
9. Feitelson, D.G., Frachtenberg, E., Beck, K.L.: Development and deployment at Facebook. IEEE Internet Computing **17**(4), 8–17 (2013)
10. O'Hearn, P.W., Reynolds, J.C., Yang, H.: Local reasoning about programs that alter data structures. In: Fribourg, L. (ed.) CSL 2001. LNCS, vol. 2142, pp. 1–19. Springer, Heidelberg (2001)
11. Reps, T.W., Horwitz, S., Sagiv, S.: Precise interprocedural dataflow analysis via graph reachability. In: Conference Record of POPL 1995: 22nd ACM SIGPLAN-SIGACT Symposium on Principles of Programming Languages, San Francisco, California, USA, January 23-25, pp 49–61 (1995)

Developing Verified Software Using Leon

Viktor Kuncak[✉]

École Polytechnique Fédérale de Lausanne (EPFL), Lausanne, Switzerland
viktorkuncak@epfl.ch

Abstract. We present Leon, a system for developing functional Scala programs annotated with contracts. Contracts in Leon can themselves refer to recursively defined functions. Leon aims to find counterexamples when functions do not meet the specifications, and proofs when they do. Moreover, it can optimize run-time checks by eliminating statically checked parts of contracts and doing memoization. For verification Leon uses an incremental function unfolding algorithm (which could be viewed as k-induction) and SMT solvers. For counterexample finding it uses these techniques and additionally specification-based test generation. Leon can also execute specifications (e.g. functions given only by postconditions), by invoking a constraint solver at run time. To make this process more efficient and predictable, Leon supports deductive synthesis of functions from specifications, both interactively and in an automated mode. Synthesis in Leon is currently based on a custom deductive synthesis framework incorporating, for example, syntax-driven rules, rules supporting synthesis procedures, and a form of counterexample-guided synthesis. We have also developed resource bound invariant inference for Leon and used it to check abstract worst-case execution time. We have also explored within Leon a compilation technique that transforms real-valued program specifications into finite-precision code while enforcing the desired end-to-end error bounds. Recent work enables Leon to perform program repair when the program does not meet the specification, using error localization, synthesis guided by the original expression, and counterexample-guided synthesis of expressions similar to a given one. Leon is open source and can also be tried from its web environment at leon.epfl.ch.

1 Overview

We present Leon, a system supporting the development of functional Scala [21] programs. We illustrate the flavor of program development in Leon, and present techniques deployed in it. Leon supports a functional subset of Scala. It has been observed time and again that one of the most effective ways of writing software that needs to be proved correct is to write it in a purely functional language. ACL2 [8] and its predecessors have demonstrated the success of this

Viktor Kuncak — This work is supported in part by the European Research Council (ERC) Grant *Implicit Programming* and Swiss National Science Foundation Grant "Constraint Solving Infrastructure for Program Analysis".

© Springer International Publishing Switzerland 2015
K. Havelund et al. (Eds.): NFM 2015, LNCS 9058, pp. 12–15, 2015.
DOI: 10.1007/978-3-319-17524-9_2

approach, resulting in verification of a number of hardware and software systems. Unlike ACL2, the input language supported by Leon has Hindley-Milner style type system [6,19]. Leon currently delegates parsing and type analysis to the existing Scala compiler front end; a Leon program is a valid Scala program. For convenience, Leon also supports local functions, local mutable variables and while loops, which are expanded into recursive functions [1]. Among related tools to Leon as far as verification functionality is concerned are liquid types [27], though Leon has a real model checking flavor in that it returns only valid counterexamples.

Leon functions are annotated with preconditions and postconditions using Scala syntax for contracts [20]. They manipulate unbounded integer and bitvector numerical quantities, algebraic data types expressed as case classes, lists, functional arrays, and maps. An ambitious research direction introduces a Real data type that compiles into a desired finite-precision data type that meets given precision guarantees [2,3]. The main challenge in this work is automatically computing the accumulation of worst-case error bounds though non-linear computations, which requires also precisely computing ranges of variables in programs using constraint solving.

Contracts in Leon can themselves refer to recursively defined functions, which makes them very expressive. Leon aims to find counterexamples when functions do not meet the specifications, and proofs when they do. For verification Leon uses an incremental function unfolding algorithm (which could be viewed as k-induction) and SMT solvers. The foundations of this work have been presented in [25], with first presentation of experimental results appearing in [26]. This algorithm simultaneously searches for proofs and counterexamples and has many desirable properties [24]. To speed up search for counterexamples, Leon also makes use of specification-based test generation, though this direction could be pushed further using, for example, techniques deployed in the domain-specific Scala language for test generation [17].

Leon has so far primarily relied on the Z3 SMT solver [4]; its performance and support for numerous theories including algebraic data types has proven to be very useful for automating a functional program verifier such a Leon. Particularly convenient have been extended array operations in Z3 [5] which have allowed us to encode Leon's sets, arrays, and maps efficiently. More recently we have built a more generic SMT-LIB interface and are exploring the possibility of using other solvers, as well as many of the unique features of CVC4, such as its increasingly sophisticated support for quantifiers [23] and automated mathematical induction [22].

We have also developed resource bound invariant inference for Leon by encoding the inference problem into non-linear arithmetic, and used this approach to check abstract worst-case execution time [18]. In this approach we have also shown that function postconditions can be inferred or strengthened automatically.

Constructs for preconditions (require) and postconditions (ensuring) have runtime checking semantics in standard Scala; they are simply particular assertions. Executing precise specifications at run time may change not only constant factors but also asymptotic complexity of the original program, changing, for example, insertion into a balanced tree from logarithmtic into quadratic operation. In Leon, even when contracts cannot be checked fully statically, they can be optimized by eliminating statically checked parts of contracts and doing memoization [12]. Using these techniques, it is often possible to speed up runtime checks and recover the asymptotic behavior of the original program.

Leon can also execute specifications alone (e.g. functions without body, given only by postconditions), by invoking a constraint solver at run time [13]. This mechanism reuses counterexample-finding ability as a computation mechanism [11]. Leon thus supports an expressive form of constraint programming with computable functions as constraints. While convenient for prototyping, constraint programming can be slow and unpredictable, often involving exponential search for solutions.

As a step towards more efficient and predictable approach, Leon supports deductive synthesis of functions form specifications. This functionality was originally aimed at being fully automated [10]. Synthesis in Leon is based on a custom deductive synthesis framework incorporating, for example, syntax-driven rules, rules supporting synthesis procedures [7,14–16], and a form of counterexample-guided synthesis [10]. Subsequently we have worked on interfaces to perform this synthesis interactively, which allows the developer both to explore different alternatives if the solution is not unique, and to guide synthesis using manual steps.

Recent work enables Leon to perform program repair when the program does not meet the specification, using error localization, synthesis guided by the original expression, and counterexample-guided synthesis of expressions similar to a given one [9].

Leon is under active development and has been used in teaching courses at EPFL. It is open source and can also be tried from its web environment at the URL http://leon.epfl.ch.

References

1. Blanc, R.W., Kneuss, E., Kuncak, V., Suter, P.: An overview of the leon verification system: verification by translation to recursive functions. In: Scala Workshop (2013)
2. Darulova, E.: Programming with Numerical Uncertainties. PhD thesis, EPFL (2014)
3. Darulova, E., Kuncak, V.: Sound compilation of reals. In: ACM SIGACT-SIGPLAN Symposium on Principles of Programming Languages (POPL) (2014)
4. de Moura, L., Bjørner, N.S.: Z3: an efficient SMT solver. In: Ramakrishnan, C.R., Rehof, J. (eds.) TACAS 2008. LNCS, vol. 4963, pp. 337–340. Springer, Heidelberg (2008)
5. de Moura, L., Bjørner, N.: Generalized, efficient array decision procedures. In: Formal Methods in Computer-Aided Design, November 2009
6. Hindley, R.: The principal type-scheme of an object in combinatory logic. Transactions of the American Mathematical Society **146**, 29–60 (1969)
7. Jacobs, S., Kuncak, V., Suter, P.: Reductions for synthesis procedures. In: Giacobazzi, R., Berdine, J., Mastroeni, I. (eds.) VMCAI 2013. LNCS, vol. 7737, pp. 88–107. Springer, Heidelberg (2013)

8. Kaufmann, M., Moore, J.S., Manolios, P.: Computer-Aided Reasoning: An Approach. Kluwer Academic Publishers, Norwell (2000)
9. Kneuss, E., Koukoutos, M., Kuncak, V.: On deductive program repair in Leon. Technical Report EPFL-REPORT-205054, EPFL, February 2014
10. Kneuss, E., Kuncak, V., Kuraj, I., Suter, P.: Synthesis modulo recursive functions. In: OOPSLA (2013)
11. Köksal, A., Kuncak, V., Suter, P.: Constraints as control. In: ACM SIGACT-SIGPLAN Symposium on Principles of Programming Languages (POPL) (2012)
12. Koukoutos, E., Kuncak, V.: Checking data structure properties orders of magnitude faster. In: Bonakdarpour, B., Smolka, S.A. (eds.) RV 2014. LNCS, vol. 8734, pp. 263–268. Springer, Heidelberg (2014)
13. Kuncak, V., Kneuss, E., Suter, P.: Executing specifications using synthesis and constraint solving. In: Legay, A., Bensalem, S. (eds.) RV 2013. LNCS, vol. 8174, pp. 1–20. Springer, Heidelberg (2013)
14. Kuncak, V., Mayer, M., Piskac, R., Suter, P.: Complete functional synthesis. In: ACM SIGPLAN Conf., Programming Language Design and Implementation (PLDI) (2010)
15. Kuncak, V., Mayer, M., Piskac, R., Suter, P.: Software synthesis procedures. Communications of the ACM (2012)
16. Kuncak, V., Mayer, M., Piskac, R., Suter, P.: Functional synthesis for linear arithmetic and sets. Software Tools for Technology Transfer (STTT) **15**(5–6), 455–474 (2013)
17. Kuraj, I., Kuncak, V.: SciFe: scala framework for effcient enumeration of data structures with invariants. In: Scala Workshop (2014)
18. Madhavan, R., Kuncak, V.: Symbolic resource bound inference for functional programs. In: Biere, A., Bloem, R. (eds.) CAV 2014. LNCS, vol. 8559, pp. 762–778. Springer, Heidelberg (2014)
19. Milner, R.: A theory of type polymorphism in programming. JCSS **17**(3), 348–375 (1978)
20. Odersky, M.: Contracts for scala. In: Barringer, H., Falcone, Y., Finkbeiner, B., Havelund, K., Lee, I., Pace, G., Roşu, G., Sokolsky, O., Tillmann, N. (eds.) RV 2010. LNCS, vol. 6418, pp. 51–57. Springer, Heidelberg (2010)
21. Odersky, M., Spoon, L., Venners, B.: Programming in scala: a comprehensive step-by-step guide. Artima Press (2008)
22. Reynolds, A., Kuncak, V.: Induction for SMT solvers. In: D'Souza, D., Lal, A., Larsen, K.G. (eds.) VMCAI 2015. LNCS, vol. 8931, pp. 80–98. Springer, Heidelberg (2015)
23. Reynolds, A., Tinelli, C., de Moura, L.M.: Finding conflicting instances of quantified formulas in SMT. In: FMCAD, pp. 195–202. IEEE (2014)
24. Suter, P.: Programming with Specifications. PhD thesis, EPFL, December 2012
25. Suter, P., Dotta, M., Kuncak, V.: Decision procedures for algebraic data types with abstractions. In: ACM SIGACT-SIGPLAN Symposium on Principles of Programming Languages (POPL) (2010)
26. Suter, P., Köksal, A.S., Kuncak, V.: Satisfiability modulo recursive programs. In: Yahav, E. (ed.) Static Analysis. LNCS, vol. 6887, pp. 298–315. Springer, Heidelberg (2011)
27. Vazou, N., Rondon, P.M., Jhala, R.: Abstract refinement types. In: Felleisen, M., Gardner, P. (eds.) ESOP 2013. LNCS, vol. 7792, pp. 209–228. Springer, Heidelberg (2013)

Regular Papers

Timely Rollback: Specification and Verification

Martín Abadi[1] and Michael Isard[2]([⊠])

[1] University of California at Santa Cruz, Santa Cruz, California, USA
[2] Microsoft Research, Mountain View, California, USA
misard@microsoft.com

Abstract. This paper presents a formal description and analysis of a technique for distributed rollback recovery. The setting for this work is a model for data-parallel computation with a notion of virtual time. The technique allows the selective undo of work at particular virtual times. A refinement theorem ensures the consistency of rollbacks.

1 Introduction

Rollback recovery plays an important role in ensuring fault tolerance in many distributed systems [7]. In this paper we initiate the development and study of a rollback technique for distributed data-parallel computing. This technique relies on the timely-dataflow model [11], in which computations are organized as dataflow graphs (e.g., [9]) and events are associated with virtual times [8] in a partial order. The technique guarantees consistency and transparency to applications while allowing the selective undo of work that corresponds to particular virtual times. For example, if a system has processed messages associated with virtual times t_1 and t_2, with $t_2 \not\leq t_1$, the work for time t_1 may be preserved while that for time t_2 may be undone, independently of the order in which the work was originally performed.

More generally, each node p in a dataflow graph may roll back to a set of times $f(p)$. This set is not necessarily the same for all nodes, but consistency constrains its choice. For example, virtual times for which a node p has produced visible external output cannot, in general, be outside $f(p)$: the output represents a commitment. Despite such constraints, the flexibility of not having the same $f(p)$ for all nodes is attractive in practice. In particular, choosing a particular $f(p)$ may imply the availability of corresponding logs or checkpoints, and allowing $f(p)$ to vary means that subsystems may adopt their own policies for logging and checkpointing.

The goal of this paper is to describe the design of our technique abstractly, and to present specifications and proofs that have been essential for this design. These specifications and proofs, which require a non-trivial use of prophecy variables [4], go beyond the analysis of internal dependencies (cf., e.g., [6]) to ensure

---

Most of this work was done at Microsoft Research. M. Abadi is now at Google.

© Springer International Publishing Switzerland 2015
K. Havelund et al. (Eds.): NFM 2015, LNCS 9058, pp. 19–34, 2015.
DOI: 10.1007/978-3-319-17524-9_3

that rollbacks are observationally correct in the sense that every execution with rollbacks is externally indistinguishable from an execution without rollbacks. We are implementing the design in the context of the Naiad system [11]; we hope to report on this implementation in the future.

The next section reviews the framework that we use for specifications and the model of computation. Section 3 motivates an assumption on buffering external outputs. Section 4 introduces auxiliary concepts and notations needed for the specification of rollback and the corresponding proofs. That specification is the subject of Section 5. Section 6 outlines the main steps of our proof that the model of Section 5, which includes rollback, is a correct refinement of the high-level model of Section 2.3. Section 7 briefly suggests four further elaborations of the rollback mechanism. Finally, Section 8 concludes, and in particular comments on the broader applicability of our ideas and results. Because of space constraints, proofs are omitted.

2 Model of Computation

This section describes our model of computation; it is based on another paper [2], which provides further details.

2.1 Basics of Specifications and Implementations

In this work, as in much work based on temporal logic (e.g., [4, 10]), specifications describe allowed behaviors, which are sequences of states. Each of the sequences starts in an initial state, and every pair of consecutive states is either identical (a "stutter") or related by a step of computation. Formally, a specification is a *state machine*, that is, a triple (Σ, F, N) where the *state space* Σ is a subset of the product of a fixed set Σ_E of externally visible states with a set Σ_I of internal states; the set F of *initial* states is a subset of Σ; and the *next-state relation* N is a subset of $\Sigma \times \Sigma$. The *complete property generated by* a state machine (Σ, F, N) consists of all infinite sequences $\langle\!\langle s_0, s_1, \ldots \rangle\!\rangle$ such that $s_0 \in F$ and, for all $i \geq 0$, either $\langle s_i, s_{i+1} \rangle \in N$ or $s_i = s_{i+1}$. This set is closed under stuttering and is a safety property. (We omit fairness conditions, for simplicity.) The *externally visible property generated by* a state machine is the externally visible property induced by its complete property via projection onto Σ_E and closure under stuttering. It need not be a safety property. A state machine **S** *implements* a state machine **S**′ if and only if the externally visible property generated by **S** is a subset of the externally visible property generated by **S**′.

2.2 Basics of Timely Dataflow

A system is a directed graph (possibly with cycles), in which nodes do the processing and messages are communicated on edges. We write P for the set of nodes. The set of edges is partitioned into input edges I, internal edges E, and output edges O. Edges have sources and destinations (but not always both): for each $i \in I$, $dst(i) \in P$, and $src(i)$ is undefined; for each $e \in E$, $src(e)$, $dst(e) \in P$, and we require that they are distinct; for each $o \in O$, $src(o) \in P$, and $dst(o)$ is undefined. We refer to nodes and edges as locations. We write M for the set of messages, and M^* for the set of finite sequences of messages.

We assume a partial order of virtual times $(T, \leq)$, and a function *time* from M to T (independent of the order of processing of messages). Each node can request to be notified when it has received all messages for a given virtual time. We allow T to include multiple time domains, that is, subsets that may use different coordinate systems or express different concerns. For example, inside loops, virtual times may be tuples with coordinates that represent iteration counters. Therefore, it is not always meaningful to compare virtual times at different graph locations. For simplicity, we assume that all inputs, notifications, and notification requests (but not outputs) at each node are in the same time domain; if inputs in different time domains are desired, auxiliary relay nodes can translate across time domains.

The state of a system consists of a mapping from nodes to their local states and outstanding notification requests plus a mapping from edges to their contents. We write $LocState(p)$ for the local state of node p, and Σ_{Loc} for the set of local states; $NotRequests(p)$ for p's outstanding notification requests, which are elements of T; and $Q(e)$ for the finite sequence of messages on edge e.

A local history for a node p is a finite sequence that starts with an initial local state that satisfies a given predicate $Initial(p)$, and a set N of initial notification requests, and is followed by events of the forms t and (e, m); these events indicate the received notifications and the received messages with corresponding edges. We write $Histories(p)$ for the set of local histories of p.

We assume that initially, in every behavior of a system, each node p is in a local state that satisfies $Initial(p)$, and p has some set of notification requests; and for each edge $i \in I$ we let $Q(i)$ contain an arbitrary finite sequence of messages, and for each edge $e \in E \cup O$ we let $Q(e)$ be empty. Thereafter, in the absence of rollback, at each step of computation (atomically, for simplicity), a node consumes a notification or a message, and produces notification requests and places messages on its outgoing edges.

The processing of events is defined by a function $g_1(p)$ for each node p, which is applied to p's local state s and to an event x (either a time t or a pair (e, m)), and which produces a new state s', a set of times N, and finite sequences of messages $\mu_1, \ldots, \mu_k$ on p's outgoing edges $e_1, \ldots, e_k$, respectively. We write:

$$g_1(p)(s, x) = (s', N, \langle e_1 \mapsto \mu_1, \ldots, e_k \mapsto \mu_k \rangle)$$

where $\langle e_1 \mapsto \mu_1, \ldots, e_k \mapsto \mu_k \rangle$ is the function that maps e_1 to μ_1, ..., e_k to μ_k. Iterating $g_1(p)$, we obtain a function $g(p)$ which takes as input a local history h and produces a new state s' and the resulting cumulative notification requests and sequences of messages $\mu_1, \ldots, \mu_k$:

$$g(p)(h) = (s', N, \langle e_1 \mapsto \mu_1, \ldots, e_k \mapsto \mu_k \rangle)$$

We let $\Pi_{\text{Loc}}(s', N, \langle e_1 \mapsto \mu_1, \ldots, e_k \mapsto \mu_k \rangle) = s'$, $\Pi_{\text{NR}}(s', N, \langle e_1 \mapsto \mu_1, \ldots, e_k \mapsto \mu_k \rangle) = N$, and $\Pi_{e_i}(s', N, \langle e_1 \mapsto \mu_1, \ldots, e_k \mapsto \mu_k \rangle) = \mu_i$ for $i = i \ldots k$.

When one event at a given virtual time t and location l in a dataflow graph can potentially result in another event at a virtual time t' and location l' in the same graph, we say that (l,t) could-result-in (l',t'), and write $(l,t) \rightsquigarrow (l',t')$. For example, when a node p forwards on an outgoing edge e all the messages that it receives on an incoming edge d, we have that $(d,t) \rightsquigarrow (e,t)$ for all t. The could-result-in relation enables an implementation of timely dataflow to support completion notifications, which tell a node when it will no longer see messages for a given time, and also to reclaim resources that correspond to pairs (l,t) at which no more events are possible. Another paper [2] gives a precise definition of $\rightsquigarrow$ and of the assumptions and properties on which we base our proofs. These include, in particular, that $\rightsquigarrow$ is reflexive and transitive.

A set $S \subseteq ((I \cup E \cup O) \cup P) \times T$ is *upward closed* if and only if, for all (l,t) and (l',t'), $(l,t) \in S$ and $(l,t) \rightsquigarrow (l',t')$ imply $(l',t') \in S$. We write $Close_\uparrow(S)$ for the least upward closed set that contains S. Since $\rightsquigarrow$ is reflexive and transitive, $Close_\uparrow(S)$ consists of the pairs (l',t') such that $(l,t) \rightsquigarrow (l',t')$ for some $(l,t) \in S$.

2.3   High-Level Specification

Throughout this paper, each element of Σ_E is an assignment of a value to $Q(e)$ for each $e \in I \cup O$ (that is, to $Q{\restriction}(I \cup O)$, where the symbol $\restriction$ denotes function restriction). In other words, the externally visible state consists of the contents of input and output channels. In the high-level specification, each element of Σ_I is an assignment of a value to $LocState(p)$ and $NotRequests(p)$ for each $p \in P$, and to $Q(e)$ for each $e \in E$ (that is, to $Q{\restriction}E$). In our lower-level specifications, below, each element of Σ_I has additional components.

Loosely adopting the TLA [10] approach, we define a high-level specification *SpecR* in Figure 1. We use the following TLA notations. A primed state function (for example, Q') in an action refers to the value of the state function in the "next" state (the state after the action); $\square$ is the temporal-logic operator "always"; given an action N and a list of expressions $v_1, \ldots, v_k$, $[N]_{v_1,\ldots,v_k}$ abbreviates $N \vee ((v'_1 = v_1) \wedge \ldots \wedge (v'_k = v_k))$. Internal state functions are existentially quantified. We also write v for the list of the state components $LocState$, $NotRequests$, and Q, and use the auxiliary state function $Clock$ which indicates pairs of a location and a time for which events may remain:

$$Clock = Close_\uparrow \left(\begin{array}{c} \{(e, time(m)) \mid e \in I \cup E \cup O, m \in Q(e)\} \\ \cup \\ \{(p,t) \mid p \in P, t \in NotRequests(p)\} \end{array} \right)$$

The predicate *InitProp* defines the initial states of a state machine, while the action *MessR* $\vee$ *Not* $\vee$ *Inp* $\vee$ *Outp* defines its next-state relation. The disjuncts *MessR*, *Not*, *Inp*, and *Outp* correspond, respectively, to processing messages, processing notification requests, external changes to input edges, and external changes to output edges. Action *Inp* could be further constrained to ensure that it only shrinks *Clock* or leaves it unchanged. Importantly, *MessR* does not strictly require FIFO behavior. Given a queue $Q(e)$, a node may process any message m

$$InitProp = \begin{pmatrix} \forall e \in E \cup O.Q(e) = \emptyset \wedge \forall i \in I.Q(i) \in M^* \\ \wedge \forall p \in P.(LocState(p), NotRequests(p)) \in Initial(p) \end{pmatrix}$$

$$MessR = \exists p \in P.MessR1(p)$$

$$MessR1(p) = \begin{pmatrix} \exists e \in I \cup E.p = dst(e) \wedge \exists m \in M.\exists u, v \in M^*. \\ Q(e) = u{\cdot}m{\cdot}v \wedge Q'(e) = u{\cdot}v \wedge \forall n \in u.time(n) \not\leq time(m) \\ \wedge Mess2(p, e, m) \end{pmatrix}$$

$$Mess2(p, e, m) = \begin{pmatrix} let \ \{e_1, \ldots, e_k\} = \{d \in E \cup O \mid src(d) = p\}, \\ s = LocState(p), \\ (s', \{t_1, \ldots, t_n\}, \langle e_1 \mapsto \mu_1, \ldots, e_k \mapsto \mu_k \rangle) = g_1(p)(s, (e, m)) \\ in \ LocState'(p) = s' \\ \wedge NotRequests'(p) = NotRequests(p) \cup \{t_1, \ldots, t_n\} \\ \wedge Q'(e_1) = Q(e_1){\cdot}\mu_1 \ldots Q'(e_k) = Q(e_k){\cdot}\mu_k \\ \wedge \forall q \in P \neq p.LocState'(q) = LocState(q) \\ \wedge \forall q \in P \neq p.NotRequests'(q) = NotRequests(q) \\ \wedge \forall d \in I \cup E \cup O - \{e, e_1, \ldots, e_k\}.Q'(d) = Q(d) \end{pmatrix}$$

$$Not = \exists p \in P.Not1(p)$$

$$Not1(p) = \exists t \in NotRequests(p).$$
$$\forall e \in I \cup E \ such \ that \ dst(e) = p.(e, t) \notin Clock \wedge Not2(p, t)$$

$$Not2(p, t) = \begin{pmatrix} let \ \{e_1, \ldots, e_k\} = \{d \in E \cup O \mid src(d) = p\}, \\ s = LocState(p), \\ (s', \{t_1, \ldots, t_n\}, \langle e_1 \mapsto \mu_1, \ldots, e_k \mapsto \mu_k \rangle) = g_1(p)(s, t) \\ in \ LocState'(p) = s' \\ \wedge NotRequests'(p) = NotRequests(p) - \{t\} \cup \{t_1, \ldots, t_n\} \\ \wedge Q'(e_1) = Q(e_1){\cdot}\mu_1 \ldots Q'(e_k) = Q(e_k){\cdot}\mu_k \\ \wedge \forall q \in P \neq p.LocState'(q) = LocState(q) \\ \wedge \forall q \in P \neq p.NotRequests'(q) = NotRequests(q) \\ \wedge \forall d \in I \cup E \cup O - \{e_1, \ldots, e_k\}.Q'(d) = Q(d) \end{pmatrix}$$

$$Inp = \begin{pmatrix} \forall p \in P.LocState'(p) = LocState(p) \\ \wedge \forall p \in P.NotRequests'(p) = NotRequests(p) \\ \wedge \forall i \in I.Q(i) \ is \ a \ subsequence \ of \ Q'(i) \\ \wedge \forall d \in E \cup O.Q'(d) = Q(d) \end{pmatrix}$$

$$Outp = \begin{pmatrix} \forall p \in P.LocState'(p) = LocState(p) \\ \wedge \forall p \in P.NotRequests'(p) = NotRequests(p) \\ \wedge \forall o \in O.Q'(o) \ is \ a \ subsequence \ of \ Q(o) \\ \wedge \forall d \in I \cup E.Q'(d) = Q(d) \end{pmatrix}$$

$$SpecR = \exists LocState, NotRequests, Q {\restriction} E.$$
$$InitProp \wedge \Box [MessR \vee Not \vee Inp \vee Outp]_v$$

Fig. 1. High-level specification

such that there is no message n ahead of m with $time(n) \leq time(m)$. This relaxation has various benefits, for example in supporting optimizations. For our purposes, it is crucial for obtaining a flexible and correct rollback technique. For example, suppose that a node receives a message for time 2 and then a message for time 1. We would like to be able to undo the work for time 2 while preserving the work for time 1. The system will then behave as though the message for time 1 had overtaken the message for time 2. Therefore, our high-level specification should enable such overtaking.

3   An Assumption on External Outputs

The model of Section 2.2 allows each node to consume and produce multiple events in one atomic action. While such behavior does not pose problems when it is limited to internal edges, it complicates selective rollback when it becomes visible on output edges, as the following example illustrates.

Example 1. Suppose that q has an outgoing edge $o \in O$. Suppose that t_1 and t_2 are incomparable times, and t_3 is greater than both. As long as q receives messages only for time t_1, it forwards them, outputting them on o, with the same "payload" but at time t_3. As soon as q receives a notification for time t_2, it stops doing any forwarding. Suppose that in a run q has received a notification for time t_2 followed by 50 messages for time t_1, so q has not output anything on o. Suppose that we wish to roll back to a state where q has received the messages for time t_1 but not the notification for time t_2. Consistency requires that there should be 50 messages on o. But a rollback action cannot put them there all atomically, since in a run without the notification for time t_2 they would have appeared one after another, not all at once.

This example suggests that rollback can benefit from buffering external outputs. Buffering may be "a simple matter of programming". Alternatively, we can achieve it "for free" by adding buffer nodes (between q and o in the example). More generally, buffer nodes can support asynchronous behavior (see, e.g., [12]). Formally, we say that $p \in P$ is a *buffer node* if there exists exactly one $e_1 \in I \cup E$ such that $dst(e_1) = p$; there exists exactly one $e_2 \in E \cup O$ such that $src(e_2) = p$; for this e_2, $g_1(p)(s,t) = (s, \emptyset, \langle e_2 \mapsto \emptyset \rangle)$; and for this e_1 and e_2, $g_1(p)(s, (e_1, m)) = (s, \emptyset, \langle e_2 \mapsto \langle\langle m \rangle\rangle \rangle)$. Such a node p is simply a relay between queues. We assume:

Condition 1.   *If $o \in O$ and $src(o) = p$ then p is a buffer node.*

4   Auxiliary Concepts

This section reviews a few auxiliary concepts and corresponding notations (introduced in the study of information-flow security properties [3]).

4.1   Sequences, Frontiers, Filtering, and Reordering

We write $\emptyset$ for the empty sequence, $\langle\!\langle a_0, a_1, \ldots \rangle\!\rangle$ for a sequence that contains a_0, a_1, ... (as above), and use $\cdot$ both for adding elements to sequences and for appending sequences. We define *subtraction* for sequences, inductively, by:

$$u - \emptyset = u \qquad\qquad \emptyset - m = \emptyset$$
$$u - m{\cdot}v = (u - m) - v \quad (m{\cdot}u - m) = u$$
$$(n{\cdot}u - m) = n{\cdot}(u - m) \text{ for } n \neq m$$

A subset S of T is *downward closed* if and only if, for all t and t', $t \in S$ and $t' \leq t$ imply $t' \in S$. We call such a subset a *frontier*, and write F for the set of frontiers; we often let f range over frontiers. (In the parlance of mathematics, a frontier might be called an ideal; in that of distributed systems, frontiers resemble consistent cuts.) When $S \subseteq T$, we write $Close_\downarrow(S)$ for the downward closure of S (the least frontier that contains S).

Filtering operations on histories and on sequences of messages keep or remove elements in a given frontier. Given a local history $h = \langle\!\langle (s, N), x_1, \ldots, x_k \rangle\!\rangle$ and a frontier f, where each x_i is of the form t_i or (d_i, m_i), we write $h@f$ for the subsequence of h obtained by removing all $t_i \notin f$ and all (d_i, m_i) such that $time(m_i) \notin f$. When u is a sequence of messages, we write $u@f$ for the subsequence obtained by removing those messages whose times are not in f. Finally, given a sequence of messages u and a frontier f, we write $u@f$ for the subsequence of u consisting only of messages whose times are not in f.

The *reordering* relation $\hookrightarrow$ on finite sequences of messages is the least reflexive and transitive relation such that, for $u, v \in M^*$ and $m_1, m_2 \in M$, if $time(m_1) \not\leq time(m_2)$ then $u{\cdot}m_1{\cdot}m_2{\cdot}v \hookrightarrow u{\cdot}m_2{\cdot}m_1{\cdot}v$. This relation models the reordering that happens in message processing according to action *MessR*, so serves in reasoning with this action.

4.2   Expressing Dependencies

Rollback can exploit information on whether a history or a part of a history at a node suffices for determining a notification request or message generated by the node. For example, if we know that p's outputs up to time 1 are determined entirely by its history up to time 1, and a rollback does not affect p's history up to time 1, then the outputs up to time 1 and their consequences downstream do not need to be retracted. Here we consider how to capture such information.

We simply assume that every node's notification requests up to time t are determined by its local history up to time t, for all t. For messages, on the other hand, many useful nodes do not satisfy an analogous property (for example, because of the use of different time domains for inputs and outputs) or satisfy stronger properties that we would want to leverage (as is the case for nodes that increment loop counters). Therefore, we make a more flexible hypothesis: for each edge $e \in E \cup O$, we assume a function $\phi(e)$ from frontiers to frontiers (a *frontier transformer*) such that h gives rise to a message on e in $\phi(e)(f)$ if and only if so does $h@f$, and with messages in the same order and multiplicity:

Condition 2. *For all $f \in F$, if $g(p)(h) = (\ldots, N, \langle \ldots e_i \mapsto \mu_i \ldots \rangle)$ and $g(p)(h@f)$ $= (\ldots, N', \langle \ldots e_i \mapsto \mu'_i \ldots \rangle)$ then $N@f = N'@f$ and $\mu_i@\phi(e_i)(f) = \mu'_i@\phi(e_i)(f)$.*

For example, when e is the output edge of a buffer node, we can let $\phi(e)(f) = f$ for all f, that is, let $\phi(e)$ be the identity function. More generally, $\phi(e)$ may be the identity function for many other edges, but this is not required. Neither is it required that $\phi(e)$ be as precise as possible, though a more precise $\phi(e)$ will generally be more useful. In this paper, we do not investigate how to check that Condition 2 holds for a given ϕ: we simply posit that we can find a correct, useful ϕ. Our experience indicates that this assumption is reasonable.

Additionally, we require that ϕ satisfy the following properties:

Condition 3. *For all $e \in E \cup O$:*

1. *$\phi(e)(f_1) \cap \phi(e)(f_2) \subseteq \phi(e)(f_1 \cap f_2)$ for all $f_1, f_2 \in F$,*
2. *$\phi(e)(T) = T$,*
3. *$\phi(e)$ is monotonic.*

Conditions 3(1) and 3(3) imply that $\phi(e)(f_1) \cap \phi(e)(f_2) = \phi(e)(f_1 \cap f_2)$. In combination with Condition 3(2), they say that $\phi(e)$ distributes over all finite intersections, including the empty intersection that yields T. (We can justify a stronger property, namely that $\phi(e)$ distributes over arbitrary intersections [3].)

5   Low-Level Specification (with Rollback)

The low-level specification, which permits rollback, has the same state components as the high-level specification plus an internal variable H that maps each $p \in P$ to a local history in *Histories*(p). The resulting state space is Σ_{Low}. Figure 2 defines the specification. There, we write v for the list of the state components *LocState*, *NotRequests*, Q, and H.

The main novelties are in the action *RollbackL*. This action creates a global state from local histories filtered down to frontiers $f(p)$ by applying the function $g(p)$, for each node p. Among other things, for each outgoing internal edge e_i this function yields messages μ_i, from which messages in $\phi(e_i)(f(p)) \cap f(dst(e_i))$ are expunged, intuitively because e_i's destination should already have them.

Crucially, the global state is completely determined by the local histories, since $g(p)$ is a function. So we are not concerned with recording non-deterministic choices, other than those encoded in local histories, in order to ensure consistency (for example, in order to ensure that any internal choices revealed by external outputs are made in the same way at each rollback). As discussed in Section 7.2, the creation of the global state may be accelerated by precomputation; the specification is silent on such implementation matters.

The choice of the frontiers $f(p)$ is subject to several constraints. (Section 7.3 briefly considers how to pick frontiers that satisfy these constraints.) A guard in *RollbackL2*(f, p) requires that $f(p)$ cannot contain times for which there are messages in transit towards p on internal edges, basically because, in practice, any messages in transit on internal edges may be lost during the failures that

$$InitPropL = InitProp \land \forall p \in P.H(p) = \langle\!\langle (LocState(p), NotRequests(p)) \rangle\!\rangle$$

$$MessL = \exists p \in P.$$
$$MessR1(p) \land H'(p) = H(p)\cdot(e,m) \land \forall q \in P \neq p.H'(q) = H(q)$$

$$NotL = \exists p \in P.NotL1(p)$$

$$NotL1(p) = \exists t \in NotRequests(p).$$
$$\begin{pmatrix} \forall e \in I \cup E \text{ such that } dst(e) = p.(e,t) \notin Clock \\ \land \ Not2(p,t) \\ \land \ H'(p) = H(p)\cdot t \land \forall q \in P \neq p.H'(q) = H(q) \end{pmatrix}$$

$$InpL = Inp \land \forall p \in P.H'(p) = H(p)$$

$$OutpL = Outp \land \forall p \in P.H'(p) = H(p)$$

$$RollbackL = \exists f \in P{\to}F.RollbackL1(f)$$

$$RollbackL1(f) = \begin{pmatrix} \forall p \in P, i \in I \text{ such that } dst(i) = p. \\ \quad \{time(m) \mid (i,m) \in H(p)\} \subseteq f(p) \\ \land \ \forall p \in P, o \in O \text{ such that } src(o) = p. \\ \quad \{time(m) \mid \exists e.(e,m) \in H(p)\} \subseteq f(p) \\ \land \ \forall p,q \in P, e \in E \text{ such that } src(e) = p \land dst(e) = q. \\ \quad \{time(m) \mid (e,m) \in H(q)\} \cap f(q) \subseteq \phi(e)(f(p)) \\ \land \ \forall p,q \in P, e_1, e_2 \in E \text{ such that } src(e_1) = p \land dst(e_2) = q, \\ \quad t_1 \in T, l_2 \in H(q)@f(q). \\ \quad \text{if } (e_1, t_1) \rightsquigarrow (e_2, l_2) \text{ then } t_1 \in \phi(e_1)(f(p)) \\ \land \ \forall e \in I \cup O.Q'(e) = Q(e) \\ \land \ \forall p \in P.RollbackL2(f,p) \end{pmatrix}$$

$$RollbackL2(f,p) = \begin{pmatrix} f(p) \cap \{time(m) \mid \exists e \in E, m \in M.dst(e) = p \land m \in Q(e)\} = \emptyset \\ \land \\ \text{let } \{e_1, \ldots, e_k\} = \{d \in E \cup O \mid src(d) = p\}, \\ h = H(p)@f(p), \\ (s', \{t_1, \ldots, t_n\}, \langle e_1{\mapsto}\mu_1, \ldots, e_k{\mapsto}\mu_k \rangle) = g(p)(h) \\ \text{in} \\ \forall i \in 1 \ldots k. \text{ if } e_i \in E \\ \qquad \text{then } Q'(e_i) = \mu_i @(\phi(e_i)(f(p)) \cap f(dst(e_i))) \\ \land \ LocState'(p) = s' \\ \land \ NotRequests'(p) = \{t_1, \ldots, t_n\} \\ \land \ H'(p) = h \end{pmatrix}$$

$$SpecL = \exists LocState, NotRequests, H, Q{\restriction}E.$$
$$InitPropL \land \Box[MessL \lor NotL \lor InpL \lor OutpL \lor RollbackL]_v$$

Fig. 2. Low-level specification

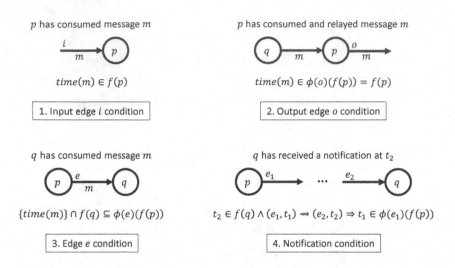

Fig. 3. The guards in $RollbackL1(f)$

cause rollbacks. One way to ensure that this guard holds is to pick $f(p)$ so that it contains only times t for which $(p, t) \notin Clock$. In addition, while the frontiers need not be the same at all nodes, guards in $RollbackL1(f)$ ensure that they are chosen to be consistent with one another and with external inputs and outputs:

1. For each node p connected to an input edge $i \in I$, $f(p)$ must contain the times of all messages that p has consumed: we do not assume any external mechanism for replaying those messages after a rollback, so p should not forget them, in general. (Optimizations may however allow p to forget many messages in practice.)

2. For each node p connected to an output edge $o \in O$, which must be a buffer node, $f(p)$ must contain the times of all messages that p has consumed and therefore relayed: they cannot be retracted.

3. For each pair of nodes p and q and edge e from p to q, $\phi(e)(f(p))$ must contain the times of all the messages that q has consumed and that are in $f(q)$: since q keeps those messages, p must keep the part of its local history that determines them.

4. Finally, an analogous but more complicated guard refers to notifications. It ensures that if a node q has received a notification for a time $t_2 \in f(q)$, then every node p that might cause events at t_2 at q keeps the part of its local history that would determine those events.
   Below, in Section 7.4, we develop a refinement of $SpecL$ that simplifies the treatment of this guard.

Figure 3 summarizes these four guards; when a message m is shown under an edge, it means that m has been transmitted on that edge (not that it is currently in transit). The following two examples illustrate the role of guards (3) and (4), respectively.

Example 2. Suppose that p has incoming edges d_0 and d_1 and outgoing edges e_0 and e_1 to q_0 and q_1, respectively; and that q_0 and q_1 are buffer nodes, with respective output edges o_0 and o_1. Suppose that p forwards all messages from d_0 on e_0 or from d_1 on e_1, but not both, depending on whether it reads first from d_0 or from d_1. For simplicity, initially, we let $\phi(e)$ be the identity function for every edge e. Assume that, in a particular run, a message with time 0 has travelled from d_0 to o_0 via p, e_0, and q_0. Upon a rollback, let $0 \in f(q_0)$, as suggested by guard (2). Guard (3) then dictates that $0 \in f(p)$. If instead we had $f(p) = \emptyset$, and upon recovery p first reads from d_1, it would cause an output on o_1, which is inconsistent with the previous output on o_0.

As a variant, suppose that p increments all virtual times, so the message from d_0 yields an output on o_0 with time 1. We take $\phi(e_0)(f) = \{0\} \cup \{t + 1 \mid t \in f\}$. Upon a rollback, we should have $1 \in f(q_0)$, but we do not need to impose that $1 \in f(p)$: the application of $\phi(e_0)$ implies that $0 \in f(p)$ suffices.

Example 3. Suppose that p_0 and p_1 each send a message to p_2, with times 0 and 1 respectively. Suppose further that, when it receives a message with time 0, p_2 forwards its "payload" with time 1 to p_3 on an edge e, but only if it has not yet processed a message with time 1. Therefore, we have that $(p_2, 0) \rightsquigarrow (p_3, 1)$ but not $(p_2, 1) \rightsquigarrow (p_3, 1)$, and we can let $\phi(e)$ be the identity function. Assume that, in a particular run, p_2 hears from p_1 first, then from p_0, so p_2 never sends anything to p_3; then p_3 receives a completion notification for time 1; and then a rollback takes place with $f(p_2) = \{0\}$. Upon recovery, it appears to p_2 that it heard from p_0 first, so it should send a message at time 1 to p_2. As this message would contradict the completion notification for time 1, we cannot have $1 \in f(p_3)$. Guard (4) prevents it.

As mentioned in Section 4.2, we need not have the most accurate function ϕ. Since the occurrences of ϕ in the guards for *RollbackL* are all in positive positions, using a more informative ϕ makes rollbacks more liberal. On the other hand, using a less informative ϕ (obtained by some under-approximation) does not compromise soundness. Section 7.1 discusses other approximations that may be attractive in practice.

6   Refinement Theorem

Our main result is that the low-level specification *SpecL* implements the high-level specification *SpecR*. In other words, the behaviors in the externally visible property of the system with rollback are all in the externally visible property of the system without rollback; so, externally, one cannot tell whether a behavior includes rollback transitions.

For safety properties, we can prove implementation relations by reasoning only about finite prefixes of behaviors: when *Spec* is a safety property, if every prefix of a behavior in *Spec'* is the prefix of a behavior in *Spec* then *Spec'* implements *Spec*. While such reasoning may not be easy, it can avoid complications related to liveness properties, such as finiteness requirements on prophecy variables [4]. Unfortunately, although *SpecR*'s body (*InitProp* ∧ □[*MessR* ∨ *Not* ∨ *Inp* ∨ *Outp*]$_v$) is clearly a safety property, *SpecR* itself need not be one, because safety properties are not closed under existential quantification. Therefore, our proof does have to address those complications.

The proof is rather long, so we cannot present it in full detail, but we hope to convey its main elements.

Invariant. As in many refinement proofs, the first step is to establish an inductive invariant of the low-level specification. In this case, the invariant, which we call *Inv*, relates the function g to elements of the state, at each node and edge. It is the conjunction of the following formulas:

$$\forall p \in P.\Pi_{\text{Loc}}g(p)(H(p)) = LocState(p)$$
$$\forall p \in P.\Pi_{\text{NR}}g(p)(H(p)) = NotRequests(p)$$
$$\forall p,q \in P, e \in E \text{ such that } src(e) = p \wedge dst(e) = q.$$
$$\Pi_e g(p)(H(p)) \hookrightarrow (\langle m \mid (e,m) \in H(q)\rangle \cdot Q(e))$$

Prophecy Variable. Constructing a refinement mapping is a sound method for proving an implementation relation. Unfortunately, it is not complete on its own [4]. Auxiliary variables are often required to complement refinement mappings. In our case, we cannot find a refinement mapping basically because we cannot predict the effects of future rollbacks, but the addition of a prophecy variable to the low-level specification can provide the required, missing information. (Another paper [1] explains this situation in detail with much smaller examples, not tied to timely dataflow.) Specifically, we add an auxiliary variable D that maps each node p to a frontier. Intuitively, $D(p)$ consists of times not affected by future rollbacks at p. Formally, $D(p)$ is subject to a number of constraints, imposed via the definition of an enriched state space Σ_{Low}^P:

Construction 1. *The enriched state space Σ_{Low}^P consists of pairs of a state from Σ_{Low} (with components LocState, NotRequests, Q, and H) and a function D from P to F such that:*

1. $\forall p \in P, \forall i \in I$ such that $dst(i) = p.\{time(m) \mid (i,m) \in H(p)\} \subseteq D(p)$,
2. $\forall p \in P, \forall o \in O$ such that $src(o) = p.\{time(m) \mid \exists e.(e,m) \in H(p)\} \subseteq D(p)$,
3. $\forall p,q \in P, \forall e \in E$ such that $src(e) = p, dst(e) = q, \forall m \in M$ such that $m \in Q(e) \vee (e,m) \in H(q)$.*if* $time(m) \in D(q)$ then $time(m) \in \phi(e)(D(p))$,
4. $\forall p,q \in P, \forall e_1, e_2 \in E$ such that $src(e_1) = p, dst(e_2) = q, \forall t_1 \in T, t_2 \in H(q)@D(q)$. *if* $(e_1, t_1) \leadsto (e_2, t_2)$ then $t_1 \in \phi(e_1)(D(p))$.

These conditions are analogous to those in the definition of the action *RollbackL*. However, they apply at all times, not just during rollbacks. This distinction largely accounts for the small differences between them.

The following specification extends *SpecL* with conjuncts that describe the changes in D. Here, v is the list of all previous state components plus D.

$$InitPropP = InitPropL$$

$$MessP = MessL \wedge D = D'$$

$$NotP = NotL \wedge D = D'$$

$$InpP = InpL \wedge D = D'$$

$$OutpP = OutpL \wedge D = D'$$

$$RollbackP = \exists f \in P{\rightarrow}F.RollbackL1(f) \wedge D = (D' \cap f)$$

$$SpecP = \exists LocState, NotRequests, H, Q{\restriction}E, D \text{ as per Construction 1.}$$

$$InitPropP \wedge \Box[MessP \vee NotP \vee InpP \vee OutpP \vee RollbackP]_v$$

Most transitions are such that $D = D'$. The exception is in rollbacks, where we have $D = D' \cap f$. In other words, at each node p, the times $D(p)$ that will survive future rollbacks, starting from before a particular rollback to $f(p)$, are those in $f(p)$ that will survive future rollbacks after the transition, that is, those in $D'(p) \cap f(p)$. Characteristically, the current value D of the prophecy variable is defined from its next value D'.

There are standard conditions on what it means to be a prophecy variable. Unfortunately, D, as we have defined it, does not quite satisfy them, because each state in Σ_{Low} may yield infinitely many states in Σ^P_{Low}. We address this difficulty by quotienting by the equivalence relation Q such that $(s_1, D_1)Q(s_2, D_2)$ if and only if $s_1 = s_2$ and D_1 and D_2 coincide on the finite set of times $ITimes(H)$, where H is the history component of s_1 and s_2, and $ITimes(H)$ consists of all $t \in T$ such that, for some p, $time(m) = t$ for some $(e, m) \in H(p)$ or $t \in H(p)$. Intuitively, $ITimes(H)$ consists of the "interesting" times given H. For each $s \in \Sigma_{\text{Low}}$, the set of equivalence classes $\{(s, D) \in \Sigma^P_{\text{Low}}\}/Q$ is finite. The soundness of prophecy variables yields that *SpecL* implements the quotient of *SpecP* by Q, which we call $SpecP_{/Q}$.

Refinement Mapping. Using the invariant *Inv* and the auxiliary variable D, we construct a refinement mapping from the low-level specification to the high-level specification. This mapping is a function from Σ^P_{Low} to Σ_{High} that preserves externally visible state components, maps initial states to initial states, and maps steps to steps or to stutters. Basically, it maps a low-level state to a high-level state by pretending that each node p did not process any events with times outside $D(p)$. Formally, it is defined by the following state functions:

$$HLocState(p) = \Pi_{\text{Loc}}g(p)(H(p)@D(p))$$

$$HNotRequests(p) = \Pi_{\text{NR}}g(p)(H(p)@D(p))$$

$$HQ(e) = Q(e) \qquad \text{for } e \in I \cup O$$

$$HQ(e) = \Pi_e g(p)(H(p)@D(p)) - \langle m \mid m \in M, (e, m) \in H(q)\rangle@D(q)$$
$$\text{where } p = src(e) \text{ and } q = dst(e), \text{ for } e \in E$$

Thus, for each node p, *HLocState*(p) and *HNotRequests*(p) are obtained by applying $g(p)$ to p's filtered local history. Similarly, for an internal edge e from a node p to a node q, $HQ(e)$ is obtained by applying $g(p)$ to p's filtered local history, but subtracting messages that q has consumed according to its filtered local history. When e is an input or an output edge, $HQ(e)$ simply equals $Q(e)$, since $Q(e)$ is externally visible.

This refinement mapping respects the equivalence relation $\mathcal{Q}$. In other words, it maps equivalent low-level states to the same high-level state. Therefore, the refinement mapping from $\Sigma_{\mathrm{Low}}^{P}$ induces a refinement mapping from $\mathcal{Q}$'s equivalence classes, and the soundness of refinement mappings yields that *SpecP*$_{/\mathcal{Q}}$ implements *SpecR*. By transitivity, we conclude:

Theorem 1. *SpecL implements SpecR.*

7   Further Refinements

In this section we consider several further refinements of the low-level specification. Our main goal is to provide evidence that the low-level specification is a useful step towards concrete, correct implementations, and to indicate some possible features of those implementations.

7.1   Approximating the Clock and the Could-Result-in Relation

The low-level specification mentions the state function *Clock* and also refers to the relation $\rightsquigarrow$ directly. Both of these may be hard to calculate precisely and efficiently. Fortunately, it is sound to replace *Clock* with any over-approximation. Using a bigger state function will mean that fewer notifications may be delivered at any point, so may result in a smaller set of behaviors. Similarly, it is sound to over-approximate the relation $\rightsquigarrow$ in its other use in the specification (since it is in a negative position).

7.2   Precomputations

While the specification of *RollbackL* suggests that a new state can be computed by applying the function g to filtered local histories, this computation may be expensive, and there is no requirement that an implementation perform it naively and on the fly. In particular, an implementation may compute and store the values of $g(p)(h)$ for certain local histories h, as it runs. For this purpose, an implementation might leverage commutativity properties that could require careful analysis. In any case, much like traditional checkpoints, these values can later facilitate rollback. Formally, the precomputation simply provides an efficient way of satisfying the equations $h = H(p)@f(p)$ and $(s', \{t_1, \ldots, t_n\}, \langle e_1 \mapsto \mu_1, \ldots, e_k \mapsto \mu_k \rangle) = g(p)(h)$ in *RollbackL*.

7.3   Choosing Frontiers

The specification of *RollbackL* does not describe how to find a function f that satisfies its constraints. A possible refinement consists in specifying that it chooses the largest solution (the function that yields the largest frontiers), which is the one that entails the least rollback. A largest solution exists because the set of functions that satisfy the constraints is closed under arbitrary unions. A further refinement consists in specifying that it chooses the largest solution that has some additional properties. For example, each processor may be willing to roll back only to some subset of "available" frontiers (possibly ones for which it has checkpoints, or ones that do not contain times of events deemed problematic for whatever reason). A largest solution will still exist as long as the set of "available" frontiers is closed under unions. We are currently exploring whether and how finding largest solutions can be practical, at least in special cases.

7.4   Implementing the Guard on Notifications

One of the guards in *RollbackL* (guard (4)) includes a relatively complex condition that refers to the relation $\rightsquigarrow$ and potentially requires some checking for all pairs of edges. We can replace that condition with one that necessitates only simpler checks. For this purpose, we introduce an additional function f_c. For all p, $f_c(p)$ is a subset of $f(p)$ and, intuitively, represents those times for which events must be preserved in order to respect notifications. The specification *SpecS* is obtained from *SpecL* by replacing that guard with the requirement that, for some $f_c : P \rightarrow F$:

1. $\forall p \in P. f_c(p) \subseteq f(p)$,
2. $\forall p \in P, t \in T.$ *if* $t \in H(p) @ f(p)$ *then* $t \in f_c(p)$, and
3. $\forall p, q \in P, e \in E$ *such that* $src(e) = p \wedge dst(e) = q. f_c(q) \subseteq \phi(e)(f_c(p))$.

We can prove that these conditions are sufficient (but not necessary). We obtain:

Theorem 2. *SpecS implies SpecL.*

8   Conclusion

This paper describes and studies, formally, the design of a technique for rollback recovery. This technique is delicate, so its rigorous development has been beneficial. The required proofs have been challenging but, in our opinion, interesting, in particular because of the advanced application of prophecy variables.

The main motivation for our work has been fault-tolerance in the timely-dataflow model of computation. However, some of the machinery that we have developed is more broadly applicable. In particular, rollbacks may arise not only because of failures but also, for example, to undo speculative computations or to revert the effects of attacks. Moreover, the use of functions on frontiers for expressing dependencies and some of the corresponding end-to-end results may be valuable even for systems without rollback. (Some of the proofs in our work on information-flow security properties [3] resemble those of this paper, but they are considerably simpler, and in particular do not include prophecy variables.) Finally, some of the ideas developed here may help explain, in a common framework, specific schemes for recovery in models less general than timely dataflow (e.g., [5]).

Acknowledgments. We are grateful to our coauthors in work on Naiad for discussions that led to this paper.

References

1. Abadi, M.: The prophecy of undo. In: Egyed, A., Schaefer, I. (eds.) FASE 2015. LNCS, vol. 9033, pp. 347–361. Springer, Heidelberg (2015)
2. Abadi, M., Isard, M.: Timely dataflow: A model, in preparation (2014). https://users.soe.ucsc.edu/~abadi/allpapers-chron.html
3. Abadi, M., Isard, M.: On the flow of data, information, and time. In: Focardi, R., Myers, A. (eds.) POST 2015. LNCS, vol. 9036, pp. 73–92. Springer, Heidelberg (2015)
4. Abadi, M., Lamport, L.: The existence of refinement mappings. Theoretical Computer Science **82**(2), 253–284 (1991)
5. Akidau, T., Balikov, A., Bekiroğlu, K., Chernyak, S., Haberman, J., Lax, R., McVeety, S., Mills, D., Nordstrom, P., Whittle, S.: MillWheel: Fault-tolerant stream processing at Internet scale. Proceedings of the VLDB Endowment 6(11), August 2013
6. Alvisi, L., Marzullo, K.: Message logging: Pessimistic, optimistic, causal, and optimal. IEEE Transactions on Software Engineering **24**(2), 149–159 (1998)
7. Elnozahy, E.N., Alvisi, L., Wang, Y., Johnson, D.B.: A survey of rollback-recovery protocols in message-passing systems. ACM Computing Surveys **34**(3), 375–408 (2002)
8. Jefferson, D.R.: Virtual time. ACM Transactions on Programming Languages and Systems **7**(3), 404–425 (1985)
9. Kahn, G.: The seantics of a simple language for parallel programming. In: IFIP Congress, pp. 471–475 (1974)
10. Lamport, L.: Specifying Systems, The TLA+ Language and Tools for Hardware and Software Engineers. Addison-Wesley (2002)
11. Murray, D.G., McSherry, F., Isaacs, R., Isard, M., Barham, P., Abadi, M.: Naiad: a timely dataflow system. In: ACM SIGOPS 24th Symposium on Operating Systems Principles, pp. 439–455 (2013)
12. Selinger, P.: First-order axioms for asynchrony. In: Mazurkiewicz, Antoni, Winkowski, J. (eds.) CONCUR 1997. LNCS, vol. 1243, pp. 376–390. Springer, Heidelberg (1997)

Sum of Abstract Domains

Gianluca Amato, Simone Di Nardo Di Maio, and Francesca Scozzari[✉]

Università di Chieti-Pescara, Pescara, Italy
{gamato,simone.dinardo,fscozzari}@unich.it

Abstract. In the abstract interpretation theory, program properties are encoded by abstract domains, and the combination of abstract domains leads to new properties to be analyzed. We propose a new method to combine numerical abstract domains based on the Minkowski sum. We provide a general framework equipped with all the necessary abstract operators for static analysis of imperative languages.

1 Introduction

The theory of abstract interpretation [8,9] is based on the notion of abstract domain. The choice of the abstract domain determines the properties to be analyzed, the precision of the analysis and, in most cases, its computational complexity. In the literature on abstract interpretation, we find a large number of numerical abstract domains, such as intervals [7], polyhedra [11], octagons [15], zonotopes [13], parallelotopes [3] and polyhedra template [16]. The choice of an abstract domain is mainly guided by a trade off between analysis precision and complexity.

Abstract domains can also be combined or refined to obtain new abstract domains. The very first and fundamental method to combine two abstract domains is Cousot and Cousot reduced product [9]. Other methods include powerset [9], quotient [6], open products [5] and donut domains [12]. In many cases domain combinators cannot be applied blindly, but the resulting domain needs some tweaking, such as the design of specific abstract operators or an ad-hoc representation for abstract objects.

In this paper we introduce a new domain combinator based on the *Minkowski sum*. Given two sets $\mathcal{A}, \mathcal{B} \subseteq \mathbb{R}^n$, the (Minkowski) sum of $\mathcal{A}$ and $\mathcal{B}$ is the subset of $\mathbb{R}^n$ given by

$$\mathcal{A} + \mathcal{B} = \{a + b \in \mathbb{R}^n \mid a \in \mathcal{A}, b \in \mathcal{B}\} \ ,$$

where $a + b$ is the vector addition of the points a and b. In other words, the Minkowski sum is the union of all the translations of the points in $\mathcal{A}$ by a point in $\mathcal{B}$. For instance, given the segments

$$\mathcal{A} = \{(x,0) \in \mathbb{R}^2 \mid 0 \le x \le 1\}$$
$$\mathcal{B} = \{(0,y) \in \mathbb{R}^2 \mid 0 \le y \le 1\}$$

© Springer International Publishing Switzerland 2015
K. Havelund et al. (Eds.): NFM 2015, LNCS 9058, pp. 35–49, 2015.
DOI: 10.1007/978-3-319-17524-9_4

the Minkowski sum $\mathcal{A} + \mathcal{B}$ is the unit square $\mathcal{C} = \{(x, y) \in \mathbb{R}^2 \mid 0 \leq x \leq 1, 0 \leq y \leq 1\}$.

In our proposal, given any two numerical abstract domains A and B, we define a new abstract domain A + B whose abstract objects are defined as the sum of an object in A and an object in B.

The Minkowski sum is well-suited to define a domain combinator, since it enjoys many geometric and algebraic properties (commutes with convex hull, distributes over the scalar product, admits an identity element and an annihilator) which greatly help in defining the abstract operators in the sum domain. Moreover, sum is not idempotent, so that, for an abstract domain A, in the general case we have that $A \neq A + A$. This allows the construction of a new domain even from a single abstract domain. In this way, the sum combinator may be used as a domain refinement operator.

Minkowski sum has also been recently used to define the numerical abstract domain of zonotopes, which are bounded polyhedra generated as the sum of a finite number of segments. In some way, the sum domain combinator may be thought of as the lifting of the zonotope construction to the level of abstract domains.

In the rest of the paper we describe the theoretical foundation of the sum of abstract domains. Its abstract operators are designed by exploiting the operators of the original abstract domains, thus ensuring ease of implementation. A prototype has been developed for the Jandom static analyzer [1, 2, 4]. We show some experiments for the special case of the sum of the interval and parallelotope domains, and discuss some heuristics which may be used to enhance precision.

2   Notations

2.1   Linear Algebra

We denote by $\overline{\mathbb{R}}$ the set of real numbers extended with $+\infty$ and $-\infty$. Addition and multiplication are extended to $\overline{\mathbb{R}}$ in the obvious way. We use boldface for elements $\boldsymbol{v}$ of $\overline{\mathbb{R}}^n$. Any vector $\boldsymbol{v} \in \overline{\mathbb{R}}^n$ is intended as a column vector, and $\boldsymbol{v}^T$ is the corresponding row vector. Given $\boldsymbol{u}, \boldsymbol{v} \in \overline{\mathbb{R}}^n$, and a relation $\bowtie \in \{<, >, \leq, \geq, =\}$, we write $\boldsymbol{u} \bowtie \boldsymbol{v}$ if and only if $u_i \bowtie v_i$ for each $i \in \{1, \ldots, n\}$. We denote by $\inf_{\boldsymbol{u} \in \mathcal{A}} f(\boldsymbol{u})$ the greatest lower bound in $\overline{\mathbb{R}}$ of the set $\{f(\boldsymbol{u}) \mid \boldsymbol{u} \in \mathcal{A}\}$ and by $\mathbb{R}(m, n)$ the set of real matrices with m rows and n columns.

2.2   Abstract Interpretation

In this paper we adopt a framework for abstract interpretation which is weaker than the common one based on Galois' connections/insertions (see [10, Section 7]). Given a poset $(\mathsf{C}, \leq^{\mathsf{C}})$ — the *concrete domain* — and a set A — the *abstract domain* — we establish an abstract–concrete relationship between them with the use of a *concretization map*, which is just a function $\gamma : \mathsf{A} \to \mathsf{C}$.

We say that $a \in \mathsf{A}$ is a *correct abstraction* of $c \in \mathsf{C}$ when $c \leq^{\mathsf{C}} \gamma(a)$. In general, a given $c \in \mathsf{C}$ has many correct abstractions. We say that $a \in \mathsf{A}$ is a *minimal correct abstraction* of $c \in \mathsf{C}$ when a is a correct abstraction of c and there is no $a' \in \mathsf{A}$ such that $c \leq^\mathsf{C} \gamma(a') <^\mathsf{C} \gamma(a)$. Moreover, $a \in \mathsf{A}$ is an *optimal* abstraction of $c \in \mathsf{C}$ when $c \leq^\mathsf{C} \gamma(a')$ implies $\gamma(a) \leq^\mathsf{C} \gamma(a')$.

A function $f^\mathsf{A} : \mathsf{A} \to \mathsf{A}$ is a correct abstraction of $f : \mathsf{C} \to \mathsf{C}$ when it preserves correctness of abstractions, i.e. when $c \leq^\mathsf{C} \gamma(a)$ implies $f(c) \leq^\mathsf{C} \gamma(f^\mathsf{A}(a))$. It is a minimal correct abstraction of $f : \mathsf{C} \to \mathsf{C}$ when it is correct and, for any $a \in \mathsf{A}$, $f^\mathsf{A}(a)$ is a minimal correct approximation of $f(\gamma(a))$. Analogously we define the concept of optimal abstraction for f. Composition preserves correctness, but not minimality and optimality. The best precision is reached when f^A is γ-complete, i.e., when $\gamma(f^A(a)) = f(\gamma(a))$.

An *abstraction function* is a map $\alpha : \mathsf{C} \to \mathsf{A}$ such that $c \leq^\mathsf{C} \gamma(\alpha(c))$. When an abstraction function exists (which is quite common), a correct abstraction of $f : \mathsf{C} \to \mathsf{C}$ may be defined as $\alpha \circ f \circ \gamma$. An abstraction function is minimal when, for each $c \in \mathsf{C}$, $\alpha(c)$ is a minimal correct abstraction of c. In this case, $\alpha \circ f \circ \gamma$ is a minimal correct abstraction of f. Analogously we define the concept of optimal abstraction function.

The abstract–concrete relationship induces a pre-order $\leq^\mathsf{A}$ on A defined as $a^1 \leq^\mathsf{A} a^2$ iff $\gamma(a^1) \leq^\mathsf{C} \gamma(a^2)$. Note that γ is a monotone map from $(\mathsf{A}, \leq^\mathsf{A})$ to $(\mathsf{C}, \leq^\mathsf{C})$. When $\leq^\mathsf{A}$ is a partial order and α is optimal, we have the classical framework based on Galois's insertions. A *widening* on A is a map $\nabla : \mathsf{A} \times \mathsf{A} \to \mathsf{A}$ such that $a, a' \leq^\mathsf{A} a \nabla a'$ and for every sequence $x^0, \ldots, x^i, \ldots$ in A, the sequence $y^0 = x^0 \leq^\mathsf{A} \cdots \leq^\mathsf{A} y^{i+1} = y^i \nabla x^{i+1} \leq^\mathsf{A} \cdots$ is not strictly increasing.

2.3   Numerical Domains

In the following, we recall the definition of several standard *numerical abstract domains*, i.e, abstractions of the concrete domain $(\wp(\mathbb{R}^n), \subseteq)$. We consider fixed the dimension n of the concrete domain. A set $\mathcal{A} \subseteq \mathbb{R}^n$ is called a *closed box* when there are $l, u \in \overline{\mathbb{R}}^n$ such that $\mathcal{A} = \{x \in \mathbb{R}^n \mid l \leq x \leq u\}$, a *parallelotope* when there are an $n \times n$ invertible matrix A and $l, u \in \overline{\mathbb{R}}^n$ such that $\mathcal{A} = \{x \in \mathbb{R}^n \mid l \leq Ax \leq u\}$, a *zonotope* when there is $A \in \mathbb{R}(m, n)$ such that $\mathcal{A} = \left\{A\binom{1}{\epsilon} \mid \epsilon \in [-1, 1]^{m-1}\right\}$ and a *polyhedral set* when there is $A \in \mathbb{R}(m, n)$ and $b \in \overline{\mathbb{R}}^m$ such that $\mathcal{A} = \{x \in \mathbb{R}^n \mid Ax \leq b\}$.

The abstract objects of the interval, parallelotope, zonotope and polyhedral domains are, respectively, closed boxes, parallelotopes, zonotopes and polyhedral sets. Abstract objects are ordered by set inclusion, and the concretization map is the identity. In actual implementations, a finite representation is used for these abstract objects, but this is not relevant to our paper.

3   Combining Domains by Minkowski Sum

One of the most important operations in geometry, in particular in convexity theory, is the *Minkowski sum* of two sets.

Definition 1 (Minkowski sum). *Given two sets* $A, B \subseteq \mathbb{R}^n$, *the* Minkowski sum $\mathcal{A} + \mathcal{B} \subseteq \mathbb{R}^n$ *is defined as:*

$$\mathcal{A} + \mathcal{B} = \{a + b \in \mathbb{R}^n \mid a \in \mathcal{A}, b \in \mathcal{B}\} .$$

It is immediate to see that every element of the interval domain is the Minkowski sum of (possibly unbounded) segments. Moreover, any zonotope is the Minkowski sum of a finite number of bounded segments.

We introduce a new operator for combining two numerical abstract domains into a new domain whose objects are the sum of the abstract objects of the constituent domains.

Definition 2 (Sum of abstract domains). *Given two numerical abstract domains* A *and* B, *we define a new abstract domain called the* (Minkowski) sum *of* A *and* B, *which is:*

$$\mathsf{A} + \mathsf{B} = \{\langle A + B \rangle \mid A \in \mathsf{A}, B \in \mathsf{B}\}$$

with concretization map:

$$\gamma^{\mathsf{A}+\mathsf{B}}(\langle A + B \rangle) = \gamma^{\mathsf{A}}(A) + \gamma^{\mathsf{B}}(B) .$$

We use the notation $\langle A + B \rangle$ instead of (A, B), since the former better conveys the real purpose of the pair. We stress out that $\langle A + B \rangle$ is only a formal sum.

Example 1. Let $\mathcal{A} \in \mathsf{Int}$ and $\mathcal{B} \in \mathsf{Parallelotope}$ with

$$\mathcal{A} = \{0 \le x \le 1, 0 \le y \le \infty\}$$
$$\mathcal{B} = \{0 \le y \le 2, 0 \le x - y \le 2\}$$

as depicted in Fig. 1(a) and 1(b). Then, $\langle \mathcal{A} + \mathcal{B} \rangle$ is an abstract object in $\mathsf{Int} + \mathsf{Parallelotope}$ such that

$$\gamma(\langle \mathcal{A} + \mathcal{B} \rangle) = \{0 \le x \le 3, 0 \le y \le \infty, x - y \le 3\}$$

as depicted in Fig. 1(c). It is neither an interval nor a parallelotope nor a zonotope (since it is unbounded and has constraints on three different linear forms).

3.1 Ordering

The subset ordering $\subseteq$ on the concrete domain induces a pre-order $\le^{\mathsf{A}+\mathsf{B}}$ on $\mathsf{A} + \mathsf{B}$. This is not a partial order, since different objects in $\mathsf{A} + \mathsf{B}$ represent the same concrete object. For example, in $\mathsf{Int} + \mathsf{Int}$, the objects $\langle [0, 1] + [0, 1] \rangle$ and $\langle [0, 0] + [0, 2] \rangle$ both represent the interval $[0, 2] \subseteq \mathbb{R}$.

Moreover, given objects $\langle A+B \rangle$ and $\langle A'+B' \rangle$, deciding whether $\langle A+B \rangle \le^{\mathsf{A}+\mathsf{B}} \langle A' + B' \rangle$ is not an easy task. There are some sufficient conditions which ensure the required property, such as $A \le^{\mathsf{A}} A'$ and $B \le^{\mathsf{B}} B'$. When A and B are both abstractions of a domain C (often C is the polyhedra domain), then we may compute, on the domain C, the representation of A, B, A', B', the Minkowski sums $A + B$ and $A' + B'$, and check if the ordering holds. However, in the general case, an algorithm for deciding $\le^{\mathsf{A}+\mathsf{B}}$ must be especially designed for a given instance of the sum combinator. In any case, we will show later that this is not required for the analysis.

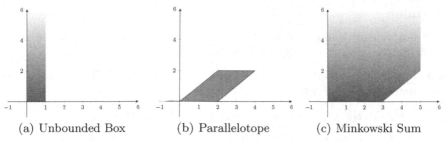

(a) Unbounded Box	(b) Parallelotope	(c) Minkowski Sum

Fig. 1. Minkowski sum of a box and a parallelotope

3.2 Sum of Standard Domains

The following proposition summarizes some basic results when combining intervals, zonotopes, parallelotopes and polyhedra. It is worth noting that, in general, for an abstract domain A we have that A+A $\neq$ A. This is the case for the abstract domain of parallelotopes, since the sum of two parallelotopes is not, in general, a parallelotope, as shown in Figure 1. Moreover, given two domains A and B such that A is an abstraction of B, it may well happen that the sum of A and B is more concrete than both domains, as shown in the next theorem.

Theorem 1. *The abstract domains* Int, Zonotope *and* Polyhedra *are closed by Minkowski sum, that is:*

- Int + Int = Int
- Zonotope + Zonotope = Zonotope
  Polyhedra + Polyhedra = Polyhedra

Moreover, the following inclusions are strict:

- Zonotope $\subsetneq$ Int + Zonotope
- Parallelotope $\subsetneq$ Int + Parallelotope
- Parallelotope $\subsetneq$ Parallelotope + Parallelotope

Figure 1 shows the counterexamples for the second part of the theorem. Note that, the box in Figure 1(a) is also a parallelotope, and the parallelotope in Figure 1(b) is also a zonotope, while their sum fails to be a zonotope.

4 Abstract Operators

We now consider the operations on $\wp(\mathbb{R}^n)$ commonly used when defining the collecting semantics of imperative programming languages, and for each of them we introduce a correct approximation. We show that some abstract operators are γ-complete, provided the corresponding abstract operators on the component domain are also γ-complete.

In the following we fix two numerical abstract domains A and B and their sum A + B.

4.1   Union

Abstract union on the sum domain can be defined component-wise from the abstract unions of the two original domains.

Definition 3 (Abstract union). *Given $A_1, A_2 \in \mathsf{A}$ and $B_1, B_2 \in \mathsf{B}$, we define the abstract union $\cup^{\mathsf{A}+\mathsf{B}}$ as:*

$$\langle A_1 + B_1 \rangle \cup^{\mathsf{A}+\mathsf{B}} \langle A_2 + B_2 \rangle = \langle (A_1 \cup^{\mathsf{A}} A_2) + (B_1 \cup^{\mathsf{B}} B_2) \rangle \ .$$

Theorem 2. *The abstract union is correct.*

4.2   Linear Transformations

A linear (homogeneous) assignment has the form $x_i := \boldsymbol{a}^T \boldsymbol{x}$ where $\boldsymbol{a} \in \mathbb{R}^n$ and $\boldsymbol{x}$ is the vector of program variables. Linear assignments (even multiple linear assignments) may be represented as linear transformations in $\mathbb{R}^n$. If M is a square real matrix of order n and $\mathcal{A} \subseteq \mathbb{R}^n$, we consider the operator

$$M \cdot \mathcal{A} = \{ M\boldsymbol{a} \mid \boldsymbol{a} \in \mathcal{A} \} \ .$$

The abstraction of $\cdot$ in $\mathsf{A} + \mathsf{B}$ may be easily recovered by its abstraction on A and B.

Definition 4 (Linear assignment). *Given $A \in \mathsf{A}$, $B \in \mathsf{B}$ and $M \in \mathbb{R}(n, n)$ we define the abstract linear transformation as:*

$$M \cdot^{\mathsf{A}+\mathsf{B}} \langle A + B \rangle = \langle M \cdot^{\mathsf{A}} A + M \cdot^{\mathsf{B}} B \rangle \ .$$

Theorem 3. *The abstract linear assignment operator is correct. Moreover, it is γ-complete if the corresponding abstract operators on A and B are γ-complete.*

4.3   Translations

Given $\boldsymbol{b} \in \mathbb{R}^n$ and $\mathcal{A} \subseteq \mathbb{R}^n$, consider the translation operator

$$\mathcal{A} + \boldsymbol{b} = \mathcal{A} + \{\boldsymbol{b}\} = \{ \boldsymbol{a} + \boldsymbol{b} \mid \boldsymbol{a} \in \mathcal{A} \} \ .$$

As for linear transformations, it is easy to determine a correct abstraction of $+$ in the abstract domain $\mathsf{A} + \mathsf{B}$ starting from correct abstractions in A and B, but there is not a single abstract version which could be considered the canonical one.

Definition 5 (Abstract translation). *Given $A \in \mathsf{A}$, $B \in \mathsf{B}$, $\boldsymbol{b} \in \mathbb{R}^n$ and $w \in \mathbb{R}$, we define the abstract sum (weighted by w) as*

$$\langle A + B \rangle +_w^{\mathsf{A}+\mathsf{B}} \boldsymbol{b} = \langle (A +^{\mathsf{A}} w\boldsymbol{b}) + (B +^{\beta} (1 - w)\boldsymbol{b}) \rangle \ .$$

In this definition, the weight w determines in which part of the two abstract objects A and B we need to apply the translation. It may be applied entirely on A ($w = 1$), entirely in B ($w = 0$) or divided between them.

Theorem 4. *The abstract translation operator is correct. Moreover, it is γ-complete if the corresponding abstract operators on A and B are γ-complete.*

4.4   Non-deterministic Assignment

Given $i \in \{1, \ldots, n\}$, we define the concrete operator $\mathsf{forget}_i : \wp(\mathbb{R}^n) \to \wp(\mathbb{R}^n)$ as

$$\mathsf{forget}_i(\mathcal{A}) = \{x \in \mathbb{R}^n \mid a \in \mathcal{A} \wedge \forall j \neq i.\ x_i = a_i\}\ .$$

This simulates the effect of a non-deterministic assignment $x_i := ?$.

Definition 6. *Given* $i \in \{1, \ldots, n\}$, *we define the non-deterministic assignment as*

$$\mathsf{forget}_i^{\mathsf{A+B}}(\langle A + B \rangle) = \langle \mathsf{forget}_i^{\mathsf{A}}(A) + B \rangle$$

or

$$\mathsf{forget}_i^{\mathsf{A+B}}(\langle A + B \rangle) = \langle A + \mathsf{forget}_i^{\mathsf{B}}(B) \rangle\ .$$

Both definitions are correct, and the choice between them follows by heuristic considerations. We will talk about this later in the paper.

Theorem 5. *The abstract non-deterministic assignment is correct. Moreover, it is γ-complete if the corresponding abstract operator on A (for the first form) or B (for the second form) is γ-complete.*

4.5   Refinement by Linear Inequality

The concrete refinement by linear inequality $\mathsf{refine}_{(a,b)}$, with $a \in \mathbb{R}^n$ and $b \in \mathbb{R}$, is the intersection of a subset of $\mathbb{R}^n$ with an half-space. Formally:

$$\mathsf{refine}_{(a,b)}(\mathcal{A}) = \mathcal{A} \cap \{x \in \mathbb{R}^n \mid a^T x \leq b\}\ .$$

In the following, we extend this definition to the case $b = \pm\infty$ with the obvious interpretation.

Definition 7. *Given* $a \in \mathbb{R}^n$ *and* $b \in \mathbb{R}$, *we define the abstract refinement by linear inequality as*

$$\mathsf{refine}_{(a,b)}^{\mathsf{A+B}}(\langle A + B \rangle) = \langle \mathsf{refine}_{(a,b-d_2)}^{\mathsf{A}}(A) + \mathsf{refine}_{(a,b-d_1)}^{\mathsf{B}}(B) \rangle$$

where $d_1, d_2 \in \overline{\mathbb{R}}$ *such that* $d_1 \leq \inf_{x \in A} a^T x$ *and* $d_2 \leq \inf_{x \in B} a^T x$. *Moreover, we define*

$$\mathsf{refine}_{(a,+\infty)}^{\mathsf{A+B}}(\langle A + B \rangle) = (\langle A + B \rangle)$$

$$\mathsf{refine}_{(a,-\infty)}^{\mathsf{A+B}}(\langle A + B \rangle) = C$$

where C is any correct approximation of $\emptyset$ (i.e., any value in $\mathsf{A} + \mathsf{B}$).

This operator needs a way to determine a lower bound for the value that a linear form may assume in every abstract object of the domains A and B. If this is not possible, both d_1 and d_2 may be considered to be $-\infty$, and the refine operator turns out to be the identity.

Theorem 6. *The operator* $\mathsf{refine}_{(a,b)}^{\mathsf{A+B}}$ *is correct.*

```
i = 0
x = 0
y = 0
while (i <= 4) {
    i = i+1
    if (?) x = i−1 else x = i
    if (?) y = i−1 else y = i
}
```

(a) Example program.

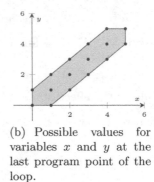

(b) Possible values for variables x and y at the last program point of the loop.

Fig. 2. Example program

4.6 Widening and Narrowing

Given $A_1, A_2 \in A$ and $B_1, B_2 \in B$ we can use the widening/narrowing operators of the individual numerical abstract domains to devise widening/narrowing operators for the Minkowski sum.

Definition 8. *The abstract widening for* $A + B$ *is defined as*

$$\langle A_1 + B_1 \rangle \nabla^{A+B} \langle A_2 + B_2 \rangle = \langle A_1 \nabla^A A_2 + B_1 \nabla^B B_2 \rangle$$

and the abstract narrowing for $A + B$ *is defined as*

$$\langle A_1 + B_1 \rangle \triangle^{A+B} \langle A_2 + B_2 \rangle = \langle A_1 \triangle^A A_2 + B_1 \triangle^B B_2 \rangle \ .$$

Theorem 7. *The abstract operator* ∇^{A+B} *is a widening and* $\triangle^{A+B}$ *is a narrowing.*

Note that widening is defined component-wise. This means that, at widening points, the increasing chains we get are of the form

$$\langle A_0 + B_0 \rangle \leq^{A+B} \langle A_1 + B_1 \rangle \leq^{A+B} \langle A_2 + B_2 \rangle \leq^{A+B} \ldots$$

with $A_0 \leq^A A_1 \leq^A A_2 \ldots$ and $B_0 \leq^A B_1 \leq^A B_2 \ldots$. Both the chains of A_i's and B_i's eventually stop increasing, since they are constrained by ∇^A and ∇^B. Therefore, if we can decide $\leq^A$ and $\leq^B$, then we known when to stop the analysis even if, in the general case, we cannot decide $\leq^{A+B}$.

5 An Example

Consider the program in Figure 2(a) and the graph in Figure 2(b) which depicts the possible values for variables x and y at the end of the loop's body. The convex hull of these points, which is the shaded area in the figure, may be described as the sum of the box $\{i = 0, -1 \leq x \leq 0, -1 \leq y \leq 0\}$ and the parallelotope $\{1 \leq i \leq 5, x = i, y = i\}$. Using the domain Int + Parallelotope, we are able to

```
i = x = y = 0
[i = 0, x = 0, y = 0] + [i = 0, x = 0, y = 0]
while (i <= 4) {
    [i = 0, x = 0, y = 0] + [i = 0, x = 0, y = 0]
    i = i+1
    [i = 0, x = 0, y = 0] + [i = 1, x = 0, y = 0]
    if (?)
        x = i−1
        [i = 0, x = −1, y = 0] + [i = 1, x = i, y = 0]
    else
        x = i
        [i = 0, x = 0, y = 0] + [i = 1, x = i, y = 0]
    [i = 0, −1 ≤ x ≤ 0, y = 0] + [i = 1, x = i, y = 0]
    if (?) y = i−1 else y = i
    [i = 0, −1 ≤ x ≤ 0, −1 ≤ y ≤ 0] + [i = 1, x = i, y = i]
}
```

Fig. 3. Annotated program after the 1st loop iteration

infer this property, although we need to refine the raw domain operators with heuristics specifically tailored for this specific combination.

The main tunable aspect of the operators we have described in the previous section is the value of the weight w in translations and abstractions. Choosing w randomly may lead to very bad precision. For the moment, assume we choose $w = 0$ for the increment $i = i + 1$ and $w = 1$ for all the other assignments. Figure 3 shows the candidate invariants reached after a single iteration of the while loop. Using the standard domain operators, before entering the while loop we get the invariant $\{i = 0, x = 0, y = 0\} + \{i = 0, x = 0, y = 0\}$ which is preserved by the loop's guard. The increment to i, according to the chosen value $w = 0$, yields $\{i = 0, x = 0, y = 0\} + \{i = 1, x = 0, y = 0\}$.

The true branch of the first non-deterministic conditional statement leads to $\{i = 0, x = −1, y = 0\} + \{i = 1, x = i, y = 0\}$ while the else branch leads to $\{i = 0, x = 0, y = 0\} + \{i = 1, x = i, y = 0\}$. The component-wise union gives $\{i = 0, −1 ≤ x ≤ 0, y = 0\} + \{i = 1, x = i, y = 0\}$. Repeating the same argument for the second conditional statement we get $\{i = 0, −1 ≤ x ≤ 0, −1 ≤ y ≤ 0\} + \{i = 1, x = i, y = i\}$.

At the second iteration, the previous while invariant $\{i = 0, x = 0, y = 0\} + \{i = 0, x = 0, y = 0\}$ is widened with $\{i = 0, −1 ≤ x ≤ 0, −1 ≤ y ≤ 0\} + \{i = 1, x = i, y = i\}$ to get $\{i = 0, −\infty < x ≤ 0, −\infty < y ≤ 0\} + \{0 ≤ i < \infty, x = i, y = i\}$. This is the fix-point of the ascending chain. The subsequent descending phase yields the while invariant $\{i = 0, −1 ≤ x ≤ 0, −1 ≤ y ≤ 0\} + \{0 ≤ i ≤ 5, x = i, y = i\}$. The program with the final annotations is shown in Figure 4. The invariant at the last program point in the loop is the one we were looking for.

Crucial in obtaining the desired result is that the parallelotope component encodes the unsound relationship $i = x = y$ while the box component contains the deviation w.r.t. this line which makes the result correct. If we use $w = 1$

$$i = x = y = 0$$
$$[i = 0, x = 0, y = 0] + [i = 0, x = 0, y = 0]$$
while (i <= 4) {
$$[i = 0, -1 \le x \le 0, -1 \le y \le 0] + [0 \le i \le 4, x = i, y = i]$$
$$i = i{+}1$$
$$[i = 0, -1 \le x \le 0, -1 \le y \le 0] + [1 \le i \le 5, x = i{-}1, y = i{-}1]$$
  if (?)
    x = i{-}1
$$[i = 0, x = -1, -1 \le y \le 0] + [1 \le i \le 5, x = i, y = i - 1]$$
  else
    x = i
$$[i = 0, x = 0, -1 \le y \le 0] + [1 \le i \le 5, x = i, y = i - 1]$$
$$[i = 0, -1 \le x \le 0, -1 \le y \le 0] + [1 \le i \le 5, x = i, y = i - 1]$$
  if (?) y = i{-}1 **else** y = i
$$[i = 0, -1 \le x \le 0, -1 \le y \le 0] + [1 \le i \le 5, x = i, y = i]$$

}

Fig. 4. Annotated program at the end of the analysis. The highlighted invariant is the one sought after.

for $i = i + 1$ instead of $w = 0$, the initial invariant $i = x = y = 0$ for the parallelotope component remains stable for the entire while loop, and all the analysis actually proceeds on the interval domain. The result is the much less precise $\{1 \le i \le 5, 0 \le x \le 5, 0 \le y \le 5\} + \{i = 0, x = i, y = i\}$. On the contrary, if we use $w = 0$ for all the assignments, the analysis actually proceeds in the parallelotope domain. The result depends on the heuristics used for parallelotopes. The Jandom static analyzer determines the following: $\{i = 0, x = 0, y = 0\} + \{1 \le i \le 6, 1.0 \le -i + x \le 0.0, -1.0 \le -i + y \le 0.0\}$. The result is qualitatively better than the one on intervals, but not as good as the one with get with the correct choices for w.

The problem is how to determine an heuristic to choose the value of w for the assignment operators. Our idea is to use the parallelotope domain to capture an "ideal" relationships between variables, and resort to the interval domain for capturing the deviation w.r.t. the ideal behavior. This means that, for a non invertible assignment $x_i = \boldsymbol{a}^T \boldsymbol{x} + b$ we use $w = 1$, in the hope that $x_i - \boldsymbol{a}^T \boldsymbol{x}$ has an almost constant value in a program point, modulo some variability captured by the interval domain. For all other assignments we use $w = 0$. In the program of Figure 2(a) this heuristic yields the optimal choice we have shown before.

6   Precision of Abstract Operators

In this section we reason about the precision of the abstract operators of the sum domain. We will see that even very precise operators (such as translations) are problematic due to the fact that many different representation exists for the same abstract object, and that the imprecise operators gives different results for different representations. Finally, we explicitly discuss the domain Int + Parallelotope.

6.1   An Approximate Ordering

The subset ordering $\subseteq$ in $\wp(\mathbb{R}^n)$ induces the pre-order $\leq^{A+B}$ on $A+B$. However, many of the operators we have defined are not monotonic w.r.t. $\leq^{A+B}$. This makes difficult to reason about the precision of analysis. We do not even know if, improving the precision of one operator, actually improves the precision of the result. However, it is possible to define a coarser ordering on $A+B$, component-wise as

$$\langle A_1 + B_1 \rangle \sqsubseteq^{A+B} \langle A_2 + B_2 \rangle \iff \exists \boldsymbol{p} \in \mathbb{R}^n \text{ s.t.}$$
$$\gamma(A_1) \subseteq \gamma(A_2) + \boldsymbol{p} \text{ and } \gamma(B_1) \subseteq \gamma(B_2) - \boldsymbol{p} \ .$$

It turns out that $\langle A_1 + B_1 \rangle \sqsubseteq^{A+B} \langle A_2 + B_2 \rangle$ implies $\langle A_1 + B_1 \rangle \leq^{A+B} \langle A_2 + B_2 \rangle$. Moreover, all operators in Section 4 (but widening and narrowing) are monotone w.r.t. $\sqsubseteq^{A+B}$. Therefore, if we replace an abstract operator with another one which is more precise w.r.t. the $\sqsubseteq^{A+B}$ ordering, we are sure we are not going to loose precision globally for the entire analysis, modulo the effect of the non-monotonic widening and narrowing operators.

6.2   Abstraction Function

Particularly critical, in the general definition of the sum domain, is the fact that we do not have a good abstraction function. Actually, a family of correct abstraction functions may be defined easily as follows.

Theorem 8. *Given abstract domain* A *and* B *with abstraction functions* α^A *and* α^B, *consider a weight* $w \in \mathbb{R}$. *Then*

$$\alpha_w^{A+B}(\mathcal{C}) = \langle \alpha^A(w\mathcal{C}) + \alpha^B((1-w)\mathcal{C}) \rangle$$

is a correct abstraction function for any $w \in \mathbb{R}$.

However, in the general case $\alpha_w(\mathcal{C})$ is not a minimal abstraction of $\mathcal{C}$ for any value of w. Even if domains A and B have good abstraction functions α^A and α^B, the abstraction function α^{A+B} may have, in general, a bad precision. For example, consider Figure 2(b) and let $\mathcal{C}$ be the set of points in the shaded area. Although $\mathcal{C}$ may be described as the sum of a box and a parallelotope, there is no choice of weight w such that $\alpha_w^{A+B}(\mathcal{C})$ returns such as description. Actually, we have

$$\alpha_w^{A+B}(\mathcal{C}) = \langle A + B \rangle$$

with

$$A = \{0 \leq x \leq 5w, 0 \leq y \leq 5w\}$$
$$B = \{-(1-w) \leq x - y \leq 1 - w, 0 \leq x + y \leq 10(1-w)\}$$

and $\gamma^{A+B}(\alpha_w^{A+B}(\mathcal{C})) \supsetneq \mathcal{C}$.

In abstraction interpretation, the abstraction function is often used to guide the definition of the abstract operators. If $f : C \to C$ is a concrete operator, $f^A = \alpha^A \circ f \circ \gamma^A$ is a correct abstract operator. However, since α^{A+B} may have such a bad precision, this approach is not applicable for the sum domain. While for most concrete operators we were nonetheless able to find good abstract counterparts, this is definitively not easy for linear refinement.

6.3   Linear Refinement

Consider the sum domain $\mathsf{Int}+\mathsf{Int}$. The box $\mathcal{B} = [0,2] \times [0,2]$ may be described in $\mathsf{Int}+\mathsf{Int}$ as $S = \langle [0,1] \times [0,1] + [0,1] \times [0,1] \rangle$. Assume we want to refine S with the linear inequality $x_1 \leq 1$, i.e., we want to compute $\mathsf{refine}_{(a,b)}(S)$ with $a = (1,0)^T$ and $b = 1$. The result is the box $[0,1] \times [0,2]$ which may be represented optimally as, for example, $\langle [0,1/2] \times [0,1] + [0,1/2] \times [0,1] \rangle$.

However, applying the definition for abstract refinement in Section 4, we get a much coarser result. Let $\mathcal{A} = [0,1] \times [0,1]$. Note that $\inf_{\boldsymbol{x}\in\mathcal{A}} \boldsymbol{a}^T\boldsymbol{x} = 0 = \inf_{\boldsymbol{x}\in\mathcal{B}} \boldsymbol{a}^T\boldsymbol{x} = 0$. By choosing $d_1 = d_2 = 0$, we get $\mathsf{refine}^{\mathsf{Int}}_{(a,b-d_1)}(\mathcal{A}) = \mathsf{refine}^{\mathsf{Int}}_{(a,b-d_2)}(\mathcal{A}) = \mathcal{A}$. Hence $\mathsf{refine}^{\mathsf{Int}+\mathsf{Int}}_{(a,b)}(\langle\mathcal{A} + \mathcal{A}\rangle) = \langle\mathcal{A} + \mathcal{A}\rangle$.

Here the problem is caused by the high redundancy in $\mathsf{Int}+\mathsf{Int}$. The constraint $x_1 \leq 2$ in $\mathcal{B}$ is divided between the two's $x_1 \leq 1$ in $\langle\mathcal{A} + \mathcal{A}\rangle$. The same may happen in $\mathsf{Int} + \mathsf{Parallelotope}$ when the parallelotope has some equations of the kind $x_i \leq b$. Therefore, in this sum, the parallelotope component should be tweaked to avoid generating constraints parallel to the axis.

Another problem caused by linear refinement is with unbounded abstract object. Consider in $\mathsf{Int}+\mathsf{Parallelotope}$ the full $\mathbb{R}^n$, represented as $\langle\mathbb{R}^n + \mathbb{R}^n\rangle$. If we want to refine with $\boldsymbol{a}^T\boldsymbol{x} \leq b$, for any $\boldsymbol{a}$ and b, we get $\inf_{\boldsymbol{x}\in\mathbb{R}^n} \boldsymbol{a}^T\boldsymbol{x} = -\infty$, hence $\mathsf{refine}_{(a,b)}(\langle\mathbb{R}^n + \mathbb{R}^n\rangle) = \langle\mathsf{refine}_{(a,+\infty)}(\mathbb{R}^n) + \mathsf{refine}_{(a,+\infty)}(\mathbb{R}^n)\rangle = \langle\mathbb{R}^n + \mathbb{R}^n\rangle$. Note that, on the contrary, if we represent $\mathbb{R}^n$ as $\langle\{0\} + \mathbb{R}^n\rangle$, then refinement works much better, essentially performing the refinement on the second component. Here $\{0\}$ may be replaced by any one-point element without affecting precision.

In some way, both problems are related and could be solved by some form of normalization which, before applying linear refinement $\mathsf{refine}_{(a,b)}$ to $\langle A + B \rangle$, transform $\langle A + B \rangle$ to $\langle A' + B' \rangle$ with the same concretization but minimizing the range of $\{\boldsymbol{a}^T\boldsymbol{x} \mid \boldsymbol{x} \in \gamma(A')\}$. There is no general method to perform such a normalization, which should be devised specifically for each instance of the sum domain.

6.4   Union and Widening

Abstract union may also be quite imprecise. Consider the abstract values $A_1 = \langle\{0\}+\{0\}\rangle$ and $A_2 = \langle\{a\}+\{0\}\rangle$ on the domain $\mathsf{Int}+\mathsf{Parallelotope}$, where $\boldsymbol{a}$ is any vector in $\mathbb{R}^n$. The concrete union $\gamma(A_1)\cup\gamma(A_2)$ is the two point set $\{0, a\}$. In the $\mathsf{Int} + \mathsf{Parallelotope}$ domain, its optimal representation is $\langle\{0\} + \mathcal{L}\rangle$ where $\mathcal{L}$ is the segment from $\boldsymbol{0}$ to $\boldsymbol{a}$. However, the abstract union gives $A_1\cup^{\mathsf{Int}+\mathsf{Int}} A_2 = \langle\mathcal{B}+\{0\}\rangle$ where $\mathcal{B}$ is the box with corners $\boldsymbol{0}$ and $\boldsymbol{a}$. This is (except for the case $\boldsymbol{a} = \boldsymbol{0}$) much worse than the optimal result.

The problem arises from the fact that abstract union cannot "restructure" the representation to use the strong points of the component domains. We believe that designing a more precise union operator is a difficult challenge. Widening, being defined component-wise as union, has similar problems.

6.5   Other Operators

The other operators are generally much more precise than linear refinement.

non deterministic assignment) Many domains have γ-complete non-deterministic assignments. When this happens, it is better to apply non deterministic assignment to this component. If the other component has a γ-complete assignment of the constant 0 to a variable, we may refine forget_i as follows:

$$\mathsf{forget}_i^{A+B}(\langle A + B \rangle) = \langle \mathsf{forget}_i^{A}(A) + M \cdot^{B} B \rangle$$

where M is the matrix whose effect is to assign 0 to the i-th variable. This is better since it smaller w.r.t. $\sqsubseteq^{A+B}$ than the one defined in Section 4.

linear assignments) This operator does not cause precision problems.

translations) Although this operator is quite precise, the choice of the weight w is crucial in obtaining good results. This is because of the imprecision of the abstract union operator. An example of this phenomenon has been shown in Section 5.

6.6   The Domain Int + Parallelotope

The domain Int + Parallelotope is one of the simplest non trivial domains which may be obtained with the sum combinator. Since translations are γ-complete both in Int and Parallelotope, the same holds for translations on Int+Parallelotope. For the same reason, non-deterministic assignment is γ-complete.

As we said before, deciding whether $\langle B_1 + P_1 \rangle \leq \langle B_2 + P_2 \rangle$ may be easily implemented by representing sums as convex polyhedra, and checking set inclusion. On the contrary, improving the abstraction function is harder. Even if the abstraction is firstly computed over polyhedra, it remains the problem of representing a polyhedron in the most effective way as sum of a box and a parallelotope. Solving the abstraction problem could lead to the design of better operators for union and refinement, which also suffer from great imprecision.

We have implemented a prototype of the sum combinator in the static analyzer Jandom and did some preliminary test of the Int + Parallelotope domain on the ALICe benchmarks [14] (plus some additional test programs). The test-suite comprises a total of 105 models with 316 program points. We have compared the results on the sum with the results on the parallelotopes (the comparison with the interval domain gives very similar results). With respect to the parallelotope domain, the sum is more precise on 53 program points and less precise in 72 program points, while in 76 cases the results are incomparable. We believe that these preliminary tests are very promising:

- The regressions w.r.t. the component domains were expected and are mainly due to the fact that some operators on the sum, like union, introduce a loss of precision.
- In addition to the cases where sum is better, we have many cases with incomparable results. This shows that the sum combinator is able to improve at least one constraint in many program points. Combining the results on the sum domain with the (incomparable) results on the component domain, we obtain more precise results in more than 40% of the program points.
- No special code has been written for the Int + Parallelotope domain: all the operators are the generic ones of the sum combinator, and the only heuristic applied is choosing w in translations as we have done in Section 5. Nonetheless, the domain was able to produce new constraints. This is in contrast with other combinators, such as reduced product, where new results always need some specific code.

We still need to do more experiments and find better heuristics, but the fact that we have found many new constraints is encouraging.

6.7 Analysis Kickoff and Non-deterministic Assignments

Some numerical abstract domains, such as template parallelotope, template polyhedra and zonotopes, need a special treatment in the starting phase of the analysis. For instance, consider the domain of template polyhedra with constraints $x + y$ and $x - y$, and assume that we start the analysis of a program whose first statement is the assignment $x = 0$. Since we cannot represent this information with the given template, we loose the information about the variable x. A similar problem arises with zonotopes, where we cannot represent an unbounded value for y. Such a situation can be easily managed using the sum combinator, by considering the sum with a simple abstract domain, like intervals, which is exploited in the starting phase of the analysis.

More generally, we can use the sum combinator to enrich a domain which may only represent bounded objects (such as the zonotope domain) summing to it a simple domain able to represent unbounded objects (such as the interval domain). The resulting domain (Int + Zonotope in our example) would be able to handle unbounded objects and non-deterministic assignment with greater precision.

7 Conclusion

We have described the theoretical foundation of the sum of abstract domains. We have defined generic abstract operators which can be easily implemented exploiting the corresponding operators on the original domains and we have discussed possible improvements.

For the sum of intervals and parallelotopes we have also discussed some heuristics to enhance the precision of the analysis and presented preliminary experimental results.

References

1. Amato, G., Di Nardo Di Maio, S., Scozzari, F.: Numerical static analysis with soot. In: Proceedings of the ACM SIGPLAN International Workshop on State of the Art in Java Program Analysis, SOAP (2013)
2. Amato, G., Scozzari, F.: Jandom. https://github.com/jandom-devel/Jandom
3. Amato, G., Scozzari, F.: The abstract domain of parallelotopes. In: Proceedings of the NSAD 2012. ENTCS, vol. 287, pp. 17–28 (2012)
4. Amato, G., Scozzari, F.: Localizing widening and narrowing. In: Logozzo, F., Fähndrich, M. (eds.) Static Analysis. LNCS, vol. 7935, pp. 25–42. Springer, Heidelberg (2013)
5. Cortesi, A., Le Charlier, B., Van Hentenryck, P.: Combinations of abstract domains for logic programming: Open product and generic pattern construction. Science of Computer Programmming **38**(1–3), 27–71 (2000)
6. Cortesi, A., Filé, G., Winsborough, W.W.: The quotient of an abstract interpretation. Theoretical Computer Science **202**(1–2), 163–192 (1998)
7. Cousot, P., Cousot, R.: Static determination of dynamic properties of programs. In: Proc. 2nd Int'l Symposium on Programming, pp. 106–130 (1976)
8. Cousot, P., Cousot, R.: Abstract interpretation: a unified lattice model for static analysis of programs by construction or approximation of fixpoints. In: Proceedings of the POPL 1977, pp. 238–252 (1977)
9. Cousot, P., Cousot, R.: Systematic design of program analysis frameworks. In: Proceedings of the POPL 1979, pp. 269–282 (1979)
10. Cousot, P., Cousot, R.: Abstract interpretation frameworks. Journal of Logic and Computation **2**(4), 511–549 (1992)
11. Cousot, P., Halbwachs, N.: Automatic discovery of linear restraints among variables of a program. In: Proceedings of the POPL 1978, pp. 84–97 (1978)
12. Ghorbal, K., Ivančić, F., Balakrishnan, G., Maeda, N., Gupta, A.: Donut domains: efficient non-convex domains for abstract interpretation. In: Kuncak, V., Rybalchenko, A. (eds.) VMCAI 2012. LNCS, vol. 7148, pp. 235–250. Springer, Heidelberg (2012)
13. Goubault, E., Putot, S., Védrine, F.: Modular static analysis with zonotopes. In: Miné, A., Schmidt, D. (eds.) SAS 2012. LNCS, vol. 7460, pp. 24–40. Springer, Heidelberg (2012)
14. Maisonneuve, V., Hermant, O., Irigoin, F.: Alice: a framework to improve affine loop invariant computation. In: 5th Workshop on Invariant Generation (2014)
15. Miné, A.: The octagon abstract domain. Higher-Order and Symbolic Computation **19**(1), 31–100 (2006)
16. Sankaranarayanan, S., Sipma, H.B., Manna, Z.: Scalable analysis of linear systems using mathematical programming. In: Cousot, R. (ed.) VMCAI 2005. LNCS, vol. 3385, pp. 25–41. Springer, Heidelberg (2005)

Reachability Preservation Based Parameter Synthesis for Timed Automata

Étienne André[1]([⊠]), Giuseppe Lipari[2], Hoang Gia Nguyen[1], and Youcheng Sun[3]

[1] Université Paris 13, Sorbonne Paris Cité, LIPN, CNRS, UMR 7030, Paris, France
Etienne.Andre@lipn.fr
[2] CRIStAL – UMR 9189, Université de Lille, USR 3380 CNRS, Lille, France
[3] Scuola Superiore Sant'Anna, Pisa, Italy

Abstract. The synthesis of timing parameters consists in deriving conditions on the timing constants of a concurrent system such that it meets its specification. Parametric timed automata are a powerful formalism for parameter synthesis, although most problems are undecidable. We first address here the following reachability preservation problem: given a reference parameter valuation and a (bad) control state, do there exist other parameter valuations that reach this control state iff the reference parameter valuation does? We show that this problem is undecidable, and introduce a procedure that outputs a possibly underapproximated answer. We then show that our procedure can efficiently replace the behavioral cartography to partition a bounded parameter subspace into good and bad subparts; furthermore, our procedure can even outperform the classical bad-state driven parameter synthesis semi-algorithm, especially when distributed on a cluster.

1 Introduction

The design of critical real-time systems is notoriously error-prone, and requires formal verification to assess the absence of undesired behaviors. The theory of timed automata (TA) [1] provided in the past two decades designers with a powerful formalism to formally verify real-time systems. TA extend finite-state automata with clocks that can be compared with integers in guards and invariants. Unfortunately, the classical definition of TA is not tailored to verify systems only partially specified, especially when the value of some timing constants is not yet known. The synthesis of timing parameters consists in deriving conditions on the timing constants of a concurrent system such that it meets its specification. Parametric timed automata (PTA) [2] extend TA by allowing the use of parameters (i.e., unknown constants) in place of integer constants in the model.

This work was partially supported by a BQR grant "SynPaTiC" and by the ANR national research program "PACS" (ANR-2014).

© Springer International Publishing Switzerland 2015
K. Havelund et al. (Eds.): NFM 2015, LNCS 9058, pp. 50–65, 2015.
DOI: 10.1007/978-3-319-17524-9_5

Related Work. The expressive power of PTA comes at the cost of the undecidability of almost all interesting problems. The EF-emptiness problem[1] ("does there exist a parameter valuation such that a control state is reachable?") is undecidable if the model contains as little as three parameterized clocks [2]. Research around PTA since then consisted mainly in either exhibiting subclasses of PTA for which interesting problems become decidable, or devising efficient semi-algorithms that would terminate "often enough" to be useful. A famous subclass of PTA is L/U PTA [8,13] where each parameter can be used only either as upper bounds or as lower bounds, and for which the EF-emptiness problem becomes decidable. In [8], further problems have been shown to be decidable for L/U PTA, including the emptiness and the universality problem for infinite runs properties ("do all parameter valuations have an infinite accepting run?"), for integer parameter valuations. In [14], however, it was shown that the solution to the EF-synthesis problem ("find all parameter valuations such that a control state is reachable") for L/U PTA cannot be represented as a finite union of polyhedra, hence strongly limiting the practical interest of L/U PTA. Orthogonal to syntactical restrictions on the model is the search for restrictions on the parameter domain: in [14], an algorithm is proposed to synthesize integer parameter valuations in a bounded domain. This is of course decidable, and the authors devise two symbolic algorithms that perform better than enumeration.

More practical research on PTA include the development of tools (e.g., Romo [16], IMITATOR [6]) and their application to several fields such as hardware verification (e.g., [10]) and parametric schedulability analysis (e.g., [12]). In [3], we proposed the inverse method IM, a procedure that takes advantage of a reference parameter valuation and generalizes it in the form of a convex constraint, such that the discrete (linear-time) behavior of the system is preserved. In [5], we proposed the behavioral cartography BC: by iterating IM on integer points in a bounded parameter domain, we decompose this domain into constraints such that, for all parameter valuations in each constraint, the discrete behavior is the same. Then, BC can give a (possibly incomplete) solution to the EF-synthesis problem, by returning the union of all constraints for which the desired control state is reachable.

Contribution. In this work, our main goal is to address the EF-synthesis problem. Instead of attacking the state space exploration in a brute force manner (like [2, 14]), we propose to perform several explorations of smaller size, taking advantage of reference valuations in the line of the inverse method. More in details, our contributions are as follows:

1. We first address the following *reachability preservation problem* for PTA: given a reference parameter valuation π and a control state, do there exist other parameter valuations that reach this control state iff π does? We show that this problem is undecidable, and we introduce a procedure PRP (parametric reachability preservation) that gives a (possibly incomplete) answer.

---

[1] "EF" comes from the CTL syntax and stands for "exists finally".

2. Then, we show that PRP can efficiently replace IM in the behavioral cartography to partition a bounded parameter subspace into good and bad subparts, and give a solution to the EF-synthesis problem.
3. We then compare the PRP-based cartography with the classical parameter synthesis semi-algorithm "EFsynth" [2,14] that solves the EF-synthesis problem: not only PRP gives a more precise result, but it also performs surprisingly well, despite its repeated analyses. Comparisons are performed using parametric schedulability problems for real-time systems.
4. We finally briefly discuss a distributed version of PRP, that is faster and almost always outperforms EFsynth.

Outline. Section 2 recalls PTA, decision problems and existing results. Section 3.1 defines the *reachability preservation problem* and proves its undecidability; Section 3.2 introduces PRP and proves its correctness; Section 3.3 shows that PRP can be used to solve the EF-synthesis problem. Section 4 discusses a distributed version of PRP, and Section 5 describes an experimental comparison with BC and EFsynth. Section 6 concludes the paper and gives perspectives.

2   Preliminaries

Throughout this paper, we assume a set $X = \{x_1, \ldots, x_H\}$ of *clocks*, i.e., real-valued variables that evolve at the same rate. A clock valuation w is a function $w : X \to \mathbb{R}_+$. We will often identify a clock valuation π with the *point* $(w(x_1), \ldots, w(x_H))$. We denote by $X = 0$ the conjunction of equalities that assigns 0 to all clocks in X. Given $d \in \mathbb{R}_+$, $w + d$ denotes the valuation such that $(w + d)(x) = w(x) + d$, for all $x \in X$.

Throughout this paper, we assume a set $P = \{p_1, \ldots, p_M\}$ of *parameters*, i.e., unknown constants. A parameter *valuation* π is a function $\pi : P \to \mathbb{Q}_+$. We will often identify a valuation π with the *point* $(\pi(p_1), \ldots, \pi(p_M))$. An *integer* point is a valuation $\pi : P \to \mathbb{N}$.

An *inequality* over X and P is $e \prec 0$, where $\prec \in \{<, \leq, \geq, >\}$, and e is a linear term $\sum_{1 \leq i \leq N} \alpha_i z_i + d$ for some $N \in \mathbb{N}$, where $z_i \in X \cup P$, $\alpha_i \in \mathbb{Q}_+$, for $1 \leq i \leq N$, and $d \in \mathbb{Q}_+$. A (linear) constraint over X and P is a set of linear inequalities over X and P. We define in a similar manner inequalities and constraints over P. A parametric guard is a set of linear inequalities where exactly one z_i is a clock. We denote by $\mathcal{L}(P)$ and $\mathcal{L}(X \cup P)$ the set of all constraints over P, and over X and P respectively. We use $K \in \mathcal{L}(P)$ and $C \in \mathcal{L}(X \cup P)$.

Given a parameter valuation π, $C[\pi]$ denotes the constraint over X obtained by replacing each parameter p in C with $\pi(p)$. Likewise, given a clock valuation w, $C[\pi][w]$ denotes the expression obtained by replacing each clock x in $C[\pi]$ with $w(x)$. We say that π *satisfies* C, denoted by $\pi \models C$, if the set of clock valuations satisfying $C[\pi]$ is nonempty. We use the notation $<w|\pi> \models C$ to indicate that $C[\pi][w]$ evaluates to true.

We denote by $\top$ (resp. $\bot$) the constraint over P that corresponds to the set of all possible (resp. the empty set of) parameter valuations. We denote by $C\downarrow_P$ the projection of C onto P, i.e., obtained by eliminating the clock variables. We define the *time elapsing* of C, denoted by $C^\uparrow$, as the constraint over X and P obtained from C by delaying an arbitrary amount of time. Given $R \subseteq X$, we define the *reset* of C, denoted by $[C]_R$, as the constraint obtained from C by resetting the clocks in R, and keeping the other clocks unchanged.

Parametric timed automata are an extension of the class of timed automata to the parametric case, where parameters can be used within guards and invariants in place of constants [2].

Definition 1. *A PTA $\mathcal{A}$ is a tuple $\mathcal{A} = (\Sigma, L, l_0, X, P, I, E)$, where:*

- *Σ is a finite set of actions,*
- *L is a finite set of locations, $l_0 \in L$ is the initial location,*
- *X is a set of clocks, P is a set of parameters,*
- *I is the invariant, assigning to every $l \in L$ a parametric guard $I(l)$,*
- *E is a set of edges (l, g, a, R, l') where $l, l' \in L$ are the source and destination locations, $a \in \Sigma$, $R \subseteq X$ is a set of clocks to be reset, and g is a parametric guard.*

Throughout this paper, we will be interested in the reachability of *bad locations*. We assume a special location $l_{bad} \in L$; without loss of generality, we assume that this location is unique (the case with several bad locations can be reduced to one only using additional transitions to l_{bad}).

Given a PTA $\mathcal{A} = (\Sigma, L, l_0, X, P, I, E)$, and a parameter valuation π, $\mathcal{A}[\pi]$ denotes the TA obtained from $\mathcal{A}$ by substituting every occurrence of a parameter p_i by the constant $\pi(p_i)$ in the guards and invariants.

We borrow from [14] and adapt to our notations the semantics of a TA.

Definition 2 (Semantics of a TA). *Given a PTA $\mathcal{A} = (\Sigma, L, l_0, X, P, I, E)$, and a parameter valuation π, the semantics of $\mathcal{A}[\pi]$ is given by the timed transition system $(Q, q_0, \Rightarrow)$, with*

- *$Q = \{(l, w) \in L \times \mathbb{R}_+^H \mid I(l)[\pi][w] \text{ evaluates to true}\}$, $q_0 = (l_0, X = 0)$*
- *$((l, w), a, (l', w')) \in \Rightarrow \text{ if } \exists w'' : (l, w) \xrightarrow{a} (l', w'') \xrightarrow{d} (l', w')$, with*
  - *discrete transitions: $(l, w) \xrightarrow{a} (l', w')$, with $a \in \Sigma$, if $(l, w), (l', w') \in Q$, there exists $(l, g, a, R, l') \in E$, $w' = [w]_R$, and $g[\pi][w]$ evaluates to true.*
  - *delay transitions: $(l, w) \xrightarrow{d} (l, w + d)$, with $d \in \mathbb{R}_+$, if $\forall d' \in [0, d], (l, w + d') \in Q$.*

A concrete run of a TA is an alternating sequence of states of Q and actions of the form $s_0 \xrightarrow{a_0} s_1 \xrightarrow{a_1} \cdots \xrightarrow{a_{m-1}} s_m$, such that for all $i = 0, \ldots, m - 1$, $a_i \in \Sigma$, and $(s_i, a_i, s_{i+1}) \in \Rightarrow$. Given a state $s = (l, w)$, we say that s is reachable (or that $\mathcal{A}[\pi]$ reaches s) if s belongs to a run of $\mathcal{A}[\pi]$; by extension, we say that l is reachable in $\mathcal{A}[\pi]$.

We now recall the semantics of PTA.

Definition 3 (Symbolic state). *A symbolic state of a PTA $\mathcal{A}$ is a pair (l, C) where $l \in L$ is a location, and $C \in \mathcal{L}(X \cup P)$ its associated constraint.*

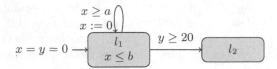

Fig. 1. An example of a PTA $\mathcal{A}_1$ [14]

A state $s = (l, C)$ is π-compatible if $\pi \models C$.

The initial state of $\mathcal{A}$ is $s_0 = (l_0, (X = 0)^\uparrow \wedge I(l_0))$.

The computation of the state space relies on the Succ operation. Given a symbolic state $s = (l, C)$, $\mathsf{Succ}(s) = \{(l', C') \mid \exists(l, g, a, R, l') \in E$ s.t. $C' = ([(C \wedge g)]_R)^\uparrow \cap I(l')\}$. By extension, given a set S of states, $\mathsf{Succ}(S) = \{s' \mid \exists s \in S$ s.t. $s' \in \mathsf{Succ}(s)\}$.

A symbolic run of a PTA is an alternating sequence of symbolic states and actions of the form $s_0 \overset{a_0}{\Rightarrow} s_1 \overset{a_1}{\Rightarrow} \cdots \overset{a_{m-1}}{\Rightarrow} s_m$, such that for all $i = 0, \ldots, m-1$, $a_i \in \Sigma$, and $s_i \overset{a_i}{\Rightarrow} s_{i+1}$ is such that s_{i+1} belongs to $\mathsf{Succ}(s_i)$ and is obtained via action a_i.

Given a (concrete or symbolic) run $(l_0, C_0) \overset{a_0}{\Rightarrow} (l_1, C_1) \overset{a_1}{\Rightarrow} \cdots \overset{a_{m-1}}{\Rightarrow} (l_m, C_m)$, its corresponding trace is $l_0 \overset{a_0}{\Rightarrow} l_1 \overset{a_1}{\Rightarrow} \cdots \overset{a_{m-1}}{\Rightarrow} l_m$. The set of all traces of a TA is called its *trace set*. Two runs (concrete or symbolic) are said to be equivalent if their associated traces are equal.

Problems for PTA. We recall below two classical problems, as formalized in [14].

Problem 1 (EF-emptiness). Let $\mathcal{A}$ be a PTA. Is the set of parameter valuations π such that $\mathcal{A}[\pi]$ reaches l_{bad} empty?

Problem 2 (EF-synthesis). Let $\mathcal{A}$ be a PTA. Compute the set of parameter valuations π such that $\mathcal{A}[\pi]$ reaches l_{bad}.

Problem 1 is undecidable [2], and the set of parameter valuations solving Problem 2 cannot be computed in general. In [14], the following semi-algorithm is proposed, that gives a complete answer to Problem 2 when it terminates.

$$\mathsf{EFsynth}_{l_{bad}}((l, C), S) = \begin{cases} C{\downarrow}_P & \text{if } l = l_{bad} \\ \emptyset & \text{if } (l, C) \in S \\ \bigcup_{s' \in \mathsf{Succ}((l,C))} \mathsf{EFsynth}_{l_{bad}}(s', S \cup \{(l, C)\}) & \text{otherwise} \end{cases}$$

Example 1. Consider the PTA $\mathcal{A}_1$ in Fig. 1 [14], with clocks x and y and parameters a and b. Then $\mathsf{EFsynth}_{l_2}(s_0, \emptyset)$ does not terminate, and neither does it if the range of the parameters is bounded from above (e.g., $a, b \in [0, 50]$).

From the proof of correctness of EFsynth in [14], one can infer that the result of EFsynth is still a (possibly incomplete) answer to Problem 2 even when the algorithm is artificially stopped before its termination. By artificially stopping

EFsynth, we mean bounding the recursion depth: when the depth indeed exceeds some bound, we replace the recursive call $\mathsf{EFsynth}_{l_{bad}}(s', S \cup \{(l, C)\})$ with $\perp$.

Proposition 1. *Let K be the result of $\mathsf{EFsynth}_{l_{bad}}(s_0, \emptyset)$ when $\mathsf{EFsynth}$ is stopped after being recursively called a bounded number of times. For all $\pi \models K$, l_{bad} is reachable in $\mathcal{A}[\pi]$.*

Behavioral Cartography. In [3], we introduced the inverse method IM. This procedure takes as input a reference parameter valuation π and outputs a constraint K such that 1) $\pi \models K$ and 2) for all $\pi' \models K$, the trace sets of $\mathcal{A}[\pi]$ and $\mathcal{A}[\pi']$ are the same; hence, the discrete (linear-time) behavior of the system is preserved. IM performs a breadth-first exploration of the symbolic state space of $\mathcal{A}$; whenever a π-incompatible state (l, C) is met, it is removed as follows: a π-incompatible inequality is selected within the projection of C onto P, and then its negation is added to a constraint maintained by IM. When a fixpoint is reached, IM returns the intersection of all parametric constraints associated to the remaining symbolic states.

A variant of IM named IM^K outputs a weaker (i.e., larger) constraint, that only guarantees that any trace of $\mathcal{A}[\pi']$ is a trace of $\mathcal{A}[\pi]$ [7]. It is similar to IM except that, instead of returning the intersection of all parametric constraints, it returns only the accumulation of π-incompatible inequalities. Hence, IM^K only forbids the traces not possible under π, without requiring that all traces of $\mathcal{A}[\pi]$ be possible in $\mathcal{A}[\pi']$.

In [5], we introduced the behavioral cartography BC: by iterating IM on the integer points in a bounded parameter domain V (usually a product of intervals in $|P|$ dimensions), one can decompose V into tiles, i.e., parametric constraints in which the discrete behavior is uniform. Hence all parameter valuations in a tile satisfy the same set of linear-time properties. Then, given such a property (expressed using, e.g., LTL), one can partition V into good and bad tiles depending whether this property is or not satisfied in each tile.

This method has two theoretical drawbacks: first, some calls to IM may not terminate and, second, BC does not formally guarantee that any "dense" part of V will be covered beside the integer points. However, in practice not only the whole dense part of V is almost always covered, but large (infinite) parts of the parameter space beyond V are often covered.

3   Solving the EF-Emptiness Problem Using Reachability Preservation

3.1   Undecidability of the Preservation of Reachability

Parameter synthesis with respect to a bad location is known to be undecidable [2]. Here, we take advantage of a reference parameter valuation π, for which it is possible to decide whether l_{bad} is reachable [1]. The assumption of a known parameter valuation seems realistic to us: in system design, it is often the case that one knows (from a previous design, of using empirical methods) a first valuation; however, finding other valuations may be much more difficult, and may require to restart the design phase from zero. Here, given a reference parameter valuation, we are interested in the preservation of the reachability of l_{bad} by other parameter valuations. Given two TA $\mathcal{A}[\pi]$ and $\mathcal{A}[\pi']$, we say that $\mathcal{A}[\pi']$ *preserves the reachability* of l_{bad} in $\mathcal{A}[\pi]$ when l_{bad} is reachable in $\mathcal{A}[\pi]$ if and only if l_{bad} is reachable in $\mathcal{A}[\pi']$. We call PREACH the problem of the preservation of reachability. In the following, we show that, given π, deciding whether at least one parameter valuation $\pi' \neq \pi$ preserves the reachability of l_{bad} in $\mathcal{A}[\pi]$ is undecidable.

Problem 3 (PREACH-emptiness). Let $\mathcal{A}$ be a PTA, and π a parameter valuation. Does there exist $\pi' \neq \pi$ such that $\mathcal{A}[\pi']$ preserves the reachability of l_{bad} in $\mathcal{A}[\pi]$?

Problem 4 (PREACH-synthesis). Let $\mathcal{A}$ be a PTA, and π a parameter valuation. Compute the set of parameter valuations π' such that $\mathcal{A}[\pi']$ preserves the reachability of l_{bad} in $\mathcal{A}[\pi]$.

We show below that Problem 3 is undecidable.

Theorem 1. *PREACH-emptiness is undecidable.*

Proof. Given a parameter valuation reaching some location, we reduce the existence of a different parameter valuation reaching the same location from the halting problem of a 2-counter machine.

1. First, recall that [2] defines the encoding of a 2-counter machine (2CM) using a PTA $\mathcal{A}_{2CM}$ that contains two parameters a and b.[2] Then [2] shows that the 2CM halts iff there exists at least one non-null parameter valuation such that a special location l_{halt} is reachable in $\mathcal{A}_{2CM}$.
2. Now, let us add a gadget to $\mathcal{A}_{2CM}$ that adds a direct transition from the initial location l_0 to l_{halt} with a guard $a = b = 0$.[3] Let $\mathcal{A}$ be this new PTA, as depicted in Fig. 2. Now, we have:
   (a) If the 2CM halts, then l_{halt} is still reachable in $\mathcal{A}$ for some non-null parameter valuation since it was already reachable in $\mathcal{A}_{2CM}$. Additionally, due to our gadget, l_{halt} is also reachable in $\mathcal{A}$ for $a = b = 0$.
   (b) If the 2CM does not halt, l_{halt} is again reachable in $\mathcal{A}$ for $a = b = 0$ due to our gadget, but no other parameter valuation can reach l_{halt}, just as in item 1.
   Hence, given $\pi : a = b = 0$, there exists a parameter valuation $\pi' \neq \pi$ such that $\mathcal{A}[\pi']$ preserves the reachability of l_{halt} in $\mathcal{A}[\pi]$ iff the 2CM halts.

---

[2] Strictly speaking, their construction uses six parameters, but it is well-known (shown, e.g., in [14]) that they can be reduced to two.

[3] This guard is not allowed in PTA, but can be simulated using an extra clock x and an urgent location followed by a transition with guard $x = a \wedge x = b$.

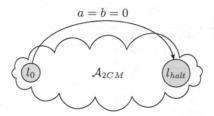

Fig. 2. Undecidability of PREACH-emptiness: PTA $\mathcal{A}$

3.2 Parameter Synthesis Preserving the Reachability

To propose a solution to Problem 4, we introduce here $\mathsf{PRP}(\mathcal{A}, \pi)$, that is inspired by two existing algorithms, viz., EFsynth and the variant IM^K of IM [7]. PRP (standing for parametric reachability preservation) is at first close to IM^K, and then switches to an algorithm that resembles EFsynth:

- As long as no bad location is reached, PRP generalizes the trace set of $\mathcal{A}[\pi]$ by removing π-incompatible states; this is done by negating π-incompatible inequalities, and returning the intersection of such negated inequalities, in the line of IM^K.
- When at least one bad location is met, PRP switches to an algorithm close to EFsynth, i.e., it simply gathers the constraints associated with the bad locations, and returns their union. However, a main difference with EFsynth is that PRP does not explore π-incompatible states: although this is not necessary to ensure correctness (in fact, this makes PRP not complete), this is a key heuristics to keep the state space of reasonable size.

We introduce PRP in Algorithm 1. It is a breadth-first exploration procedure that maintains the following variables: S (resp. S_{new}) is the set of states computed at the previous (resp. current) iterations; Bad is a Boolean flag that remembers whether a bad location has been met; K_{good} is the intersection of the negation of all π-incompatible inequalities, that will be returned if no bad state is met; K_{bad} is the union of the projection onto P of all bad states, that will be returned otherwise; i remembers the current exploration depth.

The procedure consists in a (potentially infinite) **while** loop. First, lines 3–4 take care of the π-incompatible states and resembles IM^K. These states are discarded from the exploration, i.e., they are removed from the set of new states (line 4). Then, if the exploration has not yet met any bad state, K_{good} is refined so as to prevent any such π-incompatible state (l, C) to be reached: a π-incompatible inequality J is selected within the projection of C onto P, and then its negation is added to K_{good}. This mechanism is borrowed to IM (and its variant IM^K).

Second, lines 8–9 take care of the bad states. If any bad state is reached (line 8), then the Bad flag is set to true, the union of the projection onto P of the constraints associated with these bad states is added to K_{bad}, and these states are discarded, i.e., their successor states will not be computed (line 9).

Algorithm 1. PRP($\mathcal{A}, \pi$)

---

input : PTA $\mathcal{A}$ of initial state s_0, parameter valuation π
output : Constraint over the parameters

1 $S \leftarrow \emptyset$; $S_{new} \leftarrow \{s_0\}$; $Bad \leftarrow \texttt{false}$; $K_{good} \leftarrow \top$; $K_{bad} \leftarrow \bot$; $i \leftarrow 0$
2 **while true do**
3   **foreach** π-*incompatible state* (l, C) *in* S_{new} **do**
4          $S_{new} \leftarrow S_{new} \setminus \{(l, C)\}$
5   **if** $Bad = \texttt{false}$ **then**
6   Select a π-incompatible inequality J in $C{\downarrow}_P$ (i.e., s.t. $\pi \not\models J$)
7              $K_{good} \leftarrow K_{good} \wedge \neg J$
8   **foreach** *bad state* (l_{bad}, C) *in* S_{new} **do**
9          $Bad \leftarrow \texttt{true}$; $K_{bad} \leftarrow K_{bad} \vee C{\downarrow}_P$; $S_{new} \leftarrow S_{new} \setminus \{(l_{bad}, C)\}$
10   **if** $S_{new} \subseteq S$ **then**
11   **if** $Bad = \texttt{true}$ **then return** K_{bad} **else return** K_{good} ;
12      $S \leftarrow S \cup S_{new}$; $S_{new} \leftarrow \mathsf{Succ}(S_{new})$; $i \leftarrow i + 1$

The third part is a classical fixpoint condition: if no new state has been met at this iteration (line 10), then the result is returned, i.e., either K_{bad} if some bad states have been met, or K_{good} otherwise. If new states have been met, then the procedure explores one step further in depth (line 12).

We will show in Theorem 2 that PRP outputs a sound (though possibly incomplete) answer to Problem 4. In fact, PRP verifies a stronger property: if l_{bad} is reachable in $\mathcal{A}[\pi]$, PRP outputs a constraint K guaranteeing that l_{bad} is reachable for any parameter valuation satisfying K. However, if l_{bad} is unreachable in $\mathcal{A}[\pi]$, the constraint K output by PRP satisfies the same property as IM^K, i.e., the trace set of $\mathcal{A}[\pi']$ is a subset of the trace set of $\mathcal{A}[\pi]$, for all $\pi' \models K$. This is formalized in Proposition 2.

Proposition 2. *Let $\mathcal{A}$ be a PTA, and π a parameter valuation. Suppose PRP $(\mathcal{A}, \pi)$ terminates with result K. Then, $\pi \models K$ and, for all $\pi' \models K$:*

- *if l_{bad} is reachable in $\mathcal{A}[\pi]$, then l_{bad} is reachable in $\mathcal{A}[\pi']$;*
- *if l_{bad} is unreachable in $\mathcal{A}[\pi]$, then every trace of $\mathcal{A}[\pi']$ is a trace of $\mathcal{A}[\pi]$.*

Theorem 2. *Let $\mathcal{A}$ be a PTA, and π a parameter valuation. Suppose PRP$(\mathcal{A}, \pi)$ terminates with result K. Then, $\pi \models K$ and, for all $\pi' \models K$, l_{bad} is reachable in $\mathcal{A}[\pi]$ iff l_{bad} is reachable in $\mathcal{A}[\pi']$.*

Proof. From Proposition 2.

Remark 1. PRP may not terminate, which is natural since Problem 3 is undecidable. Furthermore, even if it terminates, the result output by PRP may be non complete; in fact, this is designed on purpose (since we stop the exploration of π-incompatible states) so as to prevent a too large exploration. Enlarging the output constraint can be done by repeatedly calling PRP on other points than π, which will be done in Section 3.3.

Example 2. Let us apply PRP to the PTA $\mathcal{A}_1$ in Fig. 1. For point π_1 : ($a = 20, b = 10$), PRP outputs constraint $20 > b \wedge a > b \wedge b \geq 0$, which guarantees the unreachability of l_{bad}. For point π_2 : ($a = 30, b = 30$), PRP outputs constraint $b > 20 \wedge a \geq 0$, which guarantees the reachability of l_{bad}. For point π_3 : ($a = 0, b = 40$), PRP does not terminate.

We now state in Theorem 3 that, even when PRP is interrupted before its termination, PRP outputs a sound (though possibly incomplete) answer to Problem 4, provided some bad states have already been met. The result comes from the fact that the first item of the proof of Proposition 2 holds even if PRP has not terminated. (Note that the converse case, when $Bad =$ false, does not hold if PRP has not terminated: although no bad state has been met yet, there could be some in the future.)

Theorem 3. *Let $\mathcal{A}$ be a PTA, and π a parameter valuation. Let be K the value of K_{bad} at the end of iteration i of $PRP(\mathcal{A}, \pi)$, for some $i \geq 0$, such that $Bad =$ true. Then: 1) l_{bad} is reachable in $\mathcal{A}[\pi]$, and 2) for all $\pi' \models K$, l_{bad} is reachable in $\mathcal{A}[\pi']$.*

Example 3. Let us again apply PRP to the PTA $\mathcal{A}_1$ in Fig. 1. For this PTA and π_3 : ($a = 0, b = 40$), PRP with a depth limit of 10 terminates with $Bad =$ true. From Theorem 3, the output constraint is valid, i.e., guarantees the reachability of l_{bad}.

3.3   EF-Synthesis Using PRP

Given a bounded parameter domain, IM can be iterated on integer points to perform a behavioral cartography; then, the tiles can be partitioned in good and bad according to a linear-time property. If the property of interest is simply a (non-)reachability property, then PRP can be used in place of IM within BC, giving birth to a procedure PRPC (see Algorithm 2). PRP is called repeatedly with as an argument the first integer point not yet covered by any constraint (line 2 in Algorithm 2).

The "cartography" output by PRPC is less precise than the one output by the classical BC, because the constraints outputs by PRP are not tiles anymore: Theorem 2 only guarantees the preservation of reachability, and hence different parameter valuations within a constraint may correspond to different trace sets. To output a set of parameter valuations solving EF-synthesis, it suffices to return the union of the constraints for which l_{bad} is reachable.

Now, a key feature of PRPC is to explore a relatively small part of the whole parametric state space at a time, and to still output larger constraints than BC. We will show in Section 5 that using PRP instead of IM in the cartography indeed dramatically increases its efficiency.

Remark 2. In the general case, PRPC may not terminate, due to the non-termination of PRP. However, it is possible to set up a maximum exploration depth for PRP: when this depth is reached, the algorithm stops. If some bad states have

---

Algorithm 2. PRPC($\mathcal{A}, V$)

---

input : PTA $\mathcal{A}$, bounded parameter domain V
output : Set $\mathcal{C}$ of constraints over the parameters (initially empty)

1 **while** *there are integer points in V not covered by $\mathcal{C}$* **do**
2 │   Select an integer point π in V not covered by $\mathcal{C}$
3 └ $\mathcal{C} \leftarrow \mathcal{C} \cup \mathsf{PRP}(\mathcal{A}, \pi)$

4 **return** $\mathcal{C}$

---

been met, the resulting constraint can be safely used (from Theorem 3); otherwise the constraint is just discarded and the reference point on which PRP was called will never be covered. In this case, termination of PRPC is always guaranteed, with a partial result (some integer points may still be uncovered).

Let us now compare EFsynth and PRPC, that can both output (possibly incomplete) solutions to the EF-synthesis problem. On the one hand, EFsynth should be faster (although we will see in Section 5 that it is not even true in general), because it performs only one exploration, whereas PRPC has to launch PRP on many integer points. On the other hand, PRPC will use less memory, since a smaller part of the state space is explored at a time (due to the non-exploration of π-incompatible states). Furthermore, its main interest is that it synthesizes a more valuable result: whereas EFsynth outputs only a possibly under-approximated set of bad parameter valuations (reaching l_{bad}) and leaves the whole rest of parameter valuations unknown, PRPC outputs possibly under-approximated sets of both bad and good parameter valuations, giving much more valuable information. Finally, just as BC, PRPC can possibly cover parameter valuations beyond the limits of V, which is not possible for EFsynth.

Example 4. Consider again the PTA $\mathcal{A}_1$ in Fig. 1, and let us apply EFsynth and PRPC with a bounded exploration depth of 10; recall that this is safe from Proposition 1 and Theorem 3. We apply PRPC to an unconstrained model with $V : a, b \in [0, 50]$. We apply EFsynth to a model where a and b are constrained to be in $[0, 50]$. We give in a graphical manner in Fig. 3a (resp. Fig. 3b) the results output by PRPC (resp. EFsynth). PRPC synthesizes all the good parameter valuations (below, in green), i.e., that do not reach l_2, and all the bad parameter valuations (above, in red), i.e., that reach l_2, with the exception of a small area near $(0, 0)$ (in white). All constraints output by PRPC are infinite (which is not shown in the figure), and hence cover the whole part outside V too. As of EFsynth, the same bad valuations as for PRPC are covered, but only within V, and no information is given about the good valuations. Hence, since EFsynth was stopped prematurely, no information can be given for the non-covered part: in particular, the white part of V cannot be decided, whereas PRPC covers everything except the small area near $(0, 0)$. This is a major advantage of PRPC over EFsynth in terms of precision of the result. Also recall that EFsynth covers only (a part of) V whereas PRPC covers here the whole parameter space beyond V.

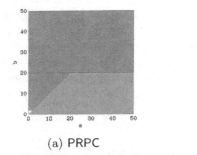

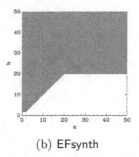

(a) PRPC   (b) EFsynth

Fig. 3. EF-synthesis using PRPC and EFsynth for $\mathcal{A}_1$

4   Towards Distributed Parameter Synthesis

In [4], we proposed two distribution algorithms to execute BC on a set of computers (e.g., on a cluster), implemented in IMITATOR using the message passing interface (MPI). Distributing BC is intrinsically easy: it is trivial that two executions of IM from two different parameter valuations can be performed on two different nodes. However, distributing it *efficiently* is challenging: calling two executions of IM from two contiguous integer points has a very large probability to yield the same tile in both cases, and hence to result in a loss of time for one of the two nodes. Hence, the critical question is how to distribute efficiently the reference valuations ("points") on which to call IM. In [4], we proposed a master-workers scheme, where a master distributes the points to the workers, using two point distribution algorithms:

1. A sequential point enumeration: each integer point not yet covered by any tile is sent to a worker, i.e., $(0,0)$, then $(0,1)$ and so on (in two dimensions). This algorithm suffers from the aforementioned problem of close integer points, but still performs reasonably well (up to 7 times faster using 36 nodes).
2. A random point distribution followed by a sequential enumeration: points are selected randomly and, when points not yet covered by any tile become scarce, the master switches to a sequential point enumeration to ensure that all integer points are covered. The fact that the points not covered by any tile become scarce is detected after the number of unsuccessful attempts to randomly choose an uncovered point goes beyond a certain threshold (e.g., 100). This algorithm performs better (up to 12 times faster using 36 nodes).

Here, we will use a third master-workers distribution method, that dynamically splits the parametric domain V in subparts: when a worker completes the covering of its subpart, the master splits another subpart into two parts, and assigns one of the two part to that worker. From our results, this algorithm (implemented in the working version of IMITATOR) is more efficient than the two algorithms of [4].

Remark 3 (Fairness). Of course, comparing a distributed algorithm (PRPC) with a monolithic one (EFsynth) is unfair. However, to the best of our knowledge, no distributed algorithm for parameter synthesis has been proposed (except [4]). One could argue that EFsynth could at least take advantage of multi-cores, e.g., using one core to compute the successor states while another performs the (costly) equality check, or by computing in parallel the successor states of several states – but PRPC could take advantage of exactly the same enhancements.

5   Experimental Comparison

We compare here several algorithms to solve the EF-synthesis problem using IMITATOR [6]. In its latest version, IMITATOR implements EFsynth, BC and PRPC, and can run PRPC in a distributed fashion. Experiments were run using IMITATOR 2.6.2 (build 845) on a Linux-based cluster. The nodes of this cluster feature two 6-core Intel Xeon X5670 running at 2.93 GHz CPUs (therefore, 12 cores in a NUMA fashion). Each node has 24 GiB of memory and runs a 64-bit Linux 3.2 kernel. The code was compiled using OCaml 3.12.1. The message-passing library we used is Bull's OpenMPI variant for Bullx, and the nodes are interconnected by a 40 Gb/s InfiniBand network.[4]

5.1   Case Studies

Our first case study is the PTA $\mathcal{A}_1$ in Fig. 1, with $V : a, b \in [0, 50]$.

Sched1 and Sched2 are two parametric schedulability problems on a single processor. The goal is to synthesize task parameter valuations guaranteeing that every task meets its relative deadline. For Sched1, we consider two parameters D_2 and T_2 that correspond to the relative deadline and the period of task 2 respectively. We set V to $D_2, T_2 \in [20, 100]$. For Sched2 (adapted from the example studied in [9,14]), we consider two parameters b and z, which correspond to upper bounds on the execution time of tasks 1 and 3, that is $C_1 \in [10, b]$ and $C_3 \in [20, z]$. A third parameter (always valuated in our experiments) is a, that is used in the relative deadline and the period of tasks 1, 2, 3. Precisely: $D_1 = T_1 = a$, $D_2 = T_2 = 2a$ and $D_3 = T_3 = 3a$. Finally, task τ_2 has a release jitter $J_2 \in \{0, 2\}$. We will study Sched2 with two different V. First, we valuate $a = 50$, we set $V : b \in [10, 50], z \in [20, 100]$ and we synthesize parameters for both $J_2 = 0$ ("Sched2.50.0") and $J_2 = 2$ ("Sched2.50.2"). Second, we valuate $a = 100$, we set $V : b \in [10, 1000], z \in [20, 1000]$ and we consider $J_2 = 0$ ("Sched2.100.0") and $J_2 = 2$ ("Sched2.100.2").

Sched5 models the schedulability of 5 fixed-priority tasks in a single processor. SPSMALL is a model of an asynchronous memory circuit [10].

---

[4] Sources, binaries, models and results are available at www.lipn.fr/~andre/PRP/.

Table 1. Comparison of algorithms to solve the EF-synthesis problem

Case study	$|H|$	$|V|$	EFsynth	BC	PRPC	PRPC distr(12)
$\mathcal{A}_1$	2	2,601	0.401*	TO	0.078*	0.050*
Sched1	13	6,561	TO	TO	1595	219
Sched2.50.0	6	3,321	9.25	990	14.55	4.77
Sched2.50.2	6	3,321	662	TO	213	84
Sched2.100.0	6	972,971	21.4	2093	116	10.1
Sched2.100.2	6	972,971	3757	TO	4557	1543
Sched5	21	1,681	352	TO	TO	917
SPSMALL	11	3,082	7.49	587	118	11.2

5.2   Summary of the Experiments and Discussion

Table 1 gives from left to right the case study, the number of clocks, the number of integer points in V and the computation time in seconds for EFsynth, BC, PRPC, and the distributed version of PRPC using the part-splitting point distribution running on 12 nodes. "TO" indicates a timeout ($> 5000\,s$).

For $\mathcal{A}_1$, none of the algorithms terminate; hence, termination is ensured by bounding the exploration depth to 10 (marked with * in Table 1). From Proposition 1 and Theorem 3, the result is still correct; however, this does not hold for BC. For the other case studies, all algorithms terminate (except in case of timeouts), and always cover entirely V. To allow a fair comparison, parameters for EFsynth are bounded in the model as in V; without these bounds, EFsynth never terminates for these case studies.

First, we see that PRPC dramatically outperforms BC for all case studies. This is due to the fact that the constraints output by PRP (that preserve only non-reachability) are much weaker than those output by IM (that preserve trace set equality). Second, we see that PRPC compares rather well with EFsynth, and is faster on three case studies; PRPC furthermore outputs a more valuable constraint for $\mathcal{A}_1$ (see Example 4). PRPC can even verify case studies that EFsynth cannot (Sched1).

The distributed version of PRPC is faster than PRPC for all case studies. Most importantly, the distributed PRPC outperforms EFsynth for all but two case studies. The good timing efficiency of PRPC is somehow surprising, since it was devised to output a more precise result and to use less memory, but not necessarily to be faster. We believe that PRPC allows to explore small state spaces at a time and, despite the repeated executions, this is less costly than handling a large state space (as in EFsynth), especially when performing equality checks when a new state is computed.

6   Conclusion

In this work, we address the synthesis of timing parameters for reachability properties. We introduce PRP that outputs an answer to the parameter synthesis problem of the preservation of the reachability of some bad control state l_{bad}, which we showed to be undecidable. By repeatedly iterating PRP on some (integer) points, one can cover a bounded parameter domain with constraints guaranteeing either the reachability or the non-reachability of l_{bad}. This approach competes well in terms of efficiency with the classical bad state synthesis EFsynth, and gives a more precise result than EFsynth while using less memory. Finally, our distributed version almost always outperforms EFsynth.

The approach recently proposed to synthesize parameters using IC3 for reachability properties [11] looks promising; it would be interesting to investigate a combination of that work with a PRP-like procedure, especially if distributed.

So far, we only investigated the preservation of the reachability; investigating infinite runs properties is of interest too. In this case, it would be interesting to combine our distributed setting with the multi-core algorithm recently proposed for (non-parametric) timed automata [15].

Acknowledgments. We thank Camille Coti for a valuable help while using the Magi cluster, and Didier Lime for useful comments on Section 3.1.

References

1. Alur, R., Dill, D.L.: A theory of timed automata. Theoretical Computer Science **126**(2), 183–235 (1994)
2. Alur, R., Henzinger, T.A., Vardi, M.Y.: Parametric real-time reasoning. In: STOC, pp. 592–601. ACM (1993)
3. André, É., Chatain, T., Encrenaz, E., Fribourg, L.: An inverse method for parametric timed automata. IJFCS **20**(5), 819–836 (2009)
4. André, É., Coti, C., Evangelista, S.: Distributed behavioral cartography of timed automata. In: EuroMPI/ASIA 201414, pp. 109–114. ACM (2014)
5. André, É., Fribourg, L.: Behavioral cartography of timed automata. In: Kučera, A., Potapov, I. (eds.) RP 2010. LNCS, vol. 6227, pp. 76–90. Springer, Heidelberg (2010)
6. André, É., Fribourg, L., Kühne, U., Soulat, R.: IMITATOR 2.5: a tool for analyzing robustness in scheduling problems. In: Giannakopoulou, D., Méry, D. (eds.) FM 2012. LNCS, vol. 7436, pp. 33–36. Springer, Heidelberg (2012)
7. André, É., Soulat, R.: Synthesis of timing parameters satisfying safety properties. In: Delzanno, G., Potapov, I. (eds.) RP 2011. LNCS, vol. 6945, pp. 31–44. Springer, Heidelberg (2011)
8. Bozzelli, L., La Torre, S.: Decision problems for lower/upper bound parametric timed automata. Formal Methods in System Design **35**(2), 121–151 (2009)
9. Bucci, G., Fedeli, A., Sassoli, L., Vicario, E.: Timed state space analysis of real-time preemptive systems. Transactions on Software Engineering **30**(2), 97–111 (2004)
10. Chevallier, R., Encrenaz-Tiphène, E., Fribourg, L., Xu, W.: Timed verification of the generic architecture of a memory circuit using parametric timed automata. Formal Methods in System Design **34**(1), 59–81 (2009)
11. Cimatti, A., Griggio, A., Mover, S., Tonetta, S.: Parameter synthesis with IC3. In: FMCAD, pp. 165–168. IEEE (2013)
12. Cimatti, A., Palopoli, L., Ramadian, Y.: Symbolic computation of schedulability regions using parametric timed automata. In: RTSS, pp. 80–89. IEEE Computer Society (2008)

13. Hune, T., Romijn, J., Stoelinga, M., Vaandrager, F.W.: Linear parametric model checking of timed automata. JLAP **52–53**, 183–220 (2002)
14. Jovanović, A., Lime, D., Roux, O.H.: Integer parameter synthesis for timed automata. IEEE Transactions on Software Engineering (2014, to appear)
15. Laarman, A., Olesen, M.C., Dalsgaard, A.E., Larsen, K.G., van de Pol, J.: Multicore emptiness checking of timed büchi automata using inclusion abstraction. In: Sharygina, N., Veith, H. (eds.) CAV 2013. LNCS, vol. 8044, pp. 968–983. Springer, Heidelberg (2013)
16. Lime, D., Roux, O.H., Seidner, C., Traonouez, L.-M.: Romeo: a parametric model-checker for petri nets with stopwatches. In: Kowalewski, S., Philippou, A. (eds.) TACAS 2009. LNCS, vol. 5505, pp. 54–57. Springer, Heidelberg (2009)

Compositional Verification
of Parameterised Timed Systems

Lăcrămioara Aştefănoaei[1,2]([⊠]), Souha Ben Rayana[1,2], Saddek Bensalem[1,2],
Marius Bozga[1,2], and Jacques Combaz[1,2]

[1] Université de Grenoble, Verimag, F-38000 Grenoble, France
lastefan@imag.fr
[2] CNRS, Verimag, F-38000 Grenoble, France
souha.benrayana@image.fr

Abstract. In this paper we address the problem of *uniform* verification of parameterised *timed* systems (PTS): *"does a given safety state property hold for a system containing n identical timed components regardless of the value of n?"*. Our approach is compositional and consequently it suits quite well such systems in that it presents the advantage of reusing existing local characterisations at the global level of system characterisation. Additionally, we show how a direct consequence of the modelling choices adopted in our framework leads to an elegant application of the presented method to topologies such as stars and rings.

1 Introduction

Swarm robots, satellite systems, multithreaded programs, ad-hoc networks, device drivers, all these applications have in common a structural characteristic: they rely on multiple copies of the same program interacting between each other, that is, they constitute systems *parameterised* by some components which are being replicated. Though the individual "replicas" may not involve a too complicated code in itself, the systems containing them are quite complex. The inherent complexity has several sources: it may come from that the systems are considerably large, as it is the case for swarm robots, or from that, effectively, their size cannot be a priori known, as it is the case for satellites. Yet another delicate matter is that these systems are highly dynamic and adaptable as their topology may change depending on initial goals, component failures, etc. All in all, the verification of such parameterised systems reveals real challenges.

There is an extensive amount of work on the verification of *untimed* parameterised systems. Some [14,17,22,26,31,32] focus on particular classes for which the problem of uniform verification is decidable. Among these classes, we name *well-structured transition systems* [1,20,21] for which decidability follows from the existence of a so-called *well-quasi ordering* between states. Two examples

Work partially supported by the European Projects 257414 ASCENS, STREP 318772 D-MILS, French BGLE Manycorelabs, and Artemis AIPP Arrowhead.

K. Havelund et al. (Eds.): NFM 2015, LNCS 9058, pp. 66–81, 2015.
DOI: 10.1007/978-3-319-17524-9_6

that fit this class are Petri nets, and lossy channel systems. Most notably, the work in [32] shows that, for *bounded-data parameterised systems* and for a restricted fragment of properties there is always a small number n (the so-called *cutoff*, later leading to *small model theorems*) such that if one can show correctness for the systems with less than n replicas then the system itself is correct. Others focus on *incomplete* but general methods: semi-automatic approaches based upon explicit induction [18] and upon network invariants [4,29,30,34] or automatic ones based upon abstraction [11,12], upon regular model-checking (for a survey [6]), or upon symmetry reduction [19].

In this paper we address the problem of uniform verification of parameterised *timed* systems (PTS). The existing approaches are less numerous than for untimed systems. The work in [3,5] concentrates on decidability: the authors show the decidability of the reachability of PTSs where processes are timed automata with either only one clock or otherwise time is discrete. These results have been later generalised to timed ad hoc networks in [2] where it is shown that even for processes as timed automata with one clock, for *star topologies* where the diameter between nodes is of length 5, the reachability problem is undecidable. It is also the case for processes with 2 clocks and *clique topologies*. Decidability holds for special topologies as stars with diameter 3 and cliques of arbitrary order for processes as timed automata with 1 clock. For discrete time, reachability is decidable for any number of clocks and topologies as graphs with bounded paths. As a side remark, all the positive results above rely on the technique of well-quasi-orderings mentioned above. The approaches in [15,16,27] are closer in spirit to ours. The work in [15,16] shows how reachability of parameterised systems where processes are timed automata can be encoded as a formula in a decidable fragment of the theory of arrays [23]. The work in [27] concentrates upon parameterised *rectangular* hybrid automata nets. They show *a small model theorem* for such systems. The proof typically follows the lines from the one showing the existence of cutoffs in [32].

Our approach borrows from [27] and builds upon the methodology described in [10]. There, a compositional method is introduced for the verification of fixed size timed systems. It did so by locally computing invariants for each component and for their interactions and checking with an SMT solver, Z3[1], if their conjunction implies the validity of a given safety property. The method being compositional suits quite well parameterised systems in that it presents the advantage of reusing existing local characterisations at the global level of system characterisation. Applying the method in the context of PTSs boils down to giving an effective method of checking the validity of quantified formulae. This is not obvious because, for instance, Z3 fails while trying to instantiate it to disprove it. At a first thought, one could apply some tactics which make extensive use of transitivity and practically reduce the formula to a tautology. However, to do this, one would need to transform the initial formula into disjunctive normal form, which is costly. At a second thought, following the reasoning from [15], we could show that the formula we feed to Z3 fits well in the theory of arrays. However,

---

[1] rise4fun.com/Z3

a simpler and more inspired solution is to make use of the small model theorem from [27]. The advantage of combining such result with the compositional method from [10] is twofold. On the one hand it can be the case that the system without replicas is big enough to make the construction of the product infeasible. On the other hand, a direct consequence of the modelling choices adopted in our framework leads to an elegant application of the presented method to parameterised timed systems where interactions are given by various types of topologies which extend the standard binary synchronous communication from [27]. With respect to the work in [15], our formulae are quite small while there the resulting formulae have a number of quantifiers proportional to the length of the fixpoint computation of the reachability set.

Organisation of the paper. Section 2 recalls the needed existing results. Section 3 introduces the semantics of PTSs while Section 4 shows how to effectively verify PTSs compositionally. Section 5 describes two applications on classical examples and Section 6 concludes.

2 Preliminaries

Following [10], our method builds upon the verification rule (VR) from [13]. Assume that a system consists of n components B^i interacting by means of an interaction set γ, and that the property that the system should satisfy is Ψ. If components B^i and interactions γ can be locally characterised by means of invariants (here denoted $CI(B^i)$, resp. $II(\gamma)$), and if Ψ can be proved to be a logical consequence of the conjunction of the local invariants, then Ψ is a global invariant. In the rule (VR) depicted in Figure 1 the symbol " $\vdash$ " is used to underline that the logical implication can be effectively proved (for instance with an SMT solver) and the notation "$B \models \Box\, \Psi$" is to be read as "Ψ holds in every reachable state of B".

$$\frac{\vdash \bigwedge_i CI(B^i) \wedge II(\gamma) \rightarrow \Psi}{\|_\gamma B^i \models \Box\, \Psi} \quad \text{(VR)}$$

Fig. 1. Compositional Verification

The method in [10] extends, in a modular manner, the above rule with the purpose of applying it to the verification of timed systems. The framework in this paper is that of *parameterised* timed systems. We show how compositional verification along the lines of the methodology of [10] works for parameterised timed systems. Before, we recall the standard concepts we make use of.

Timed Automata. We use timed automata (TA) to represent the behaviour of components. Timed automata have control locations and transitions between these locations. Transitions may have timing constraints, which are defined on clocks. Clocks can be reset and/or tested along with transition execution. Formally, a timed automaton is a tuple $(L, \Sigma, T, X, \mathsf{tpc}, s_0)$ where L is a finite set of control locations, Σ a finite set of actions, X is a finite set of clocks, $T \subseteq L \times (\Sigma \times \mathcal{C} \times 2^X) \times L$ is finite set of transitions labelled with actions, guards, and a subset of clocks to be reset, and $\mathsf{tpc} : L \rightarrow \mathcal{C}$ assigns a time progress condition to each location. $\mathcal{C}$ is the set of clock constraints and $s_0 \in L \times \mathcal{C}$ provides the initial configuration. Clock constraints are conjunctions of (in)equalities of the form $x \# ct$ or $x - y \# ct$ with $x, y \in \mathcal{X}$, $\# \in \{<, \leq, =, \geq, >\}$ and $ct \in \mathbb{Z}$. Time progress conditions are restricted to conjunctions of constraints as $x \leq ct$.

A timed automaton is a syntactic structure whose semantics is based on continuous and synchronous time progress. A state of a timed automaton is given by a control location paired with real-valued assignments of the clocks. From a given state, a timed automaton can let time progress when permitted by the time progress condition of the corresponding location, or can execute a (discrete) transition if its guard evaluates to true. The effect of time progress of $\delta \in \mathbb{R}^+$ units of time is to increase synchronously all clocks by δ. Executions of transitions are instantaneous: they keep values of clocks unchanged except the ones that are reset (i.e., assigned 0). Because of their continuous semantics, most timed automata have infinite state spaces. However, they admit finite symbolic representations of their state spaces as the so-called *zone* graphs [7,8,25,35].

T-Assertions. We use T-assertions to express local and system properties. This choice is motivated by the fact that, following a result from [27], the validity of T-assertions is decidable. T-assertions are a particular[2] case of LH-assertions. The signature of T-assertions consists of the constants 1 and n of type $\mathbb{N}$, and of a finite number of variables: (a) *index variables*: $i_1, \ldots, i_a \in \mathbb{N}$; (b) *discrete variables*: $l_1, \ldots, l_b \in L$; (c) *real variables*: $x_1, \ldots, x_c \in \mathbb{R}$; (d) *discrete array variables*: $\bar{l}_1, \ldots, \bar{l}_d : [n] \to L$; (e) *real array variables*: $\bar{x}_1, \ldots, \bar{x}_e : [n] \to \mathbb{R}^+$ where by $[n]$ we denote the set $\{1, \ldots, n\}$. Terms are given by the BNF grammar:

$$\texttt{ITerm} ::= 1 \mid n \mid i_j \qquad \texttt{DTerm} ::= L_j \mid l_k \mid \bar{l}_j[\texttt{ITerm}] \qquad \texttt{RTerm} ::= x_j \mid \bar{x}_k[\texttt{ITerm}]$$

and the formulae are structurally defined as:

$$\texttt{Atom} ::= \texttt{ITerm} < \texttt{ITerm} \mid \texttt{DTerm} = L_k \mid a \cdot \texttt{RTerm} + b \cdot \texttt{RTerm} + c < 0$$

$$\texttt{Formula} ::= \texttt{Atom} \mid \neg\texttt{Formula} \mid \texttt{Formula} \wedge \texttt{Formula}$$

with $a, b, c \in \mathbb{R}$. T-assertions are of the form $\forall i_1, \ldots, i_k \in [n] \, \exists j_1, \ldots, j_m \in [n].F$ where F is of type $\texttt{Formula}$. We note that equality and non strict comparisons between indices and real variables can be expressed by means of $\wedge, \neg, <$. For example, $i = j$ is written as $\neg(i < j) \wedge \neg(j < i)$. It is also the case that addition with constants can be expressed by means of extra quantifiers. For example, $j = i + 1$ is written as $i < j \wedge \forall k.i < k \to j \leq k$. This construction generalises to $j = i + o$ for o an integer constant. To restrict indices within bounds, we make the convention that addition is understood modulo n. For succinctness, in the rest of the paper we adopt the notation $\bar{x}[i + o]$ to stand for $\exists j.j = i + o \wedge \bar{x}[j]$.

Example 1. The following T-assertions express safety properties:

1. $\forall i \neq j. \neg(\bar{l}[i] = C \wedge \bar{l}[j] = C)$ expresses mutual exclusion for C denoting that a process is in the critical location;

---

[2] To be specific, by "particular" we mean that we do not need the so called "index-valued array variables" which in [27] model pointer variables.

2. $\forall i, j.(\bar{l}[i] = \bar{l}[j] \rightarrow | \bar{x}[i] - \bar{x}[j] | < 6)$ expresses a "maximum delay" between the timings of any two processes which are in the same location.

As in [27], the semantics of a T-assertion Φ is given by n-models, denoted as $M(n, \Phi)$, which interpret the index, the discrete and resp. the real variables in Φ as taking values in $[n]$, L, and resp. $\mathbb{R}^+$.

Example 2. A 2-model for the mutual exclusion in Example 1 is $\bar{l} = [C, I]$ where say I denotes idle locations. A 4-model for the maximum delay property is $\bar{l} = [L_1, L_2, L_1, L_2]$, $\bar{x} = [10, 8, 6, 3]$.

T-assertions have a *small model theorem*. This is a key fact that can be exploited for automatic verification in general.

Proposition 1   (Simplified from [27]). *Let Φ be a T-assertion given in the form $\forall i_1, \ldots, i_k \in [n] \exists j_1, \ldots, j_m \in [n].\phi$ where ϕ is a quantifier-free formula involving the index variables $i_1, \ldots, i_k$, $j_1, \ldots, j_m$ and array variables. We have that Φ is valid iff, for all $n \leq k + 2$, Φ is satisfied by all n-models.*

Next, we introduce our formalisation of PTSs and show how we can take advantage of the small model result to compositionally verify PTSs.

3   PTSs and Their Semantics

In our framework, PTSs are understood as consisting of possibly (but not also necessarily) a *fixed* number of components and an *arbitrary* number n of isomorphic processes P^i all given as TAs and interacting by means of an interaction set γ. In what follows, we adopt the notations C for the non parameterised part of a PTS, $C\|_\gamma^n P^i$ for a PTS itself. For ease of reference, we use Σ_C, Σ, Σ^i to denote the actions of C, of a generic process P and of a process i, P^i. Σ^i is obtained from Σ by attaching i to each action in Σ. An example of a PTS is depicted in Figure 2a. C interacts with some processes P^i by synchronising actions a and a^i while resetting clocks x^c and x^i. As Figure 2b illustrates, components P^i are obtained from the same generic timed automaton P consisting of two control locations l_0 and l_1 and one transition[3] from l_0 to l_1 labelled by action a and resetting clock x. The construction of P^i from a generic P is straightforward: each location l, clock x, and action a are mapped into l^i, x^i, a^i respectively.

Components interact by means of strong synchronisation between their actions. The synchronisations are specified in the so called *interactions* as sets of actions. An interaction can involve at most one action of each component. For the ease of reference, the whole set of interactions is denoted by γ. In a *parameterised setting*, we define γ as a set of *interaction patterns* instead. An interaction pattern α is a tuple $\left(a^c, (a_1, o_1), \ldots, (a_m, o_m)\right) \in \Sigma^c \times (\Sigma \times \mathbb{N})^m$ such that $0 = o_1 < o_2 < \cdots < o_m$. An interaction pattern describes at an abstract level a

---

[3] Non displayed guards and time progress conditions of locations are by default *true*.

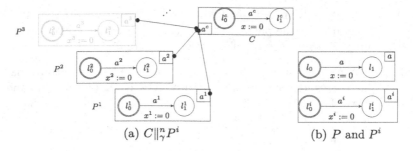

(a) $C\|_\gamma^n P^i$ (b) P and P^i

Fig. 2. An Example of a PTS and the construction of P^i

family of interactions between C and m processes[4]: $\left(a^c, (a_1, o_1), \ldots, (a_m, o_m)\right)$
generates n interactions $\alpha^i = \left(a^c, a_1^{i+o_1}, \ldots, a_m^{i+o_m}\right) \in \Sigma^c \times \Sigma^{i+o_1} \times \cdots \times \Sigma^{i+o_m}$
where all sums are understood modulo n. We use $gen(\alpha)$ to denote the interactions generated by α, that is, $\cup_{i \in [n]} \alpha^i$. By abuse of notation, we refer to γ as
either the set of interaction patterns or as $\cup_{\alpha \in \gamma} gen(\alpha)$, the set of all interactions
generated by the patterns. The distinction should be clear from the context.

Example 3. The family of interactions $\{(a^c, a^1), (a^c, a^2), \ldots, (a^c, a^n)\}$ in
Figure 2a is given by the interaction pattern $\alpha = \left(a^c, (a, 0)\right)$.

For C as $(L^c, \Sigma^c, T^c, \mathcal{X}^c, \mathsf{tpc}^c, s_0^c)$, and P^i as $(L^i, \Sigma^i, T^i, \mathcal{X}^i, \mathsf{tpc}^i, s_0^i)$, the
semantics of $C\|_\gamma^n P^i$ is given by that of the timed automaton $(L, \gamma, T_\gamma, \mathcal{X}, \mathsf{tpc}, \mathbf{s_0})$
where $L = L^c \times_i L^i$, $\mathcal{X} = \mathcal{X}^c \cup_i \mathcal{X}^i$ and:

- for $s_0^c = (l^c, C_0)$, $s_0^i = (l_0^i, C_0^i)$, $\mathbf{s_0}$ is a pair of a global location $\mathbf{l_0} = (l_0^c, l_0^1, \ldots, l_0^n)$ and the initial clock constraints given by $C_0 \wedge_i C_0^i$,
- $\mathsf{tpc}\left((l^c, l^1, \ldots, l^n)\right) = \mathsf{tpc}(l^c) \wedge_i \mathsf{tpc}(l^i)$,
- for any $\alpha = \left(a^c, (a_1, o_1), \ldots, (a_m, o_m)\right)$ with $\alpha^i = \left(a^c, a_1^{i+o_1}, \ldots, a_m^{i+o_m}\right)$ and $\mathcal{O} = \{i + o_1, \ldots, i + o_m\}$, we have that:
  - if $l^c \xrightarrow{a^c, g^c, r^c} l'^c \in T^c$ and $l^i \xrightarrow{a^i, g^i, r^i} l'^i \in T^i$ for any $i \in \mathcal{O}$, $a^i \in \Sigma^i \cap \alpha^i$
  - then $(l^c, l^1, \ldots, l^n) \xrightarrow{\alpha^i, g, r} (l'^c, l'^1, \ldots, l'^n) \in T_\gamma$ with $l'^j = l^j$ for any $j \in [n] \setminus \mathcal{O}$ and $g = g^c \wedge_{i \in \mathcal{O}} g^i$, respectively $r = r^c \cup_{i \in \mathcal{O}} r^i$.

Interaction patterns have a considerable expressiveness power to the extent
that they can encode regular topologies. Usually topologies are given by a graph
where the vertices represent the indices of the processes and the edges give the
communication between processes [2]. In our framework, the communication is
given/induced by the set of interactions. There is a close correspondence between
topologies and sets of interactions. This comes from the observation that topologies represented as graphs have a straightforward encoding as interaction sets.
As an illustration, we consider the classical topology of a *ring*[5]. Given n nodes,

---

[4] The case of PTSs without C is similar and we illustrate it only by means of examples.
[5] Rings are typically for binary communication, however broadcasts can be just as
well encoded by means of interaction patterns.

a ring topology naturally links a send from node i to a receive at node $i + 1$, that is, it is generated by the pattern $((s, 0), (r, 1))$ where s, r stand for "send", "receive". A graphical interpretation is given in Figure 3b.

Example 4. The interaction set in Figure 2a is generated by one pattern, namely $(a_c, (a, 0))$. The corresponding topology it describes is that of a *star*, another classical topology. The corresponding graphical depiction is in Figure 3a.

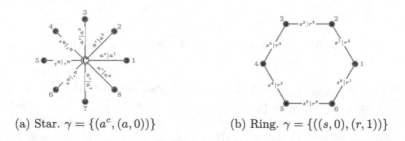

(a) Star. $\gamma = \{(a^c, (a, 0))\}$ (b) Ring. $\gamma = \{((s, 0), (r, 1))\}$

Fig. 3. Topologies & Interaction Sets

Remark 1. Thanks to the definition of γ as a set, thus implicitly nondeterministic, with our method we cover any topology which may be enforced or hard-wired in the system at a later moment of time, or stage of design. To take a concrete example, the interaction set for the star topology does not oblige all components to participate, so any star "subset" (corresponding for instance to the situation when some components are turned off) is considered. This has the implication that, with respect to deadlock freedom, if our method yields true, the system is safe, then this is the case irrespectively of how many components are interacting.

4   Compositional Verification of PTSs

To compositionally verify PTSs, our method consists of automatically generating invariants characterising components, interactions and inter-component timings. These invariants are assembled in the (VR) rule recalled in the introduction. To apply the small model result from Proposition 1, the provided invariants need to be T-assertions. Next, we take them one by one and show how they can be effectively computed and shaped into the form of T-assertions.

4.1   Component Invariants

Component invariants characterise the reachable states of components when considered alone. Such invariants can be computed from the zones of the corresponding timed automata [7,8,25,35]. More precisely, given that the set of the reachable symbolic states (l_j, ζ_j) of an arbitrary process P is finite, its invariant is defined by the disjunction $\vee_j (l_j \wedge \zeta_j)$, where by abuse of notation l_j is used to denote the predicate that holds whenever P is at location l_j.

We recall that, for a process P^i, we identify locations and clocks as l^i, x^i, for locations l and clocks x in the generic process P. To fit the formulae characterising the reachable set of states of P^i in the class of T-assertions, we indiscriminately view l^i as the ith element in the array $\bar{l}$ and similarly, x^i is equally viewed as the ith element in the array $\bar{x}$, that is, semantically we make no difference between l^i and $\bar{l}[i]$, respectively x^i and $\bar{x}[i]$.

Example 5. As an illustration, the component invariants for C, P and P^i (where C, P^i, P are the ones depicted in Figures 2a,2b) are as follows:

$$CI(C) = (l_0^c \wedge x^c \geq 0) \vee (l_1^c \wedge x^c \geq 0) \tag{1}$$
$$CI(P) = (l_0 \wedge x \geq 0) \quad \vee \quad (l_1 \wedge x \geq 0)$$
$$CI(P^i) = (\overline{l_0}[i] \wedge \overline{x}[i] \geq 0) \vee (\overline{l_1}[i] \wedge \overline{x}[i] \geq 0) \tag{2}$$

We use CI to denote the conjunction of $CI(C)$ and of all $CI(P^i)$. Extending the argument that the conjunction of invariants is an invariant itself, it can be shown that CI is an invariant characterising all components.

Proposition 2 $CI \triangleq \big(CI(C) \wedge \forall i.\, CI(P^i)\big)$ *is an invariant of* $C\|_\gamma^n P^i$.

4.2   History Clocks and Auxiliary Constraints

A direct application of the rule (VR) on PTSs may be too weak in the sense that the component and the interaction invariants alone are usually not enough to prove global properties, especially when such properties involve relations between clocks in different components. Though component invariants encode timings of local clocks, because the interaction invariant is orthogonal on timing aspects, there is no direct way to constrain the bounds on the differences between clocks in different components. History clocks allow to decouple the analysis for components and for their composition. They make it possible to derive new global constraints from the simultaneity of interactions and the synchrony of time progress.

Adding History Clocks. History clocks are associated with actions and interactions. For a process P we use P^h to denote its extension with history clocks. The extension $C^h\|_\gamma^n P^{i^h}$ of $C\|_\gamma^n P^i$ is obtained from the extensions of the components alone together with the history clocks for interactions. As an illustration, Figure 4 shows the extension of the PTS in Figure 2a.

The mechanism of history clocks is as follows. When an interaction α takes place, the history clocks h_α and h_a associated to α and to any action $a \in \alpha$ are reset. Thus they measure the time passed from the last occurrence of α, respectively of a. Since there is no timing constraint involving history clocks, the behaviour of the components is not changed by the addition of history clocks, a fact which is shown by a similar argument as in [10].

Proposition 3 $C\|_\gamma^n P^i$ *and* $C^h\|_\gamma^n P^{i^h}$ *are bisimilar.*

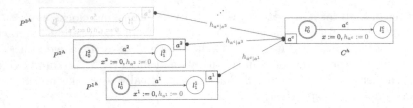

Fig. 4. Illustrating Components with History Clocks for (Inter)Actions

Generating Interaction Equalities from History Clocks. History clocks are introduced with the purpose of obtaining stronger invariants. Intuitively, the strengthening comes from the following observation. Each time an interaction α is executed, h_α and all the history clocks corresponding to the actions participating in α are reset synchronously, and then remain unchanged and *equal* until the next interaction is executed. Moreover, a history clock h_a for an action a from a last executed interaction α is necessarily *less* than any h_β with β another interaction containing a. This is because the clocks of the actions in α are the last ones being reset. Consequently, given a common action a of $\alpha_1, \alpha_2, \ldots, \alpha_p$, h_a is the minimum of h_{α_i}, $h_a = \min\limits_{i \in [p]} h_{\alpha_i}$.

In the parameterised case, the above observation is captured as follows. Each interaction pattern α and each $a \in \alpha$ are associated to the arrays $\overline{h_\alpha}$, respectively $\overline{h_a}$. Let α be of the form $(\ldots, (a, o), \ldots)$. For a given index i, a^i appears in α^{i-o}. Consequently, $\overline{h_a}[i]$ is the minimum among $\overline{h_\alpha}[i - o]$:

$$\mathcal{E}(a^i) = \left(\bigvee_{(a,o) \in \alpha} \overline{h_a}[i] = \overline{h_\alpha}[i - o] \right) \wedge \left(\bigwedge_{(a,o) \in \alpha} \overline{h_a}[i] \leq \overline{h_\alpha}[i - o] \right)$$

By switching perspective from that of P^i to that of C, we obtain, for an action a^c in Σ^c, the following quantified formula:

$$\mathcal{E}(a^c) = \exists j. \left(\bigvee_{a^c \in \alpha} h_{a^c} = \overline{h_\alpha}[j] \right) \wedge \forall i. \left(\bigwedge_{a^c \in \alpha} h_{a^c} \leq \overline{h_\alpha}[i] \right).$$

The existential quantifier is needed to express that h_{a^c} is the minimum among an unbounded number of history clocks associated to interactions containing a^c.

To combine both perspectives, we define $\mathcal{E}(\gamma) = \forall i \wedge_a \mathcal{E}(a^i) \wedge_{a^c} \mathcal{E}(a^c)$. By an inductive argument, it can be shown that these constraints are an invariant.

Proposition 4 $\mathcal{E}(\gamma)$ *is an invariant of* $C^h \|_\gamma^n P^{i^h}$.

Example 6. For the star topology $\gamma = \{\alpha\}$ with $\alpha = (a^c, (a, 0))$ we have that:

$$\mathcal{E}(\gamma) = \forall i. (\overline{h_a}[i] = \overline{h_\alpha}[i] \wedge \overline{h_a}[i] \leq \overline{h_\alpha}[i]) \wedge$$
$$\exists j. (h_{a^c} = \overline{h_\alpha}[j]) \wedge \forall i. (h_{a^c} \leq \overline{h_\alpha}[i])$$

As for the ring topology $\gamma = \{\alpha\}$ with $\alpha = ((s,0),(r,1))$ we have:

$$\mathcal{E}(\gamma) = \forall i.\left(\overline{h_s}[i] = \overline{h_\alpha}[i] \wedge \overline{h_s}[i] \leq \overline{h_\alpha}[i]\right) \wedge \left(\overline{h_r}[i] = \overline{h_\alpha}[i-1] \wedge \overline{h_r}[i] \leq \overline{h_\alpha}[i-1]\right).$$

Generating Inequalities from Conflicting Interactions. The equality constraints shown previously allow to relate local constraints obtained separately from the component invariants. Without conflicts, that is, when interactions do not share any action, the generated invariants are quite tight in the sense that $\mathcal{E}(\gamma)$ is essentially a conjunction of equalities. However, $\mathcal{E}(\gamma)$ is weaker in the presence of conflicts because any action in conflict can be used in different interactions. The disjunctions in $\mathcal{E}(\gamma)$ reflect precisely this uncertainty. History clocks on interactions are introduced to capture the time lapses between conflicting interactions. The basic information we exploit is that when two conflicting interactions compete for the same action a, no matter which one is first, the other one must wait until the component which owns a is again able to execute a. This is referred to as a "separation constraint" for conflicting interactions. Since we make the distinction between the actions in C and P, the reasoning goes as for $\mathcal{E}$, by a case distinction:

$$\mathcal{S}(a^c) = \forall i_1, i_2. \bigwedge_{\substack{\alpha \ni a^c \\ \beta \ni a^c \\ i_1 \neq i_2 \vee \alpha \neq \beta}} \left|\overline{h_\alpha}[i_1] - \overline{h_\beta}[i_2]\right| \geq k_{a^c}$$

$$\mathcal{S}(a^i) = \bigwedge_{\substack{(a,o_1) \in \alpha \\ (a,o_2) \in \beta \\ o_1 \neq o_2 \vee \alpha \neq \beta}} \left|\overline{h_\alpha}[i - o_1] - \overline{h_\beta}[i - o_2]\right| \geq k_a$$

where k_{a^c}, k_a are lower bounds of the time elapsed between two consecutive executions of a^c in C, respectively of a in P, bounds which can be statically computed from the timed automata of C, respectively of P. Similarly to $\mathcal{E}(\gamma)$, $\mathcal{S}(\gamma)$ is defined by combining $\mathcal{S}(a^c)$ and $\mathcal{S}(a^i)$: $\mathcal{S}(\gamma) = \forall i \wedge_a \mathcal{S}(a^i) \wedge_{a^c} \mathcal{S}(a^c)$. Furthermore, $\mathcal{S}(\gamma)$ can be shown to be an invariant.

Proposition 5 $\mathcal{S}(\gamma)$ is an invariant of $C^h\|_\gamma^n P^{i^h}$.

Example 7. For the star topology $\gamma = \{\alpha\}$ with $\alpha = \left(a^c, (a,0)\right)$ we have that:

$$\mathcal{S}(\gamma) = \forall i_1, i_2. \left|\overline{h_\alpha}[i_1] - \overline{h_\alpha}[i_2]\right| \geq k_{a^c} \tag{3}$$

As the ring topology $\gamma = \{\alpha\}$ with $\alpha = ((s,0),(r,1))$ does not have conflicts, for illustration purposes, we consider the following slight variation $\alpha = ((r,0),(s,1),(r,2))$ corresponding to sends being forwarded to the left and to the right. In this case, we have that:

$$\mathcal{S}(\gamma) = \forall i. \left|\overline{h_\alpha}[i] - \overline{h_\alpha}[i-2]\right| \geq k_r \tag{4}$$

with k_r being the lower bound of the time elapsed between two consecutive r.

4.3   Interaction Invariants

Interaction invariants $II(\gamma)$ are induced by the synchronisations and have the form of global conditions involving control locations of components. Previous work considered boolean conditions [13] as well as linear constraints [28] as methods for generating $II(\gamma)$. These approaches do not easily generalise to the parameterised case: applying the method of [13] boils down to transforming to conjunctive normal forms quantified formulae while the one in [28] boils down to solving an unbounded number of equations. Our solution is to adopt a k-window abstraction instead. To obtain such an abstraction, the main step is to generate interactions involving only actions from Σ_i with $i \leq k$. Let α be an interaction pattern $\left(a^c, (a_1, o_1), \ldots, (a_m, o_m)\right)$. Recall that the offsets o_i are in ascending order. We define $gen(\alpha, k)$ as $\cup_{i \in [k]} proj(\alpha^i)$ where $proj(\alpha^i) = \left(a^c, a_1^i, a_2^{i+o_2}, \ldots, a_j^{i+o_j}\right)$ and j is the last index for which $i + o_j \leq k$. We recall that addition is taken modulo n. We denote $\cup_{\alpha \in \gamma} gen(\alpha, k)$ by γ_k. Given this construction, the remaining steps for computing a k-window abstraction are:

1. use the above mentioned methods or simply compute the set of the reachable states of C interacting with k processes P^i to generate $II_k \overset{\triangle}{=} II(\gamma_k)$;
2. reindex II_k by renaming all indices $j \in [k]$ to $j + i$ to obtain II_k^* of the form $\forall i. II_k[j \leftarrow j + i]$.

We note that k-window is an abstraction of the original system $C\|_\gamma^n P^i$. Consequently, each invariant computed with respect to the k-window is also an invariant of $C\|_\gamma^n P^i$.

Proposition 6   *The formula $(k < n \vee II_k^*)$ is an invariant of $C\|_\gamma^n P^i$.*

Example 8. We consider the star topology present in the toy example shown in Figure 2a. If we abstract to a window of size 1, the first step consists in the computation of the interaction invariant for C interacting with P^1, where the interaction set after projection is $\gamma_1 = \{(a^c, a^1), a^c\}$. Using the reachable set of $C\|_{\gamma_1} P^1$, the interaction invariant for this abstraction is $II_1 = \overline{l_0}[1] = 1 \vee l_1^c = 1$. By Step 2, the interaction invariant for $C\|_\gamma^n P^i$ is $II^* = \forall i. \overline{l_0}[i] = 1 \vee l_1^c = 1$.

4.4   Parameterised (VR)

Taking into account the clock constraints $\mathcal{E}$ and $\mathcal{S}$, the generalisation of the rule (VR) recalled in the introduction to the parameterised case boils down to checking the validity of the following formula:

$$\underbrace{CI \wedge (k < n \vee II_k^*) \wedge \mathcal{E}(\gamma) \wedge \mathcal{S}(\gamma)}_{GI} \to \Psi \tag{5}$$

or equally the unsatisfiability of $GI \wedge \neg\Psi$. These formulae are T-assertions whenever Ψ is a T-assertion itself.

Proposition 7   *For Ψ a T-assertion, $GI \to \Psi$ is a T-assertion itself.*

Proof (sketch). In prenex normal form, each invariant is a T-assertion. We only detail the more interesting cases of $\mathcal{E}$ and $\mathcal{S}$:

$$\mathcal{E}(\gamma) = \forall i \wedge_a \mathcal{E}(a^i) \wedge_{a^c} \mathcal{E}(a^c)$$

$$\equiv \forall i_1, i_2. \exists j_{\Sigma^c}. \left(\bigvee_{(a,o)\in\alpha} \overline{h_a}[i_1] = \overline{h_\alpha}[i_1 - o] \right) \wedge \left(\bigwedge_{(a,o)\in\alpha} \overline{h_a}[i_1] \leq \overline{h_\alpha}[i_1 - o] \right) \wedge$$

$$\wedge_{a^c} \left(\bigvee_{a^c\in\alpha} h_{a^c} = \overline{h_\alpha}[j_{a^c}] \right) \wedge \left(\bigwedge_{a^c\in\alpha} h_{a^c} \leq \overline{h_\alpha}[i_2] \right) \tag{6}$$

$$\mathcal{S}(\gamma) = \forall i. \wedge_a \mathcal{S}(a^i) \wedge_{a^c} \mathcal{S}(a^c)$$

$$\equiv \forall i_1, i_2. \wedge_a \bigwedge_{\substack{(a,o_1)\in\alpha \\ (a,o_2)\in\beta \\ o_1\neq o_2 \vee \alpha\neq\beta}} \left| \overline{h_\alpha}[i - o_1] - \overline{h_\beta}[i - o_2] \right| \geq k_a$$

$$\wedge_{a^c} \bigwedge_{\substack{\alpha\ni a^c \\ \beta\ni a^c}} \left| \overline{h_\alpha}[i_1] - \overline{h_\beta}[i_2] \right| \geq k_{a^c}$$

where a, a^c are arbitrary actions in Σ, respectively Σ^c, $\exists j_{\Sigma^c}$ denotes $\exists j_{a_1} j_{a_2} \cdots j_{a_m}$ for $\Sigma^c = \{a_1, \ldots, a_m\}$ and j_{a^c} stands for an arbitrary element in j_{Σ^c}.

Observing that all quantified variables are not shared among invariants, we can rename these such that there are no overlappings and use the following basic equivalences where *op* denotes any logical connective and **Q** any quantifier:

$$\mathbf{Q}x\mathbf{Q}y.(P(x) \ op \ R(y)) \equiv \mathbf{Q}y\mathbf{Q}x.(P(x) \ op \ R(y))$$
$$P \ op \ \mathbf{Q}y.R(y) \equiv \mathbf{Q}y.(P \ op \ R(y))$$

to finally transform $GI \to \Psi$ itself into a T-assertion. □

Proposition 7 allows us to apply the small model theorem from Section 2.

Corollary 1. *For a PTS $C\|_\gamma^n P^i$ and a global property $\Psi \stackrel{\triangle}{=} \forall\bar{s}\exists\bar{t}.\Psi^\circ$ it is enough to check the validity of $\neg GI \vee \Psi$ for $n \leq \#\bar{s} + \#\Sigma^c + 2$ in order to assert the validity of Ψ for any n.*

Proof. By Proposition 1, the bound depends on the number of universally quantified variables in Ψ and on the size of Σ^c, by Equation (6). The latter is the number of universal quantifiers in $\neg GI$.

Example 9. As an illustration, we work through the toy example from head to tail. As a safety state property we take $\Psi \stackrel{\triangle}{=} \exists i.x^c = \bar{x}[i]$, that is, Ψ expresses that one of the clocks in $\bar{x}$ has the same value as x^c. We have already gone through the main ingredients with Equations (1)-(3) in Examples 5-8. What is left is to combine them and rename the quantified variables to obtain:

$$\forall i \, \exists j_1, j_2, j_3, j_4, j_5. \left(\neg \Big((l_0^c \wedge h_{a^c} \geq 0 \wedge x^c \geq 0 \vee l_1^c \wedge x^c = h_{a^c} \geq 0) \wedge \right.$$

$$(\overline{l_0}[j_1] \wedge \overline{h_a}[j_1] \geq 0 \wedge \overline{x}[j_1] \geq 0 \vee \overline{l_1}[j_1] \wedge \overline{x}[j_1] = \overline{h_a}[j_1] \geq 0) \wedge$$

$$(\overline{h_a}[j_2] = \overline{h_a}[j_2] \geq h_{a^c}) \wedge (h_{a^c} = \overline{h_\alpha}[i]) \wedge \big| \overline{h_\alpha}[j_3] - \overline{h_\alpha}[j_5] \big| \, \geq k_{a^c} \Big) \vee$$

$$\left. x^c = \overline{x}[j_4] \right) \tag{7}$$

Above, we have used the component invariants with respect to the extensions with history clocks[6]. By applying Corollary 1, we can assert the correctness of Ψ from the validity the formula in (7) for $n \leq 3$ processes.

5   Experiments

To illustrate the star and the ring topologies, we take the following case studies.

Train Gate Controller: This is the parameterised version of the classical example from [9]. The system is depicted in Figure 5. It is composed of a controller, a gate and an arbitrary number of trains. The controller lowers (raises) the gate when a train enters (exits). The property Ψ is that the gate enters g_1 location only if one of the trains left far location: $\exists i. \neg \overline{far}[i] \vee \neg g_1$. For this example,

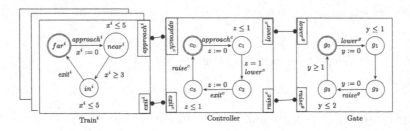

Fig. 5. A Controller Interacting with an Arbitrary Number of Trains and a Gate

$\Pi(\gamma)$ plays no role: $\mathcal{E}(\gamma)$ and $\mathcal{S}(\gamma)$ are enough to check the validity of $\neg GI \vee \Psi$ for the bound of 3. The small model result justifies this check as sufficient. As a side note, additionally, we proved deadlock-freedom (the bound was 5).

Token Ring: The protocol depicted in Figure 6 is an adaption from [33]. Every process P^i receives the token from P^{i-1} through the interaction (s^{i-1}, r^i). It then moves to t_1^i location and after passing the token, it moves from t_2^i to a^i. Once P^i sends the token, it cannot have it again before 2 time units. This constraint is expressed using clock x^i. Initially, P^1 is in t_1^1, meaning that it possesses the

---

[6] The computation is the same as the one in Example 5. For illustration, we only show the component invariant for C^h: $CI(C^h) = l_0^c \wedge h_{a^c} \geq 0 \wedge x^c \geq 0 \vee l_1^c \wedge x^c = h_{a^c} \geq 0$.

token, while all other P^i are at location a^i, waiting for the reception of the token. The property Ψ is that one and only one process possesses the token: $\Psi \overset{\triangle}{=} \exists i. \forall j \neq i. (\neg \overline{a}[i] \wedge \overline{a}[j])$.

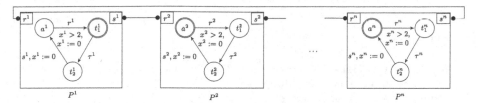

Fig. 6. An Arbitrary Number of Processes in a Ring Topology

For this example, the number of universal quantifiers in $\neg GI \vee \Psi$ is 3. As a more interesting observation from our experiments, we add that the interaction invariant as computed automatically in [10] has the form of a T-assertion: $\exists j. (\overline{t_1}[j] \vee \overline{t_2}[j])$. What it expresses is that at least one P^i is not at $\overline{a}[i]$ location, or equally, that the token is not lost. This invariant is, along with clock constraints from $CI(P^i)$, and $\mathcal{E}(\gamma)$ as $\forall i. \overline{h_s}[i] = \overline{h_\alpha}[i] \wedge \overline{h_r}[i] = \overline{h_\alpha}[i-1]$, necessary to show that exactly one P^i is at $\overline{a}[i]$ at a given time.

6   Conclusion and Future Work

We have presented a compositional method for the verification of parameterised timed systems. The key element we made use of is a typical small model theorem. The small model theorem does not hold in the context of networks of *parametric* timed automata in its most general case. If the particular case of timed automata with parameter n can be handled by extending the fragment of T-assertions with results from [24], this is no longer the case for timed automata parametric in their indices. This is because the invariant of such timed automata would involve constraints of type $x_i \geq i \cdot ct$ and such constraints are not allowed by the grammar of T-assertions. It would be of interest to investigate in this direction if possible extensions of T-assertions are foreseeable. Another possible alternative is to exploit the inherent symmetry in such systems.

Besides showing how compositional verification can benefit from small model theorems, we have also shown the close relation between interactions and topologies. In this respect, we note that tree-like topologies are more tricky to encode: offsets as constants are too weak but we intuit that the offset would need to contain offsets itself. To allow more sophisticated interaction patterns, we could also borrow some of the constructions in [24] to express constraints like periodicity on indices. That is, given an interaction pattern α, instead of generating α^i for $i \in [n]$, it would be of interest to generate α^i only for indices i satisfying a constraint like parity, or boundedness.

A third possible extension we will consider is with respect to false positives: as any incomplete method, (VR) may yield spurious counterexamples. We will look into how counterexample-based refinement techniques can in turn be applied in the context of (parameterised) timed systems. Given that the search space (of reals) is infinite, the main difficulty we envisage is the generalisation of the concrete real values from a given counterexample to a more generic characterisation which would guarantee convergence.

References

1. Abdulla, P.A., Cerans, K., Jonsson, B., Tsay, Y.: General decidability theorems for infinite-state systems. In: LICS (1996)
2. Abdulla, P.A., Delzanno, G., Rezine, O., Sangnier, A., Traverso, R.: On the Verification of Timed Ad Hoc Networks. In: Fahrenberg, U., Tripakis, S. (eds.) FORMATS 2011. LNCS, vol. 6919, pp. 256–270. Springer, Heidelberg (2011)
3. Abdulla, P.A., Deneux, J., Mahata, P.: Closed, open, and robust timed networks. ENTCS 138(3) (2005)
4. Abdulla, P.A., Jonsson, B.: On the Existence of Network Invariants for Verifying Parameterized Systems. In: Olderog, E.-R., Steffen, B. (eds.) Correct System Design. LNCS, vol. 1710, pp. 180–197. Springer, Heidelberg (1999)
5. Abdulla, P.A., Jonsson, B.: Model checking of systems with many identical timed processes. Theor. Comput. Sci. 290(1) (2003)
6. Abdulla, P.A., Jonsson, B., Nilsson, M., Saksena, M.: A Survey of Regular Model Checking. In: Gardner, P., Yoshida, N. (eds.) CONCUR 2004. LNCS, vol. 3170, pp. 35–48. Springer, Heidelberg (2004)
7. Alur, R.: Timed Automata. In: Halbwachs, N., Peled, D.A. (eds.) CAV 1999. LNCS, vol. 1633, pp. 8–22. Springer, Heidelberg (1999)
8. Alur, R., Courcoubetis, C., Dill, D.L., Halbwachs, N., Wong-Toi, H.: An implementation of three algorithms for timing verification based on automata emptiness. In: RTSS (1992)
9. Alur, R., Dill, D.L.: A theory of timed automata. Theor. Comput. Sci. (1994)
10. Aştefănoaei, L., Ben Rayana, S., Bensalem, S., Bozga, M., Combaz, J.: Compositional Invariant Generation for Timed Systems. In: Ábrahám, E., Havelund, K. (eds.) TACAS 2014 (ETAPS). LNCS, vol. 8413, pp. 263–278. Springer, Heidelberg (2014)
11. Baukus, K., Bensalem, S., Lakhnech, Y., Stahl, K.: Abstracting WS1S Systems to Verify Parameterized Networks. In: Graf, S. (ed.) TACAS 2000. LNCS, vol. 1785, pp. 188–203. Springer, Heidelberg (2000)
12. Baukus, K., Stahl, K., Bensalem, S., Lakhnech, Y.: Networks of processes with parameterized state space. ENTCS 50(4) (2001)
13. Bensalem, S., Bozga, M., Sifakis, J., Nguyen, T.-H.: Compositional Verification for Component-Based Systems and Application. In: Cha, S.S., Choi, J.-Y., Kim, M., Lee, I., Viswanathan, M. (eds.) ATVA 2008. LNCS, vol. 5311, pp. 64–79. Springer, Heidelberg (2008)
14. Bouajjani, A., Jurski, Y., Sighireanu, M.: A Generic Framework for Reasoning About Dynamic Networks of Infinite-State Processes. In: Grumberg, O., Huth, M. (eds.) TACAS 2007. LNCS, vol. 4424, pp. 690–705. Springer, Heidelberg (2007)
15. Bruttomesso, R., Carioni, A., Ghilardi, S., Ranise, S.: Automated Analysis of Parametric Timing-Based Mutual Exclusion Algorithms. In: Goodloe, A.E., Person, S. (eds.) NFM 2012. LNCS, vol. 7226, pp. 279–294. Springer, Heidelberg (2012)
16. Carioni, A., Ghilardi, S., Ranise, S.: Mcmt in the land of parametrized timed automata. In: VERIFY@IJCAR (2010)

17. Emerson, E.A., Kahlon, V.: Reducing model checking of the many to the few. In: CADE (2000)
18. Emerson, E.A., Namjoshi, K.S.: Reasoning about rings. In: POPL (1995)
19. Emerson, E.A., Sistla, A. P.: Symmetry and model checking. Formal Methods in System Design 9(1/2) (1996)
20. Finkel, A.: A generalization of the procedure of karp and miller to well structured transition systems. In: ICALP (1987)
21. Finkel, A., Schnoebelen, P.: Well-structured transition systems everywhere! Theor. Comput. Sci. 256(1-2) (2001)
22. German, S.M., Sistla, A.P.: Reasoning about systems with many processes. J. ACM 39(3) (1992)
23. Ghilardi, S., Nicolini, E., Ranise, S., Zucchelli, D.: Towards SMT Model Checking of Array-Based Systems. In: Armando, A., Baumgartner, P., Dowek, G. (eds.) IJCAR 2008. LNCS (LNAI), vol. 5195, pp. 67–82. Springer, Heidelberg (2008)
24. Habermehl, P., Iosif, R., Vojnar, T.: What Else Is Decidable about Integer Arrays? In: Amadio, R.M. (ed.) FOSSACS 2008. LNCS, vol. 4962, pp. 474–489. Springer, Heidelberg (2008)
25. Henzinger, T.A., Nicollin, X., Sifakis, J., Yovine, S.: Symbolic model checking for real-time systems. Inf. Comput. (1994)
26. Ihlemann, C., Jacobs, S., Sofronie-Stokkermans, V.: On Local Reasoning in Verification. In: Ramakrishnan, C.R., Rehof, J. (eds.) TACAS 2008. LNCS, vol. 4963, pp. 265–281. Springer, Heidelberg (2008)
27. Johnson, T.T., Mitra, S.: A Small Model Theorem for Rectangular Hybrid Automata Networks. In: Giese, H., Rosu, G. (eds.) FORTE 2012 and FMOODS 2012. LNCS, vol. 7273, pp. 18–34. Springer, Heidelberg (2012)
28. Legay, A., Bensalem, S., Boyer, B., Bozga, M.: Incremental generation of linear invariants for component-based systems. In: ACSD (2013)
29. Lesens, D., Halbwachs, N., Raymond, P.: Automatic verification of parameterized linear networks of processes. In: POPL (1997)
30. Lesens, D., Halbwachs, N., Raymond, P.: Automatic verification of parameterized networks of processes. Theor. Comput. Sci. 256(1–2) (2001)
31. Namjoshi, K.S.: Symmetry and Completeness in the Analysis of Parameterized Systems. In: Cook, B., Podelski, A. (eds.) VMCAI 2007. LNCS, vol. 4349, pp. 299–313. Springer, Heidelberg (2007)
32. Pnueli, Amir, Ruah, Sitvanit, Zuck, Lenore D.: Automatic Deductive Verification with Invisible Invariants. In: Margaria, Tiziana, Yi, W. (eds.) TACAS 2001. LNCS, vol. 2031, pp. 82–97. Springer, Heidelberg (2001)
33. Reich, J.: Processes, roles and their interactions. In: Proceedings of IWIGP (2012)
34. Wolper, P., Lovinfosse, V.: Verifying properties of large sets of processes with network invariants. In: AVMFSS (1989)
35. Yi, W., Pettersson, P., Daniels, M.: Automatic verification of real-time communicating systems by constraint-solving. In: FORTE (1994)

Requirements Analysis of a Quad-Redundant Flight Control System

John Backes[1]([⊠]), Darren Cofer[1], Steven Miller[1], and Michael W. Whalen[2]

[1] Rockwell Collins, Bloomington, MN 55438, USA
{john.backes,darren.cofer,steven.miller}@rockwellcollins.com
[2] University of Minnesota, Minneapolis, MN 55455, USA
whalen@cs.umn.edu

Abstract. In this paper we detail our effort to formalize and prove requirements for the Quad-redundant Flight Control System (QFCS) within NASA's Transport Class Model (TCM). We use a compositional approach with assume-guarantee contracts that correspond to the requirements for software components embedded in an AADL system architecture model. This approach is designed to exploit the verification effort and artifacts that are already part of typical software verification processes in the avionics domain. Our approach is supported by an AADL annex that allows specification of contracts along with a tool, called AGREE, for performing compositional verification. The goal of this paper is to show the benefits of a compositional verification approach applied to a realistic avionics system and to demonstrate the effectiveness of the AGREE tool in performing this analysis.

1 Introduction

Modern aircraft are complex cyber-physical systems with safety and security requirements that must be satisfied by their onboard software. As these systems have grown in complexity, their verification has become the single most costly development activity [1]. The verification costs of even more complex systems in the future will impact safety, not just through an increasing incidence of errors and unforeseen interactions, but by delaying and preventing the deployment of crucial safety functions.

In a NASA-funded project with University of Minnesota and University of Iowa we are addressing these challenges by developing compositional reasoning methods that will permit the verification of systems that exceed the complexity limits of current approaches. Our approach is based on:

- Modeling the system architecture using standard notations that will be usable by systems and software engineers.
- Developing a sophisticated translation framework that automates the translation of these models for analysis by powerful general-purpose verification engines such as SMT-based model checkers.

© Springer International Publishing Switzerland 2015
K. Havelund et al. (Eds.): NFM 2015, LNCS 9058, pp. 82–96, 2015.
DOI: 10.1007/978-3-319-17524-9_7

– Developing techniques for compositional verification based on the system architecture to divide the verification task into manageable, reusable pieces.

This approach has the potential to significantly reduce verification costs by identifying and correcting system design errors early in the life cycle rather than waiting until system integration. We are validating our approach and our tools on a realistic fault-tolerant flight control system model. The Quad-redundant Flight Control System (QFCS) has been designed by NASA as a suitable control system for its Transport Class Model (TCM) aircraft.

Our compositional approach is designed to exploit the verification effort and artifacts that are already part of typical software component verification processes. Each component in the system model is annotated with an assume/guarantee contract that includes the requirements (*guarantees*) and environmental constraints (*assumptions*) that were specified and verified as part of its development process. We then reason about the system-level behavior based on the interaction of the component contracts. By partitioning the verification effort into proofs about each subsystem within the architecture, the analysis will scale to handle large system designs. Additionally, the approach naturally supports an architecture-based notion of requirements refinement: the properties of components necessary to prove a system-level property in effect define the requirements for those components.

There were two objectives in using this verification approach. The first was to reuse the verification already performed on components. The second was to enable distributed, parallel development of components via *virtual integration*. In this process, we specify formal component-level requirements, demonstrate that they are sufficient to prove system guarantees, and then use these requirements as specifications for suppliers. If the suppliers' implementations meet these specifications, we have a great deal of confidence that the integrated system will work properly.

We have chosen the Architecture Analysis and Design Language (AADL) as our system architecture modeling language [2]. AADL was designed for embedded, real-time, distributed systems and so is a good fit for our domain. It provides the constructs needed to model embedded systems such as threads, processes, processors, buses, and memory. It is sufficiently formal for our purposes, and is extensible through the use of language annexes that can initiate calls to separately developed analysis tools.

We have implemented our compositional reasoning methodology in a tool called *AGREE: Assume-Guarantee Reasoning Environment*. AGREE is implemented as an Eclipse plugin and is designed to work with the open source OSATE AADL tool developed by the Software Engineering Institute [3]. AGREE is able to check the correctness of behavioral properties defined by the composition of component contracts, check component contracts for inconsistencies, and determine whether a component contract has any possible realization. AGREE makes use of the AADL annex mechanism to annotate models with contracts corresponding to formal assumptions and guarantees about their behaviors. AGREE is open source software and is available at http://github.com/smaccm.

The goal of this paper is to show the benefits of a compositional verification approach applied to a realistic avionics system and its requirements, and to demonstrate the effectiveness of the AGREE tool in performing this analysis.

2   Compositional Verification with AGREE

In this section we briefly describe the rules that AGREE uses to create compositional proofs. A more complete description is in [4] and a proof of correctness of these rules is provided in [4,5].

AGREE is a language and a tool for compositional verification of AADL models. The behavior of a model is described by *contracts* specified on each component. A contract contains a set of *assumptions* about the component's inputs and a set of *guarantees* about the component's outputs. The assumptions and guarantees may also contain predicates that reason about how the state of a component evolves over time. The state transitions of each component in the model occur synchronously with every other component (i.e., each component runs on the same clock). The guarantees of a component must be true provided that the component's assumptions have always been true. The goal of the analysis is to prove that a component's contract is entailed by the contracts of its subcomponents.

Formally, let a system $S : (A, G, C)$ consist of a set of assumptions A, guarantees G, and subcomponents C. We use the notation S_g to represent the conjunction of all guarantees of S and S_a to represent the conjunction of all assumptions of S. Each subcomponent $c \in C$ is itself a system with assumptions, guarantees, and subcomponents. The goal of our analysis is to prove that the system's guarantees hold as long as its assumptions have always held. This is accomplished by proving that Formula 1 is an invariant.

$$\mathbf{H}(S_a) \rightarrow S_g \qquad (1)$$

The predicate $\mathbf{H}$ is true if its argument has held *historically* (i.e., the expression has been true at every time step up until and including now). In order to prove that Formula 1 is invariant, we prove that the assumptions of all the subcomponents of system S hold under the assumptions of S. This invariant is shown in Formula 2.

$$\bigwedge_{c \in C} \left[\mathbf{H}(S_a) \rightarrow c_a \right] \qquad (2)$$

This formula is actually stronger than what we need to prove. It may be the case that the assumptions of certain subcomponents are satisfied by the guarantees of other subcomponents (and possibly the guarantees of the component itself at previous instances in time). This weaker invariant is shown in Formula 3.

$$\bigwedge_{c \in C} \left[\left(\mathbf{H}(S_a) \wedge \bigwedge_{w \in C} \mathbf{Z}(\mathbf{H}(w_g)) \wedge \bigwedge_{v \in C, c \neq v} \mathbf{H}(v_g) \right) \to c_a \right] \tag{3}$$

The predicate $\mathbf{Z}$ is true in the first step of a trace and thereafter is true iff its argument was true in the previous time step.

However, this formula may not be sound when the connections between components form cycles. One could imagine a scenario where the assumptions of each of two components are true precisely because of the guarantees of the other component (i.e., $w_g \to v_a$ and $v_g \to w_a$ for $w, v \in C$ and $w \neq v$). Suppose components w and v both assume that their inputs are positive, and they guarantee that their outputs are positive. If the output of w is connected to the input of v, and v's output is connected to w, the state of the system is improperly defined. To avoid this problem, AGREE creates a total ordering of a system's subcomponents. It uses this ordering to determine which subcomponent guarantees are used to prove the assumptions of other subcomponents. This slight modification of Formula 3 is shown in Formula 4.

$$\bigwedge_{c \in C} \left[\left(\mathbf{H}(S_a) \wedge \bigwedge_{w \in C} \mathbf{Z}(\mathbf{H}(w_g)) \wedge \bigwedge_{v \in C, v < c} \mathbf{H}(v_g) \right) \to c_a \right] \tag{4}$$

If Formula 4 is invariant then Formula 1 is proven to be invariant by showing that the system assumptions and subcomponent guarantees satisfy the system guarantees. Formally, if Formula 4 is invariant, then Formula 5 implies Formula 1.

$$\mathbf{H}(S_a) \wedge \bigwedge_{c \in C} \mathbf{H}(c_g) \to S_g \tag{5}$$

AGREE uses a syntax similar to Lustre to express a contract's assumptions and guarantees [6]. AGREE translates an AADL model annotated with AGREE annexes into Lustre corresponding to Formulas 4 and 5 and then queries a user selected model checker. AGREE then translates the results from the model checker back into OSATE so they can be interpreted by the user. For this project we have used both the Kind 2.0 and JKind model checkers [7,8].

In Section 3 we describe some examples of guarantees that were written in AGREE to model some of the requirements in the QFCS architecture. However, the examples are presented here in a simple first order logic syntax to make them more concise and readable.

3   Requirements Formalization

We are using NASA's TCM aircraft simulation model [9] as a realistic example to demonstrate and validate our compositional reasoning work. The TCM was not originally developed with a set of requirements, but other researchers have created a set of requirements representative of those that would be necessary to certify an aircraft for operation in the national airspace system [10]. These requirements were developed hierarchically with different requirements being assigned to different levels of the system architecture, all the way down to the major software components. The requirements hierarchy is shown in Figure 1.

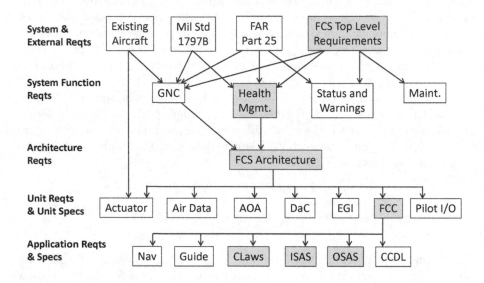

Fig. 1. The QFCS requirements hierarchy (those in grey were included in our analysis)

3.1   QFCS Architecture

The QFCS is a quad-redundant flight control system for the TCM consisting of four cross-checking flight control computers (FCC), as shown in Figure 2. The QFCS model was developed in Simulink® and includes models of the aircraft's control laws, sensors, and actuators, and interacts with the TCM aerodynamics model. The fault tolerance logic was not originally part of this model, but was added to the simulation in parallel during our project.

Our work focused on formalizing requirements for five components of the QFCS hierarchy: the Flight Control System (FCS), the Flight Control Computers (FCC), the Output Signal Analysis and Selection component (OSAS), the Input Signal Analysis and Selection component (ISAS), and the Control Laws (CLAW). The FCS consists of four individual FCCs, and each FCC includes a single OSAS, ISAS, and CLAW component, as well as several other components. We focused on formalizing the requirements for these components for a couple reasons. First, others were working to formalize some of the other components

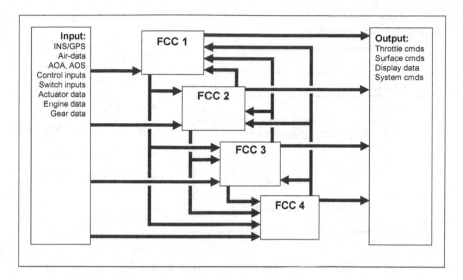

Fig. 2. The QFCS architecture with four flight control computers

using different techniques in parallel with this work [10]. Second, the requirements for these components had a much clearer path to formalization compared to the other component requirements.

The FCS component hierarchy is shown in Figure 3. These components were modeled in AADL with the same interfaces and connections described in the QFCS Simulink® model. The requirements for the QFCS were taken from the hierarchy of requirements shown in Figure 1 and were formalized and assigned as assume guarantee contracts to the relevant QFCS components in the AADL model. AGREE was used to show that the requirements at each level of the component hierarchy were satisfied by the requirements of their direct subcomponents. Explicitly, the requirements formalized for the FCS were proven to hold by the composition of the requirements of the four FCCs. Additionally, the requirements of each FCC were satisfied by the requirements of the OSAS, ISAS, and CLAW components. This section lists examples of some of the English language requirements that were formalized for some of these components. In particular, we discuss requirements related to the actuator signals that are sent from each flight control computer.

In the remainder of this section we list examples of some of the English language requirements that we formalized for some of these components. In particular, we discuss requirements related to the actuator signals that are sent from each flight control computer.   •

3.2 Flight Control System

The FCS requirements make up the "top level" properties that should be satisfied by the composition of the requirements of all of the components within the

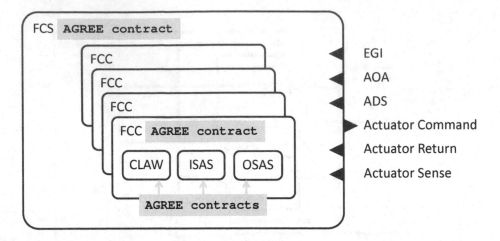

Fig. 3. The QFCS component hierarchy

FCS. Many of the FCS requirements reference functions that we have not yet modeled, including as Guidance Navigation and Control, Maintenance Function, and Status and Warning. We have chosen to focus our analysis on the fault tolerance requirements for the FCS. The top level FCS requirement for the fault handling logic is shown in Requirement FCS-120.

> **FCS-120** - The Health Management Function (HM) shall detect and mitigate Flight Control System faults.

This statement is certainly too vague to be formalized. There is no guidance given on what qualifies as "mitigating a fault". However, Requirement FCS-120 depends on many sub requirements that are more precise. Among these are Requirements HM-220 and HM-240.

> **HM-220** - The Health Management Function shall provide Cooper Harper Level 4 Handling Qualities after any single LRU, LRU function, or LRU IO signal failure.

Requirements HM-220 and HM-240 are also challenging to formalize because they require that the aircraft meet a specific Cooper Harper rating [11]. A Cooper Harper rating is a subjective measurement used to describe the ease with which a pilot is able to operate an aircraft. However, there are some objective properties that are related to these statements. We propose Requirements HM-240a and HM-240b as properties that can be stated precisely and are necessary for satisfying Requirements HM-220 and HM-240.

> **HM-240** - The Health Management Function shall provide Cooper Harper Level 4 Handling Qualities after any dual simultaneous LRU, LRU function, or LRU IO signal failures including actuator runaways and jams not shown to be extremely improbable.

> **HM-240a** - The average of the signals sent to any given actuator is bounded regardless of how many LRU failures occur.

The rationale behind Requirements HM-240a and HM-240b is that they offer some guarantee about the controllability of the vehicle. They are also written in precise language that can be verified using AGREE. We modeled Requirements HM-240a and HM-240b as Guarantees 1 and 2, respectively, in the contract of the FCS component.

$$\textbf{guarantee}: \; low \leq avg \wedge avg \leq high$$
$$avg = \frac{(act_1 + act_2 + act_3 + act_4)}{4} \tag{1}$$

The variable act_n in Guarantee 1 represents the nth signal sent to an actuator. Each of these signals comes from a set of four redundant signals. The values of low and $high$ are constant values that are determined for each actuator. This guarantee is repeated for each actuator in the FCC.

The variable num_valid_acts in Guarantee 2 represents the total number of valid actuator signals. Readers familiar with Lustre will recognize the **pre** function [6]. The **pre** function returns the value of its expression on the previous time step, in this case the previous value of num_valid_acts. This guarantee is also repeated for each set of quad redundant actuator signals.

$$\textbf{guarantee}: \; num\_valid\_acts \leq \textbf{pre}(num\_valid\_acts) \tag{2}$$

3.3 Flight Control Computer

The FCS consists of four individual FCCs. The composition of the guarantees of the four FCCs prove the guarantees of the FCS. One of the FCC requirements is shown in Requirement FCC-S-150.

This statement also lacks the precision needed to develop a direct formalization. It is not obvious what constitutes "mitigation logic" or what is considered "fault detection". This requirement needed to be linked to more precise definitions in lower level requirements. The OSAS component requirements, which are discussed in the next subsection, contain language describing how the output signal gains are computed. When the OSAS is declared faulty, its actuator

> **HM-240b** - The number of FCCs with a failed OSAS component decreases monotonically.

> **FCC-S-150** - The FCC OSAS application shall perform FCC command fault detection and mitigation logic.

signals are latched to zero. When the OSAS is behaving correctly each output signal is multiplied by a factor determined by the number of faulty FCCs.

The requirements of each FCC act as lemmas about the ISAS, OSAS, and CLAW components to prove the top level properties about the FCS component. Based on the requirements of the OSAS and Requirement HM-240a in the FCS, Requirement FCC-S-150 was modeled by Guarantees 3 and 4. These guarantees fulfill some of the "mitigation logic" and "fault detection logic" functionality mentioned in Requirement FCC-S-150. The composition of these guarantees from all four FCCs is strong enough to prove Requirements HM-240a and HM-240b in the FCS, and they are abstract enough to be proven by some of the OSAS requirements.

$$
\begin{aligned}
\textbf{guarantee:} \\
(num\_valid = 0 &\rightarrow (low \leq act \wedge act \leq 4 * high)) \wedge \\
(num\_valid = 1 &\rightarrow (low \leq act \wedge act \leq 2 * high)) \wedge \\
(num\_valid = 2 &\rightarrow (low \leq act \wedge act \leq (3/4) * high)) \wedge \\
(num\_valid = 3 &\rightarrow (low \leq act \wedge act \leq high))
\end{aligned} \tag{3}
$$

$$
\textbf{guarantee: } \mathbf{pre}(act\_fail) \rightarrow act\_fail \tag{4}
$$

Guarantees 3 and 4 are repeated for each actuator. The variable num_valid represents the number of valid actuator signals from other FCCs, act represents the signal being sent to the actuator, low represents the lower bound of the actuator signal, $high$ represents the upper bound of the actuator signal, and act_fail is a Boolean variable that is true if the actuator signal is latched failed.

3.4   Output Signal Analysis and Selection

Each actuator signal is computed by the OSAS component. The redundant actuators apply force to their associated control surface in parallel. The requirements for the OSAS component determine the gain to be applied to each actuator signal depending on whether there have been failures in the other FCCs. The OSAS component also has requirements that state how the value of an actuator signal is determined in the event of a failure in the OSAS component's own FCC. Requirements OSAS-S-180, OSAS-S-140, and OSAS-S-170 reflect some of the

> **OSAS-S-180** - OSAS shall compute the actuator command gain as the ratio of the total number of command channels to the number of valid command channels (i.e. 4/(number of valid command channels)).

> **OSAS-S-140** - When an actuator command has been latched failed, OSAS shall set that actuator command to 0 (zero).

> **OSAS-S-170** - If the local CCDL has failed, OSAS shall set the local actuator command gain to 1 (one).

requirements used to determine the gain of each actuator signal. Their formalizations are shown as Guarantees 5, 6, and 7, respectively.

$$
\begin{aligned}
\textbf{guarantee:} \\
(num\_valid = 0 \rightarrow fcc\_gain = 4) \wedge \\
(num\_valid = 1 \rightarrow fcc\_gain = 2) \wedge \\
(num\_valid = 2 \rightarrow fcc\_gain = 4/3) \wedge \\
(num\_valid = 3 \rightarrow fcc\_gain = 1)
\end{aligned}
\tag{5}
$$

$$
\textbf{guarantee:} \ (latched\_failed \rightarrow fcc\_gain = 0)
\tag{6}
$$

$$
\textbf{guarantee:} \ (ccdl\_failed \rightarrow fcc\_gain = 1)
\tag{7}
$$

There are other requirements that determine the true actuator gain value for the OSAS component, but they have been omitted here for the sake of space. These guarantees are used to prove Guarantee 3 in the FCC, and the composition of the FCC contracts are used to prove Guarantee 1 in the FCS.

In the next section we discuss errors that were discovered through the process of formalizing and analysing the QFCS requirements in AGREE.

4 Analysis Results

We ran our analysis on a laptop computer with an Intel® i5 CPU and 16GB of RAM. The tool was run inside a virtual machine running Ubuntu Linux. Using JKind as the model checker and Yices [12] as the SMT Solver, the contract for the FCS was proved in 7 seconds and the contract for the FCC (all four FCCs had identical contracts) was proven in 115 seconds. Kind 2.0 had similar performance. In Table 1 we list some information about the size of the QFCS AADL model and the number of requirements that we formalized for each component. The *Inputs* and *Outputs* columns list the number of input and output features, respectively, that are present in the AADL model. Many of these features are complex structures that consist of multiple data fields. For example, one actuator output consists of 20 real number values. The number of variables generated in the Lustre code that is sent to the model checker is on the order of hundreds for each component. The *Guarantees* column reports the number of guarantees in each component contract. This number roughly corresponds to the number of English language requirements that we formalized for each component from the requirements hierarchy described in Figure 1. The number of guarantees is not exactly the same as the number of English language requirements because the language of some of the requirements was changed somewhat during formalization (as discussed in Section 3).

Table 1. Information about the QFCS AADL Model

Component	Inputs	Outputs	Guarantees
FCS	13	12	2
FCC	11	22	9
OSAS	9	4	9
ISAS	9	18	11
CLAW	1	1	1

Through the course of our analysis, we discovered a number of problems with the QFCS requirements. These errors were discovered either through formalizing the requirements, attempting to prove properties, or using AGREE's realizability analysis (which we describe briefly later in this section). In this section we give a few examples of the kinds of problems that we found.

4.1   Errors Found During Formalization

Some requirements contained clear mistakes that were found through formalizing the English text. In our experience, this is almost always a benefit of formalizing requirements. One of these requirements is shown in Requirement ISAS-S-260.

ISAS-S-260 - ISAS shall determine the selected value for a quad digital signal using the following table:

1. 4 good values with total range less than *SignalTolerance*, average all 4
2. 4 good values with total range greater than *SignalTolerance*, average middle 2
3. 3 good values with total range less than *SignalTolerance*, average all 3
4. 3 good values with total range greater than *SignalTolerance*, select middle value
5. 2 good values with total range less than *SignalTolerance*, average values

---

Interpreting this requirement at face value would indicate that the selected signal from a set of quad redundant digital signals would be completely unconstrained in the event that the range of all four values of the quad-redundant signals were exactly equal to *SignalTolerance*. This does not seem to be the intent of the requirement as it is stated. This problem was discovered while formalizing the requirement, but it would have otherwise been discovered while verifying assumptions about the CLAW component input signal ranges.

4.2   Errors Found During Model Checking

For some QFCS components we were able to check whether or not the implementation met its requirements. In addition to the requirements for the ISAS component, we were also provided with an algorithmic specification (in tabular format) for its implementation. We formalized this specification and attempted to prove that it met its formalized requirements. This analysis can be performed in AGREE by determining if a component's guarantees are entailed by *assertions* about the component's implementation. In essence, component assertions are treated similarly to the component assumptions described in Section 2, but are not checked to determine whether they hold as result of the system level assumptions. Unlike component assumptions, which must be proven to hold by Formula 4, component assertions are thought of as "details about how a component is designed."

The ISAS component is responsible for determining a selected sensor value to send to the CLAW component from a set of redundant input signals. Some input signals are quad redundant while others are dual redundant. Among the quad redundant signals are values from the Embedded GPS/INS Sensor (EGI). For each dual redundant signal, there exists a roughly equivalent signal that can be computed from the EGI. In the event that the two values of a dual input signal miscompare (are not equal within some tolerance) the equivalent value of the EGI is selected to be sent to the CLAW component. During verification it was discovered that the implementation for the ISAS component did not correctly implement Requirement ISAS-S-220. The implementation for the ISAS component did not meet this requirement when the following scenario occurred.

- Channels 1 and 2 of a dual redundant signal are neither stale nor out-of-range
- Channels 1 and 2 of a dual redundant signal miscompare
- The equivalent value from the EGI is not declared faulty
- Channel 1 of a dual redundant signal miscompares with its equivalent EGI parameter
- Channel 2 of a dual redundant signal does not miscompare with its equivalent EGI parameter

In this scenario, the implementation selects the average of Channel 2 of a dual redundant signal with its equivalent EGI parameter. AGREE produced a counterexample showing this behavior. Through discussions with the domain experts, it was determined that the implementation was correct, and the requirement should be amended to handle this scenario in the same manner.

ISAS-S-220 - In the case of mismatched dual input signals, ISAS shall set the selected value equal to the equivalent selected value of EGI data.

4.3 Errors Found During Realizability Analysis

AGREE also has an analysis option to determine if a component's contract is *realizable*. This analysis is detailed in other work [13]. Informally, a component's contract is realizable if there exists some implementation for the component that obeys the contract. Realizability is a stronger notion than consistency. For example, consider a component with a single integer input and a single integer output. Suppose the component's contract guarantees that the output is always half the value of its input. The component's contract is consistent because there are certainly some values for the input that satisfies this contract (e.g., if the input is 2 then the output would be 1). However, if the input is an odd value then there is no corresponding integer value for the output. This contract is not realizable because there is no way to implement a component that could compute output values to satisfy this contract for every allowable input value.

A diligent reader may have noticed that Requirements OSAS-S-140 and OSAS-S-170 are stated, likewise Guarantees 6 and 7 are formulated, in a way that makes them unrealizable. What happens in the scenario where an actuator is latched failed and the CCDL fails? There is a contradiction in what the selected gain value should be (should it be 0 or 1?). This error eluded the engineers who originally drafted the requirements as well as the engineers who formalized them. However, AGREE's realizability analysis was able to identify the error and provide a counterexample with variables $latched\_failed$ and $ccdl\_failed$ set to true.

After discussing the error with the domain experts who wrote the requirements, it was determined that the solution was to set an order of precedence for how the gain value is computed. For example, Guarantees 5, 6 and 7 could be reformalized as Guarantees 8, 9 and 10.

guarantee:
$$not\ (latched\_failed \lor ccdl\_failed) \rightarrow$$
$$(num\_valid = 0 \Rightarrow fcc\_gain = 4)\land$$
$$(num\_valid = 1 \Rightarrow fcc\_gain = 2)\land \tag{8}$$
$$(num\_valid = 2 \Rightarrow fcc\_gain = 4/3)\land$$
$$(num\_valid = 3 \Rightarrow fcc\_gain = 1)$$

guarantee:
$$(latched\_failed \Rightarrow fcc\_gain = 0) \tag{9}$$

guarantee:
$$(not\ latched\_failed \land ccdl\_failed \Rightarrow fcc\_gain = 1) \tag{10}$$

5   Lessons Learned

Through the course of this project we developed a number of insights about the challenges and benefits associated with formalizing and proving requirements compositionally.

- Many of the requirements that we attempted to formalize were not conducive to compositional verification. Some of the high level requirements contained language that included details about lower level components. These types of requirements are hard to prove compositionally because they require details about components that are at a low level in the hierarchy to be exposed at a high level. Care should be taken when drafting requirements to make sure that they are precise but still abstract enough to reasoned about compositionally.
- Often when we found that a component implementation failed to meet its requirements, the requirements were amended to be satisfied by the implementation. This scenario seemed to occur frequently because the requirements were not expressed formally in the first place. The examples given in Sections 4.2 and 4.3 are illustrations of this.
- Requirements are hard to formalize without a clear description of the model's architecture. We started this project without descriptions of the component interfaces. Upon receiving the interface descriptions, it was clear that many of our original formalizations were not correct.
- Often times proof failures will expose errors in the model. For example an incorrect connection between two components will often cause the model checker to produce a counter example to properties that would normally seem trivial. Formalizing and proving requirements gives some assurance that the architectural model is correct.

6   Conclusion

Much of the effort in this work was spent trying to find reasonable formalizations for the original English language properties. The formalization process itself identified significant problems with the requirements as they were originally stated. Even after formalization, model checking and realizability analysis identified a number of other issues.

Future work includes modeling more of the QFCS architecture in AADL, and formalizing other requirements in AGREE. In this project all of the components were modeled to execute synchronously. Based on discussions with the QFCS designers this seemed to be a fair assumption. However, many systems are composed of components that execute on different clock domains. Support for modeling components that execute asynchronously (or quasi-synchronously [14]) is currently being added to AGREE.

References

1. Crum, V., Buffington, J., Tallant, G., Krogh, B., Plaisted, C., Prasanth, R., Bose, P., Johnson, T.: Validation verification of intelligent and adaptive control systems. In: Proceedings of the Aerospace Conference 2004. IEEE (2004)
2. Feiler, P.H., Gluch, D.P.: Model-Based Engineering with AADL: An Introduction to the SAE Architecture Analysis & Design Language, 1st edn. Addison-Wesley Professional (2012)
3. The Software Engineering Institute: OSATE: Plug-ins for front-end processing of AADL models (2013)
4. Cofer, D.D., Gacek, A., Miller, S.P., Whalen, M.W., LaValley, B., Sha, L.: Compositional verification of architectural models. In: Goodloe, A.E., Person, S. (eds.) Proceedings of the 4th NASA Formal Methods Symposium (NFM 2012). Berlin, vol. 7226, pp. 126–140. Heidelberg, Springer-Verlag (2012)
5. Gacek, A., Backes, J., Whalen, M.W., Cofer, D.: AGREE Users Guide[3] (2014). http://github.com/smaccm/smaccm
6. Halbwachs, N., Caspi, P., Raymond, P., Pilaud, D.: The synchronous dataflow programming language LUSTRE. In: Proceedings of the IEEE, pp. 1305–1320 (1991)
7. University of Iowa: Kind2: a multi-engine smt-based automatic model checker for safety properties of lustre programs (2014)
8. JKind: A Java implementation of the KIND model checker[4] (2013). http://github.com/agacek/jkind
9. Hueschen, R.M.: Development of the transport class model (TCM) aircraft simulation from a sub-scale generic transport model (GTM) simulation. NASA Technical Report (2011)
10. Brat, G., Bushnell, D., Davies, M., Giannakopoulou, D., Howar, F., Kahsai, T.: Verifying the saftety of a flight-critical system. NASA Technical Report (2015)
11. Cooper, G., Harper, R.: The use of pilot rating in the evaluation of aircraft handling qualities. NASA Technical Report (1969)
12. Dutertre, B., de Moura, L.: The Yices SMT solver. SRI International Tech Report (2006)
13. Gacek, A., Katis, A., Whalen, M., Backes, J., Cofer, D.: Towards realizability checking for contracts using theories. In: NASA Formal Methods Symposium (2015)
14. Caspi, P., Mazuet, C., Paligot, N.R.: About the design of distributed control systems, the quasi-synchronous approach (2001)

Partial Order Reduction and Symmetry with Multiple Representatives

Dragan Bošnački[⊠] and Mark Scheffer

Eindhoven University of Technology, Eindhoven, The Netherlands
dragan@win.tue.nl, m.scheffer@tue.nl

Abstract. Symmetry reduction is one of the most successful techniques to cope with the state explosion problem in model-checking. One of the central issues in symmetry reduction is the problem of finding unique (canonical) representatives of equivalence classes of symmetric states. This problem is equivalent to the graph isomorphism problem, for which no polynomial algorithm is known. On the other hand finding multiple (non-canonical) representatives is much easier because it usually boils down to sorting algorithms. As a consequence, with multiple representatives one can significantly improve the verification times. In this paper we show that symmetry reduction with multiple representatives can be combined with partial order reduction, another efficient state space reduction technique. To this end we introduce a new weaker notion of independence which requires confluence only up to bisimulation.

1 Introduction

Symmetry reduction [3,6,20] is one of the most successful techniques to tackle the state space explosion problem in model checking. The technique exploits the inherent symmetry of the model which is present in many systems, like mutual exclusion algorithms, cache coherence protocols, bus communication protocols, etc. After observing that the symmetry in the description of the model results in a symmetric state space, the key idea is to partition the state space into equivalence classes of (symmetric) states. Then, the state space exploration can be performed in the usually smaller quotient state space that consists only of (representatives of the) equivalence classes.

The problem of finding canonical, i.e., unique, representatives of equivalence classes is also known as the *orbit problem*. The orbit problem is equivalent to the graph isomorphism problem [3], for which no polynomial algorithm is known. As a result, often with symmetry reduction the verification time can become critical. On the other hand, finding multiple (non-canonical) representatives usually boils down to sorting algorithms [2,6]. An obvious drawback of the multiple representatives is that they provide less state space reduction compared to the canonical representatives. However, in practice it often turns out that, with an acceptable increase of the state space, the verification time can be improved significantly by using multiple representatives [2,20].

© Springer International Publishing Switzerland 2015
K. Havelund et al. (Eds.): NFM 2015, LNCS 9058, pp. 97–111, 2015.
DOI: 10.1007/978-3-319-17524-9_8

It is always an advantage if one can combine symmetry with other reduction techniques which are orthogonal to it, i.e., which exploit different aspects of the system for reduction of the state space. One such technique is partial order reduction [11, 21, 23].

Partial order reduction exploits the independence of the checked property from the execution order of the system actions. More specifically, two actions a, b are allowed to be permuted precisely when, if for all sequences v, w of actions: if $vabw$ (where juxtaposition denotes concatenation) is an accepted behavior, then $vbaw$ is an accepted behavior as well. In a sense, instead of checking all the execution sequences, the desired property is checked only on representative sequences, which results in significant savings in space and time. Thus, the corner stone of the independence relation is the confluence condition as given in Fig. 1a. The confluence requires that from each state s of the state space the permutations of two independent actions a and b will lead to the same state s'. The actual reduction of the state space is realized during the state space exploration by limiting the search from a given state s to only a subset of the actions that are executable in s.

The problem of combining symmetry based on canonical representatives with partial order reduction was solved in [9]. In fact, this paper can be seen as a continuation of [9] which also deals with multiple representatives. Following [9] we derive our result in the more general setting of bisimulation preserving reductions. As symmetry reduction is just a special case of a bisimulation preserving reduction, all results are valid for symmetry too.

The central idea of this paper is to use a new notion of independence, which is weaker than the standard one. As mentioned above, in the usual definition of independence we insist on confluence, i.e., we require that the two paths obtained by permuting the independent actions a and b meet in the same state s'. Instead, in the new definition we relax the confluence condition by allowing the permutations to lead to *bisimilar states* s'_1 and s'_2, as represented in Fig. 1b.

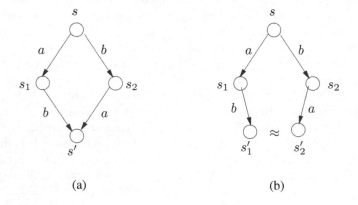

(a)   (b)

Fig. 1. Confluence of independent actions

It turns out that almost all property preservation results, like absence of deadlock, safety, and liveness (LTL and CTL^* without the next operator), that can be found in the literature can be reused with a straightforward adaptation.

Related work other than [9]. The usefulness of multiple representatives (without partial order reduction) is discussed in several papers (e.g. [20], [3]).

To the best of our knowledge only [12] tackles the problem of combining symmetry with multiple representatives and partial order reduction. The main difference compared to our work is that [12] works only with safety properties, while we also show preservation of liveness properties given in the next-free versions of LTL and CTL^*. Also the multiple representatives used in [12] are of a special kind.[1] As [12] targets software model checking, it deals with symmetry based on transitions instead of states. We believe that our concept of weak independence leads to a more seamless reusage of the results that exists in the literature. This is because the latter are mostly based on symmetry of states.

The concept of *symmetric independence* was introduced in [19]. It turns out that the concept is a special case of our weak independence. However, symmetric independence is used in [19] in a different context of combining partial order reduction with so-called heap symmetries for software model checking. Also, [19] assumes only canonical representatives.

Paper layout. The next section provides some basic definitions and terminology used in the paper. Section 3.1 recalls some of the main concepts and results from [9]. The main contributions of the paper are contained in Sections 3.2 and 4. In Section 3.2 we introduce the definition of weak independence and give the property preservation results that can be derived from it. In Section 4 we show that the combination of partial order reduction and a bisimulation preserving reduction also preserves deadlock, safety (local) properties, and next-free LTL and CTL^* formulae which are invariant under the preserved bisimulation. Section 5 deals with some experimental results that confirm the practical benefit of the presented theory. The last section concludes the paper and provides some directions for future work.

2   Preliminaries

In the paper we use temporal logics defined in the standard way. For the definitions of CTL^* and LTL, as well as their variants without the next operator CTL^*-X and LTL-X, we refer the reader to, for instance, [5].

We represent the state space of the system which is checked as a *labeled transition system* formally defined as follows:

---

[1] For the sake of truth it should be said that the derivation of the results can be done for the general case.

Definition 1. *Let Π be a set of atomic propositions. A labeled transition system (LTS) is a 5-tuple $T = (S, R, L, A, \hat{s})$, where*

- *S is a finite set of states,*
- *$R \subseteq S \times A \times S$ is a transition relation (we write $s \xrightarrow{a} s' \in R$ for $(s, a, s') \in R$),*
- *$L : S \to 2^{\Pi}$ is a labeling function which associates with each state a set of atomic propositions that are true in the state,*
- *A is a finite set of actions,*
- *$\hat{s}$ is the initial state,*

Unless stated differently, we fix T to be $(S, R, L, A, \hat{s})$ for the rest of the paper.

An action a is *enabled* in a state $s \in S$ iff $s \xrightarrow{a} s' \in R$ for some $s' \in S$. We denote the set of enabled actions in a given state s with $en_T(s)$. Similarly, for given $s \in S$ and $a \in A$ we define $a_T(s) = \{s' \mid s \xrightarrow{a} s' \in R\}$. An *execution sequence* or *path* is a finite or infinite sequence of subsequent transitions, i.e., for $s_i \in S$, $a_i \in A$, the sequence $s_0 \xrightarrow{a_0} s_1 \xrightarrow{a_1} s_2 \dots$ is an execution sequence in T iff $s_i \xrightarrow{a_i} s_{i+1} \in R$ for all $i \geq 0$. A finite execution sequence $c = s_0 \xrightarrow{a_0} s_1 \xrightarrow{a_1} \dots \xrightarrow{a_{n-1}} s_n$, $n \geq 1$ is a *cycle* iff the start and end states coincide, i.e. $s_0 = s_n$. A state s is *reachable* iff there exists a finite execution sequence that starts at $\hat{s}$ and ends in s.

Next, we define bisimulation between two LTSs:

Definition 2. *Given two LTSs $T_1 = (S_1, R_1, L_1, A, \hat{s}_1)$ and $T_2 = (S_2, R_2, L_2, A, \hat{s}_2)$, an equivalence relation $\equiv \subseteq S_1 \times S_2$ is called a bisimulation between T_1 and T_2 iff the following conditions hold:*

- *$\hat{s}_1 \equiv \hat{s}_2$;*
- *If $s \equiv s'$, then:*
  - *$L_1(s) = L_2(s')$;*
  - *Given an arbitrary transition $s \xrightarrow{a} s_1 \in R_1$, there exists $s_2 \in S_2$ such that $s' \xrightarrow{a} s_2 \in R_2$ and $s_1 \equiv s_2$;*
  - *The symmetric condition holds: given an arbitrary transition $s' \xrightarrow{a} s_2 \in R_2$, there exists $s_1 \in S_1$ such that $s \xrightarrow{a} s_1 \in R_1$ and $s_1 \equiv s_2$;*

We say that T_1 and T_2 are bisimilar *iff there exists a bisimulation between T_1 and T_2.*

3   Property Preserving Reductions

3.1   Bisimulation Preserving Reduction

In this section we recall some definitions and results from [9]. Our starting point is the idea to model check in an abstract state space, which is usually much smaller than the original one. To this end, the original state set S is partitioned into equivalence classes. The abstract state space consists of (not necessarily unique) representatives of these classes, chosen by a function h, with transitions between them as defined below.

Definition 3. *Given a function* $h : S \to S$ *on LTS* $T = (S, R, L, A, \hat{s})$, *we define the corresponding* abstract LTS T_h *to be* $(S_h, R_h, L_h, A, h(\hat{s}))$, *where*

- $S_h = h(S)$, *the set of representatives,*
- $r_1 \xrightarrow{a} r_2 \in R_h$ *iff there exists* $s \in S$ *such that* $r_1 \xrightarrow{a} s \in R$ *and* $h(s) = r_2$.
- *for all* $r \in S_h$, $L_h(r) = L(r)$.

In order to preserve the properties of interest that hold in T also in T_h we need to impose some additional constraints on the function h. In particular, we require that the equivalence class induced by the partitioning is a bisimulation.

Definition 4. *For a given LTS* T, *a function* $h : S \to S$ *is a* selection function *iff there exists a bisimulation* $\equiv \subseteq S \times S$ *between* T *and* T *such that for all* $s \in S$, $s \equiv h(s)$.

Intuitively, the function h picks one or more representatives for each equivalence class of S induced by $\equiv$. It should be emphasized that in the definition of selection function in [9] h is required to satisfy the additional property

$$s \equiv s' \text{ implies that } h(s) = h(s')$$

which in the sequel we call *canonicity requirement*. Obviously, with this requirement each equivalence class has a canonical (unique) representative. In what follows we assume that h is a selection function without the canonicity requirement, which allows multiple representatives per equivalence class.

We say that h *preserves* the bisimulation relation $\equiv$. The following result is implied by the definitions given above:

Lemma 1 ([9]). *Given an LTS* $T = (S, R, L, A, \hat{s})$ *and a selection function* h, T *and* T_h *are bisimilar.*

Lemma 1 is actually Lemma 8 from [9]. The proof of that lemma in [9] is valid in our setting too because it does not use the canonicity requirement for the representatives. (Due to lack of space most of the proofs are omitted in this version of the paper.)

The main consequence of Lemma 1 is the following result [9]:

Theorem 1. *Given a LTS* T, *let* ϕ *be a formula in* CTL^*-X *over the set of atomic propositions* Π *of* T. *Let* T' *be an LTS which is bisimilar to* T. *The formula* ϕ *is satisfied by* T *iff it is satisfied by* T'. *(See [5] for a definition of the satisfaction of an* CTL^*-X*formula by an LTS.)*

The result above implies that we can do the model checking in the reduced state space. Notice that the property ϕ is in fact not an arbitrary CTL^*-Xformula. The set of preserved formulae is limited by the choice of the set of atomic propositions Π and the bisimulation relation. Thus, there is an implicit requirement that ϕ is invariant under the bisimulation $\equiv$ which is preserved by the reduction. More precisely, if $prop(\phi) \subseteq \Pi$ is the set of atomic propositions in ϕ, we have that for all $s, s' \in S$, if $s \equiv s'$, then $L(s) \cap prop(\phi) = L(s') \cap prop(\phi)$. (The last condition is obviously trivially satisfied because we have $L(s) = L(s')$ from the definition of T_h.)

3.2   Partial Order Reduction

This section and the next one contain the main contributions of the paper. In the current section we combine the systematization of the properties which are preserved under partial order reduction from [26] with a definition of reduced LTS along the lines of [1]. After the definition of the reduced LTS modulo a reduction function r, we list some conditions on this function, which ensure preservation of particular properties. Intuitively, during the construction of the reduced LTS in each new state the function r selects only a subset of the enabled actions in that state.

Definition 5 ((Partial Order) Reduction).   *For any so-called* reduction *function* $r : S \to 2^R$, *we define the (partial-order)* reduction *of* T *with respect to* r *as the smallest LTS* $T^r = (S^r, R^r, L^r, A, \hat{s})$ *satisfying the following conditions:*

- $S^r \subseteq S$, $R^r \subseteq R$, *and* $L^r = L \cap (S^r \times 2^\Pi)$;
- *for every* $s \in S^r$, *if* $s \xrightarrow{a} s'$ *is in* $r(s)$, *then* $s \xrightarrow{a} s'$ *is in* R^r.

Note that these requirements imply that, for every $s \in S^r$ *and* $a \in A$, *if* $s \xrightarrow{a} s' \in R^r$, *then also* $s \xrightarrow{a} s' \in R$. *For every* $s \in S$ *we define* $act(r(s)) = \{a \mid \exists s'.s \xrightarrow{a} s' \in r(s)\}$.

It may be clear that not all reductions preserve all properties of interest. Thus, depending on the properties that a reduction must preserve, we have to define additional restrictions on r. To this end, we need to formally capture the notion of independence introduced earlier. Actions occurring in different processes may still influence each other, for example, when they access global variables in the specification. The following notion of independence defines the absence of such mutual influence. Intuitively, two actions are independent iff, in every state where they are both enabled, (1) the execution of one action cannot disable the other and (2) the result of executing both actions is always the same or similar state.

Definition 6 (Independence).   *Given an LTS* $T = (S, R, L, A, \hat{s})$ *and a relation* $\approx \subseteq S \times S$, *an irreflexive and symmetric relation* $I \subseteq A \times A$ *is a* $\approx$-independence relation *on actions iff for each pair of actions* $(a, b) \in I$ *(called* independent actions*) it must hold that for each* $s \in S$, *if* $\{a, b\} \subseteq en_T(s)$ *then*

- *for each state state* $s' \in a_T(s)$ *we have that* $b \in en_T(s')$.
- *there exists a path* $s \xrightarrow{a} s_1 \xrightarrow{b} s'$ *in* T *iff there exists a path* $s \xrightarrow{b} s_2 \xrightarrow{a} s''$ *in* T *and* $s' \approx s''$.

In what follows we assume that $\approx$ is either the identity or a bisimulation relation. The first version of $\approx$-independence, obtained by taking $s' \approx s''$ iff $s' = s''$, corresponds to the usual definition of independence that can be found in the literature. Therefore, throughout the paper we refer to it simply as *(standard) independence*. The second version, when $\approx$ is a bisimulation relation, we call *weak independence*. We introduce the latter in order to combine bisimulation preserving reductions with partial order reduction.

In order to reuse as seamlessly as possible the existing results about partial order reduction in the sequel we assume that T is $\approx$-*deterministic*, i.e., for any $s \in S$ and $a \in A$ it holds that if $s \xrightarrow{a} s'$ and $s \xrightarrow{a} s''$ are in R, then $s' \approx s''$. This is not a serious limitation because the symmetry reduction (or more precisely, symmetry equivalence), which is our main target, satisfies this constraint. (Nondeterminism and partial order reduction can be reconciled too with certain modifications of the criteria presented below [22, 23].)

The first class of properties we are interested in is the presence or absence of deadlocks. To preserve deadlock states of an LTS in a reduced LTS, the reduction function r must satisfy the following two conditions:

C0 $r(s) = \emptyset$ iff $en_T(s) = \emptyset$.

C1 (persistency) For any $s \in S$ and a finite execution sequence $s = s_0 \xrightarrow{a_0} s_1 \xrightarrow{a_1} \ldots \xrightarrow{a_{n-1}} s_n$ with $a_i \notin r(s)$ for all i ($0 \le i < n$), action a_{n-1} is $\approx$-independent of all actions in $act(r(s))$.

Theorem 2 (Deadlock Preservation). *Let r be a reduction function for LTS T that satisfies C0 and C1. Then the following holds:*

- *if a deadlock state s is reachable in T, then there exists a deadlock state $s' \approx s$ which is reachable in the reduced LTS T^r.*
- *if a deadlock state s' is reachable in T^r, then there exists a deadlock state $s \approx s'$ which is reachable in the original LTS T.*

Proof of the theorem for the case when $\approx$ is the identity relation (standard independence) can be found, for instance, in [11](Theorem 4.3).[2] With straightforward modifications the proof of [11] carries over to the case of weak independence.

The second class of properties we discuss are the local properties. A local property is a boolean combination of propositions in Π whose truth value cannot be changed by two $\approx$-independent actions: That is, a property ϕ is *local* iff, for all states $s, s', s'' \in S$ and $\approx$-*independent* actions $a, b \in A$ such that

- $a, b \in en_T(s)$,
- $s \xrightarrow{a} s'$, $s \xrightarrow{b} s''$ and
- ϕ has different truth values in states s and s',

the truth values of ϕ in s and in s'' are the same. An LTS satisfies a local property ϕ iff there is a reachable state that satisfies ϕ. Typical examples of local properties are properties that depend only on the state of a single process or shared object. Notice that ϕ is invariant under $\approx$, i.e., for any $s, s' \in S$ such that $s \approx s'$, and for any atomic proposition $\pi \in \Pi$ in ϕ, it holds $\pi \in L(s) \Leftrightarrow \pi \in L(s')$. To guarantee that a reduction of a state space preserves local properties, it suffices that the reduction function r satisfies the following requirement (in addition to C0 and C1).

---

[2] In [11] a slightly stronger definition of (standard) independence is used. However, the proof of Theorem 4.3 in [11] stays valid also with our definition of standard independence.

C2 (cycle proviso). For any *cycle* $s_0 \xrightarrow{a_0} s_1 \xrightarrow{a_1} \ldots \xrightarrow{a_{n-1}} s_n = s_0$ there is an i with $0 \leq i < n$ such that $r(s_i) = en_T(s_i)$.

Theorem 3 (Local-Property Preservation). *Let r be a reduction function for LTS T satisfying conditions C0, C1, and C2; let ϕ be a local property. LTS T satisfies ϕ iff the reduced LTS T^r satisfies ϕ.*

Condition C2 prevents the so-called 'ignoring problem' identified in [24]. Informally, this problem occurs when a reduction of a state space ignores the actions of an entire process. Proofs of (variants of) Theorem 3 for standard independence can be found in [11,17,24]. For weak independence the theorem can be proved in an analogous way. In fact, [11,17,24] show that C2 can be weakened if one is only interested in the preservation of local properties. The stronger proviso given above is needed for the preservation of next-time-free LTL properties, which is the third class of properties we are interested in.

For any LTL formula ϕ over the set of atomic propositions Π of a given LTS T, $prop(\phi)$ is the set of atomic propositions in ϕ.

Definition 7 (Invisibility). *An action $a \in A$ is ϕ-invisible in state $s \in S$ iff $a \notin en_T(s)$ or, for all $\pi \in prop(\phi)$ and $s' \in S$ such that $s \xrightarrow{a} s'$, $\pi \in L(s) \Leftrightarrow \pi \in L(s')$. Action a is globally ϕ-invisible iff it is ϕ-invisible for all $s \in S$.*

Informally, a globally ϕ-invisible action cannot change the truth value of the formula ϕ.

C3 (invisibility). For any state $s \in S$, all actions in $act(r(s))$ are globally ϕ-invisible or $r(s) = en_{T_h}(s)$.

Theorem 4 (Next-Time-Free LTL Preservation). *Let r be a reduction function for LTS T satisfying C0, C1, C2, and C3; let ϕ be a next-time-free LTL formula. T satisfies ϕ iff the reduced LTS T^r satisfies ϕ.*

The proof of (variants of) Theorem 4 for standard independence can be found in [4,18,21,25]. The proof of [4] is seamlessly adjusted for weak independence too. A similar remark to the one at the end of Section 3.1 for the preservation of CTL^*-X and the local properties above can also be given for LTL-X– there is an implicit requirement that ϕ is invariant under $\approx$.

In [9] it is discussed how symmetry can be combined with partial order reduction for CTL^*-X. It is shown that the algorithm [10] can be reused also in the setting of [9]. Analogously one can show that the same algorithm can be straightforwardly adapted for the case with multiple representatives. The r function for CTL^*-X differs from the one for LTL by the fact that it must satisfy an additional condition

C4 (singleton). The set $r(s)$ is a singleton set or $r(s) = en_T(s)$.

In an analogous way as for LTL we define the invisibility of actions with regard to a given formula. It can be shown that CTL^*-X formulae which are invariant under bisimulation are preserved in the reduced state space obtained with the additional condition. In the proof of the following theorem we assume that the original LTS T is deterministic, i.e., that $|a_T(s)| \leq 1$, for each $s \in S, a \in A$.

Theorem 5 (Next-Time-Free CTL Preservation). *Let r be a reduction function for LTS T satisfying C0, C1, C2, C3, and C4; let ϕ be a CTL^*-X formula. T satisfies ϕ iff the reduced LTS T^r satisfies ϕ.*

As absence of deadlock, local properties, and LTL-X formulae can be expressed in CTL^*-X, it might look like we could have shown only the preservation of the latter, or maybe only of LTL-X and CTL^*-X, as it is done in [9]. However, in practice, it is often useful to use the weaker variants on the conditions imposed on r in order to achieve a better reduction. Therefore, we opted for giving the gradual strengthening on the conditions on r, following the usual hierarchical property classification (see [26]).

4   Combining Bisimulation Preserving Reductions with Partial Order Reduction

In this section we combine the bisimulation preserving reduction with partial order reduction in two ways. In the first approach, which we introduce only for the sake of the proof and which we call *sequentially combined reduction*, we first apply the bisimulation preserving reduction in order to obtain the abstract LTS T_h. After that we apply partial order reduction on T_h. We use for $\approx$ in the definition of r the bisimulation which is preserved by h, i.e., we assume weak independence. Intuitively, the second more efficient approach corresponds to applying both partial order and bisimulation reduction simultaneously while generating (on-the-fly) the (reduced) state space. So, we refer to this approach as *simultaneously combined reduction*. We assume the same weak independence relation as in the first approach. Actually, it turns out that we can reuse the independence relation of the original LTS T, as a weak independence relation for the reduction in the reduced state space in both approaches. The correctness of the first combination follows straightforwardly from the preservation results presented in the previous section. Thus, we establish the correctness of the second approach by showing that both approaches generate the same reduced state space, provided that the same selection and reduction functions are used in both cases.

Definition 8 (Sequentially Combined Reduction). *Given a LTS T and a selection function h we define the sequentially combined reduction $(T_h)^r$ to be the LTS obtained such that partial order reduction, as defined in Def. 5, is applied on the abstract LTS T_h.*

In order to preserve properties we substitute in r for $\approx$ the bisimulation $\equiv$ which is preserved by h. The preservation of the properties (deadlock, local, LTL-X, CTL^*-X) which hold in the original LTS T is implied by the preservation results from the previous section. In particular, the preservation from T to T_h is guaranteed by Theorem 1. The preservation in the second phase, between T_h and $(T_h)^r$, follows directly from Theorems 2 to 5. Hence, we can rephrase the theorems from the previous section for the sequentially combined reduction $(T_h)^r$. We give below only the theorem for CTL^*-X. The other properties can be formulated in an analogous way – i.e., by basically only replacing T^r with $(T_h)^r$ in the corresponding texts.

Theorem 6 (Next-Time-Free CTL Preservation Under Sequentially Combined Reduction). *Given an LTS T with a selection function h which preserves the bisimulation $\equiv$, let r be a reduction function which satisfies C0, C1, C2, C3, and C4, and which is based on $\equiv$-independence. Let ϕ be a CTL^*-X formula. T satisfies ϕ iff the reduced LTS $(T_h)^r$ satisfies ϕ.*

A generic algorithm for partial order reduction is given in Fig. 2. Applied to T_h it constructs the sequentially combined reduction $(T_h)^r$. (It is trivial to write a similar algorithm which generates T_h from T according to Def. 3.)

```
1 states := unexpanded := {ŝ}; transitions = ∅
2 while unexpanded ≠ ∅ do
3     remove a state s from unexpanded;
4     for each transition s ─a→ s' in r(s) do
5         if s' ∉ states then
6             add s' to states and unexpanded;
7             add s ─a→ s' to transitions
```

Fig. 2. An Algorithm for Sequentially Combined Reduction

The following definition paves the way to a more efficient algorithm for performing combined reduction:

Definition 9 (Simultaneously Combined Reduction). *Let T be a LTS for which we are given a selection function h, which preserves the bisimulation $\equiv$, and a reduction function r. We define the simultaneously combined reduction for T with respect to r and h as the smallest LTS $T_h^r = (S_h^r, R_h^r, L_h^r, A, h(\hat{s}))$ satisfying the following conditions:*

- $S_h^r \subseteq S$, $R_h^r \subseteq R$, and $L_h^r = L \cap (S_h^r \times 2^\Pi)$;
- *for every $s \in S_h^r$, if $s \xrightarrow{a} s'$ is in $r(s)$, then $s \xrightarrow{a} h(s')$ is in R_h^r.*

The algorithm in Fig. 3 is an implementation of the above definition.

The following theorem states the equivalence of the two reduction combinations, if they are featuring the same selection and reduction functions:

1 $states := unexpanded := \{h(\hat{s})\}; transitions = \emptyset$
2 while $unexpanded \neq \emptyset$ do
3   remove a state s from $unexpanded$;
4   for each transition $s \xrightarrow{a} s'$ in $r(s)$ do
5   if $h(s') \notin states$ then
6   add $h(s')$ to $states$ and $unexpanded$;
7   add $s \xrightarrow{a} h(s')$ to $transitions$

Fig. 3. An Algorithm for Simultaneously Combined Reduction

Theorem 7. *For a LTS T with a selection function h which preserves the bisimulation $\equiv$ it holds that $(T_h)^r = T_h^r$, provided that the functions r in both reductions are defined with $\equiv$-independence and satisfy the same subset of the conditions C0 to C4.*

The theorem can be proved in a similar way as Theorem 19 in [9]. After observing that with the conditions of the theorem the functions r are the same, we show that for each run of the algorithm in Fig. 2 there exists a corresponding run of the algorithm in Fig. 3. To this end we execute lock-step both runs and show that the invariant holds that the variables *states*, *transitions*, and *unexpanded* are the same in both executions. The following observation is important from practical point of view because it solves in an elegant way the requirement that the same weak independence has to be used in both approaches:

Lemma 2. *Let I be an independence relation for a LTS $T = (S, R, L, A, \hat{s})$ and h a bisimulation preserving selection function for T which preserves the bisimulation $\equiv$. In this case, I is a weak (i.e., $\equiv$) independence relation for the corresponding abstract LTS T_h.*

Again, this can be proved like the analogous Lemma 10 from [9] which holds for unique representatives.

In conclusion, Theorem 7 leads us directly to an algorithm for checking properties in a reduced LTS which is obtained by combining partial order and bisimulation reduction (thus, also symmetry) with multiple representatives. Moreover, this can be done on-the-fly and (by Lemma 2) reusing the independence relation of the original LTS T. (Notice that this provides a practical method for computing the reduction funciton r, i.e., the persistent sets of actions in presence of symmetries.) Such an algorithm can be obtained by adjusting in a straightforward way the algorithm in Fig. 3 to various well known algorithms for verification of safety and liveness properties.

5   Experimental Support

A prototype implementation of the algorithm described in the previous sections is included in SymmSpin [2], an extension of the model checker Spin [14] (version 3.4.16) with symmetry reductions. We tried it on the case studies from [2] with encouraging results. The obtained reductions for liveness properties were usually of several orders of magnitude, very similar to the results for the same examples for safety properties, reported in [2].

For comparison we also give the results of the experiments with standard Spin with and without the partial order reduction (POR) option, but without symmetry reduction (which does not exists in the standard version of the tool). The synergy between the symmetry and the partial order reductions which was reported in [2] for safety properties is observed also for liveness. The two reduction techniques are orthogonal because they exploit different features of the concurrent systems, therefore, their cumulative effect can be used to obtain more efficient verification.

We ran the symmetry reduction algorithm with four versions of the selection function h. Two of them are canonical (denoted here with "can1" and "can2") and correspond to the "segmented" and "pc-segmented" heuristic, respectively, from [2]. The other two, "mult1" and "mult2", yield multiple representatives and correspond to the "sorted" and "pc-sorted" heuristics, respectively, from [2]. Notice that the number of states for the canonical heuristics "can1" and "can2" is the same. Although they may produce different representatives, the number of symmetry classes remains the same (minimal) in both cases.

All experiments were performed on a PC machine with 1.7 GHz Pentium processor and 256 MB of main memory, running Red Hat Linux 7.0 operating system. Verification times (in the rows labeled with "t") are given in seconds ($s.x$), minutes ($m{:}s$), or hours ($h{:}m{:}s$); the number of states (in the rows labeled with "s") is given directly or in millions (say, 9.1M); $o.m.$ stands for out of memory, and $o.t.$ denotes out of time (more than 10 hours); time 0.0 means less than 0.1 second; +POR and -POR mean with and without POR, respectively.

Table 1 contains the results for the Data Base manager example from [2]. The verified property was absence of individual starvation expressed via Spin's non-progress cycle feature, which corresponds to an LTL formula of the form $\Diamond\Box p$. One can see that the reduction factor significantly improves as N increases, which is typical for symmetry reduction. Also, for greater N the verification times with the multiple representative heuristics are clearly better than the ones with the canonical representatives.

Also, it is interesting to notice that, in this particular example, the heuristics "mult2" actually produced canonical representatives. So, within the same state space, the verification times were improved for a factor greater than 10,000. The latter was due to the fact that the algorithm for canonical representatives has significant overhead compared to the one for multiple representatives. It is difficult to say, however, how often this most favorable situation would occur in practice. We did not observe with any of the other case studies.

Multiple representative heuristics were less successful in the case of Peterson's mutual exclusion protocol (Table 2). For this example we verified a bounded response type property (LTL formula: $\Box(p \rightarrow \Diamond q)$): each process that enters its critical section will eventually leave it. Obviously, for this case, non-canonical

Table 1. Results for the Data Base Manager example

N		7		8		9		10		11		12	
		+POR	-POR	+POR	-POR	+POR	-POR	+POR	-POR	+POR	-POR	+POR	-POR
no sym.	s	1809	5120	4627	17515	11541	59070	28183	196853	67609	649564	159771	2.1M
	t	0.0	0.1	0.0	0.4	0.1	1.3	0.3	5.3	0.6	26.4	1.6	3:08
can1	s	18	33	20	41	22	50	24	60	26	71	—	—
	t	0.2	0.2	1.5	1.7	15.2	16.8	3:09	3:12	35:01	40:13	o.t.	o.t.
can2	t	0.1	0.1	0.4	0.5	4.0	4.2	40.7	44.8	7:54	8:31	o.t.	o.t.
mult1	s	60	258	76	514	94	1026	114	2050	136	4098	160	8194
	t	0.0	0.0	0.0	0.0	0.0	0.1	0.0	0.1	0.0	0.2	0.0	0.5
mult2	s	18	60	20	93	22	157	24	247	26	417	28	661
	t	0.0	0.0	0.0	0.0	0.0	0.0	0.0	0.1	0.0	0.1	0.0	0.1

Table 2. Results for Peterson's mutual excusion protocol

N		2		3		4		5		6		7	
		+POR	-POR	+POR	-POR	+POR	-POR	+POR	-POR	+POR	-POR	+POR	-POR
no sym.	s	81	149	1353	3536	32836	89137	912833	2.596M	o.m.	o.m.	o.m.	o.m.
	t	0.1	0.1	0.1	0.1	0.3	0.9	7.5	32.6	—	—	—	—
can1	s	49	77	262	656	1610	4470	10029	27800	54366	162131	279528	898344
	t	0.2	0.2	0.2	0.2	0.2	0.4	0.5	1.5	3.6	18.6	46.0	4:44.5
can2	t	0.2	0.2	0.2	0.2	0.2	0.3	0.5	1.0	3.3	10.2	50.5	2:24.1
mult1	s	61	94	541	1260	5552	15247	65987	174287	653668	1.93M	o.m.	o.m.
	t	0.2	0.2	0.2	0.2	0.3	0.4	0.8	3.0	8.0	43.9	—	—
mult2	s	50	79	301	794	2948	7560	33395	82644	471720	1.05M	o.m.	o.m.
	t	0.2	0.2	0.2	0.2	0.2	0.3	0.6	1.6	6.7	22.7	—	—

heuristics cause much larger number of states which results in worse verification times. This observation is also consistent with the results in [2] for the same protocol obtained for safety properties.

6   Conclusion and Future Work

In this paper we showed that partial order reduction is compatible with symmetry reduction with multiple representatives. The results were derived in the more general setting of bisimulation preserving reduction as defined in [9]. As symmetry reduction is only a special case of a bisimulation preserving reduction, all results were automatically valid for the former too. The central idea was to introduce a new kind of independence which is weaker than the independence usually used in the literature. In particular, we weakened the confluence condition by requiring that the permutations of independent actions lead to bisimilar states.

Our results can be readily adapted for parallel model checking algorithms, e.g. [15], as well as for arbitrary search order of the state space, e.g., along the lines of [16].

From practical point of view, a very important direction for future work is to combine partial order, symmetry and fairness. A good starting point in that direction could be the algorithms for model checking by exploiting symmetry under (weak) fairness in [7,13].

The material in this paper was instigated mainly by authors' experience in model checking with explicit state representation. However, it should be possible to apply directly the results presented here also for symbolic model checking. To this end, a promising idea looks the combination of the partial order reduction algorithm presented in [1] and the existing work on symmetry reduction with multiple representatives (e.g. [3]) in the context of symbolic model checking. For instance, the adaptation for weak independence of the cycle proviso for breadth first search – one of the crucial ideas in [1] – should be quite straightforward.

Finally, it can be interesting to identify bisimulation preserving reductions other than symmetry. The results of the paper will of course be immediately applicable. A good candidate in that direction are the "almost symmetric" systems from [8].

References

1. Alur, R., Brayton, R.K., Henzinger, T.A., Qadeer, S., Rajamani, S.K.: Partial-Order reduction in symbolic state-space exploration. In: Grumberg, O. (ed.) CAV 1997. LNCS, vol. 1254, pp. 340–351. Springer, Heidelberg (1997)
2. Bošnački, D., Dams, D., Holenderski, L.: Symmetric Spin. International Journal on Software Tools for Technology Transfer **4**(1), 65–80 (2002)
3. Clarke, E.M., Enders, R., Filkorn, T., Jha, S.: Exploiting Symmetry in Temporal Logic Model Checking. Formal Methods in System Design **19**, 77–104 (1996)
4. Clarke, Jr., E.M., Grumberg, O., Peled, D.A.: Model Checking. The MIT Press (2000)
5. Emerson, E.A.: Temporal and modal logic. In: van Leeuwen, J. (ed.) Formal Models and Semantics, pp. 995–1072. Elsevier (1990)
6. Emerson, E.A., Sistla, A.P.: Symmetry and model checking. In: Courcoubetis, C. (ed.) CAV 1993. LNCS, vol. 697, pp. 463–478. Springer, Heidelberg (1993)
7. Emerson, E.A., Sistla, A.P.: Utilizing symmetry when model checking under fairness assumptions: an automata theoretic approach. In: Wolper, P. (ed.) CAV 1995. LNCS, vol. 939, pp. 309–324. Springer, Heidelberg (1995)
8. Emerson, E.A., Trefler, R.J.: From asymmetry to full symmetry: new techniques for symmetry reduction in model checking. In: Pierre, L., Kropf, T. (eds.) CHARME 1999. LNCS, vol. 1703, pp. 142–157. Springer, Heidelberg (1999)
9. Emerson, E.A., Jha, S., Peled, D.: Combining partial order and symmetry reductions. In: Brinksma, E. (ed.) TACAS 1997. LNCS, vol. 1217, pp. 19–34. Springer, Heidelberg (1997)

10. Gerth, R., Kuiper, R., Peled, D., Penczek, W.: A partial order reduction approach to branching time logic model checking. In: Proc. of Third Israel Symposium on Theory on Computing and Systems, pp. 130–139, Tel Aviv, Israel. IEEE (1995)
11. Godefroid, P. (ed.): Partial-Order Methods for the Verification of Concurrent Systems. LNCS, vol. 1032. Springer, Heidelberg (1996)
12. Godefroid, P.: Exploiting symmetry when model-checking software. In: Proc. of FORTE/PSTV 1999, Formal Methods for Protocol Engineering and Distributed Systems, pp. 257–275, Beijing, October 1999
13. Gyuris, V., Sistla, A.P.: On-the fly model checking under fairness that exploits symmetry. In: Grumberg, O. (ed.) CAV 1997. LNCS, vol. 1254, pp. 232–243. Springer, Heidelberg (1997)
14. Holzmann, G.J.: The SPIN Model Checker - primer and reference manual. Addison-Wesley (2004)
15. Holzmann, G.J., Bošnački, D.: The Design of a Multicore Extension of the SPIN Model Checker. IEEE Trans. Software Eng. **33**(10), 659–674 (2007)
16. Bošnački, D., Leue, S., Lluch-Lafuente, A.: Partial-Order Reduction for General State Exploring Algorithms. STTT **11**(1), 39–51 (2009)
17. Holzmann, G.J., Godefroid, P., Pirottin, D.: Coverage preserving reduction strategies for reachability analysis, protocol specification, testing and verification, pp. 349–363, XII. Elsevier (1992)
18. Holzmann, G., Peled, D.: An improvement in formal verification. In: FORTE 1994. Bern, Switzerland (1994)
19. Iosif, R.: Symmetry reduction criteria for software model checking. In: Bošnački, D., Leue, S. (eds.) SPIN 2002. LNCS, vol. 2318, pp. 22–41. Springer, Heidelberg (2002)
20. Ip, C.N., Dill, D.I.: Better verification through symmetry. Formal Methods in System Design **9**, 41–75 (1996)
21. Peled, D.: Combining partial order reductions with on-the-fly model checking. In: Dill, D.L. (ed.) CAV 1994. LNCS, vol. 818, pp. 377–390. Springer, Heidelberg (1994)
22. Peled, D.: Personal communication (2001)
23. Valmari, A.: The state explosion problem. In: Reisig, W., Rozenberg, G. (eds.) APN 1998. LNCS, vol. 1491, pp. 429–528. Springer, Heidelberg (1998)
24. Valmari, A.: Stubborn sets for reduced state space generation. In: Rozenberg, G. (ed.) Advances in Petri Nets 1990. LNCS, vol. 483, pp. 491–515. Springer, Heidelberg (1991)
25. Valmari, A.: A Stubborn Attack on State Explosion. Formal Methods in System Design **1**, 297–322 (1992)
26. Willems, B., Wolper, P.: Partial order models for model checking: from linear to branching time. In: Proc. of 11th Symposium of Logics in Computer Science, LICS 1996, New Brunswick, pp. 294–303 (1996)

Statistical Model Checking of Ad Hoc Routing Protocols in Lossy Grid Networks

Alice Dal Corso[1], Damiano Macedonio[2], and Massimo Merro[1(✉)]

[1] Dipartimento di Informatica, Università degli Studi di Verona, Verona, Italy
massimo.merro@univr.it
[2] Julia Srl, Verona, Italy

Abstract. We extend recent work by Höfner and McIver con the performances of the *ad hoc routing protocols* AODV and DYMO in terms of routes established. Höfner and McIver apply *statistical model checking* to show that on arbitrary small networks (up to 5 nodes) the most recent, and apparently more robust, DYMO protocol is less efficient than AODV. Here, we reformulate their experiments on 4x3 toroidal networks, with possibly lossy communication. As a main result we demonstrate that, in this more realistic scenario, DYMO performs significantly better than AODV.

1 Introduction

Ad hoc networking is a relatively recent area in wireless communications that is attracting the attention of many researchers for its potential to provide ubiquitous connectivity without the assistance of any fixed infrastructure. A *Mobile Ad Hoc Network* (MANET) is an autonomous system composed of *mobile* devices communicating with each other via radio transceivers.

Wireless devices use radio frequency channels to *broadcast* messages to the other devices. A single transmission span over a limited area and reach only a subset of the devices in the network. As a consequence, ad hoc networks rely on multi-hop wireless communications where nodes have essentially two roles: (i) acting as end-systems and (ii) performing routing functions.

A *routing protocol* is used to determine the appropriate paths on which data should be transmitted in a network. Routing protocols for wireless systems can be classified into topology-based and position-based ones:

- *Topology-based protocols* rely on traditional routing concepts, such as maintaining routing tables or distributing link-state information.
- *Position-based protocols* use information about the physical locations of the nodes to route data packets to their destinations.

The third author is partly supported by the Joint Project 2011 "Statical Analysis for Multithreading" from Università degli Studi di Verona.

© Springer International Publishing Switzerland 2015
K. Havelund et al. (Eds.): NFM 2015, LNCS 9058, pp. 112–126, 2015.
DOI: 10.1007/978-3-319-17524-9_9

Topology-based protocols can be further divided into proactive protocols and reactive ones:

- *Proactive routing protocols* try to maintain consistent routing information within the system at any time.
- *Reactive routing protocols* establish a route between a source and a destination only when it is needed, typically when a new data packet is injected by a user. For this reason, reactive protocols are also called *on-demand* protocols.

Examples of proactive routing protocols for mobile ad hoc networks are OLSR [6] and DSDV [19], while DSR [13], AODV [17] and DYMO [18] are typical on-demand protocols.

Most of the analyses of protocols for large-scale MANETs are usually based on discrete-event simulators (e.g., ns-2, Opnet and Glomosim). However, different simulators often support different models of the MAC physical-layer yielding different results, even for simple systems. Formal analysis techniques allow to screen protocols for flaws and to exhibit counterexamples to diagnose them. For instance, *model checking* provides both an exhaustive search of all possible behaviours of the system, and exact, rather than approximate, quantitative results. As an example, Fehnker et al. [10] used the Uppaal model checker [1] to analyse basic qualitative properties of the AODV routing protocol. The authors of [10] were able to analyse systematically all network topologies up to five nodes. However, crucial aspects such as *passage of time* and *probabilities* were not considered in their analysis.

Statistical Model Checking (SMC)[20,21] is a trade off between testing and formal verification: it consists in performing an appropriate number of runs of the model under examination to check whether a given property is satisfied with a certain probability. Unlike an exhaustive approach, a simulation-based solution does not guarantee a correct result with a 100% confidence. It is only possible to bound the probability of making an error. More precisely, according to theoretical Chernoff-Hoeffding bounds, it is possible to estimate the number of runs that the simulator must perform: the higher is the precision required in the analysis and the greater must be the number of runs.

In the current paper we apply SMC-Uppaal [8] (release 4.1.19, July 2014), a statistical extension of the Uppaal model checker which supports the composition of timed and/or probabilistic automata. In SMC-Uppaal the user must fix two main statistical parameters, α and ε, both in the real interval $]0,1[$. The answer provided by the tool is a confidence interval $[p-\varepsilon, p+\varepsilon]$ for estimating the probability p of the desired property; α represents the probability of false negatives while ϵ is the probabilistic uncertainty. In the last two releases of SMC-Uppaal, the number of runs to be executed in a simulation to ensure a fixed precision is not estimated a priori anymore; instead it is continually re-computed during the simulation, taking into consideration the results of the runs executed up to that point. As a consequence, starting from SMC-Uppaal 4.1.18 there is a dramatic reduction of the average number of runs effectively executed in a simulation.

Our work has been strongly inspired by a recent comparison between the two ad hoc routing protocols AODV and DYMO, on arbitrary networks up to 5 nodes with perfect communication [12], relying on the SMC-Uppaal model checker (release 4.1.11). DYMO [18] is a recent evolution of AODV (since March 2012 it is sometimes referred to as AODVv2) that tries to populate the routing tables of each node by adopting a concept called *path accumulation*: whenever a control message travels via more than one node, information about all intermediate nodes is accumulated in the message and distributed to its recipients. In principle this should result in better performances of the routing process. However, the analysis of [12] revealed that DYMO establishes fewer routes on average than does AODV. This calculation is obtained by counting the average number of entries appearing in the routing tables of all nodes after completing routing requests. Also the average quality of the routes found by AODV seems to be better than that of DYMO. Here route quality measure the difference between the length of the routes found by the routing protocol and the length of the corresponding optimal route.

These results cast a shadow on the more recent and more sophisticated DYMO protocol. Actually, it would seem that path accumulation in DYMO constitutes more a problem rather than an help. We conjecture that the results of [12] applies only to small networks, where the proliferation of extra messages may really constitute a problem. For this reason we decided to use the most recent release of SMC-Uppaal to repeat the analysis of [12] on networks of bigger size, operating in a slightly more realistic communication scenario. Ad hoc routing protocols have been developed for networks operating in harsh operating conditions. In particular, *communication failures* are quite common in MANETs: wireless communications can easily fail due to either communication collisions or environmental conditions such as temporary obstacles or physical interferences.

We have adapted the SMC-Uppaal models of [12] to compare AODV and DYMO on 4x3 *toroid topologies*, i.e. 4x3 grids circularly connected in the two dimensions. In this manner, each of the 12 nodes is connected with exactly 4 neighbours. We have adopted a *probabilistic model* of wireless communication to take into account *message loss* at different rates. For high loss rates this allows us to emulate *scarse networks*, i.e. networks scarsely connected.

As in [12] we consider three different workbenches to compare the two protocols: i) a probabilistic analysis to estimate the ability to successfully complete the protocol; ii) a quantitative analysis to determine the average number of routes found during the routing process; iii) a qualitative analysis to verify how good (i.e. short) are the routes found by the routing protocol. In our probabilistic analysis, in the case of perfect communication, AODV and DYMO have pretty much the same performances. However, with the introduction of some loss rate, DYMO performs dramatically better than AODV: up to 20% better than AODV, with a 30% loss rate. In the quantitative analysis DYMO performs at least 24% better than AODV. Again, the gap between the two protocols is wider when increasing the loss rate. Finally, our qualitative analysis shows that, in this respect, the two protocols behave pretty much in the same manner.

$$
\begin{array}{lll}
s \longrightarrow * & : & \texttt{rreq}, s, Rid, d, Sseq, Dseq, 0 \\
l \longrightarrow * & : & \texttt{rreq}, s, Rid, d, Sseq, Dseq, 1 \\
m \longrightarrow * & : & \texttt{rreq}, s, Rid, d, Sseq, Dseq, 2 \\
d \longrightarrow m & : & \texttt{rrep}, s, d, Dseq', 0 \\
m \longrightarrow l & : & \texttt{rrep}, s, d, Dseq', 1 \\
l \longrightarrow s & : & \texttt{rrep}, s, d, Dseq', 2
\end{array}
$$

Fig. 1. The AODV routing protocol

Outline In Section 2 we describe the two protocols under examination: AODV and DYMO. In Section 3 we recall and extends the SMC-Uppaal models of [12] for the two protocols. In Section 4 we repeat the experiments of [12] in our setting. The paper ends with a discussion of the results.

2 AODV and DYMO: Two Different Generations of Ad-hoc Routing Protocols

This section provides a brief overview of both ad hoc routing protocols.

AODV [17] is one the four protocols standardised by the IETF MANET working group. The protocol is intended to first establish a route between a source node and a destination node (*route discovery*), and then maintain a route between the two nodes during topology changes caused by node movement (*route maintenance*). Since AODV works on-demand, routers only maintain distance information for nodes reached during route discovery. In this paper we focus on the route discovery process.

In the AODV protocol each node maintains a *routing table* (*RT*) containing informations about the routes to be followed when sending messages to the other nodes of the network. In particular, for each destination node n a routing table provides an entry containing the following information: (i) the name of the *destination node* (say n); (ii) the number of *hops* necessary to reach n; (iii) the *neighbour node* in the route towards n; (iv) a *destination sequence number* to represent how fresh the information is: the higher the sequence number is, the fresher the path will be; (v) a validity *flag* for that entry. The collective information in the nodes' routing table is at the best a partial representation of network connectivity as it was sometimes in the past; in the most general scenario, mobility together with node and communication failures continually modify that representation.

Each node maintains also a *local history table* (*HT*) containing pairs of the form (*source-name, request-id*) to discard request packets which have already been processed.

In Figure 1, we report a scheme of the AODV protocol on a network of four nodes in a line topology: a source s, a destination d and two intermediate nodes l and m. We also provide a graphical representation of the flow of messages: dashed arrows denote the broadcast of *route request packets* (`rreq`), while continuous arrows denote the unicast sending of *route reply packets* (`rrep`). More precisely, suppose the source node s wishes to send a message to the destination node d. In order to perform the sending, s will look up an entry for d in its routing table. If there is no such an entry it will launch a route discovery procedure to find a route to d. The protocol works as follows:

– The source s broadcasts a route request packet of the form

$$\langle \texttt{rreq}, s, Rid, d, Sseq, Dseq, hc \rangle .$$

Here, the fields s and d denote the IP addresses of source and destination, respectively. The field Rid denotes a *request-id*, that is a sequence number uniquely identifying the request. The $Sseq$ field contains the *source sequence number*, i.e. the current sequence number to be used in routing table entries pointing towards the source node s. The $Dseq$ field is the *destination sequence number* containing the latest sequence number received in the past by the source node s for any route towards the destination d; this number is 0 if d is unknown to s. The *hop-count* field hc keeps track of the number of hops from the source node to the node handling the request. Initially, this field is set to 0.

– When the intermediate node l receives the route request, it acts as follows:

  • It looks up the pair (s, Rid) in its local history table to verify whether the request has already been processed. If this is the case, the request is discarded and the processing stops. Otherwise, the pair is entered into the local history table, so that future requests from s with the same Rid will be discarded.

  • Then, l looks up an entry for d in its routing table. If there is such an entry, with destination sequence number greater than or equal to the $Dseq$, then a route reply packet is sent back to the source saying to use l itself to get to the destination d. Otherwise, it re-broadcasts the route request packet with the hc field incremented by one.

  • In any case, l compares the source sequence number $Sseq$ contained in the request with the one appearing in its routing table associated with node s. If $Sseq$ is more recent (i.e. greater) than the one in the table, l updates its routing table entry associated with s.

– Node m will repeat the same steps executed by node l.

– Whenever the destination d receives the route request, it sends to m a unicast reply packet of the form

$$\langle \texttt{rrep}, s, d, Dseq', hc, lt \rangle .$$

Here, the source address and the destination address are copied from the incoming request, while the destination sequence number is possibly updated according to d's routing table. The *hop-count* field is set to 0. The *lifetime* field *lt* contains the time expressed in milliseconds for which nodes receiving the `rrep` consider the route to be valid.

- The reply packet then follows the reverse path towards node s increasing the hc field at each hop. Each node receiving the reply packet will update the routing table entry associated with d if one of the following conditions is met:
    - No route to d is known;
    - The sequence number for d in the route reply packet is greater than that stored in the routing table;
    - The sequence numbers are equal but the new route is shorter.
  In this way, nodes on the reverse route learn the route to d.

The architecture of the DYMO protocol [18] is quite similar to that of AODV. Here we follow the explanation of [12] to highlight only the major design differences between the two protocols.

- DYMO's mechanism for managing duplicate `rreq` messages is no longer based on checking the history table. Instead DYMO check the sequence number inside a route request to judge whether that request should be forwarded or discarded. While this modification save some memory, it has been shown that the change can lead to loss of route requests [9].
- On the other hand AODV can loose route replies since `rrep` messages are only forwarded if the routing table of an intermediate node is updated (changed). To avoid this, in DYMO a node generating a route reply increments the sequence number for the destination, thereby guaranteeing that the routing tables of nodes receiving the `rrep` message will be updated, and the `rrep` forwarded.
- DYMO establishes *bidirectional* routes between originator and destination. When an intermediate node initiates a route reply, it unicasts a message back to the originator of the request (as AODV does), but at the same time it forwards a route reply to the intended destination of the route request. In this manner the destination node gets all informations about intermediate nodes.
- DYMO uses the concept of *path accumulation*: whenever a control message travels via more than one node, information about *all* intermediate nodes is stored in the message. In this way, a node receiving a message establishes routes to *all other intermediate nodes*. In AODV nodes only establish routes to the initiator and to the sender of a message.

3   A Probabilistic Model for AODV and DYMO in SMC-Uppaal

In this section we provide a slight extension of the SMC-Uppaal models of [12] for both AODV and DYMO, where probabilities are introduced to model message loss. Both protocols are represented as parallel composition of node processes,

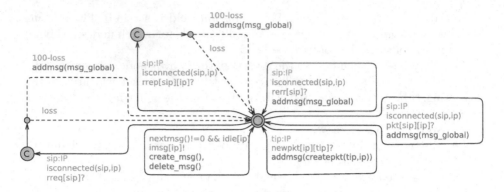

Fig. 2. `Queue(ip)` model for DYMO

where each process is a parallel composition of two timed automata, the `Handler` and the `Queue`. This is because each node maintains a message queue to store incoming messages and a process for handling these messages; the workflow of the handler depends on the type of the message. Communication between nodes `i` and `j` is only feasible if they are neighbours, i.e. in the transmission range of each other. This is modelled by predicates of the form `isconnected[i][j]` which are true if and only if `i` and `j` can communicate. Communication between different nodes `i` and `j` are on channels with different names, according to the type of the control message being delivered (`rrep`, `rreq`, `rerr`).

The `Queue` of a node `ip` for DYMO is depicted in Figure 2; the `Queue` automaton for AODV is very similar. Messages (arriving from other nodes) are stored in the queue, by using a function `addmsg()`. Only messages sent by nodes within the transmission range may be received. Unlike the model of [12] our `Queue` is essentially a probabilistic timed automata. SMC-Uppaal features branching edges with associated weights for the probabilistic extension. Thus we define an integer constant `loss`, with $0 \leq$ `loss` ≤ 100, and a node can either lose a message with weight `loss` or receive it with weight (100−`loss`). Notice that SMC-Uppaal requires input determinism to ensure that the system to be tested always produces the same outputs on any given sequence of inputs. Thus we need an extra intermediate committed location instead of branching immediately on the receiving action.

The `Handler` automaton, modelling the message-handling protocol, is far more complicated and has around 20 states. The implementation of the two protocols basically differs for this automaton. The `Handler` is busy while sending messages, and can only accept one message from the `Queue` once it has completely finished handling the previous message. Whenever it is not processing a message and there are messages stored in the `Queue`, the `Queue` and the `Handler` synchronise via channel `imsg[ip]`, transferring the relevant message data from the `Queue` to the `Handler`. According to the specification of AODV [17], the most time consuming activity is the communication between nodes, which take

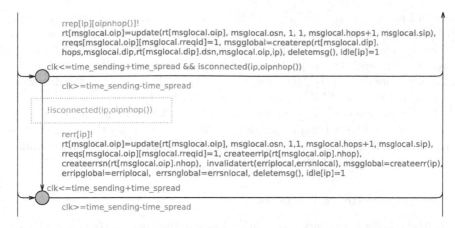

Fig. 3. Extract from Handle(ip, art[ip]) model for AODV at RREQ message

on average 40 milliseconds. This is modelled in the Handler by means of a clock variable t, set to 0 before transmission, so that a delay between 35 and 45 milliseconds is selected uniformly at random. Due to lack of space, we cannot present the full timed automaton modelling the Handler, but it is available online[1].

The Handler automata of the two protocols are exactly the same as those made available in [12] except for a few minor details. In particular, in the model for AODV of [12] we noticed a missing guard

$$!isconnected(ip, oipnhop())$$

on an arc that resulted in an rerr-message even if the networks was connected. As a consequence a node could get into a non-deterministic choice between sending a rrep-message and an rerr-message. In our model we have introduced the missing guard as depicted in Figure 3. Moreover, in order to correctly communicate the number of hops to the target node, we corrected the rrep-message rrep[ip][msg_local.tip]! as rrep[ip][rt[msg_local.tip].nhop]! in the Handler of DYMO. In both automata the constant MAX_HOP_LIMIT is now set to 100 instead of 10: in a 5-nodes network the value 10 is widely enough, but when working with bigger networks (we have worked also on 7x7 toroidals) this limitation may become a problem.

4 Experiments

We replay the experiments of [12] to compare AODV and DYMO on 4x3 toroidals (12 nodes) with possibly lossy channels. As in [12] we consider three different workbenches to compare the two protocols: i) a probabilistic analysis to estimate the ability to successfully complete the protocol finding the requested routes for a

---

[1] http://www.profs.scienze.univr.it/~merro/nfm2015/

number of properly chosen scenarios; ii) a quantitative analysis to determine the average number of routes found during the routing process in the same scenarios; iii) a qualitative analysis to verify how good (i.e. short) are the routes found by the routing protocol. Our experiment relies on the following set-up: (i) 2.3 GHz Intel Quad-Core i7, with 16GB memory, running the Mac OS X 10.9 "Maverick" operating system; (ii) SMC-Uppaal model-checker 64-bit version 4.1.19. The statistical parameters of false negatives (α) and probabilistic uncertainty (ϵ) are both set to 0.01 -yielding a confidence level of 99%. With these parameters SMC-Uppaal checks for each experiment a number of runs that can go from a few hundreds to 26492, in the worst case.

4.1   Successful Route Requests

In the first set of experiments we consider four specific nodes A, B, C and D; each with particular originator/destination roles. Our scenarios are a generalisation of those of [12] (as we consider larger networks) and assign roles as follows:

 (i)   A is the only originator sending a packet first to B and afterwards to C;
 (ii) A is sending to B first and then B is also sending to C;
 (iii) A is sending to B first and then C is sending to D.

Up to symmetry, varying the nodes A, B, C and D on a 4x3 toroidal, we have 1728 different configurations. From this number we deduct 276 configurations because they make little sense in our analysis, as the source and the destination node coincide. This calculation yields 1452 different experiments. As we will repeat our simulations for three different loss rates, this makes in total 4356 experiments.

Initially, for each scenario no routes are known, i.e. the routing tables of each node are empty. Then, with a time gap of 35-45 millisecond, two of the distinct nodes receive a data packet and have to find routes to the packet's destinations. The query in SMC-Uppaal's syntax has the following shape:

```
Pr[<=10000](<>(tester.final  &&  emptybuffers() &&
art[OIP1][DIP1].nhop!=0  &&  art[OIP2][DIP2].nhop!=0))
```

The first two conditions require the protocol to complete; here, **tester** refers to a process which injects to the originators nodes (**tester.final** means that all data packets have been injected), and the function **emptybuffers()** checks whether the nodes' message queue are empty. The third and the fourth conditions require that two different route requests are established. Here, **art[o][d].nhop** is the next hop in o's routing table entry for destination d. As soon as this value is set (is different to 0), a route to d has been established. Thus, the whole query asks for the probability estimate (Pr) satisfying the CTL-path expression within 10000 time units (milliseconds); as in [12] this bound is chosen as a conservative upper bound to ensure that the analyser explores paths to a depth where the protocol is guaranteed to have terminated.

In Table 1 we provide the results of our query on the AODV model. More precisely, we report the average probability to satisfy the required property in

Table 1. AODV: Probability analysis on 4x3 toroidals ($\alpha = \epsilon = 0.01$)

loss rate	avg probability	standard deviation	avg runs	standard deviation
0%	0.984	0.0036	583	1795
10%	0.746	0.130	11521	4486
30%	0.354	0.190	12875	2980

Table 2. DYMO: Probability analysis on 4x3 toroidals ($\alpha = \epsilon = 0.01$)

loss rate	avg probability	standard deviation	avg runs	standard deviation
0%	0.990	0.001	294	154
10%	0.818	0.090	9416	3851
30%	0.429	0.164	14571	2085

all 1452 different configurations. This is done for three different loss rates: 0% (perfect communication), 10% and 30%. Note that, in the case of perfect communication, our analysis shows that the probability to successfully establish a required route in our setting can be estimated to be at least 0.98. In the same analysis, paper [12] estimates at 0.99 the success rate for AODV on 5-nodes networks with arbitrary topologies. It should not surprise to see that the performances of AODV are strongly influenced by the message-loss rate. From a model-checking point of view, it is interesting to notice that the higher is the loss rate the greater is the number of runs required to complete the simulation. This is because with unreliable channels control messages need to be resent, making longer the whole routing process.

Table 2 presents the results for the same experiments on the DYMO protocol. In the case of perfect communication, our analysis shows that the probability of success in establishing the route requests can be estimated at around 0.99. In a similar analysis, paper [12] estimates success probably in DYMO, on arbitrary 4-nodes networks, at around 0.94.

Putting together the results of Tables 1 and 2 we can see that on 4x3 toroidals with perfect communication the reliability of the two protocols is quite similar. However, in the presence of message loss, DYMO performs much better than AODV. Actually, the higher is the loss rate the bigger is the gap between the two protocols. More precisely, with a 10% loss rate DYMO performs 10% better than AODV, whereas with a 30% loss rate DYMO performs 20% better then AODV. It should be also noticed that the results of the simulations on DYMO are more homogeneously distributed around the average probability, as it appears from the smaller standard deviation.

4.2   Number of Route Entries

The second analysis proposed in [12] compares the performances of AODV and DYMO by taking into account the capability to build other routes while establishing a route between two specific nodes. Routing tables are updated whenever

Table 3. Route quantity on 4x3 toroidals (26492 runs for each experiment)

	loss 0%	stand. dev.	loss 10%	stand. dev.	loss 30%	stand. dev.
AODV	62.30	2.79	60.89	3.11	54.79	3.48
DYMO	77.61	4.59	75.77	4.51	69.87	4.36
max	132	-	132	-	132	-

control messages are received. AODV does so only for the originator/destination node and for the sender of each message; whereas DYMO uses *path accumulation* to establish routes to all intermediate nodes of a path. This difference in design between the two protocols should make a significant difference in the number of routes computed by the two protocols. However, the analysis made in [12], for all possible topologies up to 5-nodes, provides a quite surprising result: AODV establishes more routes on average than does DYMO. The authors have obtained their results by checking the property

$$E[<=10000,26492](max:total\_knowledge())$$

where the function `total_knowledge()` counts the number of non-empty entries appearing in all routing tables built along a run of the protocol, and the function `max` returns the largest of these numbers among all runs of the simulation. This calculation is done for all different configurations; the result of the analysis is the average over all configurations. The reader should notice that this kind of query is different from the previous one. It has the form $E[..](..)$, where the letter "E" stands for *value estimation*, as the result of the query is a value and not a probability. Since value estimation does not fix the statistical parameters α and ϵ, from which it is determined the number of runs, we set 26492 runs for our simulations to guarantee a 99% confidence.

We repeat the same analysis of [12] on our 4x3 toroidals by considering three different loss rates. In total we did 4356 experiments, one for each configuration with a different loss rate. The results of our analysis are reported in Tables 3. Note that the last row shows the maximal number of routing entries which can be involved during the routing processes: this number is $n \cdot (n - 1)$ because in an n-node network each node has a routing table with $n - 1$ entries. Tables 3 shows that during the routing process DYMO establishes on average 24.5% more routes than AODV, in the absence of message loss. This gap rises up to 27.5% with a 30% loss rate. It is quite interesting to notice that in both protocols the introduction of a loss rate has a relatively small influence on the average number of established routes.

In the same analysis of [12], on arbitrary networks up to 5 nodes without message loss, the results obtained depict a complete different picture: AODV establishes on average 15% more routes than DYMO.

4.3   Optimal Routes

The results of the previous section tell us that in our 4x3 toroidals DYMO is more efficient than AODV in populating routing tables while establishing

Table 4. Höfner and McIver's route quality on 4x3 toroidals (738 runs)

	loss 0%	stand. dev.	loss 10%	stand. dev.	loss 30%	stand. dev.
AODV	0.02%	0.14	1.65%	0.68	9.10%	2.50
DYMO	1.91%	1.24	6.03%	1.45	14.58%	1.69

routing requests. In this section we provide a class of experiments to compare the ability of the two protocols in establishing optimal routes, i.e. routes of minimal length, according to the network topology. As explained in [12,16], all ad-hoc routing protocols based on rreq-broadcast can establish non-optimal routes when, for instance, the destination node does not forward the rreq-message. This phenomenon is obviously more evident in a scenario with an unreliable communication medium.

We start our analysis by replaying the same experiments of [12]. In particular, we check the property

$$E[<=10000,26492](max:quality())$$

for all possible configurations and loss rates. Again, this makes in total 4356 experiments. Here, the function quality() compares the length of the established routes with the length of the corresponding optimal routes. This is done by considering *all non-empty hops-entries of all routing tables of all nodes*. More precisely, for a given configuration, the property above returns the maximum among 738 runs (to ensure a 95% confidence) of the *average deviation* from the optimal route of all hops-entries. Then, as in [12], our experiment returns the average on all possible configurations. And as in [12], the results of Table 4 say that the established routes in AODV are significantly closer to optimal routes, when compared to DYMO. The gap between the two protocols goes from a couple of percentage points, in the case of perfect communication, up to 5 points, with a 30% loss rate. These results are not that surprising as the quality() function takes into consideration *all and only* non-empty entries, i.e. those entries which have been involved somehow in the routing process. As described in the previous section, DYMO, unlike AODV, fills routing entries of nodes which are not directly involved in the routing request. However, there is no guarantee that these entries are filled with optimal routes. Thus, if after two route requests AODV fills 62 entries while DYMO fills 78 entries, then the function quality() returns for AODV the maximum average deviation on 62 entries, while in DYMO it returns the maximum average deviation on 78 entries. We believe that the two protocols should be compared considering the same routing entries. In fact, the extra 16 non-empty entries in DYMO are not necessarily optimal but they are definitely closer to the optimal route when compared to the corresponding empty entries of AODV. Thus, perhaps the quality() function proposed by Höfner and McIver is not the best instrument to test which of the two protocols establish the better route as a result of a route request.

As a consequence, we decided to reformulate our analysis on route quality by making a different experiment. We checked the following property:

Table 5. Optimal routing on 4x3 toroidals ($\alpha = \epsilon = 0.01$)

	loss 0%	stand. dev.	loss 10%	stand. dev.	loss 30%	stand. dev.
AODV	0.980	0.042	0.696	0.119	0.280	0.161
DYMO	0.983	0.022	0.712	0.087	0.298	0.129

```
Pr[<=10000](<>(tester.final  &&  emptybuffers() &&
art[OIP1][DIP1].hops==min_path  &&  art[OIP2][DIP2].hops==min_path1)).
```

Here, the third and the fourth conditions require that two different route requests are established. In fact, `art[o][d].hops` returns the number of hops necessary to reach the destination node `d` from the originator `o`, according to `o`'s routing table. Furthermore, we require this number to be equal to the length of the corresponding optimal route (which has been previously computed).

In this experiment we are not interested in checking all non-empty routing entries but only those which are directly involved in the two routing requests. As usual this property is checked on all 4356 configurations with three different loss rates. Notice that this time we ask for a probability estimation, so the result is going to be a probability. The statistical parameters of our simulations are $\alpha = \epsilon = 0.01$, as usual.

Table 5 says that the probability to establish optimal routes in the two routing protocols is very close. Actually, in the presence of message loss, there is a small gap, between 0.01 and 0.02, in favour of DYMO. This gap would become bigger if we would focus only on the optimality of the second route request, which is lauched slightly after the first one. This is because DYMO works better then AODV when routing tables are non completely empty.

5 Conclusions, Related and Future Work

The formal analysis of MANETs and their protocols is challeging and go beyond the usual requirements for standard network protocols. In particular, the formal verification of ad hoc routing protocols received a lot of attention from the formal methods community [2,3,5,10–12,14,15].

Our work has been strongly inspired by a recent comparison of AODV and DYMO on arbitrary 5-node networks, in the ideal case of perfect communication [12]. In that analysis the DYMO protocol does not seem to perform better than the ten years older AODV protocol. In our opinion, some of the negative results of [12] about the performances of DYMO are due to the fact that 5-node networks might be too small (or scarsely connected) to allow DYMO to beneficiate of *path accumulation*.

In our paper we have carried on the analysis of [12] on 4x3 toroidals with possible lossy communication. We have extended the models of [12] to our setting and obtained a network of probabilistic timed automata [7] which has been used for doing Statistical Model Checking within the UPPAAL toolset [8] (release 4.1.19, July 2014). As a main result, in contrast with the results of [12], we have showed that on 4x3 toroidals the performances of DYMO appear to be significantly better than those of AODV. In particular, the probability to satisfy a route request in DYMO is significantly higher than in AODV in the presence of message loss: DYMO performs up to 20% better than AODV, with a 30% loss rate. In the quantitative analysis DYMO performs at least 24% better than AODV, with both loss rates. Again, the gap between the two protocols becomes larger when increasing the loss rate. Finally, the quality analysis of the established routes is a bit more delicate. We believe that the function `quality()` designed in [12] is not appropriate to estimate the quality of the requested routes, because it gives the average deviation of all non-empty entries. So, we have proposed a different query which estimates the deviation from the optimal route of the paths obtained from the required route requests. The results say that both protocols are pretty good in finding optimal routes with very small differences, depending on the loss rate. Notice that our quality analysis starts always from scratch, with empty routing tables. We conjecture that in a scenario where routing tables are non-empty DYMO will do better than AODV, also in term of route quality.

As in [12] we have assumed stationary networks. It would be interesting to compare the two protocols in a scenario with node mobility, along the lines of the work done in [11]. Moreover, we would like to extend our analysis to sparse grids affected by an increasing number of node and/or link failures. It would be interesting to check whether the robustness of DYMO makes a difference in such a kind of networks.

In order to study bigger systems with an higher confidence, paper [4] proposes a distributed implementation of UPPAAL SMC. We are planning to employ this approach to extend our results to bigger networks.

Acknowledgments. We thank Giacomo Annaloro and Marco Campion for their preliminary experiments on 7x7 toroidals. Annaloro and Campion also found some minor errors in the SMC-Uppaal models of [12], as pointed out in Section 3. We thank the anonymous referees for their constructive comments.

References

1. Behrmann, G., David, A., Larsen, K.G., Håkansson, J., Pettersson, P., Yi, W., Hendriks, M.: UPPAAL 4.0. In: International Conference on the Quantitative Evaluation of Systems (QEST), pp. 125–126. IEEE Computer Society (2006)
2. Benetti, D., Merro, M., Vigano, L.: Model checking ad hoc network routing protocols: Aran vs. endairA. In: 8th IEEE International Conference on Software Engineering and Formal Methods (SEFM), pp. 191–202. IEEE Computer Society (2010)
3. Bhargavan, K., Obradovic, D., Gunter, C.: Formal verification of standards for distance vector routing protocols. Journal of the ACM **49**, 538–576 (2002)

4. Bulychev, P., David, A., Guldstrand Larsen, K., Legay, A., Mikučionis, M., Bøgsted Poulsen, D.: Checking and distributing statistical model checking. In: Goodloe, A.E., Person, S. (eds.) NFM 2012. LNCS, vol. 7226, pp. 449–463. Springer, Heidelberg (2012)
5. Chiyangwa, S., Kwiatkowska, M.: A timing analysis of AODV. In: Steffen, M., Zavattaro, G. (eds.) FMOODS 2005. LNCS, vol. 3535, pp. 306–321. Springer, Heidelberg (2005)
6. Clausen, T., Jacquet, P.: Optimized Link State Routing Protocol (OLSR), rFC 3626 (2003)
7. David, A., Larsen, K.G., Legay, A., Mikučionis, M., Poulsen, D.B., van Vliet, J., Wang, Z.: Statistical model checking for networks of priced timed automata. In: Fahrenberg, U., Tripakis, S. (eds.) FORMATS 2011. LNCS, vol. 6919, pp. 80–96. Springer, Heidelberg (2011)
8. David, A., Larsen, K.G., Legay, A., Mikučionis, M., Wang, Z.: Time for statistical model checking of real-time systems. In: Gopalakrishnan, G., Qadeer, S. (eds.) CAV 2011. LNCS, vol. 6806, pp. 349–355. Springer, Heidelberg (2011)
9. Edenhofer, S., Höfner, P.: Towards a rigorous analysis of AODVv2 (DYMO). In: IEEE International Conference on Network Protocols (ICNP), pp. 1–6. IEEE Computer Society (2012)
10. Fehnker, A., van Glabbeek, R., Höfner, P., McIver, A., Portmann, M., Tan, W.L.: Automated analysis of AODV using UPPAAL. In: Flanagan, C., König, B. (eds.) TACAS 2012. LNCS, vol. 7214, pp. 173–187. Springer, Heidelberg (2012)
11. Höfner, P., Kamali, M.: Quantitative analysis of AODV and its variants on dynamic topologies using statistical model checking. In: Braberman, V., Fribourg, L. (eds.) FORMATS 2013. LNCS, vol. 8053, pp. 121–136. Springer, Heidelberg (2013)
12. Höfner, P., McIver, A.: Statistical model checking of wireless mesh routing protocols. In: Brat, G., Rungta, N., Venet, A. (eds.) NFM 2013. LNCS, vol. 7871, pp. 322–336. Springer, Heidelberg (2013)
13. Johnson, D.B., Maltz, D.A.: Dynamic Source Routing in Ad Hoc Wireless Networks. Kluwer Acad. Pub. (1996)
14. Liu, S., Ölveczky, P.C., Meseguer, J.: A framework for mobile Ad hoc networks in real-time maude. In: Escobar, S. (ed.) WRLA 2014. LNCS, vol. 8663, pp. 162–177. Springer, Heidelberg (2014)
15. Merro, M., Sibilio, E.: A calculus of trustworthy ad hoc networks. Formal Aspects of Computing **25**(5), 801–832 (2013)
16. Miskovic, S., Knightly, E.: Routing primitives for wireless mesh networks: design, analysis and experiments. In: IEEE International Conference on Computer Communications (INFOCOM), pp. 2793–2801. IEEE Computer Society (2010)
17. Perkins, C., Belding-Royer, E., Das, S.: Ad-hoc on-demand distance vector (AODV). RFC 3561 (Experimental) (2003). http://www.ietf.org/rfc/rfc3561
18. Perkins, C., Chakeres, I.: Dynamic MANET on-demand (AODVv2) routing. IETF Internet Draft (2012, Work in Progress)
19. Perkins, C.E., Bhagwat, P.: Highly dynamic destination-sequenced distance-vector routing (DSDV) for mobile computers. In: Conference on Communications Architectures, Protocols and Applications (SIGCOMM), pp. 234–244 (1994)
20. Sen, K., Viswanathan, M., Agha, G.: VESTA: A statistical model-checker and analyzer for probabilistic systems. In: International Conference on the Quantitative Evaluation of Systems (QEST), pp. 251–252. IEEE Computer Society (2005)
21. Younes, H., S.: Verification and Planning for Stochastic Processes with Asynchronous Events. Ph.D. thesis, Carnegie Mellon University (2004)

Efficient Guiding Strategies for Testing of Temporal Properties of Hybrid Systems

Tommaso Dreossi[1]([⊠]), Thao Dang[1], Alexandre Donzé[2], James Kapinski[3],
Xiaoqing Jin[3], and Jyotirmoy V. Deshmukh[3]

[1] Verimag, Gières, France
{tommaso.dreossi,thao.dang}@imag.fr
[2] University of California, Berkeley, USA
donze@berkeley.edu
[3] Toyota Technical Center, Ann Arbor, USA
{james.kapinski,xiaoqing.jin,jyotirmoy.deshmukh}@tema.toyota.com

Abstract. Techniques for testing cyberphysical systems (CPS) currently use a combination of automatic directed test generation and random testing to find undesirable behaviors. Existing techniques can fail to efficiently identify bugs because they do not adequately explore the space of system behaviors. In this paper, we present an approach that uses the rapidly exploring random trees (RRT) technique to explore the state-space of a CPS. Given a Signal Temporal Logic (STL) requirement, the RRT algorithm uses two quantities to guide the search: The first is a robustness metric that quantifies the degree of satisfaction of the STL requirement by simulation traces. The second is a metric for measuring coverage for a dense state-space, known as the star discrepancy measure. We show that our approach scales to industrial-scale CPSs by demonstrating its efficacy on an automotive powertrain control system.

1 Introduction

Model-Based Development (MBD) for cyberphysical systems (CPS) is a paradigm based on an end-to-end use of high-level executable models of physical systems interacting with software. These models facilitate a wide array of design and analysis techniques such as accurate simulation, control design, test generation, and code generation. This allows validating the behavior of the CPS early in development cycles, which not only enhances product reliability but also brings significant cost savings.

Techniques for testing CPSs typically employ a combination of automatic directed test generation and random testing [21,24] to detect undesirable behaviors. The prevalent practice is to use coverage metrics such as Modified-Condition Decision Coverage (MCDC) inspired from software testing [24]. Such metrics help quantify the degree to which the models of software components of the CPS (typically embedded/control software) have been tested. Models of CPS, however, often contain physics-based models (also called plant models) tightly coupled with the models of embedded software. In contrast to models of control

© Springer International Publishing Switzerland 2015
K. Havelund et al. (Eds.): NFM 2015, LNCS 9058, pp. 127–142, 2015.
DOI: 10.1007/978-3-319-17524-9_10

software (that are akin to standard computer programs), plant models typically represent behaviors that evolve over continuous time and state-space. Existing code-coverage metrics are thus not applicable when reasoning about the "coverage" of the possibly infinite state-space of a CPS. Furthermore, the idea of using temporal logic to specify behavioral specifications of CPSs has been gaining traction [12,17,25]. Existing directed testing tools are inadequate as they typically try to generate test inputs to satisfy code-coverage criteria or inputs to violate static assertions in the model [21,24].

In this paper, we propose a testing-based approach that hopes to fill these two lacunae. It builds on two recent results: the first is a hybrid systems test generation technique that is based on the rapidly exploring random trees (RRT) algorithm and guided by the star-discrepancy coverage measure [6]. The other is a technique for robust monitoring of properties expressed in Signal Temporal Logic (STL) [8,9]. The combination of coverage and robustness analysis allows increasing the effectiveness of generated test suites in terms of error detection.

Another goal of this work is to create a tool that supports industrial CPS models by considering modeling environments that are prevalent in industry, such as Simulink®. Simulink has become a *de facto* standard in the automotive engine controls domain. It is used as an MBD platform to perform system modeling, simulation, and automatic code generation. Tools that can identify design-bugs in Simulink models offer a significant benefit over testing-based techniques, as the cost of addressing problems during the later stages of development is significantly greater than at the modeling stage.

Our contribution can be summarized as follows. Given a user-provided temporal logic specification φ, our technique can automatically identify examples of system behaviors that falsify φ. Our method uses an RRT algorithm, guided by a combination of two metrics: a metric quantifying state-space coverage and a metric quantifying the robust satisfaction degree of the given specification. We provide experimental results that compare the performance of our implementation with the falsification tool S-TaLiRo.

Related Work. Our technique brings together two lines of work. The first is the development of efficient sampling-based exploration algorithms. The use of Rapidly-exploring Random Trees (RRT) has been popularized in the context of path planning in robotics [14,18] and applied and extended later for falsification of safety properties, using the observation that the latter reduces to finding a path from an initial state to some unsafe state [1,5,15,23].

The second line of work is falsifying temporal specifications on CPS models. This is a very active area of research, and tools based on search guided by stochastic and nonlinear optimization (as implemented in the tools S-TaLiRo [2] and Breach [7]) have been already applied in an industrial context to Simulink models [10,12]. There are two key differences between falsification tools and our approach. First, S-TaLiRo and Breach essentially assume a parameterized representation of input signals, and at the beginning of a simulation run, fix a valuation for the parameters.

By contrast, our RRT-based algorithm allows the flexibility to change input values based on robustness values of a partial system trajectory; in Section 5, we demonstrate how this flexibility leads to superior falsification performance

compared to S-TaLiRo for some examples. The second difference is that falsification tools typically do not measure the coverage of the hybrid state-space
by the set of test inputs explored, while our approach uses the star-discrepancy
based coverage metric to quantify coverage.

The dual of falsification, the problem of control with temporal logic specifications, has been considered recently [13,16]. The work in [4] is similar to our
work, in that RRT algorithms are considered to derive control inputs enforcing
temporal logics goals. However, most of the work in this area assumes either
simpler (linear) dynamical models, or simpler specification formalisms such as
LTL. To the best of our knowledge, our work is the first to consider the problem
of STL falsification based on a modified RRT algorithm.

2   Preliminaries

2.1   Dynamical System Model

We assume that a system model $\mathcal{M}$ is specified as a gray-box, that is, we assume
we know qualitative information about $\mathcal{M}$ (e.g., the number of state variables)
but we do not know detailed information (e.g., the closed-form analytic representation of system dynamics). We assume that the underlying system described by
the gray-box is a continuous-time hybrid system. We also assume that the system
is provided with a *simulator* that takes as input discrete-time input sequences,
and returns discrete-time output sequences.

The system model $\mathcal{M}$ is defined as a tuple $(\mathcal{X}, \mathcal{U}, \mathsf{sim})$, where $\mathcal{X}$ is a finite or
infinite set of states, $\mathcal{U}$ is a finite or infinite set of input values. Let $\boldsymbol{x}$ denote a
function that maps a given time point t over a given time domain to the state
$\boldsymbol{x}(t)$ of $\mathcal{M}$ at time t; we also call $\boldsymbol{x}$ as the *state variable*. Let $\boldsymbol{u}$ denote a function
mapping a given time point t to the input value $\boldsymbol{u}(t) \in \mathcal{U}$; we also call this
function an *input signal*. The function sim maps a state and an input at a given
time t_k, i.e., $\boldsymbol{x}(t_k)$ and $\boldsymbol{u}(t_k)$, and a rational time-step $h_k > 0$, to a new state
at time $t_{k+1} = t_k + h_k$. In other words, $\mathcal{M}$ can be viewed as a nonautonomous
discrete-time dynamical system, with the update function given by sim:

$$\boldsymbol{x}(t_{k+1}) = \mathsf{sim}(\boldsymbol{x}(t_k), \boldsymbol{u}(t_k), h_k) \tag{1}$$

In general, $\mathcal{X}$ can be a product of n different domains (such as the Boolean
$\{true, false\}$ domain, $\mathbb{Z}$, $\mathbb{R}$, etc.). We say that the state dimension of $\mathcal{M}$ is
n. Similarly, $\mathcal{U}$ can be a product of m different input domains, and the input
dimension is called m.

A *simulation trace* of the model $\mathcal{M}$ is defined as a sequence of times and
pairs of state and input values:

$$(t_0, \boldsymbol{x}(t_0), \boldsymbol{u}(t_0)), \ (t_1, \boldsymbol{x}(t_1), \boldsymbol{u}(t_1)), \ \ldots, \ (t_N, \boldsymbol{x}(t_N), \boldsymbol{u}(t_N))$$

where $\forall i : \boldsymbol{x}(t_{i+1}) = \mathsf{sim}(\boldsymbol{x}(t_i), \boldsymbol{u}(t_i), h_i)$, and $t_{i+1} = t_i + h_i$.

We stress that we do not require the function sim to be known in an analytic
or symbolic form, but assume that there is a simulator that returns the states
computed by sim. Formally, a *simulator* is a program that, given an initial time

t_0, an initial state value $\boldsymbol{x}(t_0)$, a sequence of non-zero time-steps $h_0, \ldots, h_N$, and a sequence of input values $\boldsymbol{u}(t_0), \ldots, \boldsymbol{u}(t_N)$ is able to compute the corresponding simulation trace of $\mathcal{M}$.

In the case of Simulink models, the simulator can be provided with a fixed time step h_i. Simulation traces are computed by performing numerical integration of the differential (or difference) algebraic equations corresponding to the continuous or hybrid dynamical systems that the models describe.

Simulator Assumptions. We assume that the inputs of $\mathcal{M}$ are controllable by the user and the full state of $\mathcal{M}$ is observable. We also assume that it is possible to reset any stateful element of the model to a permissible value in $\mathcal{X}$. These assumptions are meaningful in the context of model-based testing as they allow a user or a test program to start a simulation trace from an arbitrary initial state. Note that, in theory, our technique could be applied to a testing scenario, where the result of sim is provided by performing a particular test case. While our assumptions are plausible for this case, they would be quite difficult to enforce, as observing and resetting the state of the system is often difficult or impossible in a testing scenario.

2.2   Signal Temporal Logic

We require a formal language to specify how a model $\mathcal{M}$ is expected to behave and employ Signal Temporal Logic (STL) for this purpose. STL was proposed in [20] as a specification language for properties of signals (i.e., functions from a time domain to some domain of values). In the following we present the syntax and semantics of STL for a continuous time domain ($\mathbb{R}_0^+$). In practice, STL semantics have to be adapted to discrete time signals (such as the simulation traces of a system $\mathcal{M}$) on a dense time domain by use of linear interpolation (i.e., for t between t_k, t_{k+1}, we define $\boldsymbol{x}(t)$ by linear interpolation between $\boldsymbol{x}(t_k)$ and $\boldsymbol{x}(t_{k+1})$).

An STL formula is formed of *atomic predicates* connected with Boolean and *temporal* operators. Atomic predicates can be reduced to inequalities of the form $\mu = f(\boldsymbol{x}) \sim 0$, where f is a scalar-valued function over the signal $\boldsymbol{x}$, $\sim \in \{<, \leq, \geq, >, =, \neq\}$. Temporal operators are "always" (denoted as $\square$), "eventually" (denoted as $\lozenge$) and "until" (denoted as $\mathcal{U}$). Each temporal operator is indexed by intervals of the form (a, b), $(a, b]$, $[a, b)$, $[a, b]$, (a, ∞) or $[a, \infty)$ where each of a, b is a non-negative real-valued constant, and $a < b$. If I is an interval, then an STL formula is written using the following grammar:

$$\varphi := \top \mid \mu \mid \neg\varphi \mid \varphi_1 \wedge \varphi_2 \mid \varphi_1 \mathcal{U}_I \varphi_2$$

The always and eventually operators are defined as follows: $\square_I \varphi \triangleq \neg\lozenge_I \neg\varphi$, $\lozenge_I \varphi \triangleq \top \mathcal{U}_I \varphi$. When the interval I is omitted, we use the default interval of $[0, +\infty)$. The semantics of STL formulas are defined informally as follows. The signal $\boldsymbol{x}$ satisfies $f(\boldsymbol{x}) > 0$ at time t (where $t \geq 0$) if $f(\boldsymbol{x}(t)) > 0$. It satisfies $\varphi = \square_{[0,2)} (x - 1 > 0)$ if for all time $0 \leq t < 2$, $x(t) - 1 > 0$. The signal x_1 satisfies $\varphi = \lozenge_{[1,2)} x_1 + 0.5 > 0$ iff there exists time t such that $1 \leq t < 2$ and $x_1(t) > -0.5$. The two-dimensional signal $\boldsymbol{x} = (x_1, x_2)$ satisfies the formula $\varphi = (x_1 > 0) \mathcal{U}_{[2.3,4.5]} (x_2 < 0)$ iff there is some time t where $2.3 \leq t \leq 4.5$ and $x_2(t) < 0$, and $\forall t'$ in $[2.3, t)$, $x_1(t')$ is greater than 0.

Quantitative Semantics. We define a quantitative semantics of STL as a function ρ such that the sign of $\rho(\varphi, \boldsymbol{x}, t)$ determines whether $(\boldsymbol{x}, t)$ satisfies φ and its absolute value estimates the *robustness* of this satisfaction. A common way of defining such functions, as presented in [8], is as follows. For a predicate $\mu = x > 2$, one can simply use the value $x(t) - 2$ as a robustness estimate. For the conjunction of two formulas $\varphi = \varphi_1 \wedge \varphi_2$, with robustness ρ_1 and ρ_2, we can use $\rho = \min(\rho_1, \rho_2)$. For $\Diamond_{[0,2]} (x - 1 > 0)$, the robustness at time 0 can be estimated by the maximum for $t \in [0, 2]$ of $x(t) - 1$.

3   Coverage-Based Testing

The original RRT algorithm is a technique for quickly exploring the state space for systems with differential constraints [19]. In this section, we recall the gRRT version of RRT, which is a testing approach used to maximize state space coverage [6]. The gRRT algorithm stores the visited states in a tree, the root of which corresponds to the initial state. The construction of the tree is summarized in Algorithm 1.

We will now present how the algorithm is applied to a Simulink model. The procedure takes as input a Simulink model $\mathcal{M}$, an initial state value $\boldsymbol{x}_{init} \in \mathcal{X}$, and an iteration limit k_{max}. The function sample samples a goal-state $\boldsymbol{x}_{goal}$ from $\mathcal{X}$. The goal-state is intended to indicate the direction towards which the tree is expected to evolve. Then, a starting state $\boldsymbol{x}_{near}$ is determined as a neighbor of $\boldsymbol{x}_{goal}$ using some predefined distance. The point $\boldsymbol{x}_{near}$ is expanded towards $\boldsymbol{x}_{goal}$ as follows:

- The function findInput is used to select a sample from the input set $\boldsymbol{u} \in \mathcal{U}$. This can be performed by randomly selecting a point in $\mathcal{U}$.
- The initial condition for $\mathcal{M}$ is set to $\boldsymbol{x}_{near}$, and a simulation is performed for h seconds using the input $\boldsymbol{u}$. A new edge from $\boldsymbol{x}_{near}$ to $\boldsymbol{x}_{new}$, labeled with the associated input $\boldsymbol{u}$, is then added to the tree.

Unlike the original RRT algorithm, the goal state sampling in the gRRT algorithm is not uniform, and the function sample is used to guide the exploration to improve the star-discrepancy coverage, which we define below.

3.1   Star-Discrepancy Coverage

The star discrepancy is a notion in equidistribution theory (see for example [3]) that has been used in quasi-Monte Carlo techniques for error estimation. Let P be a set of k points inside $\mathcal{B} = [l_1, L_1] \times \ldots \times [l_n, L_n] \subset \mathbb{R}^n$. Let $p = (\beta_0, \ldots, \beta_n)$ be a point inside $\mathcal{B}$, this point together with the bottom left vertex of $\mathcal{B}$ forms a subbox $J = [l_1, \beta_1] \times \ldots \times [l_n, \beta_n]$. The local discrepancy of the point set P with respect to the sub-box J is:

$$D(P, J) = \left| \frac{A(P, J)}{k} - \frac{vol(J)}{vol(\mathcal{B})} \right| \qquad (2)$$

where $A(P, J)$ is the number of points of P that are inside J, and $vol(J)$ is the volume of the box J. We use $\mathcal{J}$ to denote the set of all subboxes J such that

Algorithm 1. The gRRT Algorithm	**Algorithm 2.** The RRT-REX Algorithm
1: **function** GRRT($\mathcal{M}$,$\boldsymbol{x}_{init}$,k_{max},h)	1: **function** RRT-REX($\mathcal{M}$,$\boldsymbol{x}_{init}$,φ,k_{max}, h)
2: $k \leftarrow 0$; $\mathcal{T}$.init($\boldsymbol{x}_{init}$)	2: $k \leftarrow 0$; $\mathcal{T}$.init($\boldsymbol{x}_{init}$)
3: **repeat**	3: **repeat**
4: $\boldsymbol{x}_{goal} \leftarrow \mathcal{T}$.sample()	4: $\boldsymbol{x}_{goal} \leftarrow \mathcal{T}$.sample()
5: $\boldsymbol{x}_{near} \leftarrow \mathcal{T}$.neighbor($\boldsymbol{x}_{goal}$)	5: $\boldsymbol{x}_{near} \leftarrow \mathcal{T}$.neighbor($\boldsymbol{x}_{goal}$)
6: $\boldsymbol{u} \leftarrow \mathcal{T}$.findInput($\boldsymbol{x}_{near}$, $\boldsymbol{x}_{goal}$)	6: $\boldsymbol{u} \leftarrow \mathcal{T}$.findInput($\boldsymbol{x}_{near}$, $\boldsymbol{x}_{goal}$)
7: $\boldsymbol{x}_{new} \leftarrow$ sim($\boldsymbol{x}_{near}$, $\boldsymbol{u}$, h)	7: $\boldsymbol{x}_{new} \leftarrow$ sim($\mathcal{M}$, $\boldsymbol{x}_{near}$, $\boldsymbol{u}$, h)
8: $\mathcal{T}$.addState($\boldsymbol{x}_{new}$, $\boldsymbol{u}$)	8: $traj \leftarrow \mathcal{T}$.getTrajectory($\boldsymbol{x}_{new}$)
9: $k \leftarrow k+1$	9: $v \leftarrow \rho^{est}(traj, \varphi)$
10: **until** $k \geq k_{max}$	10: $\mathcal{T}$.addState($\boldsymbol{x}_{new}$, $\boldsymbol{u}$,v)
11: **end function**	11: $k \leftarrow k+1$
	12: **until** ($v < 0$) or ($k \geq k_{max}$)
	13: **end function**

$l_i \leq \beta_i \leq L_i$ for each $i \in 1, \ldots, n$. The star discrepancy of a point set P with respect to the box $\mathcal{B}$ is defined as:

$$D^*(P,\mathcal{B}) = \sup_{J \in \mathcal{J}} D(P, J). \tag{3}$$

The star discrepancy of a point set P with respect to a box $\mathcal{B}$ satisfies $0 < D^*(P,\mathcal{B}) \leq 1$. We define the coverage of P as $\gamma(P,\mathcal{B}) = 1 - D^*(P,\mathcal{B})$. Intuitively, the star discrepancy is a measure for the irregularity of a set of points. A large value $D^*(P,\mathcal{B})$ means that the points in P are not distributed well over $\mathcal{B}$.

We use the star discrepancy to evaluate the coverage of a set of states. Since there is no efficient way to compute the star discrepancy, we approximate it with an upper and lower bound. The estimation is based on a finite box partition, $\mathcal{C}$, of the box $\mathcal{B}$ (see [6] for more detail). Below, we describe how this information is used to guide the exploration of the system behaviors to the elements of $\mathcal{C}$ that are not as well explored as other elements.

4   Combining Coverage and Robustness

In this section we show how to combine the robustness and coverage information to guide the test generation process. To guide the exploration towards the states violating the property, robustness information can be used to select a starting state with a low robustness value; however, this objective can result in poor performance, as the initial robustness values can lead the exploration to some local positive minima. The star discrepancy coverage information can be used to ameliorate this problem by steering the algorithm to other parts of the feasible space. Intuitively, the algorithm uses the robustness to bias towards critical behaviors and the coverage to explore freely in the search space.

Note that while the coverage is defined for a set of states, robustness is defined for a trace. Each state in the RRT tree stems from a unique trace from the initial state (at the root of the tree). This trace may be *incomplete*, that is, the trace is not long enough to determine the true robustness value; however, a "predictive" value can be estimated and used for the purpose of guiding the search. The estimation will be discussed in Section 4.2. When a trace is *complete*, the robustness value indicates whether it satisfies the STL property in question.

We now describe the sampling method employed by the function sample in Algorithm 1. The search space is partitioned into a set $\mathcal{C}$ of rectangular regions called *cells*. Each cell c is associated with a local star discrepancy value, denoted by $D(c)$, determined by the geometric distribution of the current set of states with respect to the cell (see the definition (2)). When a new state is added, the estimates for the affected cells are updated.

4.1 Guiding Strategies

Using the above information, the main steps of the goal state sampling process are as follows:

- Step 1: a goal cell $c_{goal} \in \mathcal{C}$ is selected, based on the coverage estimate;
- Step 2: a goal state x_{goal} is randomly selected from inside the chosen cell c_{goal}.

The goal cell selection in Step 1 is performed by defining a probability distribution for the cells in the partition. We create a discrete probability distribution by assigning a probability value to each c based on the estimated star discrepancy. Let $\mathcal{C}$ be the current set of cells. For each cell we define a weight:

$$w(c) = s(\rho(c))$$

where $s(\rho(c)) = \frac{1}{1+e^{-\rho(c)}}$ is the sigmoid function. A goal cell is then sampled according to the following probability distribution:

$$Prob[c_{goal} = c] = \frac{w(c)}{\sum_{c \in \mathcal{C}} w(c)}.$$

The computation of the neighbor is biased by the robustness. Indeed, we can choose m nearest neighbors of the x_{goal} and then pick the one with the lowest robustness estimate. So the robustness plays a role in the selection of the neighbor which determines the initial state for the next iteration.

4.2 Defining Branch Robustness

The syntax and semantics of STL introduced in Section 2.2 are defined for traces with a possibly unbounded time horizon. In practice, one usually assumes that simulation time is long enough to estimate the satisfaction of a property. However, this assumption cannot be made in our case since we construct a tree of incomplete trajectories and estimate the satisfaction of a property for each node of the tree corresponding to incomplete trajectories. In this section, we introduce an *interval* quantitative semantics which is well-defined even for partial traces.

Consider the simple property $\varphi \equiv \Box_{[10,20]}(x > 1)$ and assume that we simulated the system until some time T_{sim}. There can be three situations: $T_{sim} < 10$, $10 \leq T_{sim} < 20$ or $20 \leq T_{sim}$. In the first case, the trace does not contain any information relevant to the property, hence its satisfaction cannot be determined in any way. In the last case, the trace contains all the information needed for computing the Boolean and quantitative satisfaction. In the middle case, we cannot know what happens between T_{sim} and $20s$, but the values of x between $10s$ and T_{sim} provide some information. For instance, we have $\rho(\varphi, x, t) = \min_{t \in [10,20]}(x(t) - 1) \leq \min_{t \in [10, T_{\text{sim}}]}(x(t) - 1)$, hence the minimum of $x(t) - 1$ in $[10, T_{\text{sim}}]$ is an upper bound of $\rho(\varphi, x, t)$. If this upper bound is negative, we know that the property is falsified, even though we do not know the actual robust satisfaction value. Similarly, if $\varphi \equiv \Diamond_{[10,20]}(x > 1)$, then we can easily deduce that the *maximum* of $x(t) - 1$ over $[10, T_{\text{sim}}]$ is a *lower bound* of $\rho(\varphi, x, t)$. If it is positive, we know already that no matter what happens between T_{sim} and 20, the property will be satisfied. The computation of upper and lower bounds for ρ can be done automatically by induction on formulas. Let x be a signal defined on $\mathbb{R}^+$, $x_{|T_{\text{sim}}}$ its restriction to $[0, T_{\text{sim}}]$ for some $T_{\text{sim}} > 0$ and φ an STL formula.

Formally, we define the function $\bar{\rho}$ for $x_{|T_{\text{sim}}}$ and an arbitrary STL formula as:

$$\bar{\rho}(\mu, x_{|T_{\text{sim}}}, t) = f(x(t)) \text{ if } t \leq T_{\text{sim}}, +\infty \text{ otherwise.} \tag{4}$$

$$\bar{\rho}(\neg\varphi, x_{|T_{\text{sim}}}, t) = -\underline{\rho}(\varphi, x_{|T_{\text{sim}}}, t) \tag{5}$$

$$\bar{\rho}(\varphi_1 \wedge \varphi_2, x_{|T_{\text{sim}}}, t) = \min(\bar{\rho}(\varphi_1, x_{|T_{\text{sim}}}, t), \bar{\rho}(\varphi_2, x_{|T_{\text{sim}}}, t)) \tag{6}$$

$$\bar{\rho}(\varphi_1 \mathcal{U}_{[a,b]}\varphi_2, x_{|T_{\text{sim}}}, t) =$$
$$\sup_{t' \in [t+a,t+b]} \left(\min(\bar{\rho}(\varphi_2, x_{|T_{\text{sim}}}, t'), \inf_{t'' \in [t,t')} \bar{\rho}(\varphi_1, x_{|T_{\text{sim}}}, t'')) \right). \tag{7}$$

Then $\underline{\rho}$ satisfies the same self inductive rules except that $+\infty$ is replaced by $-\infty$ in (4) and $\bar{\rho}$ and $\underline{\rho}$ are switched in (5). The following lemma is true by construction:

Lemma 1. *Define the time horizon $T(\varphi)$ of φ inductively by $T(\mu) = 0$, $T(\neg\varphi) = T(\varphi)$, $T(\varphi_1, \varphi_2) = \max(T(\varphi_1), T(\varphi_2))$ and $T(\varphi_1 \mathcal{U}_{[a,b]}\varphi_2) = \max(T(\varphi_1), T(\varphi_2)) + b$. Then*

$$T_{sim} > 0 \Rightarrow \bar{\rho}(\varphi, x_{|T_{sim}}, 0) \geq \rho(\varphi, x, 0) \geq \underline{\rho}(\varphi, x_{|T_{sim}}, 0) \tag{8}$$

$$T_{sim} \geq T(\varphi) \Rightarrow \bar{\rho}(\varphi, x_{|T_{sim}}, 0) = \underline{\rho}(\varphi, x_{|T_{sim}}, 0) = \rho(\varphi, x, 0) \tag{9}$$

From (8), it follows that if $\bar{\rho}$ is negative for $x_{|T_{\text{sim}}}$, we can conclude that x falsifies φ. Similarly, a non-negative $\underline{\rho}$ for $x_{|T_{\text{sim}}}$ means that x satisfies φ, which means we can stop expanding the tree from $x_{|T_{\text{sim}}}$. From (9), it follows that if a trace issued from a node in the exploration tree is longer than $T(\varphi)$, its satisfaction status is fully determined. If it falsifies φ, then we are done, otherwise, the branch issued from this node does not need to be explored any further.

In practice, it is often the case that $\bar{\rho}$ and/or $\underline{\rho}$ do not provide any useful information (e.g., if they are equal to $+\infty$ or $-\infty$). For guiding purposes, we use an intermediate estimate obtained by computing ρ on the unbounded signal defined by constant extrapolation of the last value. Since such extrapolation does not provide any guarantee on the Boolean satisfaction of φ, we use ρ only for guiding, $\bar{\rho}$ to determine falsification and $\underline{\rho}$ to determine definite satisfaction.

4.3   Algorithm for Testing a Simulink Model Against an STL Formula

We describe an implementation of our approach called RRT-REX (RRT Robustness-guided EXplorer), which uses Simulink as a simulation engine. The pseudocode in Algorithm 2 summarizes the new algorithm. The algorithm receives as input a Simulink model $\mathcal{M}$, an STL formula φ, and the maximum number of iterations $k_{max} \in \mathbb{N}$. The algorithm iterates until a negative robustness estimate is found, i.e., a trace that does not satisfy the property is discovered, or the maximum number of iterations is reached. In this algorithm we use a fixed time step h for simplicity of presentation but it is possible to use a variable time step for more accurate simulation performance.

In RRT-REX, as the sim function, we use the numerical differential equation solvers within Simulink to produce an updated state x_{new}. This is performed by first resetting the solver state to x_{near} and then setting the input to u; the solver then provides a solution over h seconds. For the Simulink tool, this is computationally costly, due to a time-consuming model-compilation step that is performed before each simulation is computed. This is an inefficiency in the solver implementation, but it does not reflect a fundamental drawback of our technique.

Our implementation of the function neighbor uses the Approximate Nearest Neighbors (ANN) library [22]. The ANN library can quickly identify members of the elements of $\mathcal{T}$ in close proximity to a given point x_{near}. Also, we use a part of HTG (Hybrid Test Generation Tool [6]) to build and maintain the $\mathcal{T}$ structure, as well as to implement the function sample (sample uses coverage to bias a randomized selection of x_{goal}, as in Algorithm 1). The Breach [7] tool is used to implement the ρ^{est} function, which results in branch robustness estimates $v = (\rho, \bar{\rho})$ based on the trajectory $traj$ and the specification φ. The function addState primarily adds a new point to the RRT $\mathcal{T}$; it additionally updates the partitions in the tree with the star-discrepancy information as well as the robustness estimate. The updated star-discrepancy information is used by the sample function, and both the star-discrepancy and robustness estimates are used by neighbor to select a point in the tree (i.e., in addition to proximity, coverage and robusntess affect which point x_{near} is selected). All of the $\mathcal{T}$-related functions use the implied partition $\mathcal{C}$. We note that this partition can be dynamically refined for more accurate star discrepancy estimation, faster neighbor computation, and better cell robustness estimation.

5   Case Studies

This section discusses case studies of the application of our technique. We consider four case studies: an academic model of a system that measures how much longer a signal remains positive than it remains negative, a mode-selection example that uses a number of Boolean connectives to determine an operating regime and accordingly sets a reference value, an abstract model for the closed-loop fuel-control in an internal combustion gasoline engine, and a closed-loop model of the airpath in a diesel engine.

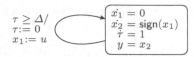

Fig. 1. Sampled polarity integrator system

For each model, we try to falsify a given STL requirement and compare the performance of RRT-REX with a state-of-the-art falsification tool: S-TaLiRo. S-TaLiRo uses robust satisfaction values of an MTL requirement computed on complete simulation traces in iteration i to guide the choice of inputs and initial conditions of the model in iteration $i+1$. This guidance is provided by stochastic optimization algorithms such as simulated annealing, cross-entropy, and ant-colony optimization. Recall that S-TaLiRo chooses a fixed parameterization of the input signal-space and at the beginning of each simulation picks a set of valuations for the parameters to define the concrete input signals.

The results of the study are summarized in Table 1. Note that for each item in the table, an average over 10 cases is reported. For the Falsified columns (denoted *Fals.*), all of the 10 cases for each item were either falsified or not, except for the footnoted item.

5.1 Sampled Polarity Integrator System (SPI)

A sampled polarity integrator is an academic model that highlights the advantages of using intermediate robustness values as a search heuristic for guiding the RRT search. As shown in Fig. 1, every Δ seconds, the system samples the input $u(t)$, and stores the value in state x_1. We assume that u is a signal that ranges over $[-v, v]$ for some real number v. The state x_2 evolves with rate -1 if $x_1(t) < 0$, and $+1$ if $x_1(t) > 0$. Finally, the output of the system (denoted y) is the state x_2. We pick $\Delta = 1$ for our experiment, and initial conditions $x_1(0) = 0$, $x_2(0) = 0$, $\tau(0) = 0$.

We introduce the following artificial safety requirement, where n, k are fixed positive integers, $k \in [-v, v]$, and $n > k$: $\Box_{[0,n\Delta]}(y < k)$. We assume the following fixed parameterization of the input signals: $u(t) = u_i$ if $(i-1)\Delta \leq t < i\Delta$ for $1 < i \leq n$, and $u_i \in [-v, v]$. Each u_i is called a control point. We observe that in order to falsify the requirement, the required input u would have to be positive at greater than $\lceil \frac{n+k}{2} \rceil$ control points. For a tool based on Markov-chain Monte-Carlo based random testing techniques, the probability of at least $\lceil \frac{n+k}{2} \rceil$ of n uniform-randomly chosen numbers in the interval $[-v, v]$ being positive is tiny (when k is comparable[1] to n). For example, for $k = 30$, and $n = 50$, the probability is about 10^{-5}.

One of the RRT-REX heuristics is to pick multiple goal points and select one based on lower branch robustness. The next step is then to perform a local optimization in order to choose an input that drives the RRT towards the goal point.

---

[1] One could use the (conservative) Chernoff bounds on the sum of binomial coefficients, which yields the following bound on probability: $\exp\left(\frac{-k^2}{2n}\right)$.

In this variant, in each step, the probability that RRT-REX selects a positive input effectively exceeds that in the previous step (starting with a probability of 0.5 in the first step). Thus, as a result of the robustness-guided goal-point selection and local optimization, the probability that RRT-REX discovers a sequence containing greater than $\frac{n+k}{2}$ positive values is much better than that for MCMC techniques. This is reflected in the experimental results shown in Table 1. For the results in the table, we use a time step of $h = 1.0$ seconds for the RRT-REX algorithm over each of the various time horizons (50,200,500). For the associated S-TaLiRo tests, the time horizon is equivalent to the dimension of the search space explored by the falsification engine.

5.2 Mode-Specific Reference Selection Model (MRS)

Next, we consider a model that selects an operating regime based on the input signals, and then sets a reference value based on the operating regime. The model takes as input 9 signals $u_1, \ldots, u_9$, where the range for each input in $u_1, \ldots, u_8$, is $[0, 100]$, and the range for u_9 is $[-5, 5]$. The model has two outputs, and we consider it a violation if any one of the outputs is less than a specified bound for that output. There are two discrete-time states for the model, the inputs of which are connected to the output signals (i.e., the states do not affect the model behaviors). We consider three requirements of the form:

$$\Box_{[\tau, T_{hoz}]}(y_i > -\rho_i). \tag{10}$$

In the above, we assume $\tau = 5$ seconds, $T_h = 10$ seconds, and $\rho_1 = 8$, $\rho_2 = 100$ and $\rho_3 = 20$. We use a slightly different version of the model for each of the three requirements. Analyzing the structure of the models, we observe that for each requirement, selection of the mode corresponding to the following condition leads to the failing case:

$$\bigwedge_{i \in [1..4]} ((u_{2i}(t) > 90) \wedge (u_{2i-1}(t) < 10)). \tag{11}$$

We thus know that is is possible to falsify each of the requirements by setting the appropriate input values, so as to enable the particular failing mode. However, such a configuration is difficult to find since the probability of finding an input at a given time t for which (11) is *true* is 10^{-8} (8 inputs, and for each input there is a probability of $\frac{1}{10}$ for choosing the right value for that input). We select a time step of $h = 2.5$ seconds for the RRT-REX algorithm over the 10 second time horizon. For the associated S-TaLiRo tests, this corresponds to 4 decision variables per each of the 9 inputs (i.e., a 36 dimension search space). As expected, neither RRT-REX nor S-TaLiRo were able to falsify any of the requirements with their default configurations.

5.3 Fuel Control System (AFC)

Next we consider a closed-loop model of an automotive powertrain control (PTC) subsystem. The system consists of two separate parts: (1) a plant model that

Table 1. Results of comparison between RRT approach and S-TaLiRo tool[a]

		RRT			S-TaLiRo		
Model	Spec.	Fals.	Time (sec)	Iter.	Fals.	Time	Iter.×Run
SPI	$\square_{[0,50]}(y < 20)$	yes	57.48	186.15	yes	104.95	1176.60
	$\square_{[0,200]}(y < 50)$	yes	421.24	492.31	no	1103.46	2000×10
	$\square_{[0,500]}(y < 150)$	yes	2970.72	2251.01	no	9771.45	5000×10
MRS	$\square_{[5,10]}(y_i > -8)$	no	376.79	5000	no	813.36	1000×10
	$\square_{[5,10]}(y_i > -100)$	no	351.81	5000	no	997.80	1000×10
	$\square_{[5,10]}(y_i > -20)$	no	313.21	5000	no	905.93	1000×10
AFC	$\square_{[5,50]}(|\lambda| \leq 0.05)$	yes	1091.76	171.34	no	5737.43	5000×10
	$\square_{[5,50]}(|\lambda| \leq 0.02)$	yes	1751.58	305.93	no	6755.09	5000×10
	$\Diamond_{[50,50]}(\lambda_{rms} \leq 0.05)$	no	6359.22	1000	yes	928.97	10.00
DAP	$\square_{[1.1,50]}(\mathbf{x} < 2)$	yes	14.23	2.3	yes	35.01	1
	$\square_{[1.1,50]}(\mathbf{x} < 4)$	yes	155.55	15.3	yes	46.30	1.4
	$\square_{[1.1,50]}(\mathbf{x} < 6)$	yes/no[b]	416.38	40.0	yes	204.36	7.6

[a] Note that the experiments involving the DAP example were performed on an Intel® Xeon® dual core (2.13 GHz, 24GB RAM) machine running Windows 7. All other experiments were performed on an Intel® Core™2 Duo (2.40 GHz, 4GB RAM) machine running the Windows 7 operating system.

[b] For this case, RRT-REX found falsifying traces 7 out of 10 times.

describes some key physical processes in an internal combustion engine, and (2) a controller model that represents the embedded software used to regulate the ratio of air-to-fuel (A/F) within the engine. A detailed description of this model can be found in [11], section 3.1.; here, we only focus on features relevant to this case study. The model has 7 continuous state variables (5 for the plant, and 2 for the controller), a *delay* function[2], 4 discrete modes of operation in the controller, and two exogenous inputs. In this case study we focus on: (1) the plant state λ denoting the measured, normalized A/F ratio, (2) a fixed engine speed $\omega \in [900, 1100]$, which is treated as a parameter, and (3) the exogenous user input θ representing the throttle angle command. We assume that $\theta(t_i) \in [0, 61.2]$, and is permitted to change value at a rate of $h = 1.0$ seconds.

We provide three requirements for the closed-loop model. The first two are specified in (12). Here, φ_1 specifies the bounds on the worst-case overshoot or undershoot on λ, while φ_2 characterizes the settling time on λ (time it requires λ to return to a small neighborhood of the reference value λ_{ref} after a perturbation). In (13), we introduce the signal λ_{rms} to help measure the RMS error between λ and λ_{ref}. In the definition of λ_{rms}, we exclude model behaviors for an initial τ_I seconds of time in order to discard transients in the startup mode and

[2] A continuous-time delay is a function described by the input/output relation $y(t) = u(t - \Delta)$ for some $\Delta \in \mathbb{R}^{\geq 0}$. Systems with delays pose a significant challenge to techniques such as RRT-REX, as they correspond to systems with infinite state variables. We assume that we can simulate such systems, but do not assume that we can measure the states associated with the delays.

transients arising from a mode switch to the normal mode of operation. Note that u(t) denotes the Heaviside step function. The third requirement (shown in (14)) specifies the bounds on the RMS error incurred in the A/F ratio state in the normal model of operation.

$$\varphi_1 \equiv \Box_{[0,T_h]}(|\lambda| \leq 0.05) \qquad \varphi_2 \equiv \Box_{[\tau,T_h]}(|\lambda| \leq 0.02) \tag{12}$$

$$\lambda_{rms}(t) = \sqrt{\frac{1}{t - \tau_I} \int_0^t (\lambda(\tau) - \lambda_{ref})^2 \cdot u(t - \tau_I) d\tau} \tag{13}$$

$$\varphi_3 \equiv \Diamond_{[T_h,T_h]}(\lambda_{rms} \leq 0.05) \tag{14}$$

In the above formulas, we select parameter values $\tau = 11$ seconds and $T_h = 50$ seconds, and we use a time step of $h = 1.0$ seconds for the RRT-REX algorithm. In this study RRT-REX and S-TaLiRo present mixed results (see Table 1). RRT-REX was able to falsify both the specifications 1) and 2) but not 3); however, S-TaLiRo was not able to falsify the properties 1) nor 2), but found a counterexample for the specification 3). The results support the theory that constructing input traces incrementally, as is the case for RRT-REX, can offer performance benefits over other approaches for some cases; however, such incremental approach may be a drawback in some instances. For instance, specification 3) imposes a constraint on a precise time instant rather then on a time interval. This does not provide RRT-REX with incremental quantitative information that will lead to the failing trace, which makes it difficult for RRT-REX to identify a falsifying instance.

5.4   Diesel Air-Path Model (DAP)

In this section, we consider an industrial closed-loop Simulink model of a prototype airpath controller for a diesel engine. The model contains more than $3,000$ blocks. It has a detailed plant model and a controller with more than 20 lookup tables and function blocks containing customized Matlab functions and legacy code. Moreover, more than half of these lookup tables are high dimensional (greater than one dimension). One of the challenges is, due to the high model complexity, obtaining simulation traces for this model is computationally expensive.

For this case study, we choose a safety property specifying upper bounds on the overshoot of a particular signal. This is represented by the following STL formula: $\Box_{[1.1,50]}(\mathbf{x} < c)$. We select a time step of $h = 5.0$ seconds, and compare the results of running RRT-REX and S-TaLiRo on this model, using three different values for c (2, 4, and 6). These values for c are not realistic, in the sense that the actual worst-case bounds on the system behavior are much larger. We select these smaller bounds due to the significant computational costs required to find falsifying traces using either RRT-REX or S-TaLiRo. The c values we select are adequate to study the performance of the RRT-REX approach versus S-TaLiRo as a function of the relative difficulty of the falsification task.

Table 1 indicates the results of the experiments. For the $c = 2$ case, RRT-REX is able to identify falsifying traces early in the simulation runs, and so explores simulation runs that are significantly shorter in length than the 50 second time horizon. By contrast, S-TaLiRo has to complete at least one simulation trace over the 50 second time horizon to determine that a trace falsifies the property. Since this requirement is easily falsified, RRT-REX is able to identify falsifying traces by exploring a small number of short simulation traces. The result is that RRT-REX performs better than S-TaLiRo for this case.

For the $c = 4$ and $c = 6$ cases, S-TaLiRo performs better than RRT-REX. The reason for this is that the requirements are such that the robustness values are sufficient to guide the global optimizer within S-TaLiRo directly to falsifying traces. This is in contrast to the RRT-REX approach, which introduces a significant amount of randomness into the search. This additional randomness incurs computational costs (due to the increased number of required simulations) that are larger than those incurred by S-TaLiRo.

6   Conclusions

In this paper we proposed a testing-based technique to find bugs in CPS systems. Given a specification expressed in terms of an STL formula, the search for an input sequence that causes the system to exhibit behaviors that violate the formula (falsifying behaviors) is guided using a combination of two criteria: the coverage of the system state space and the satisfaction robustness value of the specification. The coverage indicates "how well" we are exploring the state space of the system, while the robustness reflects "how much" the specification is satisfied, giving us the numerical intuition of how far we are from falsifying the formula. We incrementally build a simulation tree to best cover the state space, favoring those branches that correspond to low robustness value (with respect to the specification).

We implemented our framework in a prototype tool called RRT-REX, we applied it to both academic and industrial models, showing its applicability to practical systems, and we compared it with the S-TaLiRo tool.

Our experiments reveal that the relative performance of RRT-REX and S-TaLiRo depends on the nature of the model and the associated specification. We demonstrated that the incremental random RRT-REX search performs well on system with large input spaces and long input sequence; however, the RRT-REX approach is weak in the case of specifications defined of precise temporal instants. This drawback suggests directions for future developments. In subsequent work, we plan to study a dynamic exploration technique triggered by the formula itself, where the sampling space from which RRT-REX selects the exploration directions varies according to logical subformulas within the specification.

References

1. Ahmadyan, S.N., Kumar, J.A., Vasudevan, S.: Runtime verification of nonlinear analog circuits using incremental time-augmented rrt algorithm. In: Design, Automation Test in Europe Conference Exhibition (DATE), pp. 21–26, March 2013
2. Annpureddy, Y., Liu, C., Fainekos, G., Sankaranarayanan, S.: S-TaLiRo: a tool for temporal logic falsification for hybrid systems. In: Abdulla, P.A., Leino, K.R.M. (eds.) TACAS 2011. LNCS, vol. 6605, pp. 254–257. Springer, Heidelberg (2011)
3. Beck, J., Chen, W.: Irregularities of Distribution. Cambridge Studies in Social and Emotional Development. Cambridge University Press (1987)
4. Bhatia, A., Maly, M., Kavraki, E., Vardi, M.: Motion planning with complex goals. IEEE Robotics Automation Magazine 18(3), 55–64 (2011)
5. Dang, T., Donzé, A., Maler, O., Shalev, N.: Sensitive state-space exploration. In: CDC, pp. 4049–4054 (2008)
6. Dang, T., Nahhal, T.: Coverage-guided test generation for continuous and hybrid systems. Formal Methods in System Design 34(2), 183–213 (2009)
7. Donzé, A.: Breach, a toolbox for verification and parameter synthesis of hybrid systems. In: Touili, T., Cook, B., Jackson, P. (eds.) CAV 2010. LNCS, vol. 6174, pp. 167–170. Springer, Heidelberg (2010)
8. Donzé, A., Maler, O.: Robust satisfaction of temporal logic over real-valued signals. In: Chatterjee, K., Henzinger, T.A. (eds.) FORMATS 2010. LNCS, vol. 6246, pp. 92–106. Springer, Heidelberg (2010)
9. Donzé, A., Ferrère, T., Maler, O.: Efficient robust monitoring for STL. In: Sharygina, N., Veith, H. (eds.) CAV 2013. LNCS, vol. 8044, pp. 264–279. Springer, Heidelberg (2013)
10. Fainekos, G., Sankaranarayanan, S., Ueda, K., Yazarel, H.: Verification of automotive control applications using s-taliro. In: ACC (2012)
11. Jin, X., Deshmukh, J.V., Kapinski, J., Ueda, K., Butts, K.: Powertrain control verification benchmark. In: HSCC (2014)
12. Jin, X., Donzé, A., Deshmukh, J., Seshia, S.: Mining requirements from closed-loop control models. In: HSCC (2013)
13. Karaman, S., Frazzoli, E.: Linear temporal logic vehicle routing with applications to multi-UAV mission planning. Int. J. of Robust and Nonlinear Control 21(12), 1372–1395 (2011)
14. Karaman, S., Frazzoli, E.: Sampling-based algorithms for optimal motion planning. Int. J. of Robotics Research 30(7), 846–894 (2011)
15. Kim, J., Esposito, J.M., Kumar, V.: An rrt-based algorithm for testing and validating multi-robot controllers. In: RSS, pp. 249–256 (2005)
16. Kloetzer, M., Belta, C.: A fully automated framework for control of linear systems from temporal logic specifications. IEEE Trans. Auto. Control 53(1), 287–297 (2008)
17. Kong, Z., Jones, A., Ayala, A.M., Gol, E.A., Belta, C.: Temporal logic inference for classification and prediction from data. In: HSCC (2014)
18. LaValle, S.M.: Planning Algorithms, chap. 5. Cambridge University Press, Cambridge, U.K. (2006). http://planning.cs.uiuc.edu/
19. Lavalle, S.M., Kuffner, J.J., Jr.: Rapidly-exploring random trees: progress and prospects. In: Algorithmic and Computational Robotics: New Directions. pp. 293–308 (2000)
20. Maler, O., Nickovic, D.: Monitoring temporal properties of continuous signals. In: Lakhnech, Y., Yovine, S. (eds.) FORMATS 2004 and FTRTFT 2004. LNCS, vol. 3253, pp. 152–166. Springer, Heidelberg (2004)

21. Mathworks, T.: Simulink design verifier. http://www.mathworks.com/products/sldesignverifier/
22. Mount, D.M., Arya, S.: Ann: a library for approximate nearest neighbor searching. http://www.cs.umd.edu/~mount/ANN/
23. Plaku, E., Kavraki, L., Vardi, M.: Hybrid systems: from verification to falsification by combining motion planning and discrete search. Formal Methods in System Design **34**(2), 157–182 (2009)
24. Systems, R.: Model based testing and validation with reactis, reactive systems inc. http://www.reactive-systems.com
25. Yang, H., Hoxha, B., Fainekos, G.: Querying parametric temporal logic properties on embedded systems. In: Nielsen, B., Weise, C. (eds.) ICTSS 2012. LNCS, vol. 7641, pp. 136–151. Springer, Heidelberg (2012)

First-Order Transitive Closure Axiomatization via Iterative Invariant Injections

Aboubakr Achraf El Ghazi$^{(\boxtimes)}$, Mana Taghdiri, and Mihai Herda

Karlsruhe Institute of Technology, Karlsruhe, Germany
{elghazi,mana.taghdiri,herda}@kit.edu

Abstract. This paper presents an approach for proving the validity of first-order relational formulas that involve transitive closure. Given a formula F that includes the transitive closure of a relation R, our approach can deduce a complete (pure) first-order axiomatization of the paths of R that occur in F. Such axiomatization enables full automated verification of F using an automatic theorem prover like Z3. This is done via an iterative detection and injection of R-invariants —invariant formulas with respect to R-transitions in the context of F. This paper presents a proof for the correctness of the approach, and reports on its application to non-trivial Alloy benchmarks.

Keywords: First-order relational logic · Transitive closure · Axiomatization · Specification · Verification · Alloy · SMT solving

1 Introduction

Many computational problems, especially those that encode manipulations of linked data structures, can be efficiently specified in a relational first-order logic. Alloy [16] is a popular such language that has been successfully used for specifying and checking several different systems for different purposes at both the design and implementation level (see e.g. [5,17,24,26]). The transitive closure (TC) operator is a crucial, powerful tool for encoding structure-rich systems.

While the Alloy Analyzer can efficiently check Alloy specifications within a bounded scope, their full verification is a long-standing challenge. This is especially due to the known difficulty of reasoning about transitive closure —adding transitive closure even to very tame logics makes them undecidable [15]. Due to this undecidability, most attempts to verify the correctness of Alloy specifications are based on *interactive* theorem proving (e.g. [1,12,25]).

In our previous work [8], we proposed to verify Alloy specifications by first trying a fully automatic proof engine before switching to interactive theorem proving. The automatic engine, described in [9], relies on an efficient, semi-satisfiable[1] translation of Alloy into the satisfiability modulo theories (SMT)

---

[1] If the result is unsatisfiable, the input is unsatisfiable too.

© Springer International Publishing Switzerland 2015
K. Havelund et al. (Eds.): NFM 2015, LNCS 9058, pp. 143–157, 2015.
DOI: 10.1007/978-3-319-17524-9_11

language, and is able to automatically provide (full) proofs of some non-trivial Alloy specifications. Given the increasing capability of SMT solvers in handling quantifiers [4,13,14], the success of our automatic engine is not surprising at a first glance. However, given the fact that some of the proofs required transitive closure which causes undecidability, the success was thought-provoking. Since transitive closure is not expressible in pure first-order logic, in [9], we used an integer-based axiomatization. Although such axiomatization guaranties TC-satisfiability —any model of the axiomatisation is a TC model— it is not generally sufficient for refuting proof obligations; one still needs the integer induction (IND) principle. The latter claim roots in our experiments with Kelloy [25], an interactive proof engine for Alloy specifications. We observed that most specifications that require the transitive closure theory, need the IND principle and have to be proven manually.

In this paper, we investigate the following questions: (1) when can the integer based axiomatization of TC refute proof obligations without requiring the IND principle? (2) for the logic fragment of question 1, can one use an integer-free axiomatization? and (3) to refute a proof obligation outside the fragment of question 1, what kind of integer-free axiomatization can be used?

Let F be a refutable first-order relational formula in which the semantics of all symbols except for transitive closure are precisely encoded, and the transitive closure of a relation R is encoded by an uninterpreted binary relation tc_R. To answer questions (1) and (2), we use a pure first-order, weak axiomatization (WTC) which constrains tc_R to a transitive relation containing R but not the smallest one. We prove that WTC is complete for any *negative* transitive closure occurrence in the clause normal form (CNF) of F. Therefore, if the solver (falsely) reports F as satisfiable modulo WTC, it is only because of *positive* transitive closure occurrences. To extend the WTC fragment and to answer question (3), we introduce a technique which automatically detects relevant invariants about the paths of tc_R and adds them as additional assumptions to F. If any of such invariants cause contradiction, F has been refuted and the process stops. Otherwise, more invariants will be detected and added to F.

We applied our technique to a total of 20 Alloy benchmarks known to be valid, all of which require the transitive closure theory for their proof. Out of the 20 benchmarks 18 were successfully proven correct fully automatically using our invariant detection technique.

2   Background

Let $\Sigma = (Typ, \sqsubseteq, Fun, \alpha)$ be a typed *signature* consisting of a set of type symbols Typ that always includes boolean (*Bool*) and integer (*Int*) types, a partial order $\sqsubseteq$ over Typ, a set of function symbols Fun[2], and a typing function $\alpha : Fun \rightarrow Typ^+$ that gives the type of each function symbol, i.e. $\alpha(f) = (T_1, \ldots, T_n)$ iff $f : T_1 \times \cdots \times T_{n-1} \rightarrow T_n$. If $T_n = Bool$, function f can also be called a predicate

---

[2] Certain interpreted functions (e.g. equality and logical connectives) are always included and denoted in infix notation.

and the notation $f \subseteq T_1 \times \cdots \times T_{n-1}$ can be used alternatively. We assume that for each type $T \in Typ$, there exists an infinite set of variables of type T denoted by Var^T. Variable sets are mutually disjoint and their union is denoted by Var.

Terms of the logic are built recursively from variables in Var, function symbols in Fun and quantifiers. The type of a term is determined recursively based on the types of its variables and functions. Function symbols with arity 0 are constants, and denoted by the set Con. Terms without variables are ground terms, and denoted by Gr. The notation $t[x_1, \ldots, x_n]$ denotes that the variables $x_1, \ldots, x_n$ (for short $x_{1:n}$) occur in t. For two terms t and s and a variable x, the notation $t[s/x]$ denotes the result of substituting s for x in t. We use $t[S]$ for applying a set of substitutions S when the substitution order does not matter.

Formulas are boolean terms. A formula is *atomic* if it is a function application, i.e. $f(t_{1:n})$, and the top-level function f is not a logical connective. A *literal* is an atomic formula or its negation. A *clause* is a disjunction of literals. A formula F is in *clause normal form* (CNF) if it is a conjunction of clauses $C_1 \wedge \cdots \wedge C_n$, where each C_i is quantifier-free and its variables are implicitly universally quantified. We view CNF formulas as sets of clauses and clauses as sets of literals.

We extend our first-order logic to a relational one by introducing two distinct types Rel and $Tuple$, and a binary predicate $\in \subseteq Tuple \times Rel$ that represent relations, tuples, and the membership predicate respectively. We use $ar : Rel \cup Tuple \to \mathbb{N}$ to denote the arity of relations and tuples. Unary relations are called sets and unary tuples are called atoms. We use $R \subseteq T_1 \times \cdots \times T_n$ to denote that R is an n-ary relation, and that the ith element of every tuple in R is of type T_i.

Constant relations form basic relational expressions[3]. Complex relational expressions are built using the usual relational operators. Particularly, the join $R \cdot S$ of two relational expressions R and S is a relational expression Q of arity $n := ar(R) + ar(S) - 2$, such that $(a_{1:n}) \in Q$ iff there exists an atom a where $(a_{1:ar(R)-1}, a) \in R$ and $(a, a_{ar(R):n}) \in S$; the transitive closure R^+ of a binary relation R is the smallest transitive relation containing R; the restriction $R|_S$ of a relational expression R and a set of tuples S of arity $ar(R)$ is a relational expression Q such that $Q = R \cap S$. For a binary relation R, an R-path is a sequence of atoms $a_{1:n}$ where $n \geq 2$ and $(a_i, a_{i+1}) \in R$ for $1 \leq i < n$. An R-path of length $n = 2$ is an R-step. An R-path may not list the intermediate atoms explicitly. That is, $(a, b) \in R^+$ is also an R-path. For an R-path p we use p_u to denote its tuple and p_s and p_e to denote its start and end boundaries respectively.

Let $|M|^T$ denote the universe of all semantical values of a type $T \in Typ$. A model $\mathcal{M}$ for a signature Σ is a pair $(|M|, M)$ where $|M|$ is a class of universes defined as $\{|M|^T \mid T \in Typ\}$ such that if $T_i \sqsubseteq T_j$, then $|M|^{T_i} \subseteq |M|^{T_j}$, and M is an interpretation that maps every function $f : T_1 \times .. \times T_{n-1} \to T_n$ to an interpretation $M(f) : |M|^{T_1} \times \ldots \times |M|^{T_{n-1}} \to |M|^{T_n}$ and every variable $x : T$ to a value in $|M|^T$. For a relation R, we write $M(R)$ as a shorthand for $\{u \mid M(\in (u, R))\}$. By default, $|M|^{Bool} = \{true, false\}$ and $|M|^{Int} = \mathbb{Z}$. The interpretation $M(t)$ of a term t is defined recursively using the rule $M(f(t_{1:n})) = M(f)(M(t_1), \ldots, M(t_n))$ for a function symbol f. Satisfaction,

---

[3] Conventionally, relational terms are called relational expressions.

F :
    (1) $h_1 . mark = \emptyset$
    (2) $h_0 . ref \subseteq h_1 . ref$
    (3) $\forall n. \neg((root, n) \in tc_{H.ref}(h_1)) \vee n \in h_2 . mark$
    (4) $h_1 . ref \subseteq h_2 . ref$
    (5) $\forall n. \neg(n \notin h_2 . mark) \vee n . (h_3 . ref) = \emptyset$
    (6) $\forall n. \neg(n \in h_2 . mark) \vee n . (h_3 . ref) = n . (h_2 . ref)$
    (7) $(root, live) \in tc_{H.ref}(h_0)$
    (8) $live . (h_0 . ref) \not\subseteq live . (h_3 . ref)$
WTC : (9) $\forall h. h . ref \subseteq tc_{H.ref}(h)$
    (10) $\forall h. Transitive(tc_{H.ref}(h))$

(a)

Essential R-path p:
  $(root, live) \in tc_{H.ref}(h_0)$
Path invariant for p:
  $n \in h_2 . mark$

(b)

F' :
$F \wedge WTC \wedge$
  $\forall x. (root, x) \in tc_{H.ref}(h_0) \rightarrow x \in h_2 . mark$

(c)

Fig. 1. Example. (a) Original formula and a weak transitive closure theory, (b) a difficult R-path in F and its invariant, (c) augmented formula.

denoted by $\mathcal{M} \models \varphi$, for a model $\mathcal{M}$ and a formula φ is defined as usual (see elsewhere [11, p. 80]).

A theory $\mathcal{T}$ is a set of deductively closed formulas. A class of models ω induces a theory $Th(\omega)$, namely the theory of all formulas φ where $\mathcal{M} \models \varphi$ and $\mathcal{M} \in \omega$ —the resulting set is deductively closed by definition. We use $\mathcal{T}_f^g$ to denote the theory which agrees with $\mathcal{T}$ except for the interpretations $\mathcal{M}$ of f, where it is interpreted the same way as $M(g)$. A $\mathcal{T}$-model $\mathcal{M}$ is a model that satisfies all formulas of $\mathcal{T}$. Especially, a formula φ is satisfiable modulo a theory $\mathcal{T}$ if there exists a $\mathcal{T}$-model $\mathcal{M}$ where $\mathcal{M} \models \varphi$, for short $\mathcal{M} \models_{\mathcal{T}} \varphi$.

Let Ax be the finite set of axioms for all the interpreted symbols of Fun except transitive closure. Only sub-theories of the theory built by the deductive closure $Cl(Ax)$ of Ax are considered here. For the transitive closure R^+, we introduce a fresh uninterpreted binary relation tc_R.

3   Example

Figure 1(a) gives a relational first-order formula F in CNF form —lines correspond to clauses. Symbols h_0 to h_3 are constants of type H that represents the system state; $root$ and $live$ are two constants of type Obj that represents objects; $mark \subseteq H \times Obj$ represents the marked objects in each state; $ref \subseteq H \times Obj \times Obj$ represents references between objects in each state; and $tc_{H.ref} : H \rightarrow Obj \times Obj$ is a function that maps each state h to a binary relation $tc_{H.ref}(h) \subseteq Obj \times Obj$ which aims at representing the transitive closure of the relation $h . ref$. The last two lines (WTC) give a weak semantics for $tc_{H.ref}(h)$. They constrain it to be transitive and to include the base relation, but not necessarily the smallest such relation. F gives the negated proof obligation of a safety property of an extremely simplified version of mark-and-sweep algorithm. The state transition $(h_0 – h_1)$ resets all the marks (Lines 1-2), $(h_1 – h_2)$ marks objects reachable from $root$ (Lines 3-4), and $(h_2 – h_3)$ sweeps references of non-marked objects (Lines 5-6). The safety property is negated, thus it checks if in the final state, there is a $live$ object that was originally reachable from $root$ in the beginning state (Line 7), but some of its references have been swept (Line 8).

In our previous work [25], we solved such formulas by adding general axioms about transitive closure. Here, for example, F can be refuted using the subset preservation axiom, namely $R \subseteq S \rightarrow R^+ \subseteq S^+$ for binary relations R and S. The only state transition in F that allows for sweeping object references is $(h_2 - h_3)$ —Line 5. Since (5) is guarded by the condition that the objects are not marked at h_2, to refute the formula, it is sufficient to show that all live objects are marked at h_2. Applying the above axiom to Lines 2, 4 and using Line 7, we have $(root, live) \in tc_{H.ref}(h_2)$ and can easily close the proof. In [25] we collected more than 100 such transitive closure axioms, proved and added them as further deduction rules. Although the approach was useful for interactive and semi-interactive solving, the results of [3] suggest that this approach does not scale for automatic provers such as SMT solvers. [3] proposes to add these lemmas only on-demand based on some heuristics. In this paper, we go one step further and detect and add only the actually needed properties on-the-fly (as opposed to always include some general properties).

Our new approach refutes F by first solving $F \wedge WTC$ using an SMT solver. In this example, the safety property holds, and thus F must be unsatisfiable. The solver, however, (falsely) reports F as satisfiable. This is because WTC only fixes the semantics of *negative* R-paths in F —those that only appear in negated literals in CNF; *positive* R-paths remain as sources of incompleteness (thus called *difficult* R-paths). We are interested in those difficult R-paths whose refutation is mandatory for refuting F (*essential* R-paths). Fig. 1(a) contains only one difficult R-path: $(root, live) \in tc_R$ (Line 7) (denoted by p), and it is essential since it is a unit clause in F^4. We refute p by searching for some property $\varphi[x]$, called p-invariants, that (1) holds for all objects reachable from the beginning of p, namely $root$, by one R-step —p-step test— and (2) if it holds for an object x, it holds for all objects reachable from x by one R-step —R-invariant test. Given a p-invariant $\varphi[x]$, the induction principle allows us to add the assumption $\forall x_2.(root, x_2) \in tc_R \rightarrow \varphi[x_2/x]$ as an additional clause to F without affecting its validity. If one of the p-invariants is known to not hold for $live$ (the end object of p), then p is refuted and we are done. Fig. 1(b) shows the p-invariant which is sufficient to refute our essential R-path. It is the subclause of clause (3) which passes both p-step and R-invariant tests. Details on the search procedure for p-invariants are presented in sec. 6. After adding the p-invariant assumption to F (Fig. 1(c)), the SMT solver reports it as unsatisfiable, and thus the example has been verified fully automatically.

4   Weak TC Axiomatization and Its Fragment

In this section, we discuss a general[5], weak, first-order, integer-free axiomatization for transitive closure (denoted by WTC) and describe a fragment for which this is complete. The WTC axioms are given in 1. They constrain the symbol tc_R to be a transitive relation that contains R —denoted by $tr(R)$. Therefore, their

---

[4] In general the test for essential R-paths is not trivial.

[5] Independent of the considered formula.

deductive closure $Cl(WTC)$ describes $\mathcal{T}_{tc_R}^{tr(R)}$. Although the WTC is very weak, there exists a *non-trivial* fragment for which this axiomatization is complete.

$$\forall x_1, x_2.\ (x_1, x_2) \in R \rightarrow (x_1, x_2) \in tc_R$$
$$\forall x_1, x_2, x_3.\ (x_1, x_2) \in tc_R \wedge (x_2, x_3) \in tc_R \rightarrow (x_1, x_3) \in tc_R \tag{1}$$

Theorem 1 (WTC complete fragment). *Let F be a first-order relational formula, R and tc_R two binary relations, and u a tuple such that the R-path $u \in tc_R$ occurs only as negative literal in $CNF(F)$. Then, F is unsatisfiable modulo $\mathcal{T}_{tc_R|u}^{R^+}$ iff it is unsatisfiable modulo $\mathcal{T}_{tc_R|u}^{tr(R)}$.*

Proof. Let u denote a tuple (a, b) and the R-path $(a, b) \in tc_R$ be denoted by p. Assuming that p occurs only as negative literal in $CNF(F)$, we need to prove that (1) if F is unsatisfiable modulo $\mathcal{T}_{tc_R|u}^{tr(R)}$, then it is unsatisfiable modulo $\mathcal{T}_{tc_R|u}^{R^+}$ too, and (2) if F has a $\mathcal{T}_{tc_R|u}^{tr(R)}$-model, it has a $\mathcal{T}_{tc_R|u}^{R^+}$-model too. Case (1) is trivial since $R^+ \subseteq tr(R)$. For case (2) we assume that $\mathcal{M}$ is a $\mathcal{T}_{tc_R|u}^{tr(R)}$-model of F. For all clauses in $CNF(F)$ in which a literal other than $\neg p$ is satisfied, $\mathcal{M}$ is especially a $\mathcal{T}_{tc_R|u}^{R^+}$-model because $\mathcal{T}_{tc_R|u}^{tr(R)}$ and $\mathcal{T}_{tc_R|u}^{R^+}$ coincide in symbols other than $tc_R|_u$. For all other clauses C, we can assume that $C := \neg p \vee C_{rest}$ and $\mathcal{M} \models \neg(a, b) \in tc_R$. Since $\mathcal{T}_{tc_R}^{tr(R)} = Cl(WTC)$, $\mathcal{M}$ is especially a model for the second WTC axiom instantiated with a and b; $\mathcal{M} \models \forall x_2.\ (a, x_2) \notin tc_R \vee (x_2, b) \notin tc_R$. By induction, using the first axiom, there is no R-path from a to b in $\mathcal{M}$. Therefore $\mathcal{M}$ is a $\mathcal{T}_{tc_R|u}^{R^+}$-model for $\neg p$ and thus for C. □

In other words, theorem 1 states that if all R-paths in $CNF(F)$ are negative literals, then WTC is a correct and complete R^+-axiomatization of tc_R in F. It describes, therefore, a WTC complete fragment. The fragment conditions are syntactic and allow categorizing R-paths into easy —with only negative literals in the $CNF(F)$— and difficult —otherwise. Hereafter, we denote the set of all difficult R-paths by DP.

5 R-Invariants for Axiomatizing Difficult R-Paths

This section introduces R-*invariants* as a means for providing a transitive closure axiomatisation that is *context-complete*, i.e. complete with respect to the context in which the transitive closure is used. This axiomatisation handles difficult R-paths, those for which the weak axiomatisation is not complete, and thus provides a proof possibility for formulas beyond the WTC-fragment described in Sec. 4.

Definition 1 (Essential difficult R-paths). *Let R be a binary relation and F be a refutable first-order relational formula modulo $\mathcal{T}_{tc_R}^{R^+}$. Then, a difficult R-path $p \in DP$ is essential —for refuting F— if there exists a model $\mathcal{M}$ where $\forall p' \in DP \setminus p.\ M(tc_R|_{p'_u}) = M(R^+|_{p'_u}),\ M(tc_R|_{p_u}) = M(tr(R)|_{p_u})$ and $\mathcal{M} \models F$. The set of all essential (difficult) R-paths is denoted by EDP.*

Definition 1 describes difficult R-paths that require further axiomatization in order to refute F. The definition condition, however, requires a complete axiomatization of difficult R-paths, which is in fact our ultimate goal. Therefore, we will later give a practical *heuristic* to check for essential R-paths.

Definition 2 (R-invariant). *Let F be a first-order formula and R a binary relation. Then, a formula $\varphi[x]$ is a forward (resp. backward) R-invariant with respect to x, F and a theory $\mathcal{T}$ if*

$$F \models_{\mathcal{T}} \forall x_1, x_2.\ \varphi[x_1/x] \wedge (x_1, x_2)^d \in R \rightarrow \varphi[x_2/x]$$

for $d = 1$ (resp. $d = -1$) , where $(x_1, x_2)^{-1} = (x_2, x_1)$.

Definition 3 (p-invariant). *Let F be a first-order formula, R a binary relation and p an R-path of the form $(a, b) \in tc_R$. Then, a forward (resp. backward) R-invariant formula $\varphi[x]$ is forward (resp. backward) p-invariant with respect to x, F and a theory $\mathcal{T}$ if a (resp. b) is ground and*

$$F \models_{\mathcal{T}} \forall x_2.\ (a, x_2)^{-d} \in R \rightarrow \varphi[x_2/x]$$

for $d = 1$ (resp. $d = -1$).

When using def. 3 and 2, we may skip mentioning x, F and $\mathcal{T}$ when clear from the context. Unless explicitly stated, the forward definitions are meant.

Definition 4 (TC induction schema). *The first-order relational version of the induction axiom, denoted by IND^r, is a schema of axioms which states that for any closed first-order formula $\varphi[z_1, z_2]$, containing variables z_1 and z_2, the following hold:*

$$[\forall x_{1\cdot 2}.\ (x_1, x_2) \in R \rightarrow \varphi[x_1/z_1, x_2/z_2] \wedge \tag{2}$$
$$\forall x_{1\cdot 3}.\ \varphi[x_1/z_1, x_2/z_2] \wedge (x_1, x_2) \in tc_R \wedge (x_2, x_3) \in R \rightarrow \varphi[x_1/z_1, x_3/z_2]] \tag{3}$$
$$\rightarrow \quad [\forall x_{1\cdot 2}.\ (x_1, x_2) \in R^+ \rightarrow \varphi[x_1/z_1, x_2/z_2]] \tag{4}$$

For any refutable formula F modulo $\mathcal{T}^{R^+}_{tc_R|p_u}$ that contains an essential R-path p of the form $(a, b) \in tc_R$, we would like to claim the existence of a p-invariant formula φ, such that $(\forall x.(a, x) \in tc_R \rightarrow \varphi) \wedge F$ is refutable modulo $\mathcal{T}^{tr(R)}_{tc_R|p_u}$. We found it difficult to prove this claim using a $\mathcal{T}^{R^+}_{tc_R}$ theory, especially since any refutation proof of F has to be considered in a second-order proof system. Instead, we consider the $\mathcal{T}^{ind}_{tc_R}$ theory, which consists of the extension of $\mathcal{T}^{tr(R)}_{tc_R}$ with our induction schema for transitive closure (def. 4). This is indeed a restriction, since $\mathcal{T}^{ind}_{tc_R}$ only covers a recursively-enumerable set of properties — similar argument as in [19]. This is comparable to the gap between the first- and second-order Peano axiomatization of arithmetic (cf. [2, page 1133]). In practice, however, it imposes no restriction to the proof power and this is the common practice in literature (cf. [1,25]).

Theorem 2 (Main theorem). *Let R be a binary relation, F a first-order relational formula and p a difficult R-path of the form $(a, b) \in tc_R$ in a clause C of F. If F is refutable modulo $\mathcal{T}^{ind}_{tc_R|a,b}$ but satisfiable modulo $\mathcal{T}^{tr(R)}_{tc_R|a,b}$, then there exists a p-invariant $\varphi[x]$ w.r.t. x, $F \setminus C$ and $\mathcal{T}^{tr(R)}_{tc_R|a,b}$, such that*

$$F \setminus C \models_{\mathcal{T}^{tr(R)}_{tc_R|a,b}} \neg\varphi[b/x] \text{ and} \tag{5}$$

$$(\forall x_2.\ (a, x_2) \in tc_R \rightarrow \varphi[x_2/x]) \wedge F \text{ is refutable modulo } \mathcal{T}^{tr(R)}_{tc_R|a,b}. \tag{6}$$

Proof. Without lost of generality, we can assume that $\mathcal{T}^{tr(R)}_{tc_R|a,b}$ differs from $\mathcal{T}^{ind}_{tc_R|a,b}$ only in the interpretation of $tc_R|_{(a,b)}$, and p only occurs in C. Therefore, $F \setminus C$ must be satisfiable modulo $\mathcal{T}^{ind}_{tc_R|a,b}$. This means that since F is refutable modulo $\mathcal{T}^{ind}_{tc_R|a,b}$ but satisfiable modulo $\mathcal{T}^{tr(R)}_{tc_R|a,b}$, for each $\mathcal{T}^{ind}_{tc_R|a,b}$-model $\mathcal{M}$ of $F \setminus C$, $\mathcal{M} \models (a,b) \notin tc_R$, which in turn means $F \setminus C \models_{\mathcal{T}^{ind}_{tc_R|a,b}} (a,b) \notin tc_R$.

Let us further consider a proof object pr (e.g. in sequent style) for $F \setminus C \models_{\mathcal{T}^{ind}_{tc_R|a,b}} (a,b) \notin tc_R$, then the set of all formulas IP of all essential IND^r applications in pr is non-empty. Let $\Gamma := \{\phi_i[x_1, x_2] := \forall x_1, x_2. (x_1, x_2) \in tc_R \rightarrow \varphi_i(x_1, x_2) \mid \varphi_i \in IP\}$. Since IP contains all formulas of all essential IND^r applications in pr, we can conclude that $\Gamma, F \setminus C \models_{\mathcal{T}^{tr(R)}_{tc_R|a,b}} (a,b) \notin tc_R$. Note, that a proof pr' of the last sequent does not contain any IND^r application, but have to make use of Γ in order to close, since $F \setminus C \not\models_{\mathcal{T}^{ind}_{tc_R|a,b}} (a,b) \notin tc_R$. Therefore, we can assume, w.l.o.g. the existence of a formula $\psi[x_1, x_2]$ where $F \setminus C \models_{\mathcal{T}^{tr(R)}_{tc_R|a,b}} \neg\psi(a,b)$ and $\Gamma, \neg\psi(a,b) \models_{\mathcal{T}^{tr(R)}_{tc_R|a,b}} (a,b) \notin tc_R$. Because of the form of the formulas in Γ, there must exist a $\phi_i \in \Gamma$ where $\Gamma, \neg\psi(a,b) \models_{\mathcal{T}^{tr(R)}_{tc_R|a,b}} \neg\varphi_i(a,b)$. Having this, $(a,b) \notin tc_R$ can be directly concluded from ϕ_i —left to right. Note that this argument will already work if we only had the instantiation of x_1 in ϕ_i with a. Now we construct $\varphi[x_2] := \varphi_i[a/x_1]$ and prove that φ fulfills all the conditions of the theorem.

By instantiating x_1 with a in the first and second IND^r conditions (2) and (3) for $\varphi_i[x_1, x_2]$, we get directly that $\varphi[x_2]$ is a p-invariant w.r.t. x_2, F and $\mathcal{T}^{R^+}_{tc_R|a,b}$. For the theorem condition (5), let us assume that $F \setminus C \models_{\mathcal{T}^{tr(R)}_{tc_R|a,b}} \varphi_i(a,b)$, then we get that $F \setminus C \models_{\mathcal{T}^{tr(R)}_{tc_R|a,b}} \psi(a,b)$, which contradicts our earlier results. The last condition (6) holds since $F \setminus C \models_{\mathcal{T}^{tr(R)}_{tc_R|a,b}} \neg\psi(a,b)$ and $F \setminus C, \varphi(b) \models_{\mathcal{T}^{tr(R)}_{tc_R|a,b}} \psi(a,b)$. □

Theorem 2 offers a basis for a framework capable of proving the validity of transitive closure formulas beyond the WTC fragment. Especially, for each essential R-path p, the theorem guaranties the existence of a p-invariant which is deducible from F modulo $\mathcal{T}^{ind}_{tc_R}$ and can together with F refute p. In the next section we show how the conditions of the theorem on φ can be turned into practical rules and heuristic algorithms to direct the search for p-invariants.

6   Algorithm for Detecting p-invariants

In order to provide an automatic procedure capable of proving transitive closure specifications, we present an algorithm which tries to bring the theoretical results of the previous sections into action. Before discussing the actual algorithm, some definitions and lemmas are needed.

We first discuss two concepts introduced and used in the last section: (1) *essential R-paths*, and (2) *R-path isolation*, i.e. the consideration of F modulo $(\mathcal{T}^{R^+}_{tc_R})^{tr(R)}_{tc_R|p_u}$ for an R-path p (cf. proof of theorem 2). The latter concept subsumes the former one and is of particular importance for the automation process. It allows for detecting essential R-paths and for handling the WTC incompleteness for each R-path individually regardless of other paths. However, the second concept requires $\mathcal{T}_{tc_R}^{R^+}$ which is our actual goal. In order to overcome this, in def. 5, we introduce the idea of *bounded R-paths isolation*. Here, an R-path —of an arbitrary length— is replaced with a corresponding R-path of length less equal n, where n is the isolation confidence and R^i denotes joining R with itself i times.

Definition 5 (n **confident** R-**path isolation**). *Let R be a binary relation, F a first-order relational formula, p a difficult R-path in F and n a positive natural number. Then, the n confident isolation of p in F is*

$$F|_p^n := F[\{[u \in \bigcup_{i \leq n} R^i \ / \ u \in tc_R] \mid (u \in tc_R) \in DP \setminus \{p\}\}].$$

> **Data:** F : *Term*
> **Result:** *Term*
> 1 $F^{ini} \leftarrow CNF(\neg F); \ F \leftarrow F^{ini}; \ n \leftarrow 1$
> 2   **repeat**
> 3   **for** $p := (p_s, p_e) \in tc_R \in \{p \in DP(F^{ini}) \mid sat(F^{ini}|_p^n)\}$ **do**
> 4   **for** $<p_g, d> \in \{<p_s, 1>, <p_e, -1>\}$ **do**
> 5   **if** $p_g \in Gr$ **then**
> 6 $F \leftarrow pathInv(p, p, p_g, F, F^{ini}, R, d, n)$
> 7   **if** $unsat(F)$ **then**
> 8   **return** F
> 9   **else**
> 10 $x_{1:n} \leftarrow Var(p_g)$
> 11   **for** $p' := (p'_s, p'_e) \in \{p|a_{1:n}/x_{1:n}] \mid a_i \in sufGT^1(x_i)\}$ **do**
> 12   **if** $sat(F[p'/p]|_{p'}^n)$ **then**
> 13 $p'_g \leftarrow d \ ? \ p'_s : p'_e$
> 14 $F \leftarrow pathInv(p, p', p'_g, F, F^{ini}, R, d, n)$
> 15   **if** $unsat(F)$ **then**
> 16   **return** F
> 17   **if** $(\forall p'. \ unsat(F[p'/p]|_{p'}^n)) \wedge sat(F|_p^n)$ **then**
> 18   Further/General techniques are needed
> 19   **if** $\forall p : EDP. \ unsat(F|_p^n)$ **then**
> 20 $n \leftarrow n + 1$
> 21 **until** F and n are unchanged;
> 22 **return** F

Algorithm 1. Main Procedure

Algorithm 1 shows the main procedure of our approach. Given a refutable formula F modulo $\mathcal{T}_{tc_R}^{R^+}$, it will first detect all essential R-paths by checking the satisfiability of the n bounded isolation $F|_p^n$ of all difficult R-paths p (line 3). The isolation confidence n, is only increased if $F|_p^n$ is unsatisfiable for all essential R-paths in EDP but F is not (lines 19-20).

Data: p, p', p_g, F, F^{ini} : $Term, R \subseteq T \times T, d, n : Int$
Result: $Term$
1 **for** $\varphi[x_{1:n}] \in (F^{ini} \setminus C_p)$ with $p_g \equiv type(x_i)$ **do**
2   **for** $x_i \in \{x_{1:n}\}$ **do**
3      $F \leftarrow concPathInv(\varphi, p, p', p_g, F, F^{ini}, x_i, R, d, n)$
4   **if** $unsat(F[p'/p]|_{p'}^{n})$ **then**
5   **return** F
6 **return** F

Algorithm 2: *pathInv*

Data: $\varphi, p, p', p_g, F, F^{ini}$: $Term, x : Var, R \subseteq T \times T,$
   $d, n : Int$
Result: $Term$
1 **for** $\varphi_i[x] \subseteq \varphi$ **do**
2    $F \leftarrow checkPathInv(\varphi_i, x, p_g, F, R, d)$
3   **if** $unsat(F[p'/p]|_{p'}^{n})$ **then**
4   **return** F
5   **for** $\varphi'_i[x] \in abst(\varphi_i, F^{ini}, x, R, n)$ **do**
6      $F \leftarrow checkPathInv(\varphi'_i, x, p_g, F, R, d)$
7   **if** $unsat(F[p'/p]|_{p'}^{n})$ **then**
8   **return** F
9 **return** F

Algorithm 3: *concPathInv*

Data: φ, F : $Term, x : Var, R \subseteq T \times T, n : Int$
Result: $Set < Term >$
1 $S \leftarrow \{\varphi\}; A \leftarrow \emptyset$
2 **for** $\varphi_i \in S$ **do**
3   **for** $abst \in \{applicable\ abstraction\ rules\ to\ \varphi_i\}$ **do**
4      $A \leftarrow A \cup abst(\varphi_i, x, R, n); S \leftarrow S \cup abst(\varphi_i, x, R, n)$
5    $S \leftarrow S \setminus \{\varphi_i\}$
6 **return** A

Algorithm 4: *abst*

Data: φ, t, p_g, F : $Term, R \subseteq T \times T, d : Int$
Result: $Term$
1 **begin**
2    $PO_{ini} \leftarrow \forall x_2.\ (p_g, x_2)^d \in R \rightarrow \varphi[x_2/t]$
3    $PO_{ind} \leftarrow \varphi[x_2/t] \wedge (p_g, x_2)^d \in tc_R \wedge (x_2, x_3)^d \in R$
4    $PO_{ind} \leftarrow \forall x_2, x_3.\ PO_{ind} \rightarrow \varphi[x_3/t]$
5   **if** $unsat(F \wedge \neg PO_{ini}) \wedge unsat(F \wedge \neg PO_{ind})$ **then**
6      $F \leftarrow (\forall x_2.\ (p_g, x_2)^d \in tc_R \rightarrow \varphi[x_2/t]) \wedge F$
7   **return** F

Algorithm 5: *checkPathInv*

For each essential R-path p we search for forward p-invariants with respect to its start boundary p_s and backward p-invariants with respect to its end boundary p_e. If the currently handled path boundary, p_g, is ground, which corresponds exactly to the considered case in theorem 2, the search is performed for the original R-path p by algo. 2. Otherwise, instances of p are used (line 11-12). The p instances are generated by instantiating the variables of p_g with their essential ground terms of complexity 1 —constants— using a slightly modified version of the framework in [10][6]. The R-path instantiation approach is motivated by the guess that probably only a *small* finite set of p instances are refutable.

In algo. 2, each clause φ of $CNF(F)$ —after excluding p's clauses— that contains a non empty set of variables $x_{1:n}$ of a type compatible to p_g is considered for the p-invariant search, namely with respect to each x_i in $\{x_{i:n}\}$ (line 1-2). Since all variables in φ are universally quantified, φ is obviously a p-invariant with respect to any variable x_i, however, we are interested in more concrete forms of φ. This is described in algo. 3, where, each sub clause φ_i that contains x_i is considered a candidate. The actual check for p-invariance is performed in algo. 5. Depending on weather p_g is a start or end boundary, the forward or backward definition of p-invariants is used respectively. If the p-invariant check fails for a candidate φ_i, syntactically-driven abstractions are generated and tried (algo. 4). Our abstraction rules are shown in fig. 2. The first rule abstracts a φ_i by instantiating their variables —x_i excluded— with their essential ground terms of complexity equal to the current calculation round r. The second rule relaxes positive literals —conclusions— in φ_i by their *syntactic* consequences in F. The

---

[6] The essential ground terms are calculated in rounds with increasing term complexity, regardless of whether the set is finite or not.

third rule is only used if a p-invariant candidate passes the p-step test (cf. PO_{ini} in algo. 5) but fails in the R-invariant test. It then relaxes *unary* assumptions on a single path boundary such that they hold for all reachable nodes from that boundary including itself —reachability direction is stated by d. Let's assume a clause C in F of the form $(a, x_2) \in R \wedge \phi(a) \to \varphi_{rest}[x_2]$ and an R-path p of the form $(a, x_2) \in tc_R$. Then, the p-invariant candidate φ equal to $\phi(a) \to \varphi_{rest}[x_2]$ will pass the p-step check using C only. If φ does not pass the R-invariant test, then our third abstraction rule can abstract it such that it passes both tests using C only.

$Abst_1$: Variable instantiations with essential ground terms of complexity r, using [10]
$Abst_2$: $\varphi := (l \vee \varphi_{rest}), (\neg l \vee C_{rest}) \in CNF(F) \Longrightarrow \varphi \rightsquigarrow \varphi[C_{rest} / l]$
$Abst_3$: $\varphi := (\neg\phi(t) \vee \varphi_{rest}), t := p_g \Longrightarrow \varphi \rightsquigarrow \varphi[(\forall x.\ x = t \vee (t, x)^d \in tc_R \to \phi(x)) / \phi(t)]$

Fig. 2. Abstraction rules

If, in the case of a non-ground p_g, all R-path instances p' can be refuted but not the original path p, we directly switch to a more general technique (algo. 1 line 17-18). Basically, the technique is a natural extension of the framework presented in section 5 to explicitly consider R-paths with non-ground boundaries. This technique was employed in only one of our benchmarks. Details of the technique are skipped in the interest of space.

7 Evaluation

We have implemented a prototype version of the procedure described in section 6. In the current implementation, we fixed both the isolation confidence (algo. 1 line 19-20) and the ground term complexity (fig. 2 $Abst_1$) parameters to 1. To evaluate our technique, we checked 20 Alloy specifications that were expected to be correct. These benchmarks were taken from the Alloy Analyzer 4.2 distribution and involve transitive closure of varying complexities. In order to provide a fair evaluation of the technique, we have restricted the considered benchmarks to those that require the semantics of transitive closure for their correctness proof.

Since most Alloy benchmarks that involve transitive closure also involve trace specifications (based on the Alloy ordering library), we developed a reduction of Alloy trace specifications to transitive closure specifications. That is, we represent any ordered signature S which forms the base of a trace specification, as the set *first* $\cup$ *first* . $next^+$ where *first* denotes the starting atom of the trace and $next \subseteq S \times S$ is a fresh acyclic relation denoting the ordering. If a trace invariant is known, we divide the original specification to (1) an invariant proof and (2) an invariant use specification. Such reduction is used for two of our Alloy benchmarks: *addrbooktrace* and *hotelroom*.

Table 1 shows the experimental results[7] performed using Z3 4.3.1 on an Intel Xeon, 2.7 GHz, 64GB memory. For each checked benchmark, we collect the number of R-paths, difficult R-paths, essential R-paths, checked p-invariant candidates, proved and injected p-invariants and the total analysis time (in seconds). Time-out is set to 12 hours for the entire analysis and to 1 minute for each call to the SMT solver. Out of 20 benchmarks assumed to be valid, 18 were proven correct by our tool. It should be noted that these benchmarks are absolutely not trivial. For example, our previous axiomatization using Z3 could not prove any of the benchmarks with essential R-paths at all (cf. [9]), and although Kelloy could prove all benchmarks, it required substantial human interactions, even for the *com* benchmarks, which do not contains essential R-paths at all (cf. [25]).

A surprising observation is that quite a large number, 13 out of 20, of Alloy specifications, that involve transitive closure, do not contain any essential R-paths, which lets them be *effectively* in the WTC fragment, although not syntactically. This fully answers our question of why in our earlier investigation [9], some transitive closure benchmarks could be proven but not others. It shows that only a very small part of our previous [9] transitive closure axiomatization, namely the WTC axioms, was actually responsible for the success.

All of the 13 benchmarks with no essential R-paths could be proven fully automatically in less than 2 seconds using WTC and without the need of any p-invariant injection. For these examples, according to theorem 1, if the SMT solver had reported a satisfying model, it would have been a valid one. Out of the remaining 7 benchmarks containing essential R-paths, our tool could prove 5. The number of injected p-invariants varies between 1, for *soundness1*, and 159, for *completeness*. The number of injected p-invariants is not guaranteed to reflect the number of needed p-invariants since it depends very much on the ordering of essential R-paths and CNF clauses. However, it does reflect that for all of our proven benchmarks except the last two. The benchmarks *hotelroom-locking* and *javatypes-soundness* could not be proven by our tool. For both benchmarks, the main difficulty lies in the complexity of our generated SMT formulas which makes them too difficult to solve by Z3. For *hotelroom-locking*, the proof obligations for the essential R-path checks could be handled, but none of the p-invariant checks, whereas for *javatypes-soundness* every single call of the solver times-out. This shows the dependency of the current version of our approach on analysable SMT representations.

8   Related Work

Several approaches have addressed the verification of Alloy specifications in general. Due to the undecidability of the Alloy language, most of these approaches are based on interactive solving. Prioni [1] and Kelloy [25] rely on reasoning in first-order logic and integer arithmetic, Dynamite [12] chose a reasoning in fork algebras —a higher-order logic. In all these general approaches the verification of

---

[7] Benchmarks, results and tool are available at http://i12www.ira.uka.de/~elghazi/ tcAx_via_p-inv/

Table 1. Evaluation results

BENCHMARKS	RESULT	ALL/DIF/ESS PATHS	CHE. p-INV	INJ. p-INV	TIME
addrbook-addIdempotent	proved	5 / 2 / 0	0	0	0,08
addrbook-delUndoesAdd	proved	5 / 2 / 0	0	0	0,10
addrbooktrace-addIdempotent	proved	23 / 17 / 0	0	0	0,25
addrbooktrace-delUndoesAdd	proved	20 / 14 / 0	0	0	0,21
addrbooktrace-lookupYields-use	proved	22 / 13 / 0	0	0	0,24
grandpa-noSelfFather	proved	6 / 3 / 0	0	0	0.09
grandpa-noSelfGrandpa	proved	6 / 3 / 0	0	0	0.09
com-theorem1	proved	5 / 2 / 0	0	0	0,18
com-theorem2	proved	5 / 2 / 0	0	0	1.73
com-theorem3	proved	5 / 2 / 0	0	0	0.24
com-theorem4a	proved	5 / 2 / 0	0	0	0.25
com-theorem4b	proved	5 / 2 / 0	0	0	0.13
filesystem-noDirAliases	proved	7 / 4 / 0	0	0	0.12
filesystem-someDir	proved	5 / 3 / 1	2	1	0.15
marksweepgc-soundness1	proved	15 / 9 / 1	38	1	9,29
marksweepgc-soundness2	proved	16 / 10 / 2	75	2	5,92
marksweepgc-completeness	proved	16 / 8 / 2	1021	159	66,58
addrbooktrace-lookupYields-proof	proved	18 / 11 / 2	271	41	79,67
hotelroom-locking	timeout	6 / 3 / 1	–	–	–
javatypes-soundess	timeout	116 / 19 / –	–	–	–

transitive closure specifications is in general *interactive*. In addition to definition rules, an induction schema is involved either directly or indirectly —for proving general lemmas.

Closer to our approach, are the works of Nelson [23] and Ami [22]. Nelson proposes a set of first-order axioms for axiomatizing the reachability between two objects following a *functional* relation f. To handle the presence of cycles he uses a ternary predicate $a \xrightarrow{f}_{c} b$ stating that b is reachable from a via arbitrary f applications, but never going through c. Later works, as in [7,20,21], revisited and extended Nelson's ideas. The main problem with such fixed first-order axiomatizations of transitive closure is that it is unlikely that they are complete. Ami proves in [22] that Nelson's axioms are not complete even in the functional setting. More directly, we can provide a very simple refutable formula modulo transitive closure which is satisfiable in Nelson' axioms, i.e. $a \xrightarrow{f}_{b} b \wedge \forall x.\ f(x) \neq b$.

In our approach, however, the f-path from a to b can be easily refuted since the empty clause —*false*— is a backward invariant for this path. Ami's work, also motivated by Nelson's work, proposes, instead, three axiom *schemas*, which follow from a transitive closure induction schema. This is very similar to our approach in that the axiom set is not fixed, but generated on-demand. However, their approach differs significantly from ours in that: (1) only a pure syntactical notion of *difficult* R-paths is used (2) only *unary* predicates and their boolean combinations are considered as instantiation formulas for the axiom schemas, (3) the search for instantiation formulas is not R-path directed, (4) no criteria for detecting already refuted R-paths is involved, and finally (5) no abstractions are used, even not variable instantiations.

Other tools like ACL2 [18], and IsaPlanner [6] are well established in the automation of general induction schemas, for years. We think that our procedure and implementation can definitively profit from their ideas, especial their lemma discovering routine, called *lemma calculation*, and lemma abstraction ideas.

9   Conclusion

We have presented an approach capable of proving Alloy specifications that involve transitive closure fully automatically. For all transitive closure occurrences the WTC axiomatization is introduced. In case the Alloy specification includes neither *difficult R*-paths —syntactical check— nor essential *R*-path — semantical check— we have proved that WTC is a complete axiomatization of transitive closure and thus the solver result —either *sat* or *unsat*— can be trusted. Otherwise, each essential *R*-path can be handled on its own thanks to our bounded *R-path isolation* concept. The incompleteness of WTC is adjusted for an essential *R*-path p by a directed detection and injection of *p-invariants*.

Although in theory our p-invariant detection procedure is guaranteed to terminate, this has little significance in practical terms, as we could observe for some benchmarks. From both, the conceptual as well as the engineering point of view, there is plenty room for improvement. This includes (1) the reduction of redundancy w.r.t. p-invariant candidates, and instantiation of paths and formulas, (2) the introduction of heuristics for the prioritization of paths, clauses, instantiations and abstractions, and (3) the further, also conceptual, investigation of essential *R*-paths with non-ground boundaries. At least for (1) and (2) we think that we can profit from well established tools in the area of induction automation like ACL2 [18], and IsaPlanner [6], even though their focus is different.

References

1. Arkoudas, K., Khurshid, S., Marinov, D., Rinard, M.: Integrating model checking and theorem proving for relational reasoning. In: Berghammer, R., Möller, B., Struth, G. (eds.) Relational and Kleene-Algebraic Methods in Computer Science. LNCS, vol. 3051, pp. 21–33. Springer, Heidelberg (2004)
2. Barwise, J. (ed.): Handbook of mathematical logic. In: Number 90 in Studies in Logic and the Foundations of Mathematics. North-Holland Publ., Amsterdam (1977)
3. Best, J.: Proving alloy models by introducing an explicit relational theory in SMT. Studienarbeit, Karlsruhe Institute of Technology, Dec. 2012
4. Bonacina, M.P., Lynch, C., de Moura, L.: On deciding satisfiability by DPLL $(\Gamma + \mathcal{T})$ and unsound theorem proving. In: Schmidt, R.A. (ed.) CADE-22. LNCS, vol. 5663, pp. 35–50. Springer, Heidelberg (2009)
5. Dennis, G., Chang, F., Jackson, D.: Modular verification of code with SAT. In: ISSTA, pp. 109–120 (2006)
6. Dixon, L., Fleuriot, J.D.: IsaPlanner: a prototype proof planner in isabelle. In: Baader, F. (ed.) CADE 2003. LNCS (LNAI), vol. 2741, pp. 279–283. Springer, Heidelberg (2003)

7. Van Eijck, J.: Defining (reflexive) transitive closure on finite models (2008)
8. El Ghazi, A.A., Geilmann, U., Ulbrich, M., Taghdiri, M.: A dual-engine for early analysis of critical systems. In: DSCI, Berlin (2011)
9. El Ghazi, A.A., Taghdiri, M.: Relational reasoning via SMT solving. In: Butler, M., Schulte, W. (eds.) FM 2011. LNCS, vol. 6664, pp. 133–148. Springer, Heidelberg (2011)
10. El Ghazi, A.A., Ulbrich, M., Taghdiri, M., Herda, M.: Reducing the complexity of quantified formulas via variable elimination. In: SMT, pp. 87–99, July 2013
11. Enderton, H.B.: A mathematical introduction to logic. Academic Press (1972)
12. Frias, M.F., Pombo, C.G.L., Moscato, M.M.: Alloy analyzer+PVS in the analysis and verification of alloy specifications. In: Grumberg, O., Huth, M. (eds.) TACAS 2007. LNCS, vol. 4424, pp. 587–601. Springer, Heidelberg (2007)
13. Ge, Y., Barrett, C., Tinelli, C.: Solving quantified verification conditions using satisfiability modulo theories. AMAI 55(1), 101–122 (2009)
14. Ge, Y., de Moura, L.: Complete instantiation for quantified formulas in satisfiabiliby modulo theories. In: Bouajjani, A., Maler, O. (eds.) CAV 2009. LNCS, vol. 5643, pp. 306–320. Springer, Heidelberg (2009)
15. Immerman, N., Rabinovich, A., Reps, T., Sagiv, M., Yorsh, G.: The boundary between decidability and undecidability for transitive-closure logics. In: Marcinkowski, J., Tarlecki, A. (eds.) CSL 2004. LNCS, vol. 3210, pp. 160–174. Springer, Heidelberg (2004)
16. Jackson, D.: Software Abstractions: Logic, Language, and Analysis. The MIT Press, Apr. 2006
17. Kang, E., Jackson, D.: Formal modeling and analysis of a flash filesystem in alloy. In: Börger, E., Butler, M., Bowen, J.P., Boca, P. (eds.) ABZ 2008. LNCS, vol. 5238, pp. 294 308. Springer, Heidelberg (2008)
18. Kaufmann, M., Strother Moore, J., Manolios, P.: Computer-Aided Reasoning: An Approach. Kluwer Academic Publishers, USA (2000)
19. Keller, U.: Some remarks on the definability of transitive closure in first-order logic and datalog (2004)
20. Lahiri, S.K., Qadeer, S.: Verifying properties of well-founded linked lists. In: ACM SIGPLAN Notices, POPL, pp. 115–126. ACM, New York (2006)
21. Rustan, K., Leino, M.: Recursive object types in a logic of object-oriented programs. In: Hankin, C. (ed.) ESOP 1998. LNCS, vol. 1381, pp. 170–184. Springer, Heidelberg (1998)
22. Lev-Ami, T., Immerman, N., Reps, T., Sagiv, M., Srivastava, S., Yorsh, G.: Simulating reachability using first-order logic with applications to verification of linked data structures. In: Nieuwenhuis, R. (ed.) CADE 2005. LNCS (LNAI), vol. 3632, pp. 99–115. Springer, Heidelberg (2005)
23. Nelson, G.: Verifying reachability invariants of linked structures. In: POPL, pp. 38–47, ACM, New York (1983)
24. Taghdiri, M., Jackson, D.: A lightweight formal analysis of a multicast key management scheme. In: König, H., Heiner, M., Wolisz, A. (eds.) FORTE 2003. LNCS, vol. 2767. Springer, Heidelberg (2003)
25. Ulbrich, M., Geilmann, U., El Ghazi, A.A., Taghdiri, M.: A proof assistant for alloy specifications. In: Flanagan, C., König, B. (eds.) TACAS 2012. LNCS, vol. 7214, pp. 422–436. Springer, Heidelberg (2012)
26. Vaziri-Farahani, M.: Finding bugs in software with a constraint solver. Thesis, Massachusetts Institute of Technology (2004)

Reachability Analysis Using Extremal Rates

Andrew N. Fisher[1][(✉)], Chris J. Myers[1], and Peng Li[2]

[1] University of Utah, Salt Lake City, UT 84112, USA
{andrew.n.fisher,myers}@ece.utah.edu
[2] Texas A&M University, College Station, TX 77843, USA
pli@tamu.edu

Abstract. General hybrid systems can be difficult to verify due to their generality. To reduce the complexity, one often specializes to hybrid systems where the complexity is more manageable. If one reduces the modeling formalism to ones where the continuous variables have a single rate, then it may be possible to use the methods of *zones* to find the reachable state space. Zones are a restricted class of polyhedra formed by considering the intersections of half-planes defined by two variable constraints. Due to their simplicity, zones have simpler, more efficient methods of manipulation than more general polyhedral classes, though they are less accurate. This paper extends the method of zones to *labeled Petri net* (LPN) models with continuous variables that evolve over a range of rates.

Keywords: Range of rates · LPNs · Zones · Difference bound matrices

1 Introduction

A common method for modeling hybrid systems is to use *hybrid automata* [2] which combine discrete transitions with dynamics described by first-order differential equations. The full generality of hybrid automata is difficult to formally verify, and it is common for authors to restrict their attention to more restrictive subclasses, such as *linear hybrid automata* (LHA) [1]. Instead of allowing general first-order differential equations, LHA restrict the invariants, guards, and flow relations to be linear equations over the continuous variables. Even though LHA represent a restricted class of hybrid automata, they are still useful in describing systems and can approximate more general automata [16]. By the restricting to LHA, one can perform *reachability analysis* to verify that a system satisfies a given condition. Although the exact state space is undecidable [11], methods have been able to verify systems by approximating the reachable state space using classes of polyhedra [3,8,9,17,18]. The complexity of these methods comes from the choice of polyhedral class along with the methods used to

This material is based upon work supported by an ARCS Fellowship and the National Science Foundation (NSF) under Grant No. CCF-1117515 and CCF-1117660. Any opinions, findings, and conclusions or recommendations expressed in this material are those of the author(s) and do not necessarily reflect the views of the NSF.

K. Havelund et al. (Eds.): NFM 2015, LNCS 9058, pp. 158–172, 2015.
DOI: 10.1007/978-3-319-17524-9_12

update the state space. For example, SpaceEx [10] utilizes template polyhedra and updates the state space by essentially lifting a numerical integrator to the level of sets. By increasing the number of template directions, the accuracy of the approximating state space improves, but at a cost of increasing the storage requirements and the number of operations needed to update the state.

One can avoid numeric integration techniques by restricting the modeling class even further. One option is to use *labeled Petri nets* (LPNs) [13]. Although LPNs, in general, allow for a range of possible rates for each continuous variable, the authors in [12] assume a constant rate. This simplification allows them to avoid the expense of numerical integration by extending the methods used for *timed automata* (TA) [4,15] to LPNs whose rates are a single constant. The method is based on *zones*, a subclass of polyhedra formed by considering the intersection of half-planes of the form $y - x \leq c$, where x and y are continuous variables and c is a constant. A common method of representing zones is to gather the constants into a matrix that relates each pair of continuous variables. Such matrices are known as *difference bound matrices* (DBMs) [6]. One key advantage to the method of zones is that time advancements can be performed by appropriately adjusting the largest possible value for each continuous variable and then re-tightening the boundary constraints defining the zone, which has a complexity of $O(n^3)$ where n is the number of continuous variables. To handle rates other than one, the zone is *warped* [12], a process where the variables in the original zone are scaled to produce variables with a rate of 1. After scaling, the resulting $\mathbb{R}^n$-subset $\mathcal{Z}$ is, in general, no longer a zone, so the subset $\mathcal{Z}$ is replaced with the best over-approximating zone Z such that $\mathcal{Z} \subseteq Z$.

Although the methods used in [12] are straightforward, they fall short of handling the ranges of rates possible in general LPNs. To remedy this situation, a couple attempts ([5,14]) have been made to extend zones to a range of rates. Both methods are based on a translational approach whereby the original model is transformed into a single rate model, but, as explained later, neither fully handles the use of ranges of rates in models. This paper shows how a zone-based method can be extended to verify LPN models with ranges of rates. Similar to the translational approaches, this extension is based on the fact that states reachable using a rate chosen from a range of possible rates are also reachable using only the extremal rates. Moreover, since the work of [13] extends zones to capture all states reachable from a set of states advancing with a particular rate, it is only necessary to consider the rate changes at fixed discrete moments in time and allow the zones to capture the simultaneous advancement of a collection of states. This paper is organized as follows: Section 2 defines the LPN syntax and updated semantics for ranges of rates. Section 3 presents an algorithm for computing an over-approximation of the reachable state space. Section 4 presents a correctness argument for the algorithm. Section 5 discusses the related translational approaches. Section 6 provides some experimental results. Finally, Section 7 gives conclusions.

2 Labeled Petri Nets

This section provides an overview of the LPN formalism used in this paper.

2.1 LPN Syntax

An LPN is a type of Petri net that has been augmented with a set of labels for modeling continuous variables and their rates of change. This does not preclude the use of discrete (or Boolean) variables since they can be modeled using variables with a zero rate. LPNs are assumed to be safe, and continuous variables are allowed to non-deterministically choose a rate from an interval of possible rates. Formally, an LPN is a tuple $N = \langle P, T, T_f, V, F, M_0, Q_0, R_0, L \rangle$ where:

- P : is a finite set of places;
- T : is a finite set of transitions;
- $T_f \subseteq T$: is a finite set of failure transitions;
- V : is a finite set of continuous variables;
- $F \subseteq (P \times T) \cup (T \times P)$ is the *flow relation*;
- $M_0 \subseteq P$ is the set of initially marked places;
- $Q_0 : V \to \mathbb{Q}$ is the initial value of each continuous variable;
- $R_0 : V \to \mathbb{Q} \times \mathbb{Q}$ is the initial range of rates for each continuous variable;
- L : is a tuple of *labels* defined below.

Failure transitions are used to indicate when a failure has occurred. The flow relation, F, is used to describe how the places and transitions are connected. Every transition $t \in T$ has a *preset* denoted by $\bullet t = \{p \mid (p, t) \in F\}$ and a *postset* denoted by $t \bullet = \{p \mid (t, p) \in F\}$. The labels, L, for an LPN are defined by the tuple $L = \langle En, D, VA, RA \rangle$:

- $En : T \to \mathcal{P}_\phi$ labels each transition $t \in T$ with an enabling condition;
- $D : T \to \mathbb{Q} \times \mathbb{Q}$ labels each transition $t \in T$ with a minimum and a maximum delay for which a transition t must be enabled before it can fire;
- $VA : T \times V \to \mathbb{Q}$ labels each transition $t \in T$ and continuous variable $v \in V$ with a continuous variable assignment that is made to v when t fires;
- $RA : T \times V \to \mathbb{Q} \times \mathbb{Q}$ labels each transition $t \in T$ and continuous variable $v \in V$ with a range of possible rates v can have after the transition t fires.

The enabling conditions are Boolean expressions, $\mathcal{P}_\phi$, that satisfy the grammar:

$$\phi ::= \mathbf{true} \mid \neg \phi \mid \phi \wedge \phi \mid v \geq c$$

where $\neg$ is negation, $\wedge$ is conjunction, v is a continuous variable, and c is a rational constant. The expressions $\mathbf{false}$, $\vee$, and $v \leq c$ are defined from these. For simplicity, the delay, variable, and rate assignments are assumed to be constants or ranges bounded by constants, but they can, in general, be expressions that evaluate to constants (i.e., include only continuous variables whose rates are zero). All ranges are of the form $(a, b) \in \mathbb{Q} \times \mathbb{Q}$, which corresponds to the interval $[a, b]$ with the restriction that $a \leq b$ and is either non-negative (i.e., $a \geq 0$) or is

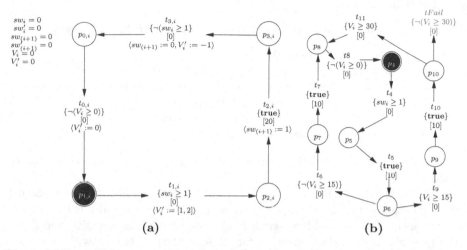

Fig. 1. LPN model for a capacitor stage with a corresponding property. (a) A model of a capacitor whose charging is turned on by sw_i. After a time delay of $20\mu s$, the switch $sw_{(i+1)}$ is turned on (i.e., set to 1), initiating the charging of the next capacitor. Note that $[d]$ is used when $d_l(t) = d_u(t) - d$. (b) A property in which, when sw_i is 1, it checks that V_i is above 15mV after $10\mu s$, and then that V_i is more than 30mV after an additional $10\mu s$. The property is violated if the fail transition, $tFail$, fires.

negative (i.e., $b \prec 0$). In the case of delay assignments, the ranges clearly must be non-negative.

As a running example, consider a sequence of capacitors that are charged sequentially. The charging phase of the first capacitor is initiated by a switch sw_0. After $20\mu s$ of charging, a switch sw_1 is turned on, initiating the second capacitor's charging phase, and so on. When the switch sw_0 is turned off, the first capacitor starts discharging and the switch sw_1 is turned off, starting the second capacitor to discharge, and so on. Fig. 1a shows an LPN model of the i-th capacitor where the charging is some uncertain rate between $1mV/\mu s$ and $2mV/\mu s$. The initial marking is $M_0 = \{p_{1,i}\}$ and is represented by the filled in circle. The values $V_i = 0$ and $V_i' = 0$ are the initial conditions for the voltage V_i. The variables sw_i and $sw_{(i+1)}$ are essentially Boolean variables with initial values of 0, representing **false**. The enabling conditions, delays, and variable assignments are in the curly braces, square brackets, and angle brackets, respectively. In this example, the delays are constants rather than bounds. Initially, the capacitor is not charging. When the signal sw_i is set to 1, charging is initiated by assigning V_i' the interval $[1, 2]$, which indicates the rate of V_i can be any rate between $1mV/\mu s$ and $2mV/\mu s$. The capacitor is allowed to charge for $20\mu s$ (given as a delay on the transition $t_{2,i}$) before setting the variable $sw_{(i+1)}$ to 1. Once the charging is turned off, that is, when sw_i is set to 0, the capacitor begins to discharge at a rate of $-1mV/\mu s$. Finally, when the capacitor is fully discharged, the $t_{0,i}$ transition fires, setting the rate to zero.

2.2   LPN Semantics

The state of an LPN is defined as a tuple $\sigma = \langle M, Q, RR, R, I, C \rangle$ where:

- $M \subseteq P$ is the set of marked places;
- $Q : V \to \mathbb{Q}$ is the value of each continuous variable;
- $RR : V \to \mathbb{Q} \times \mathbb{Q}$ is the current range of rates for each continuous variable;
- $R : V \to \mathbb{Q}$ is the current rate of each continuous variable;
- $I : \mathcal{I} \to \{\textbf{false}, \textbf{true}\}$ is the value of each inequality;
- $C : T \to \mathbb{Q}$ is the time each transition has been enabled.

The set of all inequalities of the form $v_i \geq c_i$ is denoted by $\mathcal{I}$.[1] The collection of all states is Σ.

In LPNs, the Boolean value of an inequality is evaluated in a non-standard way at the boundary. For example, if the inequality is $v \geq 5$ and v is equal to 5, then the inequality is considered **true** if the rate of v is non-negative and **false** if the rate is negative. The intuition for these semantics is that when the rate is negative and the variable is at the boundary, then the inequality is about to become **false** while when the rate is positive, then the inequality remains **true** as time progresses. Formally, the evaluation of an inequality is given by:

$$\texttt{evalInequalities}(\sigma)(v \geq c) = \begin{cases} R(v) \geq 0 & \text{if } Q(v) = c; \\ Q(v) \geq c & \text{otherwise.} \end{cases}$$

The initial state, σ_0, for an LPN consists of the initial markings, M_0, the initial value of each continuous variable, Q_0, the initial range of rates, R_0, an initial rate within this range, the initial value of the inequalities, and the time each transition has been enabled set to 0. The initial rate for each variable, v, is determined using the function $\texttt{resetRates}(RR)$, which is defined by:

$$\texttt{resetRates}(RR)(v) = r_l(v),$$

where $r_l(v)$ returns the lower bound rate. Similarly, $r_u(v)$ returns the upper bound. Requiring that the initial rate is given by the function $\texttt{resetRates}$ is not a limitation since the rate is allowed to change arbitrarily within the range at any time. The initial state, σ_0, of the LPN in Fig. 1a has $M = \{p_{1,i}\}$, $Q(V_i) = Q(sw_i) = Q(sw_{(i+1)}) = R(V_i) = R(sw_i) = R(sw_{(i+1)}) = 0$, $RR(V_i) = RR(sw_i) = RR(sw_{(i+1)}) = [0,0]$, $I(V_i \geq 0) = \textbf{true}$, $I(sw_i \geq 1) = \textbf{false}$, and $C(t_{0,i}) = C(t_{1,i}) = C(t_{2,i}) = C(t_{3,i}) = 0$.

The state σ can change to a new state $\sigma' = \langle M', Q', RR', R', I', C' \rangle$ by firing a transition, advancing time, or changing a rate. Collectively, transition firings, time advancements, and rate changes are known as *events*. A time advancement that results in the truth value of an inequality changing is an *inequality event*.

A transition $t \in T$ is *enabled* when all the places in its preset are marked (that is, when $\bullet t \subseteq M$) and the enabling condition on t evaluates to **true** (that

---

[1] Recording the inequality values is not strictly necessary. It is included as a matter of convenience so that an implementation does not need to calculate it repeatedly.

is, when $Eval(En(t), \sigma)$ is **true** where the function $Eval: \mathcal{P}_\phi \times \Sigma \to \{\textbf{false}, \textbf{true}\}$ evaluates an expression given a state $\sigma \in \Sigma$). The set of all enabled transitions in a state σ is given by $\mathcal{E}(\sigma)$. When a transition becomes enabled, it must fire after the minimum delay $d_l(t)$ and before the maximum delay $d_u(t)$, where $d_l(t)$ is the lower bound and $d_u(t)$ is the upper bound of the delay assignment $D(t)$. The state σ' created as a result of firing the transition t is defined by:

$$M' = (M - \bullet t) \cup t \bullet;$$
$$\forall v \in V.Q'(v) = VA(t, v);$$
$$\forall v \in V.RR'(v) = RA(t, v);$$
$$R' = \texttt{resetRates}(RR');$$
$$I' = \texttt{evalInequalities}(\sigma');$$
$$\forall t \in T.C'(t) = \begin{cases} 0 & \text{if } t \in \mathcal{E}(\sigma') \wedge t \notin \mathcal{E}(\sigma); \\ C(t) & \text{otherwise.} \end{cases}$$

When a transition is fired, the marking is updated and any assignments to the continuous variables and their rates are performed. The firing of a transition, t, causing a change from a state σ to a state σ' is denoted by $\sigma \xrightarrow{t} \sigma'$. As an example, consider the state σ_i, which is identical to σ_0 except $sw_i = 1$. The new state, σ_{i+1}, after $t_{1,i}$ fires in Fig. 1a is $M = \{p_{2,i}\}$, $Q(V_i) = 0$, $Q(sw_i) = 1$, $Q(sw_{(i+1)}) = 0$, $R(V_i) = 1$, $R(sw_i) = R(sw_{(i+1)}) = 0$, $RR(V_i) = [1, 2]$, $RR(sw_i) = RR(sw_{(i+1)}) = [0, 0]$, $I(V_i \geq 0) = I(sw_i \geq 1) = \textbf{true}$, and $C(t_{0,i}) = C(t_{1,i}) = C(t_{2,i}) = C(t_{3,i}) = 0$.

Time can advance by any amount τ such that $\tau \leq \tau_{\max}(\sigma)$ where $\tau_{\max}(\sigma)$ is the largest allowable time advancement before an inequality changes value or a transition is forced to fire due to its maximum delay expiring.

$$\tau_{\max}(\sigma) = \begin{cases} \frac{c - Q(v)}{R(v)} & \forall (v \geq c) \in \mathcal{I}.I(v \geq c) \neq (R(v) \geq 0); \\ d_u(t) - C(t) & \forall t \in \mathcal{E}(\sigma). \end{cases}$$

In this equation, division by 0 is interpreted as yielding ∞. Thus, a zero rate variable does not limit the maximum time advancement. The new state σ' after advancing τ time units has $M' = M$, $RR' = RR$, $R' = R$, and:

$$\forall v \in V.Q'(v) = Q(v) + \tau * R(v);$$
$$I' = \texttt{evalInequalities}(\sigma');$$
$$\forall t \in T.C'(t) = \begin{cases} C(t) + \tau & \text{if } t \in \mathcal{E}(\sigma); \\ 0 & \text{otherwise.} \end{cases}$$

A time advancement by an amount τ is denoted by $\sigma \xrightarrow{\tau} \sigma'$. If a time advancement, τ, results in the change of truth value of an inequality in the set $\mathcal{I}$ (that is, the time advancement is an inequality event), then the event is denoted by $\sigma \xrightarrow{\tau, \mathfrak{J}} \sigma'$ where $\mathfrak{J}$ is the set of inequalities that change truth value. In addition, the rates are reset to the initial conditions (i.e., $R' = \texttt{resetRates}(RR')$).

Note that a time advancement results in an inequality event, if and only if, $\tau = \tau_{\max}(\sigma)$. In state σ_{i+1} above, $\tau_{\max} = 20$, since after 20 time units the timer for the transition $t_{2,i}$ expires. The new state, σ_{i+2}, after a time advancement of 10 time units is $M = \{p_{2,i}\}$, $Q(V_i) = 10$, $Q(sw_i) = 1$, $Q(sw_{(i+1)}) = 0$, $R(V_i) = 1$, $R(sw_i) = R(sw_{(i+1)}) = 0$, $RR(V_i) = [1,2]$, $RR(sw_i) = RR(sw_{(i+1)}) = [0,0]$, $I(V_i \geq 0) = I(sw_i \geq 1) = \mathbf{true}$, $C(t_{0,i}) = C(t_{1,i}) = C(t_{3,i}) = 0$, and $C(t_{2,i}) = 10$.

The final type of state change is a rate change event. This event changes the rate of a single continuous variable $\hat{v} \in V$ to a new rate $\hat{r} \in RR(\hat{v})$. Since the truth value of an inequality depends on the rate, a rate change requires the updating of the inequalities involving $\hat{v}$. The corresponding new state has $M' = M$, $Q' = Q$, $RR' = RR$, $C' = C$, and:

$$R'(v) = \begin{cases} \hat{r} & \text{if } \hat{v} = v; \\ R(v) & \text{otherwise}; \end{cases}$$

$$I' = \mathtt{evalInequalities}(\sigma').$$

After a rate change event for a continuous variable, the rate cannot change again until another non-rate event occurs. This restriction disallows the possibility of the state changing infinitely often solely due to the rates of continuous variables changing. Generality is not sacrificed in imposing this condition since the rate can be set to any value prior to the advancing of time, which is all that matters to the final trajectory of the continuous variable concerned. A rate change for a particular variable $\hat{v}$ to the rate $\hat{r}$ is denoted by $\sigma \xrightarrow{R(\hat{v}) \leftarrow \hat{r}} \sigma'$. In the state σ_{i+2}, the state σ_{i+3} after changing the rate of V_i to a rate of 1.5 is given by $M = \{p_{2,i}\}$, $Q(V_i) = 10$, $Q(sw_i) = 1$, $Q(sw_{(i+1)}) = 0$, $R(V_i) = 1.5$, $R(sw_i) = R(sw_{(i+1)}) = 0$, $RR(V_i) = [1,2]$, $RR(sw_i) = RR(sw_{(i+1)}) = [0,0]$, $I(V_i \geq 0) = I(sw_i \geq 1) = \mathbf{true}$, $C(t_{0,i}) = C(t_{1,i}) = C(t_{3,i}) = 0$, and $C(t_{2,i}) = 10$.

3   Reachability Algorithm

The reachability algorithm presented here is an extension of the zone-based model checking algorithm used by LEMA as described in [12]. The main point of using zones (or any polyhedral method) is to reduce the infinite number of possible continuous variable states to a finite set of state sets that collect together several states into a finite representation. A state set is a tuple $\psi = \langle M, Q, RR, R, I, Z \rangle$ where:

- $M \subseteq P$ is the set of marked places;
- $Q : V \to \mathbb{Q} \times \mathbb{Q}$ is the range of values of each zero rate continuous variable;
- $RR : V \to \mathbb{Q} \times \mathbb{Q}$ is the current range of rates for each continuous variable;
- $R : V \to \mathbb{Q}$ is the current rate of each continuous variable;
- $I : \mathcal{I} \to \{\mathbf{false}, \mathbf{true}\}$ is the truth value of each inequality;
- $Z : (T \cup V \cup \{c_0\}) \times (T \cup V \cup \{c_0\}) \to \mathbb{Q} \cup \{\infty\}$ is a DBM composed of the transition clocks for the enabled transitions, the non-zero rate continuous variables, and c_0, a reference clock which is always zero.

This definition is modified from that in [12] to accommodate ranges of rates.

The basic reachability algorithm used by LEMA is shown in Algorithm 1.1. The algorithm starts by constructing the initial state set, ψ, for the LPN. In the initial state, $M = M_0$, $Q = Q_0$, $RR = R_0$, $R = \mathtt{resetRates}(RR)$, and $I = \mathtt{evalInequalities}(\psi)$. The DBM, Z, is composed of the initial values for all the continuous variables for which $R(v) \neq 0$. In addition, the DBM contains a clock initialized to 0 for every enabled transition. After adding the initial state to the set of reachable states, Ψ, the algorithm next calls the function $\mathtt{findPossibleEvents}$ which returns the set of all events, E, that are possible in the current state. The function $\mathtt{select}$ then chooses an arbitrary event, e, to be the next event to explore. If, after removing the event, e, the event set, E, still has events remaining, these remaining events are pushed onto a stack together with the current state. The next state, ψ', is computed by the $\mathtt{updateState}$ function and is the result of executing the event, e, in the current state, ψ. If the state ψ' has not been seen before, then the algorithm adds it to the set of reachable states, makes ψ' the current state to search from, and finds the possible events that can be executed from ψ' (now the current ψ). If ψ' has been seen before, then the algorithm checks if there are any event sets left on the stack to explore. If the stack is not empty, then the last record is removed and is used as the new current state, ψ, and current set of events, E. If the stack is empty, then there are no events left to explore, and the result is returned.

Algorithm 1.1. reach()

```
1  ψ := initialStateSet();
2  Ψ := {ψ};
3  E := findPossibleEvents(ψ);
4  while (true) do
5  |    e := select(E);
6  |    if (E − {e} ≠ ∅) then
7  |    |    push(E − {e}, ψ);
8  |    ψ' := updateState(ψ, e);
9  |    if (ψ' ∉ Ψ) then
10 |    |    Ψ := Ψ ∪ {ψ'};
11 |    |    ψ := ψ';
12 |    |    E := findPossibleEvents(ψ);
13 |    else
14 |    |    if (stack not empty) then
15 |    |    |    (E, ψ) := pop();
16 |    |    else
17 |    |    |    return Ψ;
```

The functions $\mathtt{findPossibleEvents}$ and $\mathtt{updateState}$ must be modified to take into account a new rate change event. The $\mathtt{findPossibleEvents}$ algorithm is shown in Algorithm 1.2. Lines 1-7 are the same as in [12] and handle determining which transitions can fire and which inequalities can change. A transition can fire as soon as the clock (stored in the zone) exceeds the lower bound of the delay assignment for that transition. The function $ub(Z,t)$ is used to obtain the largest value of the clock, t, from the zone, Z. An inequality can change if time has advanced far enough for the variable to cross the constant associated with the inequality. Lines 8-10 are added to determine if any rate events are possible. Namely, any variables that are not evolving at their upper rate bound can have a rate event to set it to its upper rate. In all cases, the function addSetItem handles the adding and removing of elements from the event set according to which events should occur first.

Algorithm 1.2. findPossibleEvents(ψ)

---

1 $E := \emptyset$;
2 **foreach** $(t \in Z)$ **do**
3 $\quad$ **if** $(ub(Z,t) \geq d_1(t))$ **then**
4 $\quad\quad$ $E := \text{addSetItem}(E,t)$;
5 **foreach** $(i \in ineq(En))$ **do**
6 $\quad$ **if** $(\text{ineqCanChange}(R,I,Z,i))$ **then**
7 $\quad\quad$ $E := \text{addSetItem}(E,i)$;
8 **foreach** $(v \in V)$ **do**
9 $\quad$ **if** $(R(v) \neq r_u(v))$ **then**
10 $\quad\quad$ $E := \text{addSetItem}(E,v)$;
11 **return** E;

The modified updateState function is shown in Algorithm 1.3. The main modifications to the original algorithm are the addition of resetRates and the rateChange event. The first step is to restrict the zone according to the knowledge provided by which event has occurred. When a transition fires, this means that the time has advanced at least to the lower bound delay and for inequalities this means that the continuous variable has reached the bounding constant. After the restriction, the bounds are re-tightened. Next, the state is updated according to whether the event is a set of inequalities changing, a transition firing, or a rate change event. In the cases of inequalities changing or transitions firing, the rates are reset via resetRates(RR), which resets the rates of each continuous variable according to its range of rates. A rate change event consists of a call to rateChange which takes the current state ψ and the rate change event, e, and makes the rate change of $R(v) = r_u(v)$. Note, this change has the effect of changing the rate for every state represented by the state set ψ. After assigning the new rate, the inequalities are updated according to any variable assignments and rate changes. Similarly, the zone is updated according to which transitions are enabled. Finally, the zone is re-warped, time is allowed to advance up to $\tau_{\max}$, and the bounds are re-tightened.

Algorithm 1.3. updateState(ψ, e)

---

1 $Z :=$ restrict(Z, e);
2 $Z :=$ recanonicalize(Z);
3 $R_{old} := R$;
4 **if** ($e \subseteq \mathcal{I}$) **then**
5 | $\psi :=$ updateInequalities(ψ, e);
6 | $R :=$ resetRates(RR);
7 **else if** ($e \subseteq T$) **then**
8 | $\psi :=$ fireTransition(ψ, e);
9 | $R :=$ resetRates(RR);
10 **else**
11 | $R :=$ rateChange(ψ, e);
12 $\psi :=$ evalInequalities(ψ);
13 **forall the** ($t \in T$) **do**
14 | **if** ($t \notin Z \wedge t \in \mathcal{E}(\psi)$) **then**
15 | | $Z :=$ addT(Z, t);
16 | **else if** ($t \in Z \wedge t \notin \mathcal{E}(\psi)$) **then**
17 | | $Z :=$ rmT(Z, t);
18 $Z :=$ dbmWarp(R_{old}, R, Z);
19 $Z :=$ advanceTime(R, I, Z);
20 $Z :=$ recanonicalize(Z);
21 **return** ψ;

---

4   Correctness

The proof that the above algorithm does over-approximate the reachable state space is done in two stages (see [7] for additional details). The first stage shows that every state set S' resulting from a transition firing or a set of inequalities changing is captured by some state set ψ'. The second stage handles the intervening rate changes and time advancements. First suppose that tr is a transition and $S \xrightarrow{tr} S'$. Since $S \in \psi$, the same transition tr is enabled in ψ and is one of the possible event firings that are explored. Thus, one has $\psi \xrightarrow{tr} \psi'$. The state S' is then in ψ', since the same operations of updating the state S to produce S' are performed for all the states in ψ to produce ψ'. For example, the markings, M, are updated in the same fashion, the zone, Z, is updated to reflect the same continuous variable assignments, etc. If S' is the result of a set of inequalities, $\mathcal{I}$, changing, then this same set of inequalities is enabled to change in the state set ψ. Furthermore, the same set of inequalities can change to produce ψ'. Since the only states that are removed from ψ to produce ψ' satisfy the condition $v \neq c$ for each $v \geq c \in \mathcal{I}$, the state S' is not removed since v must equal c for each $v \geq c \in \mathcal{I}$ owing to the fact that the inequality is changing its truth value. Next, the rate change events and time advancements are handled. Let ψ be the result of a transition firing, a set of inequalities changing, or the initial state set, and let S be a state in ψ. It is shown that if S' is a state resulting from a sequence of rate changes and time advancements up to a total time advancement of τ_{max}, then S' is in some ψ' resulting from ψ by a sequence of rate changes. For simplicity, assume that $\hat{v}$ is the only continuous variable and that $RR(\hat{v}) = [a, b]$. The argument is to first show that the state S' can be obtained by using a single rate change and then show that the resulting trace is captured by a sequence of state sets. Theorem 1 establishes the first part.

Theorem 1 ([7]). *Let $a, b \in \mathbb{R}$ with $0 \leq a \leq b$ or $a \leq b \leq 0$, $\tau \in \mathbb{R}$ any nonnegative real number, and $q \in \mathbb{R}$ any real number. Then, for any real number v such that $a\tau + q \leq v \leq b\tau + q$, there exists a $\tau' \in [0, \tau]$ such that $f(\tau) = v$ where:*

$$f(x) = \begin{cases} b(x - \tau') + a\tau' + q & \text{if } \tau' \leq x \leq \tau \\ ax + q & \text{if } 0 \leq x \leq \tau' \end{cases}.$$

Using this theorem, there exists τ_1, τ_2 such that $S \xrightarrow{\tau_1} S'' \xrightarrow{R(\hat{v}) \leftarrow b} S''' \xrightarrow{\tau_2} S'$. In like fashion, let ψ' be the state set resulting from ψ by changing the rate of $\hat{v}$ to b, and advancing time $\tau_{\max}$, that is $\psi \xrightarrow{R(\hat{v}) \leftarrow b} \psi'' \xrightarrow{\tau_{\max}} \psi'$. All that remains to show is that the states S, S', and S'' are captured by the two state sets ψ and ψ'. In [14], it is shown that the zone obtained by warping and advancing time contains all points obtained by picking a point in the original zone, changing the rate, and advancing time. This fact can be expressed formally in the following theorem:

Theorem 2 (Section 4.4 of [14]). *Let Z be a zone, let $\mathcal{Z}$ be the zone obtained by warping Z, $\tau, r \in \mathbb{R}$ such that $\tau \geq 0$ and $r \neq 0$. Then, for all $z \in Z$, $z/r + \tau \in \mathcal{Z} \oplus [0, \tau]$ where $\oplus$ is the Minkowski sum $X \oplus Y = \{x + y \mid x \in X \text{ and } y \in Y\}$. Consequently, the point $z + rt$ is represented by a point in the time-advanced warped zone $\mathcal{Z} \oplus [0, \tau_{\max}]$.*

Therefore, ψ contains all points $z \in \mathcal{Z}$ which are the result of a time advancement τ such that $\tau \leq \tau_{\max}$ when the rate of $\hat{v}$ is a. Thus, S'' is in ψ. Similarly, the construction of ψ' changes the rate of $\hat{v}$ to b for each state in ψ and captures all time advancements up to $\tau_{\max}$. So, S''' and S' are in ψ'.

Finally, extending to multiple continuous variables is a matter of finding the sequence of switching points for each of the continuous variables and applying the appropriate warping for each dimension.

5   Related Work

This paper addresses ranges of rates using an *algorithmic approach*. In contrast, the methods of [5,14] use a *translational approach* where the original LPN or automaton is transformed to replace the range of rates with single rate changes. Suppose a variable v has a range of possible rates $[a, b]$ in a given state. The method of [5] is to replace the range of rates with three stages. The first stage determines the total amount of time the system spends in the state, say τ time units. The second stage determines the value of the continuous variable v after τ

time units, provided the rate is a. The third stage determines the possible values for the continuous variable after τ time units for each of the possible rates in the interval $[a, b]$. Similar to the approach of [5], the method used in [14] replaces the state with two stages. The first stage sets the rate of v to a and then allows a transition to fire that sets the rate to b.

Both these methods break the range of rates into traces that utilize only single rates, namely, the rates a and b. However, in each case, the traces explored only allow for a single change of rate. Such a transformation is enough when the LPN or automaton is used to check a property, but it is not necessarily enough when ranges of rates are used for an LPN or automaton model. The single switching ensures that given a time τ and a range of rates $[a, b]$, every possible value of v at time τ is achievable by setting v to have rate a for some time $\hat{\tau}$, switching the rate to b and then allowing time to advance $\tau - \hat{\tau}$ (Theorem 1). This process breaks down when two sample times are involved. For example, suppose v is required to be $2b$ at time 2 and $2b + a$ after 1 more time unit, for $0 < a < b$. Then, it is no longer possible to start with the rate at a and then switch once to b since after 2 time units the rate needs to be changed back to a. As a concrete example, consider the property LPN shown in Fig. 1b. After being initiated by sw_i being set to 1, the property checks that V_i is above 15mV after $10\mu s$ and then checks that V_i is more than 30mV after an additional $10\mu s$. For V_i to be greater than 15mV at $10\mu s$, the rate of V_i must switch at or before $5\mu s$. However, since the rate has switched once, the rate must remain at $2mV/\mu s$ for the next $10\mu s$ resulting in V_i being at least 35mV. Thus, it is not possible for the failure transition to fire. However, if V_i is 15mV at $10\mu s$ and the rate is set to $1mV/\mu s$, then V_i is 25mV after an additional $10\mu s$, enabling the failure transition.

Instead of a translational approach, the method of Section 3 uses an algorithmic approach that allows the rate to switch once per transition firing and inequality changing. For LPNs, the number of times that a variable needs to be allowed to switch is the number of times that the LPN 'samples' the variable, that is, when an inequality changes or a transition fires. It is with these events that something is learned about the values of the continuous variables.

6   Experimental Results

This section compares verification results from the translational approach of [14] with results from the algorithmic approach of this paper by using models having a varying number of capacitor stages (Fig. 1a). In the translational approach of [14], the capacitor stages in Fig. 1a are modified to only use a single rate by setting the rate initially to 1 and then adding a one time transition which optionally sets the rate to 2. The algorithmic approach requires no modifications. The capacitor models are verified against the property in Fig. 1b with three different enabling conditions for $tFail$ and t_{11} using LEMA, a java-based verification tool. All experiments are run on a 64-bit machine with an 3.4 GHz Intel Core i5-3570 CPU with 4 cores and 12GB of memory with a time limit of 6 hours. In each case, the property is placed on the last stage.

Table 1. Comparison of translational approach [14] to our algorithmic approach with a tFail enabling condition of $\neg(V_i \geq -2)$ that should verify to be correct

	Translational			Algorithmic		Algorithmic (opt)		
# Caps	Time (s)	States	Correct?	Time (s)	States	Time (s)	States	Correct?
1	0.149	72	yes	0.188	59	0.108	35	yes
2	0.268	235	yes	2.01	144	0.457	56	yes
3	0.487	553	yes	40.085	279	0.941	65	yes
4	1.083	881	yes	15311.948	1148	2.954	105	yes
5	3.066	3009	yes	TIMEOUT	-	4.081	207	yes

Table 2. Comparison of translational approach [14] to our algorithmic approach with a tFail enabling condition of $V_i \geq 30$ that should not verify to be correct

	Translational			Algorithmic		
# Caps	Time (s)	States	Correct?	Time (s)	States	Correct?
100	108.686	1639	no	6.504	233	no
200	972.568	3239	no	88.599	723	no
300	3496.862	4839	no	287.089	875	no
400	10290.709	6439	no	710.162	1127	no
500	TIMEOUT	-	no	3418.39	1967	no

For the first example, the enabling condition on $tFail$ is $\neg(V_i \geq -2)$. In the capacitor models, the voltage is never negative. Thus, the failure transition should not fire. The verification results for the modified property are shown in Table 1. Both the translational approach and this paper's algorithmic approach give the correct verification result. Namely, that the model satisfies the property. The state spaces are comparable, with the algorithmic approach producing no more than a multiple of 2 more than the translational approach; however, the run time quickly explodes. This fact suggests that many new states are either subsets or supersets of previously found zones. To address this problem, addSetItem can be modified to ensure that rate events fire before all other events. The results are in the Algorithmic (opt) column in Table 1.

As a second example, the enabling condition for the failure transition $tFail$ is changed to $V_i \geq 30$. In this case, the model does not satisfy the property and both approaches correctly find this result, as is shown in Table 2. In this case, the translational approach has state counts that are four to seven times larger than the algorithmic approach for 100, 200, 300, 400, and 500 stages of capacitors. Furthermore, the translational approach is now the one experiencing the rapid increase in time. The state count for the algorithmic approach is relatively small which indicates that the failure occurs rather early in the state search.

Table 3. Comparison of translational approach in [14] to our algorithmic approach for the property shown in Fig. 1b that should not verify to be correct

# Caps	Translational			Algorithmic		
	Time (s)	States	Correct?	Time (s)	States	Correct?
1	0.162	81	yes	0.146	52	no
2	0.287	240	yes	0.534	143	no
3	0.529	622	yes	2.00	280	no
4	1.31	1550	yes	13.6	481	no
5	3.83	3710	yes	130	877	no
6	13.1	8926	yes	1047	1649	no
7	76.2	52574	yes	860	3798	no
8	410	122014	yes	29709	7489	no

The final property is the one shown in Fig. 1b. This property first checks that if the voltage V_i is at least 15mV at $10\mu s$, then the voltage must be at least 30mV after an additional $10\mu s$. If this is not true, then $tFail$ fires, indicating a failure. The results of verifying the last capacitor stage for models with one capacitor through eight are shown in Table 3. For each example, the translational approach indicates the model passes verification; however, this result is incorrect. If V_i has a rate of $1mV/\mu s$ for $5\mu s$ and then has a rate of $2mV/\mu s$ for $5\mu s$, the value of V_i at $10\mu s$ is 15mV. If the rate goes back to $1mV/\mu s$ for another $10\mu s$, then the value of V_i is 25mV. This trace results in the sequence of transitions t_5, t_9, t_{10}, and $tFail$ in Fig. 1b. Although zones over-approximate the state space, this trace is missing from the transformed model. Thus, the translational approach does not find this failure trace while the algorithmic approach does.

7 Conclusion

This paper shows how a zone-based reachability method can be extended to verify models that utilize a range of rates. Previous methods have opted for a translational approach that converts models to ones with only a single rate change. Although this approach is adequate for properties, it is not enough when used for models. By using a method that allows for multiple resets, one can recover all the necessary behaviors. One avenue of future exploration is increasing the accuracy of zones. Since zones provide an over-approximation, states are introduced into the reachable state set that are not, in fact, reachable. Thus, the verification result may indicate that the system does not meet the specification, when the system really does. In the future, this method should also be applied to more realistic examples. The experiments are shown with the aid of a toy example that gives insight into the behavior of the method; however, the applicability should be tested against examples in a real design flow.

References

1. Alur, R., Courcoubetis, C., Halbwachs, N., Henzinger, T.A., Ho, P.H., Nicollin, X., Olivero, A., Sifakis, J., Yovine, S.: The algorithmic analysis of hybrid systems. Theoretical Computer Science **138**, 3–34 (1995)
2. Alur, R., Courcoubeti, C., Henzinger, T.A., Ho, P.H.: Hybrid automata: An algorithmic approach to the specification and verification of hybrid systems. In: Grossman, R.L., Nerode, A., Ravn, A.P., Rischel, H. (eds.) Hybrid Systems. LNCS, vol. 736, pp. 209–229. Springer, Heidelberg (1993)
3. Asarin, E., Dang, T., Maler, O.: The **d/dt** tool for verification of hybrid systems. In: Brinksma, E., Larsen, K.G. (eds.) CAV 2002. LNCS, vol. 2404, pp. 365–370. Springer, Heidelberg (2002)
4. Bengtsson, J.E., Yi, W.: Timed Automata: Semantics, Algorithms and Tools. In: Desel, J., Reisig, W., Rozenberg, G. (eds.) Lectures on Concurrency and Petri Nets. LNCS, vol. 3098, pp. 87–124. Springer, Heidelberg (2004)
5. Cassez, F., Larsen, K.G.: The impressive power of stopwatches. In: Palamidessi, C. (ed.) CONCUR 2000. LNCS, vol. 1877, p. 138. Springer, Heidelberg (2000)
6. Dill, D.L.: Timing assumptions and verification of finite-state concurrent systems. In: Sifakis, J. (ed.) Automatic Verification Methods for Finite State Systems. LNCS, vol. 407, pp. 197–212. Springer, Heidelberg (1990)
7. Fisher, A.N., Myers, C.J., Li, P.: Ranges of rates (2013) [Online; accessed 31-December-2014]. http://www.async.ece.utah.edu/~andrewf/ranges_of_rates.pdf
8. Frehse, G., Le Guernic, C., Donzé, A., Cotton, S., Ray, R., Lebeltel, O., Ripado, R., Girard, A., Dang, T., Maler, O.: SpaceEx: Scalable verification of hybrid systems. In: Gopalakrishnan, G., Qadeer, S. (eds.) CAV 2011. LNCS, vol. 6806, pp. 379–395. Springer, Heidelberg (2011)
9. Frehse, G., Krogh, B., Rutenbar, R.: Verifying analog oscillator circuits using forward/backward abstraction refinement. In: DATE 2006 Proceedings of the Design, Automation and Test in Europe, vol. 1, p. 6, March 2006
10. Frehse, G.: Spaceex (2012) [Online; accessed 31-December-2012]. http://spaceex. imag.fr/documentation/publications
11. Henzinger, T.A., Kopke, P.W., Puri, A., Varaiya, P.: What's decidable about hybrid automata? In: Symposium on Theory of Computing, pp. 373–382. Association for Computing Machinery (1995). http://dl.acm.org/citation.cfm?id=225162
12. Little, S., Seegmiller, N., Walter, D., Myers, C., Yoneda, T.: Verification of analog/mixed-signal circuits using labeled hybrid petri nets. IEEE Transactions on Computer-Aided Design of Integrated Circuits and Systems **30**, 617–630 (2011)
13. Little, S., Walter, D., Jones, K., Myers, C., Sen, A.: Analog/mixed-signal circuit verification using models generated from simulation traces. The Inernational Journal of Foundations of Computer Science **21**(2), 191–210 (2010)
14. Little, S.R.: Efficient modeling and verification of analog/mixed-signal circuits using labeled hybrid petri nets. Ph.D. thesis, University of Utah (2008)
15. Myers, C.: Asynchronous Circuit Design. John Wiley & Sons, July 2001
16. Puri, A., Borkar, V., Varaiya, P.: ϵ-approximation of differential inclusions. In: Alur, R., Sontag, E.D., Henzinger, T.A. (eds.) HS 1995. LNCS, vol. 1066. Springer, Heidelberg (1996)
17. Silva, B.I., Krogh, B.H.: Formal verification of hybrid systems using checkmate: A case study. American Control Conference **3**, 1679–1683 (2000)
18. Yan, C., Greenstreet, M.: Faster projection based methods for circuit level verification. In: ASPDAC 2008 Design Automation Conference, Asia and South Pacific, pp. 410–415 (2008)

Towards Realizability Checking of Contracts Using Theories

Andrew Gacek[1]($\boxtimes$), Andreas Katis[2], Michael W. Whalen[2],
John Backes[1], and Darren Cofer[1]

[1] Rockwell Collins Advanced Technology Center,
400 Collins Rd. NE, Cedar Rapids, IA 52498, USA
{andrew.gacek,john.backes,darren.cofer}@rockwellcollins.com
[2] Department of Computer Science and Engineering,
University of Minnesota, 200 Union Street, Minneapolis, MN 55455, USA
katis001@umn.edu, whalen@cs.umn.edu

Abstract. *Virtual integration* techniques focus on building architectural models of systems that can be analyzed early in the design cycle to try to lower cost, reduce risk, and improve quality of complex embedded systems. Given appropriate architectural descriptions and compositional reasoning rules, these techniques can be used to prove important safety properties about the architecture prior to system construction. Such proofs build from "leaf-level" assume/guarantee component contracts through architectural layers towards top-level safety properties. The proofs are built upon the premise that each leaf-level component contract is *realizable*; i.e., it is possible to construct a component such that for any input allowed by the contract assumptions, there is some output value that the component can produce that satisfies the contract guarantees. Without engineering support it is all too easy to write leaf-level components that can't be realized. Realizability checking for propositional contracts has been well-studied for many years, both for component synthesis and checking correctness of temporal logic requirements. However, checking realizability for contracts involving infinite theories is still an open problem. In this paper, we describe a new approach for checking realizability of contracts involving theories and demonstrate its usefulness on several examples.

1 Introduction

In the recent years, *virtual integration* approaches have been proposed as a means to lower cost and improve quality of complex embedded systems. These approaches focus on building architectural models of systems that can be analyzed prior to construction of component implementations. The objective is to discover and resolve problems early during the design and implementation phases when cost impact is lower. Several architecture description languages such as AADL [1], SysML [2], and AUTOSAR [3] are designed to support such an engineering process, and there has been significant effort to analytically determine

© Springer International Publishing Switzerland 2015
K. Havelund et al. (Eds.): NFM 2015, LNCS 9058, pp. 173–187, 2015.
DOI: 10.1007/978-3-319-17524-9_13

system performance [4,5], fault tolerance [5], security [6], and safety [7] using these techniques.

In an ongoing effort at Rockwell Collins and The University of Minnesota, we have been pursuing virtual integration using compositional proofs of correctness. The idea is to support hierarchical design and analysis of complex system architectures and co-evolution of requirements and architectures at multiple levels of abstraction [8]. This was based on two observations about software development for commercial aircraft: first, that component-level errors are relatively rare and that most problems occur during integration [9], and second, that requirements specifications often contain significant numbers of omissions or errors [10] that are at the root of many of the integration problems. Specifically, the problem involves demonstrating *satisfaction arguments* [11], i.e., that the requirements allocated to components and the architecture connecting those components is sufficient to guarantee the system requirements. We have created the AGREE reasoning framework [12] to support compositional assume/guarantee contract reasoning over system architectural models written in AADL.

Such proof systems build from "leaf-level" assume/guarantee component contracts through architectural layers towards proofs of top-level safety properties. The soundness of the argument is built upon the premise that each leaf-level component contract is *realizable*; i.e., it is possible to construct a component such that for any input allowed by the contract assumptions, there is some output value that the component can produce that satisfies the contract guarantees.

Unfortunately, without engineering support it is all too easy to write leaf-level components that can't be realized. When applying our tools in both industrial and classroom settings, this issue has led to incorrect compositional "proofs" of systems; in fact the goal of producing a compositional proof can lead to engineers modifying component-level requirements such that they are no longer possible to implement. In order to make our virtual integration approach reasonable for practicing engineers, tool support must be provided to check whether components are *realizable*.

Realizability checking for propositional contracts has been well-studied for many years (e.g., [13–16]), both for component synthesis and checking correctness of temporal logic requirements. Checking realizability for contracts involving theories, on the other hand, is still an open problem. In this paper, we describe a new approach for checking realizability of contracts involving theories and demonstrate its usefulness on several examples. Our approach is similar to k-induction over quantified formulas. We describe two algorithms. The first is sound for both proofs and counterexamples, but computationally intractable. The second algorithm is not sound for counterexamples (i.e., it may return a 'false counterexample' to a problem that is in fact realizable), but we have found it fast and accurate in practice.

The rest of the paper is structured as follows. In Section 2 we will describe our motivation and an example to illustrate realizability, and will define realizability formally in Section 3. We next describe two algorithms for checking realizability in Section 4, our implementation in the AGREE tool suite in Section 5, and our experience using the realizability check in Section 6. Section 7 describes related work and Section 8 concludes.

2   Motivation and Example

We have been pursuing a *proof-based virtual integration* approach for building complex systems using the architecture description language AADL [1] and the AGREE compositional reasoning system [12]. We have demonstrated the effectiveness of the approach on a variety of industrial-scale systems, including the software controller for a patient-controlled analgesia (PCA) infusion pump [17], a dual flight-guidance system [12], and several more recent models, such as a quad-redundant flight control system and a quadcopter control system. We are using this approach on the DARPA HACMS program to build secure vehicles and to demonstrate how to apply virtual integration on industrial scale systems to facilitate technology transfer.

As part of the HACMS project, we attempted a feasibility test via a classroom exercise. We used the AADL and AGREE tools in a class assignment in a graduate-level software architecture class. The students were organized into six teams of four students. Each team was asked to specify the control software for a simplified microwave oven in AADL using a virtual integration approach. The software was split into two subsystems: one for controlling the heating element and another for controlling the display panel, with several requirements for each subsystem. The goal was to formalize these component-level requirements and use them to prove three system-level safety requirements.

The results of the initial experiment were sobering. All student groups were able to prove the system-level requirements starting from formalizations of the component requirements. Unfortunately, in many cases, the proofs succeeded because the components were incorrectly specified. In fact, only one of the teams had written component-level requirements that could be implemented. The other teams had requirements which were inconsistent under certain input conditions. For example, one team produced the following informal component-level requirements:

> **Microwave-1** - While the microwave is in cooking mode, seconds_to_cook shall decrease.

> **Microwave-2** - If the display is quiescent (no buttons pressed) and the keypad is enabled, the seconds_to_cook shall not change.

and then produced the following formalized requirements[1]:

> **guarantee**: is_cooking$'$ $\Rightarrow$ seconds_to_cook$'$ $\leq$ seconds_to_cook $- 1$

> **guarantee**: ($\neg$any_digit_pressed $\wedge$ keypad_enabled) $\Rightarrow$
> seconds_to_cook$'$ = seconds_to_cook

---

[1] We have translated this property and others from the higher level AGREE syntax into a two-state form that is used throughout this paper.

These formalized guarantees fail to avoid the conflict in the seconds_to_cook variable between the Microwave-1 and Microwave-2 requirements, as they cannot be both satisfied in a case where the microwave is cooking and the keypad is enabled. This error was not caught despite an analysis built into an early version of AGREE that checks contracts for *consistency*, i.e., whether the conjunction of a system's guarantees is satisfiable. We realized that consistency checking does not actually provide a trustworthy answer because it only checks whether the system works in *some* external environment, not in *all* environments. Realizability checking determines whether or not the component works in all input environments that satisfy the component assumptions.

From this experience, we decided that realizability checking was necessary for successful tech transfer of a virtual integration approach. The analysis was not only necessary for classroom settings. We also found problems with component-level requirements in two of our large-scale analysis efforts. Further, existing approaches for checking realizability do not allow predicates over infinite theories such as integers and reals, which are native to our AGREE contracts.

In the following sections, we formally define realizability over transition systems, as well as algorithms for checking realizability over infinite-state systems that are efficient and accurate in practice. A machine-checked formalization of the definitions and proofs in Coq can be found in a companion paper [18].

3   Realizability

We assume the types state and input for states and inputs. We use s for variables of type state and i for variables of type input. State represents both internal state and external outputs. A transition system is a pair (I, T) where I : state $\rightarrow$ bool holds on the initial states states and T : state $\times$ input $\times$ state $\rightarrow$ bool holds on $T(s, i, s')$ when the system can transition from state s to state s' on receipt of input i. We assume the usual notion of path with respect to a transition relation.

A contract specifies the desired behavior of a transition system. A contract is a pair (A, G) of an assumption and a guarantee. The assumption A : state $\times$ input $\rightarrow$ bool specifies for a given system state which inputs are valid. The guarantee G is a pair (G_I, G_T) of an initial guarantee and a transitional guarantee. The initial guarantee G_I : state $\rightarrow$ bool specifies which states the system may start in, that is, the possible initial internal state and external outputs. The transitional guarantee G_T : state $\times$ input $\times$ state $\rightarrow$ bool specifies for a given state and input what states the system may transition to.

We now define what it means for a transition system to realize a contract. This requires that the system respects the guarantee for inputs which satisfying the contract. Moreover, the system must always remain responsive with respect to inputs that satisfying the assumptions. In order to make this definition precise, we first need to define which system states are reachable given some assumptions on the system inputs.

Definition 1 (Reachable with respect to assumptions). *Let (I, T) be a transition system and let A : state $\times$ input $\rightarrow$ bool be an assumption. A state of*

(I, T) *is reachable with respect to A if there exists a path starting in an initial state and eventually reaching s such that all transitions satisfying the assumptions. Formally,* $\mathsf{Reachable}_A(s)$ *is defined inductively by*

$$\mathsf{Reachable}_A(s) = I(s) \vee \exists s_{\mathsf{prev}}, i.\ \mathsf{Reachable}_A(s_{\mathsf{prev}}) \wedge A(s_{\mathsf{prev}}, i) \wedge T(s_{\mathsf{prev}}, i, s)$$

Definition 2 (Realization). *A transition system (I, T) is a realization of the contract $(A, (G_I, G_T))$ when the following conditions hold*

1. $\forall s.\ I(s) \Rightarrow G_I(s)$
2. $\forall s, i, s'.\ \mathsf{Reachable}_A(s) \wedge A(s, i) \wedge T(s, i, s') \Rightarrow G_T(s, i, s')$
3. $\exists s.\ I(s)$
4. $\forall s, i.\ \mathsf{Reachable}_A(s) \wedge A(s, i) \Rightarrow \exists s'.\ T(s, i, s')$

The first two conditions in Definition 2 ensure that the transition system respects the guarantees. The second two conditions ensure that the system is non-trivial and responsive to all valid inputs.

Definition 3 (Realizable). *A contract is realizable if there exists a transition system which is a realization of the contract.*

Definitions 2 and 3 are useful for directly defining realizability, but not very useful for checking realizability. We now develop an equivalent notion which is more suggestive and amenable to checking. This is based on a notion called *viability*. Intuitively, a state is viable with respect to a contract if being in that state does not doom a realization to failure. We can capture this notion without reference to any specific realization, because condition 2 in the definition of realization tells us that G_T is an over-approximation of any T.

Definition 4 (Viable). *A state s is viable with respect to a contract $(A, (G_I, G_T))$, written $\mathsf{Viable}(s)$, if G_T can keep responding to valid inputs forever, starting from s. Informally, one can say that a state s is viable if it satisfies the infinite formula:*

$$\forall i_1.\ A(s, i_1) \Rightarrow \exists s_1.\ G_T(s, i_1, s_1) \wedge \forall i_2.\ A(s_1, i_2) \Rightarrow \exists s_2.\ G_T(s_1, i_2, s_2) \wedge \forall i_3. \cdots$$

Formally, viability is defined coinductively by the following equation

$$\mathsf{Viable}(s) = \forall i.\ A(s, i) \Rightarrow \exists s'.\ G_T(s, i, s') \wedge \mathsf{Viable}(s')$$

Theorem 1 (Alternative realizability). *A contract $(A, (G_I, G_T))$ is realizable if and only if $\exists s.\ G_I(s) \wedge \mathsf{Viable}(s)$.*

Proof. For the "only if" direction the key lemma is $\forall s.\ \mathsf{Reachable}_A(s) \Rightarrow \mathsf{Viable}(s)$. This lemma is proved by coinduction and follows directly from conditions 2 and 4 of Definition 2. Then by conditions 1 and 3 we have some state s such that $I(s)$ and $G_I(s)$. Thus $\mathsf{Reachable}_A(s)$ holds and applying the lemma we get $G_I(s) \wedge \mathsf{Viable}(s)$.

For the "if" direction, let s_0 be such that $G_I(s_0)$ and $\mathsf{Viable}(s_0)$. Define $I(s) = (s = s_0)$ and $T(s, i, s') = G_T(s, i, s') \wedge \mathsf{Viable}(s')$. Conditions 1, 2, and 3 of Definition 2 are clearly satisfied. Condition 4 follows from the observation that $\forall s.\ \mathsf{Reachable}_A(s) \Rightarrow \mathsf{Viable}(s)$ and from the definition of viability.

4 An Algorithm for Checking Realizability

In this section we develop two versions of an algorithm for automatically checking the realizability of a contract. The first version is based on Theorem 1 together with under- and over-approximations of viability. An over-approximation is useful to show that a contract is not viable, while an under-approximation is useful to show that a contract is viable. The second version of the algorithm follows from the mitigating the intractability of the first version.

We first define an over-approximation of viability called *finite viability* based on a finite unrolling of the definition of viability. Because this is an over-approximation, if a contract does not have an initial state which is finitely viable, then the contract is not viable. We formalize this when we prove the correctness of the realizability algorithm.

Definition 5 (Finite viability). *A state s is viable for n steps, written* Viable_n *(s) if G_T can keep responding to valid inputs for at least n steps. That is,*

$$\forall i_1.\ A(s, i_1) \Rightarrow \exists s_1.\ G_T(s, i_1, s_1) \ \wedge$$
$$\forall i_2.\ A(s_1, i_2) \Rightarrow \exists s_2.\ G_T(s_1, i_2, s_2) \wedge \cdots \wedge$$
$$\forall i_n.\ A(s_{n-1}, i_n) \Rightarrow \exists s_n.\ G_T(s_{n-1}, i_n, s_n)$$

All states are viable for 0 steps.

We next define an under-approximation of viability based on *one-step extension*. This notion looks if G_T can respond to valid inputs given a finite historical trace of valid inputs and states.

Definition 6 (One-step extension). *A state s is extendable after n steps, written* $\mathsf{Extend}_n(s)$*, if any valid path of length n from s can be extended in response to any input. That is,*

$$\forall i_1, s_1, \ldots, i_n, s_n.$$
$$A(s, i_1) \wedge G_T(s, i_1, s_1) \wedge \cdots \wedge A(s_{n-1}, i_n) \wedge G_T(s_{n-1}, i_n, s_n) \Rightarrow$$
$$\forall i.\ A(s_n, i) \Rightarrow \exists s'.\ G_T(s_n, i, s')$$

We now use these two notions to formally define our realizability algorithm. The core of the algorithm is based on two checks called the *base* and *extend* check.

Definition 7 (Realizability Algorithm). *Define the checks:*

$$\mathsf{BaseCheck}(n) = \exists s.\ G_I(s) \wedge \mathsf{Viable}_n(s)$$
$$\mathsf{ExtendCheck}(n) = \forall s.\ \mathsf{Extend}_n(s)$$

The following algorithm checks for realizability or unrealizability of a contract.

for $n = 0$ *to* ∞ *do*
  if not BaseCheck(n) *then*
    return *"unrealizable"*
  else if ExtendCheck(n) *then*
    return *"realizable"*
  end if
end for

Theorem 2 (Soundness of "unrealizable" result). *If* $\exists n.\ \neg$BaseCheck(n) *then the contract is not realizable.*

Proof. First we show $\forall s, n.$ Viable(s) $\Rightarrow$ Viable$_n$(s) by induction on n. The result then follows from Theorem 1.

Theorem 3 (Soundness of "realizable" result). *If* $\exists n.$ BaseCheck(n) $\wedge$ ExtendCheck(n) *then contract is realizable.*

Proof. First we show how Extend$_n$(s) can be used to shift Viable$_n$(s) forward. The following is proved by induction on n.

$$\forall s, n, i.\ \text{Extend}_n(s) \wedge \text{Viable}_n(s) \wedge A(s, i) \Rightarrow \exists s'.\ G_T(s, i, s') \wedge \text{Viable}_n(s')$$

Using this lemma we can show the following by coinduction.

$$\forall s, n.\ \text{Viable}_n(s) \wedge \text{ExtendCheck}(n) \Rightarrow \text{Viable}(s)$$

The result then follows from Theorem 1.

Corollary 1 (Soundness of Realizability Algorithm). *The Realizability Algorithm is sound.*

Due to the approximations used to define the base and extends check, the algorithm is incomplete. The following two examples show how both realizable and unrealizable contracts may send the algorithm into an infinite loop.

Example 1 (Incompleteness of "realizable" result). Suppose the type *state* is integers. Consider the contract:

$$A(s, i) = \top \qquad G_I(s) = \top \qquad G_T(s, i, s') = (s \neq 0)$$

This contract is realizable by, for example, a system that starts in state 1 and always transitions into the same state. Yet, for all n, ExtendCheck(n) fails since one can take a path of length n which ends at state 0. This path cannot be extended.

Example 2 (Incompleteness of "unrealizable" result). Suppose the type *state* is integers. Consider the contract:

$$A(s, i) = \top \qquad G_I(s) = (s \geq 0) \qquad G_T(s, i, s') = (s' = s - 1 \wedge s' \geq 0)$$

This contract is not realizable since in any realization the state 0 would be reachable, but the contract does not allow a transition from state 0. However, BaseCheck(n) holds for all n by starting in state $s = n$.

Implementing this algorithm requires a way of automatically checking the formulas BaseCheck(n) and ExtendCheck(n) for validity. This can be done in an SMT-solver that supports quantifiers over the language the contract is expressed in. Checking ExtendCheck(n) is rather nice in this setting since it has only a single quantifier alternation. Moreover, using an incremental SMT-solver one can reuse much of the work done to check ExtendCheck(n) to also check ExtendCheck($n+1$). However, BaseCheck(n) is problematic. First, it has $2n$ quantifier alternations which puts even small cases outside the reach of modern SMT-solvers. Second, the quantifiers make it impractical to reuse the results of BaseCheck(n) in checking BaseCheck($n + 1$). Finally, due to the quantifiers, a counterexample to BaseCheck(n) would be difficult to relay back to the user. Thus we need a simplification of BaseCheck(n) in order to make our algorithm practical.

Definition 8 (Simplified base check). *Define a simplified base check which checks that any path of length n from an initial state can be extended one step.*

$$\text{BaseCheck}'(n) = \forall s.\ G_I(s) \Rightarrow \text{Extend}_n(s)$$

First, note that this check has a single quantifier alternation. Second, this check can leverage the incremental features in an SMT-solver to use the results of BaseCheck$'(n)$ in checking BaseCheck$'(n + 1)$. Finally, when this check fails it can return a counterexample which is a trace of a system realizing the contract for n steps, but then becoming stuck. This provides very concrete and useful feedback to system developers. The correctness of this check is captured by the following theorem.

Theorem 4 (One-way soundness of simplified base check).

$$(\exists s.\ G_I(s)) \Rightarrow \forall n.\ (\forall k \leq n.\ \text{BaseCheck}'(k)) \Rightarrow \text{BaseCheck}(n)$$

Proof. We first prove the following by induction on n:

$$\forall s, n.\ \text{Extend}_n(s) \wedge \text{Viable}_n(s) \Rightarrow \text{Viable}_{n+1}(s)$$

The final result follows using this and induction on n.

Thus replacing BaseCheck(n) in the realizability algorithm with BaseCheck$'(n)$ preserves soundness of the "realizability" result. However, because the implication in Theorem 4 is only in one direction, the algorithm is no longer sound for the "unrealizable" result. That is, it may return a counterexample showing n steps of a realization of the contract that gets into a stuck state. The following example makes this point explicit.

Example 3. Consider again Example 1 where the type *state* is integers and the contract is:

$$A(s, i) = \top \qquad G_I(s) = \top \qquad G_T(s, i, s') = (s \neq 0)$$

As before, this contract is easily realizable. However, BaseCheck$'(n)$ fails for all n since it will consider a path starting at state n and transitioning n steps to state 0 where no more transitions are possible.

The benefits of this second version of the algorithm outweigh its costs. The cases where a contract is realizable, yet fails the modified base check seems unlikely in practice. We have encountered none in our case studies. Moreover, when a contract does spuriously fail the simplified base check, it can almost always be rewritten into a form which would pass.

5 Implementation

We have built an implementation of the realizability algorithm as an extension to JKind [19], a re-implementation of the KIND model checker [20] in Java. Our tool is called JRealizability and is packaged with the latest release of JKind. The model's behavior is described in the Lustre language, which is the native input language of JKind and is used as an intermediate language for the AGREE tool suite.

We unroll the transition relation defined by the Lustre model into SMT problems (one for the base check and another for the extend check) which can be solved in parallel. We use the SMT-LIB Version 2 format which most modern SMT solvers support. The most significant issue for SMT solvers involves quantifier support, so we use the Z3 SMT solver [21] which has good support for reasoning over quantifiers and incremental search. The tool is often able to provide an answer for models containing integer and real-valued variables very quickly (in less than a second). Because of the use of quantifiers over a range of theories, it is possible that for one of the checks, Z3 returns unknown; in this case, we discontinue analysis. In addition, because our realizability check is incomplete, the tool terminates analysis when either a timeout or a user-specified max unrolling depth (default: 200) is reached. In this case we are able to report how far the base check reached which may provide some confidence in the realizability of the system.

6 Case Studies

As a part of testing the algorithm in actual components, we examined three different cases: a quad-redundant flight control system, a medical infusion pump, and a simple microwave controller. In this section, we provide a brief description of each case study and summarize the results in Table 1 at the end of the section.

6.1 Quad-Redundant Flight Control System

We ran our realizability analysis on a Quad-Redundant Flight Control System (QFCS) for NASA's Transport Class Model (TCM) aircraft simulation. We were provided with a set of English language requirements for the QFCS components and a description of the architecture. We modeled the architecture in AADL and the component requirements as assume/guarantee contracts in AGREE. As the name suggests, the QFCS consists of four redundant Flight Control Computers (FCCs). Each FCC contains components for handling faults and computing actuator signal values. One of these components is the Output Signal Analysis and Selection component (OSAS). The OSAS component is responsible for determining the output gain for signals coming from the control laws and going to the actuators. The output signal gain is determined based on the number of other faulty FCCs or based on failures within the FCC containing the OSAS component. The OSAS component contains 17 English language requirements including the following:

> **OSAS-S-170** – If the local Cross Channel Data Link (CCDL) has failed, OSAS shall set the local actuator command gain to 1 (one).

> **OSAS-S-240** – If OSAS has been declared failed by CCDL, OSAS shall set the actuator command gain to 0 (zero).

We formalized these requirements using the following guarantees:

$$\textbf{guarantee}: \mathsf{ccdl\_failed} \Rightarrow (\mathsf{fcc\_gain}' = 1)$$
$$\textbf{guarantee}: \mathsf{osas\_failed} \Rightarrow (\mathsf{fcc\_gain}' = 0)$$

These guarantees are contradictory in the case when the local CCDL has failed and the local CCDL reports to the OSAS that the OSAS has failed. This error eluded the engineers who originally drafted the requirements as well as the engineers who formalized them. In this case, there should be an assumption that if the CCDL has failed then it will not report to the OSAS that the OSAS has failed. This was not part of the original requirements. However, AGREE's realizability analysis was able to identify the error and provide a counterexample.

6.2 Medical Device Example

Our realizability tool was also used to verify the realizability of the components in the Generic Patient Controlled Analgesia infusion pump system that was described in [22]. The controller consists of six subcomponents that were given as input for the tool to verify the requirements described inside. While five of the models were proven to be realizable, a subtly incorrect requirement definition was found in the contract for the controller's infusion manager.

> **GPCA-1** - The mode range of the controller shall be one of nine different modes. If the controller is in one of the first two modes the commanded flow rate shall be zero.

$$
\begin{aligned}
\textbf{guarantee}: \quad & \\
& (\mathsf{IM\_OUT.Current\_System\_Mode}' \geq 0) \ \wedge \\
& (\mathsf{IM\_OUT.Current\_System\_Mode}' \leq 8) \ \wedge \\
& (\mathsf{IM\_OUT.Current\_System\_Mode}' = 0 \Rightarrow \\
& \quad \mathsf{IM\_OUT.Commanded\_Flow\_Rate}' = 0) \ \wedge \\
& (\mathsf{IM\_OUT.Current\_System\_Mode}' = 1 \Rightarrow \\
& \quad \mathsf{IM\_OUT.Commanded\_Flow\_Rate}' = 0)
\end{aligned}
\tag{1}
$$

> **GPCA-2** - Whenever the alarm subsystem has detected a high severity hazard, then Infusion Manager shall never infuse drug at a rate more than the specified Keep Vein Open rate.

guarantee:

$$(\mathsf{TLM\_MODE\_IN.System\_On'} \land$$
$$\mathsf{ALARM\_IN.Highest\_Level\_Alarm'} = 3) \Rightarrow \qquad (2)$$
$$(\mathsf{IM\_OUT.Commanded\_Flow\_Rate'} = \mathsf{CONFIG\_IN.Flow\_Rate\_KVO'})$$

The erroneously defined guarantee (2) tries to assert that the IM_OUT.Commanded_Flow_Rate to some (potentially non-zero) Flow_Rate_KVO if the alarm input is 3; however, this may occur when the IM_OUT.Current_System_Mode is computed to be zero or one, in which case the flow rate is commanded to be 0. While discovering and fixing the problem was not difficult, the error was not discovered by the regular consistency check in AGREE.

6.3 Microwave Assignment

The realizability tool was used to check the contracts for the microwave models produced by the graduate student teams described in Sect. 2 that provided the initial motivation for this work. The microwave consists of two subsystems that manage the cooking element and display panel of the device. Table 1 shows the corresponding results for each team, named as MT1, MT2, etc. While every team but one managed to provide an implementable set of requirements for the microwave's mode controller, there were several interesting cases involving the display control component. For space reasons, we highlight only one here.

> **Microwave-1** - While the microwave is in cooking mode, seconds_to_cook shall decrease.

> **Microwave-3** - When the keypad is initially enabled, if no digits are pressed, the value shall be zero.

Team 6 formalized these requirements as

guarantee: $(\mathsf{cooking\_mode'} = 2) \Rightarrow (\mathsf{seconds\_to\_cook'} = \mathsf{seconds\_to\_cook} - 1)$
guarantee: $(\neg\mathsf{keypad\_enabled} \land \mathsf{keypad\_enabled'} \land \neg\mathsf{any\_digit\_pressed'}) \Rightarrow$
$(\mathsf{seconds\_to\_cook'} = 0)$

In the counterexample provided, the state where the microwave is cooking (cooking_mode = 2) and no digit is pressed creates a conflict regarding which value is assigned to the seconds_to_cook variable: should it decrease by one, or be assigned to zero? This counterexample is interesting because it indicates a missing assumption on the environment: the keypad is not enabled when the

Table 1. Realizability checking results for case studies

Case study	Model	Result	Time elapsed (seconds)	Base check depth (# of steps)
QFCS	FCS	realizable	1.762	0
QFCS	FCC	unrealizable	0.981	1
GPCA	Infusion Manager	unrealizable	0.2	1
GPCA	Alarm	realizable	0.316	0
GPCA	Config	realizable	0.102	0
GPCA	OutputBus	realizable	0.201	0
GPCA	System_Status	realizable	0.203	0
GPCA	Top_Level	realizable	0.103	0
MT 1	Mode Control	realizable	0.229	0
MT 1	Display Control	unrealizable	0.207	1
MT 2	Mode Control	realizable	0.202	0
MT 2	Display Control	unknown	1000 (tool timeout)	1
MT 3	Mode Control	realizable	0.203	0
MT 3	Display Control	unrealizable	0.202	1
MT 4	Mode Control	realizable	0.202	0
MT 4	Display Control	unrealizable	0.521	1
MT 5	Mode Control	unrealizable	0.1	1
MT 5	Display Control	unrealizable	0.222	1
MT 6	Mode Control	realizable	0.201	0
MT 6	Display Control	unknown	1000 (tool timeout)	1

cooking mode is 2 (cooking). Without this assumption about the inputs, the guarantees are not realizable.

Table 1 contains the exact results that were obtained during the three case studies. Every "realizable" result was determined to be correct since an implementation was produced for each of the components analyzed, ensuring the accuracy of the tool. Every contract that was identified as "unrealizable" was manually confirmed to be unrealizable, i.e., there were no spurious results. Additionally, the number of steps that the base check required to provide a final answer was not more than one, with the unknown results being particularly interesting, as the tool timed out before the solver was able to provide a concrete answer. This shows that there is still work to be done in terms of the algorithm's scalability, as well as an efficient way to eliminate quantifiers, making the solving process easier for Z3.

7   Related Work

The idea of *realizability* has been the subject of intensive study. Gunter et al. refer to it using the term *relative consistency* in [23], while Pnuelli and Rosner use the term *implementability* in [13] to refer to the problem of synthesis for propositional LTL. Additionally, the authors in [13] proved that the lower-bound time complexity of the problem is doubly exponential, in the worst case. In the following years, several techniques were introduced to deal with the synthesis problem in a more efficient way for subsets of propositional LTL [24], simple LTL formulas ([14], [25]), as well as in a component-based approach [16] and specifications based on other temporal logics ([26], [15]), such as SIS [27]. Finally, an interesting and relevant work has been done regarding the solution to the controllability problem using in [28] [29] and [30], which involves the decision on the existence a strategy that assigns certain values to a set of controllable activities, with respect to a set of uncontrollable ones.

Recent work in solving infinite game problems [31,32] can be specialized to the problem of realizability. In this work, the authors describe a framework for analyzing arbitrary two-player games. To provide proofs within the framework, *template formulas* must be provided by the user that describe the shape of a Skolem function that is used to explicitly define an inductive invariant that demonstrates the realizability of a model. Although this work is more general than ours, the applicability of the approach requires user-provided templates that are problem specific, so is not entirely automated.

The main contribution of our work is that it automatically checks the realizability of infinite domain systems. The problem is, in general, undecidable. Still, the application of bounded model checking can still offer an approximate answer to the realizability problem as we experienced by the fact that Z3 managed to solve the majority of our test models.

8   Conclusions and Future Work

In this paper, we have presented a new approach for determining realizability of contracts involving infinite theories using SMT solvers. This approach allows analysis of a class of contracts that were previously not solvable using automated analysis. The approach is both incomplete and conservative, i.e., it may return "false positive" results, declaring that a contract is not realizable when it could be realized. However, it has been shown to be both fast and effective in practice on a variety of models.

The results of this paper provide a good foundation towards further research in realizability. In much the same way that many properties are not *inductive*, some contracts cannot be proven realizable using one step extensions. We are examining alternate algorithms, similar to approaches such as IC3 [33], which support property-directed invariant generation, to improve the approach presented here. However, this requires generalizing the IC3 approach to solve quantified formulas (as well as to generalize counterexamples over quantified formulas). We hope to demonstrate an approach involving a IC3-like algorithm in the near future.

In addition, for realizable systems, it is likely that we want to consider the *synthesis* problem, which we have not explicitly considered in this paper. Synthesis aims to construct a concrete implementation of the contract, rather than determine its existence. It is known for propositional systems that the synthesis problem is equivalent in complexity to the realizability problem [13], but it is not known (to us) whether this equivalence is true in the infinite-state case.

Acknowledgments. This work was funded by DARPA and AFRL under contract FA8750-12-9-0179 (Secure Mathematically-Assured Composition of Control Models), and by NASA under contract NNA13AA21C (Compositional Verification of Flight Critical Systems), and by NSF under grant CNS-1035715 (Assuring the safety, security, and reliability of medical device cyber physical systems).

References

1. SAE-AS5506: Architecture Analysis and Design Language. SAE (2004)
2. Friedenthal, S., Moore, A., Steiner, R.: A Practical Guide to SysML: Systems Modeling Language. Morgan Kaufmann Publishers Inc., San Francisco (2008)
3. Consortium, A.: Automotive Open System Architecture (AUTOSAR) Revision 4.2.1. AUTOSAR (2014)
4. Varona-Gomez, R., Villar, E.: Aadl simulation and performance analysis in systemc. In: 2009 14th IEEE International Conference on Engineering of Complex Computer Systems, pp. 323–328 (2009)
5. Bozzano, M., Cimatti, A., Katoen, J.P., Nguyen, V.Y., Noll, T., Roveri, M.: Safety, dependability and performance analysis of extended aadl models. Comput. J. **54**, 754–775 (2011)
6. Apvrille, L., Roudier, Y.: SysML-Sec: A model-driven environment for developing secure embedded systems. In: SAR-SSI 2013, 8ème Conférence sur la Sécurité des Architectures Réseaux et des Systèmes d'Information, Mont-de-Marsan, France, 16–18 Septembre 2013
7. Bozzano, M., Cimatti, A., Katoen, J.P., Katsaros, P., Mokos, K., Nguyen, V.Y., Noll, T., Postma, B., Roveri, M.: Spacecraft early design validation using formal methods. Reliability Engineering and System Safety **132** (2014)
8. Whalen, M.W., Gacek, A., Cofer, D., Murugesan, A., Heimdahl, M.P., Rayadurgam, S.: Your what is my how: Iteration and hierarchy in system design. IEEE Software **30**, 54–60 (2013)
9. Rushby, J.: New challenges in certification for aircraft software. In: Proceedings of the Ninth ACM Int'l Conf. on Embedded Software, pp. 211–218. ACM (2011)
10. Miller, S.P., Tribble, A.C., Whalen, M.W., Heimdahl, M.P.E.: Proving the shalls: Early validation of requirements through formal methods. Int. J. Softw. Tools Technol. Transf. **8**, 303–319 (2006)
11. Hammond, J., Rawlings, R., Hall, A.: Will it work? [requirements engineering]. In: Proceedings of Fifth IEEE Int'l Symposium on Requirements Engineering, 2001, pp. 102–109 (2001)
12. Cofer, D.D., Gacek, A., Miller, S.P., Whalen, M.W., LaValley, B., Sha, L.: Compositional verification of architectural models. In: Goodloe, A.E., Person, S. (eds.) Proceedings of the 4th NASA Formal Methods Symposium (NFM 2012). LNCS, vol. 7226, pp. 126–140. Springer-Verlag, Heidelberg (2012)
13. Pnueli, A., Rosner, R.: On the Synthesis of a Reactive Module. In: Proceedings of the 16th ACM SIGPLAN-SIGACT Symposium on Principles of Programming Languages (POPL 1989), pp. 179–190 (1989)
14. Bohy, A., Bruyére, V., Filiot, E., Jin, N., Raskin, J.F.: Acacia+, a tool for LTL Synthesis. In: Madhusudan, P., Seshia, S.A. (eds.) Computer Aided Verification (CAV 2012). LNCS, vol. 7358, pp. 652–657. Springer, Heidelberg (2012)
15. Hamza, J., Jobstmann, B., Kuncak, V.: Synthesis for regular specifications over unbounded domains. In: Proceedings of the 2010 Conference on Formal Methods in Computer-Aided Design, pp. 101–109 (2010)

16. Chatterjee, K., Henzinger, T.A.: Assume-guarantee synthesis. In: Grumberg, O., Huth, M. (eds.) Tools and Algorithms for the Construction and Analysis of Systems (TACAS 2007). LNCS, vol. 4424, pp. 261–275. Springer, Heidelberg (2007)

17. Murugesan, A., Whalen, M.W., Rayadurgam, S., Heimdahl, M.P.: Compositional verification of a medical device system. In: ACM Int'l Conf. on High Integrity Language Technology (HILT) 2013. ACM (2013)

18. Katis, A., Gacek, A., Whalen, M.W.: Machine-checked proofs for realizability checking algorithms (2015) (submitted). http://arxiv.org/abs/1502.01292

19. Gacek, A.: JKind - a Java implementation of the KIND model checker (2014). https://github.com/agacek/jkind

20. Hagen, G.: Verifying safety properties of Lustre programs: an SMT-based approach. PhD thesis, University of Iowa (2008)

21. De Moura, L., Bjørner, N.: Z3: An efficient SMT solver. In: Ramakrishnan, C.R., Rehof, J. (eds.) Tools and Algorithms for the Construction and Analysis of Systems. LNCS, vol. 4963, pp. 337–340. Springer, Heidelberg (2008)

22. Murugesan, A., Sokolsky, O., Rayadurgam, S., Whalen, M., Heimdahl, M., Lee, I.: Linking abstract analysis to concrete design: A hierarchical approach to verify medical CPS safety. In: Proceedings of ICCPS 2014 (2014)

23. Gunter, C.A., Gunter, E.L., Jackson, M., Zave, P.: A Reference model for Requirements and Specifications. IEEE Software 17, 37–43 (2000)

24. Klein, U., Pnueli, A.: Revisiting synthesis of GR(1) specifications. In: Barner, S., Harris, I., Kroening, D., Raz, O. (eds.) Hardware and Software: Verification and Testing (HVC 2010). LNCS, vol. 6504, pp. 161–181. Springer, Heidelberg (2010)

25. Tini, S., Maggiolo Schettini, A.: Compositional Synthesis of Generalized Mealy Machines. Fundamenta Informaticae 60, 367–382 (2003)

26. Beneš, N., Černá, I.: Factorization for component-interaction automata. In: Bieliková, M., Friedrich, G., Gottlob, G., Katzenbeisser, S., Turán, G. (eds.) Theory and Practice of Computer Science. LNCS, vol. 7147, pp. 554–565. Springer, Heidelberg (2012)

27. Aziz, A., Balarin, F., Braton, R., Sangiovanni-Vincentelli, A.: Sequential synthesis using SIS. In: Proceedings of the 1995 IEEE/ACM International Conference on Computer-Aided Design (ICCAD 1995), pp. 612–617 (1995)

28. Cimatti, A., Micheli, A., Roveri, M.: Solving temporal problems using SMT: Weak controllability. In: AAAI, pp. 448–454 (2012)

29. Cimatti, A., Micheli, A., Roveri, M.: Solving temporal problems using SMT: Strong controllability. In: Milano, M. (ed.) Principles and Practice of Constraint Programming (CP). LNCS, vol. 7514, pp. 248–264. Springer, Heidelberg (2012)

30. Cimatti, A., Micheli, A., Roveri, M.: Solving strong controllability of temporal problems with uncertainty using SMT. Constraints (2014)

31. Beyene, T., Chaudhuri, S., Popeea, C., Rybalchenko, A.: A constraint-based approach to solving games on infinite graphs. In: Proceedings of the 41st ACM SIGPLAN-SIGACT Symposium on Principles of Programming Languages. POPL 2014, pp. 221–233. ACM, New York, NY, USA (2014)

32. Beyene, T.A., Popeea, C., Rybalchenko, A.: Solving existentially quantified Horn clauses. In: Sharygina, N., Veith, H. (eds.) Computer Aided Verification (CAV). LNCS, vol. 8044, pp. 869–882. Springer, Heidelberg (2013)

33. Bradley, A.: SAT-based model checking without unrolling. In: Jhala, R., Schmidt, D. (eds.) Verification, Model Checking, and Abstract Interpretation (VMCAI). LNCS, vol. 6538, pp. 70–87. Springer, Heidelberg (2011)

Practical Partial Order Reduction for CSP

Thomas Gibson-Robinson[1]([✉]), Henri Hansen[2], A.W. Roscoe[1],
and Xu Wang[1,2]

[1] Department of Computer Science, University of Oxford, Oxford, UK
{thomas.gibson-robinson,bill.roscoe}@cs.ox.ac.uk
[2] Department of Mathematics, Tampere University of Technology, Tampere, Finland
henri.hansen@tut.fi

Abstract. FDR is an explicit-state refinement checker for the process algebra CSP and, as such, is vulnerable to the state-explosion problem. In this paper, we show how a form of partial-order reduction, an automatic state reduction mechanism, can be utilised to soundly reduce the number of states that must be visited. In particular, we develop a compositional method for partial-order reduction that takes advantage of FDR's internal, compositional, process representation. Further, we develop novel methods of preserving the traces of a process which allow partial-order reduction to be applied to arbitrary FDR refinement checks. We also provide details on how to efficiently implement the algorithms required for partial-order reduction.

1 Introduction

Communicating Sequential Processes (CSP) [1–3] is one of the most widely known process algebras. FDR (Failures Divergence Refinement) [4,5] is an industrial-strength tool that can check for refinement between CSP processes described in a lazy functional language, along with other properties including deadlock-freedom and determinism. Partial-order reduction [6–8] is a technique for automatically and soundly reducing the number of states that need to be visited. In this paper we describe an extension to FDR3 that adds support for partial-order reduction, using *weak stubborn sets*, based on [9].

The stubborn sets are computed using a dependency graph that encodes information about how actions interfere. This dependency graph is computed compositionally, by taking advantage of FDR's compositional process representation using *supercombinators*. A supercombinator represents a labelled-transition system (LTS) implicitly as a set of component LTSs and a set of rules specifying how to combine the component transitions. The partial-order reduction has been designed to preserve not only deadlocks, but also traces, failures, and divergences, using theory similar to [9,10]. This means that it can be used for general refinement checks inside FDR.

This paper makes three main contributions. 1. We provide a general framework for efficiently computing weak stubborn sets, which have not been exploited

© Springer International Publishing Switzerland 2015
K. Havelund et al. (Eds.): NFM 2015, LNCS 9058, pp. 188–203, 2015.
DOI: 10.1007/978-3-319-17524-9_14

thus far due to the perceived complexity of the algorithms. 2. We show how to efficiently compute dependency information for supercombinators. 3. We develop a vastly more efficient method of preserving trace refinement violations (one of FDR's verification modes) utilising the watchdog transformation of [11].

Related Work. Recent research in partial order reduction has explored ways to expand its applications. Strong stubborn sets were proven to be optimal in a model theoretic sense [12]: if the classic dependency and enabling relations are the only things known about the system, omitting any transition from the strong stubborn set as calculated by the deletion algorithm [13], risks losing a deadlock. The result does not apply to weak sets, which use different dependency relations.

The more complicated algorithms (e.g. the deletion algorithm) we discuss in this article come at a cost in time. Approaches that target more efficient calculation have recently been explored, for instance the use of guards [14] in shared variable concurrency to control for causality. We make use of similar ideas in the implementation, though adapted for supercombinators.

The use of weak stubborn sets with the failures-divergences model was earlier explored in [9]. The work in this article provides a more general framework of parallel composition and covers reductions for several other models. Our work extends many of the ideas presented in [10], which covers computation of (strong) stubborn sets for many of the semantic models in the linear-time/branching-time spectrum. Most models require solving the so-called *ignoring problem* as defined in [6], which has recently received some attention on its own [15]. Our methods do not require global information such as cycle provisos. The approach in the watchdog transformation is similar to that in [16].

Outline. Section 2 describes FDR's LTS representations and weak stubborn sets. Section 3 formalises dependency graphs and shows how these can be computed from a supercombinator. Section 4 describes how to compute stubborn sets. Section 5 extends Section 3 to preserve the traces, failures, and divergences of a process. Section 6 presents experimental results regarding partial-order reduction, and discusses how it relates to FDR's existing state-reduction methods.

2 Background

FDR converts CSP processes to *labeled-transition systems*.

Definition 1. A *labeled transition system* (LTS) is a 4-tuple $(S, \Sigma, \Delta, \hat{s})$ where:

- S is a set of *states*;
- Σ is a finite set of *events* (such that $- \notin \Sigma$);
- $\Delta \subseteq S \times \Sigma \times S$ is a transition relation;
- $\hat{s} \in S$ is the *initial state*.

Given Σ we write $\Sigma^- = \Sigma \cup \{-\}$. If $(s, a, s') \in \Delta$ we write $s \xrightarrow{a} s'$. $s \xrightarrow{a_1 \ldots a_n} s'$ iff there exists $s_1, \ldots, s_n$ such that $s = s_1 \xrightarrow{a_1} s_2 \cdots s_n \xrightarrow{a_n} s'$. $s \xrightarrow{a}$ is true iff $\exists \cdot s \xrightarrow{a} s'$. We define $en(s) \hat{=} \{a \in \Sigma \mid \exists s' \cdot s \xrightarrow{a} s'\}$.

FDR also has an implicit LTS representation, called a *supercombinator*. It consists of a set of component LTSs along with a set of rules that describe how the transitions should be combined. The rules are partitioned into *formats*: in a state, rules from one format are active. A rule combines transitions of (a subset of) the components and determines the event the supercombinator performs. Rules may also *reset* components to their initial state, and change the format.

Definition 2. A *supercombinator* is a 3-tuple $(\mathcal{P}, \mathcal{R}, \hat{f})$ where:

- $\mathcal{P} = \{P_1, \ldots, P_n\}$ is a set of LTSs, such that $P_i = (S_i, \Sigma_i, \Delta_i, \hat{s}_i)$.
- $\mathcal{R}$ is a sequence of disjoint sets of length $|\mathcal{R}|$. The ith format is denoted by $\mathcal{R}(i)$ and is a set of *supercombinator rules* (e, a, r, f) where:
  - $e \in \Sigma_1^- \times \cdots \times \Sigma_n^-$ specifies the action each component must perform. '$-$' indicates it performs none.
  - a is an event.
  - $r \subseteq \{1, \ldots, n\}$ are the indices of the P_i that are *reset*.
  - $f \in \{1, \ldots, |\mathcal{R}|\}$ is the *result format*.
- $\hat{f} \in \{1, \ldots, |\mathcal{R}|\}$ is the *initial format*.

Given a rule α in a format $f \in \mathcal{R}$, $[\alpha] \mathrel{\hat{=}} f$. We abuse notation and write $(e, a, r, f) \in \mathcal{R}$ to mean $\exists i \cdot (e, a, r, f) \in \mathcal{R}(i)$. Further, we assume that if $(e_1, a_1, r_1, f_1), (e_2, a_2, r_2, f_2) \in \mathcal{R}$ are two different rules, then $a_1 \neq a_2$[1].

Given a supercombinator, a corresponding explicit LTS can be constructed.

Definition 3. Let $\mathcal{S} = (\{P_1, \ldots, P_n\}, \mathcal{R}, \hat{f})$ be a supercombinator where $P_i = (S_i, \Sigma_i, \Delta_i, \hat{s}_i)$. The LTS *induced by* $\mathcal{S}$ is the smallest LTS $(S, \Sigma, \Delta, \hat{s})$ such that:

- States are tuples consisting of the state of each component, plus the identifier of the format: $S \subseteq S_1 \times \cdots S_n \times \{1, \ldots, |\mathcal{R}|\}$.
- The initial state is the tuple containing the initial states of each of the components, along with the initial format: $\hat{s} = (\hat{s}_1, \ldots, \hat{s}_n, \hat{f}) \in S$.
- The action labels are the labels of the rules $\Sigma = \{a \mid \exists(e, a, r, f) \in \mathcal{R}\}$.
- The transitions correspond to the supercombinator rules firing. Let $s \mathrel{\hat{=}} (s_1, \ldots, s_n, f) \in S$, $s' \mathrel{\hat{=}} (s'_1, \ldots, s'_n, f') \in S$, and $((b_1, \ldots, b_n), a, r, f') \in \mathcal{R}(f)$. $(s, a, s') \in \Delta$ iff for each component i:
  1. If $i \notin r$, then either $b_i = -$ and $s_i = s'_i$, or $s_i \xrightarrow{b_i}_{P_i} s'_i$;
  2. If $i \in r$, $s'_i = \hat{s}_i$ and, if $b_i \neq -$ then $\exists s_i^* \cdot s_i \xrightarrow{b_i}_{P_i} s_i^*$.

---

[1] This assumption simplifies the theory by allowing supercombinator rules to be uniquely identified. This is required as the techniques we develop need to know which rule generated each transition. This is not a desirable restriction and, in practice, rules are identified by an integer and thus do not need unique events.

Weak Stubborn Sets. Our partial-order reduction technique utilises *weak stubborn sets* [9], which is the weaker form (i.e. can achieve more reduction) of the common *stubborn set* method [6]. In the stubborn set method, a *stubborn* subset of the actions in each state are selected. The main requirement is that any action from the stubborn set must commute with sequences of non-stubborn actions.

Definition 4 (From [9]). A function $T : S \mapsto 2^\Sigma$ is a *stubborn set reduction function* for a LTS $L = (S, \Sigma, \Delta, \hat{s})$ iff for every $s \in S$:

D1 For all $b_1, \ldots, b_n \notin T(s)$ and $a \in T(s)$, if $s \xrightarrow{b_1 \cdots b_n a} s'$ then $s \xrightarrow{a b_1 \cdots b_n} s'$;

D2 Either $en(s) = \{\}$, or there exists $a \in T(s)$ such that for every $b_1, \ldots, b_n \notin T(s)$, if $s \xrightarrow{b_1 \cdots b_n} s'$, then $s' \xrightarrow{a}$.

If T is a stubborn set reduction function for L, we say that the set $T(s)$ is a *stubborn set at s*. If $T(s)$ is a stubborn set and $a \in T(s)$ satisfies the second condition, we say that a is a *key action* of s.

The difference between weak and strong stubborn sets only concerns D2. In the strong stubborn set definition, every $a \in T(s)$ is required to be a key action.

The LTS induced by a stubborn set reduction function is defined as follows.

Definition 5 (From [9]). Let $L = (S, \Sigma, \Delta, \hat{s})$ be a LTS and T be a stubborn set reduction function for L. The *T-reduction* of L, denoted $T(L) \cong (S_T, \Sigma, \Delta_T, \hat{s})$, is the minimal LTS such that: 1. $\hat{s} \in S_T$; 2. $S_T \subseteq S$; 3. For every $s \in S_T$, if $(s, a, s') \in \Delta$ and $a \in T(s) \cap en(s)$, then $(s, a, s') \in \Delta_T$ and $s' \in S_T$.

Weak stubborn sets only preserve deadlocks. Section 5 considers how to strengthen Definition 4 to preserve other properties of interest to FDR.

Theorem 6 (From [9]). Let T be a stubborn set reduction function for a LTS $L = (S, \Sigma, \Delta, \hat{s})$ and $L' = (S', \Sigma', \Delta', \hat{s}')$ be the T-reduction of L. For every reachable $s' \in S$, if $en_L(s') = \{\}$ then $s' \in S'$ is reachable and $en_{L'}(s') = \{\}$.

3   Dependency Information

In this section we consider how to compute stubborn sets. Our analysis will be dynamic (i.e. we will compute stubborn sets in each state), but will be based on statically-computed information derived from supercombinators.

Supercombinators naturally suggest a compositional method of analysing the components. Firstly, we will analyse the component processes (which are small explicit LTSs) to see how events interfere. This will be used to determine how the supercombinator rules interfere, which will form the basis of our analysis.

Our definitions are not restricted to supercombinators: in Section 3.1 we will describe a general framework that can be used for computing stubborn sets, and we will then describe how to include supercombinators in this in Section 3.2.

3.1   Dependency Graphs

The static analysis will produce a *dependency graph* that indicates how actions interfere. It will be defined so that a subset of it that is *closed* (in some sense) will be a stubborn set. Before defining the dependency graph, we firstly define two dependency relations that will form the basis of the dependency graph.

Definition 7. Given a LTS $L = (S, \Sigma, \Delta, \hat{s})$, $D \subseteq \Sigma \times \Sigma$ is a *strong dependency relation* iff for all $s \in S, a, b \in \Sigma$: if $(a, b) \notin D$, $s \xrightarrow{b}$, and $s \xrightarrow{a}$, then:

1. For every s' such that $s \xrightarrow{a} s'$, $s' \xrightarrow{b}$ (and symmetrically for b);
2. For every s^*, if $s \xrightarrow{ab} s^*$ then $s \xrightarrow{ba} s^*$ (and symmetrically for ba).

Two actions are strongly dependent if either they disable each other, or do not commute. We also consider another notion, called weak dependency. Despite its name, the relation is incomparable with strong dependency.

Definition 8. Given a LTS $L = (S, \Sigma, \Delta, \hat{s})$, $W \subseteq \Sigma \times \Sigma$ is a *weak dependency relation* iff for every $s \in S$ and $a, b \in \Sigma$: if $(a, b) \notin W$ and $s \xrightarrow{ba} s'$, then $s \xrightarrow{ab} s'$.

a is weakly independent of b if the result of ba can be obtained by performing ab. Note that it is asymmetric: if a is weakly independent of b, then this prevents b from enabling a, and only prevents a from disabling b if b does not disable a, whereas strong independence prevents either from disabling the other.

The dependency graph contains three vertex types: enabled actions, disabled actions, and *guards*. The guards encode why each disabled action is disabled, whilst each action is linked to the guards it may satisfy.

Definition 9. Let $L = (S, \Sigma, \Delta, \hat{s})$ be a LTS, D be a strong dependency relation on L, W be a weak dependency relation on L, and $s \in S$. A *dependency graph* of L at s is a tuple $(X, Y, Z, \rightsquigarrow, \rightsquigarrow_W)$ where:

1. X contains the enabled actions, i.e. $X = en(s)$.
2. Y contains the disabled actions, i.e. $Y = \Sigma \setminus en(s)$.
3. Every disabled action is *guarded*: for every $a \in Y$ there is at least one $c \in Z$ such that $c \rightsquigarrow a$.
4. For all $(a, b) \in D$ such that $a \in en(s)$, $a \rightsquigarrow b$.
5. For all $(a, b) \in W$ such that $a \in en(s)$, $a \rightsquigarrow_W b$.
6. Guards of disabled actions must meet the following criterion: if $a \in Y$, and $s \xrightarrow{b_1 \cdots b_n a}$, then for every $c \in Z$ such that $c \rightsquigarrow a$, there is some $i \leq n$ such that $b_i \rightsquigarrow c$ (i.e. b_i causes the guard c to be satisfied).

Close subsets of dependency graphs are also stubborn sets, as we now show.

Definition 10. Let $(X, Y, Z, \rightsquigarrow, \rightsquigarrow_W)$ be a dependency graph of a LTS L at s, and $T \subseteq X \cup Y \cup Z$. An element $a \in X$ is *strongly closed* in T iff $\{b \mid a \rightsquigarrow b\} \cap (X \cup Y) \subseteq T$. An element $b \in X$ is *weakly closed* in T iff $\{b \mid a \rightsquigarrow_W b\} \cap (X \cup Y) \subseteq T$. T is a *result* set iff:

1. If $X \neq \{\}$ then there exists $a \in T \cap X$ such that a is strongly closed in T;
2. Every $a \in T \cap X$ is either strongly or weakly closed in T;
3. If $a \in T \cap Y$ then there is some $c \in Z$ such that $c \rightsquigarrow a$ and $c \in T$;
4. If $c \in T \cap Z$ then $\{a \mid a \rightsquigarrow c\} \subseteq T$.

Recall a stubborn set is required to commute with all sequences of non-stubborn actions. This explains the definition: a result set consists of at least one strongly closed action, along with everything that it interferes with. Further, if an action is in the result set and disabled, then no action that is not in the result set can enable the disabled action, thus ensuring D1.

Theorem 11. If T is a result set of a dependency graph $(X, Y, Z, \rightsquigarrow, \rightsquigarrow_W)$ at s, then $T \cap (X \cup Y)$ is a stubborn set at s.

The proof is very similar to the proofs in [9,12].

3.2 Supercombinator Dependency Graphs

We now consider how to construct a dependency graph for a supercombinator. As discussed above, this will be done compositionally by composing dependency information about the components using the supercombinator rules.

We firstly define strong and weak dependency relations for supercombinators.

Lemma 12. Let $\mathcal{P} = \{P_1, \ldots, P_n\}$ be a set of LTSs, D_i and W_i be strong and weak dependency relations for P_i, resp. Let $\mathcal{S} = (\mathcal{P}, R, \hat{f})$ be a supercombinator. Then, the relations D and W, defined as follows, are strong and weak dependency relations for the LTS induced by $\mathcal{S}$:

- $(a, b) \in D$ iff $\exists \alpha = ((a_1, \ldots, a_n), a, r_a, f_a), \beta = ((b_1, \ldots, b_n), b, r_b, f_b) \in \mathcal{R}$, such that $[\alpha] = [\beta]^2$ and either:
  1. The actions of a component are dependent, i.e. $\exists i \cdot (a_i, b_i) \in D_i$; or
  2. α resets a component that β requires (or vice-versa), i.e. there exists $i \in r_a$ such that $b_i \neq -$ (or symmetrically for r_b and a_i); or
  3. α or β change the format, i.e. $\neg(f_a = [\alpha] = [\beta] = f_b)$.
- $(a, b) \in W$ iff $\exists \alpha = ((a_1, \ldots, a_n), a, r_a, f_a), \beta = ((b_1, \ldots, b_n), b, r_b, f_b) \in \mathcal{R}$, such that:
  1. α and β are enabled in the same format, and one of their component events is weakly dependent, i.e. $[\alpha] = [\beta] = f_b$ and $\exists i \cdot (a_i, b_i) \in W_i$; or
  2. α and β are enabled in different formats, but β switches to α's format, i.e. $[\alpha] \neq [\beta]$ and $f_b = [\alpha]$; or
  3. $f_b = [\alpha]$ and β resets a component that α utilises to enable α, i.e. $\exists i \in r_b \cdot a_i \neq - \wedge a_i \in en_i(\hat{s}_i)$.

---

^{2} Actions in different formats can never be enabled in the same state, so cannot be strongly dependent.

Note that the above are sufficient, but not necessary conditions. For instance, requiring $f_a = [\alpha] = [\beta] = f_b$ is stronger than necessary since it may be the case that even though the formats change, there may be a rule equivalent to β in f_a, and a rule equivalent to α in f_b, in which case the actions may not interfere.

In order to construct the dependency graph for the supercombinator, another relation is required on the components. This *causality relation* indicates when actions enable others, and is used for constructing edges from actions to guards.

Definition 13. Given a LTS $P = (S, \Sigma, \Delta, \hat{s})$, a relation $C \subseteq \Sigma \times \Sigma$ is a *causality relation* iff for every $s \in S, a, b \in \Sigma$: If $(a, b) \notin C$, then $s \xrightarrow{ba} s' \Rightarrow s \xrightarrow{a}$.

We now define a dependency graph for a supercombinator, so that it satisfies Definition 9. The main decision concerns the choice of guard nodes. In a LTS induced by a supercombinator, there are two reasons why an action may be disabled: 1. The wrong format is currently selected; 2. A component is unable to perform the event required by the rule. Thus, there will be two types of guard nodes: *format guards* corresponding to a format, and *component event guards* that correspond to a component performing an event.

Theorem 14. Let $\mathcal{P} = \{P_1, \ldots, P_n\}$ be a set of LTSs, C_i be a causality relation for P_i, $\mathcal{S} = (\mathcal{P}, \mathcal{R}, \hat{f})$ be a supercombinator, and W and D weak and strong dependency relations for the LTS L induced by $\mathcal{S}$. The 5-tuple $(X, Y, Z, \leadsto, \leadsto_W)$ is a dependency graph for L at $s = (s_1, \ldots, s_n, f)$ if:

- $X = en(s)$ and $Y = \Sigma \setminus en(s)$.
- $Z = Z_F \cup Z_C$ where Z_F consists of format guards for disabled formats, and Z_C consists of component event guards for each event that each component cannot perform. Formally, $Z_F \mathrel{\hat{=}} \{f' \in \{1 \ldots |\mathcal{R}|\} \mid f' \neq f\}$ whilst $Z_C \mathrel{\hat{=}} \{(a_i, i) \mid ((a_1, \ldots, a_n), a, r, f_a) \in \mathcal{R}, a_i \neq -, a_i \notin en_i(s_i)\}$.
- For every $a \in X$ and $b \in \Sigma$, if $(a, b) \in D$ then $a \leadsto b$.
- For every $a \in X$ and $b \in \Sigma$, if $(a, b) \in W$ then $a \leadsto_W b$.
- For every disabled rule, there is an edge from every component event guard to every rule for which the component cannot perform the required event. Formally, for every $((a_1, \ldots, a_n), a, r, f_a) \in \mathcal{R}$ where $a \in Y$ and, for all i such that $a_i \neq -$ and $a_i \notin en_i(s_i)$, $(a_i, i) \leadsto a$.
- For every disabled rule of a different format, there is an edge from the format guard to the rule. Formally, for every $\alpha = (e, a, r, f) \in \mathcal{R}$ such that $a \in Y$ and $f \neq [\alpha]$, $[\alpha] \leadsto a$.
- For every rule that changes format, there is an edge from the rule to the new format guard. Formally, for all $\alpha = (e, a, r, f) \in \mathcal{R}$ where $[\alpha] \neq f$, $a \leadsto f$.
- There is an edge from every rule to every component event guard that the rule may satisfy. Formally, for every $(a_i, i) \in Z$ and $b \in \Sigma$ such that $(e, b, r_i, f_b) \in \mathcal{R}$, $b \leadsto (a_i, i)$ if:
  1. $i \in r_b$ and $a_i \in en_i(\hat{s}_i)$ (i.e. b resets i, and a_i is available in $\hat{s}_i$); or
  2. $e = (b_1, \ldots, b_n)$ and $(a_i, b_i) \in C_i$ (i.e. performing b means component i performs b_i, which enables a_i).

4 Implementing Stubborn Sets

In the previous section we showed how a dependency graph can be constructed for a supercombinator, and also proved that a subset of a dependency graph, known as a *result set*, is a stubborn set. In this section, we consider how to actually compute a result set from a dependency graph.

In order to achieve as much reduction as possible, it appears to be desirable to compute a stubborn set with as few enabled actions as possible. However, not only is this problem known to be NP-complete [17], but it is also not guaranteed to yield the best overall reduction. Clearly, if one stubborn set reduction yields a subset of another reduction, the first also results in a reduced system with a subset of the latter's states. We instead give approximation algorithms, one of which is guaranteed to give subset-minimal stubborn sets. We then explain how they can be efficiently implemented in practice, which is challenging.

4.1 Deletion Algorithm

The first algorithm we consider is an adaptation of the well-known *deletion algorithm* [13, 18]. This is a method for computing a result set of the dependency graph by progressively pruning a set. It is, essentially, an optimised least-fixed point calculation. The algorithm is guaranteed to give a subset-minimal result in the sense that no proper subset can be a result set, but its weakness is complexity: it is cubic in the number of actions and guards.

The algorithm, shown in Algorithm 1, takes a dependency graph $(X, Y, Z, \rightsquigarrow, \rightsquigarrow_W)$. It maintains two sets: $\mathcal{K}$ which initially equals X, and $\mathcal{N}$ which initially contains $X \cup Y \cup Z$. An iteration consists of a recursive operation called *deletion* of one of the elements in X. Between iterations, the algorithm maintains the following invariants:

- $\mathcal{K}$ contains enabled rules that are strongly closed with respect to $\mathcal{K} \cup \mathcal{N}$.
- $\mathcal{N}$ consists of enabled rules nodes that are weakly closed, disabled rule nodes that have a guard predecessor, and guards that have all of their predecessors.

The invariants guarantee that if $\mathcal{K} \neq \{\}$ then $\mathcal{K} \cup \mathcal{N}$ is a result set (cf. Definition 10 (1)). When deleting a node, anything that violates the definition of a result set is removed in order to maintain the invariants.

Theorem 15. Given a dependency graph $G \triangleq (X, Y, Z, \rightsquigarrow, \rightsquigarrow_W)$, the set left after deletion of every node of X, i.e. $\mathcal{T} = \mathcal{K} \cup \mathcal{N}$, is a result set of G. Further, no $\mathcal{T}' \subset \mathcal{T}$ is a result set of G.

Implementation. Efficiently implementing the algorithm is a challenge. We outline several details that were required to obtain acceptable performance.

The algorithm requires a representation of the dependency graph to be constructed in each state. Dynamically constructing a graph is clearly inefficient, and thus we statically construct a *global dependency graph* for the LTS. Any

```
 1  function Stubborn₁(s)
 2      K, N = X, X ∪ Y ∪ Z
 3      forall the b ∈ X do
 4          K', N' = Delete(K, N, b)
 5          if K' ≠ {} then  K, N = K', N'
 6      return N ∪ K
 7  function Delete(K, N, b)
 8      K, N = K \ {b}, N \ {b}
 9      if b ∈ Σ then
10          forall the a ∈ K : a ⤳ b do
11              K = K \ {a}
12              if a ∉ N then  K, N = Delete(K, N, a)
13          forall the a : a ∈ N ∩ X ∧ a ⤳_w b do
14              N = N \ {a}
15              if a ∉ K then  K, N = Delete(K, N, a)
16          forall the c : c ∈ Z ∩ N ∧ b ⤳ c do
17              K, N = Delete(K, N, c)
18      if b ∈ Z then
19          forall the a : a ∈ Y ∩ N ∧ b ⤳ a do
20              if {c ∈ Z | c ⤳ a} ∩ N = {} then  K, N = Delete(K, N, a)
21      return K, N
```

Algorithm 1. The *deletion* algorithm for finding stubborn sets.

dependency graph of the LTS is a subgraph of the global dependency graph, and can be obtained simply by selecting a subset of the guard vertices. This is a straightforward adaptation of Theorem 14.

Given a global dependency graph, instantiating it in each state requires the rule nodes to be partitioned into X and Y, and the correct guard nodes to be enabled. The latter can be expensive, and therefore we precompute for each state of each component the set of component event guards that are enabled. This reduces the computation of the enabled guards to a union operation.

Another challenge with dependency graphs concerns is that they are often very large, making traversal of the graph prohibitively expensive. To solve this we present two strategies. Firstly, we consider component event guards.

Definition 16. Let $(S, \Sigma, \Delta, \hat{s})$ be a LTS and let $a, b \in \Sigma$. a and b are *always co-enabled* iff for all $s \in S$, $s \xrightarrow{a}$ iff $s \xrightarrow{b}$.

If (a, i) and (b, i) are guard nodes such that a and b are always co-enabled in component i, they have exactly the same neighbours in any dependency graph. This means that the dependency graph can be factored by co-enabled guards, with an arbitrary representative picked for each equivalence class. In practice, CSP scripts produce components with large numbers of always co-enabled events.

The second size optimisation considers cliques of rules (i.e. sets of rules where each rule strongly conflicts with each other rule). Cliques are interesting, because when running the deletion algorithm, if a rule node is deleted (i.e. it is no longer

```
1  function Stubborn₂(s)
2      W = {a} for some a ∈ X
3      S = {}
4      while W ≠ {} do
5          S = S ∪ {a} for some a ∈ W
6          W = W \ a
7          if a ∈ X then
8              W = W ∪ {b | a ⤳ b}
9              or W = W ∪ {b | a ⤳_W b}
10         if a ∈ Y then
11             W = W ∪ {c} for some c ∈ Z such that c ⤳ a
12             if a ∈ Z then  W = W ∪ {b | b ⤳ a}
13     return S
```

Algorithm 2. The *closure* algorithm for finding stubborn sets

in $\mathcal{K} \cup \mathcal{N}$), then every other node in the clique must be removed from $\mathcal{K}$ since it is no longer strongly closed. Treating cliques as a whole, rather than traversing all edges, is advantageous since cliques contain quadratically many edges.

The other notable optimisation is the data structure used for representing $\mathcal{K}$ and $\mathcal{N}$. This is a set representation that supports $O(1)$ operations to: query membership, insert/delete, and backtrack to the last snapshot. This data structure takes advantage of the fact that all items are integers in a small range by maintaining an array that contains all the integers, along with an offset specifying the border between elements in and out of the set. Thus, backtracking can be done by simply resetting the border to its old value.

4.2 Iterative Algorithm

The second algorithm we consider is known as the *iterative algorithm* and, in contrast to the deletion algorithm, builds a result set from a single *seed*. The algorithm is linear time, but it is nondeterministic and there is no guarantee whatsoever about the size of the resulting set, unlike with the deletion algorithm.

The algorithm, shown in Algorithm 2, works as follows. A *work set* $\mathcal{W}$ is initialised with a nondeterministically chosen node from X. The algorithm proceeds to build the set by adding nodes that are required in order to make the set a result set. For example, if an enabled rule node is added then either all weakly or all strongly conflicting rule nodes must be added (which is another nondeterministic choice). In our implementation, this is resolved by choosing the set that contains the fewest nodes still outside the set; one of the choices must be the strong set. If a disabled rule node is added, then one of its guards must be added. This is the third nondeterministic choice. In our implementation we select the guard that serves as the guard for as many disabled rule nodes in the set as possible. The process ends when no new nodes need to be added.

Theorem 17. Given a dependency graph $G \cong (X, Y, Z, \leadsto, \leadsto_W)$, the set constructed is a result set of G providing one nodes from X is strongly closed.

5   Preserving CSP Models

The theory and methods explored thus far preserve deadlocks. In order to preserve the results of refinement checks, additional constraints on the stubborn set are required. A refinement assertion $S \sqsubseteq_M I$ asserts that every behaviour of I in the denotational model M is also a behaviour of the specification S. FDR supports three denotational models: the traces, failures, and failures-divergences models. In this section we discuss how to extend the existing stubborn set definition to preserve the denotational value of a process.

Definition 2 assumed supercombinator rules have unique action labels (from Σ). To discuss CSP denotational models, we need to map actions from Σ to *events*, non-injectively, as multiple supercombinator actions may generate the same event. Thus, let Σ_E be a set of *events* such that $\tau \notin \Sigma_E$ and $L = (S, \Sigma, \Delta, \hat{s})$ be a LTS. A function $f : \Sigma \rightarrow \Sigma_E \cup \{\tau\}$ is called a *naming function* for L. The naming function induces a partition of Σ into Σ_V and Σ_I, such that $\Sigma_I = \{a \in \Sigma \mid f(a) = \tau\}$ (i.e. Σ_I and Σ_V contain *invisible* and *visible* actions, respectively).

5.1   The Traces Model

The *traces* model associates each process with the set of finite linear sequences of visible events it can perform. Preserving all traces of a process [10] requires the use of *non-local* information that is unavailable during a breadth-first search. FDR uses a breadth-first search as it allows for an extremely time and space efficient implementation [4]. We instead utilise *watchdogs* [11], which allow trace checks to be converted into deadlock checks (similarly to [16]).

To check if $S \sqsubseteq_T I$, FDR converts S to a watchdog that monitors I for trace violations. This watchdog *barks* iff I's behaviour deviates from S. We define:

$$I' \mathrel{\widehat{=}} \left(I \underset{\Sigma_E \setminus \{bark\}}{\|} Watchdog(S) \right) \Theta_{\{bark\}} STOP$$

I' runs I in parallel with the watchdog, synchronising on all events that I can perform and, if the watchdog barks, I' deadlocks ($P \Theta_S Q$ behaves like P until P performs an event in S, at which point it behaves like Q). Further, $Watchdog(S)$ is defined such that I' deadlocks iff the watchdog has barked.

I' can be utilised in several ways to verify if $S \sqsubseteq_T I$. One option is to check if I' is deadlock free. This is correct since I' deadlocks iff I' performs $bark$, which is true iff I can perform a trace that is disallowed by S.

The problem with checking if I' is deadlock free is that any counterexample is of the form $tr' = tr^\frown \langle bark \rangle$ (i.e. I' deadlocks after tr') where tr is a counterexample to $S \sqsubseteq_T I$. As FDR performs a breadth-first search, this delays detection of the error until the next level of the search, increasing the search cost.

Instead, we check if $S \sqsubseteq_T I'$. If $S \sqsubseteq_T I$, then I' will not perform $bark$, and thus $S \sqsubseteq_T I'$. Otherwise, if $S \not\sqsubseteq_T I$, then there is some trace $tr \in traces(I) \setminus traces(S)$. Hence, I' will also be able to perform tr (and then perform $bark$ before deadlocking), and thus $S \not\sqsubseteq_T I'$. Further, when applying partial-order reduction to I', it is sufficient to preserve deadlocks of I' since any trace violation leads to a deadlock. This means that preserving deadlocks preserves at least one violating trace, but not necessarily all violating traces (partial-order reduction preserves the reachability of deadlock states, but not all unique paths to them).

Note that the above construction has not required us to address the ignoring problem with any global rules (unlike the majority of other techniques). Further, checking if $S \sqsubseteq_T I'$ imposes essentially no overhead versus verifying if $S \sqsubseteq_T I$.

5.2   Failures and Divergences

The *failures* model associates each process P with a set of pairs (tr, X) that indicate that after P performs tr it can reach a *stable* state (i.e. a state τ is unavailable) in which all events in X are refused. The *failures-divergences model* associates each process not only with its failures, but also a set of traces on which it can *diverge* by performing an infinite sequence of events from Σ_I.

Neither failures nor divergences are preserved by D1 and D2. [11] also defines a *failures watchdog* that can be used to monitor a process for failures violations, but unfortunately the construction is not efficient (particularly with deterministic specification). Thus, we instead require the stubborn set reduction function (Definition 4) to also satisfy the following properties from [10]:

I1. If $\Sigma_I \cap en(s) \neq \{\}$ then there is some $a \in \Sigma_I \cap T(s)$ that is a key action at s.
V2. For each $s \in S$, if $en(s) \cap T(s) \cap \Sigma_V \neq \{\}$, then $\Sigma_V \subseteq T(s)$.

The above are sufficient to preserve the failures and divergences of a process.

V2 requires that either no visible actions are stubborn, or all visible actions are. This intuitively makes sense: if an arbitrary subset of the visible actions were included, the failures of the resulting LTS could be different.

I1 requires that at least one single invisible action is key, if there is at least a single invisible action available. This ensures divergences are preserved: without it, there would be no guarantee that any invisible action would be preserved in a divergent state.

It is tempting to think that only invisible actions that are part of a divergence need to be preserved. This is actually only true when *strong* stubborn sets are being used, rather than weak stubborn sets. If an unstable state (i.e. a state with an invisible action) has all of its invisible actions elided, the state becomes stable, essentially introducing new failures which may well not be part of the specification. In the case of strong stubborn sets, this is not problematic, because the strong stubborn set properties guarantee that the current state has the same failures as any stable state that can be reached by following invisible actions, and therefore no new failures are introduced. However, when weak stubborn sets are used, this guarantee is removed. Hence, only preserving invisible actions that are part of a divergence is not sufficient.

The two algorithms of Section 4 can be efficiently altered to enforce V2. The deletion algorithm is altered so that as soon as a single visible action is deleted, all other visible actions are deleted. The iterative algorithm inserts all visible actions as soon as a single visible action is inserted. They can also be modified to enforce I1. The deletion algorithm can be modified so that as soon as the last

Table 1. Experimental results comparing the performance of the algorithms ('Normal' means partial-order reduction is deactivated). $|S|$ is the number of states, $|\Delta|$ is the number of transitions, T is the time (in seconds), and K, M, and B indicate 10^3, 10^6, and 10^9 respectively.

Input File	Normal			Deletion			Iterative		
	$|S|$	$|\Delta|$	$T(s)$	$|S|$	$|\Delta|$	$T(s)$	$|S|$	$|\Delta|$	$T(s)$
chain	100M	243M	11	1M	2M	1	73	82	< 1
ddb	26M	117M	33	8M	20M	36	6M	15M	15
inv	22M	221M	178	85K	126K	< 1	17M	169M	276
nspk	7M	114M	3	7K	25K	0.06	126K	879K	0.3
phils	915M	9,253M	338	96	118	< 1	819	1,140	< 1
swp	24M	57M	20	9M	22M	16	7M	16M	14
tokring	786M	2,319M	289	20M	22M	169	31M	35M	82
virtroute	244M	3,515M	107	3M	7M	4	589K	1M	< 1
Average	—	—	—	-89 %	-92 %	-63 %	-81 %	-83 %	-57 %

action from $\Sigma_I \cap K$ is deleted, it backtracks, whilst the iterative algorithm can be modified so that the initial selection of a key action selects one from Σ_I if one is available.

6   Experiments

To measure the effectiveness of partial-order reduction, we took the example files accompanying [3], and ran each of the 348 checks both with and without partial-order reduction. In total, when using the deletion algorithm, 17 % of assertions had some reduction, whilst 13 % achieved more than a 20 % reduction. This also illustrated the value of weak stubborn sets: with strong stubborn sets, only 11 % achieved more than a 20 % reduction, and some no longer achieved any reduction.

Table 1 gives the results of running partial-order reduction on specific examples and illustrates the differences between the algorithms. As expected, the deletion algorithm is often slower than the iterative algorithm. The iterative algorithm sometimes achieves more reduction than the deletion algorithm. This illustrates a problem with the deletion algorithm: whilst the result is subset minimal, it is not always minimal. When the experiments from Table 1 were repeated using strong stubborn sets, the number of states in swp doubled, and for phils increased by a factor of 10.

The overhead of computing stubborn sets causes FDR to visit states 2—5 times slower (i.e. between 50 %-85 % of time is spent in the partial-order reduction code). However, in cases where partial-order reduction achieves some reduction (such as those in Table 1), the reduction in the number of states almost always exceeds this factor, and thus the overall time to check an assertion is reduced. This is observed in Table 1 where the average time decreased by 63 % despite slower visiting rates. As FDR's memory usage is proportional to the number of states visited, memory requirements decreased by 90 %, on average.

Existing Reductions. FDR has long supported a simple form of partial-order reduction, known as chase. chase(P) behaves like P, except that whenever *P* offers a τ, chase(P) automatically selects an arbitrary τ and proceeds. This is only sound when *P* is deterministic. nspk exploits this to dramatically cut the state space. In our testing, we found that the version of nspk using partial-order reduction visited the same number of states in the same time as the version with chase, indicating that our technique can spot the τ-commutativity.

FDR also supports another method of visiting a subset of the states known as *compression* [19]. Compressing a LTS produces another LTS that is semantically equivalent, but is, hopefully, smaller. FDR has many different methods of compressing LTSs, including bisimulation-based techniques [20], in addition to CSP-specific compressions such as diamond, and normal. Compression is generally effective on processes that have subprocesses with complex internal state spaces that are externally very simple. Partial-order reduction instead reduces interleaving of actions. Thus, whilst it is able to reduce systems even where the external interface is highly complex, it is not able to recognise that state is redundant. They are somewhat incomparable in that regard: there are examples on which partial-order reduction works better than compression (e.g. tokring), and also conversely (e.g. SVA scripts [21]). This makes partial-order reduction complementary to compression, rather than a replacement. Indeed, there should be scripts where using partial-order reduction on compressed machines yields better reduction than using just one of the techniques.

7   Conclusions

We have shown how to efficiently implement partial-order reduction for FDR. We have extended existing theory to develop a general framework in which partial-order reduction can be expressed, and have shown how this can be used to achieve compositional partial-order reduction for supercombinators. Further, we have shown how this partial-order reduction can be efficiently implemented, and have developed new techniques for preserving the denotational value of processes that can be more efficiently implemented than previous approaches.

The partial-order reduction outlined in this paper is available in FDR 3.2, and is fully compatible with all of the other FDR3-enhancements, including the shared-memory [4] and cluster [22] refinement-checkers.

The experiments of Section 6 demonstrated that the three different algorithms can give different quantities of reduction on different problems. Therefore, we intend to consider if an algorithm that combines the three approaches can be developed. It would also be interesting to consider methods of combining partial-order reduction and compression: given that they reduce different aspects of problems, there may be a benefit to combining them. The experiments of Section 6 also revealed that partial-order reduction does not always work. It would be very useful to develop a technique to automatically determine if partial-order reduction will be effective.

The improvements in this paper are incorporated into FDR3 which is available from https://www.cs.ox.ac.uk/projects/fdr/. FDR3 is free for personal or academic use, whilst commercial use requires a licence.

Acknowledgments. Research into FDR3 has been partially sponsored by DARPA under agreement number FA8750-12-2-0247. We are grateful to the anonymous reviewers for their helpful comments.

References

1. Hoare, C.A.R.: Communicating Sequential Processes. Prentice-Hall (1985)
2. Roscoe, A.: The Theory and Practice of Concurrency. Prentice Hall (1997)
3. Roscoe, A.: Understanding Concurrent Systems (2010)
4. Gibson-Robinson, T., Armstrong, P., Boulgakov, A., Roscoe, A.W.: FDR3 — A modern refinement checker for CSP. In: Ábrahám, E., Havelund, K. (eds.) TACAS 2014 (ETAPS). LNCS, vol. 8413, pp. 187–201. Springer, Heidelberg (2014)
5. University of Oxford, Failures-Divergence Refinement–FDR 3 User Manual (2014). https://www.cs.ox.ac.uk/projects/fdr/manual/
6. Valmari, A.: Stubborn sets for reduced state space generation. In: Rozenberg, G. (ed.) Advances in Petri Nets 1990. LNCS, vol. 483, pp. 491–515. Springer, Heidelberg (1991)
7. Peled, D.: All from one, one for all: on model checking using representatives. In: Courcoubetis, C. (ed.) Computer Aided Verification (CAV). LNCS, vol. 697, pp. 409–423. Springer, Heidelberg (1993)
8. Godefroid, P.: Partial-Order Methods for the Verification of Concurrent Systems: An Approach to the State-Explosion Problem (1996)
9. Hansen, H., Wang, X.: Compositional analysis for weak stubborn sets. In: Application of Concurrency to System Design (ACSD) (2011)
10. Valmari, A.: Stubborn set methods for process algebras. In: Proceedings of the DIMACS Workshop on Partial Order Methods in Verification (1997)
11. Goldsmith, M., Moffat, N., Roscoe, A.W., Whitworth, T., Zakiuddin, I.: Watchdog transformations for property-oriented model-checking. In: Araki, K., Gnesi, S., Mandrioli, D. (eds.) FME 2003. LNCS, vol. 2805, pp. 600–616. Springer, Heidelberg (2003)
12. Valmari, A., Hansen, H.: Can stubborn sets be optimal?. Fundamenta Informaticae **113**(3) (2011)
13. Varpaaniemi, K.: On the Stubborn Set Method in Reduced State Space Generation. PhD thesis, Helsinki University of Technology (1998)
14. Laarman, A., Pater, E., van de Pol, J., Weber, M.: Guard-based partial-order reduction. In: Bartocci, E., Ramakrishnan, C.R. (eds.) SPIN 2013. LNCS, vol. 7976, pp. 227–245. Springer, Heidelberg (2013)
15. Evangelista, S., Pajault, C.: Solving the ignoring problem for partial order reduction. International Journal on Software Tools for Technology Transfer **12**(2) (2010)
16. Godefroid, P., Wolper, P.: Using partial orders for the efficient verification of deadlock freedom and safety properties. In: Larsen, K.G., Skou, A. (eds.) CAV 1991. LNCS, vol. 575, pp. 332–342. Springer, Heidelberg (1992)
17. Varpaaniemi, K.: Minimizing the number of successor states in the stubborn set method. Fundamenta Informaticae **51**(1) (2002)
18. Valmari, A.: State space generation: Efficiency and practicality. PhD thesis, Tampere University of Technology (1988)

19. Roscoe, A.W., Gardiner, P., Goldsmith, M., Hulance, J., Jackson, D., Scattergood, J.: Hierarchical compression for model-checking CSP or how to check 10^{20} dining philosophers for deadlock. In: Brinksma, E., Steffen, B., Cleaveland, W.R., Larsen, K.G., Margaria, T. (eds.) TACAS 1995. LNCS, vol. 1019, pp. 133–152. Springer, Heidelberg (1995)
20. Boulgakov, A., Gibson-Robinson, T., Roscoe, A.W.: Computing maximal bisimulations. In: Merz, S., Pang, J. (eds.) ICFEM 2014. LNCS, vol. 8829, pp. 11–26. Springer, Heidelberg (2014)
21. Roscoe, A.W., Hopkins, D.: SVA, a tool for analysing shared-variable programs. In: AVoCS (2007)
22. Gibson-Robinson, T., Roscoe, A.W.: FDR into the cloud. In Communicating Process Architectures (2014)

A Little Language for Testing

Alex Groce[✉] and Jervis Pinto

School of Electrical Engineering and Computer Science,
Oregon State University, Corvallis, OR, USA
agroce@gmail.com

Abstract. The difficulty of writing test harnesses is a major obstacle
to the adoption of automated testing and model checking. Languages
designed for harness definition are usually tied to a particular tool and
unfamiliar to programmers; moreover, such languages can limit expressiveness. Writing a harness directly in the language of the software under
test (SUT) makes it hard to change testing algorithms, offers no support
for the common testing idioms, and tends to produce repetitive, hard-
to-read code. This makes harness generation a natural fit for the use of
an unusual kind of domain-specific language (DSL). This paper defines a
template scripting testing language, TSTL, and shows how it can be used
to produce succinct, readable definitions of state spaces. The concepts
underlying TSTL are demonstrated in Python but are not tied to it.

1 Introduction

Building a test harness is an often irksome task many users of formal methods or
automated testing face from time to time [12,18]. The difficulty of harness generation is one reason for the limited adoption of sophisticated testing and model
checking by the typical developer who writes unit tests. This is unfortunate, as
even simple random testing can often uncover subtle faults.

The "natural" way to write a test harness is as code in the language of the
Software Under Test (SUT). This is obviously how most unit tests are written,
as witnessed by the proliferation of tools like JUnit [3] and its imitators (e.g.,
PyUnit, HUnit, etc.). It is also how many industrial-strength random testing
systems are written [15,17]. A KLEE "test harness" [6] for symbolic execution is
written in C, with a few additional constructs to indicate which values are symbolic. This approach is common in model checking as well: e.g., Java Pathfinder
[2,28] can easily be seen as offering a way to define a state space using Java
itself as the modeling language, and CBMC [1,24] performs a similar function
in C, using SAT/SMT-based bounded model checking instead of explicit-state
execution. JPF in particular has shown how writing a harness in the SUT's own
language can make it easy to perform "apples to apples" comparisons of various
testing/model checking strategies [29].

Unfortunately, writing test harnesses this way is a highly repetitive and error-
prone programming task, with many conceptual "code clones" (e.g. Figure 1). A
user faces difficult choices in constructing such a harness. For example, the way

© Springer International Publishing Switzerland 2015
K. Havelund et al. (Eds.): NFM 2015, LNCS 9058, pp. 204–218, 2015.
DOI: 10.1007/978-3-319-17524-9_15

```
op = choice(operations);
val1 = choice(values);
val2 = choice(values);
switch (op) {
case op1:  if (guard1)
                call1(val1);
           break;
case op2:  if (guard2)
                call2(val1,val2);
           break;
case op3:  if (guard3)
                call3(val1,val3);
           break;
```

Fig. 1. A test harness in the SUT language

```
heap()                    : returns a new heap
heap.insert(key,val)      : inserts a key with value, returning ref
heap.union(heap)          : merges two heaps
heap.extractMin()         : extracts the minimum
ref.delete()              : given a reference to a node, deletes it
ref.decreaseKey(key)      : decreases the key of ref's node
```

Fig. 2. A binomial heap to test

guards and choices are interleaved means that the state-space will be pointlessly expanded to include many action and value choices that don't produce any useful behavior. This harness also always assigns val2 even though call1 only uses val1, to avoid having to repeat the choice code for calls 2 and 3. Moreover, this harness is possibly sub-optimal for a method such as random testing, where the lack of any memory for previously chosen values can make it hard to exercise code behaviors that rely on providing the same arguments to multiple method calls (e.g., insert and delete for container classes). The construction of a harness becomes even more complex in realistic cases, where the tested behaviors involve building up complex types as inputs to method calls, rather than simple integer choices. For example, consider the problem of testing or model checking a binomial heap that supports several operations, defined in Figure 2. Such a harness must manage the creation and storage of values of multiple types, including heaps and references. Moreover, because building up heaps and references is complicated, they cannot simply be produced on each iteration, but must be remembered. As the interactions of multiple heaps (via union) and references into a heap are the source of all interesting behavior, the harness needs to decide how many heaps and references to store. The code quickly becomes hard to read, hard to maintain, and hard to debug. In some cases [15] the code for a sophisticated test harness approaches the SUT in complexity and even size! The code's structure also tends to lock in many choices (such as how to handle storing heaps and references) that would ideally be configurable.

The definition of a harness also tends to be intimately tied to a single tool, with the only testing strategies available being those provided by that tool. Writing novel testing strategies in even such an extensible platform as Java Pathfinder is hardly a task for the non-expert. The harness in Figure 1 may support random testing and some form of model checking, if it is written in Java and can use JPF or a library for adaptation-based testing [14]. Such a harness cannot support model checking or any sophisticated strategy without being re-written if it is in a language like Python without verification tool support.

What the user really wants is to simply provide the information in Figure 2, some configuration details (e.g., how many refs to keep around), and some information on which testing method to use (e.g., model checking, random test-ing, machine-learning based approaches). Some automated testing tools for Java [8,27] take a variation on this approach, automatically extracting the signatures of methods from source code and testing them. Unfortunately, completely auto-matic extraction often fails to handle the subtle details of harness construction, such as defining guards for some operations, or temporal constraints between API calls that are not detectable by simple exception behavior. The user wants declarative harnesses, but often needs to program the details of a harness.

1.1 Domain Specific Languages for Testing

The properties of the problem at hand suggest the use of a *domain-specific language* (DSL) [13]. DSLs [7] provide abstractions and notations to support a particular programming domain. The use of DSLs is a formalization of the long-standing approach of using "little languages" in computer science, as memorably advocated by Jon Bentley in one of his famous Programming Pearls columns [5] and exemplified in such system designs as UNIX. DSLs typically come in two forms: *external* and *internal*. An external DSL is a stand-alone language, with its own syntax. An internal DSL, also known as a domain-specific embedded language (DSEL), is hosted in a full-featured programming language, restricting it to the syntax (and semantics) of that language. Many attempts to define harnesses can be seen as internal DSLs [6,10,14,24,28]. Neither of these choices is quite right for harness definition. Simply adding operations for nondeterministic choice, as is done in most cases, still leaves most of the tedious work of harness definition to the user, and makes changing testing approaches difficult at best. With an external DSL, the user must learn a new language, and the easier it is to learn, the less likely it is to support the full range of features needed.

A novel approach is taken in recent versions of the SPIN model checker [23]. Version 4.0 of SPIN [21] made use of SPIN's nature as a tool that *outputs a C program* to allow users to include calls to the C language in their PROMELA models. The ability to directly call C code makes it much easier to model check large, complex C programs [15,22]. C serves as a "DSEL" for SPIN, except that, rather than having a domain-specific language inside a general-purpose one, here the domain-specific language hosts a general-purpose language. A similar embedding is used in where clauses of the LogScope language for testing Mars Science Laboratory software [16]. We adopt this approach: embed a general-purpose language (for expressiveness) in a DSL (for concision and ease-of-use).

```
@import bh
pool: %INT% 4
pool: %HEAP% 3
pool: %REF% 4
%INT%:=%[1..20]%
%HEAP%:=bh.heap()
%REF%:=%HEAP%.insert(%INT%,%INT%)
%HEAP%.insert(%INT%,%INT%)
%HEAP%.union(%HEAP%)
%HEAP%.extractMin()
%REF%.delete()
%REF%.decreaseKey(%INT%)
```

Fig. 3. A simple harness definition for a binomial heap

1.2   Template Scripting

In previous discussions, a harness has been thought of as imperative code that tests a system, even when the underlying use is more declarative, as in CBMC, or as a purely declarative model stating the available test operations, in which case the harness is often hidden from the user and generated by a tool. In this paper, we propose thinking of a harness as a *declaration of the possible actions the SUT can take*, but where these actions are *defined in the language of the SUT itself, with the full power of the programming language to define guards, perform pre-processing, and implement oracles in an imperative fashion.* Our particular approach is based on what we call *template scripting.*

The *template* aspect is based on the fact that our method proceeds by processing a harness definition file to output code in the SUT's language for a test harness, much like SPIN. The harness description file consists of fragments of code in the SUT language that are expanded, via code-generation, into executable source code. The tool that outputs code basically defines a *template* for test harnesses in a programming language, and the harness definition tells the tool how to instantiate that template. Rather than generating a testing tool, our method outputs *a class defining a search space.* The *scripting* aspect simply means that our language is meant to be very lightweight, and assumes a host language without a rigorous type system (e.g. Python) or with effective type-inference (e.g. Scala), making minimal demands on the user. The design of the language also relies on the very-high-level nature of code in scripting languages, making the harness concise but expressive, and making "one-liners" of action definition possible.

Figure 3 shows a complete harness definition for the binomial heap class defined in Figure 2. The example is easily understood by splitting it into three sections. First, the single line proceeded by an "@" is raw Python, inserted into the output harness with no modification in most cases. This section can be used not only to import the SUT's code, but to define functions to be used in the body of the harness, as we will see below. Second, the lines beginning with **pool:** define the "pool" [4,10,27] of values that will be used during testing. In model checking terms, these store the state of the SUT. There is no type information here, because the template approach simply assumes the type system of the host language, but in an informal sense each pool value typically represents its own

```
import bh as b
class t(object):
    def act0(self):
        self.p_INT[0]=1
        self.p_INT_used[0]=False
    def guard0(self):
        return (self.p_INT_used[0])
...
    def act87(self):
        self.p_REF[0]=self.p_HEAP[0].insert(self.p_INT[1],self.p_INT[0])
        self.p_INT_used[1]=True
        self.p_INT_used[0]=True
        self.p_REF_used[0]=False
        self.p_HEAP_used[0]=True
    def guard87(self):
        return (self.p_INT[1] != None) and (self.p_INT[0] != None) and
            (self.p_REF_used[0]) and (self.p_HEAP[0] != None)
...
        self.actions.append((r"self.p_INT[0]=1",self.guard0,self.act0))
```

Fig. 4. Fragments of Python code for binomial heap harness

type in the template language, as shown by its usage below (a pool value will correspond to inputs of a particular type to method calls, in the most trivial instance, but can also be used to encode more fine-grained type distinctions not present in the host language). The numbers indicate how many values of a given pool "type" are needed. Here, at least two INTs are needed, unless both values provided to insert should always be the same. Similarly, there need to be at least two HEAPs if union is to be tested effectively. Because the performance of random testing and some learning algorithms depends heavily on pool sizes, we want to make it easy to experiment with them.

Finally, the remainder of the harness definition simply gives possible actions, one on each line. Each line is expanded into Python code for 1) the actual test action represented and 2) a guard that determines if that action is enabled, as shown in Figure 4. The functions for actions and guards are then added to a list that stores all possible SUT actions, with no remaining nondeterminism unless the SUT provides it. Nondeterminism is controlled by choosing which actions (whose guards are currently satisfied) to execute. Even in the absence of user-defined guards, some guards are automatically generated. First, no *uses* of a pool value are allowed until that value has been assigned (the generated harness initializes pool values as None, a special Python value). Second, no pool value can be assigned to unless it is either uninitialized or has been *used* at least once. This is critical to avoid the potential for some test strategies (such as random testing) to repeatedly perform useless assignments to values used in the actual testing (e.g., INT[1] = 1 followed immediately by INT[1] = 2. Figure 5 shows an example of a test that can be generated by this harness. Note that assigning anything to INT[3], REF[0] or REF[1] is not valid after the final action of the test, as these pool values have been assigned but not used.

```
self.p_INT[1]=9
self.p_INT[2]=1
self.p_INT[0]=18
self.p_HEAP[0]=b.heap()
self.p_REF[2]=self.p_HEAP[0].insert(self.p_INT[0],self.p_INT[2])
self.p_INT[3]=17
self.p_INT[0]=18
self.p_REF[0]=self.p_HEAP[0].insert(self.p_INT[0],self.p_INT[1])
self.p_REF[0].decreaseKey(self.p_INT[1])
self.p_INT[1]=19
self.p_REF[1]=self.p_HEAP[0].insert(self.p_INT[0],self.p_INT[1])
self.p_REF[0]=self.p_HEAP[0].insert(self.p_INT[0],self.p_INT[1])
self.p_HEAP[1]=b.heap()
self.p_HEAP[1].union(self.p_HEAP[0])
```

Fig. 5. A valid action sequence (test) for the binomial heap harness

```
<template> ::= <template-line> EOL <template> | EOF
<template-line> ::= <raw> | <pool> | <property> | <init> |
                    <feature> | <reference> | <compare> | <action>
<raw> ::= @ <raw-code>
<pool> ::= pool: %<ID>% <INT> [REF]
<property> ::= property: <simple-code>
<init> ::= init: <simple-code>
<feature> ::= feature: <regexp>
<reference> ::= reference: <regexp> ==> <text>
<compare> ::= compare: <regexp>
<action> ::= <text> | <lhs> := <rhs> | guardedFN(<simple-code>)
<raw-code> ::= <text> | def guardedFN(<text>) | %COMMIT%
<lhs> ::= <simple-code>
<rhs> ::= <simple-code>
<simple-code> ::= <text> | <simple-code> <ID-use> <simple-code> |
                  <simple-code> <range> <simple-code>
<ID-use> ::= %<ID>% | ~%<ID>%
<range> ::= %|INT..INT]%
```

Fig. 6. The Template Scripting Testing Language in Pseudo-BNF

2   The Template Scripting Testing Language (TSTL)

Figure 6 shows a BNF-style specification of the Template Scripting Testing Language (TSTL). Processing a harness definition involves iterating through the lines in the file and performing a set of transformations that result in an output file that defines a class in the target language (Python in our current implementation). This class itself performs no testing; it instead defines an interface to a definition of the available actions of the SUT that any testing algorithm can use, shown in Table 1.[1] The methods in this interface are not defined by the user, but automatically generated by the TSTL "compilation." The basic transformation algorithm is relatively simple (our implementation for Python is less than 1,000 lines of code):

1. Output the `<raw>` Python code, transforming guarded functions into expanded Python code as described in Section 2.2.

---

[1] This is not the entire set of methods TSTL compilation automatically generates: there are also methods for swarm testing [20], generalized delta-debugging [11,30], code coverage, and other common testing needs.

Table 1. SUT Class Methods

Method	Type	Purpose
restart	()→()	resets pools, executes <init> code
actions	()→[(str,()→bool,()→())]	returns a list of all possible actions
enabled	()→[(str,()→bool,()→())]	returns actions with True guard
check	()→bool	executes <property> assertions
state	()→STATE	returns deep copy of pool values
replay	[(str,()→bool,()→())] → bool	replays a test, returns whether it failed
backtrack	STATE→()	sets pools to STATE

2. Collect the set of pool values, properties, initialization code, features, references, and comparisons.
3. Replace each pool ID in actions and properties with the pool ID plus a <range> from 0 to the pool size - 1.
4. Recursively expand each action and property range, creating copies with each value in the range instantiated. At this point all actions should be deterministic[2]
5. Collect assignments and uses from actions; assignments are IDs on the lhs of a :=; uses are IDs appearing in an action, such that ID is not an assignment or marked with a ~.
6. Generate guards for each action: first, ensure no values are used that have no value; second, ensure no assignments to values that have a value that has not been used are made; third, add any guarded function calls as extra guards (see Section 2.2).
7. For any actions involving pools marked as ref, copy with reference.
8. Apply all transformations indicated by <reference> (text matching regexp is replaced by the given text), then add an assertion of equal return values for any transformed code that matches a <compare> regexp.
9. Perform any language-specific transformations.

Due to lack of space here, we cannot elaborate on every aspect of TSTL. Instead, we present some example uses to highlight salient features.

2.1   Oracles

TSTL handles test oracles in two ways. First, users can specify properties that the check method will automatically verify using assertion statements, expanded for each pool item involved. Figure 7 shows how properties are defined, in this case with quite trivial properties. Note that because raw Python can be used, and properties can call arbitrary Python code, it is easy to encode even complex specifications by defining a Python function that takes the pool values of interest as input and returns a Boolean, then adding it as a property. A second popular approach to the oracle problem is differential testing [25], also known as testing

---

[2] Assuming the SUT itself is determinstic.

```
@def guardedAppend(l,item,limit): @
if len(l) >= limit:
@    return False
@  %COMMIT%
@  l.append(item)
property: (len(%LIST%) < 10) or (6 not in %LIST%)
property: %VAL% != -1
pool: %LIST% 1
pool: %VAL% 1
%LIST% := []
guardedAppend(~%LIST%,%VAL%,10)
%VAL% := %[1..10]%
print %LIST%
```

Fig. 7. A toy bounded list generation example (`%COMMIT%` is expanded into a check for when the function is used as a guard)

```
@import avl
@import bintree
pool: %INT% 4
pool: %AVL% 1 REF
%INT%:=%[1..20]%
%AVL%:=AvlTree()
%AVL%.insert(%INT%)
%AVL%.delete(%INT%)
%AVL%.find(%INT%)
reference: AvlTree() ==> BinTree()
compare: find
```

Fig. 8. Using a reference as oracle

with a reference. TSTL supports this by making it easy to define how to transform actions on the SUT into actions on the reference, and when to compare values from calls to the SUT and reference. Figure 8 shows a simple example, where an AVL tree in Python is tested by comparing its behavior to a simple (unbalanced) binary tree implementation. All that is required to do this is 1) to mark the AVL pool as a **ref** pool, meaning it will have a copy that contains a reference implementation 2) to explain how to transform the call that initialized the AVL tree to initialize the binary tree and 3) to indicate that results from calling **find** on the AVL and reference should be compared. TSTL automatically generates the required code based on this information.

2.2 Guards and Function Calls

As Figure 7 shows, TSTL makes it simple to define functions and call them in actions. Obviously, some actions cannot be expressed as one line of code. In these cases, we expect that the user will define a function whose inputs can be any pool values, constants, etc. and perform more complex tasks. We exploit this feature to implement user-defined guards for actions easily. If a function is named **guardedFN**, where **FN** is a function name, TSTL will automatically add an additional parameter to the function definition when it generates a harness. This parameter indicates whether the call is to actually perform the action, or simply check if the action is enabled. The function definition should check the guard and return **False** if it is not satisfied. At the point where the user indicates that a "real" action is to follow (which typically modifies SUT state) the function definition should include a %COMMIT%, which will be replaced with code that checks for a speculative call and simply returns True without proceeding if the call is in a guard context. The translation of the relevant code from Figure 7 is shown in Figure 9, with a comment to indicate where the %COMMIT% was.

```
def guardedAppend(l,item,limit, SPECULATIVE_CALL = False):
  if len(l) >= limit:
    return False
  if SPECULATIVE_CALL: return True                              # /%COMMIT/%
  l.append(item)
...
  def act1(self):
      guardedAppend(self.p_LIST[0],self.p_VAL[0],10)
      self.p_VAL_used[0]=True
  def guard1(self):
      return (self.p_LIST[0] != None) and (self.p_VAL[0] != None)
          and (guardedAppend(self.p_LIST[0],self.p_VAL[0],10,True))
```

Fig. 9. User-defined guard example, Python code generated

2.3 Miscellaneous Notes on TSTL

In order to effectively test the SUT, it is often important to build up complex values before calling the code under test. Making every appearance of a pool element in an action a use, therefore allowing the value to be reset to its initial state can "suppress" [19] behaviors, even if it does not strictly prevent them. TSTL therefore allows the use of a ~ before a use of a pool ID, as shown in Figure 7 to indicate that a reference to a pool ID should not count as a use, it is simply building up a complex input. Another mitigation for suppression effects is provided by the <feature> definitions, which allow TSTL to support swarm testing [20]. Swarm testing is a random testing approach in which each test disables some randomly chosen API calls or grammar features, in order to better explore the state space of the system. A feature definition indicates that any action matching the regexp is considered an instance of a certain feature, and is disabled if that feature is disabled. TSTL has strong out-of-the-box support for a variety of testing algorithms, some state-of-the-art like swarm testing.

Finally, we note that TSTL is not restricted to API testing. Figure 10 demonstrates TSTL's support for encoding grammars for generating strings. It also provides an example of mixing range values and explicit values in assignment.

2.4 Output Language

The language and tool presented here are not inherently tied to any language. With trivial modifications, the harness maker could output Scala code instead of Python. In principle, C or Java could also serve as the base for the DSEL. In fact, it should be simple to output PROMELA models with embedded C, given a harness with C as the base language, though maintaining the "declarative"

```
@import sys
@import calculator as c
pool: %EXPR% 7
pool: %NUM% 5
%NUM% := '%[-100..100]%'
%NUM% := str(sys.maxint)
%NUM% := str(-sys.maxint - 1)
%EXPR% := %NUM%
~%EXPR% = '(' + ~%EXPR% + ')'
~%EXPR% = ~%EXPR% + '+' + ~%EXPR%
~%EXPR% = ~%EXPR% + '*' + ~%EXPR%
~%EXPR% = ~%EXPR% + '-' + ~%EXPR%
~%EXPR% = ~%EXPR% + '/' + ~%EXPR%
c.calculate(%EXPR%)
reference: c.calculate ==> eval
compare: calculate
```

Fig. 10. Harness for a simple calculator class

```
t = SUT.t()
for ntests in xrange(1,config.maxtests+1):
    t.restart()
    test = []
    for s in xrange(0,config.depth):
        (name,guard,act) = random.choice(t.enabled())
        test.append(name)
        act()
        if not t.check():
            print "FAILED TEST:", test
            sys.exit(1)
print ntests, ''SUCCESSFUL''
```

Fig. 11. A simple random tester

approach would make the PROMELA somewhat difficult to read (each SPIN nondeterministic choice would need to pick the nth action, with the guards being the enabled check). Python was chosen for several reasons: first, it is a widely adopted language in the real world, particularly in the testing community. Second, Python programs can particularly benefit from more effective automated testing because the lack of a good type system means Python code may fail in surprising and frustrating ways.

3   Using the Harness to Test and Experiment

It is simpler to show how the interface described in Table 1 is used than to explain each method. Figure 11 shows the core of the implementation of a pure random tester for an arbitrary SUT, omitting boilerplate such as import statements, command-line option parsing, and checking for timeout. A few points are important: first, the test algorithm is entirely SUT-agnostic. All interaction with the SUT is performed through the API in Table 1. The use of pools and the (name, guard, action) tuple list reduces the complex problem of choosing values and operations as shown in Figure 1 to the uniform simplicity of picking one enabled action and calling it as a function, storing the name as a human-readable identifier for the test behavior. Note that when reference oracles are used, the call to `act` is also typically enclosed in a `try` block to record the failing test, as is done with `check`.

```
t = SUT.t()
t.restart()
visited = []
S = []
S.append(t.state(), [])
test = []
while S != []:
    (v, test) = S.pop()
    t.backtrack(v)
    if (v not in visited) and (len(test) < config.maxdepth):
        visited.append(v)
        trans = t.enabled()
        for (name, guard, act) in trans:
            test.append(name)
            act()
            if not t.check():
                print "FAILED TEST:", test
                sys.exit(1)
            S.append((t.state(), test))
```

Fig. 12. A really simple DFS-only model checker for safety properties

Perhaps more impressively, a natural consequence of encoding a state space is that we can easily implement a (very simple) model checker, as shown in Figure 12. Of course, as a model checker it is highly inefficient, since the visited check is implemented as a linear search through a list of visited states. The inefficient linear search can be easily improved through the use of a hash table for pool states. TSTL makes use of Python's `deepcopy` functionality to automatically provide backtracking for many SUTs. To our knowledge, no other frameworks makes it as easy to use either backtracking or replay for state restoration as TSTL. State copies are often more efficient than replay. However, for simple SUTs and shallow depths replay may be better, and it works for some hard-to-copy SUTs.

Exploring Novel Testing Algorithms: In order to demonstrate how TSTL facilitates the design and evaluation of testing approaches, we provide the following simple algorithm motivated by classical beam search. Note that we do not claim this algorithm is highly effective in general, the point is to show that it is extremely easy to implement and compare new algorithms using TSTL.

Figure 13 shows a modified random testing algorithm. It performs almost like traditional random testing (as shown in Figure 11) except for the following change: at each step of the test, the state is saved. Instead of randomly selecting a single enabled action at random, this strategy picks k actions at random, and tries each one (backtracking to the old state after each action but the final one). However, if any action covers a never-before-explored branch of the SUT, it is chosen and testing proceeds to the next step immediately.[3] In less than thirty

---

[3] The coverage analysis is provided in this example by a simple Python coverage instrumentation tool, but TSTL offers integration with the very popular `coverage.py` as well.

```
t = SUT.t()
coverTool.clearCoverage()
for ntests in xrange(1, config.maxtests+1):
    t.restart()
    test = []
    print ntests+1, len(coverTool.getCoverage())
    for s in xrange(0,config.depth):
        possible = t.enabled()
        random.shuffle(possible)
        old = t.state()
        cov = coverTool.getCoverage()
        last = min(config.k, len(possible))
        pos = 0
        for (name, guard, act) in possible[:config.k]:
            pos += 1
            test.append(name)
            act()
            if not t.check():
                print "FAILING TEST:", test
                sys.exit(1)
            covNew = coverTool.getCoverage()
            if (pos == last) or (len(covNew) > len(cov)):
                break
            coverTool.setCoverage(cov)
            t.backtrack(old)
```

Fig. 13. A novel random testing algorithm, which is essentially random beam search, demonstrating the use of backtracking for state restoration

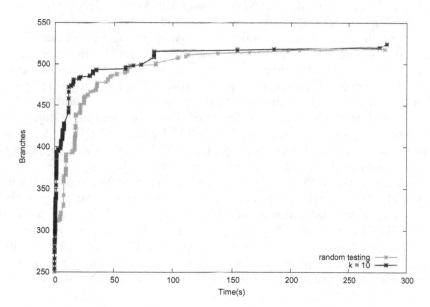

Fig. 14. Testing time vs. branches seen, traditional random testing vs. beam-search like method with $k = 10$, for Dominion simulator

minutes, we modified the random tester to perform this algorithm and both it and the default random tester to output the time at which each new branch is first covered during testing. Figure 14 shows the branch discovery rate of random testing compared to the novel test harness based on beam-search. The SUT (an implementation of strategy simulation for the card game Dominion) was taken from our work on applying machine learning to test generation, where it had proven difficult to improve on random testing. The experiment shows that, for this subject, the curve of covered code increases much more rapidly using the modified beam search than with traditional random testing. This simple experiment shows the ease with which researchers can explore novel testing strategies in TSTL. The benefits of providing backtracking are also evident here — other experiments show the same algorithm using replay performs considerably worse on average, at the test lengths required for good code coverage.

4   Related Work

To our knowledge, there has been no previous proposal of a concise *language* like TSTL to assist users in building test harnesses. One line of related work is our own previous work on building common frameworks for random testing and model checking [18] and proposing common terminology for imperative harnesses [12]. Work on domain-specific languages also informed our approach [7].

There exist various testing tools and languages of a somewhat different flavor: e.g. Korat [26], which has a much more fixed input domain specification, or the tools built to support the Next Generation Air Transportation System (NextGen) software [9]. The closest of these is the UDITA language [10], an extension of Java with non-deterministic choice operators and `assume`, which yields a very different language that shares our goal. TSTL aims more at the *generation* of tests than the *filtering* of tests (as defined in the UDITA paper), while UDITA supports both approaches. This goal of UDITA (and resulting need for first-class `assume`) means that it is hosted inside a complex (and sometimes non-trivial to install/use) tool, JPF [28], rather than generating a stand-alone simple interface to a test space, as with TSTL. Building "UDITA" for a new language is far more challenging than porting TSTL. UDITA also supports far fewer constructs to assist test harness development.

The design of the SPIN model checker [23] and its model-driven extension to include native C code [21] inspired our flavor of domain-specific language, though our approach is more declarative than the "imperative" model checker produced by SPIN. Similarly, work at JPL on languages for analyzing spacecraft telemetry logs in testing [16] provided a working example of a Python-based declarative language for testing purposes. The pool approach to test case construction is derived from work on canonical forms and enumeration of unit tests [4].

5   Conclusions and Future Work

We believe that the little language defined in this paper could be of considerable use to software developers who would like to use more automated testing, but do not want to learn complex new languages and tools. We expect that it also will prove useful to researchers who would like to rapidly prototype new testing and model checking methods and easily try their ideas out on new SUTs. The use of a template language makes it easy to exploit the usability of a scripting language, and the declarative approach makes implementing new testing algorithms easy.

Our future work is to further develop the TSTL language and tool, based on other users' experiences. One goal is to make use of TSTL easy out-of-the-box, which means including many example harnesses, SUTs, and testing algorithms. A second task is to improve the core language to include more functionality. For example, one obvious language omission is the inability to express desired probabilities for random testing. More automatic ranges, or a shorthand for including multiple concrete values as choices on one line for grammar encoding would also be useful. We also plan to extend TSTL to handle more host languages, including Scala, Java, C (possibly including use of KLEE [6]), and PROMELA. Additionally, we plan to use TSTL as a basis for further research in using machine learning techniques to improve software testing [13]. A development version of TSTL is available at https://code.google.com/p/harness-maker.

Acknowledgments. The authors would like to thank Klaus Havelund, Gerard Holzmann, Rajeev Joshi, John Regehr, Alan Fern, Martin Erwig, and the anonymous NFM'15 reviewers for their comments and ideas. A portion of this research was funded by NSF CCF-1217824 and NSF CCF-1054876.

References

1. http://www.cs.cmu.edu/~modelcheck/cbmc/
2. JPF: the swiss army knife of Java(TM) verification. http://babelfish.arc.nasa.gov/trac/jpf
3. JUnit. http://junit.sourceforce.net
4. Andrews, J., Zhang, Y.R., Groce, A.: Comparing automated unit testing strategies. Technical Report 736, Department of Computer Science, University of Western Ontario, December 2010
5. Bentley, J.: Programming pearls: little languages. Communications of the ACM **29**(8), 711–721 (1986)
6. Cadar, C., Dunbar, D., Engler, D.: KLEE: Unassisted and automatic generation of high-coverage tests for complex systems programs. In: Operating System Design and Implementation, pp. 209–224 (2008)
7. Fowler, M.: Domain-Specific Languages. Addison-Wesley Professional, (2010)
8. Fraser, G., Arcuri, A.: Evosuite: automatic test suite generation for object-oriented software. In: Proceedings of the 19th ACM SIGSOFT Symposium and the 13th European Conference on Foundations of Software Engineering, pp. 416–419. ESEC/FSE '11, ACM (2011)
9. Giannakopoulou, D., Howar, F., Isberner, M., Lauderdale, T., Rakamarić, Z., Raman, V.: Taming test inputs for separation assurance. In: International Conference on Automated Software Engineering, pp. 373–384 (2014)
10. Gligoric, M., Gvero, T., Jagannath, V., Khurshid, S., Kuncak, V., Marinov, D.: Test generation through programming in udita. In: International Conference on Software Engineering, pp. 225–234 (2010)
11. Groce, A., Alipour, M.A., Zhang, C., Chen, Y., Regehr, J.: Cause reduction for quick testing. In: Software Testing, Verification and Validation (ICST), 2014 IEEE Seventh International Conference on, pp. 243–252. IEEE (2014)

12. Groce, A., Erwig, M.: Finding common ground: choose, assert, and assume. In: Workshop on Dynamic Analysis, pp. 12–17 (2012)
13. Groce, A., Fern, A., Erwig, M., Pinto, J., Bauer, T., Alipour, A.: Learning-based test programming for programmers, pp. 752–786 (2012)
14. Groce, A., Fern, A., Pinto, J., Bauer, T., Alipour, A., Erwig, M., Lopez, C.: Lightweight automated testing with adaptation-based programming. In: IEEE International Symposium on Software Reliability Engineering, pp. 161–170 (2012)
15. Groce, A., Havelund, K., Holzmann, G., Joshi, R., Xu, R.G.: Establishing flight software reliability: Testing, model checking, constraint-solving, monitoring and learning. Annals of Mathematics and Artificial Intelligence 70(4), 315–349 (2014)
16. Groce, A., Havelund, K., Smith, M.: From scripts to specifications: The evolution of a flight software testing effort. In: International Conference on Software Engineering, pp. 129–138 (2010)
17. Groce, A., Holzmann, G., Joshi, R.: Randomized differential testing as a prelude to formal verification. In: International Conference on Software Engineering, pp. 621–631 (2007)
18. Groce, A., Joshi, R.: Random testing and model checking: Building a common framework for nondeterministic exploration. In: Workshop on Dynamic Analysis, pp. 22–28 (2008)
19. Groce, A., Zhang, C., Alipour, M.A., Eide, E., Chen, Y., Regeher, J.: Help, help, I'm being suppressed! the significance of suppressors in software testing. In: IEEE International Symposium on Software Reliability Engineering, pp. 390–399 (2013)
20. Groce, A., Zhang, C., Eide, E., Chen, Y., Regehr, J.: Swarm testing. In: International Symposium on Software Testing and Analysis, pp. 78–88 (2012)
21. Holzmann, G.J., Joshi, R.: Model-driven software verification. In: Graf, S., Mounier, L. (eds.) SPIN 2004. LNCS, vol. 2989, pp. 76–91. Springer, Heidelberg (2004)
22. Holzmann, G., Joshi, R., Groce, A.: Model driven code checking. Automated Software Engineering 15(3–4), 283–297 (2008)
23. Holzmann, G.J.: The SPIN Model Checker: Primer and Reference Manual. Addison-Wesley Professional, (2003)
24. Clarke, E., Kroning, D., Lerda, F.: A tool for checking ANSI-C programs. In: Jensen, K., Podelski, A. (eds.) TACAS 2004. LNCS, vol. 2988, pp. 168–176. Springer, Heidelberg (2004)
25. McKeeman, W.: Differential testing for software. Digital Technical Journal of Digital Equipment Corporation 10(1), 100–107 (1998)
26. Milicevic, A., Misailovic, S., Marinov, D., Khurshid, S.: Korat: A tool for generating structurally complex test inputs. In: International Conference on Software Engineering, pp. 771–774 (2007)
27. Pacheco, C., Lahiri, S.K., Ernst, M.D., Ball, T.: Feedback-directed random test generation. In: International Conference on Software Engineering, pp. 75–84 (2007)
28. Visser, W., Havelund, K., Brat, G., Park, S., Lerda, F.: Model checking programs. Automated Software Engineering 10(2), 203–232 (2003)
29. Visser, W., Păsăreanu, C., Pelanek, R.: Test input generation for Java containers using state matching. In: International Symposium on Software Testing and Analysis, pp. 37–48 (2006)
30. Zeller, A., Hildebrandt, R.: Simplifying and isolating failure-inducing input. Software Engineering, IEEE Transactions on 28(2), 183–200 (2002)

Detecting MPI Zero Buffer Incompatibility by SMT Encoding

Yu Huang$^{(\boxtimes)}$ and Eric Mercer

Brigham Young University, Provo, Utah
{yuHuang,egm}@byu.edu

Abstract. A prevalent asynchronous message passing standard is the Message Passing Interface (MPI). There are two runtime semantics for MPI: zero buffer (messages have no buffering) and infinite buffer (messages are copied into a runtime buffer on the API call). A problem in any MPI program, intended or otherwise, is zero buffer incompatibility. A zero buffer incompatible MPI program deadlocks. This problem is difficult to predict because a developer does not know if the deadlock is based on the buffering semantics or a bad program. This paper presents an algorithm that encodes a single-path MPI program as a Satisfiability Modulo Theories (SMT) problem, which if satisfiable, yields a feasible schedule, such that it proves the program is zero buffer compatible. This encoding is also adaptable to checking assertion violation for correct computation. To support MPI semantics, this algorithm correctly defines the point-to-point communication and collective communication with respective rules for both infinite buffer semantics and zero buffer semantics. The novelty in this paper is considering only the schedules that strictly alternate sends and receives leading to an intuitive zero buffer encoding. This paper proves that the set of all the strictly alternating schedules is capable of covering all the message communication that may occur in any execution under zero buffer semantics. Experiments demonstrate that the SMT encoding is correct and highly efficient for a set of benchmarks compared with two state-of-art MPI verifiers.

Keywords: MPI · SMT · Message Passing

1 Introduction

Message passing technology has become widely used in many fields such as medical devices and automobile systems. The Message Passing Interface (MPI) plays a significant role as a common standard. It is easy for a developer to implement a message passing scenario using MPI semantics, including:

- zero buffer semantics (messages have no buffering) and infinite buffer semantics (messages are copied into a runtime buffer on the API call) [21],
- MPI point-to-point operations (e.g., send and receive), and
- MPI collective operations (e.g., barrier and broadcast).

© Springer International Publishing Switzerland 2015
K. Havelund et al. (Eds.): NFM 2015, LNCS 9058, pp. 219–233, 2015.
DOI: 10.1007/978-3-319-17524-9_16

A problem in any MPI program is zero buffer incompatibility. A zero buffer incompatible program deadlocks. If there exists any feasible schedule for a program under zero buffer semantics, this program is zero buffer compatible. Note that the zero buffer incompatibility is not equivalent to deadlock that may be caused by reasons other than buffering. The zero buffer incompatibility is essential to any MPI application since it is difficult for a developer to predict. This problem is also very difficult to verify because of the complicated MPI semantics. In particular, the message passing may be non-deterministic such that a receive may match more than one send in the runtime system. Also, the MPI collective operations that synchronize the program may change how messages communicate. To address the problem of zero buffer incompatibility, this paper presents an algorithm that encodes a single-path MPI program into a Satisfiability Modulo Theories (SMT) problem [2]. This encoding is resolved by a standard SMT solver in such a way that the program is proved/disproved to be zero buffer compatible. This encoding is also adaptable to checking assertion violation caused by message non-determinism.

Several solutions were proposed to verify MPI programs. The POE algorithm is capable of dynamically analyzing the behavior of an MPI program [20]. This algorithm is implemented by a modern MPI verifier, ISP. As far as we know, there is no research proposed merely for zero buffer incompatibility. Though the works on MPI deadlock are also capable of detecting zero buffer incompatibility, they suffer from the scalability problem [10,16]. In particular, the algorithm MSPOE is an extension of POE. It is able to detect deadlock in an MPI program [16]. Forejt et al. proposed a SAT based approach to detect deadlock in a single-path MPI program [10].

The problem of generating a input match pair set is NP-Complete. The preprocessing, however, only needs to over-approximate the match pairs in quadratic time complexity. Before discussing how the new algorithm is capable of detecting zero buffer incompatibility, this paper needs to present in detail the complete list of encoding rules for several MPI operations, including a few rules that are trivial to define. In particular, the MPI non-deterministic point-to-point communication is similar to how message communicate in the Multicore Communications API (MCAPI). As such, this paper adapts the existing encoding rules for MCAPI defined in prior work [12]. This paper also presents how to encode deterministic receive operations and collective operations, which are essential to MPI semantics, into a set of SMT formulas. The formula size is quadratic. Note that the prior work also provides a list of non-intuitive and complicated zero buffer encoding rules. However, these rules are only useful for manually encoding the zero buffer semantics. The new zero buffer encoding in this paper considers only the schedules that strictly alternate sends and receives, therefore, not only is it correct and intuitive, it is easy to build automatically. The use of strict alternation is able to cover any message communication that may occur in any execution under zero buffer semantics. This strategy is inspired by Threaded-C Bounded Model Checking (TCBMC) that extends C Bounded Model Checking (CBMC) [4,5] to support concurrent C program verification

[15]. It assumes each lock operation and its paired unlock operation is ordered alternatingly in any execution.

To summarize, the main contributions of this paper include,

- a new zero buffer encoding with strict alternation of sends and receives that is capable of detecting zero buffer incompatibility,
- a new encoding algorithm that supports MPI deterministic point-to-point communication and MPI collective communication, and
- a set of benchmarks that demonstrate the new encoding is more efficient than two state-of-art MPI verifiers.

The rest of the paper is organized as follows: Sections 2 and 3 present a few trivial rules for encoding MPI operations, including the summarization of the prior work [12] in section 2 and the rules for MPI deterministic operations and collective operations in section 3; Based on these rules, section 4 discusses the new zero buffer encoding and how it is able to check zero buffer incompatibility; Section 5 gives the experiment results; Section 6 discusses the related work; and Section 7 discusses the conclusion and future work.

2   SMT Encoding for MCAPI

This section summarizes the SMT encoding rules (except the rules for zero buffer semantics) discussed in the prior work for MCAPI verification. MCAPI is a lightweight message passing interface that only uses sends and wildcard receives for message communication. A wildcard receive is a receive that can match sends from any source. These rules are used to encode MPI non-deterministic point-to-point communication. In general, the SMT encoding is generated from 1) an execution trace of a program that includes a sequence of events; and 2) a set of possible match pairs for message communication. Intuitively, a match pair is a coupling of a send and a receive.

The encoding contains a timestamp $time_e$ for every event e in a program. Intuitively, the timestamp is an integer. The event order is enforced by the *Happens-Before* (HB) operator, denoted as $\prec_{HB}$, over two events, $e1$ and $e2$ respectively, such that $time_{e1} < time_{e2}$ holds. The send and receive operations are encoded as tuples. In particular, a send operation $S = (M_S, time_S, e_S, value_S)$, is a four-tuple of variables. M_S is the timestamp of the matching receive; $time_S$ is the timestamp of S; e_S is the destination endpoint of a message; and $value_S$ is the transmitted value. The values of e_S and $value_S$ are fixed from the input trace. Similarly, a receive operation $R = (M_R, time_R, e_R, value_R, time_{W_R})$, is modeled by a five-tuple of variables. M_R is the timestamp of the matching send; $time_R$ is the timestamp of R; e_R is the destination endpoint of a message; $value_R$ is the received value; and $time_{W_R}$ is the timestamp of the nearest-enclosing wait W_R. A nearest-enclosing wait is a wait that witnesses the completion of a receive by indicating that the message is delivered and that all the previous receives on the same process issued earlier are completed as well. The value of e_R is fixed from

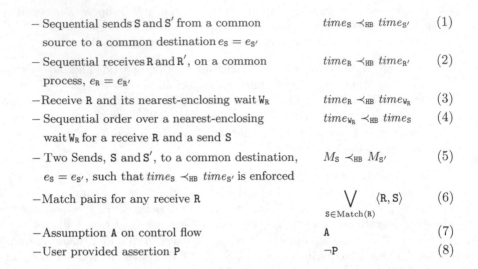

- Sequential sends S and S′ from a common source to a common destination $e_S = e_{S'}$ $time_S \prec_{HB} time_{S'}$ (1)

- Sequential receives R and R′, on a common process, $e_R = e_{R'}$ $time_R \prec_{HB} time_{R'}$ (2)

- Receive R and its nearest-enclosing wait W_R $time_R \prec_{HB} time_{W_R}$ (3)

- Sequential order over a nearest-enclosing wait W_R for a receive R and a send S $time_{W_R} \prec_{HB} time_S$ (4)

- Two Sends, S and S′, to a common destination, $e_S = e_{S'}$, such that $time_S \prec_{HB} time_{S'}$ is enforced $M_S \prec_{HB} M_{S'}$ (5)

- Match pairs for any receive R $\bigvee_{S \in Match(R)} \langle R, S \rangle$ (6)

- Assumption A on control flow   A   (7)

- User provided assertion P $\neg P$ (8)

Fig. 1. SMT encoding for MPI non-deterministic point-to-point communication

the input trace. Note that only wildcard receive is used in the MCAPI semantics. Therefore, the encoding for MCAPI does not need to specify the message source endpoints in sends and receives. The message communication topology is encoded as a set of match pairs defined in Definition 1.

Definition 1 (Match Pair). *A match pair, $\langle R, S \rangle$, for a receive* $R = (M_R, time_R, e_R, value_R, time_{W_R})$ *and a send* $S = (M_S, time_S, e_S, value_S)$, *corresponds to the following constraints:*
1. $M_R = time_S \wedge M_S = time_R$
2. $e_R = e_S \wedge value_R = value_S$
3. $time_S \prec_{HB} time_{W_R}$

We define the potential sends for a receive R, denoted as Match(R), as the set of all the sends that R may potentially match. The encoding rules are given in Figure 1: rules (1) – (5) encode the program order; rule (6) encodes the match pairs; and rules (7) and (8) encode the assumptions on control flow and the negated assertion respectively. Assume a program contains $\mathcal{N}$ API calls, the generated SMT encoding contains $\mathcal{O}(\mathcal{N}^2)$ formulas. The following sections discuss the extension to MPI semantics and more importantly zero buffer incompatibility that is not included in the prior work.

3   Extension to MPI

This section discusses the new encoding for MPI deterministic point-to-point communication and collective communication. To be precise, the encoding needs to add variables src_S and src_R to the send operation and the receive operation respectively. Intuitively, the variables src_S and src_R are the source endpoints of messages. As such, a send operation $S = (M_S, time_S, e_S, src_S, value_S)$, is now a five-tuple of variables. A receive operation $R = (M_R, time_R, e_R, src_R, value_R, time_{W_R})$, is now a six-tuple of variables. We constrain the variable src_R to be equal to $*$ for a wildcard receive R. In addition, the match pair defined in Definition 1 adds a new constraint:

$$src_R = * \lor src_S = src_R,$$

indicating that either R is a wildcard receive or the source endpoints are matched for S and R.

As discussed earlier, collective operations are used to synchronize an MPI program. To be precise, collective operations such as barriers block the execution of processes until all the members in a group are matched. In addition, some type of collective operations such as broadcast are able to send internal messages amongst its group, and/or to execute global operations. MPI semantics guarantee that messages generated on behalf of collective operations are not confused with messages generated by point-to-point operations. Therefore, the encoding in this paper puts emphasis on how to reason about the synchronization of collective operations as it affects point-to-point communication. The internal message passing and the execution of global operations by collective communication can be added as SMT constraints to the encoding. In the following discussion, we take barrier as an example. The barrier is defined as a group in Definition 2.

Definition 2 (Barrier). *The occurrence of a group of barriers, $B = \{B_0, B_1, ..., B_n\}$, is captured by a single timestamp, $time_B$, that marks when all the members in the group are matched.*

Even though barriers affect the issuing order of two events, it is hard to determine whether they prevent a send from matching a receive. As an example, the message "1" in Figure 2 may flow into R even though R is ordered before the barrier and S is ordered after the barrier. The wait W(&h2) determines the behavior. If the program had issued W(&h2) before the barrier, R would have to be completed before the barrier, meaning the message is delivered. The encoding further defines the nearest-enclosing barrier (Definition 3) for this type of interaction.

Definition 3 (Nearest-Enclosing Barrier). *For any process i, a receive R has a nearest-enclosing barrier B if and only if*

Process 0	Process 1
B(comm)	R(from P0, A, &h2)
S(to P1, "1", &h1)	B(comm)
W(&h1)	W(&h2)

Fig. 2. Message Communication with Barriers

- Any receive R that has a nearest-enclosing $time_{W_R} \prec_{HB} time_B$ (9)
  barrier B and a nearest-enclosing wait W_R
- Any barrier B and any operation O ordered $time_B \prec_{HB} time_O$ (10)
  after a member of B

Fig. 3. SMT encoding for MPI collective communication

1. *the nearest-enclosing wait,* W, *of* R *is ordered before* $B_i \in B$, *and*
2. *there does not exist any receive* R' *on process* i, *with a nearest-enclosing wait,* W', *such that 1)* W' *is ordered after* W; *and 2)* W' *is ordered before* B_i.

Based on the definitions above, the encoding defines two rules for program order in Figure 3. Rule (9) only constrains the program order over the nearest-enclosing wait and the nearest-enclosing barrier for a receive. The order over this receive and the nearest-enclosing barrier is not constrained. For rule (10), a barrier has to happen before any operation ordered after it.

4   Zero Buffer Incompability

This section presents a new zero buffer encoding that is easy to build automatically. The key insight is to order a send immediately preceding the matching receive in a match pair captured in Definition 4.

Definition 4 (Match Pair *). *A match pair,* $\langle R, S \rangle^*$, *for a receive* $R = (M_R,$ $time_R, e_R, src_R, value_R, time_{W_R})$ *and a send* $S = (M_S, time_S, e_S, src_S, value_S)$, *corresponds to the constraints:*

1. $M_R = time_S \wedge M_S = time_R$
2. $e_R = e_S \wedge value_R = value_S$
3. $src_R = * \vee src_S = src_R$
4. $\mathbf{time_S = time_R - 1}$

Intuitively, the consecutive order over a send and the matching receive is defined in the bold rule 4 of Definition 4. Any resolved execution strictly alternates sends and receives.

Definition 5 (Strict Alternation). *A set of sends,* $\mathbb{S}$, *and a set of receives,* $\mathbb{R}$, *are strictly alternated if and only if each send in* $\mathbb{S}$ *immediately precedes the matching receive in* $\mathbb{R}$ *and each receive in* $\mathbb{R}$ *immediately follows the matching send in* $\mathbb{S}$.

To further constrain the program order for zero buffer semantics, new rules are added as shown in Figure 4: on each process a send happens before a receive that is issued later (rule (11)); and similarly, on each process a send happens before a barrier that is issued later (rule (12)). In addition, Rule (1*) replaces

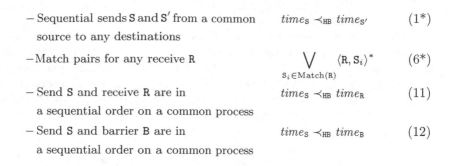

– Sequential sends S and S′ from a common source to any destinations	$time_S \prec_{HB} time_{S'}$	(1^*)
–Match pairs for any receive R	$\bigvee_{S_i \in Match(R)} \langle R, S_i \rangle^*$	(6^*)
– Send S and receive R are in a sequential order on a common process	$time_S \prec_{HB} time_R$	(11)
– Send S and barrier B are in a sequential order on a common process	$time_S \prec_{HB} time_B$	(12)

Fig. 4. SMT encoding for zero buffer semantics

rule (1) as zero buffer semantics do not allow a new send to be issued before the pending send is completed on a common process. Rule (6^*) replaces rule (6) to enforce strict alternation for every send and its matching receive.

To check zero buffer incompatibility, the encoding intends to find a feasible strictly alternating schedule by constraining the over-approximated match relation and the program order. If no feasible schedule exists, meaning there is no ordering that satisfies the happens-before relation, the program is zero buffer incompatible, and it deadlocks under zero buffer semantics; otherwise, zero buffer compatibility is proved. Since this process only relies on the event ordering, the constraints of user-provided assertions defined in rule (8) are removed.

Notice that a program with deadlock may be zero buffer compatible. Intuitively, a deadlock can be caused by an orphaned send or receive that is never matched, a dependency circuit existing in the message communication topology, the improper use of collective operations, etc.

4.1 Correctness

As discussed earlier, the zero buffer encoding only considers schedules that strictly alternate sends and receives, therefore, it makes the encoding rules intuitive and easy to build automatically. The fundamental insight is that this strict alternation is sufficient to cover all possible resolutions of message communication. We prove a theorem later that asserts this insight. Before that, we need to define a few terms.

Definition 6 (Method Invocation). *A invocation of a method,* M, *with a list of specific values of arguments,* $(args \cdots)$, *on process* P, *denoted as* $P : M_i(args \cdots)$, *is a event that occurs when* M *is invoked.*

Definition 7 (Method Response). *A response of a method,* M, *with a specific return value, resp, on process* P, *denoted as* $P : M_r(resp)$, *is a event that occurs when* M *returns.*

Based on Definition 6 and Definition 7, an operation is split into two events: invocation and response. The invocation asserts the issuing of an operation with concrete arguments. We use the notations $\mathbb{S}_i$ and $\mathbb{R}_i$ to represent the set of all the send invocations and the set of all the receive invocations respectively for an MPI program. The response asserts the completion of an operation with a concrete return value. We use the notations $\mathbb{S}_r$ and $\mathbb{R}_r$ to represent the set of all the send responses and the set of all the receive responses respectively for an MPI program. A history of an MPI program relies on method invocation and method response.

Definition 8 (History). *For an MPI program, let $\mathcal{H}$ be a history with a total order over method invocations and method responses for a set of send operations, $\mathbb{S}$, a set of receive operations, $\mathbb{R}$, and a set of barriers, $\mathbb{B}$.*

Based on Definition 8, we further define a legal history as follows.

Definition 9 (Legal History). *A history, $\mathcal{H}$, for an MPI program is legal if the total order over all the events in $\mathcal{H}$ is allowed by MPI semantics.*

A legal history defined in Definition 9 represents a total order over events for an MPI program. A legal history only takes care of sends, receives and barriers because only they matter to message communication. In other words, the events in a legal history can be used to evaluate how messages may flow in a runtime system. Since the arguments are concrete in any method invocation and the return value is also concrete in any method response, a legal history corresponds to a precise resolution of message communication. To find a feasible message communication for a receive R, one only needs to search through the preceding events and find a send S that matches the endpoints of R and obeys the non-overtaking order for all the sends to the common destination endpoint. The legal history asserts that the total order over all the events is allowed by MPI semantics. In particular, if a legal history is allowed by zero buffer semantics, we call it a zero-buffer legal history.

To prove the theorem later, we need to compare two legal histories for equivalence. The equivalence relation relies on the following definitions for projections.

Definition 10 (Projection to Process). *A projection of a legal history, $\mathcal{H}$, to a process, P, denoted as $\mathcal{H}|_P$, is a sequence of all the events on process P in $\mathcal{H}$, such that the order over any pair of events in $\mathcal{H}|_P$ is identical as in $\mathcal{H}$.*

Definition 11 (Projection to Receive Response). *A projection of a legal history, $\mathcal{H}$, to the receive responses, $\mathbb{R}_r$, denoted as $\mathcal{H}|_{\mathbb{R}_r}$, is a sequence of receive responses in $\mathcal{H}$ such that the order over any pair of receive responses in $\mathcal{H}|_{\mathbb{R}_r}$ is identical as in $\mathcal{H}$.*

Based on Definition 10 and Definition 11, a legal history can be further projected to the receive responses $\mathbb{R}_r$ on process P. We use $\mathcal{H}|_{\mathbb{R}_r,P}$ to represent this projection. The equivalence relation relies on $\mathcal{H}|_{\mathbb{R}_r,P}$.

Definition 12 (Equivalence Relation). *Two legal histories for an MPI program, say $\mathcal{H}$ and $\mathcal{L}$ respectively, are equivalent, denoted as $\mathcal{H} \sim \mathcal{L}$, if and only if their projections to the receive responses $\mathbb{R}_r$ on each single process P, $\mathcal{H}|_{\mathbb{R}_r,P}$ and $\mathcal{L}|_{\mathbb{R}_r,P}$ respectively, agree on the return values of $\mathbb{R}_r$.*

The following lemma is essential to proving that Definition 12 is a valid equivalence relation. Definition 13 defines the reachable set of legal histories for an MPI program.

Definition 13 (Reachable Legal Histories). *For an MPI program, p, let $\mathcal{RS}(p)$ be a set of all the legal histories that are reachable from p.*

Lemma 1 (Validity of Equivalence Relation). *The $\sim$-operator is an equivalence relation over the set of all legal histories.*

Proof. Proof by the definition of equivalence relation. Consider three legal histories, $\mathcal{H}, \mathcal{L}, \mathcal{T} \in \mathcal{RS}(p)$, for an MPI program, p, the equivalence relation in Definition 12 is reflexive, symmetric and transitive.

1. $\mathcal{H} \sim \mathcal{H}$. The reflexivity is true because the projection $\mathcal{H}|_{\mathbb{R}_r,P}$ to the receive responses $\mathbb{R}_r$ on any process P, and the projection itself agree on the return values of $\mathbb{R}_r$.
2. $\mathcal{H} \sim \mathcal{L}$ then $\mathcal{L} \sim \mathcal{H}$. The symmetry is also true because $\mathcal{H} \sim \mathcal{L}$ and $\mathcal{L} \sim \mathcal{H}$ both indicate that the projections $\mathcal{H}|_{\mathbb{R}_r,P}$ and $\mathcal{L}|_{\mathbb{R}_r,P}$ to the receive responses $\mathbb{R}_r$ on any process P agree on the return values of $\mathbb{R}_r$.
3. $\mathcal{H} \sim \mathcal{L}$ and $\mathcal{L} \sim \mathcal{T}$ then $\mathcal{H} \sim \mathcal{T}$. As for the transitivity, for all the receive responses $\mathbb{R}_r$ on any process P in the MPI program, $\mathcal{H} \sim \mathcal{L}$ indicates that the projections $\mathcal{H}|_{\mathbb{R}_r,P}$ and $\mathcal{L}|_{\mathbb{R}_r,P}$ to the receive responses $\mathbb{R}_r$ on any process P agree on the return values of $\mathbb{R}_r$. Further, $\mathcal{L} \sim \mathcal{T}$ indicates that $\mathcal{L}|_{\mathbb{R}_r,P}$ is also identical to $\mathcal{T}|_{\mathbb{R}_r,P}$. Therefore, $\mathcal{H}|_{\mathbb{R}_r,P}$ is identical to $\mathcal{T}|_{\mathbb{R}_r,P}$. Since P is an arbitrary process in the MPI program and $\mathbb{R}_r$ do not change on P, thus $\mathcal{H} \sim \mathcal{T}$ is implied.

Based on the reflexivity, symmetry and transitivity, this equivalence relation is able to partition the reachable set of legal histories, $\mathcal{RS}(p)$, and therefore identifies the equivalent classes among $\mathcal{RS}(p)$.

Based on Lemma 1, we further use $\mathcal{E}(\mathcal{RS}(p))$ to represent the equivalent classes for all the legal histories in $\mathcal{RS}(p)$. If an equivalent class includes zero-buffer legal histories, we call it a zero-buffer available equivalent class. The following theorem states that a representative exists for each zero-buffer available equivalent class.

Theorem 1. *For any MPI program, p, each zero-buffer available equivalent class, $E \in \mathcal{E}(\mathcal{RS}(p))$, has a representative zero-buffer legal history, T, that strictly alternates the sends, $\mathbb{S}$, and the receives, $\mathbb{R}$.*

Proof. Proof by showing the existence of a zero-buffer legal history for any equivalence class. First, assume there is a legal history $\mathcal{L} \in E$. Second, assume $\mathbb{R}_r$ is a set of all the receive responses. The projection $\mathcal{L}|_{\mathbb{R}_r}$ is a sequence of receive responses that reflects how messages are received in $\mathcal{L}$ for all the processes. Since the message communication is precisely resolved in $\mathcal{L}$, each receive in $\mathbb{R}$ is matched with a send in $\mathbb{S}$. Based on $\mathcal{L}$ and $\mathcal{L}|_{\mathbb{R}_r}$, a new sequence, $\mathcal{T}$, can be produced by two steps: 1) inserting the corresponding receive invocation immediately preceding each receive response; and 2) inserting the invocation and the response of the matching send immediately preceding each receive invocation. Based on those steps, $\mathcal{T}$ strictly alternates $\mathbb{S}$ and $\mathbb{R}$. Further, it obeys the conditions in Definition 9: first, the consecutive order over a send and the matching receive in $\mathcal{L}$ still exists in $\mathcal{T}$; second, if the matching receive is issued earlier on process P, there is no way to execute any operation after the receive on process P until it is matched with a send, therefore, postponing issuing the receive after the matching send does not violate the MPI semantics. Under zero buffer semantics, it is not possible to order a send and the matching receive other than the two stated situations above. Notice that $\mathcal{T}$ is equivalent to $\mathcal{L}$ as they receive a common sequence of messages on each process. Therefore, for any existing zero-buffer available equivalent class, the procedure above is able to find a representative zero-buffer legal history that strictly alternates sends and receives.

$\square$

Given the proof of message communication coverage, the soundness and completeness only rely on the existing proofs in the prior work. The soundness proof is consistent with the prior work: 1) the program order is precisely constrained in the encoding; and 2) any match pair used in a resolved satisfying schedule is valid. The deterministic receive operations and the collective operations for the new encoding do not violate these properties. To be precise, the first property still holds because the program order for deterministic receive operations and collective operations are precisely defined in the new encoding. The second property is also true because the set of match pairs is given as input, which is not affected by deterministic receive operations and collective operations.

The completeness proof of the new technique is similar to the prior work that uses the operational semantics to simulate the encoding during its operation to ensure that the two make identical conclusions. To prove the new encoding is complete, the operational semantics are extended to support deterministic receive operations and collective operations. A simulation of the extended operational semantics is then able to prove that any behavior of MPI semantics is encoded by the new technique in this paper. Because the soundness and completeness for the new encoding are both proved, we conclude that the encoding is correct for MPI semantics.

5   Experiment

We compare the performance of our work with two state-of-art MPI verifiers: ISP [20,16], a dynamic analyzer, and MOPPER [10], a SAT based tool. We conduct a series of experiments for five typical benchmark programs that are modified to be single-path. Assertions related to correct computation are manually inserted into each program. All the results show the comparison between

Table 1. Tests on Selected Benchmarks

Test Programs				B	Error	ZI	Our Method		ISP		MOPPER	
Name	#Procs	#Calls	Match				Mem	Time	#Runs	Time	Mem	Time
Monte	4	35	24	0	No	No†	3.62	0.02s	6	0.25s	6.09	<0.01s
				∞	No	-	3.42	0.02s	6	0.96s	-	-
	8	75	40K	0	No	No†	4.83	0.04s	>5K	TO	11.28	0.02s
				∞	No	-	4.34	0.04s	>5K	TO	-	-
	16	155	2E13	0	No	No†	8.97	0.29s	>5K	TO	24.42	0.08s
				∞	No	-	7.22	0.15s	>5K	TO	-	-
Integrate	8	36	5K	0	Yes	No	4.71	0.08s	1	0.15s	-	-ᵃ
				∞	Yes	-	4.20	0.04s	1	0.16s	-	-
	10	46	362K	0	Yes	No	5.39	0.08s	1	0.16s	-	-ᵃ
				∞	Yes	-	4.76	0.05s	1	0.26s	-	-
	16	76	1E12	0	Yes	No	8.79	0.62s	1	0.25s	-	-ᵃ
				∞	Yes	-	7.50	0.32s	1	0.54s	-	-
Diffusion2D	4	52	6E9	0	No	Yes	5.50	0.04s	90	3.09s	6.10	0.01s
				∞	No	-	4.80	0.03s	90	32.01s	-	-
	8	108	2E21	0	No	Yes	11.94	0.22s	>9K	TO	-	TO
				∞	No	-	8.51	0.12s	>9K	TO	-	-
	16	228	3E57	0	No	Yes	30.68	1.25s	>10K	TO	-	TO
				∞	No	-	30.76	5.11s	>10K	TO	-	-
Router	2	34	1	0	No	Yes	3.39	0.02s	1	0.04s	-	-ᵃ
				∞	No	-	3.37	0.02s	60	13.24s	-	-
	4	68	83K	0	No	Yes	4.18	0.02s	1	0.04s	-	-ᵃ
				∞	No	-	3.99	0.03s	>10K	TO	-	-
	8	136	7E9	0	No	Yes	5.17	0.04s	1	0.15s	-	-ᵃ
				∞	No	-	5.06	0.05s	>11K	TO	-	-
Floyd	8	120	4E29	0	No	No	13.87	0.15s	>20K	TO	18.05	0.27s
				∞	No	-	12.14	0.12s	>20K	TO	-	-
	16	256	1E58	0	No	No	21.58	0.26s	>20K	TO	67.53	43.08s
				∞	No	-	17.55	0.21s	>20K	TO	-	-
	32	528	3E137	0	No	No	252.07	439.89s	>20K	TO	212.30	476.52s
				∞	No	-	57.91	19.34s	>20K	TO	-	-

† MOPPER detects deadlock.
ᵃ MOPPER does not launch SAT analysis.

zero buffer semantics and infinite buffer semantics. The initial program trace for our approach is generated by running MPICH [14], a public implementation of the MPI standard. This program trace is encoded symbolically where each variable does not have a concrete value. A unique instance is generated for each write of a variable in the program computation (similar to the static single assignment form [6]). Our encoding is resolved by the SMT solver Z3 [13]. MOPPER also needs an initial program trace with the same input data. MOPPER launches ISP to automatically generate such a trace. Since MOPPER is designed for deadlock checking, it does not encode any computation in a program. The results only show the performance of MOPPER for zero buffer incompatibility. The experiments are run on a AMD A8 Quad Core processor with 6 GB of memory running Ubuntu 14.04 LTS. We set a time limit of 30 minutes for each test. We abort the verification process if it does not complete within the time limit.

The results of the comparison are in Table 1. The column "Match" records the approximated number of match possibilities. A program with a large number of match possibilities has a large degree of message non-determinism. The column "ZI" indicates whether the program is zero buffer incompatible or not. The column "Mem" records the memory cost in megabytes. The "Time" columns for our approach and MOPPER are only for constraint solving. As a note, our approach and MOPPER both spend less than one second to generate the trace and the encoding for every benchmark. The column "#Runs" for ISP is the number of program interleavings that ISP traverses before termination. The column "Time" for ISP is the running time of dynamic analysis. The meaning of the symbol "–" is "unavailable": either the test is not interesting for comparison or the error is detected in preprocessing.

Monte implements the Monte Carlo method to compute π [3]. It uses one manger process and multiple worker processes to send messages back and forth. In addition, barrier operations are used to synchronize the program.

Integrate uses heavy non-determinism in message communication to compute an integral of the sin function over the interval $[0, \pi]$ [1]. This benchmark also has a manger-worker pattern where the root process divides the interval to a certain number of tasks. It then distributes those tasks to multiple worker processes.

Diffusion2D has an interesting computation pattern that uses barriers to "partition" the message communication into several sections [1]. A message from a send can be only received in a common section.

Router is an algorithm to update routing tables for a set of nodes. Each node is in a ring and communicates only with immediate neighbors to update the tables. The program ends when all the routing tables are updated.

Floyd implements the Floyd's all-pairs shortest path algorithm [24]. Each node communicates only with the immediate following neighbor.

Note that all the tools are able to correctly check zero buffer incompatibility for the benchmarks above. Also, our encoding and ISP are both able to correctly check assertion violations. The results in Table 1 show that our encoding with Z3 is highly efficient compared to ISP. For the benchmark programs such as *Diffusion2D* and *Floyd*, where ISP does not terminate after traversing a large number of interleavings, our approach returns under a second in most cases. Even for the benchmark programs where ISP terminates after traversing only a small subset of all the interleavings, our approach is able to run slightly faster. Our approach is also faster than MOPPER for the benchmark programs where there is a large degree of message non-determinism. If the number of match possibilities is low, our approach runs as fast as MOPPER does. As discussed earlier, a deadlock may be caused by many ways other than zero buffer incompatibility. The program *Monte* is zero buffer compatible, but it contains a deadlock that can be detected by MOPPER. Our solution was never intended to find such a deadlock. ISP should detect it but does not. For the programs *Integrate* and *Router*, MOPPER does not launch a SAT analysis because the ISP preprocessor detects the assertion violation or deadlock, and thus, MOPPER aborts the verification process.

6   Related Work

The dynamic analyzer ISP implements the POE algorithm, a Dynamic Partial Order Reduction (DPOR) algorithm [9] applied to MPI programs [20].

An extension is the MSPOE algorithm [16]. It operates by postponing the cooperative operations for message passing in transit until each process reaches a blocking call. It then determines the potential matches of send and receive operations in the runtime. In addition to program properties, it is able to check deadlocks.

Forejt et al. proposed a SAT based approach to detect deadlock in a single-path MPI program [10]. This solution is correct and efficient for programs with a low degree of message non-determinism. However, since the size of their encoding is cubic, checking large programs is time consuming. Similar to our solution, this work requires a match pair set that can be over-approximated.

MPI-Spin is integrated into the classic model checker SPIN [11] for verifying MPI programs [18,19]. It generates a model of an MPI program and symbolically executes it. It does not scale to large programs with a large degree of message non-determinism.

Vo et al. used Lamport clocks to update auxiliary information via piggyback messages [22,23]. While completeness is abandoned in their analysis, they show the approach is useful and efficient in practice.

Sharma et al. proposed the first push button model checker for MCAPI – MCC [17]. It indirectly controls the MCAPI runtime to verify MCAPI programs under zero buffer semantics. One drawback of this work is that it does not include the ability to analyze infinite buffer semantics which is known as a common runtime environment in message passing. A key insight, though, is the direct use of match pairs – couplings for potential sends and receives.

Elwakil et al. also used SMT techniques to reason about the program behavior in the MCAPI domain [7,8]. State-based and order-based encoding techniques are both used. These techniques fail to reason about the infinite buffer semantics and require a precise match set which is non-trivial to compute beforehand.

Our prior work encodes an MCAPI execution into an SMT problem for detecting user-provided assertions [12]. The encoding is sound and complete and is easy to use to reason about infinite buffer semantics without requiring a precise match set. The work also provides an algorithm that runs in quadratic time complexity to generate a sufficiently small over-approximated match set based on the given execution trace.

7   Conclusion and Future Work

This paper presents a new algorithm that correctly encodes a single-path MPI program. This encoding, including the rules for MPI point-to-point communication and MPI collective communication, is capable of detecting zero buffer incompatibility. It is also adaptable to checking assertion violations. The key insight in this paper is that the new zero buffer encoding considers only the schedules that strictly alternate sends and receives. This strict alternation strategy makes the encoding intuitive and easy to build automatically, and is able to cover all the message communication. Experiments indicates that our solution is correct and more efficient than two state-of-art MPI verifiers.

The encoding is dependent on a single-path MPI program which can be initialized by an execution trace. Future work will explore using bounded model checking to encode all the paths of an MPI program. This technique statically unrolls an MPI program and then verifies it by constraining the semantics into an SMT encoding. Also, future work will explore using the SMT encoding to check deadlock patterns other than zero buffer incompatibility.

References

1. FEVS benchmark. http://vsl.cis.udel.edu/fevs/index.html
2. Barrett, C., Ranise, S., Stump, A., Tinelli, C.: The satisfiability modulo theories library (smt-lib). www.SMT-LIB.org (2008)
3. Burkardt, J.: MPI Examples. http://people.sc.fsu.edu/jburkardt/cpp_src/mpi/mpi.html
4. Clarke, E., Kroning, D., Lerda, F.: A tool for checking ANSI-C programs. In: Jensen, K., Podelski, A. (eds.) TACAS 2004. LNCS, vol. 2988, pp. 168–176. Springer, Heidelberg (2004)
5. Clarke, E.M., Kroening, D., Yorav, K.: Behavioral consistency of C and verilog programs using bounded model checking. In: DAC, pp. 368–371. ACM (2003)
6. Cytron, R., Ferrante, J., Rosen, B.K., Wegman, M.N., Zadeck, F.K.: Efficiently computing static single assignment form and the control dependence graph. ACM Trans. Program. Lang. Syst. 13(4), 451–490 (1991). http://doi.acm.org/10.1145/115372.115320
7. Elwakil, M., Yang, Z.: Debugging support tool for MCAPI applications. In: Lourenço, J. (ed.) PADTAD, pp. 20–25. ACM (2010)
8. Elwakil, M., Yang, Z., Wang, L.: CRI: symbolic debugger for MCAPI applications. In: Bouajjani, A., Chin, W.-N. (eds.) ATVA 2010. LNCS, vol. 6252, pp. 353–358. Springer, Heidelberg (2010)
9. Flanagan, C., Godefroid, P.: Dynamic partial-order reduction for model checking software. In: Palsberg, J., Abadi, M. (eds.) POPL, pp. 110–121. ACM (2005)
10. Forejt, V., Kroening, D., Narayanaswamy, G., Sharma, S.: Precise predictive analysis for discovering communication deadlocks in MPI programs. In: Jones, C., Pihlajasaari, P., Sun, J. (eds.) FM 2014. LNCS, vol. 8442, pp. 263–278. Springer, Heidelberg (2014)
11. Holzmann, G.J.: The model checker SPIN. IEEE Trans. Software Eng. 23(5), 279–295 (1997)
12. Huang, Y., Mercer, E., McCarthy, J.: Proving MCAPI executions are correct using SMT. In: ASE, pp. 26–36 (2013)
13. de Moura, L., Bjørner, N.S.: Z3: an efficient SMT solver. In: Ramakrishnan, C.R., Rehof, J. (eds.) TACAS 2008. LNCS, vol. 4963, pp. 337–340. Springer, Heidelberg (2008)
14. MPICH: High-Performance Portable MPI. http://www.mpich.org
15. Rabinovitz, I., Grumberg, O.: Bounded model checking of concurrent programs. In: Etessami, K., Rajamani, S.K. (eds.) CAV 2005. LNCS, vol. 3576, pp. 82–97. Springer, Heidelberg (2005)
16. Sharma, S., Gopalakrishnan, G., Bronevetsky, G.: A sound reduction of persistent-sets for deadlock detection in MPI applications. In: Gheyi, R., Naumann, D. (eds.) SBMF 2012. LNCS, vol. 7498, pp. 194–209. Springer, Heidelberg (2012)

17. Sharma, S., Gopalakrishnan, G., Mercer, E., Holt, J.: MCC: A runtime verification tool for MCAPI user applications. In: FMCAD, pp. 41–44. IEEE (2009)
18. Siegel, S.F.: Model checking nonblocking MPI programs. In: Cook, B., Podelski, A. (eds.) VMCAI 2007. LNCS, vol. 4349, pp. 44–58. Springer, Heidelberg (2007)
19. Siegel, S.F.: Verifying parallel programs with MPI-Spin. In: PVM/MPI, pp. 13–14 (2007)
20. Vakkalanka, S.S., Sharma, S., Gopalakrishnan, G., Kirby, R.M.: ISP: a tool for model checking MPI programs. In: PPOPP, pp. 285–286 (2008)
21. Vakkalanka, S.S., Vo, A., Gopalakrishnan, G., Kirby, R.M.: Reduced execution semantics of MPI: From theory to practice. In: FM, pp. 724–740 (2009)
22. Vo, A., Aananthakrishnan, S., Gopalakrishnan, G., de Supinski, B.R., Schulz, M., Bronevetsky, G.: A scalable and distributed dynamic formal verifier for MPI programs. In: SC, pp. 1–10. IEEE (2010)
23. Vo, A., Gopalakrishnan, G., Kirby, R.M., de Supinski, B.R., Schulz, M., Bronevetsky, G.: Large scale verification of MPI programs using Lamport clocks with lazy update. In: Rauchwerger, L., Sarkar, V. (eds.) PACT, pp. 330–339. IEEE Computer Society (2011)
24. Xue, R., Liu, X., Wu, M., Guo, Z., Chen, W., Zheng, W., Zhang, Z., Voelker, G.M.: MPIWiz: subgroup reproducible replay of mpi applications. In: Proceedings of the 14th ACM SIGPLAN Symposium on Principles and Practice of Parallel Programming, PPOPP 2009, Raleigh, NC, USA, February 14–18, 2009, pp. 251–260 (2009), http://doi.acm.org/10.1145/1504176.1504213

A Falsification View of Success Typing

Robert Jakob[✉] and Peter Thiemann

University of Freiburg, Freiburg, Germany
{jakobro,thiemann}@informatik.uni-freiburg.de

Abstract. Dynamic languages are praised for their flexibility and expressiveness, but static analysis often yields many false positives and verification is cumbersome for lack of structure. Hence, unit testing is the prevalent incomplete method for validating programs in such languages.

Falsification is an alternative approach that uncovers definite errors in programs. A falsifier computes a set of inputs that definitely crash a program.

Success typing is a type-based approach to document programs in dynamic languages. We demonstrate that success typing is, in fact, an instance of falsification by mapping success (input) types into suitable logic formulae. Output types are represented by recursive types. We prove the correctness of our mapping (which establishes that success typing is falsification) and we report some experiences with a prototype implementation.

1 Introduction

Dynamic languages like JavaScript, Python, and Erlang are increasingly used in application domains where reliability and robustness matters. Their advantages lie in the provision of domain specific libraries, flexibility, and expressiveness, which enables rapid prototyping. However, massive unit testing with all its drawbacks is the primary method of discovering errors: static analysis is often not applicable because it either yields many false positives or restricts the expressiveness. Verification is feasible but cumbersome (see for example the JavaScript formalization effort [3,6]). Moreover, it requires a major effort.

Unit testing with good code coverage is not straightforward to achieve, either. As the development of meaningful unit tests is also cumbersome and time consuming, the lack of static analyses that permit error detection prior to execution is one of the major drawbacks of dynamic languages.

Classical static analyses and type systems guarantee the absence of a particular class of errors: the program cannot *go wrong*. Imposing such a system on a dynamic language deprives it of its major attraction for certain programmers: the ability to write code without being restricted by a formal framework. Even suggesting such a framework would come close to treason. Furthermore, programmers are confused by false positives or error messages they do not understand [2]. However, an analysis that only reports problems that would definitely

© Springer International Publishing Switzerland 2015
K. Havelund et al. (Eds.): NFM 2015, LNCS 9058, pp. 234–247, 2015.
DOI: 10.1007/978-3-319-17524-9_17

lead to an error during execution could be acceptable. This point of view leads to the idea of a success typing.

In a standard type system, the typing $F : \tau_1 \to \tau_2$ means that an application of F to an argument v of type τ_1 yields a result of type τ_2 if $F(v)$ terminates normally. If type checking for the system is decidable, then there are programs which do not lead to type mismatches when executed, but which are rejected by the type system. A trivial example is a conditional that returns values of different types in its branches, but semantically it is clear that only the first branch can ever be executed.

In contrast, a success type system guarantees that for all arguments v **not** of type τ_1, the function application $F(v)$ leads to a run-time error (or nontermination). For an argument v of type τ_1, success typing gives the same guarantees as traditional typing: $F(v) \in \tau_2$ if it terminates normally. By necessity, the guarantee of the run-time error is also an approximation, but success typing must approximate in the other direction as a standard type system. Hence, the "standard part" of a success type usually gives a weaker guarantee than a standard type. In model checking terms, a standard type system performs verification whereas success typing seems related to falsification [1]: its goal is the detection of errors rather than proving the absence of them.

1.1   Success Typings in Erlang

Erlang is a dynamically typed functional programming language with commercial uses in e-commerce, telephony, and instant messaging. Besides the usual numeric and string types, Erlang includes an atom data type for symbols and tuples for building data structures.

Lindahl and Sagonas [10,14] designed a success typing system for Erlang which infers types with a constraint-based algorithm. Types are drawn from a finite lattice that encompasses types for various atoms (symbols, numbers, strings, etc), functions, tuple and list constructions, unions, and a type *any* that subsumes all other types. One of the major goals of their approach is the ability to automatically generate documentation for functions from the inferred success types. This goal requires small, readable types, which are guaranteed by the finiteness of the lattice. Types for data structures are made finite by cutting off at a certain depth bound. A concrete example shows where this boundedness leads to approximation.

Many Erlang programming idioms rely on named tuples, that is, tuples where the first component is an atom and the remaining components contain associated data as in {book,"Hamlet","Shakespeare"}. One can view named tuples as named constructors: book("Hamlet","Shakespeare"). Named tuples can be nested arbitrarily and created dynamically.

Lindahl and Sagonas' algorithm misses some definite errors based on nested named tuples, as can be seen by the following example. Here is an implementation of a list length function returning the zero constructor and succ constructor instead of the built-in integers.[1]

```
length([]) -> {zero};
length([_|XS]) -> {succ, length(XS)}.
```

The Dialyzer[2] infers the following success type for length:

$$\text{length} : [any] \rightarrow \text{zero} \cup \text{succ}(\text{zero} \cup \text{succ}(\text{zero}) \cup \text{succ}(any))$$

The argument part of the success type, $[any]$, describes that applying length to a non-list argument yields an error and applying it to a list of arbitrary content might succeed or fail. The result part describes the return value as either zero or as a nested tuple consisting of succ and any value. The argument part is exact: There is no argument of type $[any]$ for which length fails. However, the analyzer restricts tuples to a nesting depth of three levels.

To illustrate the problem with this approximation, consider the function check that pattern matches on a nest of named tuples, which cannot be created by the length function. Applying the check function to the result of length yields a definite error. However, the standard setting of the Dialyzer does not detect this error.

```
check({succ,{succ,{succ,{foo}}}}) -> 0.
test() -> check(length([0,0,0,0])).
```

1.2   Our Approach

We focus on errors that include the creation and destruction of data structures and thus consider programs that manipulate constructor trees, only. Our approach describes input type and output type of a function with different models. A success typing of a function comprises a recursive type describing the possible outputs and of a crash condition as a logical formula whose models are the crashing inputs of the function. This approach yields a modular definition of success typings.

Contributions.

- We propose a new formally defined view of success typing for a language with data structures. We represent the input and output types of a function differently and thus obtain a modular approach.
- Our approach is correct. We show preservation of types and crash condition during evaluation as well as failure consistency (i.e., if our analysis predicts a crash, the evaluation crashes definitely).
- We give a prototype implementation of our approach.

---

[1] The left-hand side pattern [] matches the empty list and the pattern [_|XS] matches a list with arbitrary head and tail bound to XS.

[2] The DIscrepancy AnalYZer for ERlang programs, an implementation of Lindahl and Sagonas' algorithm. http://www.erlang.org/doc/man/dialyzer.html

Outline. In Section 2 we define syntax and semantics of a constructor-based language. We introduce types and crash conditions for expressions of this language in Section 3 followed by an analysis that assigns types and crash conditions to expressions. Afterwards, we show show the correctness of the analysis. We discuss practical issues of our approach in Section 4. In Section 5 we discuss related work and conclude in Section 6.

An extended version of this article, including proofs, is available online [8].

2   Language

We illustrate our approach using a higher-order call-by-value language λ_C that comprises of explicit recursion, integer values, n-ary constructors, and pattern-matching to distinguish and destruct the previously defined constructors. We draw these constructors from a fixed, finite, and distinct ranked alphabet, that is, every constructor has a specific arity. We will denote constructors by upper case letters $A, B, C, \ldots$, and implicitly specify their arity when creating constructor terms.

Syntax. Syntactically, the language λ_C (Fig. 1) consists of values and expressions. A value v is either an integer literal n, a constructor term $C(v_1, \ldots, v_n)$ where C has arity n and v_i are values, a recursive unary[3] function **rec** $f\ x = e$, or an explicit error err. An expression e is either a value v, an identifier x, a constructor term $C(e_1, \ldots, e_n)$ where C has arity n and e_i are expressions, a function application $(e\ e)$, or a pattern-matching expression **match** e **with** P. Within the possibly empty list of patterns P, a pattern $C(x_1, \ldots, x_n) \to e$ consists of a constructor C with arity n, a list of variables $x_1, \ldots, x_n$, and a body expression e. For the list of empty patterns we write $[\ ]$ and to append lists we write $[C(x_1, \ldots, x_n) \to e] + P$. We assume that the constructors in a list of patterns occur at most once. We introduce an auxiliary definition $\hat{v}$ that represents values not containing functions. For constructor expressions with arity zero, we omit parentheses.

Semantics. In Fig. 2 we define the semantics of λ_C as a small-step operational semantics. We use $\mathcal{E}$ to describe expressions with holes $\square$ and EVAL-FINAL to evaluate expressions containing only values as subexpressions. EVAL-HOLE evaluates expressions by choosing holes. SAPP defines recursive function application by capture-avoiding substitution of the argument and function symbol. The rule SMATCH evaluates a constructor value and a list of patterns if the the constructor value matches the first pattern. If so, it extracts the values of the argument and substitutes the variables for the corresponding values in the pattern's body expression. If the first pattern in the list of patterns does not match the constructor value, the rule SMATCHNEXT applies and discards the first non-matching pattern.

---

[3] Multiple arguments can be passed by wrapping them in a constructor.

We explicitly define error creation and propagation as we want to detect definite errors in our programs. Errors occur, if the expression at the first argument of a function application is reduced to a non-function value or if a pattern matching expression occurs with an empty list either because no pattern matched or the list of patterns was initially empty. The former case, non-function values in applications, is handled by the rule SAPPERR1 and the latter case by the rule SMATCHERR both reducing to the error value err. Error propagation is handled by the rules SMATCHERR, if the argument to a pattern matching is an error, the rule SAPPERR2 if the argument to a function application is an error, and the rule SMATCHNEXTERR, if a constructor contains an error as a subexpression.

$$v ::= n \mid \mathbf{rec}\ f\ x = e \mid C(v_1, \ldots, v_n) \mid \mathrm{err}$$

$$e ::= v \mid x \mid C(e_1, \ldots, e_n) \mid (e\ e) \mid \mathbf{match}\ e\ \mathbf{with}\ \overline{[C_i(\bar{x}) \rightarrow e_i]}$$

$$\hat{v} ::= n \mid C(v_1, \ldots, v_n)$$

Fig. 1. Syntax of λ_C with values v, expressions e and non-function values $\hat{v}$

$$\mathcal{E} ::= C(v_1, \ldots, v_n, \Box, e_1, \ldots, e_m) \mid \Box\ e \mid v\ \Box \mid \mathbf{match}\ \Box\ \mathbf{with}\ [C_i(\bar{x}) \rightarrow e_i]$$

$$
\begin{array}{cc}
\text{EVAL-FINAL} & \text{EVAL-HOLE} \\
\dfrac{e \longrightarrow e'}{e \hookrightarrow e'} & \dfrac{e \hookrightarrow e'}{\mathcal{E}[e] \hookrightarrow \mathcal{E}[e']}
\end{array}
$$

SAPP	$((\mathbf{rec}\ f\ x = e)\ v)$	$\longrightarrow e[x \mapsto v, f \mapsto \mathbf{rec}\ f\ x = e]$
SAPPERR1	$(\hat{v}\ v)$	$\longrightarrow \mathrm{err}$
SAPPERR2	$((\mathbf{rec}\ f\ x = e)\ \mathrm{err})$	$\longrightarrow \mathrm{err}$
SMATCH	$\mathbf{match}\ C(\bar{v})\ \mathbf{with}\ [C(\bar{x}) \rightarrow e, \ldots]$	$\longrightarrow e[\overline{x_i \mapsto v_i}]$
SMATCHERR	$\mathbf{match}\ \mathrm{err}\ \mathbf{with}\ [\ldots]$	$\longrightarrow \mathrm{err}$
SMATCHNEXT	$\mathbf{match}\ C(\bar{v})\ \mathbf{with}\ [D(\bar{x}) \rightarrow e] \mathbin{+\!\!+} P$	$\longrightarrow \mathbf{match}\ C(\bar{v})\ \mathbf{with}\ P$
SMATCHNEXTERR	$\mathbf{match}\ C(\bar{v})\ \mathbf{with}\ [\ ]$	$\longrightarrow \mathrm{err}$
SCTORERR	$C(v_1, \ldots, v_n, \mathrm{err}, e_1, \ldots, e_m)$	$\longrightarrow \mathrm{err}$

Fig. 2. Small-step operational semantics for λ_C

3 Type and Crash Condition

The basic notion of our formalization is a type τ that represents trees created from constructors C on a type level. Furthermore, we represent function values using recursive types. To formalize success types, we represent the possible outputs of a function and the valid inputs of a function differently, thus resulting in a non-standard function type definition where the possible outputs are represented using a type τ and the possible inputs are represented using a crash condition ϕ. Types and crash conditions are defined mutually in Fig. 5. Intuitively, a crash condition for a function is a logical formula whose models are types. These types describe inputs that definitely crash the function.

Types τ comprise of type variables α, an equi-recursive function type written $\mu X.\forall \alpha\,[\phi]\,.\tau$ that includes a type variable α representing the function's argument, a return type τ, and a crash condition ϕ indicating when the function definitely crashes. Furthermore, we define a constructor type τ that captures the types of a constructor expression, a union type $\tau \cup \tau$, an integer type int, and the empty type $\perp$ that has no values. We define two operators that work on types: a type-level function application $(\tau\; @_\tau\; \tau)$, and a projection function for constructor types $\tau \downarrow_i^C$ that projects the ith component of a type τ if it is a constructor type C. The semantics of these operators is defined in Fig. 6. In our definition, the fix-point formulation μX only occurs together with a function type definition. The type operators are always implicitly applied.

Crash conditions ϕ are defined as atoms true tt and false ff, intersection $\phi \vee \phi$ and conjunction $\phi \wedge \psi$, predicates over types $C \in \tau$ symbolizing that a type τ can be a constructor C, $C \notin \tau$ symbolizing that a type τ is not a constructor type C, and $\forall \notin \tau$ symbolizing that τ is not a function. Furthermore, in Fig. 6 we define an operator $(\tau\; @_\phi\; \tau)$ that describes a crash-condition-level function application. Again, the crash condition operator is implicitly applied.

An interpretation $\mathcal{J}$ is a mapping of type variables to types. An interpretation of a type $[\![\tau]\!]_{\mathcal{J}}$ is a set of types as specified in Fig. 3.

$$
\begin{aligned}
[\![\alpha]\!]_{\mathcal{J}} &= \{\mathcal{J}(\alpha)\} \\
[\![\mu X.\forall \alpha\,[\phi]\,.\tau]\!]_{\mathcal{J}} &= \{\mu X.\forall \alpha\,[\phi]\,.\tau' \mid \tau' \in [\![\tau]\!]_{\mathcal{J}'}, \mathcal{J}' = \mathcal{J} \setminus \{\alpha\}\} \\
[\![C(\tau_1,\ldots,\tau_n)]\!]_{\mathcal{J}} &= \{C(\tau_1',\cdots,\tau_n') \mid \tau_i' \in [\![\tau_i]\!]_{\mathcal{J}}) \\
[\![\tau_1 \cup \tau_2]\!]_{\mathcal{J}} &= [\![\tau_1]\!]_{\mathcal{J}} \cup [\![\tau_2]\!]_{\mathcal{J}} \\
[\![\text{int}]\!]_{\mathcal{J}} &= \{\text{int}\} \\
[\![\perp]\!]_{\mathcal{J}} &= \{\}
\end{aligned}
$$

Fig. 3. Definition of an interpretation $\mathcal{J}$ on a type τ

In Fig. 4 we recursively define an entailment relation $\mathcal{J} \vDash \phi$ for an interpretation $\mathcal{J}$ and a crash condition ϕ.

$$\mathcal{J} \vDash \mathbf{tt}$$
$$\mathcal{J} \nvDash \mathbf{ff}$$
$$\mathcal{J} \vDash \phi_1 \vee \phi_2 \iff \mathcal{J} \vDash \phi_1 \vee \mathcal{J} \vDash \phi_2$$
$$\mathcal{J} \vDash \phi_1 \wedge \phi_2 \iff \mathcal{J} \vDash \phi_1 \wedge \mathcal{J} \vDash \phi_2$$
$$\mathcal{J} \vDash C \in \tau \iff \exists C(\overline{\tau}) \in \tau_{\mathcal{J}}$$
$$\mathcal{J} \vDash C \notin \tau \iff \nexists (C(\overline{\tau})) \in \tau_{\mathcal{J}}$$
$$\mathcal{J} \vDash \forall \notin \tau \iff \nexists (\mu X.\forall \alpha\,[\phi].\tau) \in \tau_{\mathcal{J}}$$

Fig. 4. Definition of the entailment relation $\mathcal{J} \vDash \phi$

Example 1. We take the length function of lists as an example using constructors $C_{nil}, C_{zero}, C_{succ}$, and C_{cons} with arities zero, zero, one, and two, respectively.

rec *len* $x = $ **match** x **with** $[C_{nil} \to C_{zero}, C_{cons}(x_1, x_2) \to C_{succ}((len\ x_2))]$

A possible function type for the length function is

$$\tau_{len} = \mu X.\forall \alpha \left[C_{nil} \notin \alpha \wedge \left(\left(C_{cons} \in \alpha \wedge (X\,@_\phi\,\alpha \downarrow_2^{C_{cons}}) \right) \vee C_{cons} \notin \alpha \right) \right].$$
$$C_{zero} \cup C_{succ}((X\,@_\tau\,\alpha \downarrow_2^{C_{cons}}))$$

whose type is recursively entwined with its crash condition. The derivation of this type is described in Section 3.1. We extract the crash condition that still makes use of τ_{len} via X and get a logical formula with free variable α

$$\phi_{len} = C_{nil} \notin \alpha \wedge \left(\left(C_{cons} \in \alpha \wedge (\tau_f\,@_\phi\,\alpha \downarrow_2^{C_{cons}}) \right) \vee C_{cons} \notin \alpha \right)$$

that symbolizes when the function crashes. For example the following interpretation (amongst many others)

$$\mathcal{J} = \{\alpha \mapsto \bigcup \{(((\mu X.\forall \alpha\,[\mathbf{ff}].C_{zero} \cup C_{cons}\,(\tau, (X\,@_\tau\,\alpha)))\,@_\phi\,C_{unused}) \mid \tau \in T\}$$

entails the crash condition: $\mathcal{J} \vDash \phi_{len}$. Here, C_{unused} is only needed as a dummy argument to the type-level function. When implicitly applying the type operators, we end up with the infinite type[4]

$$\{\mu X.C_{zero} \cup C_{cons}(\tau, X) \mid \tau \in T\}$$

This type represents all lists not ending with a nil but with a zero.

Before introducing the analysis that assigns types and crash conditions to expressions, please note that the question of entailment is not decidable in general.

---

[4] For the sake of a simpler type syntax, this type cannot be represented using our type syntax directly. We always have to use type-level applications.

$$\tau ::= \alpha \mid \mu X.\forall \alpha \, [\phi] \, . \tau \mid C(\tau_1, \ldots, \tau_n) \mid \tau \cup \tau \mid \text{int} \mid \bot \mid (\tau \, @_\tau \, \tau) \mid \tau \downarrow_i^C$$
$$\phi ::= \mathbf{ff} \mid \mathbf{tt} \mid \phi \vee \phi \mid \phi \wedge \phi \mid C \in \tau \mid C \notin \tau \mid \forall \notin \tau \mid (\tau \, @_\phi \, \tau)$$

Fig. 5. Definition of types τ and crash conditions ϕ

$$(\tau_1 \, @_\tau \, \tau_2) = \begin{cases} \tau_b[\alpha \mapsto \tau_2, X \mapsto \tau_1] & \text{if } \tau_1 = \mu X.\forall \alpha \, [\phi] \, . \tau_b \\ (\tau_1 \, @_\tau \, \tau_2) & \text{if } \tau_1 = \alpha \\ (\tau_{11} \, @_\tau \, \tau_2) \cup (\tau_{12} \, @_\tau \, \tau_2) & \text{if } \tau_1 = \tau_{11} \cup \tau_{12} \\ (\tau_1 \, @_\tau \, \tau_{21}) \cup (\tau_1 \, @_\tau \, \tau_{22}) & \text{if } \tau_2 = \tau_{21} \cup \tau_{22} \\ \bot & \text{otherwise} \end{cases}$$

$$\tau \downarrow_i^C = \begin{cases} \tau_i & \text{if } \tau = C(\tau_1, \ldots, \tau_n), 1 \leq i \leq n \\ \tau \downarrow_i^C & \text{if } \tau_0 = \alpha \\ \bot & \text{otherwise} \end{cases}$$

$$(\tau_1 \, @_\phi \, \tau_2) = \begin{cases} \phi[\alpha \mapsto \tau_2, X \mapsto \tau_1] & \text{if } \tau_1 = \mu X.\forall \alpha \, [\phi] \, . \tau_b \\ (\tau_1 \, @_\phi \, \tau_2) & \text{if } \tau_1 = \alpha \\ (\tau_{11} \, @_\phi \, \tau_2) \cup (\tau_{12} \, @_\phi \, \tau_2) & \text{if } \tau_1 = \tau_{11} \cup \tau_{12} \\ (\tau_1 \, @_\phi \, \tau_{21}) \cup (\tau_1 \, @_\phi \, \tau_{22}) & \text{if } \tau_2 = \tau_{21} \cup \tau_{22} \\ \mathbf{tt} & \text{otherwise} \end{cases}$$

Fig. 6. Type and crash condition operators

Lemma 1. *It is undecidable whether for an arbitrary crash condition ϕ there exists an interpretation $\mathcal{J}$ such that $\mathcal{J} \vDash \phi$.*

We discuss possible solutions to this problem in Section 4.

3.1 Analysis

We present our analysis as a type system using a judgment $\Gamma \vdash e : \tau \mathbin{\&} \phi$ that relates a type variable environment Γ, an expression e, a type τ of the expression, and a crash condition ϕ characterizing when the expression crashes. We define the derivation rules in Fig. 7.

The rule T-REC derives a recursive function type for a recursive function expression by inferring the body's type and crash condition using type variables for the argument and a recursive type formulation for recursive calls. For a function application (T-FUNAPP) we infer types and crash conditions for both the callee e_1 and the argument e_2. The result type of the function application is the type-level application of the types of the callee and the argument. The function application can crash if either e_1 or e_2 crashes, e_1 is not a function, or the application itself crashes. The latter is symbolized by a crash condition-level function application. The rule T-IDENTIFIER derives the type of a variable from the environment and never crashes. An error value err has type $\bot$ and always crashes (T-ERROR). In rule T-CONSTRUCTOR, a constructor expression has a constructor type with the types of its arguments inferred recursively. A constructor crashes if one of its arguments crashes. Integer literals are handled by T-INTEGER and always have type int and never crash.

For the pattern matching expression, the type is described by the union of the types of the expression in the patterns. The crash condition is described by the crash condition of the expression to match and the crash conditions of the cases. The crash conditions of the cases are built using an auxiliary judgment: $\phi_m; \tau_0; \Gamma \vdash_p P : \tau_p \ \& \ \phi_p$ where ϕ_m describes the crash conditions accumulated so far, τ_0 describes the type of the expression to match, P the list of patterns which are traversed and τ_p the union of the types of the pattern case's body expression. The type and crash condition of a pattern list is created by two rules: if the pattern list is empty, we return the bottom type and the crash condition accumulated to far. If the pattern list is non-empty, we create the type of the current body expression by binding the variables defined in the pattern and inductively applying the derivation. The current expression can crash, if

T-REC
$$\frac{\Gamma, x_r : \alpha_r, f_r : X \vdash e : \tau_e \ \& \ \phi_e \qquad \alpha_r \text{ fresh} \quad x_r, f_r \notin \mathbf{dom}(\Gamma)}{\Gamma \vdash \mathbf{rec} \ f_r \ x_r = e : \mu X.\forall \alpha_r \left[\phi_e \right].\tau_e \ \& \ \mathbf{ff}}$$

T-FUNAPP
$$\frac{\Gamma \vdash e_1 : \tau_1 \ \& \ \phi_1}{\Gamma \vdash (e_1 \ e_2) : (\tau_1 \ @_\tau \tau_2) \ \& \ (\tau_1 \ @_\phi \tau_2) \vee \phi_1 \vee \phi_2 \vee \forall \notin \tau_1}$$

T-IDENTIFIER
$$\frac{\Gamma(x) = \tau}{\Gamma \vdash x : \tau \ \& \ \mathbf{ff}}$$

T-ERROR
$$\frac{}{\Gamma \vdash \mathrm{err} : \bot \ \& \ \mathbf{tt}}$$

T-CONSTRUCTOR
$$\frac{\forall i \in \{1, \ldots, n\} : \Gamma \vdash e_i : \tau_i \ \& \ \phi_i}{\Gamma \vdash C(e_1, \ldots, e_n) : C(\tau_1, \ldots, \tau_n) \ \& \ \bigvee \overline{\phi}}$$

T-PATTERN-MATCHING
$$\frac{\mathbf{tt}; \tau_0; \Gamma \vdash_p P : \tau_p \ \& \ \phi_p}{\Gamma \vdash \mathbf{match} \ e_0 \ \mathbf{with} \ P : \tau_p \ \& \ \phi_0 \vee \phi_p}$$

T-INTEGER
$$\frac{}{\Gamma \vdash n : \mathrm{int} \ \& \ \mathbf{ff}}$$

T-PATTERN-NEXT
$$\frac{\phi_0 \wedge ((C \in \tau_0 \wedge \phi_e) \vee C \notin \tau_0); \tau_0; \Gamma \vdash_p P : \tau' \ \& \ \phi'}{\phi_0; \tau_0; \Gamma \vdash_p [C(x_1, \ldots, x_n) \to e] \ +\!\!+ \ P : \tau' \cup \tau_e \ \& \ \phi'}$$

T-PATTERN-EMPTY
$$\frac{}{\phi_0; \tau_0; \Gamma \vdash_p [\,] : \bot \ \& \ \phi_0}$$

Fig. 7. Derivation rules for the types and crash conditions

either the pattern matches ($C \in \tau_0$) and the body expression crashes, or if the pattern does not match at all.

Additionally, we define a subtyping relation $\leq: \tau \times \tau$ in Fig. 8 The relation is standard, except for the rule S-Fun, which requires a logical implication of the crash conditions.

The (output) types derived for an expression are over-approximations whereas the crash conditions describe the possible crashes exactly. The interplay of types and crash conditions ends up with definite errors, because the predicate $C \notin \tau$ describes the question whether it is not possible that the type τ is a constructor C, and similarly for the predicate $\forall \notin \tau$.

$$
\begin{array}{cccc}
\text{S-Bot} & \text{S-Union} & \text{S-Refl} & \text{S-Ctor} \\
 & & & \dfrac{\bar{\tau} \leq \bar{\tau}'}{} \\
\dfrac{}{\bot \leq \tau} & \dfrac{}{\tau \leq \tau \cup \tau'} & \dfrac{}{\tau \leq \tau} & \dfrac{\bar{\tau} \leq \bar{\tau}'}{C(\bar{\tau}) \leq C(\bar{\tau}')}
\end{array}
$$

$$
\begin{array}{cc}
\text{S-Fun} & \text{T-Sub} \\
\dfrac{\tau \leq \tau' \quad \phi' \to \phi}{\mu X.\forall \alpha \,[\phi].\tau \leq \mu X.\forall \alpha \,[\phi'] .\tau'} & \dfrac{\Gamma \vdash e : \tau \,\&\, \phi \quad \tau \leq \tau' \quad \phi' \to \phi}{\Gamma \vdash e : \tau' \,\&\, \phi'}
\end{array}
$$

Fig. 8. Subtyping rules

3.2 Properties

To justify our analysis, we prove the preservation of types and crash conditions and the correctness. To do so, we need several auxiliary lemma.

Weakening allows the introduction of a fresh type variable into the type environment without changing anything.

Lemma 2 (Weakening). *For expressions e, types τ, τ_y, and τ_0, an identifier y, conditions ϕ and ϕ_0, and an environment Γ, the following holds:*

1. *If $\Gamma \vdash e : \tau \,\&\, \phi$ and $y \notin \mathbf{dom}(\Gamma)$ then $\Gamma, y : \tau_y \vdash e : \tau \,\&\, \phi$*
2. *If $\phi_0; \tau_0; \Gamma \vdash_p P : \tau \,\&\, \phi$ and $y \notin \mathbf{dom}(\Gamma)$ then $\phi_0; \tau_0; \Gamma, y : \tau_y \vdash_p P : \tau \,\&\, \phi$.*

The next lemma shows that we can replace a type variable α within an environment by a concrete type a if we replace all occurrences of the type variable in the resulting type and crash condition. We need this lemma when working with the type-level function application.

Lemma 3 (Consistency of type substitution). *For a well-formed environment Γ, an identifier y, a type variable α, an arbitrary expression e, types τ and τ_α, conditions ϕ and ϕ_0 the following holds:*

1. *If $\Gamma, y : \alpha \vdash e : \tau \,\&\, \phi$ then $(\Gamma, y : \alpha)[\alpha \mapsto \tau_\alpha] \vdash e : \tau[\alpha \mapsto \tau_\alpha] \,\&\, \phi[\alpha \mapsto \tau_\alpha]$*
2. *If $\phi_0; \tau_0; \Gamma, y : \alpha \vdash_p P : \tau \,\&\, \phi$ then $\phi_0[\alpha \mapsto \tau_\alpha]; \tau_0[\alpha \mapsto \tau_\alpha]; (\Gamma, y : \alpha)[\alpha \mapsto \tau_\alpha] \vdash_p P : \tau[\alpha \mapsto \tau_\alpha] \,\&\, \phi[\alpha \mapsto \tau_\alpha]$.*

Lemma 4 shows that we can substitute a variable y in an expression e with a value of the same type without changing the type and crash condition of the whole expression. This lemma is needed for the type-level function applications later.

Lemma 4 (Consistency of value substitution). *For an environment Γ, an identifier y, types τ and τ_y, an expression e, conditions ϕ and ϕ_0, and a value v, the following holds*

1. *If $\Gamma, y : \tau_y \vdash e : \tau \ \& \ \phi$ and $\Gamma \vdash v : \tau_y \ \& \ \mathtt{ff}$ then $\Gamma \vdash e[y \mapsto v] : \tau \ \& \ \phi$.*
2. *If $\phi_0; \tau_0; \Gamma, y : \tau_y \vdash_p P : \tau \ \& \ \phi$ and $\Gamma \vdash v : \tau_y \ \& \ \mathtt{ff}$ then $\phi_0; \tau_0; \Gamma \vdash_p P[y \mapsto v] : \tau \ \& \ \phi$.*

The next lemma shows that the analysis is designed such that after a successful pattern matching, the crash conditions of the remaining pattern's body expressions cannot be satisfied anymore. The reason is that ϕ_0 in the rules T-PATTERN-NEXT and T-PATTERN-EMPTY influences the resulting crash condition of the whole expression.

Lemma 5 (Unsatisfiability after matching patterns). *For an environment Γ, types τ and τ', and conditions ϕ' it holds that if $\mathtt{ff}, \tau_0; \Gamma \vdash_p P : \tau' \ \& \ \phi'$ then $\nvDash \phi'$.*

Finally, we can establish the preservation theorem for our type system.

Theorem 1 (Preservation of types and crash conditions). *If $\Gamma \vdash e : \tau \ \& \ \phi$, $e \hookrightarrow e'$ and $\Gamma \vdash e' : \tau' \ \& \ \phi'$ then $\tau \leq \tau'$ and $\phi \leftrightarrow \phi'$.*

Furthermore, we show that our analysis is sound: if the crash conditions report an error, then there is either an error or the evaluation does not terminate.

Theorem 2 (Failure). *If $\forall \mathcal{T}, \mathcal{V}, \Gamma$ and $\forall x \in \mathbf{dom}(\Gamma) : \vdash \mathcal{V}(x) : \mathcal{T}(\Gamma(x)) \vDash \mathcal{T}(\phi)$, and*

1. *$\Gamma \vdash e : \tau \ \& \ \phi$, then $\mathcal{V}(e) \hookrightarrow^* \mathtt{err}$ or $\mathcal{V}(e) \Uparrow$.*
2. *$\phi_0; \tau_0; \Gamma \vdash_p [C_1(\bar{x} \to e_1), \ldots, C_n(\bar{x} \to e_n)] : \tau \ \& \ \phi$ and a value $C(v_1, \ldots, v_n)$ with $\Gamma' \vdash C(v_1, \ldots, v_n) : C(\tau_1, \ldots, \tau_n) \ \& \ \mathtt{ff}$, then either*
   - *$\forall i : C_i \neq C$*
   - *or $\exists i : C_i = C$ and $(\mathcal{V}'(e_i) \hookrightarrow^* \mathtt{err}$ or $\mathcal{V}(e_1) \Uparrow)$.*

4   Practical Considerations

We have shown that success typing is an instance of falsification and thus allows the detection of definite errors. However, as shown by Lemma 1, the satisfiability of ϕ is undecidable in general. Thus a direct algorithmic solution cannot exist. We implemented[5] a version of the analysis that imposes a user-definable limit of k iterations on the unfolding operations described in the operators in Section 3 and can thus check for errors up to depth k.

---

[5] http://www.informatik.uni-freiburg.de/~jakobro/stpa/

Example 2. An example for a yet problematic combination of type and crash condition we cannot solve at the moment is the following: We create a function that generates an infinite list and apply the resulting stream on the list length function.

With the list generator's type

$$\tau_{gen} = ((\mu X.\forall \alpha \, [\mathtt{ff}] . C_{cons}(C_{zero}, (X \, @_\tau \, \alpha))) \, @_\tau \, C_{unused})$$
$$= C_{cons}(C_{zero}, (\tau_{gen} \, @_\tau \, C_{unused}))$$

and the list's type from Example 1 the application of the stream to the length function has the following crash condition after type and crash condition operators are applied once (before substitution):

$$\left(C_{nil} \notin \alpha \wedge \left(\left(C_{cons} \in \alpha \wedge (X \, @_\phi \, \alpha \downarrow_2^{C_{cons}}) \right) \vee C_{cons} \notin \alpha \right) \right)$$
$$[\alpha \mapsto C_{cons}(C_{zero}, (\tau_{gen} \, @_\tau \, C_{unused}))]$$

After performing the substitution, we can evaluate the predicates that only look finitely deep into their argument. When we apply type and crash condition operators again, we end up on the same crash condition. Although we reach a fix point in this case, this is of course not the case in general.

To solve this problem in general, we need to find an approximation for the crash condition formula. As we only want to find definite errors, our approximation has to be an under-approximation. However, finding a good under-approximation, is yet an open problem.

When we view the output type of a functions as a constructor tree, we can represent it as a higher-order tree grammar, as is proposed by Ong and Ramsey [12]. The (approximated) crash condition of a function can be represented as a tree automaton. As the model checking of tree automata and higher-order tree grammars is decidable [11] we have some means of finding definite errors.

5   Related Work

The idea of finding definite errors in programs is quite old and several approaches exist.

Constraint-based analyses to detect must-information can be found in Reynolds [13] where he describes a construction of recursive set definitions for LISP programs that are "a good fit to the results of a function". However, the goal of the paper was to infer data structure declarations and not to find errors. The constraint-based analysis of Lindahl and Sagonas' [10] is a modular approach similar to ours, but does not account for data structures of arbitrary depth but instead uses k-depth abstraction as we do in our current implementation. Furthermore, the approach of Lindahl and Sagonas uses union types that are widened after a fixed size limit. These limits are to establish small and readable types whereas we focus on exact tracking of values.

Soft typing, presented by Cartwright and Fagan [4] detects suspicious expressions in a program, i.e., expressions that cannot be verified to be error-free, and adds run-time checks. Although the idea of not rejecting working programs is the same, our approach requires no changes in existing programs as we only assume programs to contain errors if we can proof it.

The line of work of Vaziri et al. [5,7] focuses on imperative first-order languages and uses user-defined specifications given in the Alloy language to state the intention of a function and then checks the implementation against its specification. Although they explicitly mention unbounded data structures in their approach, only instances up to a number of heap cells and loop iterations are considered. In contrast to our approach, they require user-defined annotations. A similar framework [15] removes the chore to define annotations and only requires the user to provide a property to be checked. Their abstraction refines specifications that describe the behavior of procedures and thus creates a refinement-based approach that ensures that no spurious errors appear if the analysis halts.

Different approaches for definite error detections are presented by Ball et al. [1] and Kroening and Weissenbacher [9] for imperative first-order languages in a Hoare-style way. However, a comparison to our approach is difficult because they rely on a transition system to model the behavior of programs whereas we use a type system.

6   Conclusion

We presented a new formal approach to success typings for a constructor-based higher-order language using different representations for the input and output type of a function. We proved that our formulation of success typings is a falsification in the sense that it only reports definite errors. We presented a prototype implementation that checks for errors up to a user-defined bound.

In future we want to look at means to model check (type) trees [11,12] with logical formula represented as higher-order tree grammars and tree automata, respectively. Thus, we hope to (partly) remove the n-bound of current approaches.

Acknowledgments. This work has been partially supported by the German Research Foundation (Deutsche Forschungsgemeinschaft, DFG) within the Research Training Group 1103 (Embedded Microsystems).

References

1. Ball, T., Kupferman, O., Yorsh, G.: Abstraction for falsification. In: Etessami, K., Rajamani, S.K. (eds.) CAV 2005. LNCS, vol. 3576, pp. 67–81. Springer, Heidelberg (2005)
2. Bessey, A., Block, K., Chelf, B., Chou, A., Fulton, B., Hallem, S., Gros, C., Kamsky, A., McPeak, S., Engler, D.R.: A few billion lines of code later: using static analysis to find bugs in the real world. Commun. ACM **53**(2), 66–75 (2010)

3. Bodin, M., Charguéraud, A., Filaretti, D., Gardner, P., Maffeis, S., Naudziuniene, D., Schmitt, A., Smith, G.: A trusted mechanised JavaSript specification. In: Jagannathan, S., Sewell, P. (eds.) POPL, pp. 87–100. ACM (2014)

4. Cartwright, R., Fagan, M.: Soft typing. In: Wise, D.S. (ed.) Proceedings of the ACM SIGPLAN'91 PLDI, Toronto, Ontario, Canada, June 26–28, 1991, pp. 278–292 (1991)

5. Dolby, J., Vaziri, M., Tip, F.: Finding bugs efficiently with a SAT solver. In: Crnkovic, I., Bertolino, A. (eds.) Proceedings of the 6th joint meeting of the European Software Engineering Conference and the ACM SIGSOFT International Symposium on Foundations of Software Engineering, 2007, Dubrovnik, Croatia, September 3–7, 2007, pp. 195–204. ACM (2007)

6. Gardner, P., Maffeis, S., Smith, G.D.: Towards a program logic for JavaScript. In: Field, J., Hicks, M. (eds.) Proc. 39th ACM Symp. POPL, pp. 31–44, Philadelphia, USA, January 2012. ACM Press

7. Jackson, D., Vaziri, M.: Finding bugs with a constraint solver. In: ISSTA, pp. 14–25 (2000)

8. Jakob, R., Thiemann, P.: A falsification view of success typings. CoRR, abs/1502.01278 (2015). extended version

9. Kroening, D., Weissenbacher, G.: Verification and falsification of programs with loops using predicate abstraction. Formal Asp. Comput. **22**(2), 105–128 (2010)

10. Lindahl, T., Sagonas, K.F.: Practical type inference based on success typings. In: Bossi, A., Maher, M.J. (eds.) PPDP, pp. 167–178. ACM (2006)

11. Ong, C.-H.L.: On model-checking trees generated by higher-order recursion schemes. In: LICS, pp. 81–90. IEEE Computer Society (2006)

12. Ong, C.-H.L., Ramsay, S.J.: Verifying higher-order functional programs with pattern-matching algebraic data types. In: Ball, T., Sagiv, M. (eds.) POPL, pp. 587–598, Austin, TX, USA, January 2011. ACM Press

13. Reynolds, J.C.: Automatic computation of data set definitions. IFIP Congress **1**, 456–461 (1968)

14. Sagonas, K.F., Silva, J., Tamarit, S.: Precise explanation of success typing errors. In: Albert, E., Mu, S.-C. (eds.) PEPM, pp. 33–42. ACM (2013)

15. Taghdiri, M.: Inferring specifications to detect errors in code. In: 19th IEEE International Conference on Automated Software Engineering (ASE 2004), 20–25 September 2004, Linz, Austria, pp. 144–153. IEEE Computer Society (2004)

Verified ROS-Based Deployment of Platform-Independent Control Systems

Wenrui Meng[✉], Junkil Park, Oleg Sokolsky,
Stephanie Weirich, and Insup Lee

University of Pennsylvania, Philadelphia, PA 19104, USA
wenrui@cis.upenn.edu

Abstract. The paper considers the problem of model-based deployment of platform-independent control code on a specific platform. The approach is based on automatic generation of platform-specific glue code from an architectural model of the system. We present a tool, ROS-Gen, that generates the glue code based on a declarative specification of platform interfaces. Our implementation targets the popular Robot Operating System (ROS) platform. We demonstrate that the code generation process is amenable to formal verification. The code generator is implemented in Coq and relies on the infrastructure provided by the CompCert and VST tool. We prove that the generated code always correctly connects the controller function to sensors and actuators in the robot. We use ROSGen to implement a cruise control system on the LandShark robot.

1 Introduction

Modern cyber-physical systems are typically constructed from individually developed components. This process involves two steps: first, developing the components in a platform independent way, and second, deploying these components on a specific architecture, using a middleware platform to implement the connections between the components.

Model-based development aids in both parts of this development process. First, in developing individual components, component behaviors are abstractly specified by data models, state charts, or diagrams. These diagrams can be expressed using design tools such as Simulink/Stateflow, UPPAAL [1], or SCADE/- Lustre [2]. Code generation tools then convert these diagrams into code, typically platform-independent C source code. This generative approach helps us to preserve properties verified at the modeling level, making sure that component implementations also satisfy these properties.

Second, system architectural models describe the relationships between the components of the system. For example, in an autonomous robotic system the

This research is supported in part by DARPA HACMS program under agreement FA8750-12-2-0247. The views expressed are those of the authors and may not reflect the official policy or position of the Department of Defense or the U.S. Government.

K. Havelund et al. (Eds.): NFM 2015, LNCS 9058, pp. 248–262, 2015.
DOI: 10.1007/978-3-319-17524-9_18

architectural model specifies (1) how each component should be executed (such as how the periodic execution within a given period may be specified), (2) how system inputs, such as sensor streams, should be routed to inputs of components processing the streams, and (3) how outputs of each component should be routed to inputs of other components or to system outputs (such as actuators). A significant part of platform configuration is providing a platform-specific wrapper for the platform-independent component implementation. The wrapper (also known as the glue code) uses platform APIs to schedule component execution, to obtain inputs for the component, and to forward its outputs. A faulty deployment undermines the benefits of provably correct implementation of individual components. Platform configurations, therefore, should be automatically generated from the architectural model to ensure correct integration of individual components.

In this paper, we address the problem of automatically generating provably correct glue code for a particular deployment platform from a given architectural model. We use the Robot Operating System (ROS)[1] as our target platform, a "thin, message-based, peer-to-peer" [3] robotics middleware designed for mobile manipulators. The ROS platform has recently gained popularity in the robotics community because it raises the level of abstraction in embedded control system development. ROS-based applications are assembled from multiple ROS nodes that run concurrently. ROS supports communication between these nodes using a publish/subscribe-based message system.

To that end, we develop a ROS glue code generator, called ROSGen, that automatically generates such glue code from system architecture specifications. The input language for our code generator is a domain-specific language, called a ROS node model, that specifies the ROS nodes that comprise the system and ROS topics that the nodes subscribe to and publish on.

Of course, by generating code we eliminate some sources of programmer error in system development. However, for safety critical systems, we want the highest level of assurance. We would like to prove that the output of our code generator satisfies strong correctness and safety requirements. One can take two approaches for the verification of generated code; first, one may verify every output individually. Alternatively, which is generally much harder, one may verify the code generator itself.

Our code generator is designed to support (both forms of) formal verification. ROSGen is implemented using the Coq proof assistant [4], making the full higher-order logic of Coq available for reasoning about both the output of the generator (represented as a Coq data structure) and the code generator itself (represented as a Coq function). In this context, we have used both approaches for verification.

We have applied ROSGen as part of a case study of glue code generation for the Black-i Robotics LandShark platform. The LandShark is an unmanned ground vehicle typically used to extend human capabilities, often in dangerous environments such as at a chemical spill or for sentry duty. ROSGen can generate glue code for this platform, and we have proven that the generated code satisfies

---

[1] www.ros.org

a crucial `Data Delivery Correctness` (DDC) property: that the arriving sensor message will be correctly delivered to the control function and that the output of the control function will be correctly delivered to the actuators. We express and prove this property using the Verified Software Toolchain (VST) tool [5], which provides a higher-order separation logic for reasoning about memory usage in C programs. Our proof has been mechanically checked by Coq.

Moreover, we prove the generalized DDC property of the code generator itself. That is, we can show that `every` output of ROSGen satisfies the same DDC property that we have shown for the LandShark instance. In general, this is a hard problem. However, in our case, because of the relatively simple code structure and because the property of interest is concerned with data transfer, we can generalize the proof of instances of the generated code to the proof of the generator itself.

In summary, this paper makes the following contributions:

- We introduce a domain specific language for describing the ROS nodes. We develop a code generator ROSGen to generate the robotics glue code according to a given ROS node model (Section 4).
- We demonstrate an application of ROSGen to a case study of a robotic control system and prove, using a suite of Coq-based tools, that the glue code correctly delivers data according to the ROS node model of the controller (Section 5).
- Finally, we verify that, given a well-formed ROS node model, ROSGen always generates code that satisfies the data delivery correctness property (Section 6).

The rest of the paper is organized as follows: we introduce the relevant work that our code generation is dependent on in Section 2. Section 3 explains the architecture of the ROS based control system and introduces the LandShark case study. In Sections 4, 5 and 6, we explain our code generation approach for ROS based control system and the verification for the generated code and code generator itself. We discuss related work in Section 7 and conclude in Section 8.

The Coq implementation of the code generator and case study can be downloaded from http://rtg.cis.upenn.edu/HACMS/codegen.html. The technical report [6] full version of this paper, including the formal VST specification and proof of DDC property, can also be found on the same webpage.

2   Proof Environment

Figure 1 shows the tools underlying ROSGen, which are briefly described below.
Coq. The Coq Proof Assistant[2] is a formal proof management system. It provides a formal language to write mathematical definitions, executable algorithms and theorems together with an environment for semi-interactive development of machine-checked proofs.

---

[2] http://coq.inria.fr/

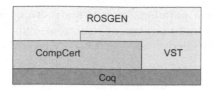

Fig. 1. ROSGen dependency structure

CompCert. CompCert [7] is a formally verified optimizing compiler for the C programming language that currently targets PowerPC, ARM and 32-bit x86 architectures. The compiler is specified, implemented and proved correct using the Coq proof assistant. It targets embedded systems programming, with stringent reliability requirements. CompCert's source language, a large subset of C called Clight, is the target language of our code generator; our generator produces abstract syntax values for Clight.

The formal semantics of Clight is mechanized using Coq. It supports many types including integral types (integers and floats in various sizes and signedness), array types, pointer types (including pointers to functions), function types, as well as struct and union types. A Clight program is composed of a list of declarations for global variables (name and type), a list of functions and an identifier naming the entry point of the program (the main function in C). *Verified software toolchain.* The goal of the Verified Software Toolchain (VST)[3] project is to verify that the assertions claimed at the top of a software toolchain really hold in the machine language program, running in the operating system context, on a weakly-consistent-shared-memory machine. It defines `Verifiable C`, a higher-order concurrent separation logic for Clight. `Verifiable C` has been proven sound with respect to the operational semantics of CompCert C [5].

The `Verifiable C` program logic extends Hoare logic by including separation logic constructs to support reasoning about mutable data structures such as arrays and pointers. In separation logic, an assertion holds on a particular subheap and assertions on different subheap are independent. As a result logical reasoning is modular. VST provides a tactic system for proving correctness properties, specified by the VST assertions, of C light programs. The most significant of these are the `forward` tactic, which symbolically executes the code, and the `entailer` tactic, which simplifies and often solves VST assertions [8].

3   ROS-Based Control System

3.1   Robot Operating System

ROS is a widely used component-based middleware for robotic system applications. A software component in ROS is called a ROS node. A ROS application usually consists of multiple ROS nodes running concurrently. The ROS nodes asynchronously communicate with each other. Communication in ROS is based

---

[3] http://vst.cs.princeton.edu/

on the Publish/Subscribe paradigm and uses structured message types. ROS Services are the mechanism to implement remote procedure calls in ROS, which are synchronous and blocking.

```
void callback(MessageType msg) { ... };
main(){
  Subscribe(..., callback);
  Advertise(...);
  while( ros_ok() ){
    SpinOnce();
      /* Process the input to the controller */
    Controller_step();
      /* Process the output of the controller */
    Publish(...); }}
```

Fig. 2. ROS-based controller system skeleton

Figure 2 shows the skeleton of a ROS-based control system. In order to subscribe to a topic in ROS, users need to define a callback function. A callback function for a topic is a message handler that is invoked to process the new messages when they arrive. `Subscribe` is a function from the ROS API that registers subscription information: a topic name, the message type, the internal buffer size and the callback function for those messages. If a new message is received, it is stored in an internal buffer. It replaces the oldest message in the buffer if the buffer is already full. When the ROS API function `SpinOnce` is invoked, all registered callback functions are invoked for every message in the internal buffers. In order to publish a topic in ROS, users should use the ROS API function `Advertise` to first create a publisher with a topic name, message type, and internal buffer size. The ROS API `Publish` function is then used to publish a message.

3.2 Case Study of LandShark Control System

In this section we illustrate a typical ROS-based control system using the Land-Shark robot. The LandShark is an electric unmanned ground vehicle, shown

Fig. 3. LandShark robot

in Figure 3, manufactured by Black-I Robotics.[4] Our case study develops a constant-speed cruise control algorithm that is resilient to attacks on vehicle sensors. The LandShark uses three sensors, GPS, a left wheel encoder and a right wheel encoder, to estimate its current velocity. These sensors can be compromised by attacks, such as GPS spoofing, that cause confusion in estimating the current velocity of the vehicle. The attack-resilient cruise controller of Land-Shark uses multiple independent sensors and the knowledge of the system model in order to correctly estimate the current velocity of the vehicle and drive the vehicle with a given constant velocity [9].

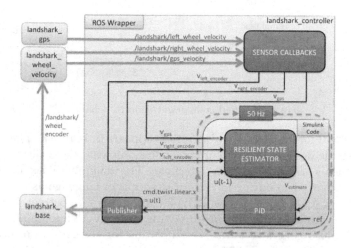

Fig. 4. LandShark control system architecture

Figure 4 shows the architecture of the LandShark control system, which consists of sensor/actuation/controller nodes and the connections between them through topic-based pub/sub communication. The ROS nodes landshark_gps and landshark_base are associated with sensors that read GPS and wheel encoder values respectively and publish them. The ROS node landshark_wheel_velocity subscribes to the series of wheel encoder values and publishes the velocity of the vehicle calculated from them. The ROS node landshark_base also plays a role as an actuation node in that it subscribes to the actuation commands and actuates the vehicle according to them. The ROS node landshark_controller is the controller node that subscribes to sensor value messages and publishes actuation commands. The landshark_controller node is periodically invoked at the rate of 50 Hz to execute the Simulink-generated step function. In each invocation, the callback functions are invoked by SpinOnce to process the messages received. The callback functions store the sensor messages in global variables. The sensor values in the global variables are transferred to the input data structure of the control algorithm function that is generated by Simulink. The step function is

---

[4] http://www.blackirobotics.com/

executed to calculate the actuation command, which is encapsulated in a ROS message variable and published by the publisher.

4   Code Generation

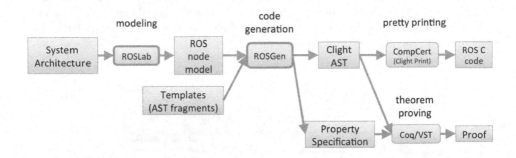

Fig. 5. Verified code generation toolchain

Our toolchain for verified code generation appears in Figure 5. The ROSLab tool supports the design of system architectures, allowing the creation of a diagram block using a graphical user interface. The diagram block in ROSLab can then be exported in our architectural description language as a ROS node model. With the ROS node model, ROSGen produces an abstract syntax tree for a subset of C called Clight, by instantiating a Clight AST template. In addition, ROSGen also generates a VST specification for each function, describing its Data Delivery Correctness DDC properties. We can prove that the generated code satisfies these specifications, as we demonstrate in Section 6. The final C code, which is run on the LandShark, is produced by the CompCert compiler using its pretty printer.

ROSLab Tool. ROSLab is a modular programming environment for robotic applications based on ROS. ROSLab enables users to model an architecture of a ROS application that consists of a set of ROS nodes and the connections between them. The interfaces of some commonly used ROS nodes such as sensor and actuator nodes are pre-defined in ROSLab. Users can define a new ROS node and its interface by selecting the pub/sub channels to add to the interface of the node.

4.1   ROS Node Model

A diagram block in ROSLab can be exported as a ROS node model. A ROS node model includes the period at which the node is to be invoked; the list of topics that the node publishes or subscribes to; the name and the I/O interface of the controller function that the node will run; and finally, a mapping from subscribed and published topics to inputs and outputs of the controller function. The ROS node model for the `landshark_controller` ROS node in Figure 4 is shown in Table 1. The name of the node, the period of the controller, and the

Table 1. ROS node model for LandShark

Node Information			
period	node name		controller name
20	landshark_controller		Controller
ROS Topics			
type	topic name	message package	message type	buffer size
S	/landshark/left_wheel_velocity	geometry_msgs	TwistStamped	1
S	/landshark/right_wheel_velocity	geometry_msgs	TwistStamped	1
S	/landshark/gps_velocity	geometry_msgs	TwistStamped	1
P	/landshark_control/base_velocity	geometry_msgs	TwistStamped	1
Controller Interface			
I/O	name		record type
I	Controller_U		(In1, double), (In2, double), (In3, double)
O	Controller_Y		(Out1, double)
Interface Relation			
type	topic		controller
SI	/landshark/left_wheel_velocity, twist, linear, x		Controller_U, In1
SI	/landshark/right_wheel_velocity, twist, linear, x		Controller_U, In2
SI	/landshark/gps_velocity, twist, linear, x		Controller_U, In3
PO	/landshark_control/base_velocity, twist, linear, x		Controller_Y, Out1

name of the controller function that the node will execute are shown at the top of the table. Published topics are indicated by the letter P and subscribed topics are indicated by the letter S. For each topic, the unique topic name and the type of messages are given. Next, the ROS node model specifies the controller function interface. In our case study, the controller function is generated from a Simulink model of the controller, and the names and types of input and output variables are following the Simulink code generator conventions. Finally, the interface relation represents the mapping from relevant fields of subscribed sensor messages to the fields in the input data structures of the controller function, and similarly for outputs of the controller function to published actuator messages.

4.2 ROSGen

Symbol Table. As the first step in code generation, ROSGen constructs a Coq data structure representing symbols to be used in the generated code. The names are obtained by parsing the ROS node model. Types for the controller function interface are given in the node model. Types for ROS messages referenced in the node model are obtained by parsing the corresponding C header files.

Code Templates. Code generation proceeds by instantiating templates that are Clight AST fragments. We use a top-level template, representing the whole program, and a set of local templates. The top-level template is shown in Figure 6. The program contains a list of global definitions and the name for the main function. A global definition can be either a variable definition or a function definition. One of the global definitions is the definition of the main function, which is partially constructed in the top-level template. Light-colored triangles in the top-level template represent holes that are filled with instantiations of local templates. Local templates are used to capture global definitions, such as callback function definitions, global variables used to transfer data from callback functions to the main function, and also glue code functions explained in more detail below. Holes in local templates can represent statements, as well as variable ids and types that are filled with references to the symbol table. Once all the templates are instantiated, the final C code is produced by CompCert pretty printing.

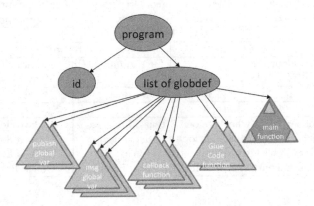

Fig. 6. Top-level template

To make proofs more efficient, we modularize the body of the main function from Figure 2 into several functions. The while loop is encapsulated as a loop function. Within the loop function, we wrap the code for transferring data from global variable to controller input and controller output to publish input as input_glue and output_glue function, respectively. Figure 7 shows the generated code for the glue functions.

```
void input_glue(){
  double temp;
  temp = landshark_left_encoder_velocity_msg.twist.linear.x;
  Controller_U.In1 = temp;
  temp = landshark_right_encoder_velocity_msg.twist.linear.x;
  Controller_U.In2 = temp;
  temp = landshark_gps_velocity_msg.twist.linear.x;
  Controller_U.In3 = temp;
  return;}
```

Fig. 7. Input glue function

5   Code Proof

We use VST to prove a DDC property for the generated Clight AST. Because VST is based on axiomatic semantics, we specify the DDC properties with pre- and post-conditions that capture the relation between the origin variables and destination variables.

5.1   Data Delivery Correctness Property of Glue Code

Fig. 8. Data delivery correctness property for ROS-based control system

The main purpose of the ROS glue code is linking the sensor input, controller function and actuator, so the critical property of glue code should capture the correctness of the linking. In ROS glue code, the linking correctness means that the sensor message is delivered into controller function input correctly. In addition, the output of the controller function correctly is delivered into the actuator input. We specify the linking correctness property of the ROS glue code as a DDC Property. This property indicates that the information from the origin should be consistent with the system specification when it arrives at the destination. For example, we design the system in the way that the sensor message is directly stored into global variables. So the DDC property of this operation is that the original value of the sensor message is equal to the value of the updated global variable. If we need to transform the original value, then the DDC property should specify the relation between the original value and destination value according to the transformation.

5.2   Generating Function Specifications

ROSGen automatically generates VST function specifications according to the ROS node model for both generated functions and ROS API functions. In VST, users specify properties through function specifications, so we wrap our glue code as functions. These functions include callback, and input and output glue functions for the controller step function.

As shown in Figure 8, the specifications of the functions capture the DDC property of the generated AST instance. The callback functions are responsible for transferring sensor messages to global message variables; the input glue function is responsible for transferring global message variable to the input parameter of controller function; and the output glue function is responsible for transferring output of controller function to the parameters of publish function. For each part, the DDC property specification defines the precondition that the original value is stored in memory and the postcondition that the destination contains the desired value according to the original value.

As shown in Figure 9, the input_glue function has precondition that there are three global message variables with values and controller input Controller_U with an unknown value. The postcondition indicates that Controller_U contains the right value from corresponding fields defined in the ROS node model and that the values of those three global variables are unchanged. By satisfying this

```
Precondition:
    {landshark_left_encoder_velocity_msg ← data1,
     landshark_right_encoder_velocity_msg ← data2,
     landshark_gps_velocity_msg ← data3,
     Controller_U ← _}
Postcondition:
    {landshark_left_encoder_velocity_msg ← data1,
     landshark_right_encoder_velocity_msg ← data2,
     landshark_gps_velocity_msg ← data3,
     Controller_U ← {data1.twist.linear.x, data2.twist.linear.x,
             data3.twist.linear.x}}
```

Fig. 9. DDC specification of input glue function

postcondition, we can guarantee that the input to the controller function is consistent to the architecture ROS node model.

Specification of ROS API Functions. For the code proof, we have to supply specifications of ROS API functions called by the code. These specifications are treated as assumptions in the proof. Here, specification of the ROS API function SpinOnce presents a challenge. The function implicitly invokes the registered callback functions to update global variables with new sensor values. The straightforward way to specify SpinOnce is to refer to the specifications of the callbacks. However, currently, VST does not support using other function specifications to construct a specification. Therefore, we specify the SpinOnce function using the global variables update essentially incorporating callback specifications directly into the SpinOnce specification. This specification has the precondition that the global variables are stored somewhere of memory and the postcondition that the global variables are updated to the provided data.

5.3   Code Proof Strategy

We use the tactics from VST proof automation to prove the DDC property. For each function, the proof starts with the function precondition as the proof context. We then apply the VST tactics for the current statement of the function body. Each tactic execution updates the proof context by calculating the postcondition of the statement and advances to the next statement, until the end of the function body is reached. At that point, the context should imply the function postcondition.

6   Code Generator Proof

6.1   Property of the Code Generator

We developed the code generator in Coq, which makes it possible to verify properties of the code generator itself. One interesting property is a generalized DDC property which states that every generated ROS glue code from a valid ROS node model will satisfy the DDC property defined in the Section 5. Intuitively, we should prove that for any input ROS node model, our function template instance satisfies our function specification instance. However, VST tactics can only reason about closed code; it cannot specify properties of our AST templates. Therefore, we cannot directly verify these templates. Instead, we analyze the properties that are required of code generation in order to guarantee the DDC property of the generated code.

The DDC property of generated code states that the destination variable holds the desired value according to the ROS node model before it is used. This DDC property is implied by three code generation properties discussed below. We use the input_glue function from Figure 7 to illustrate how the following three code generation properties imply the DDC property.

```
Definition input_glue_body_statement global_expr control_expr: statement :=
  (Ssequence
    (Sset temp_id global_expr)
    (Sassign control_expr (Etempvar temp_id temp_type))).
```

Fig. 10. Fragment of input glue function body template

Let us first look at the fragment of the template that generates statements in the body of the input_glue function that deliver the value for a single input field. The body is obtained by instantiating the template for each input field. The template has two parameters: global_expr field of message variable and control_expr field of controller input Controller_U. It generates two statements: one copies the message field value (global_expr) to the temporary variable (temp_id); the other sets one field (control_expr) of the controller variable with a temporary variable. We want to show that the DDC property of the input_glue function generated using this template will be satisfied whenever the three properties below hold.

The first code generation property is that the origin (global_expr) and the destination (control_expr) should keep the corresponding relation according to the ROS node model. It ensures that the data is delivered from the right origin to the right destination according to the ROS node model. In this case, global_expr and control_expr in the input_glue function should be consistent with the interface relation. This property guarantees that the Controller_U fields will be assigned by the values from corresponding fields shown in Table 1.

The second property is the valid assignment property, which requires only that the left and right sides of an assignment have the same type. This property implies that the destination variables receive the assigned value after this assignment according to the axiomatic semantics of VST. In this case, Controller_U will hold the value from field x of those three global message variables in Table 1. With the first and second code generation properties, the input_glue function postcondition is guaranteed.

The last code generation property is that the destination variable is not reassigned by other values before it is used. The third property guarantees that the value of `Controller_U` is preserved until the `Controller_step` function is invoked.

6.2   Proof of the Three Code Generator Properties

In this section, we discuss the proof of the three code generator properties presented above. The first property is that we instantiate the `input_glue` function assignment template correctly according to the input ROS node model interface relation. We maintain a list of expressions for each side in the resulting assignments. For the input glue function body, there are lists for `global_expr` and `control_expr`. The first property can be proven by showing that the lists of expressions are consistent with the ROS node model interface relation, as stated by the lemma in Figure 11. In this lemma, `lg_expr` is the list of expressions for `global_expr`, while `lc_expr` is the list of expressions for `control_expr`. The quantified variable `lir` is the list of interface relations from Table 1. To prove the consistency, we verify that the fields of these expression lists are identical to the fields in the interface relation.

```
Lemma relation_consistency_checking :
    forall (lir : list irelation) (lg_expr lc_expr : list expr),
      lg_expr = gen_list_global_variable_expr_input_glue lir →
      lc_expr = gen_list_controller_expr_input_glue lir →
      relation_consistency_checking lir lg_expr lc_expr.
```

Fig. 11. Relation consistency of the input glue function

For the valid assignment property, we only need to check that the lists of types for the left and right sides of the assignment are consistent. The type checking function for the `input_glue` function is shown in Figure 12. Since users may specify an inconsistent ROS node model, mapping a ROS message field with one type to controller input with a different type, the generated assignment can be invalid. The type checking function is applied before generating the `input_glue` function. If type checking returns `FALSE`, ROSGen can set the `error` flag to true and stop generating code. In this way, we guarantee that the generated code always satisfies the valid assignment property.

For the third property, we verify the preservation property by checking that there is no new assignment for the destination variable between the `input_glue` function and `Controller_step` function. This is quite straightforward, because there are no other statements between `input_glue` function and `Controller_step` function in our loop function template. Furthermore, if we were to change our template to add additional statements between the `input_glue` and `Controller_U` calling statements, we would also add the constraint that they do not involve manipulating the `Controller_U` heap. According to the separation logic of VST, the value of `Controller_U` is still preserved if those statements manipulate variables in a different heap.

```
Fixpoint type_checking_input_glue
    (ltype_global_fields ltype_controller_fields : list type) : bool :=
  match ltype_global_fields, ltype_controller_fields with
    | [], []  ⇒ true
    | tg:: ltypeg, tc:: ltypec ⇒ andb (type_equal tg tc)
      (type_checking_input_glue ltypeg ltypec)
    | _, _ ⇒ false
  end.
```

Fig. 12. Type checking for input glue function

7 Related Work

There has been much work on automatic generation of platform-specific glue code based on the architectural model of the system and the underlying platform specification. In [10,11], code generation for a variety of platforms is performed using AADL models to represent hardware and software architectures and their properties relevant for code generation. None of these papers targeted the ROS platform. More importantly, they do not consider verification of the generated code nor the code generator itself.

There is also a similarity between the intent of our approach and verification of model transformations in domain-specific languages. Most of that work, however, is done in the context of behavioral models, with the goal of ensuring that syntactic constraints are preserved by the transformation [12–14]. By contrast, we start with an architectural model, where behavior is implicit, and generate executable code.

8 Conclusions

We propose a verified framework ROSGen for generating glue code for ROS-based control systems. We start with a model of a ROS node capturing external connections of the node and parameters needed to execute the node. The code generator, implemented in Coq, uses this model to instantiate Clight templates and use the VST toolset to reason about the code. We then use CompCert utilities to generate C source code from Clight AST. We discuss how to generalize the proof of data delivery correctness for the generated code to a proof of data delivery correctness for the code generator itself. We apply the approach to the cruise control system for the LandShark robotic vehicle.

Our plans for future work include extending the proof approach to directly reason over quantified Clight templates, allowing for a more natural proof of the code generator correctness. Furthermore, we plan to extend the framework to cover the step function, to be able to reason about control-related properties of the code, in addition to the data delivery properties.

Acknowledgments. Thanks to Andrew W. Appel, Joey Dodds and Qinxiang Cao for help on applying VST and separation logic. We would like to thank the reviewers for their comments that help improve the paper.

References

1. Behrmann, G., David, A., Larsen, K.G.: A tutorial on uppaal. In: Formal methods for the design of real-time systems, pp. 200–236. Springer (2004)
2. Halbwachs, N.: A synchronous language at work: the story of lustre. In: Formal Methods for Industrial Critical Systems: A Survey of Applications, pp. 15–31 (2005)
3. Quigley, M., Conley, K., Gerkey, B., Faust, J., Foote, T., Leibs, J., Wheeler, R., Ng, A.Y.: ROS: an open-source robot operating system. In: ICRA workshop on open source software, vol. 3 (2009)
4. The Coq development team: The Coq proof assistant reference manual. LogiCal Project, Version 8.0. (2004)
5. Appel, A.W.: Verified software toolchain. In: Barthe, G. (ed.) ESOP 2011. LNCS, vol. 6602, pp. 1–17. Springer, Heidelberg (2011)
6. Meng, W., Park, J., Sokolsky, O., Weirich, S., Lee, I.: Verified ros-based deployment of platform-independent control systems. In: University of Pennsylvania Department of Computer and Information Science Technical Report No. MS-MS-CIS-15-01, February 2015
7. Leroy, X.: The compcert c verified compiler (2012)
8. Appel, A.W., Robert, D., Hobor, A., Beringer, L., Dodds, J., Stewart, G., Blazy, S., Leroy, X.: Program Logics for Certified Compilers. Cambridge University Press, UK (2014)
9. Pajic, M., Bezzo, N., Weimer, J., Sokolsky, O., Michael, N., Pappas, G.J., Tabuada, P., Lee, I.: Demo abstract: Synthesis of platform-aware attack-resilient vehicular systems. In: Cyber-Physical Systems (ICCPS), 2013 ACM/IEEE International Conference on, pp. 251–251. IEEE (2013)
10. Lasnier, G., Zalila, B., Pautet, L., Hugues, J.: OCARINA: an environment for AADL models analysis and automatic code generation for high integrity applications. In: Kordon, F., Kermarrec, Y. (eds.) Ada-Europe 2009. LNCS, vol. 5570, pp. 237–250. Springer, Heidelberg (2009)
11. Kim, B.G., Phan, L.T.X., Sokolsky, O., Lee, I.: Platform-dependent code generation for embedded real-time software. In: Compilers, Architecture and Synthesis for Embedded Systems (CASES), 2013 International Conference on, pp. 1–10. IEEE (2013)
12. Narayanan, A., Karsai, G.: Towards verifying model transformations. In: Proceedings of the 5th International Workshop on Graph Transformation and Visual Modeling Techniques (GT-VMT 2006), pp. 191–200 (2008)
13. Cabot, J., Clarisó, R., Guerra, E., de Lara, J.: Verification and validation of declarative model-to-model transformations through invariants. Journal of Systems and Software 83(2), 283–302 (2010)
14. Lucio, L., Vangheluwe, H.: Model transformations to verify model transformations. In: Proceedings of the Workshop on Verification of Model Transformations, June 2013

A Rigorous Approach to Combining Use Case Modelling and Accident Scenarios

Rajiv Murali[✉], Andrew Ireland, and Gudmund Grov

School of Mathematical and Computer Sciences,
Heriot-Watt University, Edinburgh, UK
{rm339,a.ireland,g.grov}@hw.ac.uk

Abstract. We describe an approach to embedding a formal method within UML use case modelling. Moreover, we extend use case modelling to allow for the explicit representation of safety concerns. Our motivation comes from interaction with systems and safety engineers who routinely rely upon use case modelling during the early stages of defining and analysing system behaviours. Our chosen formal method is Event-B, which is refinement based and consequently has enabled us to exploit natural abstractions found within use case modelling. By underpinning informal use case modelling with Event-B, we are able to provide greater precision and formal assurance when reasoning about concerns identified by safety engineers as well as the subsequent changes made at the level of use case modelling. To achieve this we have extended use case modelling to include the notion of an *accident case*. Our approach is currently being implemented, and we have an initial prototype.

Keywords: Formal modelling · Use cases · Hazard analysis · Model based · Refinement · Event-B

1 Introduction

UML *use cases* are an informal notation for modelling the required behaviour of a system with respect to its operational environment. They are widely used and highly accessible. Our interest in use cases has developed through interactions with systems and safety engineers at BAE Systems[1]. Use case modelling provides a basis on which initial system behaviours can be defined and analyzed by systems engineers. Moreover, safety concerns that are identified by safety engineers are mitigated via changes to the use cases, e.g. corrections, inclusion of additional behaviours, etc. The lack of formality of use case modelling means that the process of analysis is typically review-based, and thus lacks the rigour that comes from formal methods, i.e. systematic identification of ambiguities, inconsistencies and incompleteness. Moreover, use case modelling does not provide any special mechanisms for representing the concerns of safety engineers, such as accident scenarios.

---

[1] http://www.baesystems.com

© Springer International Publishing Switzerland 2015
K. Havelund et al. (Eds.): NFM 2015, LNCS 9058, pp. 263–278, 2015.
DOI: 10.1007/978-3-319-17524-9_19

We present an approach that adds rigour to use case modelling via the Event-B [1] formal modelling notation. We also extend use case modelling to include the notion of an *accident case*, which provides a way of representing accident scenarios. We selected Event-B because it promotes a layered style of formal modelling, where a design is developed as a series of abstract models – level by level concrete details are progressively introduced via provably correct refinement steps. Sometimes referred to as posit-and-prove, this style of modelling can increase the clarity of design decisions as well as simplify the complexity of the verification task. We argue that use case modelling exhibits a series of natural abstract models. Our approach exploits this mapping. That is, for a given use case we automatically generate a skeleton Event-B development. The completion of the development relies upon the user formalizing the details of their use case, e.g. constants, variables, pre-, postcondition, invariants, assignments. Our prototype tool allows the user to specify their informal and formal descriptions of the a use case side-by-side. As a consequence inconsistencies and defects identified by formal verification can be mapped back onto the informal level.

The paper is structured as follows. Sect. 2 provides background on both use case modelling and Event-B along with a case study of a simple water tank controller to describe our approach. In Sect. 3 we introduce our notion of an accident case to consider safety concerns within UML use case modelling. In Sect. 4 and 5, we provide a formal use case specification and its mapping onto an Event-B development, respectively. Sect. 6 focuses on the benefits that formal verification at the level of Event-B brings to use case modelling and describes a prototype tool support. Finally, related work and conclusions are described in Sect. 7 and 8.

2   Preliminaries

2.1   Water Tank Controller Case Study

A case study of a water tank controller is used to describe our approach on formalising UML use cases. The design intent for the *controller* is to maintain the *water level* between the high (H) and low (L) limits of a water tank, as seen in Fig. 1. To achieve this intent, the controller communicates with two external components: sensor system and pump. The sensor system monitors the water level in the tank with respect to the high threshold (HT) and low threshold (LT) sensor readings. Based on these readings, the controller either activates or deactivates the pump. When the pump is *active*, its motor is switched *on* which increases the water level in the tank, and while *inactive* the motor is switched *off* which gradually decreases the water level in the tank. The additional component *drain* is later introduced in Sect. 3.

2.2   Use Case Modelling

A use case model [2] is composed of a collection of *use cases* and *actors* that are of interest to the system being designed. A *use case diagram* describes the relationships between the actors and use cases within a system, where each use

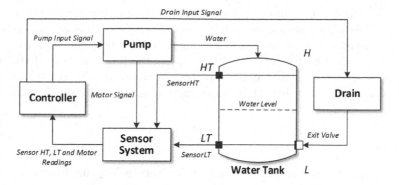

Fig. 1. A description of the water tank system

case captures the intended function of the system while the associated actors play a *role* in achieving it. Actors may represent roles played by human users, external hardware, or other subjects.

In Fig. 2a, a use case diagram for the water tank controller captures a use case, MaintainH, which denotes the desired functionality of the controller to maintain the water level below the H limit of the water tank. The pump, sensor system and water tank are represented as actors that play a role in achieving this functionality. Each use case can be further detailed in a *use case specification*[2]. The specification for MaintainH can be seen in Fig. 2b.

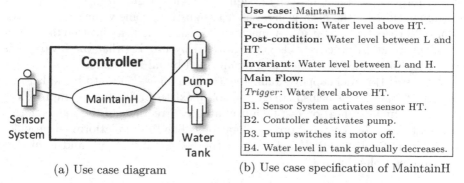

Use case: MaintainH
Pre-condition: Water level above HT.
Post-condition: Water level between L and HT.
Invariant: Water level between L and H.
Main Flow:
Trigger: Water level above HT.
B1. Sensor System activates sensor HT.
B2. Controller deactivates pump.
B3. Pump switches its motor off.
B4. Water level in tank gradually decreases.

(a) Use case diagram   (b) Use case specification of MaintainH

Fig. 2. A use case model of the water tank system

A use case specification captures a sequence of *action steps* where each step is a discrete unit of interaction between an actor and the system. This sequence of steps is known as a flow and every use case has one *main flow*. The main flow

---

[2] There is no standard template for use case specifications. The one used in the paper is kept simple as possible and is in common use in industry [3], with the exception of the invariant field.

describes a *sunny day scenario* where there are no failures or exceptions. The flow can initiate if its *trigger* condition is enabled. The specification also captures the *pre-*, *post-condition* and *invariant* for the use case. These can be described as a *contract* specified by the designer where given the pre-condition, if the main flow of the use case executes and completes, then the result described by the post-condition must be achieved. The invariant must be maintained throughout the execution of the flow.

2.3   Event-B

Event-B [1] is a refinement-based formalism for system-level modelling and analysis. An Event-B model is composed of *contexts* and *machines* where a context expresses the static information about the model while a machine represents the dynamic aspects. A machine models the state space by variables v, and state transitions are modelled by *events*. The state variables v are constrained by laws specified by invariants $I(v)$. An event *evt* is of the following form:

$$evt \,\,\widehat{=}\,\, \textbf{\textit{where}}\ G(v)\ \textbf{\textit{then}}\ S(v, v')\ \textbf{\textit{end}}$$

In event *evt*, $G(v)$ specifies the enableness conditions of the event while $S(v, v')$ defines the state transition associated with the event. A dedicated *initialisation* event with no guards defines the states of the variables v at start-up. $S(v, v')$ contains several assignments that are supposed to happen simultaneously. Each assignment may take the following forms: $v := E(v)$, $v :\in E(v)$, or $v : |P(v, v')$. The first form deterministically assigns the values of expression $E(v)$ to v, the second form non-deterministically assigns to v some value from $E(v)$. The last assignment form is the most general as it assigns to v some value satisfying the before-after predicate $P(v, v')$. A machine is consistent if its invariants hold at any given time. In practice, this is guaranteed by proving that the invariant is established by the *initialisation* and maintained by all its events.

An Event-B model supports refinement which allows detail to be added in a stepwise manner. This helps manage the complexities of design and improve the degree to which verification can be automated. Correctness of the refinement is ensured by a set of generated proof obligations. The Rodin platform [4] provides tool support for Event-B. It is based on the Eclipse framework and is further extensible via plug-ins.

3   Accident Scenarios in Use Case Modelling

Accidents, or *losses*, are considered early in the development of safety-critical systems. An accident can be defined as *"an undesired or unplanned event that result in a loss, including loss of human life or human injury, property damage, environmental pollution, mission loss, etc"* [5]. In the water tank controller case study, an accident (A1) that results in damage to the water tank is considered:

A1: Water level in tank exceeds the high (H) limit (physical damage to tank).

It is necessary for hazardous causal scenarios that lead to an accident to be considered along side the proposed system behaviour in order to agree upon appropriate design recommendations that may help mitigate them. We argue that if the design intent, i.e. the expected behaviour of a system, can be captured and conveyed via use cases (e.g. MaintainH), then it should be possible for the unexpected scenarios that result in an accident to be conveyed in a similar manner. To our knowledge, this has not yet been considered for use cases and we have extended use case modelling to incorporate a use case type known as *accident case*.

3.1 Accident Case

Leveson [5] describes the cause of an accident as follows:

Hazard (Action) + Environmental Conditions (State) $\Rightarrow$ Accident (Event)

A hazard is an *action* that together with a particular set of worst-case environmental *conditions*, constitutes an accident. What constitutes a hazard depends on where the *boundaries* of the system are drawn. The use case model establishes the actors and system boundary diagrammatically which determines what the designer has control over. If one expects the designer to create systems that eliminate or control hazards, then those hazards must be in their design space.

For the water tank controller, the designer has control over the action to either *increase* or *decrease* the water level in the tank (albeit not directly). A hazardous action would be for the water level to continue to increase in the tank even after the water level has exceeded the high threshold (HT) limit and the pump is inactive. The cause of the accident for A1 can be written as follows:

Water level increases + Water level above HT and Pump is inactive
$$\Rightarrow \text{Water level exceeds } H \text{ limit (A1)}$$

It is the role of the safety engineer to apply hazard analysis in order to determine the *hazardous causal scenarios* that can lead to the hazardous action, given the environmental conditions. We extend UML use cases with *accident cases* to help capture these hazardous causal scenarios, while relating them to use cases via a *disrupt* relationship. An accident case is defined as follows:

Definition 1 (Accident Case). *An accident case is a sequence of actions that a system or other entity can perform that result in an accident or loss to some stakeholder if the sequence is allowed to complete.*

The specification of an accident case contains the accident flow, where its trigger captures the environmental condition for the cause of an accident, while its final step captures the hazardous control action. The preceding steps capture the hazardous causal scenario identified from hazard analysis. The accident case may *disrupt* a use case by providing an alternate flow resulting in an accident if allowed to complete.

The use case model of the water tank system is updated to introduce the accident, A1, via an accident case ExceedH (Fig. 3a). ExceedH *disrupts* the MaintainH use case by introducing the accident flow. The trigger of the accident flow captures the environmental condition where the water level is above *HT* and the pump is inactive. The final step captures the hazardous control action of increasing the water level, while the preceding step capture a causal scenario leading to the hazardous action, i.e. where the motor remains switched on (Fig. 3b).

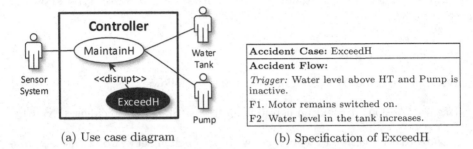

(a) Use case diagram   (b) Specification of ExceedH

Fig. 3. Use case model updated with accident case

3.2   Safety Guided Design

The purpose of the accident case is to provide a means to communicate appropriate design recommendations after hazard analysis, between system and safety engineers. One of the aims of a safety engineer is to ensure that no *single fault* or *failure* may result in an accident. In order to strengthen the safety of the water tank system an additional component *drain* is introduced, as seen in Fig. 1. The controller may activate the drain if it detects a *fault* where the motor remains switched on (motor reading from the sensor system) even after the pump has been deactivated. When the drain is activated, it opens an exit valve on the water tank which *drains* the water level to the low threshold (*LT*) limit.

In use case modelling *exceptional* behaviour can be introduced to the system via an *extension use case* [2]. An extension use case is used to describe how a system can respond to when things do not go as expected. The structure of an extension use case specification is the same as a regular use case, however it is dependant on the base use case it extends. It places an *extension-point* between the steps of the base use case, and if its trigger condition is *true* then its flow will initiate. We introduce an attribute, *return-after*, to the extension-point that captures a *step* of the use case it *extends*, which indicates where the extension flow will return to, after it completes.

An extension use case MonitorPump is introduced in the use case model of the water tank controller (see Fig. 4a). It *extends* the MaintainH use case by mitigating the accident flow provided by ExceedH. An extension-point is placed between steps F1 and F2 (as seen in Fig. 6a) of the accident flow. This captures a relationship, *mitigate*, between the extension use case and accident case. The mitigate relationship must ensure that if the accident case triggers then the extension use case will prevent its accident flow from completing. The extension-point captures a return-after step that returns the extension use case flow after the final step of the use case MaintainH.

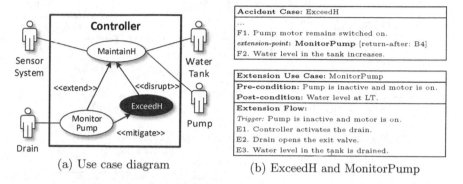

(a) Use case diagram

(b) ExceedH and MonitorPump

Fig. 4. Use case model updated with extension use case

4 A Formal Use Case Specification

We aim to perform formal verification of use cases by automatically transforming its specification to Event-B. To do so, we first introduce a *formal use case specification* to represent the informal use cases MaintainH (Fig. 2b), ExceedH (Fig. 3b) and MonitorPump (Fig. 4). These are formally written with Event-B's mathematical language [1]. Fig. 5a shows a formal use case specification of a generic use case, UC, where its pre-condition, post-condition, and invariant describe constraints on the variables i. These variables i model a state space associated to the domain of actor, A, who happens to plays a *role* in UC. Variables that are written in capital letters indicate that they are *static*, i.e. they cannot be modified by the flow of the use case. The variables, along with their types $T(i)$ for each associated actor, are provided on the left-hand side of the formal use case specification. This is done to help guide the designer when detailing the right-hand side that contains the pre-, post-condition, invariant and flow.

The flow contain steps $S_1..S_n$ that capture *actions* that describe state transition to the variables of UC. The flow is expected to reveal more of the state space, which we model by variables j. The variables i and j are kept distinct as the steps S_1 to S_{n-1} capture actions, $E(i,j,j')$, that describe some state transitions to variables j. However, we work on the assumption that there will be some step, S_n, that will capture the necessary action, $E(i,i',j)$, that modifies the variables i in order to achieve the post-condition $Q(i)$.

This template is applied to the use cases of the water tank controller. The formal use case specification can be seen for MaintainH (Fig. 5b), ExceedH (Fig. 6a) and MonitorPump (Fig. 6b). In MaintainH, the actor, Water Tank, captures the variable wl that denotes the water level in the tank. Its state space represents a numerical value hence the type $wl \in \mathbb{N}$. The pre-, post-condition and invariant

Use case: UC	
A: $i :: T(i)$ $j :: T(j)$	**Pre-condition:** $P(i)$ **Post-condition:** $Q(i)$ **Invariant:** $I(i)$
	Main Flow: $Trigger : R(i,j)$ $S_1. E_1(i,j,j')$ $\vdots$ $S_n. E_n(i,i',j)$

(a) Generic use case UC

Use case: MaintainH		
Water Tank: $wl :: wl \in \mathbb{N}$ $H :: H > HT$ $HT :: HT > LT$ $LT :: LT > L$ $L :: L < H$ $DEC ::$ $DEC \in (H - HT)..(HT - L)$ **Sensor System:** $senHT :: senHT \in BOOL$ **Controller:** $pump :: pump \in BOOL$ **Pump:** $motor :: motor \in BOOL$	**Pre-condition:** $wl > HT$ **Post-condition:** $wl \geq L \wedge wl \leq HT$ **Invariant:** $wl \in L..H$	**Main Flow:** $Trigger : wl > HT$ B1. $senHT := TRUE$ B2. $pump := FALSE$ B3. $motor := FALSE$ B4. $wl := wl - DEC$

(b) MaintainH

Fig. 5. Formal use case specification of UC and MaintainH

Accident Case: ExceedH	
Pump: $INC ::$ $INC \in (LT - L)..(H - LT)$	**Accident Flow:** $Trigger : wl > HT \wedge$ $pump = FALSE$ F1. $motor := TRUE$ $ext\text{-}point:$ MonitorPump [return-after: B4] F2. $wl := wl + INC$

(a) ExceedH

Extension Use Case: MonitorPump		
Controller: $drain :: drain \in BOOL$ **Drain:** $valve :: valve \in BOOL$ $DRN :: DRN = LT$	**Pre-condition:** $motor = TRUE \wedge$ $pump = FALSE$ **Post-condition:** $wl = LT$	**Extension Flow:** $Trigger : motor = TRUE \wedge$ $pump = FALSE$ E1. $drain := TRUE$ E2. $valve := TRUE$ E3. $wl := DRN$

(b) MonitorPump

Fig. 6. Formal use case specification of ExceedH and MonitorPump

capture the necessary constraint on wl with respect to the limits of the water tank H, HT, LT, L. The limits are written in capital to indicate that they are *static* and they cannot be modified by the flow of the use case. The static variable DEC is a discrete representation of the decrease in the water level by the water tank. The flow of MaintainH reveals more of the state space which are modelled by variables $pump$, $senHT$ (sensor reading for high threshold limit) and *motor*. They are of type $BOOL$, where $TRUE$ indicates *active* (or *on*) while $FALSE$ indicate *inactive* (or *off*), i.e. when $pump = TRUE$ denotes the pump is active. The steps B1 to B3 modify these variable, while the final step B4 captures the necessary modification to the variable wl that should achieve the post-condition. The formal use case specification helps bring the benefit of precision and clarity when detailing the use case while enabling the designer to relate informal and formal notation.

The static variable DRN in ExceedH indicates the level at which the water will be drained in the water tank. In this instance, the designer has set the drain to the low threshold limit (LT). Once the use cases are specified formally, it is possible to map their content to a formal model via refinement for purpose of verification.

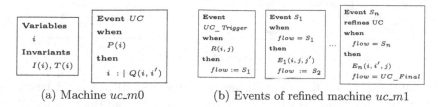

(a) Machine uc_m0 (b) Events of refined machine uc_m1

Fig. 7. Use case specification of UC mapped to an Event-B model

5   Mapping Use Cases to Event-B via Refinement

In this section we describe how the formal use case specification of UC is *mapped* to an Event-B model. We then apply this mapping to the MaintainH use case of the water tank controller. ExceedH and MonitorPump are also taken into account as they are dependent on MaintainH by providing alternate scenarios to its flow. The verification performed for the use cases from their corresponding Event-B model is discussed in Sect. 6.

5.1   Generic Use Case

We consider the use case specification to have a *contract* and *body*. The contract is composed of the pre-, post-condition and invariant, while the body contains the flow. Our mapping introduces the contract of UC in an abstract Event-B machine, uc_m0, while the body is introduced by its refinement in uc_m1. The contract is the constraint on the body of the use case, and we use refinement to relate them accordingly.

UC Contract: In uc_m0, we introduce a key abstraction of *what* is to be achieved by the use case without specifying *how*. UC's pre- and post-condition are modelled by an event, *UC*, as its guard and action, respectively (see Fig. 7a). This event introduces a state transition in the model, where given the pre-condition it is possible for the post-condition to be achieved. The event does not reveal *how* this is done and emphasises only on *what* is achieved. The variables i associated to the pre- and post-condition are introduced. The invariants, $T(i)$ and $I(i)$, ensure their constraints on i are maintained by event *UC*.

UC Body: The machine uc_m0 is refined to uc_m1, in order to introduce UC's flow which describes *how* the use case achieves and maintains its *contract*. Each step of UC's flow along with its trigger is mapped to a corresponding event in um_m1 (see Fig. 7b). The variables j (revealed by the flow) and its associated types $T(j)$ are introduced in this refinement. The flow is mediated between steps S_1 to S_n by an auxiliary variable s that act as a program counter. The event $UC\_Trigger$ initiates the use case's flow ($s := S1$) given the trigger condition $R(i,j)$. The steps S_1 to S_{n-1} capture actions that modify the variables j, however the final step S_n capture the necessary modification on variables i and

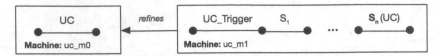

Fig. 8. Event-flow diagram of UC in Event-B

refines the abstract event *UC*. If the refinement is consistent, then the behaviour described in the body complies with the constraints specified in the contract of UC. Moreover, it allows to reason about the contract in the initial model while temporarily ignoring how they are implemented till refinement.

To illustrate the execution we use an *event-flow diagram* (see Fig. 8). The event-flow diagram is read from left-to-right, where each line is an execution of an event in the formal model. The diagram helps to illustrate the refinement, where any event in **bold** indicates it refines an event from the abstract model. However, if the name of the concrete event is different from that of its abstract counter part then we show the abstract event name in parenthesis, e.g. S_n (*UC*).

5.2 Water Tank Controller

The mapping from UC is applied to MaintainH to produce two layers of refinement mh_m0 and mh_m1. The MaintainH use case has a disrupt relationship which introduces the accident flow of ExceedH in mh_m1. This accident flow captures an extension-point that introduces the extension use case MonitorPump. The mapping from UC is applied to MonitorPump to introduce its contract in mh_m1 while its body (containing the extension flow) is introduced via refinement in mh_m2. The event-flow diagram for the Event-B model of MaintainH can be seen in Fig. 10.

Initial Model: In mh_m0, the contract of MaintainH use case is introduced. The event *MaintainH* models the pre- and post-condition as its guard ($wl > HT$) and action ($wl : | \ wl' \geq L \ \wedge \ wl' \leq HT$), respectively. The event captures *what* the use case MaintainH achieves, by allowing the water level to be reduced between the L and HT limits, if it exceeds the HT limit. The variable wl associated with the pre- and post-condition is introduced along with its type $wl \in \mathbb{N}$ and invariant $wl \in L..H$. The static variables (written in capitals) are captured in a context component of the Event-B model which can be *seen* by the machine.

First Refinement: In mh_m1, the flow of MaintainH is introduced which describes *how* the water level is reduced when it exceeds the HT limit. The trigger and steps B1 to B4 are mapped to events (as seen in machine mh_m1 in Fig. 10). The variables *pump*, *senHT* and *motor* revealed by the flow are introduced in this machine along with their types. The events $B1$ to $B3$ perform actions that modify these variables according to the behaviour specified in the main flow. The final event $B4$ describes the decrease in the water level ($wl := wl - DEC$) after the motor has been switched off. This final event $B4$ refines the abstract event *MaintainH*.

The accident flow of ExceedH is also introduced in this refinement due to the disrupt relationship with MaintainH. The accident flow of ExceedH is modelled by the events *ExceedH_Trigger*, *F*1 and *F*2. The event *ExceedH_Trigger* may initiate the accident flow at any point during the flow of MaintainH, provided its trigger condition is *true*. If the accident flow is allowed to terminate, then the water level would exceed above the H limit which would violate the invariant $(wl \in L..H)$.

The extension-point between the steps F1 and F2 introduces the extension use case MonitorPump by two events: *MonitorPump* and *MonitorPump_False*. An auxiliary boolean variable *ext* is used to insert both these events between events *F*1 and *F*2 (see Fig. 9). The event *MonitorPump* captures the contract of the extension use case. If the motor remains active while the pump has been deactivated, then the water level is reduced to the low threshold (LT) and the flow is returned after the final step B4 of the main flow. The event *MonitorPump* refines the abstract event *MaintainH*, since the post-condition describes a desired stated ($wl = LT$) on the abstract variable wl. On the other hand, *MonitorPump_False* captures the negation of the extension use case's pre-condition as its guards. Suppose if the extension use case's precondition is not *true*, then this event returns the flow back into the accident flow. This requires the right fault condition to be specified by the extension use case in order to prevent the accident flow from completing.

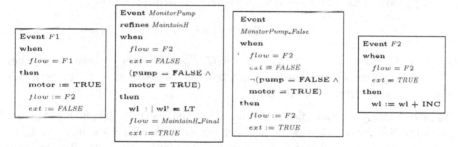

Fig. 9. Extension-point inserted between events F1 and F2 of ExceedH in Event-B

Second Refinement: In the final refinement, we introduce the body of the extension use case MonitorPump. The body reveals more of the system by introducing the variables *drain* and *valve*. The flow of MonitorPump is mapped to events *MonitorPump_Trigger*, *E*1, *E*2 and *E*3. It introduces the scenario of the controller activating the drain which opens an exit valve on the water tank. This is done to reduce the water level if the controller detects the motor remains active even after the pump being deactivated. The final event *E*3 drains the water level in the tank which refines the abstract event *MonitorPump*.

6   Verification and Tool Support

6.1   Generic Use Case

UC Contract: The main mathematical judgement in the initial model of the use case is to determine whether the invariant, $I(i)$, is guaranteed to be maintained by

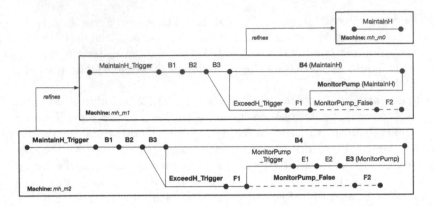

Fig. 10. Event-flow diagram for MaintainH's corresponding Event-B model

what is achieved, $Q(i, i')$, by event UC. Proving this ensures that the flow introduced by refinement will be required to meet the contract of UC.

UC Body: The model checks whether UC's flow achieves the post-condition $Q(i)$, given the pre-condition $P(i)$. We are required to prove that the precondition must be maintained before the execution of step S_1 to S_{n-1}. The following invariant is automatically introduced to help prove this:

$$\forall s \cdot s \in \{S_1, .., S_n\} \land flow = s \Rightarrow P(i) \tag{1}$$

The event S_n refines the abstract event UC. This refinement must prove that the behaviour of the abstract event, i.e. what the use case achieves, corresponds to the behaviour described in its flow.

Mitigate: For any accident flow introduced via the disrupt relationship, there is expected to be an extension-point between its steps. As discussed in Sect. 3, the extension-point in an accident flow is required to ensure the steps after its point of insertion can never be executed. In Event-B, we introduce invariants that negate the guards of the events that model these steps. This allows the model to automatically prove that the steps can never be enabled, i.e. the accident case will be unable to complete.

6.2   Water Tank Controller

Initial Model: In the initial model we are able prove what is achieved by the MaintainH use case's post-condition, i.e. the reduction of water level, is within constraints of its invariant $wl \in L..H$. The following proof is generated by the model and automatically proved:

$$wl' \geq L \land wl' \leq HT \vdash wl' \in L..H$$

First Refinement: The model is refined to introduce the flow of MaintainH which ensures that the contract introduced in the abstract model is preserved.

The invariant (1) is applied to MaintainH to produce the following invariant:

$$\forall s \cdot s \in \{B1, B2, B3, B4, F1, F2\} \wedge flow = s \Rightarrow wl > HT$$

This is used to ensure the pre-condition is *true* before the flow can execute. The event $B4$ refines the abstract event *MaintainH*. A proof obligation is generated to ensure the action of event $B4$ is maintained between L and HT limits, given that the water level is above HT. The model produces the following proof:

$$flow = B4 \vdash wl - DEC \geq L \wedge wl - DEC \leq HT$$

The event *MonitorPump*, which captures the contract of the extension use case, also refines the abstract event *MaintainH*. The model checks what the extension use case achieves, i.e. the water level reduced to LT, corresponds to what is achieved by event *MaintainH* of the abstract model. In addition, the model proves that the accident flow of ExceedH is not allowed to complete. The guards of the events after the extension-point, *MonitorPump_False*, and $F2$, are negated and introduced as invariants (3) and (2) respectively.

$$\neg(flow = F2 \wedge ext = FALSE \wedge \neg(pump - FALSE \wedge motor = TRUE)) \quad (2)$$

The model is able to prove these invariants hold as the accident flow introduces the necessary conditions for the event, *MonitorPump* to execute instead of *MonitorPump_False*.

$$\neg(flow = F2 \wedge ext = TRUE) \quad (3)$$

Second Refinement: The model is able prove that the extension use case's flow which drains the water level correspond to *MaintainH*, as the drain is set to the LT limit of the water tank $(DRN = LT)$ which is between L and HT.

6.3   UC-B Tool Support

Our approach is currently being implemented as a tool UC-B[3] (Use Case Event-B) for the Rodin platform (Fig. 11). It supports the authoring and management of UML use cases with the inclusion of accident cases. It allows the use case specifications to be detailed with Event-B's mathematical language and provides support for the automatic generation of Event-B models from a target use case. The generated

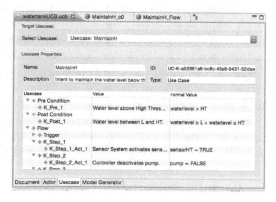

Fig. 11. UC-B tool on Rodin

[3] Tool information can be found at https://sites.google.com/site/rajivmkp/uc-b

Event-B models are immediately subjected Event-B's verification tools (syntax checks and provers) that run automatically providing an immediate display of problems. Our aim is for inconsistencies in the Event-B models to reflected back to their parent use case model. We have considered two other case studies, anti-lock braking system (ABS) and sense and avoid (SAA), that fit the same control pattern as the water tank controller.

7   Related Work

While our focus is on safety, the majority of work on representing negative scenarios within the context of use cases has targeted security issues. Ellison et al. [6] introduce *intruders* and *intrusion scenarios* in their case study as part of a large-scale distributed health care system. The intrusion scenario is similar to an accident flow, but they do not provide a diagrammatic notation, a specification, or guidelines for what constitutes an intrusion scenario. McDermott and Fox [7] propose *abuse cases* which focus on security requirements and their relation to design and testing. They capture the abuse cases and regular use cases in separate use case diagrams. This differs from our approach where we provide relationships between accident cases and regular use cases in the same use case diagram. Aside from UML use cases, Potts [8] introduces *obstacles* for goal-oriented requirements engineering (KAOS), while Harel and Marrelly [9] extend Live Sequence Chart (LSC) with *forbidden elements* (messages and condition).

Several groups have investigated a rigorous approach to capturing UML use cases [10–12]. In comparison, the novelty of our approach comes from the use of refinement to introduce key abstractions that are captured naturally by the structure of the use case specification and its relationship to other use cases. In [10], Soussa and Russo provide a mapping from the flow of a use case to operations in B. They rely upon the flow to be written in accordance to a transaction pattern between the actor and the system as follows: (1) an actors request action; (2) a system data validation action; (3) a system expletive action; and finally (4) a system response action. We consider this pattern would require the designer to focus more on the solution rather than understanding the problem domain, which steps away from some of the benefits and simplicity of using UML use cases. In [11], Whittle presents a precise notation for specifying use cases based on three levels of abstraction: use case charts, scenario charts and interaction diagrams. The motivation for this approach is similar to ours which also considers the use of negative scenarios. However, we have focused on adding rigour to the *textual* specification of use cases which is commonly used in industry.

Requirements engineering approaches such as Problem Frames[13] and KAOS[14] have been considered for formal analysis. We have deliberately focused on UML use cases in order to reach a broader audience.

8   Conclusion and Future Work

The work presented here is part of an on-going effort to help in the industrial adoption of formal methods and of a more specific effort to consider safety concerns. We have extended UML use cases to consider potential accidents via the use of accident cases, that is aimed to improve communication between system and safety engineers. For the purpose of formal analysis of use cases, we have provided a formal use case specification to detail use cases with Event-B's mathematical language. From this, we use the structure and relationship of use cases to derive a natural abstraction when mapping them to an Event-B model. Proof automation is possible which helps identify inconsistencies and defects in the formal model that can be mapped back onto the use case model. Our tool implementation supports the authoring and management of UML use cases on the Rodin, while enabling automatic generation of Event-B models.

For future work, we are investigating links between the hazard analysis techniques with our notion of an accident case. Our tool is currently being extended to support traceability between the generated Event-B model and its parent use case. Patterns of inconsistencies identified by proofs could be used to meaningfully guide an while detailing use cases.

Acknowledgments. The first author was supported by an Industrial CASE studentship funded by the EPSRC and BAE Systems (EP/J501992), while the second and third authors was partially supported by EPSRC grant EP/J001058. We also would like to thank Benjamin Gorry, Rod Buchanan and Paul Marsland from BAE Systems.

References

1. Abrial, J.R.: Modeling in Event-B: System and Software Engineering. University Press, Cambridge (2010)
2. Booch, G., Rumbaugh, J., Jacobson, I.: Unified Modeling Language. Addison-Wesley (1997)
3. Arlow, J., Neustadt, I.: UML 2 and the Unified Process: Practical Object-Oriented Analysis and Design. Pearson Education (2005)
4. Abrial, J.R., Butler, M., Hallerstede, S., Hoang, T.S., Mehta, F., Voisin, L.: Rodin: An open toolset for modelling and reasoning in event-b. International Journal on Software Tools for Technology Transfer 12(6), 447–466 (2010)
5. Leveson, N.: Engineering a Safer World: Systems Thinking Applied to Safety. Mit Press (2011)
6. Ellison, R.J., Linger, R.C., Longstaff, T., Mead, N.R.: Survivable Network System Analysis: A Case Study. IEEE Software 16(4), 70–77 (1999)
7. McDermott, J., Fox, C.: Using abuse case models for security requirements analysis. In: (ACSAC 1999) Proceedings 15th Annual Computer Security Applications Conference, pp. 55–64. IEEE (1999)
8. Potts, C.: Using schematic scenarios to understand user needs. In: Proceedings of the 1st Conference on Designing Interactive Systems: Processes, Practices, Methods, and Techniques, pp. 247–256. ACM (1995)
9. Harel, D., Marelly, R.: Come, Let's Play: Scenario-Based Programming using LSCs and the Play-Engine. Springer Science and Business Media, Vol. 1 (2003)
10. Russo Jr., A.G., de Sousa, T.: Starting B specifications from use cases. In: Abstract State Machines (ASM), Alloy, B and Z Conference (2010)

11. Whittle, J.: Precise Specification of Use Case Scenarios. In: Dwyer, M.B., Lopes, A. (eds.) FASE 2007. LNCS, vol. 4422, pp. 170–184. Springer, Heidelberg (2007)
12. Klimek, R., Szwed, P.: Formal Analysis of Use Case Diagrams. Computer Science, 115–131 (2010)
13. Jackson, M.: Problem Frames: Analysing and Structuring Software Development Problems. Addison-Wesley (2001)
14. Ponsard, C., Dieul, E.: From Requirements Models to Formal Specifications in B. ReMo2V (2006)

Are We There Yet? Determining the Adequacy of Formalized Requirements and Test Suites

Anitha Murugesan[1]([⊠]), Michael W. Whalen[1], Neha Rungta[2],
Oksana Tkachuk[2], Suzette Person[3], Mats P.E. Heimdahl[1], and Dongjiang You[1]

[1] Department of Computer Science and Engineering, University of Minnesota,
200 Union Street, Minneapolis, MN 55455, USA
{anitha,whalen,heimdahl,djyou}@cs.umn.edu
[2] NASA Ames Research Center, Mountain, USA
{neha.s.rungta,oksana.tkachuk}@nasa.gov
[3] NASA Langley Research Center, Hampton, USA
suzette.person@nasa.gov

Abstract. Structural coverage metrics have traditionally categorized code as either covered or uncovered. Recent work presents a stronger notion of coverage, *checked coverage*, which counts only statements whose execution contributes to an outcome checked by an oracle. While this notion of coverage addresses the adequacy of the oracle, for Model-Based Development of safety critical systems, it is still not enough; we are also interested in how much of the oracle is covered, and whether the values of program variables are masked when the oracle is evaluated. Such information can help system engineers identify missing requirements as well as missing test cases. In this work, we combine results from checked coverage with results from requirements coverage to help provide insight to engineers as to whether the requirements or the test suite need to be improved. We implement a dynamic backward slicing technique and evaluate it on several systems developed in Simulink. The results of our preliminary study show that even for systems with comprehensive test suites and good sets of requirements, our approach can identify cases where more tests or more requirements are needed to improve coverage numbers.

1 Introduction

Model-Based Development (MBD) refers to the use of domain-specific modeling notations to create models of a desired system early in the development lifecycle. These models can be executed on the desktop, analyzed for desired behaviors, and then used to automatically generate code and test cases. Also known as correct-by-construction development, the emphasis in model-based development is on the engineering effort invested in the early lifecycle activities of modeling, simulation, and analysis. This reduces development costs by finding defects early

This work has been partially supported by NSF grants CNS-0931931 and CNS-1035715.

© Springer International Publishing Switzerland 2015
K. Havelund et al. (Eds.): NFM 2015, LNCS 9058, pp. 279–294, 2015.
DOI: 10.1007/978-3-319-17524-9_20

in the lifecycle, avoiding rework that is necessary when errors are discovered during integration testing, and by automating the late life-cycle activities of coding and test case generation. In this way, Model-Based Development significantly reduces costs while also improving quality. There are several commercial MBD tools, including Simulink/Stateflow [19], SCADE [10], IBM Rhapsody [1] and IBM Rational Statemate [2].

An important part of MBD is automated test generation and execution. Tools such as Reactis [26], the MathWorks Verification and Validation plug-in for Simulink, and the IBM Rhapsody Automatic Test Generation add-on, as well as other tools, support automated test generation from models. These tools enable generation of structural coverage tests up to a high degree of rigor, e.g., tests satisfying the MC/DC coverage metric. In the domain of critical systems – particularly in avionics – demonstrating structural coverage is required for certification [27].

In principle, automated test generation represents a success for software engineering research: a mandatory – and potentially arduous – engineering task has been automated. However, several studies have raised questions about the effectiveness of automated test generation towards a specific structural coverage metric (e.g., [12,14,31]), in some cases finding these tests less effective than randomly generated tests of the same length in terms of fault-finding capabilities. This often has to do with the *observability* capabilities of the test oracle, which determines whether the test passes or fails. In many cases, the code structure that was examined has no measurable effect on the test outcome.

In recent work, a metric proposed by Schuler and Zeller in [29,30] addresses observability, but does so in a post-priori way: given a test suite and a set of requirements specified as assertions, it uses dynamic backward slicing from the requirements (assertions) to determine the set of program statements that affect the evaluation of the requirement. They call this metric *checked statement coverage*, because it only considers the statements that are checked (observed). They note that this metric judges the quality of the *test oracle* — a program with no assertions will have no coverage. Therefore, given any test suite, it is possible to increase coverage by adding additional oracles (requirements) to the suite. Our hypothesis is that this metric can be leveraged to better assess the quality of an automated testing process in MBD where formalized requirements serve as oracles for auto-generated tests [28].

In this work, we combine the results of checked coverage with the results of requirements coverage to determine for a given model whether its requirements and test suite are adequate. While the work in [30] focuses on whether or not the *oracles* (requirements) are adequate, we are interested in both the adequacy of the test suite and the requirements encoded as oracles: if checked coverage is low then either the requirements or the tests maybe incomplete. Specifically, we add to this notion of coverage by calculating checked coverage based on dynamic backward slicing *as well as* MC/DC masking information. Finally, we map the different forms of code coverage back to the model, and report the coverage of

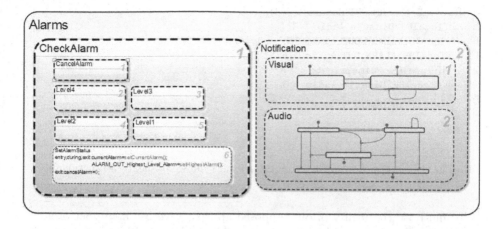

Fig. 1. Hierarchical state machine model of the ALARM subsystem

the requirements, in order to provide information to the system engineers about sources of incompleteness. Thus, the contributions of the paper are:

- An approach using checked, unchecked, and requirements coverage information to assess the adequacy of both test suites and requirements.
- An approach to calculate checked coverage based on backward dynamic slicing and MC/DC masking information, which leads to more precise checked coverage results than dynamic backward slicing alone.
- A preliminary evaluation of our technique on a set of examples that use Simulink as part of the MBD approach. In addition to computing coverage for the auto-generated code, we also map the results back to the models.

Our experience shows that even for case studies with comprehensive test suites and good sets of requirements, our approach can identify cases where more tests or more requirements are needed to improve the coverage numbers.

2   Motivation

Consider the control software for an infusion pump, a medical device that is typically used to infuse liquid drugs into a patient's body in a controlled fashion. An important subsystem of the controller is the ALARM subsystem shown in Fig. 1. The model for the system [22] was developed using MathWorks Simulink/Stateflow tool [19]. The "ALARM" subsystem is responsible for monitoring hazards (CheckAlarm state machine) with different levels of severity in the system, and alerting the clinicians (Audio and Visual state machines) to take the appropriate action when such conditions occur. We auto-generate the source code from the Simulink model, formalize the requirements as boolean expressions, and automatically generate the test cases from the model.

```
1: if(localB->ALARM_OUT_Hazard >= 3){
2:   if(localB->Disable_Audio > 1){
3:     localB->ALARM_OUT_Audio_Command = 0;
4:     localB->ALARM_OUT_Audio_Disabled = 1;
5:     if(localDW->time_minutes > 3){
6:       localB->Disable_Audio = 0;
7:     }
8:   }
9: }else ...
```

Fig. 2. Code snippet from the ALARM system's audio notification functionality

To motivate the utility of our proposed approach we use a snippet of auto-generated code from the Audio state machine in Fig. 1. The code is shown in Fig. 2. It raises an aural alert when a certain level of hazard is detected and the audio has not been disabled by the user. Assume the following oracle encodes a requirement of the system:

$$Hazard >= 3 \land Disable\_Audio = 0 \implies Audio\_Command = 1$$

Suppose we execute a test case, t, that covers program statements one to seven in Fig. 2 and the values of the variables used in the oracle are: $Hazard := 3$ and $Disable\_Audio := 2$. The corresponding checked coverage for the test does not contain the program statement at line 4 in Fig. 2; the $Audio\_Disabled$ variable defined at line 4 does not either directly or transitively impact the values used in the oracle. This example demonstrates that the *checked* coverage is lower than the set of *covered* statements.

The notion of *checked* coverage, however, does not take into account which parts of the oracle were covered and whether the values of certain program variables are masked when the oracle is evaluated. The values for variables $Hazard := 3$ and $Disable\_Audio := 2$ cause the antecedent in the requirement ($Hazard >= 3 \land Disable\_Audio = 0$) to be false; hence, the consequent of the requirement ($Audio\_Command = 1$) is not evaluated. Even though the program statement at line 3 in Fig. 2 writes to the variable $Audio\_Command$ used in the oracle, the test, t, does not evaluate $Audio\_Command$ in the oracle. We can leverage this information to define a more precise checked coverage measure by marking line 3 in Fig. 2 as unchecked. In the next section we present an overview of how we measure requirements coverage along with checked coverage to improve upon the checked coverage measure.

3   Methodology

There are three inputs to our technique: the model of the system being analyzed, a set of test cases (manual or auto-generated) that exercise the model, and a set of formalized requirements of the model as shown in Fig. 3. The requirements are

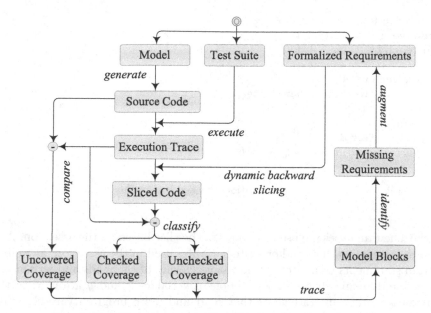

Fig. 3. Test Case Coverage Classification Approach Overview

transformed into assertions over program variables. We automatically generate the code from the model and execute the tests on the auto-generated code. The formalized requirements are used as a slicing criteria for program execution traces generated by the various tests as shown in Fig. 3. A dynamic backward slice is used to extract the set of program statements that operate on variables whose values are *checked* in the assertions. This is termed as checked coverage while all other executed statements are categorized as unchecked coverage. In addition to the code coverage we also measure the coverage of the requirements. Checked, unchecked, and uncovered code coverage are mapped back to the model to help the system engineers determine incompleteness in the requirements, tests, or the model.

We present an overview of the algorithm to partition coverage into *checked* coverage versus *unchecked* coverage in Fig. 4. The algorithm takes as input an auto-generated program M, the test suite T for exercising the behaviors of the program, and the set of assertions that encode the formalized requirements. The sets *checked* and *unchecked* are initialized as empty. We run each test, t, in the test suite T on the program and generate the set of program statements $\langle l_0, \ldots, l_n \rangle$ executed by the test. Next, we generate a dynamic slice of the trace using each assertion a as the slicing criteria. In the case that a program statement l is in the dynamic slice then it is added to the *checked* set; otherwise it is added to the *unchecked* set.

Dynamic slicing is used to compute the basic form of checked coverage. A dynamic slice of an execution trace with respect to an assertion extracts the set of program statements in the trace that *may* impact the evaluation of the assertion.

$/ * checked := \emptyset, unchecked := \emptyset * /$
procedure initialize(M, T, A)
1: **for each** $t \in T \wedge a \in A$ **do**
2:    $\langle l_0, \ldots, l_n \rangle := \texttt{execute}(P, t)$
3:    **for each** $i \in [0, n]$ **do**
4:       **if** $l_i \in \texttt{dynamicBackwardSlice}(\langle l_0, \ldots, l_n \rangle, a)$ **then**
5:          $checked := checked \cup \{l_i\}$
6:       **else**
7:          $unchecked := unchecked \cup \{l_i\}$
8:    $unchecked := unchecked \setminus checked$

Fig. 4. An algorithm to partition checked and unchecked coverage

Standard flow analyses are used to generate the slice based on the assertion. Any program statements that read or write variables used in the assertion, as well as program statements computed by transitive closure of the reads and writes, are part of the dynamic slice. Suppose, boolean variables x and y are used in the assertion; all program statements that read and write program variables that *may* be used directly or transitively by x and y are added to the dynamic slice. This notion of *checked* coverage does not however take into account which parts of the assertion are covered and whether certain values are masked when the assertion is evaluated. In the rest of the section we first present how we measure the coverage of the assertions and then leverage the information to improve the precision of the checked coverage.

3.1   Coverage of Requirements

In this work we use the Modified Decision/Condition Coverage (MC/DC) metric to evaluate the assertion coverage for a given test suite. MC/DC is commonly used to evaluate the coverage of requirements in safety-critical systems. MC/DC coverage of a requirement encoded as an assertion requires that each condition in the assertion takes on all possible outcomes at least once and each condition is shown to *independently* affect the assertion's outcome. Note that a condition is a boolean expression that contains no boolean operators. We use the masking form of MC/DC to determine the independence of the conditions in the assertion. A condition is masked if changing its value does not affect the outcome of the assertion. For example, when evaluating `assert` x `and` y, in the case when x is `false`, the value of y is masked. We need to satisfy three possible coverage obligations:

1. $x \wedge y$
2. $x \wedge \neg y$
3. $\neg x \wedge y$

In order to check the MC/DC coverage of the assertion x **and** y, we replace the assertion in A with three new assertions synthesized from the expressions shown above. If there are test cases in T that can satisfy all three assertions, then we report 100% MC/DC coverage of the assertion. But if only one is satisfied by the test, then we report 33% coverage of the assertion. We believe that measuring the MC/DC coverage of the requirements for a given test suite enables us to better characterize the quality of the test suite with respect to a given set of requirements.

3.2 A More Precise Dynamic Backward Slice

We propose a more precise dynamic backward slice that takes into account which parts of the assertion are covered and whether certain values of program variables are not used when the assertion is evaluated. We leverage the *masking* information within an assertion for a given test to generate a more precise dynamic backward slice. As stated earlier, a condition is *masked* if changing its value cannot affect the outcome of a decision. So in the assertion, x and y, if the value for x is `false`, the value of y is masked. In this more precise version of a dynamic slice we first extract the variables in the assertion that are not masked, then get all of the program statements in the execution trace that impact them. Therefore, instead of computing the slice based on both x and y, we generate a slice using x alone. Even though there are values of y being written to in the execution trace, since they are not being used in the evaluation of the assertion, they are not added to the *checked* set. We believe this will reduce the size of the *checked* set and provide a more precise characterization of parts of the program that are being checked in the assertions.

3.3 Mapping Back to the Model

In the final phase of our technique, for a given test suite, we report the following to the system engineers: (i) the precise checked coverage, (ii) the unchecked coverage, (iii) the uncovered coverage, and the (iv) coverage of the requirements. Note that we map the coverage of the code onto the model. We believe that these coverage measures help us bridge the gap between requirements, tests, and the model as discussed in [28]. The relationship between the various types of coverage can potentially help to determine the source of incompleteness in either tests, requirements, or the model. Low coverage of the requirements and high checked coverage could indicate missing functionality in the model. Low coverage of the requirements coupled with low checked coverage could be indicative of missing tests and/or missing requirements. Finally, high coverage of requirements along with low checked coverage could be indicative of missing requirements.

4 Evaluation

In this section we describe the evaluation of our approach on three systems. We first give a brief overview of the example systems, then we describe the experimental set up followed by the evaluation of the approach on the systems.

4.1   Case Examples

We consider three different systems: a medical device controller, an avionics system controller and a general appliance controller. Table 1 shows the specifics of the case examples considered. Following this section, we refer to each system and its test cases using the ID from the first column in Table 1. The second column gives the number of auto-generated source lines of code (LOC); column three presents the number of requirements available for each test suite; column 4 describes the source of the test suites. The last column shows the number of tests in each test suite.

Table 1. Case Example Artifacts Synopsis

ID	System	# LOC	# Reqs	Test Suite : Source	# Tests
ALM_1	ALARM	1950	18	Set 1 : Manual	16
ALM_2	ALARM	1950	18	Set 2 : jKind	106
DCK_1	DOCKING	2240	3	Set 1 : Reactis	32
DCK_2	DOCKING	2240	3	Set 2 : SDV	69
MCR_1	MICROWAVE	537	11	Set 1 : Reactis	39
MCR_2	MICROWAVE	537	11	Set 2 : Reactis	23

Table 2. Case Example's Test Case Coverage Metrics

ID	Statement	Condition	Requirements
ALM_1	43.65%	31.93%	65.71%
ALM_2	95.05%	95.80%	84.84%
DCK_1	39.43%	35.29%	26.66%
DCK_2	77.37%	78.89%	73.32%
MCR_1	79.07%	93.75%	60.86%
MCR_2	87.21%	100.00%	80.42%

The first system considered is the ALARM subsystem discussed in Section 2. The model of the ALARM subsystem was developed as a multi-level hierarchical state machine using the Mathworks Simulink/Stateflow tool. The source code of this model was automatically generated using MathWorks Simulink Coder [20]. The system has 18 formally verified [22] safety critical requirements. For testing the ALARM system, we created manual test cases using the requirements as a reference and also generated a test suite with high structural coverage (MC/DC) using the jKind model checker [13].

The second example we consider is a docking approach system. This system specifies the mechanism for the docking of a space vehicle. This system was also developed using Mathworks Simulink/Stateflow tool and its source code was generated using Simulink Coder. A major issue with this system is that even though it is elaborately modeled, there are only a few requirements specified. Although we know that this system lacks a complete set of requirements, our goal was to analyze the adequacy of the sparse requirements for the test cases. For the Docking example, we generated a random test suite using the Reactis tool and another test suite with high structural coverage using MathWorks Simulink Design Verifier (SDV) [21] .

The third case example is a microwave's controller system used in our previous work [28], that was also modeled as hierarchical state machines using the MathWorks Stateflow notation. The microwave controller implements the usual functions of a regular microwave. We generated code for the microwave system using the Gryphon Tool Suite [34]. The advantage with the microwave model is that it has a comprehensive set of requirements. The test cases for microwave were generated using Reactis.

4.2   Tools and Experiment Set up

We use a combination of commercially available and free open source tools to implement our approach. As previously mentioned, the test suites and the source code are generated using various sources and tools in order to generate a variety of artifacts and determine the efficacy of the different test suites based on our metrics. However, assessing the test suite generation techniques and tools is not the intent of this experiment. We used the gcov [17] tool to measure the statement and condition coverage of the test suites. In order to measure coverage of requirements we generate MC/DC obligations and replace the assertions with these obligations. The total number of obligations that are satisfied by the test suite are recorded and reported.

To generate dynamic backward slices, we use the Frama-C tool [7], an open source tool for analysis of C programs. Although Frama-C is primarily a static analysis tool, it provides the ability to construct dynamic backward slices by embedding the test vector into the program and using the `-slevel` slicing option. The Frama-C slicing plugin provides an implementation of dependence-based backward slicing. The Frama-C slicing plugin requires the slicing criterion to be expressed using ACSL [4], a formal specification language used for specifying behavioral properties of C source code. The ACSL notation allows C like syntax for specifying slicing criteria, which makes it straightforward to specify requirements as logical statements. For example, the slicing criteria for the ALARM's oracle described in Section 2 is translated into an expression for slicing as shown below:

```
//@slice pragma expr
 (!(Hazard >= 3 and Disable_Audio == 1) || (Audio_Command == 0));
```

The slice is obtained by executing each test case in the test suite and extracting the dynamic backward slice based on the slicing criterion (requirements). While executing the test, the execution trace is also obtained. Once all slices and execution traces are obtained, the slices are compared with the execution

Table 3. Coverage Metrics Partitioned based on Slicing

ID	Slicing		Precise Slicing		
	Checked	Unchecked	Checked	Unchecked	Uncovered
ALM_1	36.50%	8.65%	20.01%	23.64%	56.35%
ALM_2	75.44%	19.61%	54.35%	38.70 %	4.95%
DCK_1	23.91%	15.52%	5.49%	33.96%	60.57%
DCK_2	35.63%	41.47%	16.06%	61.31%	22.63%
MCR_1	76.70%	2.37%	56.25%	22.82%	20.93%
MCR_2	73.86 %	13.35%	65.34%	21.87%	12.79%

Table 4. Data Summary

ID	Covered	Requirements	Checked	Improve, Add
ALM_1	43.65%	65.71%	20.01%	test cases, new reqs
ALM_2	95.05%	84.84%	54.35%	new reqs
DCK_1	39.43%	26.66%	5.49%	all
DCK_2	77.37%	73.32%	16.06%	new reqs
MCR_1	79.07%	60.86%	56.25%	test cases
MCR_2	87.21%	80.42%	65.34%	new reqs

trace to identify the checked and unchecked covered lines of code. Similarly by comparing the source code and the execution trace, the uncovered lines of code are obtained.

4.3 Analysis of the Results

Table 2 shows the structural and requirements coverage metrics for the artifacts for a given test suite. The statement and condition coverage for ALM_1 and DCK_1 and the requirements coverage for DCK_1 is less than 50%. The rest of the coverage numbers are over 50%. The statement and condition coverage of ALM_2 is slightly above 95% and the requirements coverage is 84%. Similarly MCR_2 has statement and condition coverage of 87% and 100% respectively and requirements coverage of 80%. These are fairly reasonable values for traditional coverage metrics for this set of artifacts.

Table 3 shows the results obtained using the dynamic slicing based approaches. The first two columns show the checked and unchecked coverage values using the dynamic backward slicing technique as proposed by [29, 30], whereas the next two columns show the checked and unchecked coverage values using the more precise dynamic backward slicing approach presented in this paper. The results demonstrate that, overall, the checked coverage in Table 3 is lower compared to the set of covered statements shown in Table 2. Recall that the total number of checked statements plus the unchecked statements gives the covered statements. Table 3 shows that the unchecked coverage ranges from 2.37% for MCR_1 to 41.47% for DCK_2. Using the more precise dynamic slicing technique proposed in this work the checked coverage decreases even further while the unchecked coverage increases. The MCR_2 artifact has a reasonably high statement coverage of 87.21% as shown in Table 3. coverage In the MCR_1 example, the checked coverage using the slicing approach decreases from 76.70% in column one to 56.25% in column three of Table 3 when using precise slicing, because the tests are not able to exercise most variables in the requirements. The low requirements coverage of 60% as shown in Table 2 provides evidence for the same. In MCR_2, however, when more variables of the requirements are exercised by the test cases (indicated by requirements coverage of 80.42%) the decrease in the checked coverage is smaller—73.86% to 65.34%.

The results for the examples in this section provide evidence towards our hypothesis that taking into account the part of the requirements or oracle that are covered (not masked) by the tests can provide us with a stronger notion of structural coverage with respect to the requirements.

5 Discussion

We summarize the results of the empirical evaluation and provide some recommendations for improvement based on the data. Table 4 presents the three coverage metrics (i) covered, (ii) requirements, and (iii) checked, as well as the recommendations for which artifacts should be further augmented in order to improve the coverage of the code and the requirements. For example, ALM_1 has reasonable requirements coverage of 65.71% but fairly low covered program statements (43.65%) and even lower precise checked coverage (20.01%). Our recommendation is to first augment the test suite with tests that exercise additional parts of the code, then try to identify missing requirements, and finally measure the requirements coverage with the augmented test cases. DCK_1 has fairly low coverage values for all metrics, suggesting that all artifacts need to be improved. This is not surprising since there are only three requirements for the model. The ALM_2, DCK_2, MCR_2 examples have reasonable statement and requirements coverage but low precise checked coverage. This suggests that the set of requirements may be incomplete. MCR_1 also has reasonable statement coverage but the coverage of existing requirements needs to be improved prior to identifying the missing requirements.

We demonstrate using an example of how the coverage information can be used by system engineers to detect potential causes of missing requirements. The ALARM system had 19.6% unchecked coverage (see Table 3). A snippet of code from the unchecked lines of code is shown in Figure 5. The variables used in these lines are then traced back to their source blocks in the model, as shown in Figure 5. Using this information, a system engineer might want to add a requirement that would check if the system has been IDLE for more than a certain amount of time.

This overall approach can be iteratively applied until we achieve the desired coverage metrics. Although achieving 100% for all the coverage criteria is ideal, it may not be practical. However, we believe that the metrics presented in the paper help identify the specific inadequacies in the test suite, that can be analyzed by the stakeholders to determine if and how they should be addressed. In

```
switch (ALARM_Functional_DW.is_IsIdleTimeExceeded)
.....
  case ALARM_Functional_IN_No:
    else if (ALARM_Functional_B.Current_System_Mode == 1)
    ALARM_Functional_DW.idletimer = 0;
    ALARM_Functional_DW.idletimer++;
  ...
```

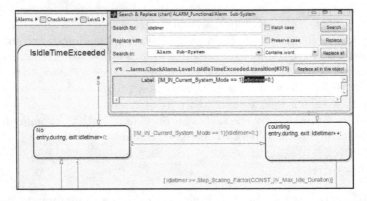

Fig. 5. Tracing unchecked lines of source code in the ALARM model

future work, we would like to assess the fault finding capability improvement by improving these artifacts.

6   Related Work

Our work is built on the checked-coverage work of Schuler and Zeller [29,30], which is in turn built upon dynamic slicing techniques [15] which follow from Weiser's original slicing work [32]. Checked coverage is in the category of *observability testing*, in which a metric tries to ensure that the code structure under test can be observed by the oracle. Often, the oracle is simply the outputs of the system under test. Observability testing has been a focus in testing of hardware logic circuits. The observability-based code coverage metric (OCCOM) attaches tags to internal states in a circuit and the propagation of tags is used to predict the actual propagation of errors (corrupted state) [9,11]. A variable is tagged when there is a possible change in the value of the variable due to a fault. The observability coverage can be used to determine whether erroneous effects that are activated by the inputs can be observed at the outputs.

For software, dynamic taint analysis, or dynamic information flow analysis, marks and tracks data in a program at runtime in order to determine observability. This technique has been used in security as well as software testing and debugging [6,18]. Taint propagation occurs in both explicit information flow (i.e., data dependencies) and implicit information flow (control dependencies). Although the way in which markings are combined varies based on the application, the default behavior is to union them [6]. Thus, dynamic taint analysis is conservative and does not consider masking. More accurate techniques for information flow modeling, such as [35], define path conditions to prove *non-interference*, that is, the non-observability of a variable or expression on a particular output. These information flow-based techniques have been used for testing in a metric called *Observable MC/DC* [33]; this work is very similar to checked coverage except that markings are *forward propagated* from observation points towards an oracle rather than (in checked coverage) *back-propagated* from the oracle towards observation points.

Mutation testing [3,8,23] is also concerned with quality of both *tests* and *oracles*. In mutation testing, one creates a set of programs that contain some small modification (*mutation*) of the original program and determines whether the discrepancy is detected (*killed*) by the test suite / oracle pair. Mutation testing suffers somewhat from the problem of *equivalent mutants*, which are program modifications that do not change the observable behavior of the program.

For requirements testing, much of the work has focused on requirements specified in temporal logic. In [24,36], a coverage metric called *Unique First Cause Coverage* is defined by expanding the MC/DC test metric to formulas involving temporal logic operators. Similar work involves *vacuity checking* of temporal logic formulas [5,16,25]. Intuitively, a model M *vacuously satisfies* property f if a sub-formula ϕ of f is not necessary to prove whether or not f is true. Formally, a formula is vacuous if we can replace ϕ by any arbitrary formula ψ in f without affecting the validity of f:

$$M \vDash f \quad \equiv \quad M \vDash f[\phi \leftarrow \psi]$$

For requirements specified as *synchronous observers*, the Simulink test generation tool Reactis and the Mathworks Verification and Validation plug-in for Simulink support MC/DC generation and coverage measurement over requirements.

7   Conclusion

There are a variety of mechanisms to generate test cases. The two main techniques for test case generation are (i) manual and (ii) automated test case generation techniques. In MBD, system engineers often write tests manually in order to cover the requirements as well as cover program statements. The system engineers study the requirements and try to determine the constraints on program inputs and their expected outputs on the model based on the statements in the requirements. This information is used to then create test inputs and a test oracle, using various techniques. Some operate on formalized requirements, some on the model, while others on the code auto-generated from the model. We can measure the structural coverage of the code when these tests are executed.

The challenge for automatically generated tests is that there is no oracle. Sometimes even in manually generated tests, defining a precise oracle for a given test is often a difficult endeavor. When present, system requirements that are either formalized or *can* be formalized serve as ideal candidates to be encoded as oracles. Even if the requirements are in a natural language such as English but describe the requirements in terms of the interface of the model, then we can convert these requirements into some formal notation.

Recent work presents a stronger notion of coverage of *checked* coverage, compared to traditional structural values of simply covered and uncovered [29, 30]. It uses dynamic backward slicing to count only statements whose execution contributes to an outcome checked by an oracle. In this work we add precision to the notion of checked coverage based on combining MC/DC masking information with dynamic backward slicing. We believe that this information can help system engineers identify missing requirements as well as missing test cases. The approach presented here allows us to connect the dots between test cases, requirements, and the model.

We demonstrated our approach using three case examples and also illustrated how the metrics can be actually used as a closed loop in identifying missing requirements and improving testing in a model-based approach. As part of future work, we would like to evaluate the proposed approach on the requirements and tests of the NASA's Lunar Atmosphere and Dust Environment Explorer (LADEE) mission.

Acknowledgments. This work was performed as part of an internship at NASA Ames Research Center funded by the Aviation Safety Program. We would like to thank Gregory Gay at University of Minnesota, for helping us measure requirements coverage of test cases.

References

1. IBM Rational Rhapsody (2014). http://www.ibm.com/developerworks/rational/products/rhapsody/
2. IBM Rational Statemate (2014). http://www-03.ibm.com/software/products/en/ratistat
3. Ammann, P., Delamaro, M.E., Offutt, J.: Establishing theoretical minimal sets of mutants. In: Proceedings of the 2014 IEEE International Conference on Software Testing, Verification, and Validation, IEEE Computer Society Washington, DC, USA (2014)
4. Baudin, P., Filliâtre, J.-C., Claude, M., Benjamin, M., Moy, Y., Virgile, P., Île-de France, I.S.: ANSI/ISO C specification language, ACSL (2008)
5. Beer, I., Ben-David, S., Eisner, C., Rodeh, Y.: Efficient detection of vacuity in ACTL formulas. In: Formal Methods in System Design, pp. 141–162 (2001)
6. Clause, J., Li, W., Orso, A.: Dytan: a generic dynamic taint analysis framework. In: Proceedings of the 2007 Int'l Symposium on Software Testing and Analysis, pp. 196–206 (2007)
7. Cuoq, P., Kirchner, F., Kosmatov, N., Prevosto, V., Signoles, J., Yakobowski, B.: Frama-c. In: Software Engineering and Formal Methods, pp. 233–247. Springer (2012)
8. DeMillo, R.A., Lipton, R.J., Sayward, F.G.: Hints on test data selection: Help for the practicing programmer. Computer **11**(4), 34–41 (1978)
9. Devadas, S., Ghosh, A., Keutzer, K.: An observability-based code coverage metric for functional simulation. In: Proceedings of the 1996 IEEE/ACM Int'l Conf. on Computer-Aided Design, pp. 418–425 (1996)

10. Esterel-Technologies. SCADE Suite product description. http://www.esterel-technologies.com/v2/scadeSuiteForSafetyCriticalSoftwareDe

11. Fallah, F., Devadas, S., Keutzer, K.: OCCOM-efficient computation of observability-based code coverage metrics for functional verification. IEEE Transactions on Computer-Aided Design of Integrated Circuits and Systems 20(8), 1003–1015 (2001)

12. Fraser, G., Staats, M., McMinn, P., Arcuri, A., Padberg, F.: Does automated white-box test generation really help software testers? In: ISSTA 2013 Proceedings of the 2013 International Symposium on Software Testing and Analysis, pp. 291–301. ACM, New York, NY, USA (2013)

13. Gacek, A.: JKind - a Java implementation of the KIND model checker. https://github.com/agacek

14. Gay, G., Staats, M., Whalen, M.W., Heimdahl, M.P.E.: Moving the goalposts: coverage satisfaction is not enough. In: Proceedings of the 7th International Workshop on Search-Based Software Testing, ACM, New York, NY, USA (2014)

15. Korel, B., Laski, J.: Dynamic program slicing. Information Processing Letters 29(3), 155–163 (1988)

16. Kupferman, O., Vardi, M.Y.: Vacuity detection in temporal model checking. Journal on Software Tools for Technology Transfer 4(2), February 2003

17. GNUGPL License. Gcov: Gnu coverage tool. https://gcc.gnu.org

18. Masri, W., Podgurski, A., Leon, D.: Detecting and debugging insecure information flows. In: Proceedings of the 15th Int'l Symposium on Software Reliability Engineering, pp. 198–209 (2004)

19. MathWorks Inc., Simulink. http://www.mathworks.com/products/simulink

20. MathWorks Inc., Simulink Coder. http://www.mathworks.com/products/simulink-coder/

21. MathWorks Inc., Simulink Design Verifier. http://www.mathworks.com/products/sldesignverifier

22. Murugesan, A., Whalen, M.W., Rayadurgam, S., Heimdahl, M.P.E.: Compositional verification of a medical device system. In: ACM Int'l Conf. on High Integrity Language Technology (HILT) 2013. ACM, November 2013

23. Offutt, A.J., Untch, R.H.: Mutation testing for the new century. chapter Mutation 2000: Uniting the Orthogonal, pp. 34–44. Kluwer Academic Publishers, Norwell, MA, USA (2001)

24. Pecheur, C., Raimondi, F., Brat, G.: A formal analysis of requirements-based testing. In: Proceedings of the Eighteenth International Symposium on Software Testing and Analysis, pp. 47–56. ACM (2009)

25. Purandare, M., Somenzi, F.: Vacuum cleaning CTL formulae. In: Brinksma, E., Larsen, K.G. (eds.) CAV 2002. LNCS, vol. 2404, p. 485. Springer, Heidelberg (2002)

26. Reactive systems inc. http://www.reactive-systems.com/index.msp

27. RTCA/DO-178C. Software considerations in airborne systems and equipment certification

28. Rungta, N., Tkachuk, O., Person, S., Biatek, J., Whalen, M.W., Castle, J., Gundy-Burlet, K.: Helping system engineers bridge the peaks. In: TwinPeaks 2014 Proceedings of the 4th International Workshop on Twin Peaks of Requirements and Architecture, pp. 9–13. ACM, New York, NY, USA, (2014)

29. Schuler, D., Zeller, A.: Assessing oracle quality with checked coverage. In: ICST 2011 Proceedings of the 2011 Fourth IEEE International Conference on Software Testing, Verification and Validation, pp. 90–99. IEEE Computer Society, Washington, DC, USA (2011)

30. Schuler, D., Zeller, A.: Checked coverage: an indicator for oracle quality. Software: Testing, Verification and Reliability **23**(7), 531–551 (2013)

31. Staats, M., Gay, G., Whalen, M.W., Heimdahl, M.P.E.: On the danger of coverage directed test case generation. In: 15th Int'l Conf. on Fundamental Approaches to Software Engineering (FASE), April 2012

32. Weiser, M.: Program slicing. IEEE Transactions on Software Engineering **10**(4), 352–357 (1984)

33. Whalen, M., Gay, G., You, D., Heimdahl, M.P.E., Staats, M.: Observable modified condition/decision coverage. In: Proceedings of the 2013 Int'l Conf. on Software Engineering. ACM, May 2013

34. Whalen, M.W., Cofer, D.D., Miller, S.P., Krogh, B.H., Storm, W.: Integration of Formal Analysis into a Model-Based Software Development Process. In: Leue, S., Merino, P. (eds.) Formal Methods for Industrial Critical Systems. LNCS, vol. 4916, pp. 68–84. Springer, Heidelberg (2007)

35. Whalen, M.W., Greve, D.A., Wagner, L.G.: Model Checking Information Flow. Springer-Verlag, Berlin Germany (2010)

36. Whalen, M.W., Rajan, A., Heimdahl, M.P.E.: Coverage metrics for requirements-based testing. In: Proceedings of Int'l Symposium on Software Testing and Analysis, pp. 25–36. ACM, July 2006

A Greedy Approach for the Efficient Repair of Stochastic Models

Shashank Pathak[1], Erika Ábrahám[2], Nils Jansen[2]($\boxtimes$),
Armando Tacchella[1], and Joost-Pieter Katoen[2]

[1] University of Genova, Genova, Italy
[2] RWTH Aachen University, Aachen, Germany
nils.jansen@cs.rwth.aachen.de

Abstract. For discrete-time probabilistic models there are efficient
methods to check whether they satisfy certain properties. If a property is
refuted, available techniques can be used to explain the failure in form of
a counterexample. However, there are no *scalable* approaches to *repair* a
model, i.e., to modify it with respect to certain side conditions such that
the property is satisfied. In this paper we propose such a method, which
avoids expensive computations and is therefore applicable to large models. A prototype implementation is used to demonstrate the applicability
and scalability of our technique.

1 Introduction

Discrete-time Markov chains (DTMCs) are a widely used modeling formalism for
systems that exhibit probabilistic behavior, some typical application areas being
distributed computing, security, hardware, and systems biology. DTMCs can
be seen as directed graphs whose transitions are equipped with probabilities. A
popular language to specify properties of such models is *probabilistic computation
tree logic (PCTL)* [1]. Model checking PCTL properties or ω-regular properties
can be reduced to *reachability problems*, i.e., checking whether the probabilities of
reaching a set of distinguished target states are within some required thresholds.
Efficient probabilistic model checkers like PRISM [2] or MRMC [3] are available.

In the recent past, much effort has been made in automatically generating
explanations for the failure of a property in the form of *counterexamples*. For an
overview on different approaches and literature we refer to [4]. In spite of various
efficient methods for counterexample generation, a still open problem is how to
automatically repair a DTMC model that does not meet a certain requirement.

A first approach, referred to as *model repair for DTMCs*, was presented in [5].
Basically, the models are *parametrized* using linear combinations of real-valued
parameters in the transition probabilities of a DTMC that violates a desired
reachability property. Additionally, a *cost-function* over the parameters is given.

This work was partially supported by the Excellence Initiative of the German federal
and state government, the FP7-IRSES project MEALS, and the EU FP7 project
SENSATION.

© Springer International Publishing Switzerland 2015
K. Havelund et al. (Eds.): NFM 2015, LNCS 9058, pp. 295–309, 2015.
DOI: 10.1007/978-3-319-17524-9_21

The goal is to find an parameter valuation which on the one hand induces the satisfaction of the property and on the other hand minimizes the value of the cost-function, i.e., changing the transition probabilities and thereby *repairing* the DTMC with minimal costs.

Formally, the underlying model is a *parametric discrete-time Markov chain* (*PDTMC*). Such models are also used in early system development stages, where the parameters represent design parameters whose values should be fixed later such that the resulting instantiated model satisfies some properties within a fixed probability range while being optimal (or nearly optimal) with respect to a given objective function under some realizability conditions. Recently some approaches were proposed to represent the probability that a PDTMC satisfies a required property in the form of a rational function over the parameters [6,7], as being implemented in the tool PARAM [8].

In [5], such a rational function is computed for the PDTMC underlying the model repair problem. Then a non-linear optimization problem [9] is solved implying that the desired property is satisfied for this formula while the cost-function is minimized. This can be done, e.g., via IPOPT [10]. If satisfiable, the resulting valuation is a solution for the model repair problem. Also a method for Markov decision processes (MDPs) was proposed, encompassing approximative methods [11]. Statistical model checking combined with reinforcement learning was used in [12] for a related problem on robustness. Model repair for non-stochastic systems has, e.g., been studied in [13].

The main practical obstacle of using non-linear optimization, be it using a dedicated optimization algorithm or using an SMT-solver for non-linear real algebra [14] coupled with a binary search towards the optimal solution, is *scalability*. As the optimization involves costly computations of greatest common divisors of polynomials, approaches like [6,7] are inherently restricted to small PDTMCs with just a few parameters.

In this paper we present a new technique which we call *local repair*. Our method starts from an initial parameter assignment and iteratively changes the parameter values by *local repair steps*. To illustrate the basic idea, assume a model in which the probability to reach some "unsafe" states is above an allowed bound. Using model checking we know for each state the probability to reach "unsafe" states from it. The higher this probability, the more dangerous it is to visit this state. To repair the model, we iteratively consider single probability distributions in isolation, and modify the parameter values such that we decrease the probability to move to more dangerous successor states. We show our approach to be *sound and complete* in the sense that each local repair step improves the reachability probability towards a desired bound for a repairable PDTMC, and under some reasonable conditions on the applied heuristics, the repair algorithm always terminates with an optimal solution.

We implemented our approach in a prototype and tested it thoroughly using a robotics application scenario, where the given environment is modeled by a Markov Decision Process (MDP) and where a controller is synthesized via reinforcement-learning [15], which is modeled by a DTMC. This controller shall be repaired until a certain property is satisfied. Furthermore, we present well-known benchmarks from the PRISM benchmark suite and categorize each of them into one of our three PDTMC subclasses. The experiments show the feasibility of our approach, where the method as proposed in [5] immediately fails even for very small systems.

2 Preliminaries

Definition 1 (Discrete-time Markov chain). *A discrete-time Markov chain (DTMC) is a tuple $D = (S, s^I, P)$ with S a finite non-empty set of states, $s^I \in S$ an initial state, and $P \colon S \times S \to [0,1] \subseteq \mathbb{Q}$ a transition probability function with $\sum_{s' \in S} P(s, s') = 1$ for all $s \in S$.*

We assume the states to be encoded by natural numbers, i.e., $S = \{1, \ldots, k\}$ for some $k \in \mathbb{N}$, $k > 0$. The transition probability function P can be seen as a *probability matrix* of size $k \times k$, where the entry in row $s_i \in S$ and column $s_j \in S$ is the probability $P(s_i, s_j)$ of the transition from s_i to s_j in S.

A *path* of a DTMC $D = (S, s^I, P)$ is a non-empty (finite or infinite) sequence $\pi = s_0 s_1 \ldots$ of states $s_i \in S$ such that $P(s_i, s_{i+1}) > 0$ for all i. Let Paths_{fin}^D denote the set of all finite paths of D, $\text{Paths}_{fin}^D(s)$ those starting in $s \in S$, and $\text{Paths}_{fin}^D(s, t)$ those starting in s and ending in t. A state $t \in S$ is called *reachable* from $s \in S$ iff $\text{Paths}_{fin}^D(s, t) \neq \emptyset$.

The *cylinder set* $\text{Cyl}(\pi)$ for $\pi \in \text{Paths}_{fin}^D$ is the set of all infinite paths of D with prefix π. As usual, we associate to D the smallest σ-algebra that contains all cylinder sets of all finite paths of D. This gives us a unique probability measure Pr^D on the σ-algebra, where the probabilities of the cylinder sets are given by

$$\text{Pr}^D(\text{Cyl}(s_0 \ldots s_n)) = \prod_{i=0}^{n-1} P(s_i, s_{i+1}) \ .$$

We write short $\text{Pr}^D(s, t)$ for the probability $\text{Pr}^D(\cup_{\pi \in \text{Paths}_{fin}^D(s,t)} \text{Cyl}(\pi))$ of reaching t from s in D. These probabilities $\text{Pr}^D(s, t)$ can be computed as the unique solution for the variables p_s of the following equation system:

$$p_s = \begin{cases} 1 & \text{for } s = t, \\ 0 & \text{if } t \text{ is not reachable from } s \text{ in } D, \\ \sum_{s' \in S} P(s, s') \cdot p_{s'} & \text{else}. \end{cases} \tag{1}$$

In [6], *parametric DTMCs (PDTMCs)* are introduced. Instead of constants, the transition probabilities in PDTMCs can be specified by *rational functions* (fractions of polynomials) over a set of parameters.

Let in the following $Var = \{x_1, \ldots, x_n\}$ be a finite set of variables with domains $dom(x_i) = [a_i, b_i] \subseteq \mathbb{R}$ for some $a_i, b_i \in \mathbb{Q}$, $i \in \{1, \ldots, n\}$. A *valuation*

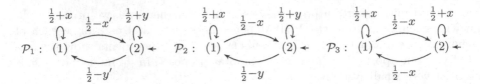

Fig. 1. Type-I PDTMC $\mathcal{P}_1$, Type-II PDTMC $\mathcal{P}_2$, and Type-III PDTMC $\mathcal{P}_3$

for Var is a function $v\colon Var \to \mathbb{R}$ such that $v(x_i) \in dom(x_i)$ for each $i \in \{1,\dots,n\}$. Let V be the set of all valuations for Var.

Transition probabilities in PDTMCs will be specified by *rational functions* $f = p_1/p_2$ over Var, where p_1 and p_2 are polynomials over Var with rational coefficients. Let F be the set of all rational functions over Var. By $Var(p)$ we refer to the set of variables appearing in the polynomial p, write $p = 0$ if p can be reduced to 0, and $p \neq 0$ otherwise. Using $p(x_1,\dots,x_n)$ we explicitly refer to the variables of p. We use similar notations for rational functions. The *value* of a polynomial $p(x_1,\dots,x_n)$ under a valuation $v \in V$ is $v(p(x_1,\dots,x_n)) = p(v(x_1),\dots,v(x_n))$, and analogously $v(p_1(x_1,\dots,x_n)/p_2(x_1,\dots,x_n)) = v(p_1)/v(p_2)$ if $v(p_2) \neq 0$ and undefined otherwise for rational functions.

Definition 2 (Parametric DTMC). *A parametric DTMC (PDTMC) is a tuple* $\mathcal{P} = (S, s^I, P)$ *with* S *a finite non-empty set of states,* $s^I \in S$ *an initial state, and* $P\colon S \times S \to F$ *a transition probability function.*

Note that, as DTMCs are a special case of PDTMCs, we use the same notations. The work [5] on model repair considers a subclass of these models, where the involved rational functions are *linear terms*. We call such models *linear PDTMCs*. We now identify the following *subclasses* of PDTMCs:

Type-I: PDTMCs where each variable appears on at most one transition:

$$\forall s_1, s_2, s_1', s_2' \in S.\; Var(P(s_1,s_2)) \cap Var(P(s_1',s_2')) \neq \emptyset \to s_1 = s_1' \wedge s_2 = s_2'\,.$$

Type-II: PDTMCs where each variable appears in at most one distribution:

$$\forall s_1, s_2, s_1', s_2' \in S.\; Var(P(s_1,s_2)) \cap Var(P(s_1',s_2')) \neq \emptyset \to s_1 = s_1'\,.$$

Type-III: Unrestricted PDTMCs, allowing each variable to appear several times possibly in different distributions.

Example 1. Figure 1 shows examples for the three PDTMC classes. Note that sometimes Type-II PDTMCs can be transformed to Type-I PDTMCs. In this example, $\mathcal{P}_1$ and $\mathcal{P}_2$ are equivalent, because they have the same set of valid valuations (up to renaming).

Let $\mathcal{P} = (S, s^I, P)$ be a PDTMC. A valuation $v \in V$ is *valid* for $\mathcal{P}$ iff $v(P(s,s')) \in [0,1]$ and $\sum_{s'' \in S} v(P(s,s'')) = 1$ for all $s, s' \in S$. Each valid valuation v for a $\mathcal{P}$ *induces* a DTMC $D(\mathcal{P},v) = (S, s^I, P_v)$ with $P_v(s,s') = v(P(s,s'))$

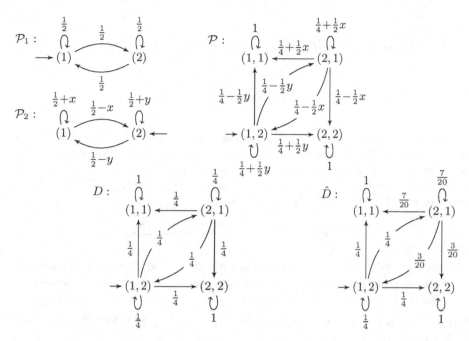

Fig. 2. Example: DTMC $\mathcal{P}_1$; PDTMC $\mathcal{P}_2$ with $dom(x) = dom(y) = [-0.4, 0.4]$; PDTMC $\mathcal{P} = \mathcal{P}_1 || \mathcal{P}_2$ where $(1, 1)$ and $(2, 2)$ are made absorbing and $(2, 2)$ is the target; $D = D(\mathcal{P}, v)$ for $v(x) = v(y) = 0$; $\hat{D} = D(\mathcal{P}, \hat{v})$ for repaired valuation $\hat{v}(x) = 0.2$, $\hat{v}(y) = 0$

for all $s, s' \in S$. The PDTMC $\mathcal{P}$ is called *realizable* iff it has a valid valuation. In the following we assume all PDTMCs to be realizable, which can be checked by solving the following equation system:

$$\bigwedge_{s \in S} \bigwedge_{s' \in S} P(s, s') \in [0, 1] \wedge \sum_{s'' \in S} P(s, s'') = 1 \quad \wedge \quad \bigwedge_{x_i \in Var} x_i \in dom(x_i). \quad (2)$$

Each solution for the above problem gives us a valid valuation for $\mathcal{P}$. For non-linear PDTMCs the check is of exponential complexity in the number of parameters, however, for linear PDTMCs it can be done in polynomial time.

Example 2. Figure 2 illustrates our running example. Assume two places (1) and (2) and an object moving between them according to the DTMC model $\mathcal{P}_1$. To catch the object, a robot moves between the places according to a strategy modeled by $\mathcal{P}_2$ with parameter domains $dom(x) = dom(y) = [-0.4, 0.4]$. In the synchronous parallel composition[1] $\mathcal{P}$ of $\mathcal{P}_1$ and $\mathcal{P}_2$ we made the states $(1, 1)$ and $(2, 2)$, in which the robot succeeds to catch the ball, absorbing. The valid valuation v with $v(x) = v(y) = 0$ induces the DTMC D.

---

[1] For the parallel composition of probabilistic automata see, e.g., [16].

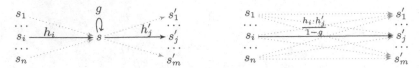

Fig. 3. State elimination

The (parametric) probability to reach a target state $t \in S$ from the initial state s^I in a PDTMC $\mathcal{P}$ can be computed as a rational function over Var (along with some side conditions) using *state elimination* [17], illustrated in Figure 3. Eliminating a non-initial non-absorbing state $s \in S$ in PDTMC $\mathcal{P} = (S, s^I, P)$ results in PDTMC $\mathcal{P}' = (S', s^I, P')$ with $S' = S \setminus \{s\}$ and

$$P'(s_i, s_j) = P(s_i, s_j) + \frac{P(s_i, s) \cdot P(s, s_j)}{1 - P(s, s)}$$

for all $s_i, s_j \in S'$. This state elimination procedure is analogous to the specification of the equation system according to Equation (1) and the elimination of the variables p_s for all $s \in S \setminus \{s^I, t\}$.

Example 3. The probabilities to reach the state $(2, 2)$ in PDTMC $\mathcal{P}$ in Figure 2 are described by:

$$p_{(2,2)} = 1$$
$$p_{(1,1)} = 0$$
$$p_{(1,2)} = (\frac{1}{4} - \frac{1}{2}y)p_{(1,1)} + (\frac{1}{4} + \frac{1}{2}y)p_{(1,2)} + (\frac{1}{4} - \frac{1}{2}y)p_{(2,1)} + (\frac{1}{4} + \frac{1}{2}y)p_{(2,2)}$$
$$p_{(2,1)} = (\frac{1}{4} + \frac{1}{2}x)p_{(1,1)} + (\frac{1}{4} - \frac{1}{2}x)p_{(1,2)} + (\frac{1}{4} + \frac{1}{2}x)p_{(2,1)} + (\frac{1}{4} - \frac{1}{2}x)p_{(2,2)}$$

Eliminating $p_{(1,1)}$, $p_{(2,1)}$ and $p_{(2,2)}$ yields the probability $p_{(1,2)} = \frac{-x+y+1}{-x-y+2}$ to reach $(2, 2)$ from $(1, 2)$. In this simple example this function is linear, however, this is not necessarily the case for real applications and our approach is not restricted to linear functions.

3   Local Model Repair

After a description of the model repair problem in Section 3.1, we propose a solution in Section 3.2. Soundness and completeness proofs are given in Section 3.3.

3.1   The Problem

Let $\mathcal{P} = (S, s^I, P)$ be a PDTMC with state set $S = \{1, \ldots, k\}$, $k \geq 1$, and let $t \in S$ be a dedicated *target* state. We assume that t is *absorbing* in $\mathcal{P}$, i.e., $P(t, t) = 1$ (otherwise we make it absorbing by changing P to P' with $P'(t, t) = 1$, $P'(t, s) = 0$ and $P'(s, s') = P(s, s')$ for all $s \in S \setminus \{t\}$ and $s' \in S$).

Given a $\lambda \in (0, 1) \subseteq \mathbb{Q}$, our aim is to determine a valid valuation v such that the probability to reach t from s^I in the induced DTMC $D(\mathcal{P}, v)$ is at most λ.

Example 4. In our running example depicted in Figure 2, assume that catching the ball at place (2) is dangerous. We declare $(2,2)$ as target state and try to find a valid valuation for $\mathcal{P}$ such that the probability to visit $(2,2)$ is below a given threshold λ.

To check whether this problem is solvable, the function p_{s^I} of the probability of reaching t from s^I in $\mathcal{P}$ can be computed, e.g., by state elimination using the PARAM tool [8]. Alternatively, satisfiability of $p_{s^I} \leq \lambda$ under Equation (1) (and potential side conditions) can be decided by SMT solvers for real arithmetic such as Z3 [18]. Even an optimal valuation minimizing the probability to reach t from s^I could be theoretically determined using an optimization algorithm for real algebra [5].

However, these are very costly procedures, which are not applicable in practice even for medium-size models with a few parameters. The reason is that the rational function p_{s^I} is usually very complex for non-trivial problems and of high degree.

Furthermore, given a parametric model and an initial valid valuation v, we are often not interested in an arbitrary solution but rather in one that is "close" to v, i.e., which changes the distributions as smoothly as possible. A reasonable measure could be the number of distributions differing from v or the maximal difference in the transition probabilities. In general, such measures can be formalized in the form of *cost functions*.

3.2 The Algorithm

For the above reasons, instead of hard algebraic computations, we aim at defining a *greedy method* to stepwise improve a given initial valuation. More precisely, given an initial valid valuation v for $\mathcal{P}$, our goal is to iteratively manipulate the valuation such that in the induced DTMC the probability of reaching t from s^I is successively reduced as long as its value exceeds the required threshold λ. (First we neglect the cost function and will embed it into our procedure later.) Another concept that we need for our repair procedure is the notion of structural equivalence.

Definition 3 (Structural equivalence). *Two DTMCs $D_1 = (S_1, s_1^I, P_1)$ and $D_2 = (S_2, s_2^I, P_2)$ are structurally equivalent, denoted $D_1 \equiv_S D_2$, if $S_1 = S_2$, $s_1^I = s_2^I$, and $P_1(s, s') = 0$ iff $P_2(s, s') = 0$ for all $s, s' \in S_1$.*

Example 5. The DTMCs D and $\hat{D}$ in Figure 2 induced by the two different valuations v and $\hat{v}$ for $\mathcal{P}$ are structurally equivalent.

Definition 4 (Partial order over valuations). *We define the relation $\prec_{\mathcal{P},t} \subseteq V \times V$ such that for all valuations $v, \hat{v} \in V$, $\hat{v} \prec_{\mathcal{P},t} v$ iff v and $\hat{v}$ are both valid for $\mathcal{P}$, $D(\mathcal{P}, v) \equiv_S D(\mathcal{P}, \hat{v})$, and*

$$(\exists s \in S.\ \hat{p}_s < p_s) \wedge (\forall s' \in S.\ \hat{p}_{s'} \leq p_{s'}),$$

where $p_s = \mathrm{Pr}^{D(\mathcal{P},v)}(s,t)$ and $\hat{p}_s = \mathrm{Pr}^{D(\mathcal{P},\hat{v})}(s,t)$ for all $s \in S$.

Example 6. For the valid valuations v and $\hat{v}$ for $\mathcal{P}$ in Figure 2 it holds that $\hat{v} \prec_{\mathcal{P},(2,2)} v$, since $\hat{p}_{(1,1)} = 0 = p_{(1,1)}$, $\hat{p}_{(2,2)} = 1 = p_{(2,2)}$, $\hat{p}_{(1,2)} = \frac{4}{9} < \frac{1}{2} = p_{(1,2)}$ and $\hat{p}_{(2,1)} = \frac{1}{3} < \frac{1}{2} = p_{(2,1)}$.

The relation $\prec_{\mathcal{P},t}$ is a strict partial order on $V \times V$. Our greedy method will apply *local repair* steps (defined below) iteratively on a valid initial valuation (or analogously on the induced DTMC) until the probability of reaching t from s^I is reduced to a value at most λ (if possible). Each local repair step results in a smaller valuation with respect to the above-defined partial order.

Assume for the rest of this section a PDTMC $\mathcal{P} = (S, s^I, P)$, an absorbing target state $t \in S$, and an arbitrary valid valuation v for $\mathcal{P}$ with $D(\mathcal{P}, v) = (S, s^I, P_v)$ (e.g., computed using Equation (2)). Let $p_s = \mathrm{Pr}^{D(\mathcal{P},v)}(s, t)$ for all $s \in S$ denote the probabilities to reach t from s in $D(\mathcal{P}, v)$; these values can be computed by applying probabilistic model checking.

Assume that in $D(\mathcal{P}, v)$ the probability to reach t is above λ (otherwise the problem is already solved). Our iterative approach modifies the valuation stepwise, satisfying the following *local repair* condition. As we will show, local repairs step change a valuation v to $\hat{v}$ such that $\hat{v} \prec_{\mathcal{P},t} v$ holds.

Definition 5 (Local repair). *A valuation $\hat{v} \in V$ is a* local repair *of v for PDTMC $\mathcal{P}$ and target state t iff there exists $\emptyset \neq S_r \subseteq S$ such that*

- *v and $\hat{v}$ are valid for $\mathcal{P}$,*
- *$D(\mathcal{P}, v) = (S, s^I, P_v) \equiv_S D(\mathcal{P}, \hat{v}) = (S, s^I, P_{\hat{v}})$ are structurally equivalent,*
- *$\sum_{s' \in S} P_{\hat{v}}(s, s') \cdot p_{s'} < \sum_{s' \in S} P_v(s, s') \cdot p_{s'}$ for all $s \in S_r$, and*
- *$P_{\hat{v}}(s, s') = P_v(s, s')$ for all $s \in S \setminus S_r$ and $s' \in S$,*

where $p_s = \mathrm{Pr}^{D(\mathcal{P},v)}(s, t)$ is the probability to reach t from s in $D(\mathcal{P}, v)$ for all $s \in S$. We say that $\hat{v}$ is a local repair of v on S_r, and call

$$\delta_{v,\hat{v}} = \sum_{s \in S_r} \sum_{s' \in S,\, P_v(s,s') < P_{\hat{v}}(s,s')} P_{\hat{v}}(s, s') - P_v(s, s')$$

the mass of the repair.

A *(finite or infinite) sequence $v_1, v_2, \ldots$ such that v_{i+1} is a local repair of v_i for $i \geq 1$ is called a* local repair sequence, *and v_j with $j > 1$ a* repair *of v_1.*

Example 7. In Figure 2, $\hat{v}$ is a local repair of v for $\mathcal{P}$ and state $(2, 2)$.

Let us come back to the integration of a cost function. As we use a greedy algorithm, we can support only cost functions for which the effect of a repair step can be estimated just by knowing the local modifications. Furthermore, a non-linear cost function would cause a significant computation effort. In our algorithm we aim at keeping the changes in the parameter values of the initial valuation v_0 small, expressed by the cost function $\sum_{x_i \in Var} |v(x_i) - v_0(x_i)|$. Assume a single repair step on state s with distribution variables $Var(s) = \bigcup_{s' \in S'} Var(P(s, s'))$, changing the values of the variables $x_i \in Var(s)$ from $v(x_i)$

Input: Realizable PDTMC $\mathcal{P} = (S, s^I, P)$, absorbing target state $t \in S$,
        upper bound $\lambda \in (0, 1) \subseteq \mathbb{Q}$, initial valid valuation v_0 for $\mathcal{P}$, (cost function f)
Output: A valid repair v of v_0 such that either $\mathrm{Pr}^{D(\mathcal{P},v)}(s^I, t) \leq \lambda$ or v is final.

1. Let $v = v_0$.
2. Compute for each $s \in S$ the probabilities p_s to reach t from s in $D(\mathcal{P}, v)$.
3. If $p_{s^I} \leq \lambda$ then return v.
4. Try to find a local repair v' of v (optimizing a cost function f under all repairs).
5. If no such repair exists, return v.
6. Set v to v'.
7. Goto 2.

Fig. 4. Model repair algorithm for PDTMCs

to $v(x_i) + \delta_i$. We prefer such a local repair step that minimizes the related component $\sum_{x_i \in Var(s)} |(v(x_i) + \delta_i) - v_0(x_i)|$ of the cost function. As the cost function is linear, such a local optimum leads also globally to a smaller cost function value. However, to reduce computational effort, the selection of a distribution for repair does not consider the cost function, therefore our greedy method is heuristic and does not guarantee to reach the global optimum.

We formalize the local model repair algorithm for PDTMCs in Figure 4. Note that the algorithm can be used also without involving a cost function. For termination, we have to assure that the mass of the repair sequence does not converge to 0 (see Sec. 3.3 for soundness and completeness). Note that for Type-I and Type-II PDTMCs we can always repair just a single distribution, what is in general not possible for Type-III PDTMCs, making the search for a repair harder. We also remark that all the benchmarks we will use for evaluation are linear, for which the repairability checks are much simpler than for general PDTMCs.

In Step 4, any heuristics could be used to find a suitable repair. In our implementation for Type-I and Type-II PDTMCs we use k-shortest path search: We determine the most probable path from the initial to the target state and check the distributions along this path whether they are repairable. If it is not the case, we continue with the next most probable path etc., until either we find a repairable distribution or we have checked all of them (in which case we have reached a final valuation).

It is also important to mention that the order in which states (respectively their distributions) are repaired is highly relevant for the efficiency of the method. Intuitively, if we repair a state s and then a state s' that is reachable from s then the second repair changes the probabilities to reach t for the successors of s; this might trigger a new repair on s, basically undoing the first one. Therefore, when using shortest paths as heuristics, we prefer to repair states at the end of the path, rather than at the beginning.

To reduce the model checking effort, we can repair several distributions before applying model checking to re-compute the reachability probabilities. Type-I benchmarks often have quite simple transition terms, for which the equation system in Step 4 can be solved without invocating an LP solver. Note that for

Type-II PDTMCs we can apply the same algorithm as for Type-I PDTMCs. The only difference is that, since each variable can appear on several transitions in the same distribution, changing the probability of one transition might cause a change of the probabilities of other transitions (in the same distribution). Therefore, the computations in Step 4 are more involved and might an LP solver.

3.3   Soundness and Completeness

The following theorem states the *correctness* of our approach, i.e., that repairing a valuation brings us closer to the goal of getting the reachability probability of t below λ.

Theorem 1 (Soundness).   *If $\hat{v} \in V$ is a local repair of v for $\mathcal{P}$ and t then $\hat{v} \prec_{\mathcal{P},t} v$.*

Proof. Let $\hat{v}$ be a local repair of v for $\mathcal{P}$ and t on $\emptyset \neq S_r \subseteq S$, $D(\mathcal{P}, v) = (S, s^I, P_v)$ and $D(\mathcal{P}, \hat{v}) = (S, s^I, P_{\hat{v}})$. Let $p = (p_{s_1}, \ldots, p_{s_k})^T \in \mathbb{Q}^k$ be the vector of the probabilities $p_{s_i} = \Pr^{D(\mathcal{P},v)}(s_i, t)$ to reach t from $s_i \in S$ in $D(\mathcal{P}, v)$. It holds that $p = P_v\, p$ (see Equation (1)).

Note that $p_t = 1$ (recall that t is absorbing) and $p_{s'} = 0$ for all states $s' \in S$ from which t is not reachable in $D(\mathcal{P}, v)$. Since reachability coincides in $D(\mathcal{P}, v)$ and the structurally equivalent $D(\mathcal{P}, \hat{v})$, it holds also for reachability in $D(\mathcal{P}, \hat{v})$. Thus for the analogous steady-state distribution $\hat{p}$ in $D(\mathcal{P}, \hat{v})$ with $\hat{p} = P_{\hat{v}}\hat{p}$, it holds that $\hat{p} = \lim_{i \to \infty} P_{\hat{v}}^i\, p$.

For two k-dimensional vectors q and q' we write $q < q'$ iff there is an $s_i \in S$ such that $q_{s_i} < q'_{s_i}$ and $q_{s_j} \leq q'_{s_j}$ for all $s_j \in S \setminus \{s_i\}$.

We show that $P_{\hat{v}}^i\, p < p$ for all $i > 0$ by induction. For $i = 1$, by the definition of $P_{\hat{v}}$ we have $P_{\hat{v}}\, p < p$. Assume now that $P_{\hat{v}}^i\, p < p$ for some $i \geq 1$. Then

$$P_{\hat{v}}^{i+1}\, p = P_{\hat{v}}\, P_{\hat{v}}^i\, p \overset{ass.\ for\ i}{<} P_{\hat{v}}\, p \overset{case\ i=1}{<} p.$$

Having shown $P_{\hat{v}}^i\, p < p$ for all $i > 0$, from $\hat{p} = \lim_{i \to \infty} P_{\hat{v}}^i\, p$ we conclude $\hat{p} < p$, i.e., $\hat{v} \prec_{\mathcal{P},t} v$, what was to be shown. $\square$

Next we show *completeness*, i.e., that if we repair a valuation such that for each distribution we repair either with at least a given minimal mass or with as much mass as the variable domains allow then our repair sequences *will always terminate with a minimal valuation*.

Definition 6 (Final and minimal valuations).

- A valuation $v \in V$ is final *for $\mathcal{P}$ and t iff it is valid for $\mathcal{P}$ and there exists no local repair of v for $\mathcal{P}$ and t.*
- A valuation $v \in V$ is minimal *for $\mathcal{P}$ and t iff it is valid for $\mathcal{P}$ and $\Pr^{D(\mathcal{P},v)}(s^I, t) \leq \Pr^{D(\mathcal{P},v')}(s^I, t)$ for all valuations $v' \in V$ that are valid for $\mathcal{P}$ and whose induced DTMCs $D(\mathcal{P}, v')$ are structurally equivalent to $D(\mathcal{P}, v)$.*

Theorem 2 (Completeness). *For each $\mathcal{P} = (S, s^I, P)$, $t \in S$, and for each valuation $v \in V$ which is valid for $\mathcal{P}$ the following holds:*

i) The masses in each infinite local repair sequence $v = v_0, v_1, \ldots$ for $\mathcal{P}$ and t converge to 0.

ii) Every final and valid valuation v for $\mathcal{P}$ and t is minimal.

Proof. Assume $\mathcal{P} = (S, s^I, P)$, $t \in S$ and a valuation $v \in V$ that is valid for $\mathcal{P}$. If the initial state is absorbing, v is final and minimal. Thus assume that the initial state is not absorbing. We prove the theorem by induction over the number of non-initial non-absorbing states in $D(\mathcal{P}, v)$.

If there is no non-initial non-absorbing state then we can repair only on the initial state, whose transitions are either

1. leading from the initial to the target state t,
2. or a self-loop on the initial state s^I,
3. or leading from s^I to non-target absorbing states.

Each local repair moves some mass from lower to higher transition types (i.e., from 1 over 2 to 3), but never back. Because the domains are finite, this process can lead to an infinite local repair sequence only if the repair masses converge to 0, thus $i)$ in Theorem 2 holds. Furthermore, if the last valuation of a local repair sequence is final then the probability of transition 1. cannot be reduced, and the probabilities of transitions of type 3. cannot be increased. This final valuation induces a DTMC with minimal reachability probability from s^I to t under all structurally equivalent instantiations of $\mathcal{P}$.

Assume now that the theorem holds for each PDTMC $\mathcal{P}_n = (S_n, s^I, P_n)$, absorbing target state $t \in S_n$, and $\mathcal{P}_n$-valid valuation $v \in V$ with $D(\mathcal{P}_n, v) = (S_n, s^I, P_{n,v})$, if the number of non-initial non-absorbing states in $D(\mathcal{P}_n, v)$ is at most n. Let $\mathcal{P}_{n+1} = (S_{n+1}, s^I, P_{n+1})$ with absorbing target state $t \in S_{n+1}$ and $\mathcal{P}_{n+1}$-valid $v \in V$, such that the number of non-initial non-absorbing states in $D(\mathcal{P}_{n+1}, v) = (S_{n+1}, s^I, P_{n+1,v})$ is $n + 1$.

i) Assume an infinite repair sequence $v = v_0, v_1, \ldots$ for $\mathcal{P}_{n+1}$ and t. We select in $\mathcal{P}_{n+1}$ a non-initial non-absorbing state s and eliminate it as shown in Figure 3 from all PDTMCs in the infinite repair sequence. Let $\mathcal{P}_n$ denote $\mathcal{P}_{n+1}$ after the elimination of s. For each $s', s'' \in S_n$ we have that

$$P_n(s', s'') = P_{n+1}(s', s'') + \frac{P_{n+1}(s', s) \cdot P_{n+1}(s, s'')}{1 - P_{n+1}(s, s)}.$$

We show that each repair step for v_i on $\mathcal{P}_{n+1}$ and t is also a repair step for v_i on $\mathcal{P}_n$ and t. The valuations $v_0, v_1, \ldots$ for $\mathcal{P}_{n+1}$ are also valid for $\mathcal{P}_n$ and they induce structurally equivalent DTMCs. The cases for the states that are not predecessors of s, and the case where no repair on any predecessor of s took place, are straightforward. Thus the only interesting condition to be checked is that when a predecessor of s is repaired, it satisfies the repair conditions for the ith repair from v_i to v_{i+1}:

$$\sum_{s'' \in S_n} P_{n,v_{i+1}}(s',s'') \cdot p_{s''} \overset{elim.prop.}{\underset{assumption}{\overset{}{=}}} \sum_{s'' \in S_{n+1}} P_{n+1,v_{i+1}}(s',s'') \cdot p_{s''}$$
$$\overset{assumption}{<} \sum_{s'' \in S_{n+1}} P_{n+1,v_i}(s',s'') \cdot p_{s''}$$
$$\overset{elim.prop.}{=} \sum_{s'' \in S_n} P_{n,v_i}(s',s'') \cdot p_{s''}$$

Thus the infinite repair sequence for $\mathcal{P}_{n+1}$ and v after the elimination of s is an infinite repair sequence for $\mathcal{P}_n$ and v. By assumption the masses in the repair of $\mathcal{P}_n$ converge to 0. Therefore, also the mass of the original sequence for $\mathcal{P}_{n+1}$ converges to 0.

ii) Assume a valid valuation v for $\mathcal{P}_{n+1}$. We select again a non-initial non-absorbing state s and eliminate it from $\mathcal{P}_{n+1}$, resulting in $\mathcal{P}_n$. Then v is also final for $\mathcal{P}_n$ and by induction minimal. Thus v is minimal also for $\mathcal{P}_{n+1}$.

4   Evaluation

In this section we present an empirical evaluation of our approach. We developed a C++ prototype implementation capable of performing repair as described in Section 3. For building the explicit state space of our benchmarks we used PRISM [2], while MRMC [3] serves as black-box probabilistic model checker. For every iteration of the repair, we maintain a priority queue indicating which state shall be repaired next. As mentioned before, this order is determined by a heuristic, the best one so far being to take for each state the probability of reaching a target state into account. After each repair step, we perform model checking. As mentioned before, it is possible to suspend model checking for a number of steps which can significantly decrease the time needed for model repair while needing the possibility to backtrack to a previous repair step in case the result is too far below the threshold.

We demonstrate the feasibility of the repair by an experimental setting incorporating three benchmarks, one of Type-I and two of Type-III. For all experiments we give the system parameters as well as the number of states and transitions. "mc" describes the overall time spent on model checking, "sn" the time spent on selecting the next state to repair, and "rn" the time needed for repair. All experiments were run on Linux using an Intel I7 CPU 3.4 GHz with 32 GB of memory. We defined a timeout (-TO-) of 2700 seconds.

First, the ROBOT benchmark consists of an *environment* modeled as a square grid of size $N \times N$ with $N \in \mathbb{Z}^+$ by means of an MDP. The goal is for a robot to reach a set of target states from a set of initial states without visiting a certain set of "fatal" states. The interaction between the robot and the environment—the *strategy*—is modeled as a DTMC. This DTMC is repaired with the goal to guarantee that the probability to end up in a fatal state ($\Pr^D$) is reduced to at most 0.001, yielding $\Pr^{\hat{D}}$. As in each state of the MDP the strategy is independent from other states, this is a Type-I repair problem which

Table 1. Results for the Type-I benchmark ROBOT

| N | model | | | time | | | quality | | | |
	states	trans	mc	sn	rn	Pr^D	$\mathrm{Pr}^{\hat{D}}$	$|E|$	steps
48	2305	17859	0.76	1.050	0.001	0.159	0.001	621	77
64	4097	32003	1.58	1.657	0.001	0.182	0.001	427	53
96	9217	72579	7.17	6.004	0.002	0.189	0.001	657	82
128	16385	129539	15.29	8.456	0.002	0.150	0.001	640	80
256	65537	521219	129.32	63.6	0.003	0.130	0.000	888	111
512	262145	2091011	-TO-	-TO-	-TO-	0.168	0.101	480	60
512 ($\mathcal{N} = 20$)	262145	2091011	144.79	21.734	0.002	0.168	0	1760	11
1024	1048577	8376323	-TO-	-TO-	-TO-	0.105	0.104	24	3
1024 ($\mathcal{N} = 100$)	1048577	8376323	377.99	28.907	0.002	0.105	0.036	2400	3

we perform for different values of N. Table 1 shows the results obtained for the ROBOT benchmark. We measure the quality of the results by giving the original and repaired probabilities (Pr^D and $\mathrm{Pr}^{\hat{D}}$). We also measure the number of edges $|E|$ that were changed. For most of the instances, model checking was performed in each step. In some cases we mention a value $\mathcal{N}$ which indicates the number of local repair steps before model checking was invoked.

The measurements show that the time spent on repair is negligible. Most time is spent on model checking. For the grid sizes $N = 512$ and $N = 1024$ we get a timeout due to model checking. In case of $N = 1024$, it was only possible to perform three iterations, as both PRISM and MRMC performed very slow on this benchmark. By repairing 20 states before calling the model checker, we obtained results for $N = 512$ within the time limit. For $N = 1024$, with $\mathcal{N} = 100$ the repair also terminated within time.

The CROWDS protocol [19] is designed for anonymous network communication using random routing. There are N nodes in a network that with probability p_f forward a message to another—again randomly chosen node—or directly deliver it. Each member is "good" or "bad" described by probability p_{bad}. The number of protocol runs is parametrized by K. The property, called *probable innocence*, of the real sender being no more likely than others to have sent the message, is formulated as a reachability property on the underlying DTMC. Here, dependencies exist between transitions yielding Type-III benchmarks. The standard instantiations are $p_f = 0.8$ and $p_{bad} = 0.091$ which induce the probability Pr^{D_0} for probable innocence for fixed values of N and K. We introduce "errors" by choosing a smaller value $p_f = 0.1$, inducing probability Pr^D and repair towards the original model checking result Pr^{D_0} as bound. Repairing only the transitions where the parameters occurred results in the parameter value $\hat{p}_f$ and probability $\mathrm{Pr}^{\hat{D}}$. Table 2 shows the results for CROWDS.

First note that in all cases the resulting probability $\mathrm{Pr}^{\hat{D}}$ and the parameter value $\hat{p}_f$ are very close to the original values Pr^{D_0} and p_f. This means that the model was *successfully repaired* which shows the applicability of our approach to very common benchmarks. Concerning the running times, most of the time was spent on searching the next state to repair while again the time for repair is negligible. We are able to

Table 2. Results for Type-III benchmarks CROWDS and NAND

Model				time[1]			quality					
N	K	states	trans	mc	sn	rn	$\Pr^D$	$\Pr^{\hat{D}}$	$\hat{p}_f/\hat{p}_{err}$	$\Pr^{D_0}$	$|E|$	steps
CROWDS 5	4	3515	6035	0.226	0.204	0	0.316	0.27	0.81	0.26	32	16
CROWDS 6	8	164308	308452	5.09	11.251	0.001	0.519	0.327	0.813	0.316	32	16
CROWDS 8	10	3058199	6558839	75.836	1194.742	0.002	0.59	0.416	0.64	0.332	32	16
CROWDS 9	10	6534529	14848549	237.162	451.931	0.001	0.589	0.332	0.82	0.323	32	16
CROWDS 10	6	352535	833015	11.48	21.093	0.001	0.424	0.249	0.807	0.231	32	16
CROWDS 12	6	829669	2166277	32.591	55.961	0.001	0.423	0.239	0.807	0.22	32	16
NAND 6	6	8426	12209	0.990	0.628	0.004	0.746	0.583	0.020	0.586	54	29
NAND 10	8	55902	83727	14.380	4.898	0.008	0.727	0.514	0.020	0.519	54	29
NAND 12	6	77294	116972	19.390	7.032	0.006	0.800	0.621	0.020	0.625	54	29
NAND 12	8	102842	155564	33.120	9.436	0.005	0.808	0.623	0.020	0.628	54	29
NAND 12	10	128390	194156	50.210	11.958	0.005	0.810	0.623	0.020	0.627	54	29
NAND 12	12	153938	232748	71.670	14.788	0.006	0.811	0.621	0.020	0.625	54	29

repair instances with millions of states within the time limit. Note that the number of changed transitions and steps is constant for all instances.

NAND [20] models how reliable computations are obtained using unreliable hardware by having N number of copies of a NAND unit all doing the same job. Parameters are the probabilities of the units p_{err} and the error input probabilities p_{Ierr}. The original value is $p_{err} = 0.02$. Consider again Table 2. K denotes the number of *restorative stages* where the possibly erroneous results is corrected. We basically make the same observations as for CROWDS, i.e., we get the desired result for the repaired parameter $\hat{p}_{err} = 0.02$ and the probability $\Pr^{\hat{D}}$.

5   Conclusion and Future Work

Summing up, our main contribution is a sound and complete greedy local-repair algorithm for repairing large stochastic models efficiently. Our experimental results confirm that greedy repair is feasible even for models with millions of states, which are beyond the reach of other comparable state-of-the-art techniques and that we are able to repair common benchmarks in a reasonable way.

Topics in our current research agenda that are yet to be explored include experimenting other node selection and repair heuristics. More in general, we believe it would be interesting also to explore the connections between our greedy method and local optimization of probability functions in the space defined by multiple parameters (e.g., establishing a formal analogy with multivariable optimization based on gradient descent methods). Finally, we would like to lift the assumption of linear local repair to see whether our method could also be applied to more complex parameter dependencies.

References

1. Hansson, H., Jonsson, B.: A logic for reasoning about time and reliability. Formal Aspects of Computing **6**(5), 512–535 (1994)
2. Kwiatkowska, M., Norman, G., Parker, D.: PRISM 4.0: verification of probabilistic real-time systems. In: Gopalakrishnan, G., Qadeer, S. (eds.) CAV 2011. LNCS, vol. 6806, pp. 585–591. Springer, Heidelberg (2011)

3. Katoen, J.P., Zapreev, I.S., Hahn, E.M., Hermanns, H., Jansen, D.N.: The ins and outs of the probabilistic model checker MRMC. Performance Evaluation **68**(2), 90–104 (2011)
4. Ábrahám, E., Becker, B., Dehnert, C., Jansen, N., Katoen, J.-P., Wimmer, R.: Counterexample generation for discrete-time markov models: an introductory survey. In: Bernardo, M., Damiani, F., Hähnle, R., Johnsen, E.B., Schaefer, I. (eds.) SFM 2014. LNCS, vol. 8483, pp. 65–121. Springer, Heidelberg (2014)
5. Bartocci, E., Grosu, R., Katsaros, P., Ramakrishnan, C.R., Smolka, S.A.: Model repair for probabilistic systems. In: Abdulla, P.A., Leino, K.R.M. (eds.) TACAS 2011. LNCS, vol. 6605, pp. 326–340. Springer, Heidelberg (2011)
6. Hahn, E.M., Hermanns, H., Zhang, L.: Probabilistic reachability for parametric Markov models. Software Tools for Technology Transfer **13**(1), 3–19 (2010)
7. Jansen, N., Corzilius, F., Volk, M., Wimmer, R., Ábrahám, E., Katoen, J.-P., Becker, B.: Accelerating parametric probabilistic verification. In: Norman, G., Sanders, W. (eds.) QEST 2014. LNCS, vol. 8657, pp. 404–420. Springer, Heidelberg (2014)
8. Hahn, E.M., Hermanns, H., Wachter, B., Zhang, L.: PARAM: a model checker for parametric markov models. In: Touili, T., Cook, B., Jackson, P. (eds.) CAV 2010. LNCS, vol. 6174, pp. 660–664. Springer, Heidelberg (2010)
9. Bradley, S., Hax, A., Magnanti, T.: Applied Mathematical Programming. Addison-Wesley Pub. Co. (1977)
10. Biegler, L.T., Zavala, V.M.: Large-scale nonlinear programming using IPOPT: An integrating framework for enterprise-wide dynamic optimization. Computers & Chemical Engineering **33**(3), 575–582 (2009)
11. Chen, T., Hahn, E.M., Han, T., Kwiatkowska, M., Qu, H., Zhang, L.: Model repair for markov decision processes. In: Proc. of TASE, pp. 85–92. IEEE (2013)
12. Bartocci, E., Bortolussi, L., Nenzi, L., Sanguinetti, G.: On the robustness of temporal properties for stochastic models. In: Proc. of HSB 2013. EPTCS, vol. 125, pp. 3–19 (2013)
13. Chatzieleftheriou, G., Bonakdarpour, B., Smolka, S.A., Katsaros, P.: Abstract model repair. In: Goodloe, A.E., Person, S. (eds.) NFM 2012. LNCS, vol. 7226, pp. 341–355. Springer, Heidelberg (2012)
14. Jovanović, D., de Moura, L.: Solving non-linear arithmetic. In: Gramlich, B., Miller, D., Sattler, U. (eds.) IJCAR 2012. LNCS, vol. 7364, pp. 339–354. Springer, Heidelberg (2012)
15. Sutton, R., Barto, A.: Reinforcement Learning - An Introduction. MIT Press (1998)
16. Sokolova, A., de Vink, E.P.: Probabilistic automata: system types, parallel composition and comparison. In: Baier, C., Haverkort, B.R., Hermanns, H., Katoen, J.-P., Siegle, M. (eds.) Validation of Stochastic Systems. LNCS, vol. 2925, pp. 1–43. Springer, Heidelberg (2004)
17. Daws, C.: Symbolic and parametric model checking of discrete-time markov chains. In: Liu, Z., Araki, K. (eds.) ICTAC 2004. LNCS, vol. 3407, pp. 280–294. Springer, Heidelberg (2005)
18. de Moura, L., Bjørner, N.: Z3: an efficient SMT solver. In: Ramakrishnan, C.R., Rehof, J. (eds.) TACAS 2008. LNCS, vol. 4963, pp. 337–340. Springer, Heidelberg (2008)
19. Reiter, M.K., Rubin, A.D.: Crowds: Anonymity for web transactions. ACM Trans. on Information and System Security **1**(1), 66–92 (1998)
20. Han, J., Jonker, P.: A system architecture solution for unreliable nanoelectronic devices. IEEE Transactions on Nanotechnology **1**, 201–208 (2002)

Integrating SMT with Theorem Proving for Analog/Mixed-Signal Circuit Verification

Yan Peng[✉] and Mark Greenstreet

University of British Columbia, Vancouver, British Columbia, Canada
{yanpeng,mrg}@cs.ubc.ca

Abstract. We present our integration of the Z3 SMT solver into the ACL2 theorem prover and its application to formal verification of analog-mixed signal circuits by proving global convergence for a state-of-the-art digital phase-locked loop (PLL). SMT (satisfiability modulo theory) solvers eliminate much of the tedium associated with detailed proofs by providing automatic reasoning about propositional formulas including equalities and inequalities of polynomial functions. A theorem prover complements the SMT solver by providing a proof structuring and proof by induction. We use this combined tool to show global convergence (i.e. correct start-up and mode-switching) of a digital PLL. The PLL is an example of a second-order hybrid control system; its verification demonstrates how these methods can address challenges that arise when verifying such designs.

1 Introduction

We present our integration of the Z3 SMT solver [1] into the ACL2 theorem prover [2]. With this approach, high-level proof structure and proof techniques such as induction can be handled by the theorem prover while many tedious details for verifying real-world designs discharged by the SMT solver. The implementation presented in this paper supports booleans, integers, and rationals/reals, and our approach could be readily extended to other types including arrays, lists, strings, and more general algebraic data types. For soundness, we want to rely on ACL2, Z3, and as little other code as possible. We also want Z3 to be easily used from within ACL2; thus, our interface performs many, automatic transformations of ACL2 formulas to convert them into the restricted form required by Z3. We resolve these seemingly conflicting objectives with a software architecture that divides the ACL2-to-Z3 translation process into two phases: most of the transformations are performed in the first phase, and the result is verified by ACL2. The second phase is a very simple direct translation from the s-expressions of ACL2 into their counterparts for Z3's Python API.

This research was supported by grants from NSERC Canada and Intel.

© Springer International Publishing Switzerland 2015
K. Havelund et al. (Eds.): NFM 2015, LNCS 9058, pp. 310–326, 2015.
DOI: 10.1007/978-3-319-17524-9_22

We demonstrate our approach by using it to verify global convergence for an all-digital phase-locked loop (PLL). The PLL is an example of an analog-mixed signal (AMS) design. The AMS approach has emerged as the dominant paradigm for implementing analog operations where digital circuits replace many analog functions and provide adaptation functions to compensate for variations in process, device, and operating conditions. AMS designs play an important role in nearly every computing, communication, and cyber-physical systems. These designs pose serious simulation challenges because they involve an extremely wide range of time-scales from sub-picosecond (e.g. for oscillator jitter) to milliseconds or longer for software controlled adaptation loops or interactions with mechanical sensors and systems. Formal methods can verify properties that are intractable or impossible to show with simulation. We consider global convergence: showing that an AMS circuit converges to the intended operating mode from all initial conditions. This requires modeling the large-scale, non-linear behavior of the analog components. If such non-linearities create an unintended basin of attraction, then the AMS circuit may fail to converge to the intended operating point. AMS circuits may make many mode changes per second to minimize power consumption, adapt to changing loads, or changes in operating conditions. Each of these mode changes requires the AMS circuit to converge to a new operating region. Once the AMS circuit is in the small operating region intended by the designer, small-signal analysis based on linear-systems theory is sufficient to show correct operation [3, 4].

The key contributions of this paper are:

- A demonstration that the arithmetic decision procedures of an SMT solver can be exploited effectively when verifying properties of physical systems with continuous models.
- A description of the challenges that arise when using a SMT solver with a theorem prover and present our solutions to these issues.
- the first integration of an SMT solver into the ACL2 theorem prover.
- A model for a state-of-the art digital PLL with recurrences using rational functions that can be used for evaluating other verification approaches.
- A proof of global convergence of the digital PLL.

2   Related Work

There has been extensive work in the past decade on integrating SAT and SMT solvers into theorem provers including [5–11]. Many of these papers have followed Harrison and Théry's "skeptical" and focused on methods for verifying SMT results within the theorem prover using proof reconstruction, certificates, and similar methods. Several of the papers showed how their methods could be used for the verification of concurrent algorithms such as clock synchronization [6], and the Bakery and Memoir algorithms [9]. While [6] used the CVC-Lite [12] SMT solver to verify properties of simple quadratic inequalites, the use of SMT in theorem provers has generally made light use of the arithmetic capability of such solvers. In fact [10] reported *better* results for SMT for several sets of benchmarks when the arithmetic theory solvers were disabled!

The work that may be the most similar to ours is [11] that presents a translation of Event-B sequents from Rodin [13] to the SMT-LIB format [14]. Like our work, [11] verifies a claim by using a SMT solver to show that its negation is unsatisfiable. They address issues of types and functions. They perform extensive rewriting using Event-B sequents, and then have simple translations of the rewritten form into SMT-LIB. While noting that proof reconstruction is possible in principle, they do not appear to implement such measures. The main focus of [11] is supporting the set-theoretic constructs of Event-B. In contrast, our work shows how the procedures for non-linear arithmetic of a modern SMT solver can be used when reasoning about VLSI circuits.

Our work demonstrates the value of theorem proving combined with SMT solvers for verifying properties that are characterized by functions on real numbers and vector fields. Accordingly, the linear- and non-linear arithmetic theory solvers have a central role. As our concern is bringing these techniques to new problem domains, we deliberately take a pragmatic approach to integration and trust both the theorem prover and the SMT solver.

Prior work on using theorem proving methods to reason about dynamical systems includes [15] which uses the Isabelle theorem prover to verify bounds on solutions to simple ODEs from a single initial condition. In contrast, we verify properties that hold from *all* initial conditions. Harutunian [16] presented a very general framework for reasoning about hybrid systems using ACL2 and demonstrated the approach with some very simple examples. Here we demonstrate that by discharging arithmetic proof obligations using a SMT solver, it is practical to reason about much realistic designs.

The past decade has also seen a rapidly growing interest in applying formal methods to analog and mixed-signal designs. Much of this work goes back to early model-checking results by Kurshan and MacMillan [17]. Other early work includes [18–21]. To verify phase-locked loops, Dong *et al.* [22] proposed using property checking for AMS verification, including PLLs. Shortly after the work by Dong *et al.*, Jesser and Hedrich [23] described a model-checking result for a simple analog PLL. Althoff *et al.* [24] presented the verification of a charge-pump PLL using an approach that they refer to as "continuization." They use a purely linear model for the components of their PLL, and their focus is on the switching activities of the phase-frequency detector, in particular, uncertainties in switching delays.

More recently, Lin et al. [25, 26] developed an approach for verifying a digital PLL using SMT techniques. To the best of our knowledge, they are the first to claim formal verification of a digital PLL. They consider a purely linear, analog model and then reason about the discrepancies between this idealized model and a digital implementation. They use the KRR SMT solver to verify bounds on this discrepancy. They verify bounds on the lock time of a digitally intensive PLL assuming that most of the digital variables are initialized to fixed values, and that only the oscillator phase is unknown. Our work shows initialization for a different PLL design over the complete state space.

Using the SpaceEx [27] reachability tool, Wei *et al.* [28] presented a verification of the same digital PLL as described in this paper. That work made a over-approximation of the reachable space by over-approximating the recurrences of the digital PLL with linear, differential inclusions. As SpaceEx could not verify convergence property for the entire space in a single run, [28] broke the problem into a collection of lemmas that were composed manually. Their work demonstrated the need for some kind of theorem-proving tool to compose results. Furthermore, they could not show the limit cycles that our proof does; therefore their proof does not provide as tight of bounds on PLL jitter and other properties as can be obtained with our techniques.

3   Integrating Z3 into ACL2

Theorem provers and SMT solvers provide complementary reasoning capabilities. The main challenge is connecting the two with an interface that is both useful and trustworthy. We achieve these goals by using a two-step translation process. The first step translates the user-provided goal into a minimal subset of operations that all have direct counterparts in the logic of the SMT solver. The second step performs a direct translation of this expanded and simplified version of the goal into the syntax and logic of the SMT solver. The SMT solver then proves the goal, provides a counter-example, or reports that it could not decide. A key feature of this architecture is that most of the complexity of the translation process is in the first step. The first step translates a goal in the theorem prover logic to an equivalent or stronger goal, still in the theorem prover logic. We use the theorem prover to verify this implication for each translated goal. Thus, the first step does not introduce any soundness assumptions beyond our existing faith in the theorem prover. The second step provides the translation between the theorem prover and SMT solver. This is trusted code, and our design allows it to be very simple and easily reviewed by other humans.

This section describes our solution to integrating Z3 into ACL2 in more detail. We describe the issues that arose to ensure the soundness of our implementation and features that we've included to make the combination easy to use. First, Section 3.1 gives a very brief description of the key features of ACL2 and Z3 used in our design.

3.1   ACL2 and Z3

ACL2 [2] is a theorem prover for programs written in a comprehensive, applicative subset of Common Lisp. ACL2 provides a very general notion of induction based on recursive function definition in lisp: every recursive function defines a corresponding induction schema. This is ideal for our application where we are using a theorem prover to compensate for the lack of induction capabilities in SMT solvers. While ACL2 supports many other methods for proving goals in its

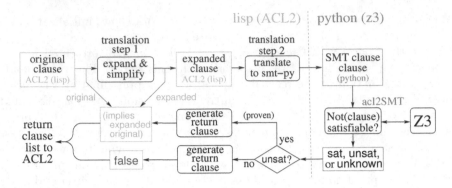

Fig. 1. The Clause Processor

"waterfall", our approach is to allow ACL2 to automate a proof where it can, and use an integrated SMT solver to discharge tedious obligations, especially those involving systems of non-linear inequalities that frequently arise when reasoning about AMS circuits or other physical systems. ACL2 supports the integration of external decision procedures through its clause processor mechanism described below.

ACL2 represents a proof goal as a conjunction of clauses, where each clause is a disjunction of terms. The terms can be arbitrary s-expressions. ACL2 supports the inclusion of user-defined "clause processors". A clause processor takes an ACL2 clause (i.e. proposition) as an argument and returns a list of clauses with the interpretation that the conjunction of the result clauses implies the original clause. In particular, if the result list is empty, then the clause processor is asserting that the original clause is true for all valuations of any free variables. ACL2 supports two types of clause processors: verified and trusted. A *verified* clause processor is written in the ACL2 subset of Common Lisp and proven correct by ACL2. A *trusted* clause processor does not require a correctness proof; instead, all theorems are tagged to identify the trusted processors that they may depend on. The soundness of the trusted clause processor becomes, in effect, a hypothesis of any theorem that uses the clause processor. We connected the Z3 SMT solver to ACL2 by writing a trusted clause processor.

Z3 [1] is a SMT solver developed at Microsoft Research that has been used in many software verification tools. Z3 combines procedures for boolean combinations of linear equalities and inequalities over linear, polynomial, and rational functions along with and operations on arrays and algebraic data types within the framework of a CDCL satisfiability solver [29]. We make incidental use of some of the other capabilities of Z3 such as lists to simplify the implementation of our interface. Formulas for Z3 can be written using the SMTLIB format [14], an Ocaml API, or a Python API (z3py). We used z3py for the ease of prototyping in Python.

3.2   The Clause Processor

Figure 1 shows the architecture of our clause processor. The critical part of this design for soundness is the second translation step. This step supports a very small subset of the ACL2 logic consisting of nineteen functions:

- five arithmetic functions – binary plus, minus, and times; and unary negation, and reciprocal.
- five comparison functions – equal, $<$, $\leq$, $\geq$, and $>$.
- three more logical operations – if, not, and implies.
- three functions for declaring the types of Z3 variables – booleanp, integerp, and rationalp.
- three functions to support other ACL2 constructions – array, lambda, and nth.

This translation step is implemented using 220 lines of lisp code (translate step 2 in the figure), and 130 lines of python (class acl2SMT in the figure). The lisp code is driven by an association list to map lisp functions to their python counterparts. The python code defines an object whose methods call the appropriate Z3 functions. As classes implementing the same interface could be defined for other SMT solvers, our architecture is largely solver agnostic. The code is straightforward and easily inspected.

In principle, a user could transform a more general ACL2 clause into one that uses the minimal set of operators described above by guiding ACL2's rewriting process. The tedious effort of doing so would largely nullify the advantages promised by using an external decision procedure. To make the SMT solver of practical use, the first step of the translation process converts a richer subset of the ACL2 logic into the minimal form accepted by the final translation. As described below, the user can provide hints that produce a translated clause that is *stronger* than the original clause. Further strengthening of the clause can occur because of the way we handle the connection between ACL2's use of rational numbers and the use of real numbers in the logic of Z3.

Once the clause has been translated into the logic of the SMT solver, we ask the SMT solver to prove it by showing that the negation of the clause is unsatisfiable. If the expanded clause is proven to be a theorem by the SMT solver, then the clause processor returns (implies expanded original) to ACL2. In other words, the original clause is a theorem if ACL2 can show that the expanded clause implies the original. The soundness of the connection to the SMT solver does not depend on the first step of the translation. If the SMT solver finds a satisfying assignment to the negated clause, the original claim *might* not be a theorem. Presently, we report the failure, but do not provide any proposed counter-example to ACL2.

Given this framework, the remainder of this section describes the logical issues that arose when integrating Z3 into ACL2 and presents our solutions.

3.3   Connecting the Logics

The logic of ACL2 is much more expressive than that of SMT solvers such as
Z3. In particular,

- ACL2 is untyped, but Z3 requires a declared sort (i.e. type) for each variable.
- ACL2 supports rational numbers, but Z3 uses reals.
- Users of ACL2 usually make extensive use of user-defined, recursive functions. Z3 only provides uninterpreted functions.
- The antecedent of an ACL2 clause may imply other facts that can be proven by ACL2 and are needed by the SMT solver but that cannot be derived by the SMT solver.
- Substitutions: a clause may include (in)equalities over terms that are neither polynomials nor rational functions and thus outside the domain of Z3's non-linear solver.
- Hints: our clause processor may return clauses for ancillary conditions that ACL2 cannot discharge without further guidance.

We show in the remainder of this section how each of these issues are naturally addressed within the clause processor architecture described above.

Typed vs. untyped logics: ACL2 is untyped and all functions are total. However, ACL2 does provide type predicates, and it is common to write theorems of the form:

```
(thm (implies (and (and type − assertion₁ type − assertion₂ ...)
                   (and other-hypotheses))
              conclusion))
```

where *type-assertions* are of the form (rationalp x), (integerp n), etc. We simply require that theorems be stated with this structure. Our clause processor checks for this structure, identifies the type assertions, and generates the corresponding variable declarations for the SMT solver. This is done in the second translation step, and soundness requires *exact* correspondence between the ACL2 and Z3 types. This is the case for booleans and integers (e.g. ACL2 and Z3 have the same definition of integer additions, etc.). However, it raises an issue for ACL2 rationals vs. Z3 reals which we discuss next.

Real Numbers and Rationals: Our translator represents variables that are restricted to rational number values in ACL2 to ones that are real valued in Z3. We need to ensure that results from Z3 are sound in ACL2. For example, in ACL2 can prove that there is no (rational) number x such that $x^2 = 2$. On the other hand, Z3 can prove that there is a (real) number x such that $x^2 = 2$. To preserve soundness, we restrict the use of the SMT solver to discharging clauses where all variables are universally quantified, noting that

$$\forall x \in \mathbb{R}.\, p(x) \;\Rightarrow\; \forall x \in \mathbb{Q}.\, p(x)$$

because $\mathbb{Q} \subset \mathbb{R}$. In practice, this is not a serious restriction.

Another consequence of this difference in representation is that Z3 may produce a counter-example where some variables are assigned irrational (in particular, algebraic) values. As illustrated by the $x^2 = 2$ example above, such a counter-example is not valid in ACL2. When Z3 produces a model for a formula, each value can be identified as being integer, rational, or algebraic. Thus, we could check if a counter-example generated by Z3 could be used in ACL2. We have not needed existential witnesses, and restricting the SMT solver as described above has been completely satisfactory.

An alternative would be to use ACL2r[30]. We have used our clause processor with both ACL2 and ACL2r, and the same proof of convergence for the digital PLL works in both systems. Presently, ACL2r is not fully upward compatible with ACL2, and we chose to start with ACL2 because of its more comprehensive environment for proof development.

Another difference between ACL2 and Z3 for numerical problems is division by zero. While ACL2 and Z3 require all operations to be total, ACL2 defines (/ x 0) to be 0 for all x; where as Z3 considers the quotient to be an unspecified number. Our solution is implement reciprocal in the acl2SMT module to match the ACL2 definition:

```
def reciprocal(self, x): self.ifx(x == 0.0, 0.0, 1.0/x)
```

Functions. ACL2 users naturally use the expressiveness of lisp to write concise theorem statements. This includes user-defined and library functions. While Z3 and other SMT solvers support uninterpreted functions, this is almost always too imprecise to prove real theorems. Many functions that appear in proofs are non-recursive; in other words, they are macros. These are easily eliminated by expanding the function. Of course, clauses can also include recursive functions.

Our clause processor accepts a user-provided "hint" called :functions that says what functions should be expanded, to what depth they should be expanded, and the type of the value produced by the function. These hints are used in the first translation step to expand function calls to the specified depth. Any deeper calls are replaced by an unconstrained variable of the specified return type. These transformations are performed in the first translation step; therefore, ACL2 verifies the soundness of this transformation.

The expansion of function calls replaces (f actual1 actual2 ...) with
    ((lambda (newVar1, newVar2, newVar3) rewritten-body-of-f)
      (actual1 actual2 ...))
where the body of f is rewritten by replacing formal parameters with the fresh variables (i.e. names that don't otherwise appear in the clause) and recursively expanding any function calls in the body. The second step translates this into the corresponding Python lambda expression. The acl2SMT object provides a method that creates names for the SMT solver for fresh variables.

This mechanism for supporting functions is also used to support let operations in the user-provided clause – in fact, the ACL2 macro expansion turns them into the form described above without any assistance from our clause processor.

Adding Hypotheses: The hypotheses of a clause may imply other facts that are not derivable by the SMT solver but that can be readily shown within the theorem prover. These include previously established theorems and claims that have straightforward induction proofs. The SMT solver may need these additional facts to prove a clause.

Our clause processor accepts a user-provided hint called :hypothesize to add additional hypotheses to the clause. The hypotheses are added in the first translation step; therefore, ACL2 verifies the soundness of this transformation.

Non-polynomials: the non-linear arithmetic procedures in Z3 only support polynomials and rational functions. For example, our reasoning about the digital PLL uses the Common Lisp function (expt r n) which computes r^n for integer n. Our clause processor accepts a user-provided hint called :let to replace all occurrences of given subexpression with a new unconstrained variable of the user specified type. Our clause processor then adds a proof obligation (to be returned to ACL2) that the type of the subexpression always matches the user specified type. These substitutions are performed in the first translation step; therefore, ACL2 verifies the soundness of this transformation. Typically, the user will also use :hypothesize hints to state constraints that must hold for the value of this new variable. For example, we might include the hint

    :hypothesize (equal (expt x (+ n 2)) (* x x (expt x n)))

As noted above, the soundness of these added hypotheses are verified by ACL2.

Nested Hints: as described above, our clause processor returns a new clause to check the soundness of the translation and any user-provided assertions. In practice, this means that Z3 establishes the truth of a complicated system of equalities and inequalities, and ACL2 is required to discharge a handful of much simpler conditions. Occasionally, these returned clauses can be non-trivial, and our clause processor accepts a user-provided hint called :use that allows the user to attach hints to the clauses returned to ACL2. A common form of this is to prove a lemma within ACL2 that corresponds to a :hypothesize hint. The user may then employ a :use hint to tell ACL2 how to instantiate the lemma to discharge the added hypothesis. Proof hints in ACL2 do not change the meaning of the formula that ACL2 is attempting to prove; they only guide the theorem prover to use proof methods that the user believes will succeed. Thus, these hints do not affect the soundness of our implementation.

3.4   Soundness of the Connection

The previous section described the main issues that arose when integrating an SMT solver into the ACL2 theorem prover. The two-step translation process allows the more complicated transformations to be performed in the first step, and the result is verified by ACL2. The second step is very simple, and that is the only part that is trusted for soundness. This section summarizes how a clause is discharged using our clause processor by showing the logical transformations that are performed at each step.

Originally, the clause processor is asked to prove

$$(antecedent \land typePredicates) \rightarrow claim \tag{1}$$

Let *Goal* denote this proposition. Furthermore, the user may provide the clause processor with various hints about function expansion, subexpression substitution, additional hypotheses, and hints to give back to ACL2. The first translation step of the clause processor rewrites *antecedent* to *antecedent'* and *claim* to *claim'*. It also introduces new hypotheses, both from :hypothesize hints and the type assumptions for functions and :let hints. Let *moreHyps* denote these added hypotheses. The SMT solver attempts to prove:

$$(antecedent' \land typePredicates \land moreHyps) \rightarrow claim' \tag{2}$$

Let *Goal'* denote this "expanded" proposition. If the SMT solver proves *Goal'*, then the clause processor returns the following clauses to ACL2:

$$\begin{array}{c} Goal' \rightarrow Goal \\ (antecedent \land typePredicates) \rightarrow moreHyps \end{array} \tag{3}$$

Where the last line is one clause for each added hypothesis in the actual implementation. The original claim (Eq. 1) is an immediate consequence of the clause established by the SMT solver (Eq. 2) and the clauses subsequently discharged by ACL2 (Eq. 3).

4   Verifying a Digital PLL

Figure 2 shows the digital phase-locked-loop (PLL) verified in this paper; it is a simplified version of the design presented in [31]. The purpose of this PLL is to adjust the digitally-controlled oscillator (DCO) so that its output, Φ_{DCO} has a frequency that is N times that of the reference input, Φ_{ref} and so that their phase match (i.e. each rising edge of Φ_{ref} coincides with a rising edge of Φ_{DCO}). The three control-paths shown in the figure make this a third-order digital control system. By design, the lower two paths dominate the dynamics making the system effectively second-order.

The DCO has three control inputs: ϕ, c, and v. The ϕ input is used by a proportional control path: if Φ_{ref} leads $\Phi_{DCO/N}$ then the PFD will assert **up**, and the DCO will run faster for a time interval corresponding to the phase difference. Conversely, if Φ_{ref} lags $\Phi_{DCO/N}$, the **dn** signal will be asserted, and the DCO will run slower for a time interval corresponding to the phase difference. If the frequencies of Φ_{ref} and $\Phi_{DCO/N}$ are not closely matched, then the PFD simply outputs **up** (resp. **dn**) if the frequency of $\Phi_{DCO/N}$ is lower (resp. higher) than that of Φ_{ref}.

The c input of the DCO is used by the integral control path. The DCO in [31] is a ring-oscillator, and the c input controls switched capacitor loads on the oscillator – increasing the capacitive load decreases the oscillator frequency.

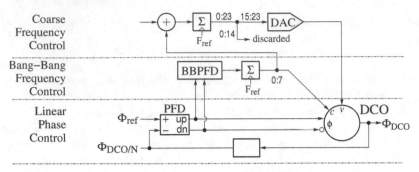

Φ_{ref} is the reference signal whose frequency is denoted by f_{ref}.
Φ_{DCO} is the output of the digitally controlled oscillator whose frequency is denoted by f_{DCO}.
Labels of the form lo:hi denote bits lo through hi (inclusive) of a binary value.

Fig. 2. A Digital Phase-Locked Loop

The bang-bang phase-frequency detector (BBPFD) controls whether this capacitance is increased one step or decreased one step with for each cycle of Φ_{ref}. The c input provides a fast tracking loop.

The v input of the DCO is used to re-center c to restore tracking range. This input sets the operating voltage of the oscillator – the oscillator frequency increases with increasing v. The accumulator for this path is driven by the difference between c and its target value c_{center}.

As a control system, the PLL converges to a switching surface where c and ϕ fluctuate near their ideal values. As presented in [31] these limit-cycle variations are designed to be slightly smaller than the unavoidable thermal and shot-noise of the oscillator. Furthermore, the time constants of the three control loops are widely separated. This facilitates intuitive reasoning about the system one loop at a time – it also introduces stiffness into the dynamics that must be considered by any simulation or reachability analysis. We believe that these characteristics of convergence to a switching surface and stiffness from multiple control loops with widely separated tracking rates are common in digitally controlled physical systems. This motivates using the digital PLL as a verification example and challenge.

4.1   Modeling the Digital PLL

From Spectre simulations, we observe that the oscillator frequency is very nearly linear in v and nearly proportional to the inverse of c for a wide range of each of these parameters. The phase error, ϕ is a continuous quantity, but the values of c and v are determined by the digital accumulators that are updated on each cycle of the reference clock, f_{ref}. This motivates modeling the PLL using a discrete-time recurrence for real-valued variables:

$$
\begin{aligned}
c(i+1) &= \min(\max(c(i) + g_c\,\mathrm{sgn}(\phi), c_{min}), c_{max}) \\
v(i+1) &= \min(\max(v(i) + g_v(c_{center} - c(i)), v_{min}), v_{max}) \\
\phi(i+1) &= \mathrm{wrap}(\phi(i) + (f_{DCO}(c(i), v(i)) - f_{ref}) - g_\phi\phi(i)) \\
f_{DCO}(c, v) &= \tfrac{1+\alpha v}{1+\beta c} f_0 \\
\mathrm{wrap}(\phi) &= \mathrm{wrap}(\phi + 1), \text{ if } \phi \le -1 \\
&= \phi, \qquad\qquad \text{ if } -1 < \phi < 1 \\
&= \mathrm{wrap}(\phi - 1), \text{ if } 1 \le \phi
\end{aligned}
\tag{4}
$$

where g_c, g_v, and g_ϕ are the gain coefficients for the bang-bang frequency control, coarse frequency control, and linear phase paths respectively. The coefficient α is the slope of oscillator frequency with respect to v, and β is the slope of oscillator period with respect to c; both are determined from simulation data. We measure phase leads or lags in cycles: $\phi = 0.1$ means that $\Phi_{DCO/N}$ leads Φ_{ref} by 10% of the period of Φ_{ref}. We say that c is "saturated" if $(c = c_{min}) \wedge (\phi < 0)$ or $(c = c_{max}) \wedge (\phi > 0)$. Likewise, v is saturated if $(v = v_{min}) \wedge (c > c_{center})$ or $(v = v_{max}) \wedge (c < c_{center})$. In this paper, we scale f_{ref} to 1. With similar scaling, we choose $g_c = 1/3200$, $g_v = -gc/5$, and $g_\phi = 0.8$. We assume bounds for c of $c_{min} = 0.9$ and $c_{max} = 1.1$ with $c_{center} = 1$ and bounds for v of $v_{min} = 0.2$ and $v_{max} = 2.5$. With these parameters, the PLL is intended to converge to a small neighbourhood of $c = c_{center} = 1$; $v = f_{ref}c_{center} = 1$ and $\phi = 0$.

4.2   Proving Global Convergence

Our verification proceeds in three phases as depicted in Fig. 3.a. First we show that for all trajectories starting with $c \in [c_{min}, c_{max}]$, $v \in [v_{min}, v_{max}]$, and $\phi \in [-1, +1]$ (the blue regions 3.a) the trajectory eventually reaches a relatively narrow stripe (the red and green regions) for which $f_{DCO} \approx f_{ref}$. The proof is based on a simple ranking function that Z3 easily verifies. By proving this we've shown that the non-linearities of the global model do not create unintended stable modes.

The second part of the proof pertains to the small, red stripes where $f_{DCO} \approx f_{ref}$ but c is close enough to c_{min} or c_{max} that saturation remains a concern. Consider the red stripe near $c = c_{min}$. We use Z3 as a bounded model checker to show that v increases, and that c "tracks" v to keep f_{DCO} close to f_{ref} and θ small. Together, these results show that all trajectories eventually enter the region shown in green in Fig. 3.

The final part of the proof shows convergence to the limit-cycle region, shown in yellow in Fig. 3.a. The key observation here is that ϕ repeatedly alternates between positive and negative values. For any given value of v, we can calculate the value of c for which $f_{DCO}(c, v) = f_{ref}$ — call this $c_{eq}(v)$. Figure 3.b depicts a trajectory from a rising zero-crossing of ϕ to a falling crossing. Let c_1 be the value of c following a rising zero-crossing of ϕ, and let c_2 be the value of c at the subsequent falling crossing. We note that $c_1 < c_{eq}(v) < c_2$.

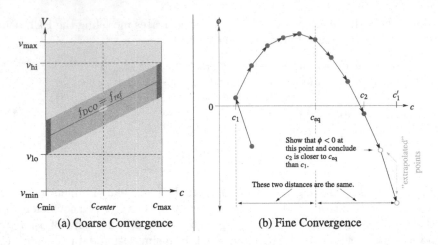

(a) Coarse Convergence | (b) Fine Convergence

Fig. 3. Global Convergence Proof

The obvious way to show convergence is to show that c_2 is closer to c_{eq} than c_1 is. However, this involves calculating the recurrence step at which ϕ makes its falling crossing of zero, and that involves solving a non-linear system of equations. Although Z3 has a non-linear arithmetic solver, it does not support induction as would be required with an arbitrary choice for c_1. Instead, we extrapolate the sequence to the last point to the right of c_{eq} that is closer to c_{eq} than c_1 is. We use formula from Eq. 4 for computing $c(i+1)$ assuming that $\operatorname{sgn} \phi = 1$; either this assumption is valid for the whole sequence, or ϕ had a falling crossing even earlier. Either is sufficient to show convergence. The proof involves solving the recurrence, and rewriting the resulting formula. The key inequality has exponential terms of the form $(1 - g_\phi)^n$ multiplied by rational function terms of the other model parameters. We use the substitution technique from Section 3.2 to replace these non-polynomial terms, and add a :`hypothesize` hint that $0 < (1 - g_\phi)^n < 1$. ACL2 readily discharges this added hypothesis using a trivial induction.

Our proof is based on a 13-page, hand-written proof. The ACL2 version consists of 75 lemmas, 10 of which were discharged using the SMT solver. Of those ten, one was the key, polynomial inequality from the manual proof. The others discharged steps in the manual derivation that were not handled by the standard books of rewrite rules for ACL2. ACL2 completes the proof in a few minutes running on a laptop computer. We found one error in the process of transcribing the hand-written proof to ACL2.

We completed much of the proof using ACL2 alone while implementing the clause processor. We plan to rewrite the proof to take more advantage of the SMT solver and believe that the resulting proof will be simpler, focus more on the high-level issues, and be easer to write and understand. When faced with proving a complicated derivation, one can guide ACL2 through the steps of the derivation, or just check the relationship of the original formula to the final one using the SMT solver. The latter approach allows novice users (including the authors of this paper) to quickly discharge claims that would otherwise take a substantial amount of time even for an expert. As noted before, if Z3 finds a counter-example, we do not return it as a witness for ACL2. However, our clause processor prints the counter-example (in its Z3 representation) to the ACL2 proof log. The user can examine this counter-example; in practice, it often points directly to the problem that needs to be addressed.

The ACL2 formulation enabled making generalizations that we would not consider making to the manual proof. In particular, the manual proof assumed that $c_{eq} - c_1$ was an integer multiple of g_1. After verifying the manual proof, we removed this restriction – this took about 12 hours of human time, most of which was to introduce an additional variable $0 \leq d_c < 1$ to account for the non-integer part. We also generalized the proof to allow v to an interval whose width is a small multiple of $|g_2(c_{max} - c_{min})|$. This did not require any new operators and took about 3 hours of human time. The interval can be anywhere in $[v_{lo}, v_{hi}]$. This shows that the convergence of c and ϕ continues to hold as v progresses toward $f_{ref}c_{center}$. It also sets the foundation for verifying the PLL with a more detailed model including the $\Delta\Sigma$ modulator in the c path, an additional low-pass filter in the v path, and adding error terms in the formula for $f_{DCO}(c, v)$.

5   Conclusions

This paper presented the integration of the Z3 SMT solver into the ACL2 theorem prover and demonstrated its application for the verification of global convergence for a digital PLL. The proof involves reasoning about systems of polynomial and rational function equalities and inequalities, which is greatly simplified by using Z3's non-linear arithmetic capabilities. ACL2 complements Z3 by providing a versatile induction capability along with a mature environment for proof development and structuring. Section 3 described technical issues that must be addressed to ensure the soundness, of the integrated prover, usability issues that are critical for the tool to be practical, and our solutions to these challenges.

Section 4 showed how this integrated prover can be used to verify global convergence for a digital phase-locked loop from all initial states to the final limit-cycle behaviours. The analysis of the limit cycle behaviour requires modeling the PLL with recurrences. Such limit cycles are not captured by continuous approximations used in [24,28]. Our approach allowed uncertainty in the model parameters and not just in the signal values. The reachability tools cited above require fixed model parameters. Our approach shows much more promise for verification that accounts for device variability and other uncertainties.

Prior work on integrating SMT solvers into theorem provers has focused on using the non-numerical decision procedures of an SMT solver. Our work demonstrates the value of bringing an SMT solver into a theorem prover for reasoning about systems where a digital controller interacts with a continuous, analog, physical system. The analysis of such systems often involves long, tedious, and error-prone derivations that primarily use linear algebra and polynomials.

We have shown that these are domains where SMT solvers augmented with induction and proof structuring have great promise. We are currently exploring using our methods to verify other AMS designs as well as to similar problems that arise in hybrid control systems and machine learning.

Acknowledgments. We thank Leo Moura, David Rager, Jijie Wei, and Ge Yu for helpful discussions about this research.

References

1. de Moura, L., Bjørner, N.S.: Z3: An efficient SMT solver. In: Ramakrishnan, C.R., Rehof, J. (eds.) TACAS 2008. LNCS, vol. 4963, pp. 337–340. Springer, Heidelberg (2008). http://dx.doi.org/10.1007/978-3-540-78800-3_24
2. Kaufmann, M., Moore, J., Manolios, P.: Computer-Aided Reasoning: An Approach. Kluwer (2000)
3. Kundert, K.S.: Introduction to RF simulation and its application. IEEE J. Solid-State Circuits **34**(9), 1298–1319 (1999). http://dx.doi.org/10.1109/4.782091
4. Kim, J., Jeeradit, M., Lim, B., Horowitz, M.A.: Leveraging designer's intent: a path toward simpler analog CAD tools. In: Custom Integrated Circuits Conf., pp. 613–620, September 2009. http://dx.doi.org/10.1109/CICC.2009.5280741
5. McLaughlin, S., Barrett, C., Ge, Y.: Cooperating theorem provers: A case study combining HOL-Light and CVC Lite. In: 3rd Workshop on Pragmatics of Decision Procedures in Automated Reasoning, pp. 43–51. http://dx.doi.org/10.1016/j.entcs.2005.12.005
6. Fontaine, P., Marion, J.-Y., Merz, S., Nieto, L.P., Tiu, A.F.: Expressiveness + automation + soundness: towards combining SMT solvers and interactive proof assistants. In: Hermanns, H., Palsberg, J. (eds.) TACAS 2006. LNCS, vol. 3920, pp. 167–181. Springer, Heidelberg (2006). http://dx.doi.org/10.1007/11691372_11
7. Besson, F.: Fast reflexive arithmetic tactics the linear case and beyond. In: Altenkirch, T., McBride, C. (eds.) TYPES 2006. LNCS, vol. 4502, pp. 48–62. Springer, Heidelberg (2007). http://dx.doi.org/10.1007/978-3-540-74464-1_4
8. Armand, M., Faure, G., Grégoire, B., Keller, C., Théry, L., Werner, B.: A modular integration of SAT/SMT solvers to Coq through proof witnesses. In: Jouannaud, J.-P., Shao, Z. (eds.) CPP 2011. LNCS, vol. 7086, pp. 135–150. Springer, Heidelberg (2011). http://dx.doi.org/10.1007/978-3-642-25379-9_12
9. Merz, S., Vanzetto, H.: Automatic verification of TLA$^+$ proof obligations with SMT solvers. In: Bjørner, N., Voronkov, A. (eds.) LPAR-18 2012. LNCS, vol. 7180, pp. 289–303. Springer, Heidelberg (2012). https://hal.inria.fr/hal-00760570/document
10. Blanchette, J.C., Böhme, S., Paulson, L.C.: Extending Sledgehammer with SMT solvers. J. of Automated Reasoning **51**(1), 109–128 (2013). http://dx.doi.org/10.1007/s10817-013-9278-5
11. Déharbe, D., Fontaine, P., Guyof, Y., Voisin, L.: Integrating SMT solvers in Rodin. Science of Computer Programming 94(pt. 2), 130–143 (2014). http://www.sciencedirect.com/science/article/pii/S016764231400183X
12. Barrett, C.W., Berezin, S.: CVC lite: A new implementation of the cooperating validity checker category B. In: Alur, R., Peled, D.A. (eds.) CAV 2004. LNCS, vol. 3114, pp. 515–518. Springer, Heidelberg (2004)

13. Abrial, J.-R., Butler, M., Hallerstede, S., Voisin, L.: An open extensible tool environment for Event-B. In: Liu, Z., Kleinberg, R.D. (eds.) ICFEM 2006. LNCS, vol. 4260, pp. 588–605. Springer, Heidelberg (2006). http://dx.doi.org/10.1007/11901433_32

14. Barrett, C., Stump, A., Tinelli, C.: The SMT-LIB standard version 2.0. In: 8th SMT Workshop (2010). http://smtlib.cs.uiowa.edu/papers/smt-lib-reference-v2.0-r10.12.21.pdf

15. Immler, F.: Formally verified computation of enclosures of solutions of ordinary differential equations. In: Badger, J.M., Rozier, K.Y. (eds.) NFM 2014. LNCS, vol. 8430, pp. 113–127. Springer, Heidelberg (2014). http://home.in.tum.de/immler/documents/immler2014enclosures.pdf

16. Harutunian, S.: Formal verification of computer controlled systems. Ph.D. dissertation, University of Texas, Austin, May 2007. http://www.lib.utexas.edu/etd/d/2007/harutunians68792/harutunians68792.pdf

17. Kurshan, R., McMillan, K.: Analysis of digital circuits through symbolic reduction. IEEE Trans. CAD 10(11), 1356–1371 (1991). http://dx.doi.org/10.1109/43.97615

18. Hedrich, L., Barke, E.: A formal approach to nonlinear analog circuit verification. In: ICCAD, pp. 123–127 (1995). http://dl.acm.org/citation.cfm?id=224841.224870

19. Greenstreet, M. R.: Verifying safety properties of differential equations. In: Alur, R., Henzinger, T.A. (eds.) CAV 1996. LNCS, vol. 1102, pp. 277–287. Springer, Heidelberg (1996). http://dx.doi.org/10.1007/3-540-61474-5_76

20. Hartong, W., Hedrich, L., Barke, E.: Model checking algorithms for analog verification. In: 39th DAC, pp. 542–547, June 2002. http://dx.doi.org/10.1109/DAC.2002.1012684

21. Dang, T., Donzé, A., Maler, O.: Verification of analog and mixed-signal circuits using hybrid system techniques. In: Hu, A.J., Martin, A.K. (eds.) FMCAD 2004. LNCS, vol. 3312, pp. 21–36. Springer, Heidelberg (2004). http://dx.doi.org/10.1007/978-3-540-30494-4_3

22. Dong, Z.J., Zaki, M.H., Al-Sammane, G., Tahar, S., Bois, G.: Checking properties of PLL designs using run-time verification. In: Int'l. Conf. Microelectronics, pp. 125–128 (2007). http://dx.doi.org/10.1109/ICM.2007.4497676

23. Jesser, A., Hedrich, L.: A symbolic approach for mixed-signal model checking. In: ASPDAC, pp. 404–409 (2008). http://dl.acm.org/citation.cfm?id=1356802.1356903

24. Althoff, M., Rajhans, A., et al.: Formal verification of phase-locked loops using reachability analysis and continuization. Comm. ACM 56(10), 97–104 (2013). http://doi.acm.org/10.1145/2507771.2507783

25. Lin, H., Li, P., Myers, C. J.: Verification of digitally-intensive analog circuits via kernel ridge regression and hybrid reachability analysis. In: 50th DAC, pp. 66:1–66:6 (2013). http://doi.acm.org/10.1145/2463209.2488814

26. Lin, H., Li, P.: Parallel hierarchical reachability analysis for analog verification. In: 51st DAC, pp. 150:1–150:6 (2014). http://doi.acm.org/10.1145/2593069.2593178

27. Frehse, G., et al.: SpaceEx: scalable verification of hybrid systems. In: Gopalakrishnan, G., Qadeer, S. (eds.) CAV 2011. LNCS, vol. 6806, pp. 379–395. Springer, Heidelberg (2011). http://dx.doi.org/10.1007/978-3-642-22110-1_30

28. Wei, J., Peng, Y., Yu, G., Greenstreet, M.: Verifying global convergence for a digital phase-locked loop. In: 13th FMCAD, pp. 113–120, October 2013. http://dx.doi.org/10.1109/FMCAD.2013.6679399

29. Marques-Silva, J., Sakallah, K.: GRASP: a search algorithm for propositional satisfiability. IEEE Trans. Computers **48**(5), 506–521 (1999). http://dx.doi.org/10.1109/12.769433

30. Gamboa, R.: Mechanically verified real-valued algorithms in ACL2. Ph.D. dissertation, University of Texas at Austin (1999)

31. Crossley, J., Naviasky, E., Alon, E.: An energy-efficient ring-oscillator digital PLL. In: Custom Integrated Circuits Conf. (September 2010). http://dx.doi.org/10.1109/CICC.2010.5617417

Conflict-Directed Graph Coverage

Daniel Schwartz-Narbonne[1], Martin Schäf[2]([✉]), Dejan Jovanović[2],
Philipp Rümmer[3], and Thomas Wies[1]

[1] New York University, New York, USA
[2] SRI International, Menlo Park, USA
martin.schaef@sri.com
[3] Uppsala University, Uppsala, Sweden

Abstract. Many formal method tools for increasing software reliability
apply Satisfiability Modulo Theories (SMT) solvers to enumerate feasible paths in a program subject to certain coverage criteria. Examples
include inconsistent code detection tools and concolic test case gener-
ators. These tools have in common that they typically treat the SMT
solver as a black box, relying on its ability to efficiently search through
large search spaces. However, in practice the performance of SMT solvers
often degrades significantly if the search involves reasoning about complex control-flow. In this paper, we open the black box and devise a
new algorithm for this problem domain that we call conflict-directed
graph coverage. Our algorithm relies on two core components of an SMT
solver, namely conflict-directed learning and deduction by propagation,
and applies domain-specific modifications for reasoning about control-
flow graphs. We implemented conflict-directed coverage and used it for
detecting code inconsistencies in several large Java open-source projects
with over one million lines of code in total. The new algorithm yields significant performance gains on average compared to previous algorithms
and reduces the running times on hard search instances from hours to
seconds.

1 Introduction

Inconsistent code represents a class of program abnormalities whose detection
has attracted considerable attention over the past years [4,15,18,20,28,29]. A
statement in a program is considered inconsistent if it never partakes in any
properly terminating execution of the program. That is, the statement is either
unreachable or any execution passing through it must inevitably lead to an
unrecoverable error.

Detecting inconsistent statements is important for several reasons. First,
inconsistent code is closely correlated with the existence of real bugs and is
difficult to detect using testing. For example, Wang et al. [29] have used code
inconsistency detection to identify optimization-unstable code in C programs[1]

---

[1] The C standard allows compilers to eliminate code with undefined behavior. Such
code can be formalized as being inconsistent.

© Springer International Publishing Switzerland 2015
K. Havelund et al. (Eds.): NFM 2015, LNCS 9058, pp. 327–342, 2015.
DOI: 10.1007/978-3-319-17524-9_23

and discovered previously unknown optimization-related bugs in the Linux kernel. The inconsistency detection tool Joogie developed by some of the authors [4] has revealed several new bugs in open-source Java programs, including Apache Tomcat and Ant [25]. Second, code inconsistencies can be detected statically and locally by checking individual procedures in isolation, without requiring precise procedure contracts. This enables the use of theorem provers to obtain a fully automated analysis that scales to entire programs. Well, not entirely ... A small number of indomitable inconsistencies still holds out against efficient detection.

In this paper, we present a new algorithm for detecting inconsistencies efficiently, realizing considerable performance improvements over existing algorithms in practice.

Most existing algorithms implement variations of the following basic idea: for a given procedure, one first computes an abstraction to obtain an acyclic control-flow graph (see, e.g., [18]). This graph is then encoded into a first-order logic formula whose models can be mapped back to the feasible executions of the procedure. Then, an SMT solver is repeatedly queried to obtain such feasible executions. For each obtained execution, the statements on the corresponding control-flow path are marked as consistent and a condition is added to prevent the prover from finding other executions of the same path. The algorithm terminates once the formula becomes unsatisfiable and all program statements that have not been covered by a feasible path are reported as inconsistent.

All the variations of this basic algorithm have in common that they treat the SMT solver as a black box. They completely rely on the solver's ability to (1) efficiently reason about the propositional encoding of the control-flow graph; and (2) learn theory conflicts from the constraints on infeasible paths to avoid enumerating them one at a time. However, the interplay between propositional reasoning and theory reasoning in a general purpose SMT solver is complex. In particular, for search-intensive problems, it is unavoidable that the solver will end up doing theory reasoning across many different paths at once, even if the application only requires reasoning about individual paths. We have observed that this can lead to severe performance degradation during inconsistent code detection, in particular, if inconsistent statements participate in many paths of a control-flow graph.

Our new algorithm builds upon the basic search loop of an SMT solver. That is, we use (1) a DPLL-style SAT procedure to search for individual paths; and we rely (2) on conflict-driven clause learning (CDCL) [27] to detect inconsistent statements efficiently by generalizing theory conflicts. However, we propose several important application-specific modifications to the standard CDCL and DPLL procedures. First, we completely separate the search for paths in the control-flow graph from checking feasibility of these paths. That is, theory reasoning and conflict learning are always restricted to single complete paths. Second, we exploit that the propositional formula given to the DPLL procedure encodes a control-flow graph. Namely, we devise specialized propagation rules that accelerate the search for individual paths. Together, these modifications ensure that none of the solver components gets confused by the complex propositional structure of the control-flow graph encoding.

```
1   boolean equals(MyClass other) {
2     if (this == other) return true;
3     if (other == null) return false;
4     if (getClass() != other.getClass()) return false;
5     if (bases == null) {
6       if (other.bases != null) return false;
7       //inconsistent with line 9
8     }
9     if (bases.hashCode() != other.bases.hashCode())
10      return false;
11    return true;
12  }
```

Fig. 1. A method with inconsistent code taken from the Bouncy Castle library. Any path through line 7 (i.e., the implicit else block of line 6) requires that `bases` and `other.bases` are `null`, which is inconsistent with the fact that these objects are dereferenced in line 9.

We have implemented our algorithm in the tool GraVy [26] and applied it to several open-source Java projects consisting of more than thirty thousand methods and over one million lines of code in total. Our evaluation shows that, even though difficult search-intensive problem instances are relatively rare, our new algorithm leads to considerable performance improvements on average. For individual difficult instances, we have observed performance improvements of up to two orders of magnitude, reducing the running times of the analysis from hours to seconds.

2   Overview

We explain our Conflict-Directed Coverage algorithm along the code snippet in Fig. 1. The snippet shows an occurrence of inconsistent code that we found and fixed in the cryptography library Bouncy Castle [1]. In this example, line 7 can only be reached by executions where `other.bases` is `null`. Further, any such execution must also reach line 9 which dereferences `other.bases`. Thus, there can be no normally terminating execution going through line 7 since any such execution will throw a null pointer exception in line 9. Therefore, line 7 is inconsistent.

To find this inconsistency, existing algorithms translate the program into a formula in first-order logic whose models encode the feasible complete executions of the program. The formula is sent to an SMT solver. Once a model is found, the formula is extended to block all other models that can be mapped to the same control-flow path. This way, each time the theorem prover is queried, it has to find a new feasible complete path. Once this formula becomes unsatisfiable, we know that all statements that occur on feasible complete paths have been covered and the remaining statements are inconsistent.

```
try {
  ...
  while((obj = ois.x()) != null) {
    if (obj instanceof SampleEvent)
        {
      try {
        ...
      } catch (...Exception err) {
        if (...){
          throw new ...;
        }
      }
    } else {...}
  }
} catch (EOFException err) {...
} catch (IOException err) { ...
} catch (...Exception err) { ...
} finally {
  try {...}
  catch (...Exception e) {...}
  if (!temporaryFile.delete())
      {...}
}
```

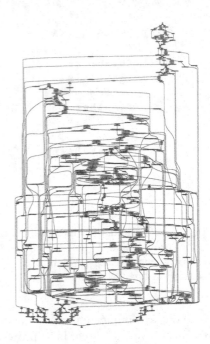

Fig. 2. The CFG of the method `testEnded` from `DiskStoreSampleSender` in the Apache `jMeter` project. The listing on the left shows an excerpt of the Java code. The method consists of only 55 lines but a combination of switch-cases, loops, and complex exception handling results in complex control-flow. The right-hand side shows the CFG. Each of the 659 nodes represents a block of straight-line bytecode instructions.

This approach is efficient as long as it is easy to find new models. In our example, we would quickly cover everything other than line 7. In order to show that line 7 is inconsistent, however, the theorem prover still has to show that all complete paths through that line are infeasible. In this example, there are only two such paths, so the prover will not struggle to solve this quickly. In practice, however, the number of paths can be prohibitively large.

Fig. 2 shows an excerpt of a method from the Apache `jMeter` project and its control-flow graph. This example shows that even a relatively small Java method (here 55 lines) can result in very complex control-flow graphs. Our previous algorithm is very fast at finding feasible paths through the first 600 of 659 nodes in the graph. Finding paths for the remaining nodes, however, takes over 90 minutes, because the solver starts enumerating all paths through these nodes to show the absence of feasible paths.

To avoid this worst-case enumeration of all paths, we propose a new algorithm that learns conflict clauses from each infeasible path. These clauses then prune entire subgraphs to show that no further models exist. We explain this approach using the simple example from Fig. 1. Let us assume that we have already covered all feasible paths in the method. What is left are two paths, one passing the lines 7 and 10, and the other passing the lines 7 and 11. Let us further assume that the SMT solver first checks feasibility of the path through the lines 7 and 10. The query for this check looks roughly as follows:

```
        ...
    bases = null ∧
    other ≠ null ∧
    other ≠ null ∧
    other.bases = null ∧
    bases ≠ null ∧
    other.bases ≠ null ∧
    bases.hashCode() = other.bases.hashCode() ∧
    ret = false
```

This formula is unsatisfiable because of the contradicting clauses other.bases = null generated from line 7 and other.bases ≠ null generated from line 10. Our algorithm extracts this conflict by computing a minimal unsatisfiable core of the formula.[2]

A theorem prover would learn this conflict as well, however, it would be unable to infer the clause other.bases ≠ null in the conflict also guards the other path through line 7 directly. When reasoning about the control-flow, which is typically implemented through Boolean variables intertwined with the actual transition relations (e.g.,[6]), the solver would not consider the information that it should not attempt any further path containing the learned conflict. In the worst-case, this causes the theorem prover to enumerate many paths that are known to be infeasible already. This problem has, e.g., been described in [10,13].

To avoid enumerating all paths, our algorithm checks if all paths through line 7 must contain the clauses from this unsatisfiable core. To that end, it turns the problem of finding the next path into a SAT problem. The structure of the control-flow graph is encoded into a SAT formula which is constrained by the fact that the node we want to cover must be used, that source and sink of the graph must be used, and that no model is allowed that contains any of the learned conflicts. Further, we give the solver additional propagation rules presented in [3] that simplify reasoning about graphs. E.g., if the solver picks a transition through one side of a diamond, we enforce that no transition on the other side of the diamond can be chosen.

Using the learned conflicts and the knowledge about the structure of the control-flow graph, we are able to establish the inconsistency of line 7 immediately without analyzing any further path and our algorithm terminates, reporting line 7 to be inconsistent. We discuss our algorithm in more detail in Section 4.

Note that for a small example such as the one shown in Fig. 1, our algorithm will typically be less efficient than a simple algorithm that enumerates

---

[2] The following argument is unchanged if the solver instead found the unsat core bases = null and bases ≠ null.

all infeasible paths explicitly because computing unsatisfiable cores is relatively expensive. Our algorithm targets big problems where existing algorithms fail because of the enormous number of paths. In particular, for the example shown in Fig. 2, our new algorithm manages to identify infeasible subgraphs efficiently using the computed conflict clauses, ruling out many complete infeasible paths simultaneously. The method `testEnded` can therefore be analyzed in less than 1 minute compared to the 90 minutes with our previous algorithm. This example shows that our new approach leads to a significant performance improvement if inconsistencies can be detected locally. If inconsistencies can not be generalized to larger subgraphs, we will not see any performance gain as our algorithm will fall back to enumerating individual infeasible paths. However, our evaluation in Section 5 shows that, in practice, inconsistencies in real code often generalize and, hence, our new algorithm works much better.

3   Preliminaries

We represent programs as control-flow automata where program statements are encoded directly in terms of their transition relations, expressed as formulas in first-order logic. We assume standard syntax of such formulas and we assume that their semantics is given by some appropriate first-order theory that we leave unspecified. We only assume that all values used for the interpretation of formulas are drawn from a fixed set V. As usual, for a formula ϕ with free variables X and a valuation $\sigma : X \rightarrow V$, we write $\sigma \models \phi$ to indicate that σ satisfies ϕ.

We fix a set of variables X, which we call *program variables*. In order to be able to reason over the states in a program execution, we define a sequence of variable sets $\{X^{\langle i \rangle}\}_{i \in \mathbb{N}}$. We use the variables in $X^{\langle i \rangle}$ to describe a program state that has been reached after executing i statements in the program. Note that for a loop free program, $X^{\langle i \rangle}$ is effectively equivalent to SSA form [7,12]. Formally, define $X^{\langle 0 \rangle} = X$ and for all $i > 0$, let $X^{\langle i \rangle}$ be a set of variables that is of equal cardinality than X and pairwise disjoint from all other $X^{\langle j \rangle}$, $j \neq i$. Let $\cdot^{\langle 1 \rangle}$ be a bijective function that maps the variables $X^{\langle i \rangle}$ to the variables $X^{\langle i+1 \rangle}$, for all $i \in \mathbb{N}$. For a variable x we denote by $x^{\langle i \rangle}$ the result of applying this function i times to x. We extend this *shift* function to formulas as expected.

Now, a program P is formally defined as a tuple (L, T, ℓ_0, ℓ_f) where

- L is a finite set of control locations,
- T is a finite set of statements (ℓ, φ, ℓ') with $\ell, \ell' \in L$ and φ a formula over the variables $X \cup X'$,
- $\ell_0 \in L$ is the initial location, and
- $\ell_f \in L$ is the final location.

For a statement $\tau = (\ell, \varphi, \ell')$ we define $\mathsf{start}(\tau) = \ell$, $\mathsf{end}(\tau) = \ell'$, and $\mathsf{tr}(\tau) = \varphi$. We call $\mathsf{tr}(\tau)$ the *transition formula* of τ.

A state $s = (\ell, \sigma)$ of a program P consists of a program location ℓ and a valuation of the program variables $\sigma : X \rightarrow V$. We denote the location of a state

s by $\mathsf{loc}(s)$ and its valuation by $\mathsf{val}(s)$. For a valuation $\sigma : X \rightarrow V$ and $i \in \mathbb{N}$, we define $\sigma^{\langle i \rangle} : X^{\langle i \rangle} \rightarrow V$ such that for all $x \in X$, $\sigma^{\langle i \rangle}(x^{\langle i \rangle}) = \sigma(x)$. Similarly, we define $s^{\langle i \rangle} = (\ell, \sigma^{\langle i \rangle})$ for a state $s = (\ell, \sigma)$.

A path π of program P is a finite sequence $\tau_0, \ldots, \tau_n$ of P's statements such that $\mathsf{start}(\tau_0) = \ell_0$, $\mathsf{end}(\tau_n) = \ell_f$, and for all $i \in [0, n)$, $\mathsf{end}(\tau_i) = \mathsf{start}(\tau_{i+1})$. We extend transition formulas from statements to paths by defining

$$\mathsf{tr}(\pi) = \mathsf{tr}(\tau_0)^{\langle 0 \rangle} \wedge \cdots \wedge \mathsf{tr}(\tau_n)^{\langle n \rangle} .$$

We call $\mathsf{tr}(\pi)$ the *path formula* of π. A path formula encodes the executions of the path. That is, projecting a model σ_π of π onto the variables $X^{\langle i \rangle}$ yields $\mathsf{val}(s^{\langle i \rangle})$, the valuation of the i-th state s in the execution.

We call a path π *feasible* if its path formula is satisfiable. A statement $\tau \in T$ is *inconsistent* if it does not occur on any feasible path of P.

Finally, we define a preorder $\preceq$ on statements that captures the notion of domination in control flow graphs: for $\tau_1, \tau_2 \in T$ we have $\tau_1 \preceq \tau_2$ iff for every path π of P, if τ_2 occurs on π, then so does τ_1. We write $\tau_1 \sim \tau_2$ if $\tau_1 \preceq \tau_2$ and $\tau_2 \preceq \tau_1$. Finally, for $\tau \in T$, we denote by $[\tau]_\sim$ the equivalence class of τ in the quotient set that is induced by the equivalence relation $\sim$. The following lemma states that inconsistency propagates along the domination relation, which gives rise to certain optimizations during inconsistency detection.

Lemma 1. *Let τ_1 and τ_2 be statements of a program. If $\tau_1 \preceq \tau_2$ and τ_1 is inconsistent, then so is τ_2.*

4 Algorithm

Our method for detection of infeasible code operates over loop-free graphs, and we assume that the input programs are loop-free. We refer the reader to existing work (e.g. [18] and [28]) that describes the algorithms for sound loop abstraction in the context of inconsistent code detection. Program statements are encoded in SSA form [7,12].

4.1 Main Procedure

The main procedure Cover is described in Algorithm 1. Cover takes a loop-free control-flow graph as input and returns the set of statements C that can occur on feasible paths.

The procedure Cover starts by collecting the set of all statements that need to be discharged (i.e., proven inconsistent, or covered by a feasible path) in the set S, and setting the set C to empty.

In each iteration of the main loop, the procedure then tries to cover a statement τ from S, or prove that it is inconsistent. The statement τ is picked using the procedure **FindMaxElement**. This procedure takes the set of not-yet-covered statements S, the control-flow graph cfg, and returns the statement $\tau \in S$ that is maximal with respect to the pre-order $\preceq$ defined in Section 3. The

---

Algorithm 1. Cover

Input: The control-flow graph cfg.
Output: The set C of statements that occur on feasible complete paths in cfg.
begin
    $S \leftarrow$ **GetStatements**(cfg) ;
    $C \leftarrow \emptyset$;
    repeat
        $\tau \leftarrow$ **FindMaxElement**(cfg, S);
        $\pi \leftarrow$ **FeasiblePath**(cfg, τ) ;
        if $\pi = \bot$ **then**
            $S \leftarrow S \setminus [\tau]_\sim$;
        else
            $S \leftarrow S \setminus \pi$;
            $C \leftarrow C \cup \pi$;
        end if
    until $S = \emptyset$;
    return C;
end

---

intuition behind this choice is two-fold. First, we aim at covering a particular node, and we focus the underlying solver on the sub-graph of paths that contain it. Second, by picking a τ to be $\preceq$-maximal, we make sure that this sub-graph is indeed reduced since it will exclude the nodes that are $\preceq$-sibling to τ (i.e. branches adjacent to τ).

The statement τ returned by **FindMaxElement** is then delegated to the FeasiblePath procedure that checks whether there exists a feasible path through this particular statement. If such a path π exists, all statements in π are then removed from S, since they are also covered by π. Otherwise, if no such path exists, the statement τ is discharged as inconsistent along with all the nodes in its equivalence class $[\tau]_\sim$ (by Lemma 1).

This procedure repeats this loop until the set of statements S becomes empty, implying that it has discharged all statements. Since in each loop iteration at least one statement is removed from S, the procedure is guaranteed to terminate.

4.2   Finding Feasible Paths

Algorithm 2 describes the FeasiblePath procedure that discharges inconsistency of a particular statement τ. The procedure takes as input the loop-free control-flow graph cfg, and the statement τ in cfg, and either returns $\bot$, if τ is inconsistent in cfg, or a feasible full path π that contains τ.

Algorithm 2 implements a typical CDCL-style search loop where path candidates are generated, while learning from unsuccessful attempts, until either a full solution is found (a feasible path), or it can be shown that no such path can exist. The set of conflicts encountered during the search is kept in the set conflicts that is initialized to the empty set. Each conflict is a set of statements

---

Algorithm 2. FeasiblePath

Input: The control flow graph cfg and the statement τ to be discharged.
Output: A feasible complete path π that covers τ, or $\bot$ if τ is inconsistent.
begin
   | conflicts ← ∅ ;
   | **while** true **do**
   | π ← **FindPath**(cfg, τ, conflicts) ;
   | **if** $\pi = \bot$ **then**
   | | **return** $\bot$
   | **if** **CheckSat**(π) **then**
   | | **return** π ;
   | **else**
   | | core ← **UnsatCore**(π) ;
   | | conflicts ← conflicts ∪ {core} ;
   | **end if**
   | **end while**
end

---

such that any full path that includes all statements of the conflicts can not be feasible.

In each iteration of the loop, the procedure first picks *a candidate* path π from the cfg using the procedure **FindPath**. The procedure **FindPath** takes as input the control-flow graph, the statement τ, and the set of learned conflicts, and returns a complete path through τ that does not contain any of the already known conflicts. This path need not be feasible, i.e. the only requirement on **FindPath** is that the path must be complete and not pass through any of the conflicts discovered so far. This can be implemented using a simple call to a SAT-solver, and does not require any SMT reasoning, making it very efficient. Our implementation uses a dedicated path solver for control-flow graphs [3] available in the Princess theorem prover.

If **FindPath** returns that no path through τ exists, we have a proof that τ is inconsistent, and we return $\bot$. Otherwise, we take the candidate path π and check whether it is feasible by calling the Princess theorem prover [24] to check if the formula $\mathsf{tr}(\pi)$ is satisfiable. If so, we know that τ is not inconsistent and the algorithm returns the path π. If $\mathsf{tr}(\pi)$ is unsatisfiable, the procedure computes a minimal unsatisfiable core of $\mathsf{tr}(\pi)$. [3] Since any path that includes all statements from the core will also be infeasible, the core is then added to the conflict set.

The **FeasiblePath** procedure terminates because each iteration of the loop either leaves the loop directly, or learns one new conflict. Each conflict eliminates a set of paths from the control-flow graph (in the worst-case only π). That is,

---

[3] Our current implementation finds the minimal core by taking the full path and then removing each statement that can be removed while keeping unsatisfiability. This is feasible only because path satisfiablity is very efficient to check.

since the set of paths in the control-flow graph is finite, the algorithm terminates eventually.

If the unsatisfiable cores that the procedure computes always contain the full paths, the procedure can diverge into complete path enumeration. However, in practice, our algorithm detects inconsistent code without enumerating all paths, as shown in our evaluation on some challenging real-world problems.

4.3   Details of the FindPath Function

Our algorithm works for any implementation of **FindPath** that computes, given the control-flow graph, the statement τ to be covered, and the set of conflicts, a single complete path through τ. Computing such paths reduces to the well-known problem of finding *hitting sets,* and is in general NP-hard [21]; it is therefore meaningful to employ a theorem prover or SAT solver for computing such paths.

Our implementation of **FindPath** uses the control-flow theory developed in [3], which provides a tailor-made propagator for reasoning about control-flow graphs. This propagator can be loaded as a plug-in into a theorem prover, and ensures that only models are computed that correspond to single, complete paths in the graph, reducing the number of explicit Boolean clauses needed to encode those constraints.

5   Evaluation

We evaluated our algorithm by comparing it against the algorithm from our Joogie tool [4]. The algorithm in Joogie uses a greedy path cover strategy to find all feasible paths. To that end, it used a special theory in the SMT solver that allows it to reason about the control-flow more efficiently [3]. Our implementation uses the same theory when searching for new paths. For comparability, both algorithms use Princess as the underlying SMT solver. The code of all algorithms and all benchmark problems are available online [26].

Setup. We compare the two algorithms on a set of open-source programs. Both algorithms are applied to each procedure in these programs. That is, the algorithms do not perform inter-procedural analysis. The task is to find all inconsistent statements in each individual procedure. Since both algorithms use the same front-end and the same loop abstraction, the set of inconsistent statements is the same in both cases.

Each algorithm is given ten minutes per procedure before it is stopped by a timeout. Procedures that timeout are counted as ten minutes computation time. The goal of the experiment is to show that our algorithm times out less often and is able to analyze the benchmark programs faster. We do not discuss the inconsistent code that was found as this would exceed the scope of this paper. For the interested reader, we provide some examples of inconsistent code that we found and fixed in our wiki.[4]

---

[4] https://github.com/martinschaef/gravy/wiki/Bugs-found-so-far

Table 1. Results of running the Conflict-Directed Inconsistency Detection algorithm against the optimized algorithm from [3]. The algorithms are applied to each procedure in isolation. The timeout per procedure is 10 minutes. The time shown is the overall running time from start to end including logging, etc. All experiments are carried out on a 2.8 GHz i7 with 16GB memory. The JVM is started with `-Xmx4g -Xms4g -Xss4m`.

Benchmark	# procedures	KLOC	Joogie Algorithm		New Algorithm	
			time	timeouts	time	timeouts
Ant	10,563	271	23,150s	34	13,136s	12
Bouncy Castle	10,692	461	8,002s	7	8,499s	6
Cassandra	1,110	237	1,073s	1	969s	1
jMeter	3,712	114	7,302s	11	2,833s	2
Log4j	2,836	65	2,950s	4	1,960s	1
Maven (Core)	2,307	43	2,793s	4	1,192s	1

Our benchmark suite consists of a variety of open-source Java programs (see Table 1). For each benchmark program, we used the source code available from GitHub at the day of submission for our experiments. Benchmark programs are translated into Boogie [23] which serves as the input language to our algorithm. The translation is sound for large parts of the Java language but abstracts certain language features such as multithreading and reflection. Looping control-flow and procedure calls are eliminated using the sound abstraction described in [18]. We do not discuss translation and abstraction in further detail. However, we emphasize that both algorithms in our experiments use the exact same code for the abstraction to ensure that the results are comparable. Details on the translation can be found on the website mentioned above.

Results. Table 1 shows the results of our experiment. The first three columns show the name of each benchmark, the total number of analyzed procedures, and the number of lines of code in thousands (excluding comments). Column four and five show the computation time and the number of timeouts for the Joogie algorithm, and the last two columns show the same for our Conflict-Directed Inconsistency Detection Algorithm.

For all benchmarks, we can see a reduction in the number of timeouts. For all benchmarks other than Bouncy Castle, the new algorithm was also faster then the old algorithm; for Bouncy Castle, it took slightly longer but succeeded on more procedures. For Ant, our new algorithm is almost twice as fast and only has one third of the timeouts. The large difference in computation time can mostly be attributed to the number of timeouts. Without considering the procedures that timeout, both algorithms take roughly the same amount of time. Most of the procedures for which the old algorithm timeouts are of a similar nature to the one in Fig. 2 of Section 2: a large control-flow graph, where a small subgraph is inconsistent. Our algorithm can establish the inconsistency after learning clauses from a few infeasible paths (in our experiments, the algorithm never needed to learn more than 10 conflicts). The old algorithm, on the other

Table 2. Distribution of timeouts per benchmark. Column 2 is the number of procedures where the old algorithm succeeded within 10 minutes, but the new algorithm timed out. The third column shows the number of procedures in that benchmark where the new algorithm succeeded within 10 minutes, but the old algorithm timed out. The final column shows the number of examples where both algorithms timed out.

Benchmark	# Joogie Better	# New Algorithm Better	Both timeout
Ant	1	23	11
Bouncy Castle	0	1	6
Cassandra	0	0	1
jMeter	0	9	2
Log4j	1	4	0
Maven (Core)	0	3	1

Table 3. Distribution of computation time per benchmark. For the respective algorithm, we show the percentage of procedures that can be analyzed in less than a second, more than one second, more than 100 seconds, and more than 300 seconds.

Benchmark	Joogie Algorithm				New Algorithm			
	$\leq$ 1s	> 1s	> 100s	> 300s	$\leq$ 1s	> 1s	> 100s	> 300s
Ant	97.73 %	2.26 %	0.35 %	0.33 %	97.88 %	2.11 %	0.23 %	0.16 %
Bouncy Castle	98.87 %	1.11 %	0.18 %	0.09 %	98.88 %	1.12 %	0.16 %	0.08 %
Cassandra	98.46 %	1.53 %	0.27 %	0.09 %	98.46 %	1.53 %	0.18 %	0.09 %
jMeter	98.16 %	1.83 %	0.32 %	0.32 %	98.27 %	1.72 %	0.18 %	0.13 %
Log4j	98.80 %	1.19 %	0.17 %	0.14 %	98.80 %	1.19 %	0.17 %	0.14 %
Maven (Core)	97.83 %	2.16 %	0.17 %	0.17 %	98.17 %	1.82 %	0.08 %	0.04 %

hand, starts enumerating all paths which is impractical for problems of that size and therefore leads to a timeout after ten minutes.

Table 2 shows the relative timeouts between the two algorithms. The first column shows the name of the benchmark. The second column shows the number of procedures in that benchmark where the old algorithm succeeded within 10 minutes, but the new algorithm timed out. The third column shows the number of procedures in that benchmark where the new algorithm succeeded within 10 minutes, but the old algorithm timed out. The final column shows the number of examples where both algorithms timed out. For all benchmarks, the new algorithm had significantly fewer timeouts than the old algorithm.

Table 3 shows the distribution of computation time per benchmark in more detail. For both algorithms, the table shows the fraction of procedures that can be analyzed in less than a second, over a second, over 100 seconds, and over 300 seconds (with a timeout of 600 seconds). The table shows that our new algorithm has the most impact on procedures in the range above 100 or 300 seconds. That is, while we see improvements across all columns, our algorithm is particularly strong on procedures where the old algorithm struggles.

The performance difference between the two algorithms would become more visible if we would not timeout the algorithms after 10 minutes. For example, for the procedure from Fig. 2 of Section 2 the old algorithm took over 90 minutes where the new algorithm took less than one minute. However, running the experiments without timeout on such a large corpus of benchmarks seemed impractical.

Threats to Validity. Although the benchmark applications is a potential threat to validity, we tried to select a diverse set of benchmark programs ranging from desktop applications (Log4j and Ant), over web applications (Cassandra), to cryptographic code (Bouncy Castle). Further, since both algorithms share a common front-end, we are confident that neither the selection of benchmarks nor the infrastructure is biased towards one of the algorithms.

Another potential threat to validity is the choice of the SMT solver. We chose Princess because it is the only solver that provides the CFG-theory [3], which we found to be vital for finding paths efficiently. During the development of our algorithm we tested whether the timeouts that we encountered in the old algorithm are specific to Princess. To that end, we exported several of our hard queries into the SMT-LIB format and checked them with Z3 [14], which also timed out.

6 Related Work

The concept of inconsistent code has been presented in several works (e.g., [4, 15, 28]), sometimes under different names such as infeasible code [9], doomed program points [18], or deviant behavior [16]. The approaches in [4, 9, 18, 28] and a similar approach in [20] are based on deductive verification. In [4] and on our website [25] we demonstrate that these approaches can identify relevant coding mistakes even in mature code.

The algorithm presented in this paper can extend any of these approaches. The approach in [15] is based on a type-checking approach but unfortunately, no tool is available for comparison. Most compilers have built in data-flow and type-checking tools as well to detect inconsistent code. For example, most compilers do not allow the use of uninitialized variables, which can be seen as a form of inconsistency. Due to the simpler reasoning, these tools only detect a subset of what can be detected with deductive verification-based approaches but are also significantly faster.

The approach of Engler et al. in [16] uses syntactic pattern matching and is therefore not directly comparable. Other syntactic tools, such as Findbugs [19] also detect a certain set of inconsistencies but have the usual limitations in terms of precision.

Inconsistent code detection has several other applications beyond finding coding mistakes. For example, [20] uses a variation of our algorithm to check reachability of annotated code. Our algorithm can be used in the same way and, beyond that, can identify code that must violate other specification statements. That is, our approach can be extended to debug functional specification in the spirit of [17], [11], and [8].

Identifying all statements in a program that occur on feasible paths also has applications for the generation of verification counterexamples. Usually, deductive verification returns only one counterexample if the proof of the desired property fails. This can be time consuming as the verification has to be re-run very often. In [2], we have presented an approach how a coverage algorithm like the one presented in this paper can be used to identify all assertions in a procedure that may fail. This is closely related to other techniques that find multiple counterexamples for one verification attempt, such as [5], and also related to the problem extracting error traces from theorem prover models as presented in [22].

7   Conclusion

We have proposed a new algorithm for finding feasible paths in a program that satisfy certain coverage criteria. The algorithm makes application-specific modifications to the core components of an SMT solver in order to accelerate the search in complex control-flow graphs. We have used our algorithm to find code inconsistencies in large Java programs and showed that we gain significant performance improvements compared to previous algorithms. We believe that the usefulness of our algorithm extends beyond inconsistent code detection to applications with different coverage notions such as those used in concolic testing.

Acknowledgments. This work was in part supported by the NASA contract NNX14-AI05A and the NSF grant CCS-1350574. The content is solely the responsibility of the authors and does not necessarily represent the official views of NASA or NSF.

References

1. The legion of the bouncy castle. https://www.bouncycastle.org/
2. Arlt, S., Rubio-González, C., Rümmer, P., Schäf, M., Shankar, N.: The gradual verifier. In: Badger, J.M., Rozier, K.Y. (eds.) NFM 2014. LNCS, vol. 8430, pp. 313–327. Springer, Heidelberg (2014)
3. Arlt, S., Rümmer, P., Schäf, M.: A theory for control-flow graph exploration. In: Van Hung, D., Ogawa, M. (eds.) ATVA 2013. LNCS, vol. 8172, pp. 506–515. Springer, Heidelberg (2013)
4. Arlt, S., Schäf, M.: Joogie: infeasible code detection for java. In: Madhusudan, P., Seshia, S.A. (eds.) CAV 2012. LNCS, vol. 7358, pp. 767–773. Springer, Heidelberg (2012)
5. Ball, T., Naik, M., Rajamani, S.K.: From symptom to cause: localizing errors in counterexample traces. SIGPLAN Not., 97–105 (2003)
6. Barnett, M., Leino, K.R.M.: Weakest-precondition of unstructured programs. SIGSOFT Softw. Eng. Notes, 82–87 (2005)
7. Barnett, M., Leino, K.R.M.: Weakest-precondition of unstructured programs. ACM SIGSOFT Software Engineering Notes 31, 82–87 (2005)

8. Beer, I., Ben-David, S., Eisner, C., Rodeh, Y.: Efficient detection of vacuity in ACTL formulas. In: Grumberg, O. (ed.) CAV 1997. LNCS, vol. 1254, pp. 279–290. Springer, Heidelberg (1997)

9. Bertolini, C., Schäf, M., Schweitzer, P.: Infeasible code detection. In: Joshi, R., Müller, P., Podelski, A. (eds.) VSTTE 2012. LNCS, vol. 7152, pp. 310–325. Springer, Heidelberg (2012)

10. Bjørner, N., Dutertre, B., de Moura, L.: Accelerating lemma learning using joins-DPLL (join). In: Int. Conf. Logic for Programming, Artif. Intell. and Reasoning, LPAR (2008)

11. Chockler, H., Kupferman, O., Vardi, M.Y.: Coverage metrics for temporal logic model checking. In: Margaria, T., Yi, W. (eds.) TACAS 2001. LNCS, vol. 2031, pp. 528–542. Springer, Heidelberg (2001)

12. Cytron, R., Ferrante, J., Rosen, B.K., Wegman, M.N., Zadeck, F.K.: Efficiently computing static single assignment form and the control dependence graph. TOPLAS, 451–490 (1991)

13. de Moura, L., Bjørner, N.: Relevancy propagation. Technical Report MSR-TR-2007-140, Microsoft Research (2007)

14. de Moura, L., Bjørner, N.S.: Z3: An efficient SMT solver. In: Ramakrishnan, C.R., Rehof, J. (eds.) TACAS 2008. LNCS, vol. 4963, pp. 337–340. Springer, Heidelberg (2008)

15. Dillig, I., Dillig, T., Aiken, A.: Static error detection using semantic inconsistency inference. In: PLDI (2007)

16. Engler, D., Chen, D.Y., Hallem, S., Chou, A., Chelf, B.: Bugs as deviant behavior: A general approach to inferring errors in systems code. In: Proceedings of the Eighteenth ACM Symposium on Operating Systems Principles, SOSP 2001, pp. 57–72. ACM, New York (2001)

17. Gheorghiu, M., Gurfinkel, A.: Vaquot: A tool for vacuity detection. Technical report. In: Proceedings of Tool Track, FM 2006 (2005)

18. Hoenicke, J., Leino, K.R., Podelski, A., Schäf, M., Wies, T.: Doomed program points. Formal Methods in System Design (2010)

19. Hovemeyer, D., Pugh, W.: Finding bugs is easy. ACM Sigplan Notices 39(12), 92–106 (2004)

20. Janota, M., Grigore, R., Moskal, M.: Reachability analysis for annotated code. In: SAVCBS (2007)

21. Karp, R.M.: Reducibility among combinatorial problems. In: Symposium on the Complexity of Computer Computations, The IBM Research Symposia Series, pp. 85–103. Plenum Press, New York (1972)

22. Leino, K.R.M., Millstein, T.D., Saxe, J.B.: Generating error traces from verification-condition counterexamples. Sci. Comput. Program. 55(1–3), 209–226 (2005)

23. Leino, K.R.M., Rümmer, P.: A Polymorphic intermediate verification language: design and logical encoding. In: Esparza, J., Majumdar, R. (eds.) TACAS 2010. LNCS, vol. 6015, pp. 312–327. Springer, Heidelberg (2010)

24. Rümmer, P.: A constraint sequent calculus for first-order logic with linear integer arithmetic. In: Cervesato, I., Veith, H., Voronkov, A. (eds.) LPAR 2008. LNCS, vol. 5330, pp. 274–289. Springer, Heidelberg (2008)

25. Schäf, M.: Bixie: Find contradictions in java code (2014). http://www.csl.sri.com/bixie-ws/
26. Schäf, M.: Gravy website (2014). https://github.com/martinschaef/gravy
27. Silva, J.P.M., Lynce, I., Malik, S.: Conflict-driven clause learning SAT solvers. In: Handbook of Satisfiability. Frontiers in Artificial Intelligence and Applications, vol. 185, pp. 131–153. IOS Press (2009)
28. Tomb, A., Flanagan, C.: Detecting inconsistencies via universal reachability analysis. In: ISSTA, pp. 287–297 (2012)
29. Wang, X., Zeldovich, N., Kaashoek, M.F., Solar-Lezama, A.: Towards optimization-safe systems: analyzing the impact of undefined behavior. In: SOSP, pp. 260–275. ACM (2013)

Shape Analysis with Connectors

Holger Siegel and Axel Simon[(✉)]

Institut für Informatik II, Technische Universität München, Garching, Germany
{holger.siegel,axel.simon}@in.tum.de

Abstract. We extend off-the-shelf shape analyses with the ability to infer numeric relations between directly or indirectly connected heap cells. Specifically, we introduce the concept of *connectors*, an instrumentation that retains relations between heap cells even if these cells are merged into summary nodes. Managing connectors is based on applying generic *fold* and *expand* operations on a numeric abstract domain. Connectors are thus a universal tool to enhance shape analyses with any numeric analysis. We show how connectors provide the ability to infer invariants of non-trivial heap structures such as sorted/skip lists and search trees.

1 Introduction

Proving the absence of NULL and dangling pointer dereferences in heap-manipulating programs requires the ability to deal with an a priori unbounded number of heap cells. The problem of summarizing these heap cells into a finite set of abstract heap cells is known as shape analysis. Traditionally, the shape of the heap is described using a logic such as separation logic [14] or three-valued logic analysis (TVLA) [15]. The challenge of both approaches is the synthesis of appropriate predicates that are able to express the invariants in the program.

While this challenge has been addressed quite successfully for the synthesis of shape predicates, the synthesis of numeric invariants remains a stronghold of numeric abstract domains. This paper therefore addresses how to combine an analysis of heap shapes with the inference of numeric relations on the contents of heap cells. Such a combination is a prerequisite to expressing invariants for sorted lists, search trees and other common data structures. The presented analysis extends any shape analysis that summarizes and materializes nodes in a graph that represents the abstracted heap. We therefore consider the actual shape analysis to be an oracle that informs our analysis about nodes that are combined into summaries and about accesses to nodes. In the latter case, we assume that a summarized node is being materialized. For the sake of the introduction, we also assume that the underlying shape analysis removes infeasible points-to edges.

Consider the sorted list in Fig. 1a) that is summarized into a single summary node in Fig. 1b). When analyzing the numeric content using the abstract domain

This work was supported by DFG Emmy Noether programme SI 1579/1.

© Springer International Publishing Switzerland 2015
K. Havelund et al. (Eds.): NFM 2015, LNCS 9058, pp. 343–358, 2015.
DOI: 10.1007/978-3-319-17524-9_24

a)

b)

c)

Fig. 1. Summarizing a linked list

of polyhedra [2], the cell content reduces to $1 \leq x \leq 3$ that we abbreviate by the interval notation $x \in [1,3]$. Note that summarizing the heap has discarded any information about the order of list elements. Figure 1c) shows one possible materialization of this summary where the order of list elements is not preserved.

The central idea is to construct so-called connectors between heap nodes that allow numeric domains to infer numeric relations between the nodes. Figure 2a) shows the connectors attached to the same three-element list as in Fig. 1a). Each connector holds copies of the contents of the cells that it connects. When summarizing the cells containing one and two, the connector between them stays on the edge that thereby points from the summary node to itself. When folding the next node onto the summary, the cell content and the connector are folded in unisono, yielding the state in Fig. 2b). The connector retains the invariant that the successor of each node contains the next larger value. When a cell is materialized from the summary, the corresponding connector is expanded too, as done in Fig. 2c). Once it is certain that one cell points to another, the content of the corresponding connector is equated to the two cells it connects. For instance, upon accessing the second list node, another cell and connector is materialized before the first connector $a, a+1$ is equated with the first and the new second heap cell. The equated connector can now be removed, yielding the heap in Fig. 2d). Note how equating the connector has restricted the content of the first cell to $a \in [1,2]$ and that of the second cell to $a+1 \in [2,3]$.

The connectors presented so far are *one-step* connectors. They are sufficient to express relations between neighboring nodes like sortedness properties, but they cannot express invariants of search trees, namely, that e.g. all elements reachable via the right branch of a node contain a greater value than the node itself. transitive properties like reachability. In order to express these reachability invariants, we additionally introduce *transitive* connectors that express a numeric relation between a cell and all cells that are transitively reachable from this cell.

In summary, we present an inference of numeric heap invariants that is generic in the shape analysis and in the numeric domains, based on these novel ideas:

- We use generic relational *fold* and *expand* operators [16] to infer numeric relations using any numeric domain. This improves over the state-of-the-art of tracking a fixed set of predicates as part of the shape analysis.
- We introduce the concepts of one-step and transitive connectors that express the relation between nodes on the heap. The handling of connectors is linked to the operations of a shape analysis which is a parameter of our framework.
- We illustrate how several important data structure invariants can be inferred.

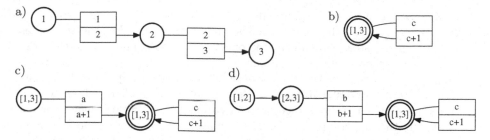

Fig. 2. Summarizing a linked list with one-step connectors

After presenting an interface to existing shape analyses and numeric domains, Section 3 introduces one-step connectors and details the interaction between the shape analysis and our connectors. Section 4 presents transitive connectors, followed by an example of their application to complex data strutures. Section 6 presents experimental results before Section 7 discusses related work and concludes.

2   Preliminaries

This section introduces the interface to an off-the shelf shape analysis and details necessary operations on the numeric domain.

2.1   Interface to the Shape Analysis

Let M denote a set of non-overlapping memory regions, consisting of heap-allocated cells and stack variables. Each region contains of a set of non-overlapping fields that are written $A.l$ with $A \in M$ and $l \in \Sigma$ where Σ denotes the set of all field names. As a convention, we write $A.x$, $A.y$ for fields containing numeric values and $A.p$, $A.q$ for fields containing pointers, although a field may contain either, a pointer or a value. For brevity, a stack variable $S.x$ is also written as x.

In order to be agnostic to the employed shape analysis, we define an interface that the shape analysis must implement and that is sufficient to infer connectors. Let S denote the set of abstract heap shapes and N denote an abstract numeric domain. Each state $s \in S$ of the shape analysis is paired with a numeric state $n \in N$ that holds valuations for all fields that contain numeric values, that is, $A.x$ and $A.y$ are variables in the numeric domain. We assume that the transfer function of assignment, tests etc. modify the numeric domain accordingly.

The interface between the shape analysis and our connector inference is given by only four functions. These may already be implemented by the shape analysis in order to summarize the numeric content of a cell. In this case, they have to be redirected to our connector inference. The four operations are as follows:

- Operation $fold_{S,C}$ merges the content of C (usually a concrete node) with that of S (usually a summary node), thereby removing all information on C. In the numeric domain, all fields $C.x_i$ are folded onto the respective fields $S.x_i$. The connector inference translates each call $fold_{S,C}$ to a call $fold_{S\ S_1...S_n, C\ C_1...C_n}$ that simultaneously folds nodes S and C and the nodes S_i, C_i that are stored in the connectors attached to S and C. By this, the numeric invariant of Fig. 2b) is inferred.

- Operation $expand_{S,C}$ is the inverse of operation $fold$. It duplicates the information in memory region S to a new memory region C. Its effect on the numeric domain and the connectors are symmetrical to those of $fold$, allowing to restore the numeric properties of the expanded memory region as shown in Fig. 2c). Both, the $fold$ and $expand$ mechanisms, are detailed below.
- Operations $assume(C.f \mapsto D)$ and $assume(C.f \not\mapsto D)$ informs the numeric domain (and the connector inference) that field $C.f$ definitely contains (respectively: does not contain) a pointer to region D.

Moreover, we require that the shape analysis provides a set $\mathcal{E} \subseteq Edges$ of possible edges where $Edges = \{A.l \mapsto B \mid A, B \in \mathcal{M}, l \in \Sigma\}$. In other words, $\mathcal{E}$ over-approximates all possible points-to configurations of the current abstract state. We now detail how two common shape analyses can provide the interface of $fold$, $expand$ and $assume$.

2.2   Separation Logic

Separation logic [14] describes a heap using a first order logic formula over heap assertions $A.l \mapsto B$, stating that the heap consists of a cell A with field l pointing to a cell B that is not necessarily part of this heap. A *separating conjunction* $h_1 * h_2$ states that the heap cells in h_1 and h_2 live in *separate* heaps. Thus, the heap described by formula $A.l \mapsto B * B.l \mapsto A$ consists of two different nodes pointing to each other. In contrast, both arguments of a logical disjunction describe the *same* heap, so that a expression $A.l \mapsto C \vee B.l \mapsto$ **null** stands for a single heap node which is named A or B. In the following, we associate each heap node with a distinct and unique name, so that each node in the heap is accompanied by exactly one node A in the numeric state. A set of possible edges $\mathcal{E}$ is then given by the set of all points-to terms $A.l \mapsto B$ in the formula.

Separation logic allows to summarize sets of similar heap cells by recursively defined predicates. For instance, a list from node A ending at B can be characterized by the predicate $ls(A, B) = (A.n \mapsto B) \vee (\exists C . A.n \mapsto C * ls(C, B))$. Each occurence of predicate $ls(A, \cdot)$ in a heap formula represents a list that is summarized into one summary node A. In the numeric domain, node A holds the summarized numeric content of this list. When a list element is accessed, the predicate $ls(A, B)$ is *unfolded* by replacing it with its right hand side. Since the right hand side consists of a disjunction $(A.n \mapsto B) \vee (\exists C . A.n \mapsto C * ls(C, B))$ of different heap shapes, both alternatives have to be considered separately in the numeric domain: replacing $ls(A, B)$ with $(A.n \mapsto B)$ just turns the summary node into a concrete node, so we do not need to adjust the numeric state. Replacing $ls(A, B)$ with $(\exists C . A.n \mapsto C * ls(C, B))$ introduces a new node C, therefore a new node is also introduced in the numeric domain via operation $expand_{A,C}$. Symmetrically, a formula that matches the right hand side of a predicate definition can be replaced by its left hand side. In this case a corresponding operation *fold*$_{A,C}$ is executed on the numeric domain. This mechanism allows to summarize any heap shape for which a recursive separation logic predicate exists.

Whenever a points-to relation $A.n \mapsto B$ is unconditionally true, operation *assume*$(A.n \mapsto C)$ should be executed on the numeric domain. Analogously, if a points-to relation $A.n \mapsto B$ is definitely unsatisfiable, then an *assume*$(A.n \not\mapsto B)$ operation should be executed.

2.3   Three-Valued Logic Analysis (TVLA)

The TVLA framework for shape analysis [15] represents the heap by a finite set of abstract summary nodes, each of them representing a set of concrete nodes. The shape of the heap is characterized by a set of user-supplied predicates. Usually, at least a *next*$(A.l, C)$ predicate is given, indicating whether a points-to edge $A.l \mapsto C$ exists. The set of *next*-predicates that occur in the current state defines the set of edges $\mathcal{E}$. A valuation function takes each predicate to a value in $\{0, \frac{1}{2}, 1\}$. Whenever the valuation of *next*$(A.l, C)$ changes to zero or one, a corresponding *assume*$(A.l \not\mapsto C)$ or *assume*$(A.l \mapsto C)$ operation is performed on the numeric state. Folding and expanding corresponds to summarizing and materializing a node in TVLA. During updating a cell, all involved predicates must map to zero or one in order to determine the semantics of an access. To this end, the state is temporarily duplicated for each involved predicate with value $\frac{1}{2}$. The task of updating a numeric state in the presence of a set of formulae has been addressed elsewhere [3]. Variants of TVLA refine the three-valued mapping with a Boolean formula, avoiding the duplication of the TVLA formula for $\frac{1}{2}$ values [13]. Moreover, the information in the Boolean formula can be folded and expanded in the same way as the numeric information [17], thereby giving a unified formulation of shape analysis as an analysis over numeric variables.

Given the interface to the shape analysis, we now turn to numeric domains.

2.4   Numeric Domain Operations

We illustrate our analysis on $N_{\mathcal{X}} := Poly_{\mathcal{X}}$, the numeric domain of convex polyhedra [2] over variables $\mathcal{X}$, although any other abstract domain may be used. In the context of our analysis, $\mathcal{X} = \{A.x, A.y, \ldots \mid A \in \mathcal{M}\}$, and we write N instead of $N_{\mathcal{X}}$ where the support set is clear from the context. We define the following three functions that return a new numeric state:

- Function $copy_{A,B} : N \to N$ adds a copy B of region A to a numeric state $n \in N$ by performing the assignment $B.l := A.l$ for all $A.l$ currently in n.
- Function $drop_A : N \to N$ eliminates all variables $A.l$ from a state $n \in N$. In the abstract domain of polyhedra, elimination of a variable x corresponds to a projection onto the Euclidian subspace without dimension x.
- Function $[\![A = B]\!] : N \to N$ restricts a state $n \in N$ by adding the constraint $A.l = B.l$ for every field $l \in \Sigma$, such that $A.l$ or $B.l$ occurs in n.

We require two more numeric domain functions that mirror the effect of *fold* and *expand* on memory regions. To this end, we recall the following definition [16]:

Definition. *Given the m dimensions* $ab\ldots \in \mathcal{X}^m$ *and m dimensions* $a'b'\ldots \in \mathcal{X}^m$, *define* $fold_{ab\ldots,a'b'\ldots} : N \to N$ *and* $expand : N \to N$ *as follows:*

$$fold_{ab\ldots,a'b'\ldots}(n) = drop_{a'b'\ldots}(n \sqcup swap_{ab\ldots,a'b'\ldots}(n))$$
$$expand_{ab\ldots,a'b'\ldots}(n) = n \sqcap swap_{ab\ldots,a'b'\ldots}(n)$$

where operation $drop_{a'b'\ldots}$ *eliminates the given variables (analogous to* $drop_A$) *and* $swap_{ab\ldots,a'b'\ldots}$ *exchanges the given primed and unprimed identifiers.*

The *fold* function merges the information over $a'b'\ldots$ with that over $ab\ldots$ and then removes $a'b'\ldots$. Intuitively, *fold* discards all relations between $ab\ldots$ and $a'b'\ldots$ but retains any relational information that $ab\ldots$ and $a'b'\ldots$ have with other variables. Symmetrically, *expand* duplicates relations within $ab\ldots$ to $a'b'\ldots$ but, unlike an assignment $a := a'$, induces no equality between a and a'. For instance, $expand_{ab,a'b'}(n)$ on a polyhedron n defined by the vertices $\langle a, b\rangle \in \{\langle 0,0\rangle, \langle 1,1\rangle\}$ yields $\langle a, b, a', b'\rangle \in \{\langle 0,0,0,0\rangle, \langle 0,0,1,1\rangle, \langle 1,1,0,0\rangle, \langle 1,1,1,1\rangle\}$. Note that the equality $a = b$ in the input state n has been preserved and duplicated to $a' = b'$ in the expanded state, but that $a = a'$ does not hold.

Applying *fold* and *expand* on memory regions S and C naturally translates to applying the corresponding numeric operations on the sequences of numeric variables $S.x\, S.y\ldots$ and $C.x\, C.y\ldots$. Care must be taken that both sequences contain the same sequence of field indices by possibly inserting lacking fields. In the sequel, we write $n := fold_{S,C}(n)$ to update a numeric state and assume that the translation to sequences of numeric variables is done implicitly.

These preliminary definitions suffice to introduce the connector inference.

3   One-Step Connectors

The connector inference tracks relational information between heap cells that preserves certain information that may otherwise be lost when heap cells are summarized. This section addresses the key questions about connectors, namely how to create them and how to use their information, by first introducing *one-step connectors* that are generalized to *transitive connectors* in the next section.

A one-step connector tracks the relation between two cells that are directly connected via a points-to edge. Thus, we define the state of the connector inference as a partial map $o : Edges \nrightarrow \mathcal{M} \times \mathcal{M}$. A connector between a field $A.l$ and a memory region B exists iff $o(A.l \mapsto B)$ is defined. In this case the tuple $\langle A', B'\rangle := o(A.l \mapsto B)$ is a connector that describes the contents of A and B in all states where the edge $A.l \mapsto B$ exists. Valuations for all fields $A'.x_i$, $B'.x_i$ are held in the numeric domain, so that relations between these fields can be inferred. Suppose that the summary node in Fig. 2b) is S and that its self-edge is $S.next$, the heap consists of a summary node S and a connector $S.next \mapsto S$ with $o(A.l \mapsto B) = \langle\langle S'.x, S'.next\rangle, \langle S''.x, S''.next\rangle\rangle$. Then the numeric domain holds the constraints $S.x \in [1,3]$, $S'.x = c$ and $S''.x = c + 1$ for some $c \in [1,2]$.

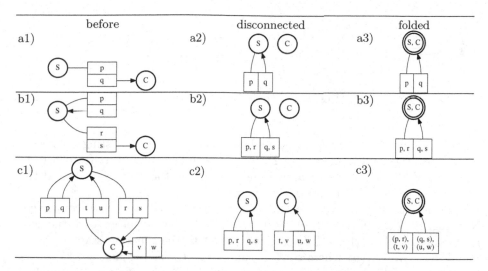

Fig. 3. Folding two cells. The result of simultaneously folding r onto p and s onto q is denoted by p, r and q, s. Folding t, v onto p, r is denoted by $(p, r), (t, v)$.

Creating Connectors. In order to curtail an information loss due to summarization, connectors have to be created before a memory region C is folded onto region S by intercepting the operation $fold(S, C)$. Based on the set of may-edges $\mathcal{E}$, we identify all edges $E \subseteq \mathcal{E}$ that are connected to S or to C and for which no connector exists. For each such edge $A.l \mapsto B \in E \setminus dom(o)$, we create two memory regions A', B', update the numeric state to $n := copy_{A,A'}(copy_{B,B'}(n))$ and extend o with the mapping from $A.l \mapsto B$ to $\langle A', B' \rangle$.

Folding Cells. When two regions S and C are folded using $fold(S, C)$, the connectors attached to S and C also have to be folded onto each other. A connector represents values of nodes *in case they are connected*, so for a non-existing edge arbitrary connectors may be introduced, as they will never be applied. Thus, when two nodes A and B are summarized where a connector $C.l \mapsto A$ but no corresponding connector $C.l \mapsto B$ exists, the connector $o(C.l \mapsto A)$ becomes the connector of the summarized node. Analogously for connectors $A.l \mapsto C$ and $B.l \mapsto C$. Connectors may be absent in two contexts, namely for connectors to other nodes than S or C and for edges between S and C, as detailed now.

The first step in folding two regions S and C is to ensure that no connectors between S and C exist, as these would be dangling once C is removed. Hence, any connector on the edge $C.l \mapsto S$ is "bent" to the edge $C.l \mapsto C$ as shown in Fig. 3a2). If a connector already exists for edge $C.l \mapsto C$, it is folded onto the bent connector as shown in Fig. 3b2). The edges from S to C are treated symmetrically, thereby giving a strategy for removing all edges between S and C. Figure 3 illustrates this strategy: In a2), the connector from S to C of the heap in a1) is bent to S, giving the heap in a3). In b1), the connector reaching from S to C is turned into a self-looping connector that reaches from S to S. This

a)

b)

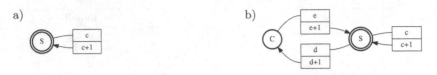

Fig. 4. Expanding a list element

requires its numeric content to be folded onto the already existing connector from S to itself, giving the heap b2). In c1), both the connectors from S to C and from C to S have to be folded onto the connector from S to S and the connector from C to C, respectively, giving the heap in c2).

The intermediate result are two nodes S and C that are not connected. Now regions S and C have to be folded onto each other together with the connectors attached to them. The goal is to update the numeric state to $n := fold_{S\,S_1...S_n,\,C\,C_1...C_n}(n)$ where $S_1...S_n$ and $C_1...C_n$ are sequences of connectors that are folded alongside the actual cells S and C. To this end, define sequences s and c as $s := S$ and $c := C$ and extend them with connectors:

- For each node $A \notin \{S, C\}$ for which connectors $\langle A', S' \rangle := o(A.l \mapsto S)$ and $\langle A'', C' \rangle := o(A.l \mapsto C)$ exist, add them to s and c by updating $s := sA'S'$ and $c := cA''C'$ and remove connector $A.l \mapsto C$ from o.
- For each node $A \notin \{S, C\}$ for which connectors $\langle S', A' \rangle := o(S.l \mapsto A)$ and $\langle C', A'' \rangle := o(C.l \mapsto A)$ exist, add them to s and c by updating $s := sA'S'$ and $c := cA''C'$ and remove connector $C.l \mapsto A$ from o.
- If there exist connectors $\langle S', S'' \rangle := o(S.l \mapsto S)$ and $\langle C', C'' \rangle := o(C.l \mapsto C)$, add them to s and c by updating $s := sS'S''$ and $c := cC'C''$ and remove connector $C.l \mapsto C$ from o.

Finally, the numeric content is folded by updating the numeric state to $n := fold_{s,c}(n)$. Now all connectors attached to C that had a corresponding connector attached to S are removed from o and their numeric contents are summarized.

Note that there may still be connectors attached to C that have no corresponding connector attached to S. These are "moved" to region S by updating o so that every connector $\langle A', C' \rangle := o(A.l \mapsto C)$ is replaced with a connector $A.l \mapsto S$ such that $\langle A', C' \rangle = o(A.l \mapsto S)$. Analogously, every connector $\langle A', C' \rangle := o(C.l \mapsto A)$ originating from C is replaced by a connector $S.l \mapsto A$ originating from S. The third column of Fig. 3 illustrates this situation. In a3) and b3) the connectors attached to S remain unchanged during summarization, whereas in c3) the connector attached to C is folded onto the connector attached to S together with the numeric contents of the nodes.

Expanding Summaries. Expanding a summary node S to a concrete node C is done by simply reverting the steps of folding two nodes to one summary node: First, S is expanded to an exact copy C, then each self-looping connector at S is expanded to a connector from S to C and finally each self-looping connector at C is bent to S. Figure 4a) shows a summary S of a consecutively numbered

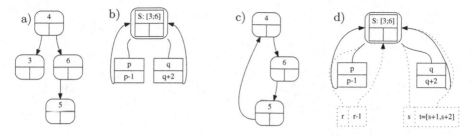

Fig. 5. summarizing a binary search tree

list. In Fig. 4b), a node C has been materialized and the connector $S.next \mapsto S$ has been expanded to connectors $S.next \mapsto C$ and $C.next \mapsto S$, describing every edge from C to S or vice versa, provided that it exists, points to the next higher value.

Applying Connectors. The information contained in a connector can be utilized whenever the shape analysis determines that an edge $A.l \mapsto B$ definitely exists. In this case, the connector $\langle A', B' \rangle := o(A.l \mapsto B)$ can be applied by updating state n to state $n := [\![A = A', B = B']\!](n)$. This operation is triggered by the shape analysis via operation $assume(A.l \mapsto B)$. In contrast, operation $assume(A.l \not\mapsto B)$ informs the connector inference that a connector is spurious and that the relations it expresses do not hold. In the first case, the information in the connector is redundant after applying it, whereas in the second case its information is not applicable. Hence, in both cases we remove the connector $A.l \mapsto B$ from o and A', B' from n using $drop_{A'} \circ drop_{B'}$.

Since relations between neighboring nodes are not always sufficient for describing complex heap structures, we now turn to *transitive* connectors.

4 Transitive Connectors

Consider summarizing the search tree in Fig. 5a). One-step connectors can express relations between a node and its left or right child. This is shown in Fig. 5b) where connector $S.l \mapsto S$ indicates that the left child is exactly one smaller and connector $S.r \mapsto S$ indicates that the right child is exactly one greater. However, the concrete heaps modeled by this abstraction include the heap shown in Fig. 5c), which obviously violates the search tree invariant as it is cyclic.

Since one-step connectors are insufficient for expressing certain invariants such as that of search trees, we now address how to generalize them to connectors that relate nodes that are indirectly connected via arbitrary paths. Considering the set of field names Σ as an alphabet, then the words over Σ describe possible paths that may connect one node with another. Suppose that we annotate each connector with the formal language that describes the set of possible paths for

a) $y \in \{x+1,\, x+2\}$
   $s \in \{r+1,\, r+2\}$

b) $y \in \{x+1,\, x+2\}$
   $t = q-1 \wedge t \in \{x+1,\, x+2\}$

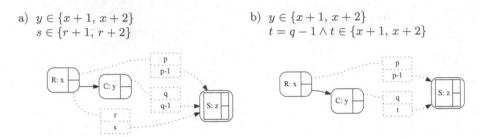

Fig. 6. Expanding a summarized tree with transitive connectors

which the connector models a relation. Then a one-step connector $A.l \mapsto B$ can be considered as tracking a relation for the one-elemented language $\{l\}$.

In principle, one can track connectors for any set of paths. For simplicity, we will confine this presentation to connectors that capture the relation between node A and all nodes reachable from A via some arbitrary path beginning in field $A.l$. Thus, we partition the possible paths into languages $\omega_l = l\Sigma^*$ for all field names $l \in \Sigma$. In the following, we will denote the set of paths connecting node A with node B via ω_l by $A.l \rightsquigarrow B$. The operations presented for these paths ω_l can straightforwardly be adopted to more specific paths.

Figure 5d) shows the summarized tree of Fig. 5a) with a dotted transitive connector $\langle r, r-1 \rangle$ for $S.l \rightsquigarrow S$, stating that, for each tree element, the nodes in the left subtree are exactly one smaller (implying at most one node), and a transitive connector $S.r \rightsquigarrow S$ whose content $\langle s, t \rangle$ with $t \in [s+1,\, s+2]$ states that all contents of a node's right subtree are strictly greater than that of S.

Creating Transitive Connectors. Transitive connectors are created in the same way as one-step connectors: For every pair of heap cells A and B and field $l \in \Sigma$ for which the set $\mathcal{E}$ of possible edges contains a path $p \in l\Sigma^*$ from A to B starting with field l, a transitive connector $A.l \rightsquigarrow B$ is created by copying the numeric contents of A and B into regions A' and B' in the numeric state, and a mapping from $(A.l \rightsquigarrow B)$ to $\langle A', B' \rangle$ is tracked. Since overapproximating the set of possible paths introduces connectors between unrelated heap cells, the precision of the transitive connectors crucially depends on the accuracy of set $\mathcal{E}$.

Folding and Expanding. Transitive connectors are folded and expanded in the same way as one-step connectors. Figure 6a) shows the tree of Fig. 5d) after expanding the summary two times and then following path r, that is, accessing contents of the root node's right child. The connector of path $R.r \rightsquigarrow C$ has been applied to the numeric content of R and C, forcing the numeric content y of C to be greater than the numeric content x of R. For the sake of presentation, we have omitted connectors originating at S and those targeting R.

Applying Transitive Connectors. In Fig. 6a), the connector for $R.r \rightsquigarrow S$ states that those nodes summarized in S that are reachable via the r field of R have greater numeric content that node R itself. We cannot apply this information directly to summary node S, since at this point the nodes abstracted in S that are reachable from node R via field r cannot be distinguished from those that are reachable from $R.l$. However, we know that $R.r$ definitely points to C, and so all fields reachable via $R.r$ are also reachable via node C, in particular, via fields $C.l$ and $C.r$. More generally, every node A that is reachable from C via paths $C.l \rightsquigarrow A$ or paths $C.r \rightsquigarrow A$ is also reachable via paths $R.r \rightsquigarrow A$. Thus, the information in connector $R.r \rightsquigarrow S$ is valid for $C.l \rightsquigarrow S$ and $C.r \rightsquigarrow S$.

Hence, we restrict the connectors $C.l \rightsquigarrow S$ and $C.r \rightsquigarrow S$ by expanding the connector $R.r \rightsquigarrow S$ as necessary and equating the instance. (Expansion is not necessary in our example, as there is only $C.l \rightsquigarrow S$.) This is done by equating the "source" value r of connector $R.r \rightsquigarrow S$ with x and equating the "target" value s of connector $R.r \rightsquigarrow S$ with the target value $q-1$ of connector $C.l \rightsquigarrow S$. The resulting state is shown in Fig. 6b), where target value t of connector $C.l \rightsquigarrow S$ is now restricted by $t = q - 1$ and $t \in \{x + 1, x + 2\}$, maintaining the invariant that the values of the left subtree of C are between the values of R and C.

5   Inferring Relational Heap Invariants

Since the numeric contents of all connectors are stored in a single domain, connector inference does not only infer relations between the heap cells a connector is attached to, but also between different connectors. This allows to infer invariants for more complex shapes like lists of lists. This section illustrates one such example.

Figure 7a) shows a linked list of sub-lists, each of them containing a numeric field, a pointer to the next list element and a pointer to a sub-list with numeric content. Similar to a skip list, this data structure fulfills the invariant that the entries of each sub-list are between the values of its own and the next list head. Figure 7b) shows the data structure with one-step connectors for the **next** fields and transitive connectors for the **sub** fields of the outer list after the sub-lists are summarized into one node S. For node A, the invariant restricting the entries of its sub-list is expressed by the transitive connector originating in A. Analogously for B, C and D. Summarizing node A with node B *simultaneously* folds node B and the two connectors attached to B onto A and the two connectors attached to A, thereby inferring the relation between the two connectors originating from each node. Summarizing the outer list yields the heap shown in Fig. 7c) where $q < t$ is inferred for the transitive connector $\langle p, q \rangle$ of $A.sub \rightsquigarrow S$ where t is in the one-step connector $A.next \mapsto A$, thereby enforcing the desired sub-list invariant. This example shows that, although being agnostic of the analyzed heap shapes, the combination of connectors and relational numeric domains can even infer properties of hierarchical data structures.

6   Experimental Work

Our prototype implementation consists of the shape analysis described in [17], extended with one-step and transitive connectors. As the numeric domain, we

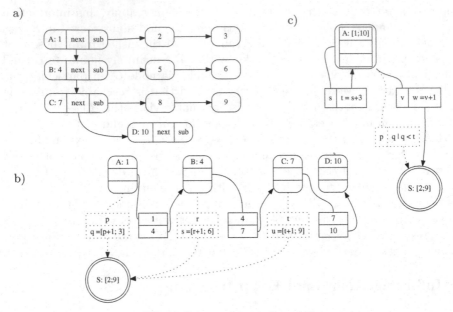

Fig. 7. Summarizing a list of lists

use the implementation of the Octagon domain [11]. While the shape analysis is written in Java, the Octagon domain is taken from the Apron library [8].

Figure 8 shows the experimental results measured on an Intel Core i7 with 1.6 Ghz. All programs are evaluated in three variations: without connectors, with one-step connectors and with transitive connnectors. The first program creates a six-elemented linked list with values in ascending order that is abstracted into one summary node by the analyzer. By inspecting the resulting state, we have verified, whether the sortedness of the list is still maintained by the summarized heap. Without connectors, all relational information between the summarized nodes is lost, whereas in the variants with one-step and transitve connectors, a connector establishes the relation between each node and its successor. The second program accesses and thereby materializes the first three nodes of a summarized sorted list, verifying that they are indeed in ascending order. As before, both one-step and transitive connectors are able to maintain sortedness.

Similarly to the first and second program, the third and fourth program of Fig. 8 summarize and expand a list of consecutive numbers. By inspecting the summarized state and by materializing list elements, we have checked whether the invariant that all list elements are increasing by one is inferred. Here, transitive connectors are not sufficient to verify that the difference between each node and its successor is exactly one, because the transitive connector models the numeric relation between a node and *all* following nodes.

The last two programs of Fig. 8 summarize the binary search tree of Fig. 9. Although the one-step connectors express that the left child of each node has a

	connectors	time (s)	verified
summarize sorted list	—	0.48	✗
	one-step	0.88	✓
	transitive	1.64	✓
unroll sorted list	—	0.73	✗
	one-step	2.68	✓
	transitive	6.49	✓
summarize numbered list	—	0.52	✗
	one-step	0.86	✓
	transitive	1.70	✗
unroll numbered list	—	0.76	✗
	one-step	2.73	✓
	transitive	6.61	✗
summarize tree	—	0.69	✗
	one-step	2.21	✗
	transitive	4.38	✓
access leaf	—	1.20	✗
	one-step	64,84	✗
	transitive	673,60	✓

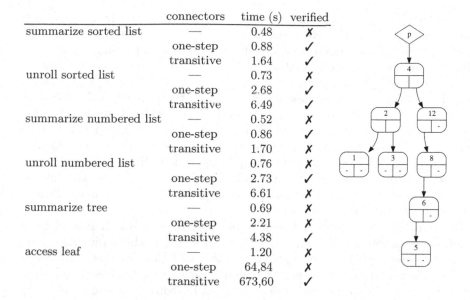

Fig. 8. Evaluation of our implementation   **Fig. 9.** The search tree

lower value and, respectively, that the right child of each node has greater value, they cannot express the crucial invariant that all nodes in the right subtree are greater than the root node. The last program descends into the right subtree and checks whether its leftmost leaf has value 5, which amounts to evaluating the C-like assertion `assert(p->r->l->l->val == 5)`. Indeed, transitive connectors succeed in proving this property. The timings show a drawback of our implementation: The complexity of the Octagon domain is quadratic in the number of variables, so that the runtime becomes cubic in the number of connectors that have to be applied. Moreover, computing the set of all transitive connectors is costly, since in the best case it is based on the Floyd-Warshall algorithm that runs in n^3 steps when creating the n^2 connectors where n is the number of reachable nodes.

7   Related Work

Ferrara et al. [3] extend a TVLA shape analysis with a numeric abstract domain. They address the challenge of modifying the single numeric domain when the TVLA analysis has inferred several possible heaps at a given program point. Their work thereby shows how TVLA can be combined with our connector inference. However, they use a one-dimensional *fold* and *expand* operation [5] that cannot retain relations between variables in a heap cell. In our context, this is particularly critical, as a connector needs to express relations between at least two variables to be of use. Thus, the use of relational *fold* and *expand* operations [16] is a prerequisite for tracking summarized relations.

Magill et al. [9] enhance a separation logic based shape analysis with a numeric analysis. The idea is to generate an arithmetic program from counterexamples that the shape analysis provides. Thus, the result of the shape analysis is refined whenever the numeric analysis infers that a counterexample is spurious.

Nguyen et al. [12] use predefined numeric predicates in a separation-logic based verification tool. They can verify various various length and sortedness properties, but they cannot infer any numeric relations and rely on user-supplied predicates. Inlining (unfolding) shape definitions creates a new instance of a numeric relation and thereby corresponds to our *expand* operation. Analogously, their fold operation corresponds to our *fold* operation. However, note that a fold operation in separation logic may fail if no predicate matches the current formula. The advantage of using *fold* on numeric domains is that new relations and hence new invariants can be inferred.

Bouajjani et al. [1] introduce *data words abstract domains* that model the numeric contents of linked lists. While their approach is able to infer numeric invariants like sortedness, it is limited to sequential data structures.

McCloskey et al. [10] implement a similar invariant checker based on canonical abstraction [15]. While the set of user-defined predicates is fixed, they infer numeric invariants using numeric abstract domains. Their approach is able to handle complex hierarchical shapes such as lists of trees. Creating hierarchical invariants amounts to summarizing a group of heap nodes onto another group. While the generic *fold* and *expand* operations would, in principle, allow this, our handling of edges between objects that are to be folded currently only caters for two single objects to be folded. Future work will address this shortcoming.

Further afield is the work of Fu [4] that focuses on scalability. Here, an upfront points-to analysis is run to obtain an approximation of possible heap structures. He shows that on this approximated structure a numeric analysis can be implemented efficiently.

Gulwani et al. [6] infer sizes and offsets into memory partitions by combining a generic shape analysis with relational numeric abstract domains. Their approach is based on an on-demand reduction between both domains. Our method of combining shape analysis with numeric analysis merely refines the shape analysis and in particular does not need to use a reduction operator in order to propagate information. Instead, all information is propagated towards the numeric domain. This alleviates the implementor from deciding when to apply the reduction.

Halbwachs et al. [7] verify algorithms that iterate over some arrays A and B simultaneously. They abstract each array A as a current element $A[i]$ at position i and summaries for the partitions before and after position i. Whenever index variable i changes, the summaries are weakly updated *simultaneously* with the current values of $A[i]$ and $B[i]$. In our approach, this simultaneous weak update corresponds to folding a connectors that spans between $A[i]$ and $B[i]$ onto a summarized connector.

Several analyses address the inference of metaproperties such as the length of lists [6, 9, 12]. Our connector inference is a universal refinement technique that also applies to these analyses. For instance, the size of a list can be analyzed by tracking the length of the remaining list in each list element. Analogously, the depth of a tree can be tracked by annotating each node with the distance to its leaves.

8 Conclusion

We proposed an analysis of the numeric contents of heap shapes that is able to infer numeric relations between different but related heap cells. Based on generic relational *fold* and *expand* operations, any numeric abstract domain can be used for this inference. We illustrated that invariants of complex data structures can be inferred automatically and described how established shape analyses like separation logic and TVLA can be enhanced with the proposed connector inference.

References

1. Bouajjani, A., Drăgoi, C., Enea, C., Rezine, A., Sighireanu, M.: Invariant synthesis for programs manipulating lists with unbounded data. In: Touili, T., Cook, B., Jackson, P. (eds.) CAV 2010. LNCS, vol. 6174, pp. 72–88. Springer, Heidelberg (2010)
2. Cousot, P., Halbwachs, N.: Automatic discovery of linear constraints among variables of a program. In: Principles of Programming Languages, Tucson, Arizona, USA, pp. 84–97. ACM, January 1978
3. Ferrara, P., Fuchs, R., Juhasz, U.: TVAL+: TVLA and value analyses together. In: Eleftherakis, G., Hinchey, M., Holcombe, M. (eds.) SEFM 2012. LNCS, vol. 7504, pp. 63–77. Springer, Heidelberg (2012)
4. Fu, Z.: Modularly combining numeric abstract domains with points-to analysis, and a scalable static numeric analyzer for java. In: McMillan, K.L., Rival, X. (eds.) VMCAI 2014. LNCS, vol. 8318, pp. 282–301. Springer, Heidelberg (2014)
5. Gopan, D., DiMaio, F., Dor, N., Reps, T., Sagiv, M.: Numeric domains with summarized dimensions. In: Jensen, K., Podelski, A. (eds.) TACAS 2004. LNCS, vol. 2988, pp. 512–529. Springer, Heidelberg (2004)
6. Gulwani, S., Lev-Ami, T., Sagiv, M.: A combination framework for tracking partition sizes. In: Principles of Programming Languages, Savannah, Georgia, USA. ACM, January 2009
7. Halbwachs, N., Péron, M.: Discovering properties about arrays in simple programs. In: Gupta, R., Amarasinghe, S.P. (eds.) Programming Language Design and Implementation, Tucson, Arizona, USA, pp. 339–348. ACM, June 2008
8. Jeannet, B., Miné, A.: Apron: a library of numerical abstract domains for static analysis. In: Bouajjani, A., Maler, O. (eds.) CAV 2009. LNCS, vol. 5643, pp. 661–667. Springer, Heidelberg (2009)
9. Magill, S., Berdine, J., Clarke, E., Cook, B.: Arithmetic strengthening for shape analysis. In: Nielson, H.R., Filé, G. (eds.) SAS 2007. LNCS, vol. 4634, pp. 419–436. Springer, Heidelberg (2007)
10. McCloskey, B., Reps, T., Sagiv, M.: Statically inferring complex heap, array, and numeric invariants. In: Cousot, R., Martel, M. (eds.) SAS 2010. LNCS, vol. 6337, pp. 71–99. Springer, Heidelberg (2010)
11. Miné, A.: The Octagon Abstract Domain. Higher-Order and Symbolic Computation **19**, 31–100 (2006)

12. Nguyen, H.H., David, C., Qin, S.C., Chin, W.-N.: Automated verification of shape and size properties via separation logic. In: Cook, B., Podelski, A. (eds.) VMCAI 2007. LNCS, vol. 4349, pp. 251–266. Springer, Heidelberg (2007)
13. Podelski, A., Wies, T.: Boolean heaps. In: Hankin, C., Siveroni, I. (eds.) SAS 2005. LNCS, vol. 3672, pp. 268–283. Springer, Heidelberg (2005)
14. Reynolds, J.C.: Separation logic: a logic for shared mutable data structures. In: Logic in Computer Science, Copenhagen, Denmark, pp. 55–74. IEEE (2002)
15. Sagiv, M., Reps, T., Wilhelm, R.: Parametric Shape Analysis via 3-Valued Logic. Transactions on Programming Languages and Systems **24**(3), 217–298 (2002)
16. Siegel, H., Simon, A.: Summarized dimensions revisited. In: Mauborgne, L. (ed.) Workshop on Numeric and Symbolic Abstract Domains, ENTCS, Venice, Italy. Springer, Heidelberg, September 2011
17. Siegel, H., Simon, A.: FESA: fold- and expand-based shape analysis. In: Jhala, R., De Bosschere, K. (eds.) Compiler Construction. LNCS, vol. 7791, pp. 82–101. Springer, Heidelberg (2013)

Automated Conflict-Free Concurrent Implementation of Timed Component-Based Models

Ahlem Triki[1]([✉]), Borzoo Bonakdarpour[2],
Jacques Combaz[1], and Saddek Bensalem[1]

[1] University Grenoble Alpes/CNRS, VERIMAG, Grenoble, France
ahlem.triki@imag.fr
[2] McMaster University, Hamilton, ON, Canada

Abstract. Correct implementation of concurrent real-time systems has always been a tedious task due to their inherent complex structure; concurrency introduces a great deal of non-determinism, which can potentially conflict with meeting timing constraints. In this paper, we focus on model-based concurrent implementation of timed models. Our *abstract* models consist of a set of components interacting with each other using multi-party interactions. Each component is internally subject to a set of timing constraints. We propose a chain of transformations that starts with an abstract model as input and generates correct-by-construction executable code as output. We show that all transformed models are observationally equivalent to the abstract model through bisimulation proofs and, hence, all functional properties of the abstract model are preserved. To facilitate developing the proofs of correctness, each transformation obtains a model by incorporating a subset of *physical* constraints (e.g., type of communication and global clock synchronization).

1 Introduction

Although concurrent computing is widely used nowadays, especially due to the recent advances in the multi-core and GPU technologies, implementation and deployment of correct concurrent applications are still time-consuming, error-prone, and hardly predictable tasks. This problem becomes even more challenging when the concurrent application is required to meet a set of timing constraints as well, for instance, in computation-intensive real-time embedded systems. This is due to the fact that the developer of a real-time concurrent application not only has to consider typical problems in concurrency (e.g., deadlock/livelock freedom, race conditions, etc), but also should ensure that all subtle interleavings of the application meet the timing constraints.

Model-based software development is a promising approach, where a chain of steps starting from a specification leads to an implementation on a given

---

This research was partially funded by projects Artemis AIPP Arrowhead and French BGLE Manycorelabs.

K. Havelund et al. (Eds.): NFM 2015, LNCS 9058, pp. 359–374, 2015.
DOI: 10.1007/978-3-319-17524-9_25

execution platform. It involves the use of transformation methods and tools for progressively deriving the implementation by making adequate design choices. Such transformations ensure functional correctness, software line productivity, and incorporate extra-functional properties such as timing constraints. Although there have recently been plausible efforts in model-based automated implementation of distributed (e.g., [7,13]) and real-time (e.g., [1,11]) systems, we currently lack techniques that obtain executable real-time concurrent code from an abstract model of a system. This problem is particularly challenging, as one has to develop transformations for different levels of abstractions, each taking into account certain physical constraints (e.g., time, communication, synchronization, etc), and each transformation should add minimal overhead while maintaining a high level of parallelism. With this motivation, in this paper, we propose an automated method for producing efficient and correct-by-construction multi-threaded real-time implementation from an abstract component-based timed model. Our abstract models are expressed in the timed BIP (Behavior, Interaction, Priority) formalism [5]. BIP is a well-founded component-based framework, where the *behavior* of each component (similar to timed automata [2]) is a Petri net or transition system subject to local timing constraints expressed by Boolean expressions over logical dense-time clock variables. A BIP model encompasses high-level multi-party *interactions* for synchronizing components (e.g., rendezvous and broadcast) and dynamic *priorities* for scheduling between interactions.

Our method consists of successive transformations that starts with a timed BIP model and terminates with an implementation. Intermediate transformation steps augment the output model with communication constraints and a physical time watching mechanism, such that each step results in a model closer to an actual implementation. These transformations are described as follows:

Decentralization. In the abstract model, each component may depend upon global synchronization with other components to execute a local step. Indeed, executing a component transition is possible only when an interaction involving that transition is executed. To decide whether an interaction can be executed, one has to consider all participating components. In a concurrent setting, however, each component can only rely on its local knowledge to decide whether to execute a transition. Thus, our first transformation builds a model where additional components are responsible for scheduling interactions, based on the information received from the input model's components. Our transformation creates *conflict-free* schedulers, where schedulers do not need to interact with each other in order to resolve distributed conflicts. A distributed conflict refers to the situation where two or more interactions are enabled in the distributed implementation, but the abstract model semantics allows execution of only one.

Logical Clock Removal. This transformation step builds a model that is robust to execution delay. This is done through decoupling logical and physical time. At this step, the two of them are assumed to be identical; i.e., communication occurs instantaneously (no delay) and component clocks are perfect (no drifts). This is the main reason that our target concurrent execution platform is *multi-process* applications, where all processes reside in the same machine and share a single clock. Unlike the logical clocks, the single clock introduced in this step is never reset and measures the absolute real time elapsed since the system starts executing. This transformation step is parametrized by a set of (observable) interactions whose constraints have to be met. We show that the model obtained in this step is observationally equivalent to the input abstract model through a bisimulation proof and, hence, all functional properties of the abstract model are preserved.

Implementation. This transformation creates a set of independent executables that communicate through asynchronous message passing and may read the value of the single global hardware clock of the platform.

The rest of this paper is structured as follows. In Section 2, we present the preliminary concepts on timed BIP models. Section 3 formalizes the point-to-point communication physical constraints. Our step-wise transformations are formally described in Sections 4 and 5. Related work is discussed in Section 6. Finally, we make concluding remarks in Section 7. For reasons of space, all proofs, implementation and experimental results appear in the appendix.

2 Basic Semantic Model of BIP

In this section, we present the operational *global state* semantics of BIP [4]. BIP is a component framework for constructing systems by superposing three layers of modeling: Behavior, Interaction, and Priority. In this paper we do not consider priorities. In Subsection 2.2, we formally define atomic components. The notion of composite components is presented in Subsection 2.3.

2.1 Notations

Given a variable x, the *domain* of x is the set $\mathcal{D}(x)$ of all values possibly taken by x. Given a set of variables X, a *valuation* of X is a function $v : X \to \bigcup_{x \in X} \mathcal{D}(x)$ assigning a value to each variable of X, that is, such that for all x $v(x) \in \mathcal{D}(x)$. We denote by $\mathcal{V}(X)$ the set of all possible valuations of X. The restriction of $v \in \mathcal{V}(X)$ to a subset of variables $X' \subseteq X$ is the valuation $v_{|X'} \in \mathcal{V}(X')$ that coincides with v on X', that is, $v_{|X'}(x) = v(x)$ for all $x \in X'$. When it is not ambiguous, we write v also for $v_{|X'}$.

Given valuations $v \in \mathcal{V}(X)$ and $v' \in \mathcal{V}(X')$ of variables X and X' such that $X' \subseteq X$, we denote by $v[X' \leftarrow v']$ the valuation of X that coincides with v' for all variables of X', and with v for all variables of $X \setminus X'$. It is defined by:

$$v[X' \leftarrow v'](x) = \begin{cases} v'(x) \text{ if } x \in X' \\ v(x) \text{ otherwise.} \end{cases}$$

When all variables in X have the same domain $\mathcal{D}$, and given value $k \in \mathcal{D}$, we also denote by k the constant valuation assigning k to all variables of X.

A *guard* is a predicate on a set of variables X. Given a guard g on X and a valuation $v \in \mathcal{V}(X)$, we denote by $g(v) \in \{\texttt{false}, \texttt{true}\}$ the evaluation of g for v. An *update function* $f : \mathcal{V}(X) \to \mathcal{V}(X)$ for variables X is used to assign new values $f(v)$ to variables in X from their current values v. It extends to any larger set of variables $X' \supseteq X$ considering that extra variables $X' \setminus X$ are unchanged, i.e., f transforms $v \in \mathcal{V}(X')$ into $v[X \leftarrow f(v)]$.

Timing Constraints and Time Progress Conditions. In order to measure time progress, we use *clocks* that are variables advancing with the same rate [2] and ranging over real numbers. We denote by $\mathbb{R}_{\geq 0}$ the set of non-negative reals, and by $\mathbb{Z}_{\geq 0}$ the set of non-negative integers.

Timing constraints are used to specify when actions of a system are enabled. Given a set of clocks C, we consider atomic constraints $c \sim k$ where $c \in \mathsf{C}$, $k \in \mathbb{Z}_{\geq 0}$, and $\sim$ is a comparison operator such that $\sim \in \{\leq, =, \geq\}$. They are used to build *timing constraints* defined by the following grammar: $\mathsf{tc} := \mathsf{true} \mid \mathsf{false} \mid c \sim k \mid \mathsf{tc} \wedge \mathsf{tc}$. Notice that any timing constraint tc can be put into a conjunction of the form:

$$\mathsf{tc} = \bigwedge_{c \in \mathsf{C}} l_c \leq c \leq u_c, \tag{1}$$

such that for all $c \in \mathsf{C}$, $l_c \in \mathbb{Z}_{\geq 0}$ and $u_c \in \mathbb{Z}_{\geq 0} \cup \{+\infty\}$. The evaluation of a timing constraint tc for a valuation $t \in \mathcal{V}(\mathsf{C})$ of clocks C is the Boolean value $\mathsf{tc}(t)$ obtained by replacing in tc each clock c by its value $t(c)$.

Time progress conditions are used to specify whether time can progress at a given state of the system. They correspond to a special case of timing constraint in which atomic constraints are restricted to the form $c \leq k$. Notice that a time progress condition put in the form of (1) is such that for all $c \in \mathsf{C}$, $l_c = 0$.

2.2   Atomic Components

An *atomic component* is described as a *1-Safe Petri net* extended with local *variables* and clocks, consisting of a set of *places* and a set of *transitions*. Each transition is labeled by a *port*, a *guard* on local variables combined with a timing constraint on clocks, and an update function. Ports are used for communication among different components. Each port *exports* a subset of variables of the component.

Definition 1. *A Petri net is defined by a triple* $S = (L, P, T)$, *where* L *is a set of places,* P *is a set of ports, and* $T \subseteq 2^L \times P \times 2^L$ *is a set of transitions. A transition* τ *is a triple* $(^\bullet\tau, p, \tau^\bullet)$, *where* $^\bullet\tau$ *is the set of* input places of τ *and* $\tau^\bullet$ *is the set of* output places of τ. ∎

A Petri net is often modeled as a directed bipartite graph $G = (L \cup T, E)$. Places are represented by circular vertices and transitions are represented by rectangular vertices (see Figure 1). The set of directed edges E is the union of the sets $\{(\ell, \tau) \in L \times T \mid \ell \in {}^\bullet\tau\}$ and $\{(\tau, \ell) \in T \times L \mid \ell \in \tau^\bullet\}$. We depict the *state* of a Petri net by marking its places with tokens [12]. We say that a place is *marked* if it contains a token. A transition τ is *enabled* at a state if all its input places $^\bullet\tau$ are marked. Upon the execution of τ, tokens of input places $^\bullet\tau$ are removed and tokens in output places in $\tau^\bullet$ are added.

Given an initial state $m_0 \subseteq L$, a Petri net (L, P, T) is *1-Safe* if for any execution from m_0, output places of enabled transitions are never marked. The

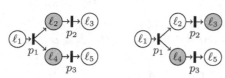

Fig. 1. A simple Petri net

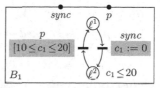

Fig. 2. An atomic component

behavior of a 1-Safe Petri net (L, P, T) is defined as a finite labeled transition system $(2^L, P, \rightarrow)$, where 2^L is the set of states, P is the set of labels, and $\rightarrow \subseteq 2^L \times P \times 2^L$ is the set of transitions defined as follows. We have $(m, p, m') \in \rightarrow$, denoted by $m \xrightarrow{p} m'$, if there exists $\tau = ({}^\bullet\tau, p, \tau^\bullet) \in T$ such that ${}^\bullet\tau \subseteq m$ and $m' = (m \backslash {}^\bullet\tau) \cup \tau^\bullet$. In this case, we say that p is *enabled* at m. We say that the Petri net (L, P, T) is *deterministic*, if for any execution from m_0 any two transitions $\tau_1 \neq \tau_2$ labeled by same port p are not simultaneously enabled at any state.

An *atomic component* is essentially a timed automaton [2] labeled by ports and extended with variables, whose states and transitions are given by the behavior of a deterministic 1-Safe Petri net.

Definition 2 (Atomic Component). *An atomic component B is defined by $B = (L, P, T, \mathsf{C}, X, \{X_p\}_{p \in P}, \{g_\tau\}_{\tau \in T}, \{\mathsf{tc}_\tau\}_{\tau \in T}, \{f_\tau\}_{\tau \in T}, \{\mathsf{tpc}_\ell\}_{\ell \in L})$ where:*

- *(L, P, T) is a deterministic 1-Safe Petri net*
- *C is a set of clocks.*
- *X is a set of discrete variables.*
- *For each port $p \in P$, $X_p \subseteq X$ is the set of variables exported by p (i.e., variables visible from outside the component through port p).*
- *For each transition $\tau \in T$, g_τ is a guard on X, tc_τ is a timing constraint over C, and $f_\tau : \mathcal{V}(X) \times \mathcal{V}(\mathsf{C}) \rightarrow \mathcal{V}(X) \times \mathcal{V}(\mathsf{C})$ is a function that updates the set of variables X and may reset a subset of clocks $\mathsf{R}_\tau \subseteq \mathsf{C}$.*
- *For each place $l \in L$, tpc_l is a time progress condition.* ∎

Example 1. Figure 2 shows an atomic component. The set of clocks is $\{c_1\}$. The set of places is $\{\ell^1, \ell^2\}$ where ℓ^1 has time progress condition $c_1 \leq 20$. The set of ports is $\{p, sync\}$ and there is no discrete variable. There are two transitions: $\tau_1 = (\ell^1, sync, \ell^2)$ and $\tau_2 = (\ell^2, p, \ell^1)$. The transition τ_1 resets clock c_1 and the transition τ_2 is guarded by a timing constraint on clock c_1.

Definition 3 (Atomic Component Semantics). *The semantics of an atomic component $B = (L, P, T, \mathsf{C}, X, \{X_p\}_{p \in P}, \{g_\tau\}_{\tau \in T}, \{\mathsf{tc}_\tau\}_{\tau \in T}, \{f_\tau\}_{\tau \in T}, \{\mathsf{tpc}_l\}_{l \in L})$ is defined as the labeled transition system $(Q_B, P_B, \xrightarrow{B})$, where*

- *$Q_B = 2^L \times \mathcal{V}(X) \times \mathcal{V}(\mathsf{C})$ is the set of states.*
- *$P_B = P \cup \mathbb{R}_{\geq 0}$ is set of labels: ports or time values.*
- *$\xrightarrow{B} \subseteq Q_B \times P_B \times Q_B$ is the set of labeled transitions defined as follows. Let (m, v, t) and (m', v', t') be two states, $p \in P$, and $\delta \in \mathbb{R}_{\geq 0}$ be a delay.*

Jump transitions. *We have* $(m, v, t) \xrightarrow[B]{p} (m', v', t')$, *iff transition* $\tau = (^\bullet\tau, p, \tau^\bullet)$ *is enabled at* m *in the Petri net* (L, P, T) *and* $g_\tau(v) \wedge \mathsf{tc}_\tau(t)$ *is* true. *In this case, we say that* p *is enabled from* (m, v, t). *Notice that* t' *satisfies* $t' = t[\mathsf{R}_\tau \leftarrow 0]$, *where* R_τ *is the set of clocks reset by* τ.

Delay transitions. *We have* $(m, v, t) \xrightarrow[B]{\delta} (m, v, t+\delta)$ *if we have* $\bigwedge_{\ell \in m} \mathsf{tpc}_\ell(t+\delta)$ *is* true, *where* $t + \delta$ *is the usual notation for the valuation defined by* $(t + \delta)(c) = t(c) + \delta$ *for any* $c \in \mathsf{C}$. ∎

An atomic component B can execute a transition $\tau = (^\bullet\tau, p, \tau^\bullet)$ from a state (m, v, t) if its guard is met by the valuation v and its timing constraint is met by the valuation t. From state (m, v, t), B can also wait for $\delta > 0$ time units if $\bigwedge_{\ell \in m} \mathsf{tpc}_\ell(t + \delta)$ stays true. Waiting for δ time units increases all the clock values by δ. Notice that the execution of a jump transition is instantaneous and time elapses only on states. The semantics presented here is slightly different from the one found in [2], as we consider time progress conditions instead of invariants. Unlike invariants, an atomic component B may reach a state (m, v, t) violating the corresponding time progress condition $\bigwedge_{\ell \in m} \mathsf{tpc}_\ell$. In this case B cannot wait and is forced to execute a transition from (m, v, t). In the following, we consider systems that cannot reach states violating time progress conditions.

2.3   Composite Components

A composite component is built from a set of n atomic components $\{B_i = (L_i, P_i, T_i, \mathsf{C}_i, X_i, \{X_p\}_{p \in P_i}, \{g_\tau\}_{\tau \in T_i}, \{\mathsf{tc}_\tau\}_{\tau \in T_i}, \{f_\tau\}_{\tau \in T_i}, \{\mathsf{tpc}_\ell\}_{\ell \in L_i})\}_{i=1}^n$, such that their respective sets of places, ports, clocks, and discrete variables are pairwise disjoint; i.e., for any two $i \neq j$ from $\{1, \ldots, n\}$, we have $L_i \cap L_j = \emptyset$, $P_i \cap P_j = \emptyset$, $\mathsf{C}_i \cap \mathsf{C}_j = \emptyset$, and $X_i \cap X_j = \emptyset$. We denote $P = \bigcup_{i=1}^n P_i$ the set of all the ports in the composite component, $L = \bigcup_{i=1}^n L_i$ the set of all places, $\mathsf{C} = \bigcup_{i=1}^n \mathsf{C}_i$ the set of all clocks, and $X = \bigcup_{i=1}^n X_i$ the set of all variables.

Definition 4 (Interaction). *An* interaction a *between atomic components* $\{B_i\}_{i=1}^n$ *is a subset of ports* $a \subseteq P$, *such that it contains at most one port of every component, that is,* $|a \cap P_i| \leq 1$ *for all* $i \in \{1, \ldots, n\}$.
The set X_a *of variables available to an interaction* a *is given by* $X_a = \bigcup_{p \in a} X_p$. *We associate to* a *its guard* G_a *and its update function* F_a *over* X_a. ∎

Since an interaction a uses at most one port of every component, we denote $a = \{p_i\}_{i \in I}$, where $I \subseteq \{1, \ldots, n\}$. A component B_i is *involved* in a if $i \in I$.

Definition 5 (Composite Component). *We denote by* $B \stackrel{def}{=} \gamma(B_1, \ldots, B_n)$ *the* composite component *obtained by applying a set of interactions* γ *to the set of atomic components* $\{B_i\}_{i=1}^n$. *It is defined by the atomic component* $B = (L, \gamma, T, \mathsf{C}, X, \{X_a\}_{a \in \gamma}, \{g_\tau\}_{\tau \in T}, \{\mathsf{tc}_\tau\}_{\tau \in T}, \{f_\tau\}_{\tau \in T}, \{\mathsf{tpc}_\ell\}_{\ell \in L})$ *as follows.*

- *Given an interaction* $a = \{p_i\}_{i \in I}$ *of* γ, *a transition* $\tau = (\ell, a, \ell')$ *is in* T *if its projection* $\tau_i = (\ell_i, p_i, \ell'_i) = (\ell \cap L_i, a \cap P_i, \ell' \cap L_i)$ *on* B_i *is a transition of* B_i *(i.e.* $\tau_i \in T_i$), *for all* $i \in I$.

- The guard g_τ of transition τ is $g_\tau = G_a \wedge \bigwedge_{i \in I} g_{\tau_i}$.
- The timing constraint tc_τ of τ is $\mathsf{tc}_\tau = \bigwedge_{i \in I} \mathsf{tc}_{\tau_i}$.
- We have $f_\tau(v, t) = (f_{\tau_1} \circ \cdots \circ f_{\tau_n})(F_a(v), t)$, where f_{τ_i} is the identity function, for $i \notin I$. Notice that functions f_{τ_i} modify disjoint sets of variables and clocks and, hence, can be composed in any order.
- For a control location $\ell = (\ell_1, \ldots, \ell_n) \in L$, the time progress condition tpc_ℓ is $\mathsf{tpc}_\ell = \bigwedge_{i \in \{1..n\}} \mathsf{tpc}_{\ell_i}$. ∎

A composite component $B = \gamma(B_1, \ldots, B_n)$ can execute an interaction $a = \{p_i\}_{i \in I} \in \gamma$ from a state (m, v, t) iff (1) for each port p_i, the corresponding atomic component B_i can execute a transition labeled by p_i from the projection $(m_i, v_i, t_i) = (m \cap L_i, v_{|X_i}, t_{|C_i})$ of (m, v, t) on B_i, and (2) the guard G_a of the interaction evaluates to true on the variables exported by the ports participating in interaction a. Execution of interaction a triggers the function F_a which modifies the variables of the components exported by ports p_i. The new values obtained are then processed by the components' transitions. Note that the components also reset clocks according to the update function associated to their transition. The states of components that do not participate in the interaction remain unchanged. We say that an interaction $a \in \gamma$ is *enabled* at state $q \in Q_B$ of B, if there exists state $q' \in Q_B$ such that $q \xrightarrow{a}_B q'$.

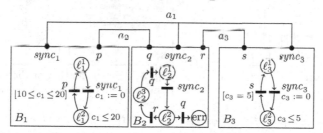

Fig. 3. Example of BIP composite component

Example 2. Figure 3 illustrates a composite component $\gamma(B_1, B_2, B_3)$. The set γ of interactions is $\{a_1, a_2, a_3\}$ with no guards nor update functions. Initially, the system is in state $(\ell_1^1, \ell_2^1, \ell_3^1)$, where c_1 and c_3 are set to 0. The only enabled interaction is a_1. Since time progress condition at this state is true, any delay $\delta \in \mathbb{R}_{\geq 0}$ can be taken. If interaction a_1 is executed, the next state is $(\ell_1^2, \ell_2^1, \ell_3^2)$ and clocks c_1 and c_3 are reset. At this state, the time progress condition and the timing constraint in B_3 impose that a_3 has to be executed after a delay of $\delta = 5$ time units. Once a_3 is executed, a_2 can execute after a delay of $\delta \in [5, 15]$ time units according to the time progress condition and the timing constraint in B_1.

3   Target Architecture

In this section, we describe the overall architecture of the source-to-source transformation of BIP models. Since we target concurrent execution of interactions, if two interactions are simultaneously enabled, they can be executed in parallel only if the semantics of the initial global state model is met. That is, if they involved disjoint sets of components. This leads to the notion of *conflict* between interactions. Two interactions are conflicting if they involve a shared component and they are potentially enabled at the same time.

Definition 6. *Let $\gamma(B_1, \ldots, B_n)$ be a BIP model. We say that two interactions a and b of γ are in structural conflict iff there exists an atomic component B_i that has two transitions $\tau_1 = ({}^{\bullet}\tau_1, p_1, \tau_1^{\bullet})$ and $\tau_2 = ({}^{\bullet}\tau_2, p_2, \tau_2^{\bullet})$ such that (1) $p_1 \in a$ and $p_2 \in b$, and (2) there exists a reachable state in the Petri net (L_i, P_i, T_i) of B_i at which both τ_1 and τ_2 are enabled.* ∎

Note that structural conflicts as defined in Definition 6 are an over-approximation of conflicts, since some structural conflicts may not be reachable due to guards and timing constraints. A special case of conflict is when two interactions a and b share a common port, that is, $a \cap b \neq \emptyset$. As already discussed, handling conflicting interactions in a BIP model executed by a centralized Engine is quite straightforward [4,15]. However, in a concurrent setting, detecting and avoiding conflicts is not trivial [7].

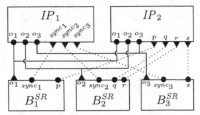

Fig. 4. Concurrent model of Figure 3

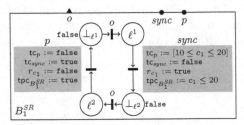

Fig. 5. Transformation of the atomic component in Figure 2

Consider a composite component $B = \gamma(B_1 \cdots B_n)$ in the BIP model and a *partition* of the set of interactions $\{\gamma_j\}_{j=1}^m$ (i.e., m *classes* of interactions γ_j are disjoint and cover all the interactions of γ). In our target concurrent model, atomic components B_i are transformed into atomic components B_i^{SR}. We also add *Interaction Protocol* components to implement interactions, such that each class of interaction γ_j is handled by a single Interaction Protocol component IP_j. The partition $\{\gamma_j\}_{j=1}^m$ allows the designer to enforce load-balancing and to improve the performance of the given model when running in a concurrent fashion. It also determines whether or not a conflict between interactions can be resolved locally. Consider conflicting interactions $a \in \gamma_j$ and $b \in \gamma_k$. We distinguish between two types of conflict for a and b, according to the partition $\{\gamma_j\}_{j=1}^m$. A conflict is *internal* if a and b belong to the same class of the partition, i.e., $j = k$. In this case, it can be resolved by the Interaction Protocol component IP_i responsible for a and b. A conflict is *external* if a and b belong to the different classes of the partition, i.e., $j \neq k$. External conflicts cannot be resolved by a single Interaction Protocol component IP_j, and requires additional synchronizations and components [7]. This is beyond the scope of this paper.

Consider again the example from Figure 3. Interaction a_1 is conflicting with neither a_2 nor a_3. However, a_2 and a_3 are conflicting because port q involved in a_2 and port r involved in a_3 are both enabled from place ℓ_2^2. Partition $\gamma_1 = \{a_1\}$ and $\gamma_2 = \{a_2, a_3\}$ is such that all conflicts between interactions are internal. The overall architecture of the concurrent model built for this partition is given in Figure 4. Notice that IP_1 and IP_2 share B_2^{SR}, as the later is involved in both $a_1 \in \gamma_1$ and $a_2 \in \gamma_2$. However, this is not a problem since a_1 and a_2 are never enabled at the same time.

From now on, we consider partitions $\{\gamma_j\}_{j=1}^m$ of interactions γ such that conflicts are always *internal*, that is, if two interactions $a, b \in \gamma$ are conflicting, then they belong to the same class γ_j. We also target Send/Receive BIP models. Intuitively, a *Send/Receive* model is a set of independent components communicating through asynchronous message passing defined next.

Definition 7. *We say that $B^{SR} = \gamma^{SR}(B_1^{SR}, \ldots, B_n^{SR})$ is a Send/Receive BIP composite component iff we can partition the set of ports of B^{SR} into three sets P_s, P_r, and P_u that are respectively the set of* send-ports, receive-ports, *and* unary interaction ports, *such that:*

- *Each interaction $a \in \gamma^{SR}$, is either (1) a Send/Receive interaction with $a = (s, r_1, r_2, \ldots, r_k)$, $s \in P_s$, $r_1, \ldots, r_k \in P_r$, $G_a = \mathtt{true}$ and F_a copies the variables exported by port s to the variables exported by ports $r_1, r_2, \ldots, r_k$, or, (2) a unary interaction $a = \{p\}$ with $p \in P_u$, $G_a = \mathtt{true}$, F_a is the identity function.*
- *If s is a port in P_s, then there exists one and only one Send/Receive interaction $a \in \gamma^{SR}$ with $a = (s, r_1, r_2, \ldots, r_k)$ and all ports $r_1, \ldots, r_k$ are receive-ports. We say that $r_1, r_2, \ldots, r_k$ are the receive-ports associated to s.*
- *If $a = (s, r_1, \ldots, r_k)$ is a Send/Receive interaction in γ^{SR} and s is enabled at some global state of B^{SR}, then all its associated receive-ports $r_1, \ldots, r_k$ are also enabled at that state.* ∎

Definition 7 defines a class of BIP models for concurrent implementation based on asynchronous message passing. In such systems, communication is sender-triggered, where a message is emitted by the sender, regardless of the availability of receivers. The third property of the definition, requires that all receivers are ready to receive whenever the sender may send a message. This ensures that the sender is never blocked and triggers the Send/Receive interaction.

Intuitively, a model that meets properties of Definition 7 can be seen as a set of independent process, communicating through asynchronous message passing. However, execution of this model according to the BIP semantics assumes that clocks of these components advance at the same rate and communication is instantaneous.

4   Step 1: BIP to Send/Receive-BIP

In this section, we describe a method for automated transformation of a timed BIP model $B = \gamma(B_1, \ldots, B_n)$ into a timed *Send/Receive*-BIP model $B^{SR} = \gamma^{SR}(B_1^{SR}, \ldots, B_m^{SR})$ that meets restrictions of Definition 7. Correctness of this transformation could be found in [15].

4.1   Atomic Components

For the sake of simplicity and clarity, we present the transformation for an atomic component such that its Petri net is an automaton, that is, each of its transitions has a single source and single target place, and its initial state consists in a single place. Notice that the behavior of a 1-Safe Petri net defines a finite automaton, allowing us to apply the following transformation to any arbitrary atomic component.

We transform an atomic component B of a BIP model into a Send/Receive atomic component B^{SR} that is capable of communicating with the Interaction Protocol component(s). To communicate, B^{SR} sends *offers* to the Interaction Protocol that are acknowledged by a *response*. An offer includes necessary information for computing enabled interactions from the current state of B^{SR}, i.e., values of variables exported by the ports, timing constraints of transitions, and resets of clocks. When the interaction protocol selects an interaction involving B^{SR} for execution, B^{SR} is notified by a response sent on the chosen port.

Since each notification from the Interaction Protocol triggers an internal computation in a component, following [4], we split each place ℓ into two places, namely, ℓ itself and a *busy place* $\perp_\ell$. Intuitively, reaching $\perp_\ell$ marks the beginning of an unobservable internal computation. We are now ready to define the transformation from B into B^{SR}.

Definition 8. *Let* $B = (L, P, T, \mathsf{C}, X, \{X_p\}_{p \in P}, \{g_\tau\}_{\tau \in T}, \{tc_\tau\}_{\tau \in T}, \{f_\tau\}_{\tau \in T}, \{tpc_\ell\}_{\ell \in L})$ *be an atomic component. The corresponding Send/Receive atomic component is* $B^{SR} = (L^{SR}, P^{SR}, T^{SR}, \emptyset, X^{SR}, \{X_p^{SR}\}_{p \in P}, \{g_\tau\}_{\tau \in T^{SR}}, \emptyset, \{f_\tau\}_{\tau \in T^{SR}}, \emptyset)$, *such that:*

- $L^{SR} = L \cup L^\perp$, *where* $L^\perp = \{\perp_\ell | \ \ell \in L\}$.
- $X^{SR} = X \cup \{tc_p\}_{p \in P} \cup \{tpc_{B^{SR}}\} \cup \{r_c\}_{c \in \mathsf{C}}$, *where* r_c *are Boolean variables,* tc_p *are timing constraint variables and* $tpc_{B^{SR}}$ *is time progress condition variable.*
- $P^{SR} = P \cup \{o\}$, *where the* offer *port* o *exports the variables* $X_o^{SR} = \bigcup_{p \in P} X_p \cup \{tc_p\}_{p \in P} \cup \{r_c\}_{c \in \mathsf{C}}$. *For all other ports* $p \in P$, *we define* $X_p^{SR} = X_p$.
- *For each place* $\ell \in L$, *we include an intermediate place* $\perp_\ell$ *and an* offer *transition* $\tau_\ell = (\perp_\ell, o, \ell)$ *in* T^{SR}. *The time progress condition* tpc_{τ_ℓ} *is* false, *both the guard* g_{τ_ℓ} *and the timing constraint* tc_{τ_ℓ} *are* true, *and the update function* f_{τ_ℓ} *is the identity function.*
- *For each transition* $\tau = (\ell, p, \ell') \in T$, *we include a response transition* $\tau_p = (\ell, p, \perp_{\ell'})$ *in* T^{SR} *with no guard and timing constraint.*
  The function f_{τ_p} *first applies function* f_τ *of* τ, *and then sets time progress condition variable to the time progress condition of next location (i.e.* $tpc_B := tpc_{\ell'}$) *and updates the timing constraint and reset variables:* $\forall p' \in P$ $tc_{p'} :=$

$$\begin{cases} tc_{\tau'} & \text{if } g_{\tau'} \wedge \tau' = (\ell', p', \ell'') \in T \\ \text{false} & \text{otherwise.} \end{cases}$$

$$\forall c \in \mathsf{C} \quad r_c := \begin{cases} \text{true} & \text{if } f_\tau \text{ resets } c \\ \text{false} & \text{otherwise.} \end{cases} \qquad \blacksquare$$

In the above definition, the execution of a transition $\tau = (\ell, p, \ell')$ of a component B corresponds to the following two execution steps in B^{SR}. Firstly, an offer transition $\tau_\ell = (\perp_\ell, o, \ell)$ transmits for each port $p' \in P$ the current values of its variables $X_{p'}$, the timing constraint $tc_{p'}$ corresponding to the enabledness of p' at ℓ, as well as the time progress condition tpc_ℓ. These are used by the Interaction Protocol for computing guards and timing constraints of interactions involving B^{SR}. The transition τ_ℓ also transmits for each clock $c \in C$ the value of its reset variable r_c, such that $r_c = \texttt{true}$, if c has been reset by the previous transition execution. Variables r_c are used to reset clocks in the Interaction Protocol before computing timing constraints of interactions.

Secondly, a response transition $\tau_p = (\ell, p, \perp_{\ell'})$ is executed once the Interaction Protocol decides to execute an interaction involving port p. Similar to τ in B, τ_p updates values of variables X according to f_τ. It also updates variables $tpc_{B^{SR}}$, $tc_{p'}$ and r_c to set up-to-date values for the next offer (i.e. starting from ℓ'). Since (L, P, T) is a deterministic 1-Safe Petri net, a port $p' \in P$ enables at most one transition at ℓ'. If no transition labeled by p' is enabled at ℓ', or if the guard $g_{\tau'}$ of the transition τ' enabled by p' at ℓ' evaluates to $\texttt{false}$, $tc_{p'}$ is set to $\texttt{false}$ to disable interactions involving p'. Otherwise, $tc_{p'}$ is set to the timing constraint $tc_{\tau'}$ of transition τ' enabled by p' at ℓ'.

Notice that time progress conditions and timing constraints of B^{SR} do not involve clocks C. Thus, according to [9] clocks are no longer *active* and can be removed from B^{SR}. Original time progress conditions and timing constraints of B are stored in variables of B^{SR}, and transmitted to the Interaction Protocol which is responsible for enforcing timeliness in interactions execution. Figure 5 illustrates the transformation of the component B_1 of Figure 2 into its corresponding Send/Receive component B_1^{SR}.

4.2   Interaction Protocol Layer

The Petri net that defines the behavior of an Interaction Protocol component IP_j handling a class γ_j of interactions is constructed as follows. Figure 6 illustrates the construction of the Petri net of component IP_2 handling interaction a_2 and a_3 in example of Figure 4.

Variables and Clocks.   For each component B_i, we include a time progress condition variable tpc_{B_i}. For each port p involved in interactions γ_j, we include a timing constraint variable tc_p and a local copy of the variables X_p exported by p. We also include for each clock a Boolean variable r_c that indicates whether clock c has to be reset.

The set of clocks of IP_j contains all the clocks defined initially in components B_i involved in γ_j before being transformed into B_i^{SR}.

Places.   The Petri net has two types of places:

- For each component B_i involved in interactions of γ_j, we include *waiting* and *received* places w_i and rcv_i, respectively. Place rcv_i has a time progress condition defined by the variable tpc_{B_i}. Initially the IP_j remains in a waiting place until it receives an offer from the corresponding component. When an offer from component B_i^{SR} is received, IP_j moves from w_i to rcv_i.

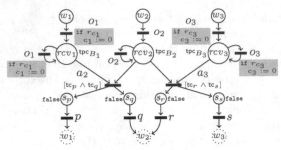

Fig. 6. Component IP_2 handling interactions a_2 and a_3 from Figure 3

- For each port p involved in interactions of γ_j, we include a *sending* place s_p. The time progress condition of s_p is `false`. The response to an offer of a component B_i^{SR} is sent from this place to port p of B_i^{SR}.

Ports. The set of ports of IP_j is the following:

- For each component B_i, we include a receive-port o_i, to receive offers. Each port o_i is associated to the variables tc_p, and X_p associated to each port p of B_i, the variables r_c for each clock c of B_i as well as the variable tpc_{B_i} of B_i. These variables are updated whenever an offer from B_i is received.
- For each port p involved in interactions γ_j, we include a send-port p, which exports the set of variables X_p.
- We include a unary port for each interaction $a \in \gamma_j$.

Transitions. IP_j receives offers from SR components and responds to them. The following set of transitions of IP_j performs these two tasks:

- In order to receive offers from a component B_i, we include transition (w_i, o_i, rcv_i). We also include a transition (rcv_i, o_i, rcv_i) to receive new offers when B_i takes part in an external interaction. This transition resets all clocks c such that r_c is `true`.
- For each interaction $a = \{p_i\}_{i \in I}$ in γ_j, we include the transition $(\{rcv_i\}_{i \in I}, a, \{s_{p_i}\}_{i \in I})$. This transition is guarded by the predicate G_a, has the timing constraint $\bigwedge_{i \in I} tc_{p_i}$ and moves the tokens from receiving to sending places. This transition triggers function F_a.
- Finally, for each port p involved in interactions γ_j, we include a transition (s_p, p, w_i). This transition notifies the corresponding component to execute the transition labeled p.

Note that in Interaction Protocol components, time progress conditions, timing constraints and resets of clocks depend on variables, which are not permitted by Definition 2. However, there is only a finite number of configurations for the values of these variables, as the number of transitions and states in atomic components B_i is finite. In IP_j, we could include multiple transitions for offers o_i and interactions a to encode all possible combinations of these configurations. In this case, an atomic component B_i^{SR} would send offers indicating in which configuration are its reset, time progress conditions and timing constraints variables, and appropriate guards in IP_j would enable the corresponding transitions.

4.3   Send/Receive Interactions

In this subsection, we define the interactions between the components defined thus far. Following Definition 7, we introduce Send/Receive interactions by specifying only the sender. Given a BIP model $\gamma(B_1 \cdots B_n)$, a partition $\gamma_1 \cdots \gamma_m$ of γ, the transformation gives a Send/Receive BIP model $B^{SR} = \gamma^{SR}(B_1^{SR}, \ldots, B_n^{SR}, IP_1, \ldots, IP_m)$. We define the Send/Receive interactions of γ^{SR} as follows:

- For each component B_i^{SR}, let $IP_{j_1}, \ldots, IP_{j_l}$ be the Interaction Protocol components handling interactions involving B_i^{SR}. We include in γ^{SR} the *offer interaction* $(B_i^{SR}.o, IP_{j_1}.o_i, \ldots, IP_{j_l}.o_i)$.
- For each port p in component B_i^{SR} and for each Interaction Protocol component IP_j handling an interaction involving p, we include in γ^{SR} the *response interaction* $(IP_j.p, B_i^{SR}.p)$.
- For each interaction $a \in \gamma$, we add the unary interaction $(IP_j.a)$ to γ^{SR}, where IP_j is the Interaction Protocol component handling the interaction a.

The concurrent version obtained from the model depicted in Figure 3 is shown in Figure 4. The transformation is parametrized by the partition of the interaction $\gamma_1 = \{a_1\}$ and $\gamma_2 = \{a_2, a_3\}$, yielding two interaction protocol components.

Theorem 1.   Given a timed BIP model B, we have $B^{SR} \sim B$, where $\sim$ denotes observational equivalence.

5   Step 2: Use of a Single Clock

In this section, we explain how we refine Send/Receive-BIP models presented in Section 4 into *Single-Clock* Send/Receive-BIP. In a *Single-Clock* Send/Receive-BIP, all the time progress conditions and timing constraints of the model are expressed based on a single global clock g that is never reset. This clock measures the absolute time elapsed since the system starts executing.

The transformation from a Send/Receive model to a *Single-Clock* Send/Receive-BIP model involves the following steps:

1. We add the global clock g to each component.
2. For each clock c of a component B, we introduce a real variable ρ_c in order to store the absolute time of the last reset of the clock c with respect to the clock g. Whenever the clock c is reset by a transition of B, we assign to ρ_c the current value of g, denoted by $\rho_c := t(g)$, where $t(g)$ represents the valuation of the clock g at the current state of the system. Notice that the value of c can be computed from the current value of g and ρ_c by using the equality $c = g - \rho_c$.
3. We express any timing constraints tc using the clock g instead of clocks C. Using (1) we rewrite tc as follows: $\text{tc} = \bigwedge_{c \in C_i} l_c + \rho_c \leq g \leq u_c + \rho_c$. That is, tc is an interval constraint on g of the form: $\text{tc} = \max\{l_c + \rho_c\}_{c \in C_i} \leq g \leq \min\{u_c + \rho_c\}_{c \in C_i}$.
4. Due to the previous transformation, local clocks C are no longer used by timing constraints, that is, they are not active [9]. Thus, we keep only the global clock g and the variables ρ_c.

Notice that steps 2, 3, and 4 apply only to Interaction Protocol components, since distributed atomic components have no clock.

Single-Clock Send/Receive-BIP models are easier to map on a platform than Send/Receive-BIP, as they require a single real-time clock to be implemented. However, they are based on the fact that atomic components respond instantaneously to notification of Interaction Protocol components by sending offers. This assumption cannot be met in practice since execution of transitions as well as transmission of messages may take significant time.

6 Related Work

LOTOS [10] is a specification language based on process algebra, that encompasses multiparty interactions. In [16], the authors describe a method of executing a LOTOS specification in a distributed fashion. This implementation is obtained by constructing a tree at runtime. The root is the main connector of the LOTOS specification and its children are the subprocesses that are connected. A synchronization between two processes is handled by their common ancestor. Another framework that offers automatic distributed code generation is described in [13]. The input model consists of composition of I/O automata, from which a Java implementation using MPI for communication is generated. The model, as well as the implementation, can interact with the environment. However, connections between I/O automata (binary synchronization) are less expressive than BIP interactions, as proved in [6]. Finally, the framework in [13] requires the designer to specify low-level elements of a distributed system such as channels and schedulers.

In the context of the framework, automated implementation of distributed applications from BIP models has been addressed in [7,8]. The authors propose a 3-layer architecture or, where the first layer is concerned with behavior of components, the second layer handles execution of interactions, and the third layer resolves distributed conflicts. However, this line of work is not concerned with notion of time and timing constraints. On the timed models side, in [1], the authors study the problem of model-based implementation of sequential timed BIP models. The closest work to this paper is the approach in [15]. This technique transforms a timed BIP model into a parallel time-aware code. The main difference is unlike our approach, the method in [15] augments the code with only one centralized engine. Such an engine can potentially become a bottleneck and consequently make the generated code inefficient.

Finally, TIMES is a tool for modelling and schedulability analysis of embedded real-time systems [3]. The tool is featured with a code generator for sequential C-code synthesis on LegoOS platform from the input model. Unlike our approach in this paper, TIMES is not able to generate concurrent code.

7 Conclusion

Concurrent real-time systems have numerous applications in today's embedded computing systems. However, correct development of such systems is known to be a notoriously difficult problem. In this paper, we focused on model-based automated and correct-by-construction development of multi-process applications that are subject to timing constraints. We proposed a chain of transformations that starts from an abstract model of the application expressed in terms of a set of interacting components. Each component is constrained by a set of local logical timing requirements. In each step, a transformation obtains a model that encompasses platform constraints, such as point-point communication and physical real time. Each transformation ensures that all functional properties of the input model are preserved. Our transformations are fully implemented and validated on a framework for real-time image reconstruction system. For reasons of space implementation and experiments parts appear in [14].

For future work, there are several research directions. An important extension of this work is to design transformations, in which schedulers are not necessarily conflict-free. Such schedulers potentially result in better levels of parallelism. A more challenging (but highly needed) research direction is model-based development of distributed real-time applications, where a global perfect clock cannot be assumed.

References

1. Abdellatif, T., Combaz, J., Sifakis, J.: Model-based implementation of real-time applications. In: ACM International Conference on Embedded Software (EMSOFT), pp. 229–238 (2010)
2. Alur, R., Dill, D.: A theory of timed automata. Theoretical Computer Science **126**(2), 183–235 (1994)
3. Amnell, T., Fersman, E., Mokrushin, L., Pettersson, P., Yi, W.: TIMES - a tool for modelling and implementation of embedded systems. In: Katoen, J.-P., Stevens, P. (eds.) Tools and Algorithms for the Construction and Analysis of Systems (TACAS). LNCS, vol. 2280, pp. 460–464. Springer, Heidelbeeg (2002)
4. Basu, A., Bidinger, P., Bozga, M., Sifakis, J.: Distributed semantics and implementation for systems with interaction and priority. In: Suzuki, K., Higashino, T., Yasumoto, K., El-Fakih, K. (eds.) FORTE. LNCS, vol. 5048, pp. 116–133. Springer, Heidelberg (2008)
5. Basu, A., Bozga, M., Sifakis, J.: Modeling heterogeneous real-time components in BIP. In: Software Engineering and Formal Methods (SEFM), pp. 3–12 (2006)
6. Bliudze, S., Sifakis, J.: A notion of glue expressiveness for component-based systems. In: Bliudze, S., Sifakis, J. (eds.) Concurrency Theory (CONCUR). LNCS, vol. 5201, pp. 508–522. Springer, Heidelberg (2008)
7. Bonakdarpour, B., Bozga, M., Jaber, M., Quilbeuf, J., Sifakis, J.: A framework for automated distributed implementation of component-based models. Springer Journal on Distributed Computing (DC) **25**(1), 383–409 (2012)
8. Bonakdarpour, B., Bozga, M., Quilbeuf, J.: Automated distributed implementation of component-based models with priorities. In: ACM International Conference on Embedded Software (EMSOFT), pp. 59–68 (2011)
9. Daws, C., Yovine, S.: Reducing the number of clock variables of timed automata. In: RTSS, pp. 73–81. IEEE Computer Society (1996)
10. ISO/IEC. Information Processing Systems - Open Systems Interconnection: LOTOS, A Formal Description Technique Based on the Temporal Ordering of Observational Behavior (1989)

11. Jee, E., Wang, S., Kim, J.-K., Lee, J., Sokolsky, O., Lee, I.: A safety-assured development approach for real-time software. In: Proceedings of the 16th IEEE International Conference on Embedded and Real-Time Computing Systems and Applications (RTCSA), pp. 133–142 (2010)
12. Murata, T.: Petri nets: Properties, analysis and applications. Proceedings of the IEEE **77**(4), 541–580 (1989)
13. Tauber, J.A., Lynch, N.A., Tsai, M.J.: Compiling IOA without global synchronization. In: Symposium on Network Computing and Applications (NCA), pp. 121–130 (2004)
14. Triki, A., Bonakdarpoor, B., Combaz, J., Bensalem, S.: Automated conflict-free concurrent implementation of timed component-based models. Technical report, Verimag Research Report
15. Triki, A., Combaz, J., Bensalem, S., Sifakis, J.: Model-based implementation of parallel real-time systems. In: Cortellessa, V., Varró, D. (eds.) FASE. LNCS, vol. 7793, pp. 235–249. Springer, Heidelberg (2013)
16. von Bochmann, G., Gao, Q., Wu, C.: On the distributed implementation of lotos. In: FORTE, pp. 133–146 (1989)

Formal API Specification of the PikeOS Separation Kernel

Freek Verbeek[1,2]($\boxtimes$), Oto Havle[3], Julien Schmaltz[4], Sergey Tverdyshev[3],
Holger Blasum[3], Bruno Langenstein[5], Werner Stephan[5], Burkhart Wolff[6],
and Yakoub Nemouchi[6]

[1] Open University of The Netherlands, Heerlen, The Netherlands
fvb@ou.nl
[2] Radboud University Nijmegen, Nijmegen, The Netherlands
[3] SYSGO AG, Klein-winternheim, Germany
[4] Eindhoven University of Technology, Eindhoven, The Netherlands
[5] DFKI GmbH, Kaiserslautern, Germany
[6] University Paris-Sud, Orsay, France

Abstract. PikeOS is an industrial operating system for safety and security critical applications in, for example, avionics and automotive contexts. A consortium of several European partners from industry and academia works on the certification of PikeOS up to at least Common Criteria EAL5+, with "+" being applying formal methods compliant up to EAL7. We have formalized the hardware independent security-relevant part of PikeOS that is to be used in a certification context. Over this model, intransitive noninterference has been proven. We present the model and the methodology used to create the model. All results have been formalized in the Isabelle/HOL theorem prover.

1 Introduction

Separation kernels are at the heart of many modern security-critical systems. Safety-critical embedded systems become more and more connected, requiring an operating system that provides clear separation between the subjects running on top of it. A separation kernel is an operating system providing such an environment [1]. A crucial security property of separation kernels is *intransitive noninterference* [2,3]. This property is typically a base for the MILS[1] architectural approach [4] and enforced by separation kernel. It ensures that a given security policy over different subjects of the system is obeyed. Such a security policy dictates which subjects may flow information to which other subjects.

Software embedded in safety- and security-critical applications needs to be of the highest quality. Formal methods are a means to meet the necessary stringent

---

[1] We use MILS as a proper noun, historically MILS stood for multiple independent levels of security.

© Springer International Publishing Switzerland 2015
K. Havelund et al. (Eds.): NFM 2015, LNCS 9058, pp. 375–389, 2015.
DOI: 10.1007/978-3-319-17524-9_26

assurance standards. Regarding PikeOS, a separation kernel used in the EURO-MILS project, an objective is to undergo an evaluation under the Common Criteria (CC) to a high evaluation assurance level (EAL5+) with "+" addressing the formal models for up to EAL7. This level requires a formal model of PikeOS and the proof that this model possesses the intransitive noninterference property. The environment in which this project is performed imposes several constraints.

If formal methods are used in the CC, then the CC obliges the developer to demonstrate a correspondence between the model (in our case: CISK, Sect. 2.1) and the functional specification. When the developer chooses to do this by a formal functional specification, then the correspondence shall be backed by a formal proof (CC, Part 3, work unit ADV_SPM.1.3D). We describe a formal model of a generic separation kernel (Sect. 3), with a selection of features that is motivated from a subset of PikeOS features, and thought to be applicable for a larger set of separation kernels. Moreover, we describe the proof that this model ensures intransitive noninterference. The environment in which this project is performed imposes several constraints. The approach shall be executable in a typical resource restricted environment of an SME (small and medium enter-prise). Usually, the CC certificate expires and the product has to undergo a maintenance evaluation. Thus, the formal model shall be feasibly adaptable if any changes are required. Previous formal efforts about separation kernels – including the verification of seL4 [5,6] – require changes in the product to ease the application of formal methods. Such changes may unnecessarily restrict the flexibility, performance, and maintainability of the product. Moreover, these modifications constitute huge obstacles to the integration with the company's Verification&Validation activities. Finally, the source code used to build the product should not contain any formal modelling artifacts.

Our main contribution is to propose a methodology (Sect. 2) supporting the development of high-level functional specifications of separation kernels under the aforementioned constraints. Our main result (Sect. 3) is the formalization in the logic of Isabelle/HOL [7] of API calls of PikeOS important for secure information flow and the proof that they ensure intransitive noninterference[2]. In this paper, we illustrate our methodology on a simplified version of the IPC (Inter Process Communication) API. The entire model includes a much more realistic version of IPC and several other calls, like an event mechanism, and file transfers. The end of Sect. 3 gives more details about these different calls.

2   Methodology

Fig. 1 shows an overview of our methodology. The starting point is a generic model of a Controlled Interruptible Separation Kernel (CISK). This model defines a state machine with some facets that are commonly present in separation ker-nels, such as different subjects running code consisting of kernel API calls, an information flow policy, interrupts and context switches. It includes a notion of time, so that it can be used to model time partitions and can model and show the

---

[2] Source code is available upon request.

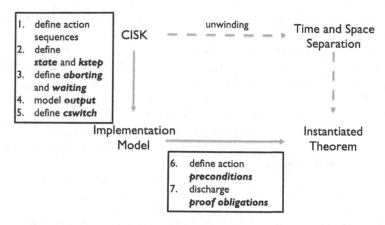

Fig. 1. CISK Methodology

absence of covert channels via common data structures. Finally, it also includes two constituents modelling the control of the kernel over its subjects. The kernel can decide to *abort* and *delay* the API calls of the subjects.

We have defined a set of nine assumptions over the CISK constituents (we will refer to these assumptions as *proof obligations*). From the proof obligations, we prove intransitive noninterference. This is commonly referred to as the unwinding of the proof obligations. This proof is done once and for all, i.e., when using CISK to make an implementation model, one does not have to consider any details of this proof. Sections 2.1 and 2.2 present an overview.

To create an implementation model, five constituents have to be defined. Subsequently, one has to discharge all proof obligations for those constituents. More details will be given below. After these steps, one automatically obtains a proof of intransitive noninterference over the implementation model.

2.1 CISK

In CISK, the entire system consists of several domains running on top of the kernel. A domain is an entity executing actions and making calls to the kernel. Actions represent atomic instructions that are executed by the kernel. As kernel actions are assumed to be atomic, an interrupt may occur after each kernel action. Each API call that a domain can execute is represented by a *sequence of atomic actions*.[3] The *program code* of a domain is thus a list of action sequences. The *system code* is a mapping of program codes to domains, i.e., it assigns to each domain its program code. The state of the kernel is assumed to contain information about the resources of the system, as well as which domain is currently active. A state does not need to include the program code of the domains, as in our model the actions that are executed are modelled separately. The observable output of the system includes, e.g., the output of executing actions and the error codes returned when aborting API calls. Time is modelled using

---

[3] We will use the terms 'sequence' and 'list' synonymously.

natural numbers. Each atomic kernel action can be executed within one or more time units. We define an enriched state to be a triple containing the state, the current system code and the current time.

The deterministic execution by the kernel of action a in state s is defined by $\mathbf{kstep}(s, a)$. The behavior observed by executing action a in state s is noted $\mathbf{out}(s, a)$. When a domain instructs the kernel to execute an atomic action, it is up to the kernel whether that action is executed, aborted or delayed. This decision is modelled by predicates $\mathbf{aborting}(a, s)$ and $\mathbf{waiting}(a, s)$. When an atomic action is aborted, the entire action sequence that it belongs to is aborted. The currently active domain is noted $\mathbb{D}(s)$.

Each step of CISK takes the current enriched state and yields the next state. Three cases can occur:

1. An interrupt occurs. In this case, a context switch is executed, changing the currently active domain.
2. The next atomic action to be executed fits in the current time partition, i.e., it can be executed *before* the next interrupt. In this case, the kernel fetches the next atomic action a from the domain code. Three cases can occur. First, based on the current state and the current action, the current API call can be aborted. The kernel updates the domain code by removing the entire API call. Secondly, the action can be executed. Thirdly, based on the current state, the current action can be in a waiting state. No state change occurs.
3. The next atomic action to be executed does *not* fit the current time partition. In this case, the kernel prevents execution of this action, as otherwise an information flow can occur as the execution of the next domain is influenced.

Non-determinism is modelled using oracles, which are functions resolving choices. Interrupts can occur at any time. Oracle $\mathbf{interrupt}(n)$ returns true if an interrupt occurs at time n. The duration of action a in state s is given by oracle $\mathbf{duration}(s, a)$.

A consequence of allowing interruptible action sequences is that it is no longer the case that any system code, i.e., any combination of atomic kernel actions, is realistic. We let AS_set(d) denote for domain d the list of kernel actions of each system call made by domain d. We restrict our model to *well-formed* executions, i.e., executions where atomic kernel actions are according to AS_set.

2.2 Intransitive Noninterference

An *information flow policy* (denoted $\rightsquigarrow$) is a relation over domains. It dictates which domains may flow information to which other domains. We assume an intransitive security policy that allows, e.g., a configuration in which $w \rightsquigarrow v \rightsquigarrow u$, but $w \not\rightsquigarrow u$. In such a configuration, domain w may flow information to u but *only* through v.

We define separation by considering the system as a Moore machine. Delay bisimulation is used to formulate that a normal run of the system executes similarly to a system in which some domains are replaced by attackers. A delay bisimulation shows that each *delay step* in one run can be simulated by a *delay step* in the other. A delay step is a step preceded by zero or more steps over *silent* states, i.e., states that produce no output.

Figure 2 explains this informally. Let u be some domain of interest and let x be the system code (we quantify over all possible u and x). We prove the existence of a bisimulation relation R. The left hand side of relation R is a normal run of the system. The right hand side of relation R is a run where domains that may not influence u have been replaced by some attacker (we quantify over all possible attackers). We will call this run a *littered run*. At all times, we only look at the output of u; whenever u is inactive the output is considered to be $\bot$.

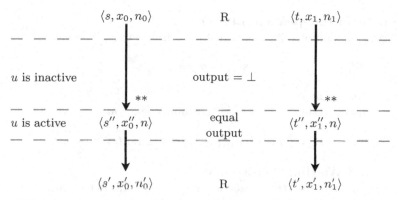

Fig. 2. Delay bisimulation showing intransitive noninterference. The double stars denote zero or more steps.

Let $\langle s, x_0, n_0 \rangle$ be the current enriched state of the normal run. Domain u either is currently active or not. Within zero or more steps, state $\langle s'', x_0'', n \rangle$ is reached in which u is active. In this state, the time is some n and the output observed is some $o \neq \bot$. This state can be simulated by the littered run. That run first executes zero or more steps over silent states (i.e., it runs the littered system until u is active), followed by a state in which u is active. That state produces the same output o at the same time n. The next states again are related by R.

What the existence of bisimulation R shows is that whenever u is active, it produces the exact same output in both runs, at the exact same time. Domain u is undisturbed, regardless of the presence of the attacker. Whenever u is inactive, no output or time is observed.

2.3   Proof Obligations and Their Unwinding

We introduce the proof obligations on the CISK constituents. Subsequently, we explain the extra assumptions that are required to finish the proof.

First, we adopt Rushby's assumptions [2]. Since these are well-known, we introduce them only informally. Rushby defines assumptions using an equivalence relation called *view-partitioning*. The intuition behind this relation is that whenever two states s and t are in the same view-partitioning for domain u, they produce the same output. We will call such states u-*equivalent* (notation: $\overset{u}{\simeq}$).

The step function must be *weakly step consistent*: let s and t be two u-equivalent states. Weak step consistency states that s and t remain u-equivalent after executing an action a, i.e., after completion of a call to function *kstep*. The property *locally respects* states that when a state s executes an action a and the current domain is not allowed to influence domain u, the next state remains u-equivalent, i.e., $s \overset{u}{\simeq} kstep(s, a)$. *Output consistency* formalizes the fact that two u-equivalent states produce the same output when u is active.

In addition to Rushby's assumptions, we require the following proof obligations:

Active Domain Independent of Step:
A regular action cannot influence which domain is currently active.

$$\mathbb{D}(\text{kstep}(s, a)) = \mathbb{D}(s)$$

Cswitch Consistency:
A context switch preserves the view-partitioning relation.

$$s \overset{u}{\simeq} t \implies \text{cswitch}(s) \overset{u}{\simeq} \text{cswitch}(t)$$

Aborting and Waiting Consistency:
When two u-equivalent states execute action a (with u the currently active domain), the aborting (waiting) condition is equal.

$$s \overset{\mathbb{D}(s)}{\simeq} t \implies \text{aborting}(s, a) = \text{aborting}(t, a)$$

$$s \overset{\mathbb{D}(s)}{\simeq} t \implies \text{waiting}(s, a) = \text{waiting}(t, a)$$

Context switch is state-independent:
For any two states s and t, the domain that is active after a context switch is equal.

$$\mathbb{D}(s) = \mathbb{D}(t) \implies \mathbb{D}(\text{cswitch}(s)) = \mathbb{D}(\text{cswitch}(t))$$

Besides these proof obligations, we require additional assumptions on the oracles.

Duration Consistency:
When two u-equivalent states execute action a (with u the currently active domain), then the duration of action a is equal.

$$s \overset{\mathbb{D}(s)}{\simeq} t \implies \text{duration}(s, a) = \text{duration}(t, a)$$

Duration Consistency, Aborting Consistency and Waiting Consistency are the major proof obligations to ensure time separation. Consider a situation in which the current domain u executes a synchronous IPC to a domain d that has no rights to influence u. If d is somehow able to let u wait, then it might be able to exploit that for a timing attack. The IPC action sequence will be aborted, since the information flow policy does not allow the communication. Aborting Consistency ensures that this happens, regardless of the state of domain d. Waiting consistency gives us that whenever the kernel delays some atomic stage of the IPC call, it will do so *not* based on information of d. Finally, duration consistency gives us that each atomic stage, if executed, has the same duration regardless of the state of d.

State-Independent Interrupts:
Whether an interrupt occurs at a given time, is independent of the state.

$$interrupt :: time\_t \mapsto \mathbb{B}$$

Oracle function *interrupt* takes as input the current time and decides whether an interrupt occurs solely on that. We assume that there is some at-beforehand fixed schedule dictating when which domain is active. This scheduler cannot base its decisions on the current state.

Theorem 1. *Let* PO *denote the set of proof obligations and assumptions defined above.* PO *implies intransitive noninterference for CISK:*

$$PO \implies separation$$

2.4 Discharging Proof Obligations

CISK supports the discharging of the proof obligations with a proof method based on *preconditions*. Preconditions are especially important due to the introduction of interrupts. We explain this using a simple example. Consider an artificial API call *write(m, u)* which triggers an action sequence of two atomic actions. First, action w_1 performs a security check whether the current domain can write into the memory of domain u. If so, then the second atomic action w_2 writes message m. Without interrupts, the property Locally Respects is easily proven: the state changes only when the communication is allowed, so quite trivially we have:

$$\mathbb{D}(s) \not\hookrightarrow u \implies s \overset{u}{\simeq} kstep(s, write(m, u))$$

However, locally respects is required for all *atomic actions*. We are therefore required to prove:

$$\mathbb{D}(s) \not\hookrightarrow u \implies s \overset{u}{\simeq} kstep(s, w_2(m, u))$$

This statement, however, is false, as atomic action w_2 writes m into the memory of u. The traditional formulation of Locally Respects is thus unprovable when interrupts are added. In general, adding interrupts can invalidate security properties [8,9].

Action w_2 is always executed after successful (non-aborting) execution of w_1. Since w_1 aborts whenever $\mathbb{D}(s) \not\rightsquigarrow u$, we can safely assume that whenever action w_2 is executed, the precondition $\mathbb{D}(s) \rightsquigarrow u$ holds. Using this precondition, discharging locally respects for action w_2 becomes trivial.

In order to use preconditions, one must first define a function *precondition* that takes the current state, an action and the domain executing that action. It returns a Boolean indicating that the precondition holds. For example:

$$precondition(s, w_2(m, u), d) = d \rightsquigarrow u$$

Let $\alpha = [a_0, a_1, a_2]$ be an action sequence. The precondition for action a_0 must always be true (note that this does not mean that a_0 cannot be aborted). Successful execution of atomic action a_i must ensure the precondition for action a_{i+1} ($0 \leq i < 2$). If an interrupt happens, then other domains are active between actions a_i and a_{i+1}. Those domains must not be able to influence the preconditions for u. These properties have been formalized as three additional proof obligations. All other proof obligations, e.g., Locally Respects, have been weakened by adding the assumption that the preconditions for the next action hold.

3   Application to the Separation Kernel

3.1   An Illustrative Example

To illustrate the application of our methodology, we use a highly simplified version of the IPC API. The IPC (for: inter process communication) provides domains with a synchronous message passing system. Algorithm 1 presents pseudo code of the simplified IPC implementation. The API provides IPC functions *ipc_send* and *ipc_rec*. The sender provides the id of the receiver thread t' and the message m. The receiver only provides the id of the sender thread t'.

Initially, communication rights are checked. If bidirectional communication is not allowed, the entire API call is aborted and some error code is produced. Otherwise, a flag *rdy* is set to true. This flag indicates that the current thread is ready for the communication and thus waiting for the partner. Once both threads are ready, the actual data transfer occurs. Finally, the flag is set to false.

Remark 1. As mentioned, in this paper, we present a simplification of our entire formalization in Isabelle/HOL. Some of the simplifications are:

- the separation kernel supports bidirectional IPC calls, that perform both sending and receiving. This leads to action sequences with more stages.
- The *rdy* variable is actually an abstraction of preparations for the IPC operation, e.g. scheduler invocations.
- the separation kernel contains partition daemons which can do restricted IPC calls.
- The security checks are more complicated than shown here. Also, we have modelled a *dynamic* state-dependent security policy.
- In our example we used only one error code, but in the real model there are many more.

Algorithm 1. Pseudo code of the IPC send and receive operation

ipc_send(t', m) =	ipc_rec(t') =
if $t \not\leftrightarrow t'$ **or** $t' \not\leftrightarrow t$ **then**	**if** $t \not\leftrightarrow t'$ **or** $t' \not\leftrightarrow t$ **then**
abort	abort
error code IPC_ERROR	error code IPC_ERROR
else	**else**
s.t.rdy = True	s.t.rdy = True
end if	**end if**
preemption point	preemption point
while s.t'.rdy = False **do**	**while** s.t'.rdy = False **do**
preemptive wait	preemptive wait
end while	**end while**
preemption point	preemption point
send IPC data	receive IPC data
preemption point	preemption point
s.t.rdy = False	s.t.rdy = False
preemption point	preemption point

3.2 Isabelle Prerequisites

Isabelle/HOL is a theorem prover with higher order logic and facilities for data types, records, inductive sets and recursive functions [7]. New datatypes are introduced using command **datatype**. Functions can be defined over datatypes using primitive recursion. For sake of presentation, we define all definitions and functions using the Isabelle command **fun**. The commands below introduce a simple binary tree type and a function computing the sum of all leaves:

datatype tree-t = LEAF nat | EMPTY | BRANCH tree-t tree-t
fun tree-sum :: tree-t $\Rightarrow$ nat **where**
      tree-sum (BRANCH t_0 t_1) = tree-sum t_0 + tree-sum t_1
  | tree-sum (LEAF n) = n
  | tree-sum - = 0

Records are datatypes generalizing tuples. Components are addressed via a label instead of their position. An important feature of records is to be extensible. We will use records to model the state. Adding new actions to the implementation model typically introduces new parts of the state. The extensibility of records is key in supporting the modular development of the separation kernel model. The commands below introduce a record representing a 2D-point. This record is then extended to a 3D-point.

record point-2d-t = x :: nat y :: nat
record point-3d-t = point-2d-t + z :: nat

3.3   Identifying Atomic Actions

The first step of the implementation model is to identify each preemption point in the C code with a stage. This yields the following five possible stages:

#	Stage	Description
1	CHECK	Check the communications rights of the sender
2	SYNC	Wait for the partner
3	SEND	Send the data
4	REC	Receive the data
5	END	Finish the IPC operation

In Isabelle, this is modelled by a datatype.

datatype ipc-stage-t = CHECK | SYNC | SEND | REC | END

An atomic action consists of a stage and the id of the intended partner t'. When a partition executes an IPC kernel call, the arguments of the call are copied to the thread state. Thread IDs are represented by type *thread_id_t*. Messages are modelled by type *msg_t*. The type of actions *ipc_action_t* is defined as either the IPC kernel call or one of the five atomic stages. We define a type for calling *ipc_send* which takes the id of the partner thread and the message that is to be transmitted. The type for calling *ipc_rec* only takes the id of the partner thread.

datatype ipc-action-t =   CALL-SEND thread-id-t msg-t
                    | CALL-REC thread-id-t
                    | STAGE ipc-stage-t thread-id-t

Obviously, these actions are always executed in a specific order. We define the possible action sequences of atomic actions that can occur due to the IPC operations. In this definition, the lambda expressions create an action sequence out of a given communication partner t' and (in case of the send operation) a message m. The set of possible action sequences are those lists that can be created by these lambda expressions, i.e., their range.

fun ipc-AS-set :: thread-id-t ⇒ ipc-action-t list set **where**
    ipc-AS-set t =
        range ($\lambda(t', m)$. [CALL-SEND t' m,
    STAGE CHECK t', STAGE SYNC t', STAGE SEND t', STAGE END t'])
        ∪
        range ($\lambda t'$. [CALL-REC t',
    STAGE CHECK t', STAGE SYNC t', STAGE REC t', STAGE END t'])

3.4   State and State Transformations

The basic state, i.e., before any action has been modelled, contains one field storing which thread is active. Currently, we assume that only one thread is active at all times. Secondly, we have a model of the memory used by the kernel and the user applications. Our memory includes both virtual and physical memory addresses. Threads may access memory in their own partition or in shared memory. We consider the details of the memory model out of the scope of this paper. In Isabelle, the default state is the following record:

record state-t =
    active-thread :: thread-id-t
    memory :: memory-t

The IPC model extends this state record with those parts that are specific to the IPC call. An *ipc_send* kernel call starts with storing the given message into a specific part of the state. The *rdy* variable is used to implement waiting. Therefore, the following record extension is used to model IPC calls:

record ipc-state-t =
    state-t + msg :: thread-id-t $\Rightarrow$ msg-t rdy :: thread-id-t $\Rightarrow$ bool

We model the semantics of the IPC actions by defining a step function that takes as input an action and a state and returns a new state. We have implemented a function *store_ipc_msg* that takes the message of the IPC call and stores it into a specific part of the memory. Also, we have implemented a function *ipc_data_transfer* that performs the actual data transfer. This function assumes that both partners are ready for the data transfer.

fun ipc-step :: ipc-action-t $\Rightarrow$ thread-id-t $\Rightarrow$ state-t $\Rightarrow$ state-t **where**
    ipc-step (CALL-SEND t′ m) t s = store-ipc-msg m s
    | ipc-step (STAGE CHECK t′) t s = set-rdy s t True
    | ipc-step (STAGE SEND t′) t s = ipc-data-transfer t t′ s
    | ipc-step (STAGE END   t′)   t s = set-rdy s t False
    | ipc-step - - s = s

The execution of an *ipc_send* kernel call first results in storing the message into the state. Then, a check occurs. The only state transformation that results from this check is that the *rdy* flag is to to true. Note that this state transformation will only happen when the action is not aborted or delayed. During the SEND stage, actual data transmission occurs. Finally, the END stage completes the IPC kernel call and sets the *rdy* flag to false.

Note that not all stages actually do a state transformation. For example, the SYNC stage just consists of waiting and therefore no change to the state occurs. Also, in this model during the SEND stage the sender executes the data transfer but in the REC stage the receiver only waits for the sender.

3.5 Aborting and Waiting

During the CHECK stage it might be possible that the IPC operation is not allowed. In that case, the entire IPC operation is aborted. This is expressed by function *ipc_aborting*. During the CHECK stage, it is checked whether the domain is doing an IPC call to itself (i.e., whether $t = t'$) and whether the IPC is not allowed by the information flow policy. In both cases, the action sequence is aborted. In all other stages, the action will not be aborted.

fun ipc-aborting :: ipc-action-t $\Rightarrow$ thread-id-t $\Rightarrow$ state-t $\Rightarrow$ bool **where**
      ipc-aborting (STAGE CHECK t') t s $= (t = t' \vee \neg\, t \rightsquigarrow t' \vee \neg\, t' \rightsquigarrow t)$
  | ipc-aborting - - - = False

When the SYNC stage is reached, the current thread has set its *rdy* variable to true. It waits until the other thread t' has done this as well. In other words, as long as (get-rdy s t') is false, the IPC call waits in its SYNC stage. In the REC stage, the receiver waits until the sender is done sending data. When the sender finished, it set its *rdy* flag to false. The receiver has to wait for this. As long as (get-rdy s t') is true, data transmission is going on and the receiver waits in its REC stage. In all other stages, the action will not be delayed.

fun ipc-waiting :: ipc-action-t $\Rightarrow$ thread-id-t $\Rightarrow$ state-t $\Rightarrow$ bool **where**
      ipc-waiting (STAGE SYNC t') t s $= (\neg\text{get-rdy s } t')$
  | ipc-waiting (STAGE REC t') t s = get-rdy s t'
  | ipc-waiting - - - = False

3.6 Output

The observable output of an IPC kernel call consists of the error codes that it generates and the effects it has on the memory. In our implementation model, we have defined an output function that considers all operations that read or write into memory. Since the IPC uses those operations, it is not necessary to explicitly model the output of the sending and receiving stages. However, for sake of presentation, we define an output function that yields both the error codes and the data transfer.

The first case of function *ipc_output* defines the observable output when the action sequence is aborted in the CHECK stage. In that case, the error code IPC_ERROR is returned. The second case models the observations when data transfer occurs. For sake of presentation, we simply retrieve the message that has been stored into the state using function *get_ipc_msg*. In all other cases, there is no observational output, represented by $\perp$.

fun ipc-output :: state-t $\Rightarrow$ ipc-action-t do $\Rightarrow$ ipc-output-t **where**
      ipc-output s (Abort (STAGE CHECK t')) = IPC-ERROR
  | ipc-output s (Do   (STAGE SEND t')) = get-ipc-msg s
  | ipc-output - - = $\perp$

3.7 Discharging Proof Obligations

In the full implementation model, many preconditions are used to complete the proofs. A precondition takes as parameters the current state s, an action, and

Table 1. Overview of our separation kernel model: "Large" is larger than 1000 Isabelle/HOL LoC in the model, "Small" is less than 250 lines of codes in the model

Description	Size	Description	Size
Configuration and policies	Medium	File providers API	Medium
State definition	Small	IPC API	Large
Proof obligations	Large	Port API	Medium
Memory API	Large	Event API	Medium

the thread t executing that action. For the simplified example, the following preconditions suffice:

1. The duration of the SYNC stage depends on the communication partner. To show the absence of timing attacks, we need to establish that whenever the current thread t is waiting for communication partner t', thread t' is allowed to interfere with thread t. This is expressed by the first line of function *ipc_precondition*.
2. In the SEND stage, the sender t starts transmitting data. At that stage, both thread t and the partner t' have to be ready to receive that data, i.e., both their *rdy* state variables have to be true. This is expressed by the second line of function *ipc_precondition*.

fun ipc-precondition :: state-t $\Rightarrow$ ipc action-t $\rightarrow$ thread-id-t $\Rightarrow$ bool **where**
  ipc-precondition s (STAGE SYNC t') t = $t' \rightsquigarrow t$
  | ipc-precondition s (STAGE SEND t') t — (get-rdy s t $\wedge$ get-rdy s t')
  | ipc-precondition - - - — True

3.8   Separation Kernel Model Details

Table 1 gives an impression about the formalized parts of PikeOS. The size indications include the modelled functions together with the proof of the associated proof obligations. A separate file (proof obligations in the table) handles the linking of all the local proofs into an instantiation of our generic model CISK. In particular, every function has its own extension of the state record. We need to prove that these extensions do not influence each other. Our separation kernel model includes five key API call groups, namely, memory based file providers, memory operations, ports, events, and IPC calls. We also modelled configuration files defining the control access matrix making up the Partitioned Information Flow Policy (PIFP) of the separation kernel. For each of these separation kernel components, we have 1.) identified the atomic stages, 2.) modelled the relevant part of the state and the state transformations, 3.) defined the aborting and waiting predicates and 4.) modelled the observable output. Subsequently, we have discharged all proof obligations.

4   Related Work and Discussion

Intransitive noninterference (NI) has been an active research field for many years [2,3,10–13]. Several methodologies are based on *unwinding*, which is also the basis of our methodology [2,13–15]. This breaks down the proof of NI into smaller proof obligations. These proof obligations can be checked by some manual proof [2,16], model checking [17] or dedicated algorithms [18].

Our work closely relates to the abstract layers of the verification of seL4 [5, 6,19,20]. These abstract layers consist in a high-level specification on which the main security properties are proven. This abstract model is then refined into an abstract specification. This specification is then linked to the actual source code. On the one hand, our model is smaller because it includes fewer API calls. On the other hand, it is more detailed because it models time and interrupts explicitly. Note that our approach considers an abstract specification directly extracted from the source code. We have no counterpart to the high-level specification of seL4.

Even if the objective and the size of our proof largely differs from the verification of seL4, there are several common aspects in both approaches. Similarly to Klein et al. [20], API calls are divided into a checking phase and an execute phase. The former validates the arguments and confirms the authority to execute. The latter executes "and never fails". Functions **aborting** and **waiting** represent the first phase. Function **kstep** represents the second phase. In our methodology, this structure is reverse engineered from the requirements and the source code. Informal arguments need to be made to ensure soundness of the abstraction. [4]

As pointed out by Klein et al., avoiding global variables to model state variables in a modular way is key. In our methodology, this is achieved using extensible records. The global state contains a very limited number of variables. For each API call, this global state is locally extended as necessary. The drawback is that one needs to prove independence between these local extensions. This can lead to a quadratic increase in the number of proof obligations to discharge.

5   Conclusion

We presented a pragmatic approach to the development of formal models of separation kernels. We applied our methodology to all security relevant parts of a separation kernel. Our effort currently focuses on extending our generic model to multi-core processors and using this extension in the Common Criteria evaluation of the industrial separation kernel PikeOS.

References

1. Kaiser, R., Wagner, S.: Evolution of the PikeOS microkernel. In: First International Workshop on Microkernels for Embedded Systems, p. 50 (2007)
2. Rushby, J.: Noninterference, transitivity, and channel-control security policies. SRI International, Computer Science Laboratory (1992)

---

[4] This is part of the CC process.

3. van der Meyden, R.: What, indeed, is intransitive noninterference? In: Biskup, J., López, J. (eds.) Computer Security ESORICS 2007. LNCS, vol. 4734, pp. 235–250. Springer, Heidelberg (2007)
4. EURO-MILS: MILS architecture (2014). http://www.euromils.eu/downloads/2014-euro-mils-mils-architecture-white-paper.pdf
5. Klein, G., Elphinstone, K., Heiser, G., Andronick, J., Cock, D., Derrin, P., Elkaduwe, D., Engelhardt, K., Kolanski, R., Norrish, M., et al.: seL4: Formal verification of an OS kernel. In: Proceedings of the ACM SIGOPS 22nd symposium on Operating systems principles, pp. 207–220. ACM (2009)
6. Murray, T., Matichuk, D., Brassil, M., Gammie, P., Bourke, T., Seefried, S., Lewis, C., Gao, X., Klein, G.: seL4: from general purpose to a proof of information flow enforcement. In: 34th IEEE Symposium on Security and Privacy (2013)
7. Nipkow, T., Paulson, L.C., Wenzel, M.: Isabelle/HOL: a proof assistant for higher-order logic (2012)
8. Jacob, J.: On the derivation of secure components. In: Proceedings of the IEEE Symposium on Security and Privacy, pp. 242–247, May 1989
9. Mantel, H., Sudbrock, H.: Comparing countermeasures against interrupt-related covert channels in an information-theoretic framework. In: Proceedings of 20th IEEE Computer Security Foundations Symposium (CSF 2007), pp. 326–340, July 2007
10. Goguen, J.A., Meseguer, J.: Unwinding and inference control (1984)
11. Mantel, H.: Information flow control and applications - bridging a gap -. In: Oliveira, J., Zave, P. (eds.) Formal Methods for Increasing Software Productivity (FME 2001). LNCS, vol. 2021, pp. 153–172. Springer, Heidelberg (2001)
12. Roscoe, A.W., Goldsmith, M.H.: What is intransitive noninterference? In: Proceedings of the 12th IEEE Computer Security Foundations Workshop, pp. 228–238 (1999)
13. von Oheimb, D.: Information flow control revisited: Noninfluence = noninterference + nonleakage. In: Samarati, P., Ryan, P., Gollmann, D., Molva, R. (eds.) Computer Security - ESORICS 2004. LNCS, vol. 3193, 225th edn, p. 243. Springer, Heidelberg (2004)
14. Leslie, R.: Dynamic intransitive noninterference. In: IEEE International Symposium on Secure Software Engineering (2006)
15. Engelhardt, K., van der Meyden, R., Zhang, C.: Intransitive noninterference in non-deterministic systems. In: Proceedings of the 2012 ACM Conference on Computer and Communications Security, pp. 869–880. ACM (2012)
16. Haigh, J.T., Young, W.D.: Extending the noninterference version of MLS for SAT. IEEE Trans. Softw. Eng. 13(2), 141–150 (1987)
17. Whalen, M., Greve, D., Wagner, L.: Model checking information flow. In: Hardin, D.S. (ed.) Design and Verification of Microprocessor Systems for High-Assurance Applications, pp. 381–428. Springer, US (2010)
18. Eggert, S., van der Meyden, R., Schnoor, H., Wilke, T.: The complexity of intransitive noninterference. In: 2011 IEEE Symposium on Security and Privacy (SP), pp. 196–211 (2011)
19. Murray, T., Matichuk, D., Brassil, M., Gammie, P., Klein, G.: Noninterference for operating system kernels. In: Hawblitzel, C., Miller, D. (eds.) Certified Programs and Proofs. LNCS, vol. 7679, pp. 126–142. Springer, Heidelberg (2012)
20. Klein, G., Andronick, J., Elphinstone, K., Murray, T.C., Sewell, T., Kolanski, R., Heiser, G.: Comprehensive formal verification of an OS microkernel. ACM Trans. Comput. Syst. 32(1), 2 (2014)

Short Papers

Data Model Bugs

Ivan Bocić[✉] and Tevfik Bultan

Department of Computer Science,
University of California, Santa Barbara, USA
{bo,bultan}@cs.ucsb.edu

Abstract. In today's internet-centric world, web applications have replaced desktop applications. Cloud systems are frequently used to store and manage user data. Given the complexity inherent in web applications, it is imperative to ensure that this data is never corrupted. We overview existing techniques for data model verification in web applications, list bugs discovered by these tools, and discuss the impact, difficulty of detection, and prevention of these bugs.

1 Introduction

Software applications have migrated from desktops to the cloud, with many benefits such as, continuous accessibility on a variety of devices, and elimination of software installation, configuration management, updates and patching. These benefits come with a cost in increased complexity.

In order to reduce the complexity and achieve modularity, most modern application frameworks use the Model-View-Controller (MVC) pattern to separate the code for the data model (Model) from the user interface logic (View) and the navigation logic (Controller). Examples of these frameworks include Ruby on Rails (Rails for short), Zend for PHP, Django for Python and Spring for J2EE.

Since modern web applications serve to store and manage user data, the *data model* is a key component of these applications. Data models are responsible for defining the *data model schema,* i.e., the sets of objects and the relations (associations) that describe the stored data format, and *data model actions* which describe the methods used to update the data. For many high profile applications such as HealthCare.gov, DMV, and consumer applications such as Facebook and Gmail, user data is the most valuable asset. Data model correctness is the most significant correctness concern for these applications since erroneous actions can lead to unauthorized access or loss of data.

In this paper we discuss and characterize data model bugs in modern software applications, and the impact of such bugs using concrete examples discovered in open source applications. We show that these bugs have the potential for causing severe and potentially irreparable damage to the data. We discuss the difficulty and plausibility of recovering from these bugs, and survey the known techniques that can help in detecting and preventing these bugs from occurring.

This work is supported in part by the NSF grant CCF-1423623.

K. Havelund et al. (Eds.): NFM 2015, LNCS 9058, pp. 393–399, 2015.
DOI: 10.1007/978-3-319-17524-9_27

2   Data Model Verification Methods

In modern software applications the interactions between the server and the back-end data store is typically managed using an object-relational mapping (ORM) library that maps the object-oriented view of the data model at the server side to the relational database view of the data model at the back-end data store. Since the ORM configuration defines the entity types managed by an application, and actions are implemented using the ORM library, investigation of the data model is largely equivalent to investigating the ORM. We overview the results of using three approaches to data model verification, all of which conform to the same overall architecture presented in Figure 1. Note that this is different from verification techniques that are based on formal specifications [2] which impose a semantic gap between the specification and actual source. These techniques do not ensure that the actual implementation conforms to the specification, making them less useful in detecting existing bugs and unable to verify that no bugs exist in the implementation.

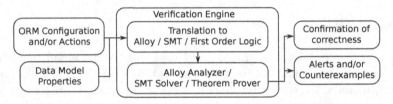

Fig. 1. Overview of Data Model Verification

For example, investigating the ORM configuration is useful for finding bugs in the data model [5]. This technique translates the ORM configuration (schema) into SMT and Alloy for unbounded and bounded verification. Real bugs were found by using this technique, as well as many misuses of different ORM constructs. However, it has a more limited scope of looking at the configuration only, which allows for false positives in case an invalidation (corruption) is possible in the database, but not possible to create using the actions.

We previously extended this work to include action verification as well [1]. Our technique translates the ORM schema, as well as all the actions, into first order logic. A first order logic theorem prover is then used to verify whether model invariants are preserved by the actions, assuming that actions are executed atomically and in any order (a reasonable assumption for RESTful applications). This technique has found other bugs in real world web applications.

Finally, Rubicon [4] is a library for specifying generalized unit tests. These unit tests are not specified with concrete ORM entities, but with quantification over entity types instead. These tests are automatically translated into Alloy for verification. Using this technique, a security vulnerability was found in a real world web application.

3   Reported Data Model Bugs

Before we proceed to discuss data model bugs in general, we will list three web applications and show examples of data model bugs that were found in them [1,4,5]. These bugs vary in nature, severity and potential for recovery, presenting useful background for a deeper discussion.

FatFreeCRM[1] is an application for customer-relation management. It allows for storing and managing customer data, leads that may potentially become customers, contacts, campaigns for marketing etc. It spans 30359 lines of code, 30 model classes and 167 actions. Using action verification [1], we found two bugs in FatFreeCRM that we reported to the developers, who confirmed them and immediately fixed one of them. In future discussion we refer to these two bugs as F1 and F2. Rubicon [4] is a tool for verification of Ruby of Rails applications that translates abstract unit tests to Alloy [3], with the goal of ensuring that these tests would pass when given any set of concrete objects. Bug F3, related to access control, was detected using this technique.

Bug F1 is caused by `Todo` objects, normally associated with a specific `User`, not being deleted when their `User` is deleted. We call these `Todo` objects *orphaned*. Orphaned `Todo` objects are fundamentally invalid because the application assumes that their owner exists, causing crashes whenever an orphaned `Todo`'s owner is accessed. Because of the severity, this bug was acknowledged and repaired immediately after we submitted a bug report.

Bug F2 relates to `Permission` objects. `Permission` objects serve to define access permissions for either a `User` or a `Group` to a given `Asset`. Our tool has found that it is possible to have a `Permission` without associated `User` or `Group` objects. This bug is replicated by deleting a `Group` that has associated `Permissions`. Although similar to F1 in causality, the repercussions of this bugs are very different. If there exists an `Asset` object whose all `Permission` objects do not have associated `Users` or `Groups`, it is possible to expose these assets to the public without any user receiving an error message, and without any `User` or `Group` owning and managing this asset.

Bug F3 is an access control bug that exposes a `User`'s private `Opportunity` objects to other `Users`. This bug is exploited by registering a new `User` in a way that it shares some of the target `User`'s `Contacts`, giving access to private `Opportunity` objects through these `Contacts`. This bug was caused by a false assumption by the developers that all `Opportunity` and `Contact` objects that belong to the same person will have the same `Permissions`. This bug was reported and acknowledged by the developers.

Tracks[2] is an application for organizing tasks, to-do lists etc. This application spans 18023 lines of code, 11 model classes and 70 actions. We identify four bugs in Tracks, which we refer to as T1, T2, T3, and T4. Bug T3 was detected using

---

[1] www.fatfreecrm.com

[2] getontracks.org

data model schema verification [5]. Bugs T1, T2 and T4 were discovered using action verification [1], and were reported to and, since, fixed by the developers.

Bug T1 is related to the possibility of orphaning an instance of a `Dependent` class. This bug is similar to bugs F1 and F2, except that the orphaned objects cannot be accessed by actions in any way. Therefore, this bug does not affect the semantics of the application. However, it does present a memory-leak like bug, affecting performance by unnecessarily populating database tables and indexes.

Bug T2 is very similar in nature to T1. When a `User` is deleted, all `Projects` of the `User` are deleted as well, but `Notes` of deleted `Projects` remain orphaned. These orphaned `Note` objects are not accessible in any way, however, the orphaned `Todos` take up space in the database and inflate indexes.

Bug T3 is caused by deleting a `Context` without correctly cleaning up related `RecurringTodo` objects. This is similar to bug F1 because the orphaned `RecurringTodo` objects are accessible by the application and cause the application to crash.

We found bug T4 when the action verification method [1] reported an inconclusive result within the action used to create `Dependent` instances between two given `Todos`. Semantically, there must not be dependency cycles between `Todos`; this is a structural property of the application. Our method could not prove or disprove that cycles between `Todos` cannot be created. Upon manual inspection we found that, while the UI prevents this, HTTP requests can be made to create a cycle between `Todos`. The repercussions of this bug are potentially enormous. Whenever the application traverses the predecessor list of a `Todo` inside a dependency cycle it will get stuck in an infinite loop, eventually crashing the thread and posting an error to the `User`. No error is shown when the user *creates* this cycle, only later upon accessing it. This creates a situation when repairing the state of the data may be impossible, as discussed in Section 4.

LovdByLess[3] is a social networking application. It allows people to create accounts, write posts and comment on posts of other users, upload and share images etc. It contains 29667 lines of code, 12 model classes and 100 actions.

Data model schema analysis [5] was used to find bug L1 where the `Comments` of a `User` were not cleaned up properly when a `User` is deleted. The orphaned `Comments`, however, remain connected to the `Post` they belong to, and are visible from the said `Post`. The application previews these `Comments`, along with their content and other data, except for the author. The author's name field remains blank. This is not expected behavior: either the `Comments` are supposed to be deleted, or they are supposed to remain, in which case the author's data is lost.

4   Discussion on Data Model Bugs

We identified two types of bugs: access control bugs and data integrity bugs. Access control bugs give access to data to users with insufficient privileges. Data integrity bugs are bugs that allow invalidation of the application's data. Note

---

[3] github.com/stevenbristol/lovd-by-less

that we draw a distinction between bugs that allow data to be invalidated and bugs that are caused by data that has been invalidated. The latter bug is a symptom of the former.

Severity. Access control policies are hard to correctly specify and hard to correctly enforce [4]. Access control bugs are severe bugs. Exposing private information is not permissible in any application that stores and manages private information, nor is allowing access to admin or root level operations.

The severity of data integrity bugs varies on the specifics of the bug, spanning from benign bugs that at most cause minor performance problems, over bugs causing crashes in the application, to bugs causing data loss and corruption from which recovery is exceptionally difficult or impossible.

We identified several data integrity bugs that allow invalid data to exist in the database, but in such a way that this invalid data is never used by the application. We refer to these bugs as *data model leaks.* They are usually caused by incorrect cleanup of related entities when an entity is deleted. This category is demonstrated by bugs T1 and T2. These bugs are hard to detect unless the leaked data accumulates to a certain point. Their impact is limited to performance, not affecting the semantics of the program. They negatively impact performance by taking up space in the database and populating indexes unnecessarily.

In most cases, the corrupted data can be accessed by the application, causing the application to misbehave in some way. We identified a wide range of misbehavior severity. For example, orphaned objects may be visible to the user as empty fields on the webpage (L1), allow operations and further data updates that should not be allowed (F2), or crash the web application (F1, T3, T4).

Recovery. Access control bugs allow no recovery. Once private information has been exposed, fixing the bug only prevents future threats. No measure exists to make the exposed information private again. However, data integrity bugs have recovery potential. Repairing a data integrity bug involves two steps: repairing the data and preventing future invalidation.

In some cases, data is recoverable. For example, once a data model leak is discovered, leaked entities can be identified and removed. The same applies in the case of data being incorrectly deleted: bugs F1, F2, T3 are recoverable from because the original intent of the developer was to delete data. Removing the invalid data not only removes the corruption, but also brings the data store to the state that was originally expected by the developers.

Data integrity bugs that do not manifest themselves through improper deletion are far more difficult to recover from. Repairing the corruption implies modifying the corrupted data into valid data, which may be impossible. T4 is an example of a bug in which valid data is not distinguishable from invalid data. Even clearly distinguishable corrupted data may be unrecoverable if, for example, invalid data has overwritten correct data.

Backups can be used to recover corrupted data in certain cases. This would be a manual and error prone effort, however, and it would rollback the user's data to a previous point which may be undesirable. To make matters worse, since data integrity bugs are observable only if the data has already been invalidated, the corruption may have been backed up in the time frame between the cause of the corruption and the escalation of the bug, making backups unusable.

Detection and Prevention. Data model bugs are hard to anticipate, and addressing them after being detected by users is undesirable because recovery may be extremely difficult. Detection of access control bugs is difficult since a malicious user may leave no trace when accessing restricted information. Similarly, data integrity bugs are hard to detect. They are not observed until the application accesses the invalidated (corrupted) data and misbehaves, which may not be possible (as is the case with bugs T1 and T2). If a user does access the invalidated data, the resulting faulty behavior cannot be replicated by the developer without being given access to the same invalidated data. Furthermore, even given access to this data, the code causing this strange behavior may be correct. No trace exists on how the data was originally invalidated.

Runtime validation is a commonly used technique for the prevention of potential data model integrity bugs. We define runtime validation as any runtime check that aborts the operation with the goal of preventing invalidation. In web application frameworks, validation can be done in the web application layer automatically (both Rails and Django support user definable model validators), or could be manually implemented in actions (in form of conditional branches that abort unless a specific condition is met), or in the database by defining constraints. Frequently multiple approaches are used: for example, the database may validate the integrity of foreign keys, whereas the application layer may validate that email strings adhere to a given format. Runtime validation alone provides an insufficient solution to the problem. This is demonstrated by the fact that we found serious bugs in applications that heavily rely on runtime validation, and have attempted enforcing security policies. For all the bugs we found, the problem was caused by incorrect implementation.

Considering the difficulty of detection, potential severity and unrecoverability of these bugs, we strongly believe that automated verification techniques should' be used to prevent data model bugs. Besides ensuring that static and runtime constraints are sufficient, verification could also be used to detect unnecessary validation. Supported by verification, runtime validation can be more effective in successfully preventing data model bugs.

5   Conclusions

Cloud-based modern software applications store and manipulate their data on remote servers as defined by the data model. We argue that the correctness of the data model is an essential difficulty in building modern software applications. We have demonstrated data model bugs in several open source applications. We have discussed the difficulties in detection, severity, and the potential for recovery from these bugs. Although there have been automated verification techniques proposed for detecting data model bugs, they all have their limitations. Detection and prevention of data model bugs remains to be an important research direction.

References

1. Locić, I., Bultan, T.: Inductive verification of data model invariants for web applications. In: Proceedings of the 36th International Conference on Software Engineering (ICSE 2014), May 2014
2. Deutsch, A., Sui, L., Vianu, V.: Specification and verification of data-driven web applications. Journal of Computer and System Sciences **73**(3), 442–474 (2007)
3. Jackson, D.: Alloy: a lightweight object modelling notation. ACM Transactions on Software Enginnering and Methodology (TOSEM 2002) **11**(2), 256–290 (2002)
4. Near, J.P., Jackson, D.: Rubicon: bounded verification of web applications. In: Proceedings of the ACM SIGSOFT 20th Int. Symp. Foundations of Software Engineering (FSE 2012), pp. 60:1–60:11 (2012)
5. Nijjar, J.: Analysis and Verification of Web Application Data Models. PhD thesis, University of California, Santa Barbara, January 2014

Predicting and Witnessing Data Races Using CSP

Luis M. Carril[✉] and Walter F. Tichy

Institute for Program Structures and Data Organization (IPD), Karlsruhe Institute of Technology (KIT), Am Fasanengarten 5, 76131 Karlsruhe, Germany
{luis.carril,walter.tichy}@kit.edu

Abstract. Detecting and debugging data races is a complex task due to the large number of interleavings possible in a parallel program. Most tools can find the data races reliably in an observed execution, but they miss errors in alternative reorderings of events. In this paper we describe an automated approach to generate, from a single program trace, a model in CSP with alternative interleavings. We check for data races patterns and obtain a witness that allows the reproduction of errors. Reproduction reduces the developer effort to correct the error.

Keywords: Data race · Concurrent programs · Debug · CSP

1 Introduction

Finding and debugging synchronization errors such as data races is a daunting task. As multicore processors become common, tools that help developers cope with data races are desperately needed. A data race happens when two threads access the same variable concurrently and at least one performs a write operation.

Usually, dynamic approaches to race detection are based on happens-before or lockset algorithms. Happens-before detectors [2](based on the Lamports relationship [8]) only cover a specific observed interleaving. They are conservative and need to run multiple times to cover unexplored interleavings. Some works [14] relax the happens-before relationship under certain conditions to cover more cases. The lockset algorithm [12] checks for consistent locking of shared objects, but produces a high number of false positives. Hybrid approaches alse exists [7,10], combining advantages of both.

The interleaving presented in listing 1.1 are difficult to detect. Only if the exact timing in listing 1.2 occurs, a happens-before detector reports the race. Additionally, typical approaches only provide the location of the error, but no context about thread state or how they reached that particular point.

Our approach infers alternative interleavings from an observed program trace and finds data race patterns in these reorderings. Once a pattern matches in one

© Springer International Publishing Switzerland 2015
K. Havelund et al. (Eds.): NFM 2015, LNCS 9058, pp. 400–407, 2015.
DOI: 10.1007/978-3-319-17524-9_28

reordering, these reordering is a story on how the program reaches the erroneous state. We infer the interleavings by constructing a model that combines the independent actions of the threads and the semantic behavior of the synchronization operations (e.g.: a mutex can only be held by one thread at a time). This model is described with the process algebra CSP (Communicating Sequential Processes [5]) and the pattern search is done with CSP refinement relationships. This approach not only allows the prediction races, but also provides the steps which lead to that race.

Similar work is found in the maximal causal model [6] and witness generation [11]. These works can also predict races and provide counterexamples from a single observation using a read-write consistency model implemented with SMT.

<table>
<tr><td colspan="2">Listing 1.1. Original captured trace</td><td colspan="2">Listing 1.2. Reordering with data race</td></tr>
</table>

	Thread 1	Thread 2		Thread 1	Thread 2
1:	y++		1:		lock (m)
2:	lock (m)		2:		x++
3:	x++		3:		unlock (m)
4:	unlock (m)		4:		y++
5:		lock (m)	5:	y++	
6:		x++	6:	lock (m)	
7:		unlock (m)	7:	x++	
8:		y++	8:	unlock (m)	

2 Detecting Races with CSP

CSP is a formal language to describe a system composed by processes (in uppercase), each process is a sequence of atomic events (in lowercase). Then processes communicate with each other and the environment (which can be another process) sharing events synchronously.

Our approach consists of defining a CSP process $PROGRAM$, that represents all alternative interleavings of a captured trace. Using a CSP refinement relationship we check if the $PROGRAM$ process matches a data race pattern (defined as a CSP process). When the relationship does not hold, a data race is revealed along with a counterexample, that allows to reproduce the scenario with the data race.

2.1 Modeling Events

A captured trace consists of a sequence of the following events: $read$, $write$, $start$, end, $fork$, $join$, $lock$ and $unlock$. The events $start$ and end have a single parameter: the thread identifier. The other events have two parameters: a related thread identifier and a relevant object for the operation: a child thread, a mutex or a variable. We map each captured event directly to a CSP event; e.g. a lock by thread t_1 on lock l_1 is represented $lock.t_1.l_1$. A symbol ? represents any valid value for a parameter; then $lock?t.l_1$ is a lock event on l_1 by any thread.

2.2 Modeling the Program

To construct the process $PROGRAM$ which represents all possible reorderings of the trace, we model the behavior of the different threads and the semantics of the synchronizing operations independently with CSP processes.

Each thread is modeled using the events that it had performed in the captured trace. We only keep one access to a variable per thread between two synchronizing operations. The corresponding events in CSP are concatenated using the prefix operator $\rightarrow$, which creates a total order for the thread trace as it has been observed; e.g. for the thread 1 in the listing 1.1:

$$THREAD_1 = write.t_1.y \rightarrow lock.t_1.m \rightarrow write.t_1.x \rightarrow unlock.t_1.m \rightarrow STOP$$

The process $STOP$ denotes a process which performs no actions (is a reserved CSP process). All these thread processes are combined with the CSP interleaving operator $|||$. The resulting process contains all reorderings of events of the thread processes, but obeying the total order corresponding to each thread:

$$T\_INTER = |||_{i \in Threads}\ T_i$$

This operation is agnostic of the semantic meaning of the events, so the process also contains a lot of traces that would not be possible in the original program, for example the order $..., lock.t_1.m, lock.t_2.m, ...$ We avoid these illegal interleavings modeling the semantic restrictions of synchronizing operations: forking, joining and mutex accesses.

The restrictions are modeled in the process $SYNC$. We compose the previous T_INTER process with the $SYNC$ process using the generalized parallel operator:

$$PROGRAM = T\_INTER \underset{sync\_set}{\|} SYNC$$

$$sync\_set = \{\!| start, end, fork, join, lock, unlock |\!\}$$

Where $\{\!|x|\!\}$ denotes all events derived from x. The parallel operator ensures that if a process wants to execute an event in the set, the other process must be ready to execute it too, otherwise it will be blocked until the second process is also ready. The T_INTER and $SYNC$ processes synchronize in all events with the exception of $read$ and $write$ events. This combination ensures that all traces of process $PROGRAM$ are traces that follow the order restrictions of T_INTER (total order per thread) and the order restrictions of $SYNC$ (order of the synchronization operations). The process $PROGRAM$ reflects all the interleavings possible by our original program in the path covered by the initial observation.

The $SYNC$ process describes the following synchronizations: thread creation, thread joining, mutex locking and unlocking. We define and interleave a process for each specific synchronization class.

$$SYNC = FORKS \;|||\; JOINS \;|||\; MUTEXES$$
$$FORKS = |||_{i \in Threads} \; FORK(i)$$
$$JOINS = |||_{i \in Threads} \; JOIN(i)$$
$$MUTEXES = |||_{i \in Mutexes} \; MUTEX(i)$$

Each of these processes represent a subgroup of restrictions on the order of the synchronization operations.

The creation of each thread is defined by a process

$$FORK(i) = fork?t.i \rightarrow start.i \rightarrow STOP$$

The *start* event cannot happen if any other thread has not realized a *fork* on the created thread. This process finally stops without doing anything else.

The *join* of each thread is defined by a process

$$JOIN(i) = end.i \rightarrow join?t.i \rightarrow STOP$$

Similar to the previous process, this is a one-shot process where any *join* on i cannot be complete until the corresponding process executes its *end* event.

A mutex process is described as a recursive process:

$$MUTEX(i) = lock?t.i \rightarrow unlock.t.i \rightarrow MUTEX(i)$$

For a specific mutex i this process is the only one capable of executing *lock* and *unlock* events on it, after one thread process executes the *lock.t.i* operation, the other thread processes are blocked until the corresponding *unlock* event occurs. Afterwards the process returns to the initial point where it accepts the *lock* event for any thread.

2.3   Detecting Races in CSP

With a CSP process representing the observed trace and the alternative reorderings along the same path, we check the model for data races. A race is the concurrent execution of two events from different threads on the same variable, where at least one is a write. Then a trace containing a data race has one of the following subtraces:

$read.t_1.v, write.t_2.v$	$write.t_1.v, read.t_2.v$	$write.t_1.v, write.t_2.v$
$read.t_2.v, write.t_1.v$	$write.t_2.v, read.t_1.v$	$write.t_2.v, write.t_1.v$

The two conflicting events can be observed consecutively and without any synchronization between them. We build a process $PATTERN$ which executes an event *race* when it performs one of these subtraces for a specific t_1, t_2 and v. The *race* event works as an indicator that a race has been found. The process $PATTERN$ is defined as:

$$PATTERN(t_1, t_2, v) = PATT\_ERR(t_1, t_2, v)$$
$$\triangle\,(\square\; x : sync\_set \cup rw\_set@x \rightarrow PATTERN(t_1, t_2, v))$$
$$rw\_set = \{read.t_1.v, write.t_1.v, read.t_2.v, write.t_2.v\}$$
$$PATT\_ERR(t_1, t_2, v) = read.t_1.v \rightarrow write.t_2.v \rightarrow race \rightarrow STOP$$
$$\square\; read.t_2.v \rightarrow write.t_1.v \rightarrow race \rightarrow STOP$$
$$\square\; write.t_1.v \rightarrow read.t_2.v \rightarrow race \rightarrow STOP$$
$$\square\; write.t_1.v \rightarrow write.t_2.v \rightarrow race \rightarrow STOP$$
$$\square\; write.t_2.v \rightarrow read.t_1.v \rightarrow race \rightarrow STOP$$
$$\square\; write.t_2.v \rightarrow write.t_1.v \rightarrow race \rightarrow STOP$$

The $PATT\_ERR$ process is the combination of the six cases described, it can perform any of them. Only when one of the cases (one option of $PATT\_ERR$) is completed, the $race$ event is fired. The process can be restarted in any state (with the $\triangle$ interrupt operator), to permit any other event combination being the prefix of the racy subtraces.

We verify a property in CSP describing it in terms of a refinement relationship $S \sqsubseteq_T I$. A refinement relationship holds if the *behavior* of the implementation process I is a subset of the *behavior* of the specification process S. *Behavior* means the set of all possible traces. We compose the $PATTERN$ process in parallel with the $PROGRAM$ process, so the process $PATTERN$ participates in the execution of all events of $PROGRAM$. But $PATTERN$ is always available to perform any event, so it will not interfere with $PROGRAM$ process orderings. Using the hiding operator $\backslash$ all events become non-observable, with the exception of the $race$ event, the one that reveals a matching pattern. We check if the resulting process refines the process $STOP$.

$$STOP \sqsubseteq_T (PROGRAM \underset{rw\_set \cup sync\_set}{\|} PATTERN(t_1, t_2, v)) \setminus \Sigma - \{race\}$$

Σ denotes all the events in the model. If the process composed of $PROGRAM$ and $PATTERN$ reaches the event $race$ then the refinement does not hold and there is a data race between t_1 and t_2 for variable v. But if there is no path to reach the $race$ event, then the composition behaves exactly like $STOP$ and the refinement holds.

The corresponding model and assertions for the trace in listing 1.1 is:

$$THREAD_1 = write.t_1.y \rightarrow lock.t_1.m \rightarrow write.t_1.x \rightarrow unlock.t_1.m \rightarrow SKIP$$
$$THREAD_2 = lock.t_2.m \rightarrow write.t_2.x \rightarrow unlock.t_2.m \rightarrow write.t_2.y \rightarrow SKIP$$
$$PROGRAM = (THREAD_1 \;|||\; THREAD_2) \underset{sync\_set}{\|} MUTEX(m)$$
$$STOP \sqsubseteq_T (PROGRAM \underset{rw\_set \cup sync\_set}{\|} PATTERN(t_1, t_2, x)) \setminus \Sigma - \{race\} \quad (1)$$
$$STOP \sqsubseteq_T (PROGRAM \underset{rw\_set \cup sync\_set}{\|} PATTERN(t_1, t_2, y)) \setminus \Sigma - \{race\} \quad (2)$$

The refinement on x (1) holds but the refinement on y (2) not.

When the refinement is violated, at least one sequence of events in the composition leading to the *race* event exists. We focus only on the trace performed by the *PROGRAM* process, as the process representing the original program. The counterexample takes the form of a sequence of only the synchronization events. For the violated refinement (2) on x in the example, a counterexample is:

$$lock.t_2.m, unlock.t_2.m$$

If we replay the program only allowing the synchronizations operations in the counterexample and in the specified order, we reach a state where all actions performed by the threads are happening concurrently, exposing the data race. For example the case shown in listing 1.2.

3   Preliminary Evaluation

We implemented an automatic tool that generates the corresponding model for a given trace. Our target programs are binaries of multithreaded C programs using the pthread library [1]. We developed a Valgrind [9] plug-in to capture the trace, through a combination of binary instrumentation and library hooks. The trace is post-processed to simplify it and detect shared variables. For each shared variable, a CSP model is built ignoring the events of other variables so it contains the minimum number of events necessary. A refinement check is build for each combination of two threads and shared variable. The model and assertions are coded in CSP_M (machine readable CSP) and fed to the Failures-Divergences Refinement 3 model checker[4]. The evaluation has been done on a dual core machine with 1.4GHz processor and 1GB RAM.

Table 1. Preliminary evaluation

Scenarios	LOC	Real races	Trace size	Checks	Races	HG-Races
20	952	14	20289	28	14	11

Table 1 shows the preliminary evaluation, as the aggregate values of a set of small scenarios. The scenarios are a collection from multiple sources[13–15]. Scenarios from papers have been coded explicitly. Some scenarios are specially complicated for a happens-before detector to reason about, as the cases in [14]. The first column is the number of scenarios, the second column the aggregated lines of code. The third column is the total number of real races in all the scenarios (one per location). The fourth column is the total size (number of events) of the post-processed traces after a single execution. The fifth column is the number of checks (refinements) made. The sixth column shows how many races have been confirmed by the refinements and generated a counterexample. Finally the seventh column shows how many races Helgrind finds in average of 10 executions.

The results show that from a single execution our approach can find more races than Helgrind in multiple executions. A non-predictive race detector relies on reaching a specific timing to be able to see some races. But our solution is time-agnostic finding the races along the same path in the program.

Also race detectors usually provide only the localization of the race, but no information on when and how the program has reached that position. Mixing the race detector with interactive debugging can make the erroneous state difficult to reach, because the probe effect [3]. Our tool provides a step by step counterexample of the synchronization steps that can be use to reproduce the observed data race.

A pure happens-before tool cannot provide false positives. Although not shown in these examples, our approach can provide false positives; if a reordering of the synchronization operations leads to a different path in the program that has not been observed, the race could not exist and the counterexample is infeasible. To tackle this cases, we plan to prune this cases with automatic enforcement and checking of the counterexample. Also improving the model with control flow information as in [6] and implementing more synchronization primitives.

The scalability of the approach is limited by two factors: length of the trace and number of shared variables. A longer trace produces a more complex model, and the model checker needs more time. But our model increases in complexity only with the number of synchronization operations in the trace, which is expected to be a small fraction of the whole program trace. Further improvement can be done by partitioning the trace in windows and checking only one partition at a time. This increases the number of false negatives, as interactions between windows are lost. The number of checks also increases with the number of variables, but we can reduce this cost with a previous filtering step using a cheaper algorithm, that does not produce false negatives but reduces the number of candidates, e.g.: a relaxed happens-before without mutex edges.

4   Conclusion

This paper describes a work-in-progress approach to predict data races and generate a trace witness. We capture a single trace of a multithreaded application and model it in CSP. This model not only includes the observed interleaving but also the alternative reorderings of other possible executions. Using the capabilities of the process algebra we find data race patterns and generate the corresponding counterexamples. These counterexamples reflect how the program reached the erroneous states, and greatly facilitate the debugging process.

Acknowledgments. The authors would like to thank Siemens Corporate Technology for their financial support. We also appreciate the support of the Initiative for Excellence at the Karlsruhe Institute of Technology.

References

1. Barney, B.L.L.N.L.: POSIX Threads Programming. https://computing.llnl.gov/tutorials/pthreads/

2. Flanagan, C., Freund, S.N.S.: FastTrack: efficient and precise dynamic race detection. In: PLDI 2009 Proceedings of the 2009 ACM SIGPLAN Conference on Programming Language Design and Implementation, PLDI 2009, pp. 121–133. ACM, New York (2009). http://doi.acm.org/10.1145/1542476.1542490, http://dl.acm.org/citation.cfm?id=1542490

3. Gait, J.: A probe effect in concurrent programs. Software: Practice and Experience **16**(3), 225–233 (1986)

4. Gibson-Robinson, T., Armstrong, P., Boulgakov, A., Roscoe, A.W.: FDR3 — a modern refinement checker for CSP. In: Ábrahám, E., Havelund, K. (eds.) TACAS 2014 (ETAPS). LNCS, vol. 8413, pp. 187–201. Springer, Heidelberg (2014)

5. Hoare, C.: Communicating Sequential Processes. Communications of the ACM **21**(8), 666–677 (1978). http://www.cs.ucf.edu/courses/cop4020/sum2009/CSP-hoare.pdf

6. Huang, J., Meredith, P., Rosu, G.: Maximal sound predictive race detection with control flow abstraction. In: PLDI 2014 Proceedings of the 35th ACM SIGPLAN Conference on Programming Language Design and Implementation, pp. 337–348 (2014). http://dl.acm.org/citation.cfm?id=2594315

7. Jannesari, A., Tichy, W.F.: On-the-fly race detection in multi-threaded programs. In: Proceedings of the 6th Workshop on Parallel and Distributed Systems: Testing, Analysis, and Debugging, PADTAD 2008, pp. 6:1–6:10. ACM, New York (2008). http://doi.acm.org/10.1145/1390841.1390847, http://www.cs.umd.edu/pugh/ISSTA08/padtad2008/papers/a8-jannesari.pdf

8. Lamport, L.: Time, clocks, and the ordering of events in a distributed system. Communications of the ACM **21**(7), 558–565 (1978). http://dl.acm.org/citation.cfm?id=359563

9. Nethercote, N., Seward, J.: Valgrind: a framework for heavyweight dynamicbinary instrumentation. ACM Sigplan Notices, 89–100 (2007). http://dl.acm.org/citation.cfm?id=1250746

10. Pozniansky, E., Schuster, A.: MultiRace: efficient on the fly data race detection in multithreaded C++ programs. Concurrency and Computation: Practice and Experience **19**(3), 327–340 (2007). http://onlinelibrary.wiley.com/doi/10.1002/cpe.1064/abstract

11. Said, M., Wang, C., Yang, Z., Sakallah, K.: Generating data race witnesses by an SMT-based analysis. In: Bobaru, M., Havelund, K., Holzmann, G.J., Joshi, R. (eds.) NFM 2011. LNCS, vol. 6617, pp. 313–327. Springer, Heidelberg (2011)

12. Savage, S., Burrows, M., Nelson, G., Sobalvarro, P., Anderson, T.: Eraser: a dynamic data race detector for multithreaded programs. ACM Transactions on Computer Systems **15**(4), 391–411 (1997). http://doi.acm.org/10.1145/265924.265927, http://portal.acm.org/citation.cfm?doid=265924.265927

13. Serebryany, K., Iskhodzhanov, T.: ThreadSanitizer: data race detection in practice. In: WBIA 2009 Proceedings of the Workshop on Binary Instrumentation and Applications, pp. 62–71 (2009). http://dl.acm.org/citation.cfm?id=1791203

14. Smaragdakis, Y., Evans, J., Sadowski, C., Yi, J., Flanagan, C.: Sound predictive race detection in polynomial time. In: Proceedings of the 39th Annual ACM SIGPLAN-SIGACT Symposium on Principles of Programming Languages, POPL 2012, p. 387 (2012). http://dl.acm.org/citation.cfm?doid=2103656.2103702

15. Valgrind: Helgrind: a data-race detector (2007). http://valgrind.org/docs/manual/hg-manual.html

A Benchmark Suite
for Hybrid Systems Reachability Analysis

Xin Chen[1], Stefan Schupp[1]([✉]), Ibtissem Ben Makhlouf[1], Erika Ábrahám[1],
Goran Frehse[2], and Stefan Kowalewski[1]

[1] RWTH Aachen University, Aachen, Germany
[2] Verimag, Gières, France
stefan.schupp@cs.rwth-aachen.de

Abstract. Since about two decades, formal methods for continuous and hybrid systems enjoy increasing interest in the research community. A wide range of analysis techniques were developed and implemented in powerful tools. However, the lack of appropriate benchmarks make the testing, evaluation and comparison of those tools difficult. To support these processes and to ease exchange and repeatability, we present a manifold benchmark suite for the reachability analysis of hybrid systems. Detailed model descriptions, classification schemes, and experimental evaluations help to find the right models for a given purpose.

1 Introduction

Recent advances in algorithms have turned reachability analysis into a powerful method for continuous and hybrid systems. Techniques are available that can compute approximations of the reachable states for systems with linear dynamics and more than 200 variables [11,16], and for complex non-linear dynamics [5,6,12]. Without any claim for completeness, some prominent tools based on different techniques are SPACEEX [11], FLOW* [6], DREACH [12], KEYMAERA [17], ISAT [10], HSOLVER [18], HYCREATE [14], ARIADNE [7] and CORA [1]. Since in general the reachability problem is undecidable for hybrid systems, and even the one-step successors can only be computed approximately, experimental results are essential for validating algorithms, detecting their shortcomings, and identifying where further research is necessary.

Experiments in reachability require not only algorithms, but also models of systems and specifications that are to be verified. Such benchmarks are not easy to come by, in particular when looking for high-dimensional systems. Research papers typically include a small number of proprietary benchmarks, or modified versions of benchmarks published in other papers. A notable exception is a small collection of benchmarks in [8], and the benchmark collection of the ARCH

This work was partially supported by the German Research Council (DFG) in the context of the HyPro project.

K. Havelund et al. (Eds.): NFM 2015, LNCS 9058, pp. 408–414, 2015.
DOI: 10.1007/978-3-319-17524-9_29

workshop series, which is tailored to industrial applications [2]. Using just a small number of benchmarks for test and evaluation comprehends the risk to tune tools to be efficient for certain application types only.

In this paper, we present a manifold collection of benchmarks for evaluating tools and algorithms for hybrid systems reachability, and to the best of our knowledge it is the first of this kind. It consists of system models along with property specifications, includes detailed descriptions, references to prior work, input files and exemplary results for some tools. Apart from making the benchmarks readily available in a unified form, the benchmark collection intends to make the following contributions:

Classification: The benchmarks originate from a variety of domains and serve a variety of purposes, e.g., testing scalability with respect to the number of variables or locations. Identifying a benchmark that suits a particular tool and helps to evaluate a certain property is non-trivial. The collection is organized by the model type (continuous/hybrid, linear/non-linear), which roughly corresponds to the kind of tool to which it is applicable. Within each class, benchmarks are listed by complexity (scalability, number of variables, locations, transitions). We intend to identify further attributes that help to find benchmarks with certain requested properties.

Specification: To ensure comparability of results between different tools, the specification needs to be unambiguous and formal. We provide such formal model specifications for all included benchmarks. Note that not all benchmarks easily lend themselves to specifications in the typical form of a given set of "bad states". For example, some benchmarks for testing the accuracy of approximations give quantitative results. Finding a unified form for specifying systems as well as their specifications is one of the long-term goals of the collection.

Evaluation criteria: Measuring the efficiency of algorithms can be done by measuring the running time and memory requirements of tools implementing them. Though comparing such measurements for different technologies is not objective, because the results are machine- and implementation-dependent, considering a larger experimental setting with a wider range of benchmarks allows to implicitly incorporate also other aspects such as accuracy, scalability and convergence rate (which in general influence running time and memory consumption).

Identifying challenges: Though state-of-the-art hybrid systems reachability analysis tools are impressively successful and can solve a wide range of interesting problems, they are still rarely applied outside their own community. Driving research directions towards the needs of other scientific areas and application domains would push this process forwards. Therefore, one of our long-term goals is to identify benchmarks suitable for this purpose, even if current tools do not exhibit sufficient functionalities yet.

Clearly, some of the above points will need to evolve while our benchmark suite grows and feedback from experiments becomes available.

The remainder of the paper is organized as follows: In the next section, we provide a brief overview of the benchmark collection. In Section 3, we show and discuss results for three tools on the benchmark suite, and conclude the paper in Section 4. The complete benchmark collection is available at [4].

2   The Benchmark Suite

Our benchmark suite currently covers 28 benchmarks. The included benchmarks are selected to cover different levels of expressivity in their components.

- We provide both pure *continuous* benchmarks as well as *hybrid* models.
- The continuous dynamics is described by either *linear* or *non-linear* ordinary differential equations.
- A further classification is provided according to the *number of variables* and, for hybrid behavior, the *number of locations* and the *number of discrete transitions*. One of the benchmarks is *scalable*, allowing the generation of high-dimensional models.
- The hybrid models specify *transition guards* varying in their form from half-spaces or hyperplanes over linear conditions up to non-linear ones.
- *Reset conditions* can be absent or described by linear terms.
- *Invariants* are boxes in some benchmarks and polyhedra in others.
- Reachability analysis is hindered by *Zeno behavior*, which is present in some of the models.

Our collection of linear benchmarks includes well-known smaller models such as the *bouncing ball* or the *two tank system*, as well as less known benchmarks, such as the *vehicle platoon* [3]. For the sake of completeness and for testing purposes we have decided to include also small but frequently referenced benchmarks. For the future it would be nice to have an even larger collection of small benchmarks that set traps for the reachability analysis through various model properties such as instability, Zeno behavior or deadlocks.

The non-linear models in our collection include benchmarks from different research fields such as mechanics, biology or electrical engineering. We have managed to extract benchmarks such as the *non-holonomic integrator* [13], the *spiking neurons* [15], *glycemic control* [9], or the *non-linear transmission line circuits* [19] from external sources, thus enhancing the collection by relevant, non-artificial benchmarks which are of interest in the previously mentioned fields and are now open to the formal methods community. Such non-artificial models are important for driving tool development towards being capable to solve real-world problems of different types.

The web page presentation [4] lists all benchmarks along with their property specifications, classified into linear continuous, non-linear continuous, linear hybrid, and non-linear hybrid models. For each model we list also measures regarding their size. We explain each of the benchmarks in our collection on its own web page, reference originating literature, provide a model description for downloading in SPACEEX and/or FLOW* input format, and show example plottings of the reachable state set generated by those tools. In the future we plan to provide such information also for other tools.

Table 1. Linear hybrid benchmark results. Legends: **var**: #variables, **unsafe**: unsafe conditions, t: running time in secs, δ: time-step size, k: Taylor model order, **T.O.**: > 900 secs, **fail**: fail to prove the safety with $\delta \geq$ 1e-14.

benchmarks	var	unsafe	SpaceEx					Flow*		
			STC		LGG					
			t (s)		t (s)		δ	t (s)	δ	k
			box	oct	box	oct				
bouncing ball	2	$v \geq 10.7$	0.13	0.15	**0.02**	0.05	0.1	0.3	0.1	5
two tank system	2	$x_2 \leq -0.76$	*fail*	0.15	*fail*	**0.05**	0.01	5.3	0.01	10
rod reactor	3	location: shutdown	0.63	2.16	**0.09**	0.26	0.1	2.3	0.1	5
cruise control	3	$v \leq -2$	*fail*	*fail*	**0.08**	0.24	0.1	3.5	0.1	5
5-D lin. switch	5	$x_1 \leq -1.2$	0.06	0.79	**0.01**	9.23	0.01	1.8	0.01	15
3 vehicle platoon	9	$e_1 \geq 1.7$	0.19	9.4	**0.11**	10.28	0.1	20.3	0.02	10
filt. oscillator 4	6	$y \geq 0.5$	0.11	1.22	**0.09**	1.1	0.1	1.4	0.05	8
filt. oscillator 8	10	$y \geq 0.5$	0.32	13.9	**0.15**	10.5	0.1	4.1	0.05	8
filt. oscillator 16	18	$y \geq 0.5$	1.1	280	**0.2**	201	0.1	13.7	0.05	8
filt. oscillator 32	34	$y \geq 0.5$	**3.28**	*T.O.*	3.8	*T.O.*	0.1	70	0.05	8
5 vehicle platoon	16	$e_1 \in [-0.5, -0.2]$	**0.1**	1.54	*fail*	*fail*	1e-14	3.6	0.5	16
10 vehicle platoon	31	$e_1 \in [-0.5, -0.2]$	**0.29**	6.38	*fail*	*fail*	1e-14	44	0.5	20

3   Experimental Results

In this section we demonstrate the advantages of our benchmark suite by using hybrid models for the comparison of the tools SpaceEx, Flow* and dReach. Since different tools are devoted to different problem types, we distinguish between linear and non-linear hybrid benchmarks. All experiments were run on a Intel Core I-7 quad-core CPU with 4.0 GHz and 16 GB memory.

3.1   Linear Hybrid Benchmarks

SpaceEx [11] and Flow* [6] are two established tools for the reachability analysis of hybrid systems. SpaceEx is well-suited to analyze linear hybrid systems, whereas Flow* is specialized in non-linear systems but with a recent enhancement for dealing with linear systems.

SpaceEx has two scenarios. One of them is based on the LGG algorithm using support functions. The second one is the STC scenario, a recent enhancement of the LGG algorithm that produces fewer convex sets for a given accuracy and computes more precise images of discrete transitions. In SpaceEx, flowpipes are over-approximated by boxes or octagons, both of which are computed based on the same support functions. On the other hand, Flow* only uses Taylor Models for over-approximations.

In Table 3, we specify for each benchmark an unsafe condition, and use both of the tools to prove the safety of the system. For SpaceEx, we consider both of box and octagon, because the overall accuracy of octagons are better than that of boxes in general. From the table, it can be seen that the performance of the tools gradually becomes worse when the benchmark scale grows. On the

Table 2. Non-linear hybrid benchmark results. Legends: **var**: #variables, **unsafe**: unsafe conditions, δ: time-step size, k in FLOW*: Taylor-model order, t: running time in secs, N: #subdivisions on the initial set, k in DREACH: unrolling depth of bounded model checking, p: value of numerical perturbation, **T.O.**: > 3600 secs.

benchmark	var	unsafe	FLOW*			DREACH			
			δ	k	t (s)	N	k	p	t (s)
non-holonomic integrator	3	$x \geq 3$	0.01	$5 \sim 8$	**201**	$1 \sim 10$	≤ 1	0.001	$T.O.$
spiking neuron I	2	$u \leq -25$	0.02	$4 \sim 6$	**367**	≥ 100	≤ 15	0.0001	$fail$
spiking neuron II	2	$u \geq 250$	0.02	$4 \sim 6$	**70**	$1 \sim 10$	≤ 15	0.001	$T.O.$
glycemic control I	3	$G \leq -2$	0.05	$2 \sim 5$	64	5	≤ 2	0.01	**1.1**
glycemic control II	3	$G \leq -2$	0.05	$2 \sim 5$	**95**	$1 \sim 5$	≤ 2	0.01	$T.O.$
glycemic control III	3	$G \leq -2$	0.05	$2 \sim 5$	**46**	$1 \sim 5$	≤ 1	0.01	$T.O.$
line circuit n = 2	2	$v_1 \geq 0.21$	0.01	$3 \sim 6$	2.3	1	≤ 2	0.01	**0.2**
line circuit n = 4	4	$v_1 \geq 0.21$	0.01	$3 \sim 6$	48	4	≤ 2	0.01	**9.6**
line circuit n = 6	6	$v_1 \geq 0.21$	$0.0002 \sim 0.02$	4	**243**	4	≤ 2	0.01	$T.O.$

other hand, some of the safety properties can not be proved (with "fail" in the table) due to the inaccuracy. Hence, the linear benchmarks from our collection are well-suited to evaluate tools in the aspects of accuracy and scalability.

3.2   Non-linear Hybrid Benchmarks

Since SPACEEX cannot work with non-linear models, we evaluate the performance of FLOW* [6] and DREACH [12] on the non-linear models in our benchmark suite. The main motivation to choose these tools is that FLOW* is a typical safety verification tool based on flowpipe computation, while DREACH is based on bounded model checking using constraint solving techniques. Thus we expect them to perform differently on different benchmarks.

We selected 12 non-linear benchmark instances from our benchmark suite for this experiment. The experimental results are listed in Table 2. The purpose of each experiment is to prove the safety. Since DREACH cannot integrate large initial sets, for each benchmark, we divide the initial set into N parts in each dimension. Then for n variables, there are N^n subdivisions. Unlike the linear cases, the dynamics defined by a non-linear ODE can be very hard to handle. It can be seen that FLOW* outperforms DREACH on hard dynamics, while DREACH works better when the dynamics is moderate. Therefore, our collection of non-linear benchmarks may provide a reasonable evaluation of a tool in not only scalability but also the ability to deal with hard dynamics.

4   Conclusion

The presented benchmark suite is an important first step to support the testing, evaluation and comparison of hybrid systems reachability analysis tools. Next steps will cover the extension with further benchmarks, including models with more expressive power like, e.g., continuous dynamics involving transcendental functions, urgent locations and transitions, or non-convex location invariants and transition guards. We will also investigate further classification criteria, with special interest in providing measures for the hardness of the problems. These steps are not only helpful for finding appropriate benchmarks and for evaluating tools, but also for the identification of interesting future research directions towards challenging unsolved problems.

References

1. Althoff, M., Dolan, J.M.: Online verification of automated road vehicles using reachability analysis. IEEE Trans. on Robotics **30**(4), 903–918 (2014)
2. Althoff, M., Frehse, G.: Benchmarks of the Workshop on Applied Verification of Continuous and Hybrid Systems (ARCH) (2014). http://cps-vo.org/group/ARCH/benchmarks
3. Ben Makhlouf, I., Diab, H., Kowalewski, S.: Safety verification of a controlled cooperative platoon under loss of communication using zonotopes. In: Proc. of ADHS 2012, pp. 333–338. IFAC-PapersOnLine (2012)
4. Benchmarks of continuous and hybrid systems. http://ths.rwth-aachen.de/research/hypro/benchmarks-of-continuous-and-hybrid-systems/
5. Bouissou, O., Chapoutot, A., Djoudi, A.: Enclosing temporal evolution of dynamical systems using numerical methods. In: Brat, G., Rungta, N., Venet, A. (eds.) NFM 2013. LNCS, vol. 7871, pp. 108–123. Springer, Heidelberg (2013)
6. Chen, X., Ábrahám, E., Sankaranarayanan, S.: Flow*: an analyzer for non-linear hybrid systems. In: Sharygina, N., Veith, H. (eds.) CAV 2013. LNCS, vol. 8044, pp. 258–263. Springer, Heidelberg (2013)
7. Collins, P., Bresolin, D., Geretti, L., Villa, T.: Computing the evolution of hybrid systems using rigorous function calculus. In: Proc. of ADHS 2012, pp. 284–290. IFAC-PapersOnLine (2012)
8. Fehnker, A., Ivančić, F.: Benchmarks for hybrid systems verification. In: Alur, R., Pappas, G.J. (eds.) HSCC 2004. LNCS, vol. 2993, pp. 326–341. Springer, Heidelberg (2004)
9. Fisher, M.: A semiclosed-loop algorithm for the control of blood glucose levels in diabetics. IEEE Trans. on Biomedical Engineering **38**(1), 57–61 (1991)
10. Fränzle, M., Herde, C., Ratschan, S., Schubert, T., Teige, T.: Efficient solving of large non-linear arithmetic constraint systems with complex Boolean structure. Journal on Satisfiability, Boolean Modeling and Computation **1**, 209–236 (2007)
11. Frehse, G., et al.: SpaceEx: scalable verification of hybrid systems. In: Gopalakrishnan, G., Qadeer, S. (eds.) CAV 2011. LNCS, vol. 6806, pp. 379–395. Springer, Heidelberg (2011)
12. Gao, S.: Computable Analysis, Decision Procedures, and Hybrid Automata: A New Framework for the Formal Verification of Cyber-Physical Systems. Ph.D. thesis, Carnegie Mellon University (2012)
13. Hespanha, J., Morse, A.: Stabilization of nonholonomic integrators via logic-based switching. Automatica **35**(3), 385–393 (1999)
14. HyCreate: A tool for overapproximating reachability of hybrid automata. http://stanleybak.com/projects/hycreate/hycreate.html
15. Izhikevich, E.: Dynamical Systems in Neuroscience. MIT Press (2007)
16. Le Guernic, C., Girard, A.: Reachability analysis of linear systems using support functions. Nonlinear Analysis: Hybrid Systems **4**(2), 250–262 (2010)

17. Platzer, A., Quesel, J.-D.: KeYmaera: a hybrid theorem prover for hybrid systems (system description). In: Armando, A., Baumgartner, P., Dowek, G. (eds.) IJCAR 2008. LNCS, vol. 5195, pp. 171–178. Springer, Heidelberg (2008)
18. Ratschan, S., She, Z.: Safety verification of hybrid systems by constraint propagation based abstraction refinement. In: Morari, M., Thiele, L. (eds.) HSCC 2005. LNCS, vol. 3414, pp. 573–589. Springer, Heidelberg (2005)
19. Rewienski, M., White, J.: A trajectory piecewise-linear approach to model order reduction and fast simulation of nonlinear circuits and micromachined devices. IEEE Trans. on Computer-Aided Design of Integrated Circuits and Systems 22(2), 155–170 (2003)

Generalizing a Mathematical Analysis Library in Isabelle/HOL

Jesús Aransay and Jose Divasón[(✉)]

Departamento de Matemáticas y Computación,
Universidad de La Rioja, Logroño, Spain
{jesus-maria.aransay,jose.divasonm}@unirioja.es

Abstract. The HOL Multivariate Analysis Library (*HMA*) of Isabelle/HOL is focused on concrete types such as $\mathbb{R}$, $\mathbb{C}$ and $\mathbb{R}^n$ and on algebraic structures such as real vector spaces and Euclidean spaces, represented by means of type classes. The generalization of *HMA* to more abstract algebraic structures is something desirable but it has not been tackled yet. Using that library, we were able to prove the Gauss-Jordan algorithm over real matrices, but our interest lied on generating verified code for matrices over arbitrary fields, greatly increasing the range of applications of such an algorithm. This short paper presents the steps that we did and the methodology that we devised to generalize such a library, which were successful to generalize the Gauss-Jordan algorithm to matrices over arbitrary fields.

Keywords: Theorem proving · Isabelle/HOL · Type classes · Linear Algebra

1 Introduction

The importance and use of theorem provers grow day to day, not only involving strictly the formalization of mathematical results but also in the verification of software and hardware. Isabelle is one of the most used and well-known theorem provers, on top of which different logics are implemented; the most explored of these varieties of logics is higher-order logic (or HOL), and it is also the one where the greatest number of tools (code generation, automatic proof procedures) are available. It has been successfully used, for instance, in the Flyspeck project (the largest formal proof completed to date) and in the formal verification of seL4, an operating-system kernel.

The HOL Multivariate Analysis Library (or, *HMA* for short) is a set of Isabelle/HOL theories that has been sucessfully used in concrete developments in Analysis, Topology and Linear Algebra. It contains about 2500 lemmas and

This author is sponsored by a research grant FPI-UR-12 of Universidad de La Rioja.

© Springer International Publishing Switzerland 2015
K. Havelund et al. (Eds.): NFM 2015, LNCS 9058, pp. 415–421, 2015.
DOI: 10.1007/978-3-319-17524-9_30

150 definitions and is based on the impressive work of J. Harrison in HOL Light [1]. Formalization of algorithms in Linear Algebra and code generation from datatypes and such algorithms had not been explored in *HMA*. To fulfill this goal, in [5] we presented a formalization of the Gauss-Jordan algorithm based on *HMA*. In that development, we set up Isabelle to generate code from the matrix representation presented in *HMA*. A refinement to immutable arrays was carried out to improve performance. We also formalized some of its well-known applications: computation of ranks, inverses, determinants, dimensions and bases of the four fundamental subspaces of a matrix and solutions of systems of linear equations. Verified code of these computations is generated to both SML and Haskell.

However, while formalizing the previous results we found a limitation in *HMA*: some important results that we needed were only proven for real matrices or for real vector spaces. Due to this fact, we were only able to generate verified code of the Gauss-Jordan algorithm for real matrices. But we were especially interested in matrices whose coeffients belong to some other fields. For instance, the rank over $\mathbb{Z}_2$ matrices permits the computation of the number of connected components of a digital image. In Neurobiology, this technique can be used to compute the number of synapses in a neuron (see [2] for details). This limitation arises since *HMA* derives from earlier formalizations limited to concrete types, such as $\mathbb{R}$, $\mathbb{C}$ and $\mathbb{R}^n$. Many results presented in *HMA* are ported from J. Harrison's work in HOL Light [1], where most theorems are proven only for $\mathbb{R}^n$. Another interesting application is the computation of determinants of $\mathbb{Q}$ matrices: commercial software performs such computations wrong (see [12]) in cases that could be critical in cryptology.

J. Hölzl et al. [4] improved significantly the *HMA*. They presented a new hierarchy of spaces based on type classes to represent the common structures of Multivariate Analysis, such as topological spaces, metric spaces and Euclidean spaces. This improvement showed the power of Isabelle's type system. Some limitations still remain; for instance, most properties about vector spaces are only demonstrated in *HMA* over real vector spaces, impeding us from working with matrices whose elements belong to other fields. Generalizing the results in *HMA* is a known problem but has not been tackled. J. Harrison already pointed it out in his work [1]: "many proofs are *morally the same* and it would be appealing to be able to use similar technology to generalize the proofs". J. Avigad also found this limitation when working with *HMA* in his formalization of the Central Limit Theorem [3]; he said that some concepts "admit a common generalization, which would unify the library substantially".

This short paper presents a work in progress which aims at being the foundation stone to get such a generalization. The final aim would be to generalize the library as far as possible. As work done, we present the generalizations and the methodology that permitted us to prove the Gauss-Jordan algorithm over matrices whose elements belong to an arbitrary field.

2   Generalization of HMA

Mathematical structures presented in *HMA* are defined by means of *type classes*; type classes are provided by Isabelle and have great advantages: they allow to organize polymorphic specifications, to create a hierarchy among different classes, to provide instances, to produce a simple sintax and to simplify proofs thanks to the Isabelle type inference mechanism. A type class C specifies assumptions $P_1, \ldots, P_k$ for constants $c_1, \ldots, c_m$ (that are to be overloaded) and may be based on other type classes $B_1, \ldots, B_n$. Only one type variable α is allowed to occur in the type class specification. Hence, if we want to prove properties of arbitrary vector spaces (where two type variables appear), we have to use locales instead.

Locales are an Isabelle approach for dealing with parametric theories and they are specially suitable for Abstract Algebra as they allow to talk about carriers, sub-structures and existence of structures. On the other hand, code generation within locales with assumptions essentially does not work. Locales enable to prove theorems abstractly, relative to sets of assumptions. These theorems can then be used in other contexts where the assumptions themselves, or instances of the assumptions, are theorems. This form of theorem reuse is called *interpretation*. Locales generalize interpretation from theorems to conclusions, enabling the reuse of definitions and other constructs that are not part of the specifications of the locales.

We are on the borderline: our work requires to use abstract structures such as vector spaces or modules (we have to use locales) but we aim to preserve the executability (code generation). Our proposal is to work with a mix between locales and type classes: every possible lemma is generalized to newly introduced locales, but lemmas required in type classes are kept (because they belong there, or because they are obtained thanks to interpretation of the corresponding abstract locale).

2.1   An Example of Generalization

Let us illustrate the previous methodology with an example. A key lemma in *HMA* is the one which states the link between matrices and linear maps:

```
theorem matrix_works:
assumes "linear f"
shows "matrix f *v x = f (x::real^'n)"
```

It is stated for linear maps between real vector spaces. The *linear* predicate in the premise is introduced by the following locale definition:

```
locale linear = additive f for f :: "'a::real_vector ⇒ 'b::real_vector"
+ assumes scaleR: "f (scaleR r x) = scaleR r (f x)"
```

One parameter is only required: a map f. In the heading, the type of f is fixed as a map between two real vector spaces (*real_vector* class). In order to generalize it to *arbitrary* vector spaces over the same field, we propose the following definition:

```
locale linear = B: vector_space scaleB + C: vector_space scaleC
  for scaleB :: "('a::field ⇒ 'b::ab_group_add ⇒ 'b)" (infixr "*b" 75)
  and scaleC :: "('a ⇒ 'c::ab_group_add ⇒ 'c)" (infixr "*c" 75) +
  fixes f :: "('b ⇒ 'c)"
  assumes cmult: "f (r *b x) = r *c (f x)"
  and add: "f (a + b) = f a + f b"
```

This new locale has three parameters, instead of one: the scalar multiplications *scaleB* and *scaleC*, which fix both the vector spaces and the field, and the map f. Now we can interpret $\mathbb{F}^n$ (where $\mathbb{F}$ is a field) as a vector space over $\mathbb{F}$ and prove the linear interpretation for $\mathbb{F}^n$ (the corresponding linear map is the multiplication of a matrix by a vector):

```
interpretation vec: vector_space "op *s :: 'a::field ⇒ 'a^'b ⇒ 'a^'b"
interpretation vec: linear "op *s" "op *s" "(λx. A *v (x::'a::field^_))"
```

After reproducing in the new locale the lemmas involved in the proof, we prove the generalized version. Note the differences between both statements:

```
theorem matrix_works:
assumes "linear (op *s) (op *s) f"
shows "matrix f *v x = f (x::'a::field^'n)"
```

2.2   The Generalization of the Gauss-Jordan Algorithm

Our aim is to generalize the Gauss-Jordan algorithm to generate verified code for matrices with elements belonging to a generic field. The algorithm itself just requires type classes (the *field*) so code generation will work; nevertheless, proving its correctness needs generalizations of properties using locales. In Section 2.1, we have shown an example of how to carry out this generalization. As Harrison pointed out [1], in many cases the proof is essentially the same. However, the procedure is not immediate and almost every demonstration involves subtle design decisions: introduce new locales, syntactic details, interpretations inside the lemma to reuse previous facts, change the types properly and so on. In broad terms, we have carried out four kinds of generalizations in the *HMA* to achieve verified execution over matrices with elements belonging to a field:

1. Lemmas involving real vector spaces (a type class) are generalized to arbitrary vector spaces (a locale).
2. Lemmas involving Euclidean spaces (a type class) are generalized to finite-dimensional vector spaces (a locale).
3. Lemmas involving real matrices are generalized to matrices over any field (thanks to the previous two points).
4. Lemmas about determinants of matrices with coefficients in a real vector space are proven for matrices with coefficients in a commutative ring.

In *HMA* the first time that the notion of a finite basis appeared was in the *euclidean_space* class. Now, we have introduced a new locale *finite_dimensional_vector_space* and generalized several proofs from the *euclidean_space* class to that locale. Thanks to those generalizations, some lemmas that were stated in *HMA* only over real matrices are now proven over more general types. Let us take a look at the following lemma, which claims that a matrix is invertible iff its determinant is not null. The following version is the original one available in *HMA*, stated for integral domains:

```
lemma det_identical_rows:
    fixes A :: "'a::linordered_idom^'n^'n"
    assumes ij: "i ≠ j" and r: "row i A = row j A"
    shows "det A = 0"
proof-
    have tha: "⋀(a::'a) b. a = b ⟹ b = - a ⟹ a = 0"  by simp
    have th1: "of_int (-1) = - 1" by simp
    let ?p = "Fun.swap i j id"
    let ?A = "χ i. A $ ?p i"
    from r have "A = ?A" by (simp add: vec_eq_iff row_def Fun.swap_def)
    then have "det A = det ?A" by simp
    moreover have "det A = - det ?A" by (simp add: det_permute_rows[OF
      permutes_swap_id] sign_swap_id ij th1)
    ultimately show "det A = 0" by (metis tha)
qed
```

The original statement comes from Harrison's formalization [1], where the lemma is demonstrated over real matrices. The previous proof follows the one presented in most of the literature. Essentially, in the proof it is deduced that $\det A = -\det A$ and thus $\det A = 0$. But such a property does not hold in rings which characteristic is 2 (such as $\mathbb{Z}_2$). For instance, in [6] the statement is presented for commutative rings but it is proven without taking into account rings with characteristic 2. The same appears in [7], but the author warns that the demonstration fails in the case of $\mathbb{Z}_2$ matrices. To generalize the result to an arbitrary ring, we had to change totally the proof and work over permutations.[1]

Not only change some proofs, sometimes we have to introduce new definitions. For instance, to multiply a matrix by a scalar. *HMA* works with real matrices, so the next operation is used: (op $*_R$)::real ⇒ 'a ⇒ 'a. In the generalization, we would like to multiply a matrix of type 'a^'n^'m by an element of type 'a. We cannot use (op $*_R$) to do that. The most similar operation presented in *HMA* is: (op *s)::'a ⇒ 'a^'n ⇒ 'a^'n.

We cannot reuse it because is thought to multiply a vector (and not a matrix) by a scalar. Then, we define the multiplication of a matrix by a scalar as follows:
definition matrix_scalar_mult :: "'a ⇒ 'a^'n^'m ⇒ 'a^'n^'m"
(**infixl** "*k" 70) **where** "k *k A ≡ (χ i j. k * A $ i $ j)"

The statements for the real matrix version and the general one are different:
lemma scalar_matrix_vector_assoc:

---

[1] We followed the proof presented in http://hobbes.la.asu.edu/courses/site/442-f09/dets.pdf

```
fixes A :: "real^'m^'n"
shows "k *_R (A *v v) = k *_R A *v v"
```

lemma scalar_matrix_vector_assoc:
  fixes A :: "'a::field^'m^'n"
  shows "k *s (A *v v) = k *k A *v v"

Some other particularities arose in the generalization. For instance, we had to completely change other demonstration: the *row rank* and the *column rank* of a matrix are equal. We had followed an elegant proof but only valid for real matrices, see [9]. We based its generalization on the output of the Gauss-Jordan algorithm (a reduced row echelon form) following [11]. This change forced us to completely reorganize the files of our development. Another example arises in systems of linear equations: in the real field there could be infinite solutions, but in other fields such as $\mathbb{Z}_2$ there is always finitely many solutions.

Finally, we have generalized more than 2500 lines of code: about 220 theorems and 9 definitions, introducing 6 new locales, 3 new sublocales and 8 new interpretations. The generalized version of the Gauss-Jordan formalization was published in the AFP [10]. Moreover, the generalizations are useful for another contribution of ours: the Rank-Nullity Theorem [8].

3   Conclusions

The generalization of *HMA* is useful and desirable, but doing it can be overwhelming at a first glance. The process can be partially automated with suitable scripts, but the full goal cannot be discharged automatically and it requires to make some design decisions. The careful combination of locales, type classes and interpretations has been shown to be a sensible methodology. A remarkable number of proofs have been reused in this way. This contribution shows that the aim is feasible and the generalization has served for our purposes of executing a verified version of the Gauss-Jordan algorithm over fields such as $\mathbb{Z}_2$ and $\mathbb{Q}$.

References

1. Harrison, J.: The HOL Light Theory of Euclidean Space. J. Autom. Reasoning. **50**(2), 173–190 (2013)
2. Heras, J., Dénès, M., Mata, G., Mörtberg, A., Poza, M., Siles, V.: Towards a certified computation of homology groups for digital images. In: Ferri, M., Frosini, P., Landi, C., Cerri, A., Di Fabio, B. (eds.) CTIC 2012. LNCS, vol. 7309, pp. 49–57. Springer, Heidelberg (2012)
3. Avigad, J., Hölzl, J., Serafin, L.: A formally verified proof of the Central Limit Theorem. CoRR (2014)
4. Hölzl, J., Immler, F., Huffman, B.: Type classes and filters for mathematical analysis in Isabelle/HOL. In: Blazy, S., Paulin-Mohring, C., Pichardie, D. (eds.) ITP 2013. LNCS, vol. 7998, pp. 279–294. Springer, Heidelberg (2013)
5. http://www.unirioja.es/cu/jodivaso/Isabelle/Gauss-Jordan-2013-2/
6. Axler, S.: Linear Algebra Done Right, 2nd edn. Springer (2004)

7. Strang, G.: Introduction to Linear Algebra. Wellesley - Cambridge Press (2009)
8. Aransay, J., Divasón, J.: Rank-Nullity Theorem in Linear Algebra. AFP (2013)
9. Mackiw, G.: A Note on the Equality of the Column and Row Rank of a Matrix. Mathematics Magazine **68**(4), 285–286 (1995)
10. Aransay, J., Divasón, J.: Gauss-Jordan Algorithm and its Applications. AFP (2014)
11. http://www.math4all.in/public_html/linearalgebra/chapter3.4.html
12. Durán, A.J., Pérez, M., Varona, J.L.: The Misfortunes of a Trio of Mathematicians Using Computer Algebra Systems. Can We Trust in Them? Notices of the AMS **51**(10), 1249–1252 (2014)

A Tool for Intersecting Context-Free Grammars and Its Applications

Graeme Gange[1], Jorge A. Navas[2]([⊠]), Peter Schachte[1],
Harald Søndergaard[1], and Peter J. Stuckey[1]

[1] The University of Melbourne, Melbourne, VIC 3010, Australia
{gkgange,schachte,harald,pstuckey}@unimelb.edu.au
[2] NASA Ames Research Center, Moffett Field, CA 94035, USA
jorge.a.navaslaserna@nasa.gov

Abstract. This paper describes a tool for intersecting context-free grammars. Since this problem is undecidable the tool follows a refinement-based approach and implements a novel refinement which is complete for regularly separable grammars. We show its effectiveness for safety verification of recursive multi-threaded programs.

1   Introduction

Checking emptiness of intersections of context-free grammars is a well-known undecidable problem. However, the fact that this problem is equivalent to safety verification of recursive multi-threaded programs has kept motivating the design of semi-decision procedures that can still be effective in practice.

In this paper, we describe COVENANT, a tool for checking whether the languages of an arbitrary number of context-free grammars are disjoint and show its role as a component in the analysis of recursive multi-threaded programs. The tool takes a *grammatical* approach [7], in the sense that it is formalized in terms of context-free grammars rather than pushdown automata [1,2,10]. It implements a *counter-example guided abstraction refinement (CEGAR)* of regular over-approximations and integrates a *complete* refinement procedure that guarantees termination if the context-free grammars are *regularly separable*.[1] We show its application to safety verification of recursive multi-threaded programs.

To the best of our knowledge, our tool is the only publicly available implementation tackling the problem of intersecting *unbounded* context-free grammars.

2   Approach

The tool discussed in this paper follows the so-called *counter-example guided abstraction refinement (CEGAR)* of regular over-approximations. Without loss

---

[1] Two context-free grammars G_1 and G_2 are *regularly separable* if there exist two regular languages L_1 and L_2 such that $\mathcal{L}(G_1) \subseteq L_1$, $\mathcal{L}(G_2) \subseteq L_2$ and $L_1 \cap L_2 = \emptyset$.

© Springer International Publishing Switzerland 2015
K. Havelund et al. (Eds.): NFM 2015, LNCS 9058, pp. 422–428, 2015.
DOI: 10.1007/978-3-319-17524-9_31

of generality, in this presentation we consider the intersection of just two context-free grammars G_1 and G_2. The scheme is based on an initial abstraction which is repeatedly refined until either the languages are proven disjoint, an intersection witness has been found, or resources have been exhausted:

1. *Abstraction:* compute *regular approximations* R_1 and R_2 such that $\mathcal{L}(G_1) \subseteq \mathcal{L}(R_1)$ and $\mathcal{L}(G_2) \subseteq \mathcal{L}(R_2)$.
2. *Verification:* using a decision procedure for regular languages (and writing $\dagger$ for disjointness), if $\mathcal{L}(R_1) \dagger \mathcal{L}(R_2)$ then $\mathcal{L}(G_1) \dagger \mathcal{L}(G_2)$, so answer "the languages are disjoint." If $w \in \mathcal{L}(R_1) \cap \mathcal{L}(R_2)$, $w \in \mathcal{L}(G_1)$, and $w \in \mathcal{L}(G_2)$ then $\mathcal{L}(G_1) \cap \mathcal{L}(G_2) \neq \emptyset$, so answer "the languages are not disjoint" and provide w as a witness. Otherwise, go to step 3.
3. *Refinement:* produce new regular approximations R'_1 and R'_2 such that for each R'_i, $i \in \{1, 2\}$, we have $\mathcal{L}(G_i) \subseteq \mathcal{L}(R'_i) \subseteq \mathcal{L}(R_i)$, and $\mathcal{L}(R'_i) \subset \mathcal{L}(R_i)$ for some i. Update the approximations $R_1 \leftarrow R'_1, R_2 \leftarrow R'_2$, and go to step 2.

Abstraction. Note that a regular approximation always exists for any grammar G since we can use Σ^*, where Σ is the alphabet of G. However, the precision of the initial abstraction often has a significant impact on the convergence of the refinement loop, so non-trivial initial abstractions such as the ith-prefix abstraction [1,2] and the *downward closure* with a *cycle-breaking heuristic* [7] are more suitable candidates.

Verification. This step assumes a decision procedure that returns "no" if $\mathcal{L}(A_1) \dagger \mathcal{L}(A_2)$ or returns a witness w if $w \in \mathcal{L}(A_1) \cap \mathcal{L}(A_2) \neq \emptyset$, where A_1 and A_2 are finite state automata recognizing regular languages R_1 and R_2, respectively (that is, $\mathcal{L}(A_1) = R_1$ and $\mathcal{L}(A_2) = R_2$). This can be solved using, for instance, the classical product construction. Note that a different approach would make use of the fact that the class of context-free languages is closed under intersection with regular languages. However, one advantage of our approach is that we are able to leverage the latest advances made in string solving [4,6,11].

Refinement. At this point, the regular solver has found some witness w such that $w \in (\mathcal{L}(A_1) \cap \mathcal{L}(A_2))$, but $w \notin (\mathcal{L}(G_1) \cap \mathcal{L}(G_2))$. There are three cases: (1) $w \notin \mathcal{L}(G_1) \wedge w \in \mathcal{L}(G_2)$, (2) $w \notin \mathcal{L}(G_1) \wedge w \notin \mathcal{L}(G_2)$, and (3) $w \in \mathcal{L}(G_1) \wedge w \notin \mathcal{L}(G_2)$. For (1) and (3) we should refine A_1 and A_2, respectively. For (2) we could choose to refine either A_1 or A_2, or both. COVENANT aggressively refines both.

We say a language L is a *safe generalization* of a witness w with respect to a context-free grammar G if (a) $L \supseteq \{w\}$ and (b) $L \dagger \mathcal{L}(G)$. If $w \notin \mathcal{L}(G_i)$ then a straightforward refinement is to produce a new abstraction that recognizes $\mathcal{L}(A_i) \setminus \{w\}$ in place of A_i. However, that refinement process will rarely converge, as it excludes only finitely many examples. Instead, we would like to produce safe generalizations of w containing an infinite number of words, to hasten convergence. For this purpose, our tool implements the concept of *star-generalization* [5]. Informally, a *star-generalization* of a word w is a language that applies the Kleene $*$ operator (*i.e.*, unbounded repetition) to any number of non-overlapping, but possibly nested, subsequences of w, while ensuring the resulting augmented language remains disjoint with the language of G.

3   Covenant

The tool is publicly available at https://github.com/sav-tools/covenant.

3.1   Design and Implementation Choices

The tool is implemented in C++ and parameterized by the initial approximation, the regular solver, and the refinement procedure.

Abstraction. One advantage of having a grammatical view is that COVENANT can easily leverage the advances made in areas such as speech processing where precise abstraction of context-free grammars into regular grammars is an active topic of research. COVENANT implements the method described by Nederhof [8] for approximating context-free grammars with strongly regular languages.

We say a grammar is *strongly regular* if all productions are of the form: $A \to B\ w \mid w$ or $A \to w\ B \mid w$, where $w \in \Sigma^*$ and A, B are nonterminals. The abstraction relies on the following observation: a grammar with productions of the form $A \to \alpha A \beta$ with both α, β non-empty might not be represented as a strongly regular grammar because α and β might be related through an "unbounded" communication not expressible by regular languages. The abstraction consists of conservatively breaking those unbounded communications in such a way that the grammar becomes regular while preserving the original grammar structure as far as possible. Nederhof [8] also proposed a transformation from strongly regular grammars to finite automata, also implemented in COVENANT.

Regular Solver. COVENANT currently implements only the naive product construction for intersecting finite automata but other regular solvers can easily be plugged in. In fact, an initial implementation of COVENANT was tested using REVENANT [4], an efficient regular solver based on bounded model checking with interpolation, though the released version does not incorporate it.

Refinement. COVENANT implements both the greedy and maximum star-epsilon generalizations of [5]. We explain these by example—[5] has details. Consider witness $w \equiv \mathsf{aab}$ and context-free language $L = \{\mathsf{a}^i\mathsf{b}^{i+1} \mid i \geq 0\}$. The greedy algorithm starts by checking whether $W_1 \equiv \mathsf{a}^*\mathsf{ab} \nmid L$. As the query succeeds, W_1 is a safe generalization of w *wrt.* L so we could stop here. However, we can continue and next ask whether $W_2 \equiv \mathsf{a}^*\mathsf{a}^*\mathsf{b} \nmid L$; but $\mathsf{b} \in L$ so W_2 is discarded. Next, we try whether $W_3 \equiv \mathsf{a}^*\mathsf{ab}^* \nmid L$; but $\mathsf{abb} \in L$ and so W_3 too fails to be a safe generalization. Finally, we query $W_4 \equiv \mathsf{a}^*(\mathsf{ab})^* \nmid L$ and $W_5 \equiv (\mathsf{a}^*(\mathsf{ab})^*)^* \nmid L$ which both succeed. Thus, starting from aab, we can produce the safe generalization $(\mathsf{a}^*(\mathsf{ab})^*)^*$. In fact, COVENANT generates three safe generalizations: $W_1 \subseteq W_4 \subseteq W_5$. Although this greedy method is reasonably cheap ($O(|w|^2)$), if resources are scarce it can stop any time, returning the weaker W_1 or W_4.

The maximum star-epsilon version is similar to the greedy one except it will compute the union of all possible safe generalizations without committing to any successful partial generalization. That is, the greedy version started by checking W_1 and since W_1 succeeded the rest of queries were relative to W_1.

The non-greedy version will not commit to W_1 but also try other possibilities. For instance, aa*b, (aa)*b, (aab)*, and a(ab)* are also safe generalizations from which we can keep generalizing. Although more expensive, it is worth mentioning that this version ensures termination of the CEGAR loop whenever the context-free grammars are regularly separable.

For the implementation, two operations are important: (a) intersection between a context-free grammar and a finite automaton for checking safe generalizations, and (b) automata difference for refining the current abstraction by discarding a safe generalization W of w. For (a), COVENANT uses a modified version of the efficient pre^* algorithm [3] and for (b) it intersects the current abstraction with the complement of the determinization of W. Although determinization of automata can have an exponential size blowup, this behavior is rare; we have not seen it during experiments. Based on our experience, it is also useful to minimize after (b) has been performed, to keep the abstraction small.

3.2 Preprocessing and Output

We require that the input grammars are in the following normal form: $A \to BC \mid B \mid a \mid \varepsilon$, where A, B, C are nonterminals and $a \in \Sigma^+$, where Σ is the alphabet of the grammar. Any context-free grammar can be converted to this form by a linear increase in terms of the size of the original grammar. COVENANT performs this normalization as a preprocessing step but it does not require any further (more expensive) normalizations, such as Chomsky Normal Form.

If COVENANT proves that the language of the grammars are not disjoint it will return a witness. The user can set the option --solutions n to ask the solver for n solutions. The option --dot will output the automata resulting from the initial abstraction, each of the safe generalizations, and the final abstractions when emptiness was proven, all in the dot language of the Graphviz package.

4   Safety Verification of Multithread Programs

Bouajjani et al. [1] pioneered safety verification of recursive multi-threaded programs by reduction to checking the intersection of context free languages for emptiness. For lack of space, we refer to [1, 2, 7] for details of the encoding.

We have tested COVENANT and compared with LCEGAR [7] using two classes of programs: textbook Erlang programs and several variants of a real Bluetooth driver. A detailed description of the programs as well as the safety properties can be found in [2, 7, 9]. We ran LCEGAR with the setting provided by the authors and tried with the two available initial abstractions: *pseudo-downward closure* (PDC) and *cycle breaking* (CB). Table 1 shows the results. The symbol ∞ means a timeout expired after 2 hours. We ran COVENANT with the greedy refinement.

5   Related Work

To the best of our knowledge, COVENANT is the first publicly available implementation for intersecting context-free grammars ensuring termination for regularly

Table 1. Comparison of COVENANT with LCEGAR; times in seconds. All experiments ran on a single core of a 2.4GHz Core i5-M520 with 8GiB of memory.

(a) Verification of multi-thread Erlang programs

Program		COVENANT	LCEGAR	
			PDC	CB
SharedMem	safe	0.01	14.37	24.75
Mutex	safe	0.04	6.12	0.14
RA	safe	0.01	∞	0.39
Modified RA	safe	0.03	∞	27.90
TNA	unsafe	0.01	0.02	0.25
Banking	unsafe	0.01	∞	3.36

(b) Verification of multi-thread Bluetooth drivers

Program		COVENANT	LCEGAR	
			PDC	CB
Version 1	unsafe	0.84	19.74	21.04
Version 2	unsafe	0.25	5560.00	4852.00
Version 2 w/ Heuri	unsafe	0.11	44.68	38.89
Version 3 (1A2S)	unsafe	0.12	217.74	217.27
Version 3 (1A2S) w/ Heuri	unsafe	0.05	6.68	11.37
Version 3 (2A1S)	safe	0.27	4185.00	3981.00

separable grammars. Several CEGAR approaches have been proposed before. Here, we do not consider the effect of initial approximations, as they do not affect the expressiveness of the refinement loop and are easily interchangeable.

The first CEGAR approach was proposed in [1] based on the concept of *refinable finite-chain abstraction* which consists of computing the series $(\alpha_i)_{i \geq 1}$ overapproximating the language of a CFG G such that $\mathcal{L}(\alpha_1(G)) \supset \mathcal{L}(\alpha_2(G)) \supset \cdots \supseteq \mathcal{L}(G)$. Several refinable abstractions were described in [1] although no experimental data was provided. Instead, we compare here with the ith-*prefix abstraction*[2] implemented in [2]. In this, $\alpha_i(G)$ is the set of words of G of length less than i, together with the set of prefixes of length i of G. We argue that the refinement implemented in COVENANT is more expressive as it is not hard to find regularly separable languages that cannot be proven so by the ith-prefix abstraction. For instance, with $R_1 \equiv \mathsf{a^*b}$ and $R_2 \equiv \mathsf{a^*c}$, we have $R_1 \nmid R_2$, while for every length i, the string a^i forms a prefix to words in both R_1 and R_2. Therefore the intersection of the two abstractions will always be non-empty.

The LCEGAR method described in [7] is based on a similar refinement framework, but the approach differs radically. LCEGAR maintains a pair of context-free grammars A_1, A_2, over-approximating the intersection of the original languages. At each refinement step, an *elementary bounded language* B_i is generated from

---

[2] [2] also implemented the ith-*suffix abstraction* which suffers from same limitations.

each grammar A_i.[3] The refinement ensures $B_i \cap A_i \neq \emptyset$, but B_i is not necessarily either an over- or under-approximation of A_i. After that, $I = B_i \cap L_1 \cap L_2$ is computed. If I is non-empty, $L_1 \cap L_2$ must also be non-empty. If I is empty, then the approximations can safely be refined by removing B_i.

Here a comparison between methods is more involved, and we refer to [5] for details. Suffice it to say that the refinements done by LCEGAR and COVENANT are incomparable. That is, there are grammars which are not regularly separable for which LCEGAR can terminate but COVENANT cannot, and there are also grammars which are regularly separable but LCEGAR cannot terminate.

Finally, the verification phase in COVENANT consists of intersecting finite automata, for which efficient solvers are available. Instead, LCEGAR intersects several context-free grammars and a bounded language which, although decidable, is NP-Complete. In our experience, LCEGAR makes a smaller number of refinements than COVENANT, but each refinement in COVENANT is considerably cheaper than in LCEGAR, resulting in the better performance.

6 Conclusions

The main contributions of this work have been to describe and implement a tool for intersecting context-free grammars, and to show it can be effective for safety verification of recursive multi-threaded programs.

Acknowledgments. Partially funded by the ARC through grant DP140102194.

References

1. Bouajjani, A., Esparza, J., Touili, T.: A generic approach to the static analysis of concurrent programs with procedures. In: POPL, pp. 62–73 (2003)
2. Chaki, S., Clarke, E., Kidd, N., Reps, T., Touili, T.: Verifying concurrent message-passing c programs with recursive calls. In: Hermanns, H., Palsberg, J. (eds.) TACAS 2006. LNCS, vol. 3920, pp. 334–349. Springer, Heidelberg (2006)
3. Esparza, J., Rossmanith, P., Schwoon, S.: A uniform framework for problems on context-free grammars. Bulletin of the EATCS **72**, 169–177 (2000)
4. Gange, G., Navas, J.A., Stuckey, P.J., Søndergaard, H., Schachte, P.: Unbounded model-checking with interpolation for regular language constraints. In: Piterman, N., Smolka, S.A. (eds.) TACAS 2013. LNCS, vol. 7795, pp. 277–291. Springer, Heidelberg (2013)
5. Gange, G., Navas, J.A., Stuckey, P.J., Søndergaard, H., Schachte, P.: A complete refinement procedure for regular separability of context-free languages (2014). http://people.eng.unimelb.edu.au/gkgange/pubs/cfg_preprint.pdf
6. Hooimeijer, P., Weimer, W.: StrSolve: Solving string constraints lazily. ASE **19**(4), 531–559 (2012)

---

[3] An elementary bounded language is a language of the form $B = w_1^* \ldots w_k^*$, where each w_i is a (finite) word in Σ^*.

7. Long, Z., Calin, G., Majumdar, R., Meyer, R.: Language-theoretic abstraction refinement. In: de Lara, J., Zisman, A. (eds.) FASE 2012. LNCS, vol. 7212, pp. 362–376. Springer, Heidelberg (2012)
8. Nederhof, M.-J.: Regular approximation of CFLs: a grammatical view. In: Advances in Probabilistic and Other Parsing Technologies, vol. 16, pp. 221–241 (2000)
9. Qadeer, S., Wu, D.: KISS: keep it simple and sequential. In: PLDI, pp. 14–24 (2004)
10. Suwimonteerabuth, D., Schwoon, S., Esparza, J.: jMoped: a java bytecode checker based on moped. In: Halbwachs, N., Zuck, L.D. (eds.) TACAS 2005. LNCS, vol. 3440, pp. 541–545. Springer, Heidelberg (2005)
11. Veanes, M., de Halleux, P., Tillmann, N.: Rex: symbolic regular expression explorer. In: ICSTVV, pp. 498–507 (2010)

UFIT: A Tool for Modeling Faults in UPPAAL Timed Automata

Reza Hajisheykhi[1]([✉]), Ali Ebnenasir[2], and Sandeep S. Kulkarni[1]

[1] Michigan State University, East Lansing, USA
{hajishey,sandeep}@cse.msu.edu
[2] Michigan Technological University, Houghton, USA
aebnenas@mtu.edu

Abstract. We present the tool UFIT (*Uppaal Fault Injector for Timed automata*). In UFIT, we model five types of faults, namely, message loss, transient, byzantine, stuck-at, and fail-stop faults. Given the fault-free timed automata model and the selection of a type of fault, UFIT models the faults and generates the fault-affected timed automata model automatically. As a result, the designer can analyze the behavior of the model in the presence of faults. Moreover, there are several tools that extract timed automata models from higher-level programs. Hence, the designer can use UFIT to inject the faults into the extracted models.

1 Introduction

In this paper, we present the tool UFIT for modeling different types of faults in UPPAAL timed automata. Timed automata are important abstractions that are able to both capture real-time behavior and be verified algorithmically (model-checked). Moreover, there are several methods that propose how to extract a timed automata model from higher-level programs such as SystemC programs, hybrid systems, real-time communication protocols, digital circuits, timed asynchronous circuits, etc. [1,2]. These programs/systems are usually subject to faults and it is necessary to see how they behave in the presence of faults.

There are several techniques for injecting faults into high-level programs such as C, C++, SystemC, etc. [3,4]. However, such programs are getting more complex and more difficult to get verified. The faults injected also introduce some time overhead and make the verification time even worse. A solution to that would be extracting abstract models from the programs and inject the faults into the extracted models. Nevertheless, most of the algorithms for extracting the models are untimed and do not consider timing constraints. Having a timed model extracted (e.g. timed automata) from higher-level programs, there are several methods/tools for verifying the models in the literature [1,5,6]. However, these methods/tools verify the models in the absence of faults. Thus, there

This work is supported by NSF CCF-1116546, NSF CNS 1329807, and NSF CNS 1318678.

K. Havelund et al. (Eds.): NFM 2015, LNCS 9058, pp. 429–435, 2015.
DOI: 10.1007/978-3-319-17524-9_32

is a need for a tool that models and injects faults into timed systems automatically yet does not add too much overhead into the models. UFIT targets timed automata models and considers five types of faults, namely, message loss, transient, byzantine, stuck-at, and fail-stop faults. It automates the injection of the faults into the model and generates a fault-affected model. Hence, this model can be analyzed with UPPAAL tool-set. In this paper, we illustrate how to use UFIT to model the faults on the well-known Fischer's mutual exclusion problem and analyze the behavior of the fault-affected model. UFIT is written in Python and its source code is available freely and can be downloaded from https://www.cse.msu.edu/~hajishey/ufit.html.

2 Modeling and Analysis Using UFIT

In this section, first, we explain UPPAAL timed automata and the input of UFIT. Thereafter, using a runtime example, we introduce our fault modeling approach and inject five types of faults into the example. Finally, we utilize the output of UFIT to analyze the behavior of the model in the presence of faults.

2.1 Input of UFIT

The input of UFIT is a fault-intolerant timed automata model in XML format and a set of parameters. Next, we explain the timed automata and the input XML format. We describe the set of parameters in Section 2.2.

UPPAAL and Timed Automata. A timed automaton (TA) is a classical finite automaton which can manipulate clocks, evolving continuously and synchronously with the absolute time. Each transition (edge) of such an automaton is labeled by a guard, or a constraint over clock values, which indicates when the transition can be fired, and a set of clocks to be reset when the transition is fired. Each location (vertex) is constrained by an invariant. The invariant restricts the possible values of the clocks for being in the state, which can then enforce a transition to be taken. UPPAAL [7] is an integrated tool environment for modeling, simulation, and verification of real-time systems modeled as networks of timed automata, extended with data types.

XML Format. Like the TA model, the XML file has a set of locations and transitions, which are respectively defined by the following tags: "$< location >$ statements $< /location >$" and "$< transition >$ statements $< /transition >$". The statements can be a name, an invariant, or a type (e.g., urgent, committed) for locations, and a source, a target, or labels for transitions. The source and target tags represent the position of the transition. The label tag shows whether the transition has a synchronization channel, an assignment operation, or a guard condition.

   We illustrate the set of parameters and our fault modeling approach used in UFIT utilizing a running example from the literature of UPPAAL timed automata, the Fischer's mutual exclusion protocol [7] (Figure 2(a)).

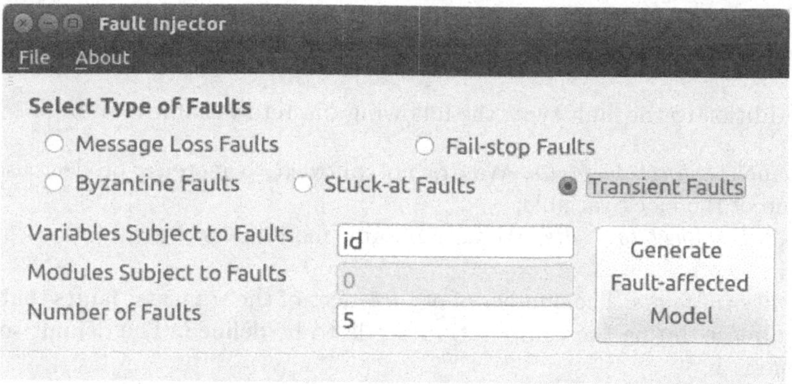

Fig. 1. The GUI of UFIT

The Running Example. Fischer's protocol is designed to ensure mutual exclusion among several processes (5 processes here) competing for a critical section using timing constraints and a shared variable *id*. In each process P, the process goes to a request location req if it is the turn for no process to enter the critical section (id=−0). After x time units in req ($0 \leq x \leq k$), P goes to the wait location and sets id to its process ID. Finally, after at least k time units, P enters the critical section cs if it is its turn. The Fischer's protocol satisfies the following set of requirements/properties in the absence of faults:

```
SPEC1: A[] not deadlock
SPEC2: P(i).req --> P(i).wait
SPEC3: A[] P1.cs + P2.cs + P3.cs + P4.cs + P5.cs <=1
```

where SPEC1 checks wether the system is deadlock-free. The liveness property SPEC2 checks that whenever a process tries to enter the critical section, it will always eventually enter the waiting location. The safety property SPEC3 checks for mutual exclusion of the location cs.

2.2 Internal Functionality

To generate the fault-affected model, in addition to the fault-free model, we need to specify the type of the faults and a set of parameters (see Figure 1). The fault types that UFIT considers are as follows.

- *Message faults,* where a message may be lost while forwarding from one module to another;
- *Fail-stop* faults, where a module fails functionally and the other modules cannot communicate with it;
- *Byzantine* faults, where the faulty component continues to run but produces incorrect results;
- *Stuck-at* faults, where a signal gets stuck-at a fixed value (logical 0, 1, or X) and cannot switch its value, and

– *Transient faults,* where the state of system components is perturbed without causing any permanent damage.

In addition to the fault type, the following discrete variables can be specified:

– *Variable subject to faults.* We are not allowed to increase or decrease the value of the clock variable;
– *Module subject to faults.* We assume any module can be subject to faults, and
– *Number of faults.* The number of occurrences of the transient faults that may take place during the computation needs to be defined. The default setting value is 1.

Remark 1. If any of the above variables is not specified, UFIT will set a value for them arbitrarily. For instance, if the module subject to fail-stop faults is not specified, UFIT will fail one of the modules non-deterministically.

Brief Discussion About Modeling of Faults in UFIT. Given the parameters and the fault type, intuitively we model the faults as follows. To model a message fault, we inject a new transition into the module subject to faults in parallel to a transition that has a synchronization channel. The set of assignments/guards of the new transition is similar to that of the original transition except that the synchronization channel is changed. To model a fail-stop fault, we define a variable *down* that shows if a module is failed (down=1). For example, Figure 2(b) illustrates that automaton $P1$ is failed since $P1$ cannot go to location wait and has to stay at location req forever. To model stuck-at faults, UFIT finds the location of the variable subject to faults and changes it to a random value. For example, in Figure 2(c), the value of id is stuck at 5, thereby $P1$ cannot enter the critical section. For modeling byzantine faults, UFIT adds a transition in parallel to that of the original automaton that updates the variable subject to faults and changes its value arbitrarily. Figure 2(d) shows injecting a byzantine faults that changes the value of id, if the faults occur. Modeling of transient faults is similar to that of byzantine faults except that the occurrence of transient faults is limited. UFIT utilizes the number of faults defined in the GUI to limit the number of occurrence of this type of faults.

Extending UFIT. UFIT is easily extensible to cover more types of faults. Specifically, UFIT is written in Python (utilizing PyQt and PySide packages [8]) and uses *XML ElementTree* library to parse the XML file. Thus, to add a new class of faults, only the modeling of that class needs to be added to UFIT.

2.3   Analysis of Results

In this section, we analyze the fault-affected models. Also, in addition to Fischer's protocol, we include the results of the *Viking problem* adapted from [7]. In the Vikings problem, four Vikings want to cross a bridge at night, but they have

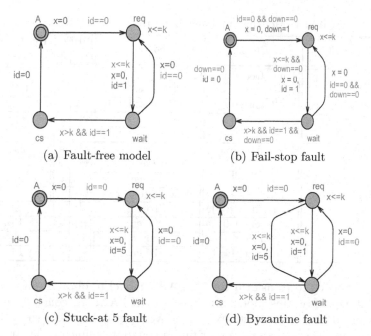

Fig. 2. Fault-free and fault-affected models of Fischer's mutual exclusion protocol. The green texts show either the *guards* or *synchronization*, the blue texts show the *updates*, and the pink texts represent the *names*.

only one torch and the bridge can only carry two of them. Thus, they can only cross the bridge in pairs and one has to bring the torch back to the other side before the next pair can cross. Each viking has different speed. The question is whether it is possible that all the vikings cross the bridge within a certain time. This example is comparable to the question if a packet can reach its receiver in a given time limit in a communication network/Network on Chip (NoC) system. The TA model satisfies the following properties in the absence of faults:

```
SPEC1: A[] not deadlock
SPEC2: E<> Viking1.safe
SPEC3: E<> Viking1.safe and Viking2.safe and Viking3.safe
       and Viking4.safe
```

where SPEC2 illustrates that the first viking eventually gets to the other side of the river and SPEC3 shows that all the vikings are in their safe location.

The results of analyzing the examples are as shown in Table 1. In this table, if requirement x is satisfied, we include s in the table, otherwise v.

3   Conclusions and Future Work

In this paper, we presented the tool UFIT and explained how it models different types of faults in timed automata models. For each type of faults, we utilized

Table 1. Modeling and analyzing the impact of faults

Protocol	Cause	Affected Locations	SPEC 1	2	3	Total Time (ms)
Fischer's protocol	Fault-free model	–	s	s	s	1250
	Fail-stop	Process P1	v	v	s	143
	Transient	Process P1	v	s	s	79
	Stuck-at	Process P1	v	s	s	81
	Byzantine	Process P1	v	s	s	149
Viking protocol	Fault-free model	–	s	s	s	25
	Fail-stop	Viking 0	v	v	v	23
		Torch	v	v	v	15
	Message loss	Viking to Torch	v	v	v	17
	Byzantine (L=1)	Torch	v	s	v	29
	Stuck-at 0	Torch	v	s	s	15
	Stuck-at 1	Torch	v	s	v	15
	Transient (L=1)	Torch	v	s	v	14

a generic approach to transform the UPPAAL model to obtain a fault-affected model. Subsequently, this model was used in UPPAAL to conclude tolerance to faults or to obtain a counterexample. We were either able to verify that the original specification is satisfied or find a counterexample demonstrating the violation of the original specification. Moreover, the time for evaluating the effect of faults was comparable ($< 165\%$) to the verification in the absence of faults.

Future Work. Having a fault-affected timed automata mode and a set of properties which are violated, we are working on repairing the model automatically to generate a model that eventually satisfies the set of violated properties while preserving the set of satisfied properties. Moreover, we are working on injecting timing faults utilizing UFIT.

References

1. Herber, P., Pockrandt, M., Glesner, S.: Transforming SystemC Transaction Level Models into UPPAAL timed automata. In: Singh, S., Jobstmann, B., Kishinevsky, M., Brandt, J. (eds.) MEMOCODE, pp. 161–170. IEEE (2011)
2. Olivero, A., Sifakis, J., Yovine, S.: Using abstractions for the verification of linear hybrid systems. In: Computer Aided Verification, CAV, pp. 81–94 (1994)
3. Lisherness, P., Cheng, K.T.: SCEMIT: a systemc error and mutation injection tool. In: Design Automation Conference, DAC, pp. 228–233 (2010)
4. Giovanni, B., Bolchini, C., Miele, A.: Multi-level fault modeling for transaction-level specifications. In: Great Lakes Symposium on VLSI, pp. 87–92 (2009)
5. Kwiatkowska, M.Z., Norman, G., Parker, D.: PRISM 4.0: Verification of probabilistic real-time systems. In: Gopalakrishnan, G., Qadeer, S. (eds.) CAV 2011. LNCS, vol. 6806, pp. 585–591. Springer, Heidelberg (2011)

6. Springintveld, J., Vaandrager, F.W., D'Argenio, P.R.: Testing timed automata. Theor. Comput. Sci. 254 (1–2), 225–257 (2001)
7. Behrmann, G., David, A., Larsen, K.G.: A tutorial on uppaal. In: Bernardo, M., Corradini, F. (eds.) SFM-RT 2004. LNCS, vol. 3185, pp. 200–236. Springer, Heidelberg (2004)
8. Summerfield, M.: Rapid GUI Programming with Python and Qt. Prentice Hall, California (2008)

Blocked Literals Are Universal

Marijn J.H. Heule[1](✉), Martina Seidl[2], and Armin Biere[2]

[1] Department of Computer Science, The University of Texas at Austin, Austin, USA
marijn@cs.utexas.edu
[2] Institute for Formal Models and Verification, JKU Linz, Linz, Austria
{martina.seidl,biere}@jku.at

Abstract. We recently introduced a new proof system for Quantified Boolean Formulas (QBF), called QRAT, that opened up a variety of new preprocessing techniques. This paper presents a concept that follows from the QRAT proof system: blocked literals. Blocked literals are redundant universal literals that can be removed or added to clauses. We show that blocked literal elimination (BLE) and blocked literal addition are not confluent. We implemented BLE in the state-of-the-art preprocessor bloqqer. Our experimental results illustrate that the BLE extension improves solver performance on the 2014 QBF evaluation benchmarks.

1 Introduction

Preprocessing a *quantified Boolean formula* (QBF) is crucial to effective QBF solving, but often tricky to implement. That motivated us to develop a new proof system for QBF [1], called QRAT, which facilitates expressing all state-of-the-art QBF preprocessing techniques in a uniform manner. By these means, the correctness of the output of a preprocessor can be checked efficiently. Moreover, the QRAT proof system opened up a variety of new preprocessing techniques. In this paper, we study two of such new preprocessing techniques.

Universal pure literal elimination [2] and *blocked clause elimination* (BCE) [3] are important QBF preprocessing techniques. The QRAT proof system revealed that universal pure literals can be generalized in a similar way as existential pure literal elimination, i.e, via BCE. We call this new generalized concept *blocked literals*. We study two new QBF preprocessing techniques: *blocked literal elimination* (BLE) and *blocked literal addition* (BLA). BLE is the dual of BCE. We show that neither BLE nor BLA are confluent, in contrast to BCE.

Additionally, this paper presents the first implementation and evaluation of a new preprocessing technique that originated from the QRAT proof system. The general rules in the QRAT proof system are very expensive to implement.

This work was supported by the Austrian Science Fund (FWF) through the national research network RiSE (S11408-N23), Vienna Science and Technology Fund (WWTF) under grant ICT10-018, DARPA contract number N66001-10-2-4087, and the National Science Foundation under grant number CCF-1153558.

© Springer International Publishing Switzerland 2015
K. Havelund et al. (Eds.): NFM 2015, LNCS 9058, pp. 436–442, 2015.
DOI: 10.1007/978-3-319-17524-9_33

However, by focusing on BLE, a restricted version of the one of the QRAT rules, we were able to extend the state-of-the-art preprocessor bloqqer [3] is such a way that its performance is clearly improved.

2   Preliminaries

The language of QBF extends the language of propositional logic by existential and universal quantifiers over the propositional variables. As usual, we assume a QBF to be in *prenex conjunctive normal form* (PCNF). Note that any QBF of arbitrary structure can be efficiently transformed to a satisfiability equivalent formula in PCNF [4]. A QBF in PCNF has the structure $\Pi.\psi$ where the prefix Π has the form $Q_1 X_1 Q_2 X_2 \ldots Q_n X_n$ with disjoint variable sets X_i and $Q_i \in \{\forall, \exists\}$. The matrix ψ is a propositional formula in conjunctive normal form, i.e., a conjunction of clauses. A clause is a disjunction of literals and a literal is either a variable x (positive literal) or a negated variable $\bar{x}$ (negative literal). The variable of a literal is denoted by $\mathsf{var}(l)$ where $\mathsf{var}(l) = x$ if $l = x$ or $l = \bar{x}$. The negation of a literal l is denoted by $\bar{l}$. The quantifier $\mathsf{Q}(\Pi, l)$ of a literal l is Q_i if $\mathsf{var}(l) \in X_i$. Let $\mathsf{Q}(\Pi, l) = Q_i$ and $\mathsf{Q}(\Pi, k) = Q_j$, then $l \leq_\Pi k$ iff $i \leq j$. We consider only closed QBFs, so ψ contains only variables which occur in the prefix. For a clause C, we denote by $\overline{C}$ the assignment that falsifies all literals in C, i.e., $\overline{C} = \{(\bar{l}) \mid l \in C\}$. By $\top$ and $\bot$ we denote the truth constants *true* and *false*. QBFs are interpreted as follows: a QBF $\forall x \Pi.\psi$ is false iff $\Pi.\psi[x/\top]$ or $\Pi.\psi[x/\bot]$ is false where $\Pi.\psi[x/t]$ is the QBF obtained by replacing all occurrences of variable x by t. Respectively, a QBF $\exists x \Pi.\psi$ is false iff both $\Pi.\psi[x/\top]$ and $\Pi.\psi[x/\bot]$ are false. If the matrix ψ of a QBF ϕ contains the empty clause after eliminating the truth constants, then ϕ is false as usual. Accordingly, if the matrix ψ of QBF ϕ is empty, then ϕ is true. Two QBFs ϕ_1 and ϕ_2 are *satisfiability equivalent* (written as $\phi_1 \sim \phi_2$) iff they have the same truth value.

3   Universal Blocked Literals

This section presents the new concept of blocked literals; redundant universal literals that can be removed or added to clauses. Removing blocked literals from clauses is a generalization of *universal pure literal elimination*, which removes universal literals that are pure, i.e., occur either only positively or only negatively in the formula. In the popular game-based view of QBF [5][1], the optimal strategy for the universal player is to assign pure literals to false. Such a move will only shrink clauses and not satisfy clauses. The preprocessing techniques presented here will have the same property, but it is literal-based instead of variable-based.

---

[1] The evaluation of a QBF is described as a game between the existential player who owns the existential variables and the universal player who owns the universal variables of the formula. The existential player wants to satisfy the formula, while the universal player wants to falsify the formula.

We explain the new concept of blocked literal using the previous concepts of blocked clauses, outer clauses, and outer formulas. These previous concepts are defined slightly differently (i.e., simplified) compared to earlier work [1] to make them easier to understand for readers that are less familiar with QBF.

Definition 1 (Outer Clause [1]): Let C be a clause occurring in QBF $\Pi.\psi$. The *outer clause* of C on literal $l \in C$, denoted by $\mathcal{OC}(\Pi, C, l)$, is given by the clause $\{k \mid k \in C, k \leq_\Pi l, k \neq l\}$.

Definition 2 (Outer Formula [6]): Let l be a literal occurring in QBF $\Pi.\psi$. The *outer formula* of $\Pi.\psi$ on l, denoted by $\mathcal{OF}(\Pi, \psi, l)$, is given by the unquantified formula $\{\mathcal{OC}(\Pi, C, l) \mid l \in C, C \in \psi\}$.

Definition 3 (Blocking Literal and Blocked Clause, see also [3]): Let C be a clause occurring in QBF $\Pi.\psi$. An existential literal $l \in C$ is called a *blocking literal* with respect to $\Pi.\psi$ if and only if $\overline{C}$ satisfies $\mathcal{OF}(\Pi, \psi, \bar{l})$. Clause C is called a *blocked clause* if and only if there exists a blocking literal $l \in C$.

Definition 4 (Blocked Literal, instance of [1]): Let C be a clause occurring in QBF $\Pi.\psi$. Universal literal l is called a *blocked literal* with respect to C and $\Pi.\psi$ if and only if $\overline{C}$ satisfies $\mathcal{OF}(\Pi, \psi, \bar{l})$.

Notice the subtle difference in the names of the concepts: the new *blocked* literals are always universal literals, while *blocking* literals are always existential literals. This naming convention is motivated as follows: blocked literals are redundant –like blocked clauses– while blocking literals [3] are *not* redundant, but the reason why the clauses, in which they occur, are blocked and thus redundant.

3.1   Blocked Literal Elimination

We refer to *blocked literal elimination* (BLE) as removing blocked literals in a formula until fixpoint. For the formal proof of the soundness of (a generalization of) BLE, we refer to Theorem 2 of our IJCAR'14 paper [1]. From that theorem it follows that BLE preserves satisfiability, but not logical equivalence. In the game-based view of QBF, blocked literals can be ignored by the universal player, so it makes sense to remove them to simplify the formula at hand.

Theorem 1. *Blocked literal elimination is not confluent.*

Proof. Consider the true QBF $\Pi.\psi_{\text{SAT}} := \forall a, b \exists x.(a \vee b \vee x) \wedge (\bar{a} \vee \bar{b} \vee \bar{x})$. The outer formula $\mathcal{OF}(\Pi, \psi_{\text{SAT}}, \bar{a}) = (\bar{b})$ and $\mathcal{OF}(\Pi, \psi_{\text{SAT}}, b) = (a)$. BLE can remove literal a from $(a \vee b \vee x)$ because $\overline{(a \vee b \vee x)} = (\bar{a}) \wedge (\bar{b}) \wedge (\bar{x})$ satisfies $\mathcal{OF}(\Pi, \psi_{\text{SAT}}, \bar{a})$. Similarly, BLE can remove literal $\bar{b}$ from $(\bar{a} \vee \bar{b} \vee \bar{x})$ because $\overline{(\bar{a} \vee \bar{b} \vee \bar{x})} = (a) \wedge (b) \wedge (x)$ satisfies $\mathcal{OF}(\Pi, \psi_{\text{SAT}}, b)$. None of the other literals in ψ_{SAT} is blocked (although all x and $\bar{x}$ literals are blocking). BLE can remove either a from $(a \vee b \vee x)$ or $\bar{b}$ from $(\bar{a} \vee \bar{b} \vee \bar{x})$, but not both. Notice that removing both is also unsound as the resulting formula is unsatisfiable.

3.2   Blocked Literal Addition

Apart from eliminating blocked literals, one might also extend clauses by adding blocked literals in a similar fashion as adding hidden literals [7] or covered literals [8]. We will refer to *blocked literal addition* (BLA) as a procedure that adds blocked literals until fixpoint to a given formula.

We expect that BLA will be less useful in practice compared to BLE, because it weakens the formula. Weakening a formula is typically only useful when the formula is reduced in size. This is not the case for BLA. However, one could use BLA in combination with hidden literal and covered literal addition to check whether a clause is redundant.

Theorem 2. *Blocked literal addition is not confluent.*

Proof. Let $\Pi.\psi_{\text{UNSAT}} := \exists x, y \, \forall a \, \exists z.(x \lor a) \land (y \lor \bar{a}) \land (\bar{x} \lor z) \land (\bar{y} \lor \bar{z})$ be a false QBF. Further let ψ^C_{UNSAT} be ψ_{UNSAT} with $(\bar{x} \lor z)$ replaced by $C = (\bar{a} \lor \bar{x} \lor z)$, ψ^D_{UNSAT} be ψ_{UNSAT} with $(\bar{y} \lor \bar{z})$ replace by $D = (a \lor \bar{y} \lor \bar{z})$. Then $\mathcal{OF}(\Pi, \psi^C_{\text{UNSAT}}, a) = (x)$ and $\mathcal{OF}(\Pi, \psi^D_{\text{UNSAT}}, \bar{a}) = (y)$. Then $\overline{C} = (a) \land (x) \land (\bar{z})$ satisfies $\mathcal{OF}(\Pi, \psi^C_{\text{UNSAT}}, a)$. So BLA can add literal $\bar{a}$ to $(\bar{x} \lor z)$ in ψ_{UNSAT}. Further BLA can add literal a to $(\bar{y} \lor \bar{z})$, since $\overline{D} = (\bar{a}) \land (y) \land (\bar{z})$ satisfies $\mathcal{OF}(\Pi, \psi^D_{\text{UNSAT}}, \bar{a})$. Adding one of these blocked literals changes the other outer formula and *unblocks* the other literal.

Adding one literal does not only unblock the other, but adding both $\bar{a}$ to $(\bar{x} \lor z)$ and a to $(\bar{y} \lor \bar{z})$ is unsound as it results in a satisfiable formula.

3.3   Universal Expansion

In general, we expect that BLE is more effective than BLA. However, in the context of *universal expansion*, an effective preprocessing technique [9], the opposite is true. Universal expansion eliminates the innermost universal variable by duplicating some clauses containing innermost existential literals. More formally, universal expansion applies the following rule [1, 9]:

$$\frac{\Pi \forall x \exists Y.\psi, C_1 \lor \bar{x}, \dots, C_n \lor \bar{x}, D_1 \lor x, \dots, D_m \lor x, E_1, \dots, E_p}{\Pi \exists Y Y'.\psi, C_1, \dots, C_n, E_1, \dots, E_p, D'_1, \dots, D'_m, E'_1, \dots, E'_p}$$

A copy Y' of the set of innermost existential variables Y is introduced. In the primed clauses, variables from Y are replaced by variables from Y'. For applying universal expansion on variable x, the clauses of the formula are partitioned into four groups: (i) those that contain literal x; (ii) those that contain literal $\bar{x}$; (iii) clauses that contain at least one innermost existential literal (i.e., from Y), but not x nor $\bar{x}$; and (iv) the others. Notice that only the clauses in the third group are duplicated, so one would like to have that group as small as possible. Yet BLE may remove x (or $\bar{x}$) literals from clauses, thereby moving them from the first group (or second group) to the third group. BLA on the other hand will add literals x (or $\bar{x}$), thereby moving clauses from the third group to the first (or second group). Therefore, applying BLA to add x and $\bar{x}$ literals to clauses is a useful pre-step before universal expansion.

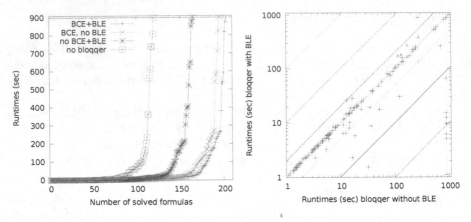

Fig. 1. Runtimes on Formulas from QBFLib Benchmark Set 2014

4   Evaluation

We extended our state-of-the-art preprocessor bloqqer v35[2] with blocked literal elimination such that BLE complements bloqqer's preprocessing techniques.

We evaluated the impact of BLE on the QBFLib 2014 Benchmarks[3] which were used in the QBF Gallery 2014, the competition of the QBF solving community. This benchmark set consists of 345 formulas stemming from various problem families mainly encoding verification and planning problems. The various problem families differ strongly in their formula structure, in particular in the number of quantifier alternations. Our experiments were run on a cluster of 31 nodes with Intel Q9550 CPUs and 8 GB of memory. The memory limit was never reached. We set an overall timeout of 900 seconds for preprocessing and solving, and we limited the memory consumption to 7 GB. The formulas, which could not be solved directly by bloqqer, were handed over to DepQBF 3.04[4], one of the most successful solvers of the QBF Gallery 2014.

We considered different configurations of bloqqer to evaluate if and how BLE influences the solving runtime. We ran DepQBF alone and with the following configurations of bloqqer: (i) all options enabled, (ii) BLE disabled, and (iii) BCE and BLE disabled. The results of our experiments are summarized in the left diagram of Fig. 1. Combining BLE and BCE leads to the best results, i.e., solving 202 formulas (102 true, 100 false). When BLE is disabled, 194 formulas are solved (98 true, 96 false). A detailed comparison is given by the scatter plot of Fig. 1. Whereas the majority of the formulas remains unaffected by BLE, for some formulas the runtime improves noticeably. Only one formula (test4_quant_squaring2) could be solved with BLE disabled, but not without. The average preprocessing time is 42 seconds without BLE and BCE, and 44 seconds

[2] http://fmv.jku.at/bloqqer
[3] http://qbf.satisfiability.org/gallery/
[4] http://lonsing.github.io/depqbf/

Table 1. Formulas solved exclusively due to BLE. The columns show the number of variables (#vars), clauses (#cl), quantifier alternations (#Q), blocked literals (#bl).

formula	original formula			preprocessing					solving	
	#vars	#cl	#Q	#bl	#vars	#cl	#Q	time	time	val
adder-6-sat	1727	1259	4	1278	2157	5401	2	0.74	0.36	T
C88020_0_0_inp	1046	2644	21	3	1306	3466	15	0.2	874.32	F
cache-coh-2-fixp-5	9604	28198	2	3599	–	–	–	9.32	–	F*
ethernet-fixpoint-3	12514	33884	2	3879	–	–	–	9.76	–	F*
k_branch_n-14	7068	33865	33	389	–	–	–	5.09	–	T*
k_branch_n-20	13821	78949	44	1397	–	–	–	12.45	–	T*
k_branch_p-15	8035	39595	34	239	–	–	–	6.12	–	F*
k_branch_p-21	15161	88627	46	1532	–	–	–	15.12	–	F*
s820_d7_s	24757	26960	3	5365	25115	12869	3	54.7	11.44	T

* solved directly by bloqqer

if they are enabled. Table 1 shows statistics on formulas which can only be solved if BLE is turned on. With BLE, bloqqer itself (i.e., without DepQBF) solves 78 formulas (37 true, 41 false), compared to 68 formula (33 true, 35 false) without BLE. The truth value of these formulas is certified by our checking tool [1].

5   Conclusion

We showed that blocked literal elimination—a special case of a rule in the QRAT proof system—can be applied as preprocessing technique for QBFs. We integrated BLE in our preprocessor bloqqer. Experiments showed the impact of this technique. We further proposed and motivated a technique called blocked literal addition where blocked literals are introduced to the formulas. However, the implementation of BLA is more involved because its application bears the danger of annihilating the effects of other preprocessing techniques. Further, we did not investigate the impact of the asymmetric variant of BLE yet nor the application of the general QRAT rules. Both will be subject to future work.

References

1. Heule, M.J.H., Seidl, M., Biere, A.: A unified proof system for QBF preprocessing. In: Demri, S., Kapur, D., Weidenbach, C. (eds.) IJCAR 2014. LNCS, vol. 8562, pp. 91–106. Springer, Heidelberg (2014)
2. Cadoli, M., Schaerf, M., Giovanardi, M., Giovanardi, M.: An algorithm to evaluate quantified boolean formulae and its experimental evaluation. Journal of Automated Reasoning, 262–267 (1999)
3. Biere, A., Lonsing, F., Seidl, M.: Blocked clause elimination for QBF. In: Bjørner, N., Sofronie-Stokkermans, V. (eds.) CADE 2011. LNCS, vol. 6803, pp. 101–115. Springer, Heidelberg (2011)
4. Tseitin, G.S.: On the complexity of derivation in propositional calculus. In: Automation of Reasoning 2, pp. 466–483. Springer (1983)

5. Ansótegui, C., Gomes, C.P., Selman, B.: The Achilles' Heel of QBF. In: AAAI 2005, pp. 275–281. AAAI Press / The MIT Press (2005)
6. Heule, M.J.H., Seidl, M., Biere, A.: Efficient Extraction of Skolem Functions from QRAT Proofs. In: FMCAD 2014, pp. 107–114. IEEE (2014)
7. Heule, M.J.H., Järvisalo, M., Biere, A.: Clause elimination procedures for CNF formulas. In: Fermüller, C.G., Voronkov, A. (eds.) LPAR-17. LNCS, vol. 6397, pp. 357–371. Springer, Heidelberg (2010)
8. Heule, M.J.H., Järvisalo, M., Biere, A.: Covered clause elimination. In: LPAR-17-short. EPiC Series, vol. 13, pp. 41–46. EasyChair (2013)
9. Biere, A.: Resolve and expand. In: H. Hoos, H., Mitchell, D.G. (eds.) SAT 2004. LNCS, vol. 3542, pp. 59–70. Springer, Heidelberg (2005)

Practical Formal Verification of Domain-Specific Language Applications

Greg Eakman[1], Howard Reubenstein[1]([✉]), Tom Hawkins[1],
Mitesh Jain[2], and Panagiotis Manolios[2]

[1] BAE Systems, Burlington, MA 01803, USA
hbr@alum.mit.edu
[2] Northeastern University, Boston, MA 02115, USA

Abstract. An application developer's primary task is to produce performant systems that meet their specifications. Formal methods techniques allow engineers to create models and implementations that have a high assurance of satisfying a specification. In this experience report, we take a model-based approach to software development that adds the assurance of formal methods to software construction while automating over 90% of the formal modeling. We discuss a software development methodology and two specific examples that illustrate how to integrate formal methods and their benefits into a traditional (testing-based) software development process.

1 Introduction

Domain-Specific Languages (DSLs) provide expressive semantics for defining computational behavior while insulating the application developer from many sources of error inherent in programming in the underlying target programming language (e.g., C or Java). A DSL can be transformed using a code generator into a traditionally compilable source language where the full expressivity of that language can be used, assuming that the transformation technology respects the execution semantics of the target language (Figure 1). The semantics of the DSL, despite the intentions of the DSL designer, are really defined in the translation rules of the code generator. In this paper, we apply formal semantics to two DSLs: a Haskell-based text DSL (Ivory developed by Galois) and a graphical DSL based on a UML profile. We augment the code generation strategy to include generation of a shallow embedding of the target DSL program in ACL2s. We prove application level properties of the DSL program and demonstrate correspondence of the ACL2s model with the source code implementation through testing for equivalent behavior.

This work is motivated by the difficulties observed in accelerating the adoption of formal methods techniques in the practicing software engineering community responsible for deploying systems. The barriers to application developers using formal tools to get their jobs done include: the need to build a constructive proof of correctness before extracting an implementation, unfamiliarity with

© Springer International Publishing Switzerland 2015
K. Havelund et al. (Eds.): NFM 2015, LNCS 9058, pp. 443–449, 2015.
DOI: 10.1007/978-3-319-17524-9_34

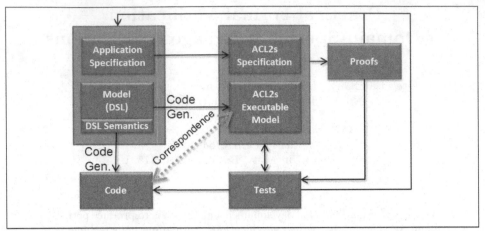

Fig. 1. Properties of the application, developed in the model and proven in ACL2s, are shown to hold in deployed code through correspondence testing

the syntax and development methodology of formal languages, the difference in semantic models (imperative versus logical/inductive), the difficulty in extracting implementations that interface with existing systems (e.g., those written in C, C++, Java), and the difficulty in obtaining performant implementations.

2   FORMED and UML

Project FORMED (Formal Methods Engineering Desktop)[1] combines software design in the Unified Modeling Language (UML) with formal methods in a way that allows application developers to create formal models. The FORMED DSL is built on the fUML profile [7] which provides executable semantics to class, operation, and association UML elements, and includes semantics for a model-level programming language [2]. This executable UML profile is a graphical DSL, albeit for a very broad domain. From this profile, we build on existing model transformation and code generation tools such as PathMATE [11] to generate a shallow mapping of an application model into ACL2s, the ACL2 Sedan [5]. ACL2s extends ACL2, an industrial strength, semi-automated theorem prover, with a powerful termination analysis engine, a data definition framework, and counterexample generation capabilities. Properties of the application are then specified and proven using ACL2s. We focus on application correctness as part of high assurance software development, rather than on general properties of memory safety or security, which depend on the implementation language, compiler, operating system, and CPU architecture.

The execution semantics of the FORMED UML profile operates on a stack and a heap, modeled in ACL2s with a reusable *context* data definition. The context and the functions that operate on it form the platform model that supports

---

[1] Sponsored by OSD under contract FA8750-14-C-0024.

the operation of the UML semantics and the execution of the application. Each context function has an associated input-output contract (proved automatically by ACL2s) that provides assurance on the correctness of the function implementation. We specify and prove many other theorems that axiomatize the semantics of operations on the context. These theorems assist us in abstracting the reasoning about UML semantics. This hierarchical approach to reasoning not only provides a reasoning structure but it also reduces the time taken by ACL2s. For example, it reduced a proof of an application level property from 20 minutes to less than 15 seconds.

The code generator produces ACL2s code that stores the application state in the stack/heap context. The imperative nature of the FORMED profile maps to ACL2s's functional language by providing the context as one of the input arguments for an operation and requiring the operation to return an updated context. Templates map the UML elements to ACL2s constructs. A UML class, for example, gets mapped to an ACL2s data definition using the defdata framework, which supports automated type-like reasoning [6]. Rather than validate the transformation, we generate theorems based on the UML profile's semantics, such as inheritance, associations, pointers, and class extents, to reason about the ACL2s code.

We have identified common properties of application models and formalized the semantics of each into a theorem template to produce an instance of the theorem for each model location where the property holds. For example, all rooms within a hotel must have a unique room number. The application developer marks the number attribute of the Room class with an «Identifier» stereotype indicating that all instances should have a unique value. We generate an ACL2s theorem that proves by induction that this invariant holds for all operations from any valid state of the application. The code generator statically analyzes the application to assist theorem proving. The unique room number invariant can only be invalidated by operations that write the room number attribute or create a new room. Thus, our proof only needs to consider those critical functions identified through static analysis.

Table 1. Just 6% of the Hotel application's formal verification code is hand-written

Hotel Locking Example Metrics		
	UML Classes	13
Source UML	Lines Action Language	220
	Operations	26
Java	Generated Java	3895
ACL2s	ACL2s SLOC	1284
Context	Theorems	132
	SLOC Theorems	998
Generated	Executable Code	5652
UML	Theorem Code	4078
Semantics	Theorems Generated	175
Hand-written ACL2s	Application Theorems	18
	SLOC Theorems	806

FORMED proves properties about the shallow embedding of the application in ACL2s, but the formal model is not the deployed code. DSLs, including this UML profile, can generate source in multiple languages (Java in this case), that are deployed as a real application. We build an assurance case argument based on correspondence testing that the properties proven in the ACL2s representation also exist in the deployed code. Since both the ACL2s and deployed code are executable representations generated from the same model, and since we apply the same test cases to each version and verify the corresponding results, we gain confidence that the properties also hold in the deployed code.

We have applied this process to a model of the Hotel Locking problem [9], which describes a protocol for managing room keys to secure hotel rooms between guests. Some metrics from the Hotel application are shown in Table 1. Preliminary results indicate that only about 6% of the ACL2s code, the Application Theorems, need to be hand written. Specifying these theorems in ACL2s requires only moderate knowledge of formal logic. Most of the theorems were automatically proved by ACL2s and some of them required us to guide the theorem prover with appropriate *lemmas*.

3   SITAPS and Ivory DSL

Ivory is a DSL undergoing development by Galois for UAV control systems used on DARPA's HACMS program. Ivory code is currently flying on a quadcopter UAV, running flight control algorithms and data link processing.

Embedded in Haskell, Ivory relies on Haskell's type system to ensure type and memory safety of the generated runtime code (Ivory compiles to C). Though it is a language similar to C, Ivory purposely limits expressiveness to provide memory safety. For example, Ivory does not provide pointer types, nor does it allow arbitrary pointer operations, but it does provide mutable references that are stack allocated and can be passed as procedure arguments. References are ensured not to escape the enclosing stack frame, which is enforced by Haskell types. To prevent buffer overflows, Ivory provides indexing types and bounded loop operations to ensure array accesses are within bounds.

To increase assurance of Ivory programs, we developed a proof framework[2], based on a compilation of Ivory into ACL2s, that verifies user specified and compiler generated assertions. In addition to assertions, Ivory also provides input and output contracts on procedures. Using these contracts to abstract procedure calls, this proof framework is able to perform an efficient interprocedural analysis that scales well with larger programs. The analysis walks through each procedure, generating verification conditions (VCs) for each assertion, each sub input contract at every sub procedure call, and each output contract at every return point. These VCs, which are captured in a VC DSL, are optimized and translated to ACL2s for verification. Verified assertions are removed from the program to lower the runtime overhead and those that fail to prove remain in

[2] Supported by DARPA under the SITAPS project under contract FA8750-13-C-0240.

place to serve as runtime checks. An example Ivory procedure and translation are illustrated below:

```
retractLandingGear :: Def ('[IBool, Sint32] :-> ())
retractLandingGear = proc "retractLandingGear" $
 \ weightOnWheels airspeed -> body $ do
    ifte_ (iNot weightOnWheels .&& airspeed >? 120) -- Better than spec
      (do
         assert $ iNot weightOnWheels  -- Spec guarding
         assert $ airspeed >? 80       -- call to GearUp
         call_ commandLandingGearUp
         retVoid)
      retVoid
```

Procedure Translated to VC DSL to Verify the First Assertion:

```
let stack0=[] in                          -- Initial stack. forall
free0 in                                  -- Free variables for forall
free1 in                                  -- arguments var0,var1. let
env0={var0 : free0, var1 : free1} in      -- Bind args into env. let
bc0=((!env0.var0)&&(env0.var1>70)) in     -- Branch condition. let
vc0=(bc0->(!env0.var0)) in   vc0          -- VC:not weightOnWheels.
```

During the development of the Ivory-ACL2s interprocedural analyzer, we established a suite of tests to cover the interesting corners of the language. Combining both assertions and procedure contracts, the test suite comprised 61 checks of which 54 were verified automatically by the analyzer. One set of tests of specific interest are Ivory compiler generated assertions, which protect loop bounds, index casting, numerical overflows, and other security impinging aspects of the language. Our limited test suite produced 6 compiler generated assertions, 5 of which were verified automatically. The one that failed verification was bounds checking an index type, though it can be argued this check is not necessary because the index's bounds is enforced by the Ivory type system. Further investigation is warranted to determine verification performance on larger, real-world examples.

4 Formal Methods to Support Application Developers

Both the FORMED and SITAPS projects demonstrate the effective use of DSLs and code generation to make formal methods accessible to developers.

Our approach in both of these projects has been to start with the goal of supporting a developer in creating high assurance software from an environment that includes the normal tools they are used to working with and that also supports a development process that is a consistent superset of the normal process they might use. The development methodology we advocate consists of:

1. Model - capture the software specification in a DSL that can be used to generate code and additional software artifacts

2. Test - perform simple unit testing to ascertain that the model properly captures the most important properties of the specification
3. Plan Proofs - define invariants, pre and post conditions, that are important to obtaining confidence in the implementation
4. Prove - prove properties (only after initial testing indicates proof is likely to succeed) or generate counter-examples. Repair model as needed.
5. Correspondence test - confirm correspondence of model and code and provide traditional visible testing evidence that software meets specification

Correspondence testing is an important aspect of this approach that varies from proof-first development approaches that derive executable code from formal models. The derivation guarantees that the implementation refines the model and thus that proofs at the model level apply to the implementation. This approach, while principled, places the modeling and proof task ahead of the application developer's primary implementation task. It also exposes the development to a common problem that formal methods do not provide an "anytime confidence" approach to development. When proving properties using formal reasoners your confidence is either 0% (unproven) or 100% (proven). The methodology described above provides increasing confidence as more proofs and tests pass and limits the proof effort while focusing on producing an executable software artifact.

5   Related Work and Conclusion

Kestrel Institute's Specware [10] tool synthesizes deployable code from formal specifications by process of successive refinements, with proofs of each refinement step, but requires a proof-first approach. Coq is another, more common, proof first language that has the ability to generate code.

Other efforts have mapped UML to various formal methods languages, such as CSP [1], Z [3], and Alloy [4]. AADL is another example of a graphical language used in both development and formal verification. In [8], the LLVM intermediate language is translated into ACL2 for both testing and low-level theorem proving.

Domain-specific languages enable application development at a higher conceptual level than general purpose languages, but hide their real semantics within the code generator. A shallow embedding of these languages in a formal language like ACL2s enables DSL semantics to be specified, reasoned about, and used to prove properties about applications. The executability of ACL2s also allows it to be used to verify the correct operation of deployable code through test correspondence. Shallow embedding also broadens the user base of formal methods, giving application developers the ability, through the DSL, to create formal models.

References

1. Abdelhalim, I., Schneider, S., Treharne, H.: Towards a practical approach to check UML/fUML models consistency using CSP. In: Qin, S., Qiu, Z. (eds.) ICFEM 2011. LNCS, vol. 6991, pp. 33–48. Springer, Heidelberg (2011)

2. http://www.omg.org/spec/ALF
3. Amálio, N., Stepney, S., Polack, F.: Formal proof from UML models. In: Davies, J., Schulte, W., Barnett, M. (eds.) ICFEM 2004. LNCS, vol. 3308, pp. 418–433. Springer, Heidelberg (2004)
4. Anastasakis, K., Bordbar, B., Georg, G., Ray, I.: UML2Alloy: a challenging model transformation. In: Engels, G., Opdyke, B., Schmidt, D.C., Weil, F. (eds.) MoDELS 2007. LNCS, vol. 4735, pp. 436–450. Springer, Heidelberg (2007)
5. Chamarthi, H.R., Dillinger, P., Manolios, P., Vroon, D.: The ACL2 sedan theorem proving system. In: Abdulla, P.A., Leino, K.R.M. (eds.) TACAS 2011. LNCS, vol. 6605, pp. 291–295. Springer, Heidelberg (2011)
6. Chamarthi, H.R., Dillinger, P.C., Manolios, P.: Data definitions in the ACL2 Sedan. In: ACL2 Workshop. EPTCS, vol. 152, pp. 27–48 (2014)
7. http://www.omg.org/spec/FUML
8. Hardin, D.S., Davis, J.A., Greve, D.A., McClurg, J.R.: Development of a translator from LLVM to ACL2. EPTCS, vol. 152
9. Jackson, D.: Software Abstractions: logic, language, and analysis. MIT press (2012)
10. Jüllig, R., Srinivas, Y., Liu, J.: SPECWARE: an advanced environment for the formal development of complex software systems. In: Nivat, M., Wirsing, M. (eds.) AMAST 1996. LNCS, vol. 1101, pp. 551–554. Springer, Heidelberg (1996)
11. http://www.pathmate.com

Reporting Races
in Dynamic Partial Order Reduction

Olli Saarikivi[✉] and Keijo Heljanko

Department of Computer Science and Engineering,
Aalto University School of Science, Espoo, Finland
{olli.saarikivi,keijo.heljanko}@aalto.fi

Abstract. Data races are a common type of bug found in multithreaded programs. The dynamic partial order reduction algorithm (DPOR) is an efficient algorithm for exploring a reduced set of interleavings that guarantees all assertion errors and deadlocks to be found. However, while DPOR does in effect explore different outcomes of data races, it was not originally designed to report them. In this paper a method for reporting data races during DPOR is presented. This allows data races to be found even when they do not trigger assertion errors or deadlocks. Additionally, for programs written in C++11 and a large subset of Java, the presented method allows DPOR to warn the user when it can not guarantee completeness due to the program having data races that trigger weak memory model semantics for it.

Keywords: Race detection · Partial order reduction · C++ · Java · DPOR

1 Introduction

A *data race* is a situation where two threads access the same variable at the same time and at least one of the accesses is a write. Unintentional data races are notoriously common in multithreaded programs. Furthermore, the fact that data races may only be present in some rare interleavings of a program makes finding them challenging.

The dynamic partial order reduction algorithm (DPOR) [5] is an efficient algorithm for exploring a reduced set of interleavings of a concurrent program while still ensuring that all assertion errors and deadlocks will be found. It executes a concurrent program while tracking the dependencies between operations executed to identify alternate interleavings that could lead to different behavior. Alternate interleavings are explored by adding backtracking points to a tree of scheduling decisions that is constructed over multiple executions. The program is repeatedly executed with alternate interleavings until no more assertion errors or deadlocks can remain unfound.

To find all assertion errors and deadlocks DPOR essentially explores different outcomes of interleaving concurrent operations. This includes exploring different

© Springer International Publishing Switzerland 2015
K. Havelund et al. (Eds.): NFM 2015, LNCS 9058, pp. 450–456, 2015.
DOI: 10.1007/978-3-319-17524-9_35

outcomes of data races. However, in the original approach data races themselves are not reported. As a data race typically is a programming error, it would make sense to report them alongside any other errors detected.

One technical issue with DPOR is that it was designed for a memory model with sequential consistency and is not complete for weaker memory models without modification [9]. However, Java programs with data races follow a weaker memory model (for which DPOR is not complete), and C++11 gives no semantics to programs with data races [1]. Therefore, given a concurrent program of which it is unknown whether it contains data races or not, if DPOR is to be employed it would be useful for data races to be reported. This would inform the user both of data races that should be considered bugs, and of benign races that trigger a weak memory model for which DPOR can not guarantee completeness.

One way to detect races would be to employ an existing dynamic race detection tool alongside DPOR. There are two main approaches to dynamic race detection: computing *locksets* [11] and tracking the *happens-before* relation [6]. Using a race detection tool based on locksets could be attractive, because they can have low overhead. However, lockset-based tools are not precise and can report false alarms for programs that communicate with, for example, Java's volatile variables. False alarms require manual work for checking them and in our use case also remove confidence in the testing tool's completeness.

Tools that track the happens-before are precise. However, they typically have higher overhead than lockset-based tools, with some tools being able to approach the same overhead levels [4]. This overhead also seems redundant, as DPOR already keeps track of a happens-before relation.

This paper presents a way to retrofit DPOR for race detection. It is shown that the proposed method is precise, and has negligible overhead over that of DPOR itself. The method is also shown to be sound for the C++11 memory model and a large subset of Java.

A related approach was described in a technical report by Elmas, Qadeer and Tasiran [2], where a new sound and precise data race detection algorithm was used to develop a partial order reduction algorithm similar to DPOR.

In Section 2 background and definitions are introduced. Section 3 gives a proof that DPOR can find all races and describes a race detection method implied by the proof. In Section 4 a brief evaluation is presented and finally Section 5 provides discussion and concluding remarks.

2   Preliminaries

This section contains definitions and background necessary for understanding Section 3. DPOR will not be fully described. Instead, only the properties of DPOR that are required for understanding this paper are introduced. For a full description of DPOR, see [5].

The execution model used here is a simplified version of the one in [5]. A concurrent program is composed of a set of *threads*, each executing a sequence of operations written in an imperative programming language (e.g., Java). The threads communicate by performing operations on shared variables and synchronization constructs. The state of the program consists of the local states of all threads and the states of all shared variables and synchronization constructs. Programs are assumed to have no infinite executions. This assumption is required due to DPOR being a stateless method.

All operations executed are considered atomic. The program induces a transition system $A = (S, \delta, s_0)$, where S is the set of states, $\delta \subseteq S \times S$ and $(s, s') \in \delta$ if and only if in state s the next operation of some thread will take the program to s', and s_0 is the initial state.

Additionally, there exists a labeling function $L : \delta \to O$, where O is the set of operations from all threads in the program. Each thread has a distinct set of operations. Given an operation $o \in O$ and states s and s', we write $s \xrightarrow{o} s'$ if and only if $(s, s') \in \delta$ and $L(s, s') = o$. We write the execution of a sequence of operations $w \in O^*$ as $s \xRightarrow{w} s'$. Given a state s we say that an operation o is *enabled in* s if and only if $\exists s' : s \xrightarrow{o} s'$. Given two operations a and b we say that a *enables* b in some state s if b is not enabled in s and there exists a state s' such that $s \xrightarrow{a} s'$ and b is enabled in s'. *Disabling* is defined in an analogous manner. Two operations a and b are said to be *co-enabled* in state s if both a and b are enabled in s.

DPOR is given a dependency relation between pairs of operations. The relation is reflexive and symmetric. For all pairs (a, b) *not* in the relation the following must hold:

1. If $s \xrightarrow{a} s'$ then b is enabled in s' if and only if it is enabled in s.
2. If a and b are enabled in s then there exists a unique s' such that $s \xRightarrow{ab} s'$ and $s \xRightarrow{ba} s'$.

Two operations a and b are *dependent* if (a, b) is in the dependency relation. Otherwise a and b are *independent*.

A *Mazurkiewicz trace* is a set of complete executions obtainable from each other by swapping adjacent independent operations. Consider a program with two threads, where the first thread always executes the operations x and a (in this order), and the second thread executes the operations y and b. Assume that only a and b are dependent. One complete execution is $xayb$. Swapping the adjacent independent operations a and y produces $xyab$, which therefore belongs to the same Mazurkiewicz trace. The Mazurkiewicz traces for this program are $\{xayb, xyab, yxab\}$ and $\{ybxa, yxba, xyba\}$. DPOR is guaranteed to explore at least one complete execution from each Mazurkiewicz trace of the program.

Given a state s and the set of operations E which are enabled in s, a set of operations $P \subseteq E$ is *persistent in* s if and only if for all nonempty sequences of operations $o_1, o_2, \ldots, o_n \notin P$ such that $s \xrightarrow{o_1 o_2 \ldots o_n} s'$ it holds that o_n is independent with all operations in P.

DPOR explores a persistent set of operations from each visited state.

3   Detecting Races

Definition 1 (Data race). *A program has a data race if there exists a reachable state s such that two operations on the same shared variable are co-enabled in s and at least one of the operations is a write.*

Let a and b be the operations of a data race. Given an integer $n \geq 0$, let $R_n^{a,b}$ be the set of states such that for each $s \in R_n^{a,b}$ the operation a is enabled in s and there exists a sequence of operations $t_1 \ldots t_n$ such that $s \xrightarrow{t_1 \ldots t_n} s'$ and the operations a and b are co-enabled in s'. As a special case $R_0^{a,b}$ is the set of states where a and b are co-enabled.

Lemma 1. *Assume the program has a data race. Let a and b be the operations in race. DPOR will at some point reach a state $s \in R_n^{a,b}$ for some $n \geq 0$.*

Lemma 2. *Assume DPOR explores a state $s \in R_n^{a,b}$. DPOR will explore a state $s' \in R_m^{a,b}$ such that $m \leq n$ and a is explored from s' (i.e. $s' \xrightarrow{a} s''$ and s'' is explored by DPOR).*

Lemmas 1 and 2 follow from the fact that DPOR explores all Mazurkiewicz traces and a persistent set of operations from each visited state. The proofs have been omitted for brevity.

Theorem 1. *If there exists a data race between two operations a and b, then DPOR will reach a state in which a and b are co-enabled.*

Proof. Let $s_1 \in R_n^{a,b}$ be a state from which DPOR explores a. By Lemmas 1 and 2 such a state must exist. From this state there exists a sequence of operations $t_1 \ldots t_n$ such that $s_1 \xrightarrow{t_1 \ldots t_n} s_1'$ and a and b are co-enabled in s_1'. If $n = 0$ then $s_1 = s_1'$ and we are done. Otherwise, because DPOR explores a persistent set of operations from s_1 then $s_1 \xrightarrow{t_1} s_1''$ will be explored. Now $s_1'' \in R_{n-1}^{a,b}$ and by Lemma 2 there exists a state $s_2 \in R_m^{a,b}$ such that $m \leq n - 1$. By iteratively applying this procedure we can prove that DPOR will reach some state $s_k \in R_0^{a,b}$ in which a and b are co-enabled.   □

Theorem 1 directly leads to a method for detecting data races during DPOR. Whenever a state is reached the set of enabled operations can be searched for two operations that constitute a data race. However, this method could potentially have a significant overhead if each pair of enabled operations is inspected. For a more efficient method, observe that when DPOR reaches a state in which two operations a and b are in a race, by Lemma 2 it will then in some state s explore one of those operations. Because DPOR explores a persistent set of operations then both a and b will be explored from s. Therefore instead of searching all enabled operations, whenever an operation is explored from a state it is sufficient to check this operation against any operations previously executed from the same state.

To check whether there is a race between two operations Definition 1 can be used. Alternatively, the dependency relation in use can also be reused if it is such that two reads on the same shared variable are considered independent. In [10] such a variation of DPOR with independent reads is presented.

This method is precise because a data race is only reported when a state matching Definition 1 is reached. This method is also sound w.r.t. Definition 1, because Theorem 1 guarantees that if there exists a race then it will be found.

4   Evaluation

Race detection with DPOR was implemented as a modification to the existing DPOR implementation in the testing tool LCT [10]. The tool warns whenever a data race between two operations is found. Due to LCT's client-server model, where state that persists across test executions is stored on the server, we found it more convenient to check executed operations against all enabled operations instead of just previously executed ones (thus avoiding additional client-server communication). This method could in principle have higher overhead.

Benchmark	No race detection	With race detection
Szymanski small	89.55 s	**89.41 s**
Pi	**7.00 s**	7.02 s
File system	**1.57 s**	1.61 s
Indexer	11.12 s	**11.07 s**
Synthetic	28.13 s	**28.12 s**

Fig. 1. Running times with race detection and without

A small set of benchmarks was used to evaluate the runtime overhead of race detection. "Szymanski small" is a simplified version of a benchmark from [7]. "Pi", "File system" and "Indexer" are from [10]. "Synthetic" has multiple threads accessing a single shared variable. The benchmarks were run on a Intel Core 2 Q9550 quad core CPU @ 2.83 Ghz with 4 GB of RAM. For each benchmark the time required for a full DPOR exploration is reported. The results can be seen in Section 4. The reported running times are averages of five test runs after a discarded initial test run to get rid of cache effects.

5   Conclusions

Looking at the results it can be seen that almost no additional overhead can be observed when race detection is enabled. This is as expected, as the method for reporting races should be a very lightweight addition to DPOR.

In this paper a method for reporting data races in the DPOR algorithm has been presented and proved sound and precise. The method guarantees that if there is an interleaving of the program with a data race then DPOR will report it. Additionally, reporting data races is useful because DPOR was designed for sequential consistency, which both C++11 and Java guarantee only for race-free programs. With the method presented in this paper, DPOR is guaranteed either to find all assertion violations and deadlocks, or to report a data race (see Definition 1). This is due to the fact that in both C++11 and a large subset of Java a program is race free if and only if no sequentially consistent execution has a race as defined by Definition 1 [1,8].

Very recent work on formalizing the Java memory model has revealed new subtleties in the way data races may be defined for Java. A *happens-before race* is present if there exists an execution where two dependent operations on a shared variable are concurrent in the happens-before relation induced by the synchronization operations executed. For C++11 happens-before races and Definition 1 are equivalent [1]. The proof has been claimed to generalize for Java [3], but due to subtleties in the Java memory model it does not [8]. The problem arises from the fact that Java's language specification requires threads to communicate in ways that are not covered by the memory model. This establishes *covert communication channels* that allow threads to communicate reliably without introducing synchronization in the memory model's happens-before relation. By exploiting these discrepancies it is possible to write a program that has a happens-before race but does not have a race matching Definition 1 [8]. For such programs the method proposed in this paper is not guaranteed to find all races. We find these subtleties extremely confusing and note that according to Lochbihler [8] the Java memory model could be changed to cover the covert communication channels making the two different notions of races equivalent for Java.

In addition to the synchronization constructs that enable sequential consistency, C++11 offers *low-level atomics* that follow a weaker memory model [1]. This does not affect the soundness of our data race detection approach due to the aforementioned equivalence of happens-before races and Definition 1. However, tools implementing DPOR for C++11 should warn about possible incompleteness when encountering low-level atomics.

Acknowledgments. We would like to thankfully acknowledge the funding from the SARANA project in the SAFIR 2014 program and the Academy of Finland projects 139402 and 277522.

References

1. Boehm, H.J., Adve, S.V.: Foundations of the C++ concurrency memory model. SIGPLAN Not. **43**(6), 68–78 (2008)
2. Elmas, T., Qadeer, S., Tasiran, S.: Precise race detection and efficient model checking using locksets. Tech. Rep. MSR-TR-2005-118, Microsoft Research (2005)
3. Elmas, T., Qadeer, S., Tasiran, S.: Goldilocks: A race and transaction-aware Java runtime. SIGPLAN Not. **42**(6), 245–255 (2007)

4. Flanagan, C., Freund, S.N.: FastTrack: Efficient and precise dynamic race detection. SIGPLAN Not. **44**(6), 121–133 (2009)
5. Flanagan, C., Godefroid, P.: Dynamic partial-order reduction for model checking software. SIGPLAN Not. **40**(1), 110–121 (2005)
6. Itzkovitz, A., Schuster, A., Zeev-Ben-Mordehai, O.: Toward integration of data race detection in DSM systems. J. Parallel Distrib. Comput. **59**(2), 180–203 (1999)
7. Kähkönen, K., Heljanko, K.: Lightweight state capturing for automated testing of multithreaded programs. In: Seidl, M., Tillmann, N. (eds.) TAP 2014. LNCS, vol. 8570, pp. 187–203. Springer, Heidelberg (2014)
8. Lochbihler, A.: Java and the java memory model — a unified, machine-checked formalisation. In: Seidl, H. (ed.) ESOP 2012. LNCS, vol. 7211, pp. 497–517. Springer, Heidelberg (2012)
9. Norris, B., Demsky, B.: CDSchecker: Checking concurrent data structures written with C/C++ atomics. SIGPLAN Not. **48**(10), 131–150 (2013)
10. Saarikivi, O., Kähkönen, K., Heljanko, K.: Improving dynamic partial order reductions for concolic testing. In: 12th International Conference on Application of Concurrency to System Design, ACSD 2012, Hamburg, Germany, June 27–29, 2012, pp. 132–141 (2012)
11. Savage, S., Burrows, M., Nelson, G., Sobalvarro, P., Anderson, T.: Eraser: A dynamic data race detector for multithreaded programs. ACM Trans. Comput. Syst. **15**(4), 391–411 (1997)

Author Index